THE OXFORD

POLITICAL PHILOSOPHY

THE OXFORD HANDBOOK OF

POLITICAL PHILOSOPHY

Edited by

DAVID ESTLUND

OXFORD
UNIVERSITY PRESS

Oxford University Press is a department of the University of Oxford.
It furthers the University's objective of excellence in research, scholarship,
and education by publishing worldwide.

Oxford   New York
Auckland   Cape Town   Dar es Salaam   Hong Kong   Karachi
Kuala Lumpur   Madrid   Melbourne   Mexico City   Nairobi
New Delhi   Shanghai   Taipei   Toronto

With offices in
Argentina   Austria   Brazil   Chile   Czech Republic   France   Greece
Guatemala   Hungary   Italy   Japan   Poland   Portugal   Singapore
South Korea   Switzerland   Thailand   Turkey   Ukraine   Vietnam

Oxford is a registered trade mark of Oxford University Press
in the UK and certain other countries.

Published in the United States of America by
Oxford University Press
198 Madison Avenue, New York, NY 10016

© Oxford University Press 2012

First issued as an Oxford University Press paperback, 2017.

All rights reserved. No part of this publication may be reproduced, stored in a
retrieval system, or transmitted, in any form or by any means, without the prior
permission in writing of Oxford University Press, or as expressly permitted by law,
by license, or under terms agreed with the appropriate reproduction rights organization.
Inquiries concerning reproduction outside the scope of the above should be sent to the Rights
Department, Oxford University Press, at the address above.

You must not circulate this work in any other form
and you must impose this same condition on any acquirer.

Library of Congress Cataloging-in-Publication Data
The Oxford handbook of political philosophy / edited by David Estlund.
p. cm.—(Oxford handbooks)
ISBN 978-0-19-537669-2 (hardcover : alk. paper); 978-0-19-024633-4 (paperback : alk. paper);
1. Political science—Philosophy. I. Estlund, David M.
II. Title: Handbook of political philosophy.
JA71.O949   2012
320.01—dc23   2011036651

Contents

Contributors ix

Introduction 3
David Estlund

Part I. Classic Questions

1. Authority 23
   A. John Simmons

2. Equality 40
   Elizabeth Anderson

3. Justice 58
   Richard J. Arneson

4. Freedom 76
   Philip Pettit

5. Property 93
   Gerald Gaus

Part II. Approaches

6. Classical Liberalism 115
   Jason Brennan and John Tomasi

7. Social Contract Approaches 133
   Samuel Freeman

8. Left-Libertarianism 152
   Peter Vallentyne

9. Marxist and Socialist Approaches   169
   Andrew Levine

Part III. Democracy

10. Democracy   187
    Jeremy Waldron

11. Deliberation   204
    Robert B. Talisse

12. Religion and Politics   223
    Robert Audi

13. Money in Politics   241
    Thomas Christiano

Part IV. The Globe

14. Global Justice   261
    Mathias Risse

15. Human Rights   279
    Allen Buchanan

16. War   298
    Jeff McMahan

Part V. Injustice

17. Historical Injustice   319
    Jeff Spinner-Halev

18. Race   336
    Tommie Shelby

19. Gender   354
    Debra Satz

20. Ideal and Nonideal Theory   373
    Zofia Stemplowska and Adam Swift

Part VI. In Retrospect

21. Rawls   393
    Leif Wenar

22. Nozick   411
    David Schmidtz and Christopher Freiman

    Index   429

Contributors

Elizabeth Anderson is Arthur F. Thurnau Professor and John Rawls Collegiate Professor of Philosophy and Women's Studies at the University of Michigan, Ann Arbor.

Richard J. Arneson is Distinguished Professor of Philosophy at the University of California, San Diego.

Robert Audi is John A. O'Brien Professor of Philosophy at the University of Notre Dame.

Jason Brennan is Assistant Professor of Business and Philosophy at Georgetown University.

Allen Buchanan is James B. Duke Professor of Philosophy and Professor of Law at Duke University, where he is also an Investigator at the Institute of Genome Sciences and Policy.

Thomas Christiano is Professor of Philosophy and Law and Associate Director of the Freedom Center at the University of Arizona.

David Estlund is Lombardo Family Professor of Humanities in the Department of Philosophy at Brown University.

Samuel Freeman is Avalon Professor in the Humanities and Professor of Philosophy and Law at the University of Pennsylvania.

Christopher Freiman is Assistant Professor of Philosophy at the College of William and Mary.

Gerald Gaus is the James E. Rogers Professor of Philosophy at the University of Arizona, where he directs the program in Philosophy, Politics, Economics, and Law.

Andrew Levine taught philosophy at the University of Wisconsin-Madison and at the University of Maryland-College Park. He is presently a Senior Scholar at the Institute for Policy Studies in Washington, D.C.

Jeff McMahan is Professor of Philosophy at Rutgers University.

Philip Pettit is L.S. Rockefeller University Professor of Politics and Human Values at Princeton University.

Mathias Risse is Professor of Philosophy and Public Policy at the John F. Kennedy School of Government at Harvard University.

Debra Satz is the Marta Sutton Weeks Professor of Ethics in Society, and Professor of Philosophy at Stanford University. She is also the faculty director of the McCoy Family Center for Ethics in Society.

David Schmidtz is Kendrick Professor of Philosophy and Director of the Center for Philosophy of Freedom at the University of Arizona.

Tommie Shelby is Professor of African and African American Studies and Professor of Philosophy at Harvard University.

A. John Simmons is Commonwealth Professor of Philosophy and Professor of Law at the University of Virginia.

Jeff Spinner-Halev is the Kenan Eminent Professor of Political Ethics at the University of North Carolina at Chapel Hill.

Zofia Stemplowska is Associate Professor of Political Theory at the University of Warwick.

Adam Swift is Fellow and Tutor in Politics and Sociology at Balliol College, Oxford.

Robert B. Talisse is Professor of Philosophy and Professor of Political Science at Vanderbilt University.

John Tomasi is Professor of Political Science at Brown University.

Peter Vallentyne is Florence G. Kline Professor of Philosophy at the University of Missouri-Columbia.

Jeremy Waldron is University Professor at New York University School of Law, and Chichele Professor of Social and Political Theory at the University of Oxford (All Souls College).

Leif Wenar holds the Chair of Ethics at King's College London.

THE OXFORD HANDBOOK OF
POLITICAL PHILOSOPHY

INTRODUCTION

DAVID ESTLUND

SEVERAL people, taking a single photograph at the same place and the same time, will produce as many images as there are photographers, each differing from the others, each freezing a passing moment, and all of them leaving most of the scene outside the frame.[1] My role in commissioning and introducing these articles is similar. The issues that occupy political philosophers change over time and are always broader and more various than can be captured in any survey of the field. Still, a volume such as this one might serve as a sort of snapshot of one stage in this evolution. It is a record and a description, from certain points of view, of part of the shifting intellectual landscape at a certain point in time. The pieces in this volume, written by leaders in the field, are intended both as introductions and as substantial statements that will be of interest to even the most advanced scholars. My aim in this introduction is not to engage in detail with the individual pieces but rather to set out some of the objectives I had in selecting topics and to reflect on what we can learn from these chapters about how the field of political philosophy has evolved and is still evolving.

Political philosophy maintains closer contact, I believe, with the history of its subject than many other areas of philosophy do. Perhaps this is due to the close intermingling of political philosophy with "political theory" (as practiced in departments of politics, political science, or government) where the historical dimension is especially prominent. I have chosen, nevertheless, to concentrate on the kinds of issues with which the canonical theorists themselves were concerned (when they weren't interpreting their own predecessors).[2] The only concession to the historical view of the subject is the chapters on the thought of Rawls and of Nozick.[3] So many of the other chapters make contact with their work that it seemed appropriate to include an overview of these two defining figures now that they are sadly gone and their bodies of work complete.

Political philosophy takes place across several conventional disciplinary boundaries, including, at least, philosophy, political science, law, and economics. While there are some significant and principled methodological differences, there are also many differences that are simply path-dependent—because of the ways universities have been organized and the ways predecessors have proceeded (Rehfeld 2010). Political theorists (the counterparts in politics departments to those who do similar work in philosophy departments) tend to stay in closer touch with empirical political history, while political philosophers care more about implications for and from general moral theory and the other branches of philosophy, such as metaphysics, epistemology, and philosophy of mind. Political theorists tend more often to take the actual and probable facts as constraints on their normative theorizing, while political philosophers may be less sure their project is a practical rather than an intellectual one.[4] These are matters of degree, and there is no clean division, with each approach (or family of approaches) having much to learn from the other. That said, the authors in this volume are, by any measure, weighted toward the philosophy side of the scale, as measured at least by departmental affiliations but also, probably, by approach and method in ways that we can recognize but not explicitly define. This respects the assigned title for the volume and is one way to maintain unity and mutual engagement among the pieces, but it is not meant to suggest that the best work on all of these topics is being done in philosophy departments.[5]

1. The Era of Rawls

The work of John Rawls, even more than that of Robert Nozick, continues to exert enormous influence and is mentioned in the text or bibliography of about two-thirds of the chapters in this volume.[6] The pieces were commissioned, of course, and so it is not a random sample of any kind, but I believe this reflects the continuing importance of Rawls's thought in current work in the field of political philosophy. It is certainly central (sometimes, of course, as a foil) to the current debates, as we can see from the chapters in this volume, about equality (see Anderson), justice (see Arneson), classical liberalism (see Tomasi and Brennan), social contract approaches (see Freeman), global justice (see Risse), and ideal and nonideal theory (see Swift and Stemplowska).

Rawls has long figured prominently in a certain received view, which I describe later, of how political philosophy has developed since the 1960s. As time goes on, that familiar story is looking less plausible, or at least greatly exaggerated in certain ways.[7] What accounts for the monumental reputation and influence of *A Theory of Justice* (Rawls 1971; hereafter *TJ*)? One common explanation is that the book appeared in 1971, when those on college campuses were feeling disconnected from urgent matters of gender, race, and war. Rawls's approach to political philosophy turned away from the academically fashionable view that philosophy was limited to logical and conceptual clarification. He confronted the great question of social justice head on, striking a chord with activists who were fighting against the sterility of academe.

But there is a puzzle about this story, this emphasis on Rawls's direct engagement with moral issues. When the book came out, students and faculty were clamoring for "relevance" in their studies. It is true that *TJ* was less sterile than most philosophy (written in English) of the preceding decades. On the other hand, Rawls himself studiously avoided joining the controversies that rocked American society in the 1960s. His defense of civil disobedience and conscientious refusal to obey certain laws was an exception; even there, he never said how these principles applied to current events. The book (unlike the man, I'm told) said nothing directly about the current civil rights controversies, the Vietnam war (the book was mostly finished by the time that war sent students into the streets), or feminism. Yet intellectuals moved by those events were galvanized by the idea that questions of social justice might be situated in such a broad and deep philosophical account, supported by powerful arguments drawing on the whole Western philosophical tradition from Socrates through Rousseau, Kant, Hegel, Marx, and Mill. The puzzle is this: How did such an abstract and learned treatment of the idea of social justice meet the needs of that turbulent and impatient time?

From his very earliest writing, Rawls wondered whether the contenders in certain reasonable but intractable controversies could be brought to see that they shared many important assumptions. If they could, then they might pursue their differences more productively on that common basis. At the beginning, the controversies he tried to steer around were esoteric philosophical disputes about the nature and knowability of moral claims in general. (Are all moral claims merely subjective in some way? Is there a moral reality independent of our moral thoughts? Can moral claims be logically derived from nonmoral ones?) In his later writing, the contentious disputes he sought to circumvent were those that arose when political actions were defended on the basis of sectarian religious principles or other deep convictions about the meaning of life.

In his other major book, *Political Liberalism*, Rawls (1993) spoke of philosophy's potential for reconciliation, though this can easily be misunderstood. Reconciliation can be a tepid, shameful stance when some of the contenders in the conflict are contemptible. Rawls loved the example of Lincoln's decision to go to war as the only way to prevent the spread of slavery and the splitting of the nation. But—and here is the familiar moral fact at the very center of Rawls's thought over the years—controversies arise even among reasonable, informed, morally decent people. In that case, Rawls thought, there are probably important issues that all sides agree on and important commitments on which their shared decency and reasonableness depend. The identification of that common ground, if it is possible, would promote a kind of reconciliation, although we still could not just retreat to our shared assumptions and avoid the need to make the difficult decisions about which we initially disagreed. The goal was not to banish conflict. But, Rawls thought, if we can find and articulate our shared principles and convictions, adjusting them when necessary to accommodate more specific convictions, at least we might narrow the range of disagreement. Some of the original contending views might turn out to be indefensible; new views might emerge that make better sense of the basic principles. Disagreement might then be pursued more productively.

The search for common ground is an exercise in abstraction, the bracketing of specifics to identify more general similarities and affinities among differing worldviews. The principles Rawls arrives at, then, are more or less familiar and unspecific in practice. This is, in my view, no indictment, but I doubt that Rawls can be appropriated by authors who believe that proper political philosophy should always be addressed to pressing problems and offer practical solutions. Rawls's two principles are, of course, in need of practical interpretation, and his own interpretation includes elements that are less familiar and more controversial than the principles themselves. He writes that "justice as fairness leaves open the question whether its principles are best realized by some form of property-owning democracy or by a liberal socialist regime" (Rawls 1990, xv). Each of these is conceived as an alternative to capitalism, and he goes to great lengths to distinguish property-owning democracy from the more familiar idea of a welfare state. However, the idea of property-owning democracy was not clarified and elaborated on by Rawls until many years after the publication of *TJ*. He admitted that it was not sufficiently distinguished from the conventional idea of a welfare state. The more radical ideas, then, had little to do with the overwhelming reception of the original book, even if they were already present in a nascent form.

Certainly, many have recognized the abstraction and generality of the two principles, including those who have objected to Rawls's emphasis on "ideal theory," which operates on unrealistic assumptions such as full compliance and a shared conception of justice that is public knowledge. This last set of issues is attracting new attention, partly owing to G. A. Cohen's fundamental critique of Rawlsian theory's contingency on nonmoral facts (Cohen 2008). I return to this issue later.

In a couple of other ways as well, a familiar narrative about Rawls's impact has failed to hold up over time. For example, Rawls developed an alternative to utilitarianism, and many seem (or seemed) to think that the victory was more or less complete and that utilitarianism was, for the most part, relegated to the history of thought. In recent decades, however, much of utilitarian thought has developed under the broader umbrella of "consequentialism," and there is no sign that it is an exhausted paradigm. Another example of premature obituaries some had written in the wake of Rawls's work is that many had come to think that Rawls's construction of a powerful normative theory of social justice without (so he thought) needing to take controversial stands on the metaphysics, semantics, or epistemology of moral claims showed that meta-ethics was, more or less, an irrelevancy bound to fade away.[8] Yet there is no doubt that while its dominance in the middle of the twentieth century is gone, it continues to thrive as a central area of moral philosophy well represented in the top philosophy journals.[9]

Rawls did not develop any detailed theory of whether and when there is an obligation to obey the law, one of the central questions in political philosophy since the subject's birth in ancient Greece. In work preceding *TJ*, Rawls (1964) had advanced a "principle of fair play," deriving from early work of H. L. A. Hart (1955) that was meant to explain political obligation, but this was largely abandoned in *TJ*. As a substitute, Rawls offered what he called a "natural duty of justice." The idea was not developed in any detail, and, as Simmons emphasizes in this volume, it faces important difficulties in explaining why a person might have stronger obligations to obey the laws of her own state than those of other just states (the "particularity problem").[10]

With the Rawlsian corpus now complete, it is possible to discern several of the main lines of inquiry that his work stimulated. An overview of developments in political philosophy since Rawls's *TJ* is hardly possible except through a lens with a Rawlsian tint. From the early reactions all the way to the most recent developments, the agenda has largely been set by Rawls's conception of the enterprise of political philosophy. As with any agenda, it has been a continuing occasion for debate rather than an uncontroversial blueprint, and much of the ensuing work has been highly original. In roughly chronological order, I briefly mention important strands of work that have focused around Nozick's libertarianism, the communitarian critique of liberalism, Marxist and egalitarian developments, the idea of deliberative democracy, the rise of global justice, and the debate about ideal theory. I begin out of order, however, with the communitarian critique, allowing the pairing of Nozick's libertarianism with the ensuing revitalization of Marxist and socialist perspectives.

2. The Communitarian Critique

One of the traditional criticisms of liberalism is that it places inappropriate emphasis on the individual person and her choices, to the neglect of social structures and their governing ideas into which every individual is already born. This line of critique is often traced to Hegel and has clear resonance in Marx, but its political implications might, in the hands of some authors, be either left-leaning or right-leaning as these ideas are normally conceived. Some communitarian authors have argued for a conservative respect for traditions, or for protection of communal groups and identities in their customary forms, while others have suggested that due respect for socially shared forms of life militates against the idea of "free markets" in which individuals' own ends drive change unfettered by any collective convictions about either justice or the good life. The several communitarian authors during this period differed from each other in many ways, and there is a large literature made up of responses and rejoinders.[11]

Michael Sandel's (1982) line of argument has become the best known, probably partly because it is aimed directly at Rawls, and it is relatively easy to explain how Rawls might reply (which is not to prejudge whether the reply is successful). Sandel argued that Rawls was committed to a false view of the nature of moral agents, one that understood them as little more than choosers. If, as Sandel argued, people are always already committed to various aims and ends inherited from the social settings in which they are born, the Rawlsian (and, so Sandel thought, Kantian) conception of a person was suspect. In turn, it would be confused to try social norms, such as a public conception of justice, at the bar of rational individual choice in the way the Rawls's famous original position proposed to do.

In the same period that Sandel was writing, Rawls's thought was undergoing an important development. Rawls came to believe that it was inappropriate to ground a public conception of justice on any "comprehensive" doctrines—including those about the metaphysical nature of persons or agents—when these were subject to reasonable controversy. He endeavored to reconstruct his justification for his theory of justice in a way that respected this new (or at least more explicit) constraint and so eschewed any foundations in such controversial philosophical views as the nature of persons, the existence or nature of a divine order, and much more. Sandel's own conception of persons as essentially "situated" would then be ineligible for inclusion in a justification of a public conception of justice, which must be a "political conception" of justice—devised for purposes of political justification but without trampling on matters of reasonable controversy. This does not yet explain, of course, how the device of the original position finds its way back in, and Rawls offers an elaborate account in *Political Liberalism*. The critique of liberalism as overly individualistic can take numerous forms and has hardly gone away, but relatively little recent work is framed in terms of debate between liberalism and communitarianism.

Important strands of feminist philosophy resonated with the critique of liberalism's individualism (Nussbaum 1999, 2002), although much of the feminist critique—again, taking Rawls as the focus—alleged that it was not individualistic enough because it subsumed women in "the family" (Okin 1989, Kymlicka 1990; also see Satz on gender in this volume). Important debates about the tension, as some believe, between liberal principles and the claims of culture interacted with the literatures stemming from the feminist and communitarian critiques of liberalism, though, for better or worse and not necessarily forever, all three of these have noticeably died down considerably in the past ten years.

3. Nozick and Liberty

In the 1970s and into the 1980s, the names of Rawls and Robert Nozick were tightly linked, as scholars worked through the direct challenges that Nozick's *Anarchy, State, and Utopia* (Nozick 1977) and Rawls's *TJ* posed to each other.[12] From the beginning, liberal political philosophy asserted strong individual property rights and other economic liberties, and the definition of proper limits, and their moral grounds, has always been an important question.[13] Nozick, while following a Lockean tradition, developed a distinctive version of liberal thought in which justice required that individuals be free to give or exchange goods and labor as they freely choose, with any resulting distribution owing to its history in free exchange. Nozick, of course, criticized what he took to be Rawls's emphasis on coercively maintaining a certain egalitarian distributive pattern of economic goods, even though Nozick's own view of property rights was constrained by an important proviso (to leave, in Locke's phrase, "enough and as good for others"; Locke 1980[1689], 19; Nozick 1977, 178). Nozick's thought became an important stimulus to the thought of G. A. Cohen, who took its challenge to socialist and egalitarian political philosophy to be among the most important ever devised (Cohen 1995, 4). Cohen's persistent interrogation of Nozick's emphasis on the idea of self-ownership contributed to a novel approach to property rights labeled "left-libertarianism," according to which even as each person is their own owner, the world and its resources are naturally owned in common. Self-ownership, on that view, no longer grounds the laissez-faire economic arrangements to which Nozick was led.

The moral value of individual freedom, which was central to Nozick's approach, has been a perennial topic in Western political philosophy and was especially active for a period in the mid-century during which Isaiah Berlin's analysis of the concept exerted broad influence. Berlin (2002) famously distinguished between "negative liberty," in which a person is free, in certain choices, from the coercive interference of others, and "positive freedom" in which a person has the capacity and opportunity to do or choose certain things. Cohen's critique of Nozick explored these notions of freedom in illuminating ways, especially as part of his critique of capitalism. More recently, Philip Pettit has influentially proposed a third form of freedom conceived as "nondomination."[14]

4. Marx and Equality

In addition to Cohen's important assessment of the arguments of Nozick and Rawls, his first prominent work considered the central themes in the thought of Karl Marx. Marxism and socialism was a prominent ingredient in Anglophone political philosophy in the 1950s and 1960s, and after the appearance of Rawls's *TJ*, this quieted, to some extent, until the emergence of the important school of thought pioneered by, especially, Cohen, Roemer, and Elster.[15] The so-called analytical Marxists brought techniques from contemporary analytic philosophy and social science to central themes inspired rather directly from the writings of Marx. It is a puzzle (and one that is confronted head-on in Levine's chapter on "Marxist and Socialist Approaches" in this volume) that this line of work has virtually disappeared since around the early 1990s.[16] If, as some have suggested, this is partly explained by the fall of the Berlin Wall and the demise of the Soviet Union, that is perplexing. The failure of Soviet communism, morally, economically, and in other ways, had been widely acknowledged and was accepted even by the founders of analytic Marxism.[17] How, then, could the eventual crumbling of that system plausibly dampen the intellectual enterprise of defending Marxian or socialist principles and ideals? Levine offers a far more nuanced story and one that might lead us to expect some significant rebirth for work in that tradition, even if the nomenclature is likely to change in response to the pejorative connotations that now accompany the terms *communism*, *Marxism*, and, often, *socialism*.[18]

The language of *egalitarianism* is still, so far, entirely reputable, even though many would hotly dispute the value of its ideals. Large literatures have grown up in the past twenty years debating and developing the merits of various interpretations of distributive equality, including both the variety of egalitarian distributive principles and the goods that would be equally distributed according to those principles.[19] Some of the energy that had gone into frankly socialist and even Marxian studies has shifted into the study of egalitarian principles, and despite the linguistic advantage this provides, the shift is not only terminological, leaving largely behind the centrality of such concepts as class, exploitation, theories of economic history, and materialist theories of social explanation.

Among the authors spearheading the massive literature on the ideal of equality during this period (e.g., the 1970s to the present) is Ronald Dworkin (1977, 1981a, 1981b). Dworkin has always worked on a broad front, with ground-breaking work across the disciplines of moral and political philosophy, in addition to his canonical standing in the field of legal philosophy.[20] (Legal philosophy is a vast field in its own right, too large to be squeezed into a chapter or two in this volume, and so I have left it aside in the choice of topics.)

5. Deliberative Democracy

Just as the rise of egalitarian studies may have peeled away some of the interest in socialist ideas, the rise of theoretical interest in "deliberative democracy" also stems from, and has to some extent supplanted, some lines of work with more frankly Marxist or socialist roots—roots that are now nearly invisible if not entirely excised.

Beginning around 1971, when Rawls's *TJ* was published, the prevailing economic model of political agency, rationality, and morality in democratic theory came under increasing challenge. Rawls's own theory still owed much to that individual maximizing model, and yet it vividly presented a "veil of ignorance" as a normative device whose value did not rest on its ability to satisfy anyone's preferences but lay in its usefulness as a representation—or so Rawls hypothesized—of widely and firmly held convictions about freedom, equality, and justification. The enormous influence of Rawls's book revived a traditional approach to politics in which it was assumed that ascertaining the most effective means to satisfying people's desires was not the only way to reason about political matters. It reasserted the traditional objection to utilitarianism: that it could not seem to account for justice.

There are still many writers inclined to the narrower conception of reason and value characteristic of the economic approach, and there is no shortage of brilliant utilitarian moral philosophers. But the broader view of reason and value characteristic of Rawls now plays a much larger role than before.

Around this same time, the economists' conception of agency and value was influentially challenged by Amartya Sen (e.g., 1977). Sen's main challenge did not lie in the presentation of a moral alternative to utilitarianism (though he also has offered such an alternative [e.g., 1984]). Rather, Sen's greatest influence on current political philosophy has been to challenge the narrow economic emphasis on the satisfaction of an agent's preferences. One side of the challenge, pursued also by others, is to argue that certain common ways of emphasizing preference satisfaction give rise to an odd and incoherent view of human agency. Another side is to note the obvious ways in which a person's preferences can be nosy or trivial (Scanlon 1975), uninformed (many emphasized), or irrationally formed in other ways (Elster 1983).

Attention to preference formation may seem to call for theoretical and empirical investigations into individual and social psychology and pathology, a route that Elster and others pioneered to important effect. But thinking about preference formation was led in a different direction by the work of Habermas. Habermas's normative vision began in an "ideal discourse" in which all affected parties join to discuss the merits of practical proposals under conditions of severe deliberative equality. The preferences that ought to matter, this tempts many to say, are those that are formed under that kind of egalitarian practical deliberation. However, Habermas's work and its suggestiveness for democratic theory required intermediaries, because, first of all, he wrote in German and his work was translated into English only after significant delays. In addition, while many of Habermas's concerns were shared by philosophers writing in English, his work drew on many less familiar sources and proceeded in a style that many found overly complex and obscure. Nevertheless, his influence has been profound. Perhaps the most important intermediary was Joshua Cohen (1986), whose early papers drew parallels and built bridges between several central themes of Habermas and the ideas of Rawls. Cohen's emphasis on democratic ideals, which are not prominent in Rawls, drew illuminating links between Rawls's liberalism and Habermas's socialism and also between Rawls's emphasis on substantive justice and Habermas's emphasis on legitimate procedure. The ensuing literature on democratic political deliberation is large and still growing.[21]

6. Public Reason

Closely associated with these deliberative themes in democratic theory is a new emphasis on "public reason." Rawls, again, largely pioneered this direction with his elaboration of the connection between the core ideas of justification in a liberal philosophical framework on one hand and the proper nature and content of public political discourse aimed at justifying laws and policies on the other. The core of the Rawlsian approach is a principle of political justification, with secondary implications about the proper conduct of citizens and officials in public political discourse. It would be possible to take up, in a more independent way, ethical questions about how to conduct oneself in public discussion. There is work, for example, on the question of "civility"—whether public discourse should remain within certain limits of politeness and mutual respect, and what sorts of behavior fall outside these limits. Despite some common misunderstandings of Rawls encouraged by his discussion of what he calls "the duty of civility," the questions about public reason arising from his underlying conception of political justification are quite different and have little to do with some political counterpart of norms of politeness. That conflation has led to exaggerated concerns that a Rawlsian approach leads to excessive limits and restrictions on what may properly take place in the public sphere. Nothing in the Rawlsian account of public reason has any particular implications, for example, about whether public political discourse may properly be sharp, discomfiting, or confrontational, nor does it imply that everyone's view ought to be treated with equanimity, as if any view has as much merit as any other. It implies only that, first, a political justification fails in its moral task if it draws on doctrines that are open to reasonable disagreement (where "reasonable" is a term of art with its meaning given by theory, not by ordinary language). If this first step is accepted, then a further corollary about conduct might follow quite naturally: Citizens and officials ought to refrain from offering such specious justifications as if they were genuine justifications. Whether or not one accepts this view about justification and public conduct, it hardly implies that controversial worldviews are to be kept out of public discourse, as many have thought.

Even with that clarification of the Rawlsian approach to public reason, there is plenty of room for dispute about it. Much of the opposition has come from authors concerned that it may be incompatible with some forms of religious conviction. Questions about the proper place of religious thought and discourse in a liberal and democratic political system are traditional, but they have become more prominent since Rawls's influential reformulation of liberal political philosophy in *Political Liberalism*.[22] Certainly, some liberal approaches to political justification are frankly secularist, denying that political arrangements can have their moral ground ultimately in the realm of the divine. The Rawlsian view, however, hopes to avoid that view. Because, as Rawls and many followers assume, a religious comprehensive outlook need not be unreasonable from a political point of view, such views are among those that may not be assumed or contradicted within the terms of a genuine and sound political justification. The aim, then, is not a secular one, and it is allowed that the principles of justification and public reason could themselves have a theistic metaphysical and moral basis. But, of course, this may not be assumed any more than it may be denied without transgressing the bounds of public reason—the fund of doctrines available for use in political justification.

7. Ideal Theory

Rawls's privileging of ideal theory (for methodological reasons) has long drawn criticism, but the work of G. A. Cohen (for several decades, but culminating in Cohen 2008) cast a new light on the question of ideal and nonideal theory generally, and on Rawls's method in particular. Cohen argues, in effect, that Rawlsian method (deeply and irretrievably) traffics in brute facts, incongruously (he thinks) folding them into the very mortar from which the conception of justice is constructed. This critique of Rawls goes to the heart of the enterprise of political philosophy and strikingly calls for an even more idealized approach than the Rawlsian ideal theory can accommodate. (See Stemplowska and Swift's chapter, "Ideal and Nonideal Theory," in this volume.)

8. Global Justice

Foundational questions in philosophy are among the most abstract questions there are, such as what kinds of things exist, what counts as knowing something, and whether anything is objectively wrong. But, of course, philosophers are, as much as anyone, challenged, inspired, frightened, and otherwise moved by the whole range of human experience. Thus, even as some lines of inquiry are driven at least partly intellectually, many are also driven partly by other factors, including events in the world outside the academy. Just one vivid example is the increased attention by philosophers to moral questions around the rise of human interaction across national boundaries and around the world. One traditional set of such questions has concerned the moral problems raised by war, and there have been small waves of important new work stimulated by the Second World War, the war in Vietnam, and more recently the several wars that followed on the terrorist attacks on the United States in 2001.[23]

Perhaps the most historically important development in political philosophy in recent years has been the new embrace of the global level of analysis. There is more intense philosophical discussion, for example, about whether the idea of social justice applies at the global level than there has probably ever been before. While there is a long history of reflection on such questions, prior to about 1990 this literature was small compared with work in which the single nation-state was assumed to be the unit whose political arrangements were in question.[24]

This new activity is often referred to under the rubric of "global justice," but that might misleadingly suggest a narrower inquiry than is intended. There is new attention to such issues as relations between nations, limited autonomy or secession of subnational communities, the legitimate structures and powers of governmental and nongovernmental institutions that operate internationally, the proper principles of just policies of immigration, and more. Among these topics, the question of justice across generations has been increasingly active as well, and many of these questions, though not all, involve questions about interactions between distinct nations. Sometimes, for example, the question is whether a later generation is responsible or liable (for, say, apologies, reparations, or affirmative action policies) in certain ways for unjust imperialistic abuses. In other cases, as in the oppression of certain domestic minority groups, there is no international element.[25] A related question that has also attracted much interest recently is whether and in what ways justice is owed to future generations. A central puzzle is that which actions are taken now will often influence not just how future people will fare but also which people will exist at all—a special complication that is not present in questions about duties of justice to past or present people.[26] One area in which activity is rapidly increasing is the set of moral and moral/political questions around the problem of climate change. If burdens must be endured to slow or reverse the human-made damage that is producing climate changes, there are difficult questions about how they should be distributed. Certain countries have certainly produced disproportionate amounts of the damage, and this is true even after such time as they should have well understood the general nature of the effects of their uses of carbon-producing energy. The questions about justice across generations are salient in this case. Are those who were not yet alive during the offending periods still morally liable to have the greater burdens imposed on them? And, insofar as certain consumption-reducing policies will result in different individuals being born in the future than otherwise would have been, who are the individuals to whom an improved system of environmental practices is owed?[27]

9. New Directions

In a spirit of adventure, we might wonder where the field will head in the next decade or two. In the spirit of cowardice, I refrain from predicting. Still, it does seem to me that there is room for reflection about some developments that would make sense in one way or another.

As is often said, there is an expanding circle of equality in Western moral and political philosophy. Yet even as the circle moves outward from blinkered beginnings, it is important not to ignore the progress that continues to be made (and that which needs yet to be made) well within what is now familiar territory. We are long past the time in which racial and gender divisions are frankly posited as the outer limit of moral or political equality.[28] The circle of equality is expanding further to break down invidious discrimination on grounds of sexual orientation. In a different way, because the relevant scope of equality is bound to be different in this case, the circle is expanding to bring the interests of animals within the ambit of moral and political thought. The question of the significance of national boundaries also sometimes takes the form of an expanding circle, as when some "cosmopolitan" authors argue that a proper moral egalitarian philosophy is committed to conceptions of justice at (at least) the global level.

Reflection on injustices done by one people to another in the past is a kind of expansion of the circle of moral concern as well. Such injustice, much of it imperialistic, has often been committed in the thrall of inegalitarian views about certain racial or cultural groups. Even if the time has long since passed when such bigoted views would be broadly embraced—that circle expanded long ago—there is always more work to be done within the new and better radius, as I have said. One such project has been to take some present action on grounds of apology, reparation, or other kinds of remedy or contrition. As rich and difficult as these ideas are even in relations among individuals, further difficulties surround the arguably collective nature of the victims and the associated questions about how long that entity, and indeed the perpetrating collective, continue to exist over time. Whether collectives themselves are moral agents or subjects at all, and, if they are, what correctly defines their identity conditions constitute difficult questions about where the circle is to be drawn.

Obviously, expansion of the circle (to stick with that oversimplified image) is not worthwhile merely as such. There would (I think) be no value to recognizing forks or asteroids as within the scope of individuals who are owed respectful treatment. Still, it is not difficult to anticipate several of the directions of expansion that might become increasingly significant, such as children (Archard 2011), the disabled (Nussbaum 2006 and Silvers 1994), the elderly (Gheaus 2009 and Cupit 1998). the natural environment (including both flora and fauna; Regan 2001 and Fox 2007), extraterrestrial life (if any; Werth 1998), and artificial minds, if such a thing is possible (Lin, Abney and Bekey in press and Bostrom and Yudkowsky 2011).

Putting aside the expanding circle of beings whose interests and agency are brought into the ambit of moral concern, there are other frontiers in political philosophy. Rather than predict, with inevitable failure, what will happen next, I simply note a few issues that seem poised for fruitful engagement in new ways.

"The state" may be an area that deserves revival in light of accelerated globalization of our legal, cultural, and economic lives. It is a traditional topic, but the traditional emphasis on the nation-state is increasingly disputed. What would count as a "world state?" What forms might a stateless political order take? What structures other than the state provide appropriate units or levels for normative political analysis?

As of this writing, the Arab Spring of 2011 continues.[29] This might well stimulate reflection on subversion and revolution, a quiet topic since the 1970s,[30] as well as questions about whether it is in the nature of liberalism and democracy to spread.

Since the attack on the World Trade Center on September 11, 2001, there has been more work on questions around terrorism and counterterrorism, a set of questions closely connected to the traditional and renewed literature on moral questions of war. Warfare has changed, but "asymmetrical" conflicts may call for reflection going well beyond that paradigm.

The explosion of new methods for storing, processing, and communicating information associated with, especially, cable and satellite television, personal computers, the Internet, and cellular phones might naturally give rise to fundamental revisions in the traditional paradigms of political communication and deliberation. How do candidates and officials communicate with each other and with voters and constituents, and how should this affect our conceptions of political legitimacy? How should the concept of distribution of communicative resources be formulated?[31] What new modes are there for the expression of dissent and for the dissemination of propaganda, and what institutional innovations, if any, do these changes call for?

10. Reading Suggestions

Few, I'm afraid, will read this book cover to cover. I close with some reading suggestions, pulling together several of the chapters in potentially fruitful ways that I have not been able to indicate by my groupings in the table of contents.

- *Property, Nozick, Left-Libertarianism, Justice, Classical Liberalism*
- *Equality, Marxist and Socialist Perspectives, Global Justice*
- *Rawls, Deliberation, Religion and Politics*
- *Race, Gender, Historical Injustices*

I encourage the reader to devise others.

NOTES

1. I am grateful to Tim Syme for excellent research assistance and to John Simmons and Leif Wenar for comments on an earlier draft.
2. For a more historical approach, see Klosko 2011, as well as several recent "companion" volumes to figures such as Mill (Skorupski 1998), Arendt (Villa 2001), Smith (Haakonssen 2006), Dewey (Cochran 2010), and Hobbes (Lloyd in press).
3. See Wenar on "Rawls" and Schmidtz and Freiman on "Nozick" in this volume.
4. This set of issues is canvassed in Stemplowska and Swift's chapter on "Ideal and Nonideal Theory" in this issue.
5. See Dryzek 2006.
6. See Wenar's chapter on "Rawls" in this volume.
7. I draw here on one of my earlier articles (Estlund 2003).
8. In Darwall, Gibbard, and Railton (1992, 140), the authors discuss several ways in which Rawls's method might be seen as circumventing meta-ethics.
9. A few illustrative examples are Darwall (2003), Gibbard (2007), Railton (in press), Schroeder (2008), and Street (2006).
10. See Simmons' chapter, "Authority," in this volume.
11. For a bibliography that includes many of these pieces see Bell (2009).

12. See the chapter on "Nozick" by Schmidtz and Freiman in this volume.
13. See the chapter by Gaus, "Property," and the chapter by Tomasi and Brennan, "Classical Liberalism," in this volume.
14. See the chapter by Petti, "Freedom," in this volume.
15. See pertinent references in Levine (this volume).
16. In addition to Cohen (1995), two important works in the "analytical Marxism" school are Elster (1985) and Elster (1982). The shift in focus over time is illustrated by the work of John Roemer. In the 1980s, Roemer published explicitly Marxist works, while the 1990s saw him shift emphasis to general questions of distributive justice such as equality of opportunity (Roemer 1989). Roemer published no papers explicitly about Marxist economic theory after 1992.
17. Roemer demonstrates his ambivalence, if not actual antipathy, towards the Soviet regime when he suggests that it is an open question for Marxists such as himself whether the Soviet Union qualifies as "capitalist, socialist or something else" (Roemer 1989, 5). Elster notes that the Soviet regime has "manifestly" failed to realize the type of regime Marx himself favored and denies that armed revolution could ever bring about such a regime (Elster 1986, 5).
18. See Wolff (2002) for an argument that Marx's ideas continue to have relevance in the twenty-first century.
19. See Anderson's chapter on "Equality" and Arneson's chapter on "Justice" in this volume.
20. I cite here only some seminal early work on equality. Dworkin's thinking continues to develop, and his many themes are given a comprehensive treatment in his most recent book (Dworkin 2011).
21. See Waldron on "Democracy," Talisse on "Deliberation," and Christiano on "Money and Politics" in this volume.
22. See Audi on "Religion and Politics" and Wenar on "Rawls" in this volume.
23. See McMahon on "War" in this volume.
24. See the chapters on "Global Justice" by Risse and "Human Rights" by Buchanan in this volume. The massive increase in scholarly work on global justice since 1990 is clearly illustrated by a search for the term on JSTOR, one of the main databases of academic work: There are 678 such references from the years 1900 to 1989 and 3,551 from 1990 to 2010.
25. See Spinner-Halev on "Historical Injustice" in this volume.
26. See, for example, Gosseries and Meyer (2009) and Meyer (2010).
27. See Gardiner (2004), Gardiner (2011), and Bou-Habib (2010).
28. See the chapters by Satz on "Gender" and Shelby on "Race" in this volume.
29. See the excellent and substantial timeline of these events in the Bligh and Pulham (2011).
30. Though see Noah Smith(2008).
31. See Christiano's chapter on "Money and Politics" in this volume.

REFERENCES

Archard, David W. 2011. "Children's Rights." In *The Stanford Encyclopedia of Philosophy*. Edited by Edward N. Zalta. Stanford, CA: Stanford University.
Bell, Daniel. 2009. "Communitarianism." In *The Stanford Encyclopedia of Philosophy*. Edited by Edward N. Zalta. Stanford, CA: Stanford University.

Berlin, Isaiah. 2002. "Two Concepts of Liberty." In *Liberty: Incorporating Four Essays on Liberty*. Edited by Henry Hardy. Oxford: Oxford University Press.

Bligh, Garry, and Sheila Pulham. 2011. "Arab Spring: An Interactive Timeline of Middle East Protests." *The Guardian* (June 8). Available from http://www.guardian.co.uk/world/interactive/2011/mar/22/middle-east-protest-interactive-timeline.

Bostrom, Nick, and Eliezer Yudkowsky. 2011. "The Ethics of Artificial Intelligence." In *The Cambridge Handbook of Artificial Intelligence*. Edited by William Ramsey and Keith Frankish. Cambridge, UK: Cambridge University Press.

Bou-Habib, Paul. 2010. "Climate Change, Justice and Future Generations." *Journal of Moral Philosophy* 7(1): 151–53.

Cochran, Molly, ed. 2010. *The Cambridge Companion to Dewey*. Cambridge, UK: Cambridge University Press.

Cohen, Gerald A. 1995. *Self-ownership, Freedom and Equality*. Cambridge, UK: Cambridge University Press.

Cohen, Joshua. 1989. "The Economic Basis of Deliberative Democracy." *Social Philosophy and Policy* 6: 25–50.

Cohen, Gerald A. 2008. *Rescuing Justice and Equality*. Cambridge, MA: Harvard University Press.

Cupit, Geoffrey.1998. "Justice, Age, and Veneration." *Ethics* 108(4): 702–18.

Darwall, Stephen. 2003. "Moore, Normativity, and Intrinsic Value." *Ethics* 113(3): 468–89.

Darwall, Stephen, Allan Gibbard, and Peter Railton. 1992. "Toward Fin de siècle Ethics: Some Trends." *The Philosophical Review* 101(1): 115–89.

Dryzek, John, ed. 2006. *The Oxford Handbook of Political Theory*. Oxford: Oxford University Press.

Dworkin, Ronald. 1977. *Taking Rights Seriously*. Cambridge, MA: Harvard University Press.

Dworkin, Ronald. 1981a. "What is Equality? Part 1: Equality of Welfare." *Philosophy and Public Affairs* 10(3): 185–246.

Dworkin, Ronald. 1981b. "What is Equality? Part 2: Equality of Resources." *Philosophy and Public Affairs* 10(4): 283–345.

Dworkin, Ronald. 2011. *Justice for Hedgehogs*. Cambridge, MA: Harvard University Press.

Elster, John. 1982. *A General Theory of Exploitation and Class*. Cambridge, MA: Harvard University Press.

Elster, John. 1983. *Sour Grapes*. Cambridge, UK: Cambridge University Press.

Elster, John. 1985. *Making Sense of Marx*. Cambridge, UK: Cambridge University Press.

Elster, John. 1986. *An Introduction to Karl Marx*. Cambridge, UK: Cambridge University Press.

Estlund, David. 2003. "The Audacious Humility of John Rawls." *Dissent* 50(2): 89–91.

Fox, Warwick. 2007. *A Theory of General Ethics: Human Relationships, Nature and the Built Environment*. Cambridge, MA: MIT Press.

Gardiner, Stephen M. 2011. "Climate Justice." In *The Oxford Handbook of Climate Change and Society*. Edited by John S. Dryzek, Richard B. Norgaard, and David Schlosberg. Oxford: Oxford University Press.

Gardiner, Stephen M. 2004. "Ethics and Global Climate Change." *Ethics* 114(3): 555–600.

Gheaus, Anca. 2009. "The Challenge of Care to Idealizing Theories of Distributive Justice." In *Feminist Ethics and Social and Political Philosophy: Theorizing the Non-Ideal*. Edited by Lisa Tessman. New York: Springer.

Gibbard, Allan. 2007. "Thinking How to Live Together." In *The Tanner Lectures on Human Values*, Vol. 27. Edited by Grethe B. Peterson, 165–226. Salt Lake City: University of Utah Press.

Gosseries, Axel, and Lukas Meyer. 2009. *Intergenerational Justice*. Oxford: Oxford University Press.
Haakonssen, Knud, ed. 2006. *The Cambridge Companion to Adam Smith*. Cambridge, UK: Cambridge University Press.
Hart, Herbert. L. A. 1995. "Are There Any Natural Rights?" *The Philosophical Review* 64: 175–91.
Klosko, George, ed. 2011. *The Oxford Handbook of the History of Political Philosophy*. Oxford: Oxford University Press.
Kymlicka, W. 1989. *Liberalism, Community, and Culture*. Oxford: Oxford University Press.
Kymlicka, W. 1990. "Feminism." In *Contemporary Political Philosophy: An Introduction*. Oxford: Oxford University Press.
Lin, Patrick, Keith Abney, and George A. Bekey, eds. 2011 *Robot Ethics: The Ethical and Social Implications of Robotics*. Cambridge, MA: MIT Press.
Lloyd, Sharon A. In press. *Continuum Companion to Hobbes*. New York: Continuum Press.
Locke, John. 1980. *Second Treatise on Government*. Edited by Crawford. B. Macpherson. London: Hackett. (Originally published 1689)
Meyer, Lukas. 2010. "Intergenerational Justice." In *The Stanford Encyclopedia of Philosophy*. Edited by Edward N. Zalta. Stanford, CA: Stanford University.
Noah Smith, Matthew. 2008. "Rethinking Sovereignty, Rethinking Revolution." *Philosophy & Public Affairs* 36(4): 405–40.
Nozick, Robert. 1977. *Anarchy, State and Utopia*. New York: Basic Books.
Nussbaum, Martha. 1999. "The Feminist Critique of Liberalism." In *Sex and Social Justice*. Oxford: Oxford University Press.
Nussbaum, Martha. 2002. "Rawls and Feminism." In *Cambridge Companion to Rawls*. Edited by Samuel Freeman. Cambridge, UK: Cambridge University Press.
Nussbaum, Martha. 2006. *Frontiers of Justice: Disability, Nationality, Species Membership*. Cambridge, MA: Belknap Press of Harvard University Press.
Okin, S. M. 1989. *Justice, Gender, and the Family*. New York: Basic Books.
Railton, Peter. In press. "Staying in Touch with Normative Reality." *Philosophical Studies*.
Rawls, John. 1964. "Legal Obligation and the Duty of Fair Play." In *Law and Philosophy: A Symposium*. Edited by Sydney Hook, 3–18. New York: New York University Press.
Rawls, John. 1971. *A Theory of Justice*. Cambridge, MA: Belknap Press.
Rawls, John. 1983. *Political Liberalism*. New York: Columbia University Press.
Rawls, John. 1990. *A Theory of Justice*, 2d ed. Cambridge: MA: Belknap Press.
Regan, Tom. 2001. *Defending Animal Rights*. Champaign: University of Illinois Press.
Rehfeld, Andrew. 2010. "Offensive Political Theory." *Perspectives on Politics* 8: 465–86.
Roemer, John. 1989. *Analytical Foundations of Marxian Economic Theory*. Cambridge, MA: Press Syndicate of Cambridge University.
Sandel, Michael. 1982. *Liberalism and the Limits of Justice*. New York: Cambridge University Press.
Scanlon, Thomas. M. 1975. "Preference and Urgency." *Journal of Philosophy* 72(19): 655–69.
Schroeder, Mark. 2008. "Expression for Expressivists." *Philosophy and Phenomenological Research* 76(1): 86–116.
Sen, Amartya K. 1977. "Rational Fools: A Critique of the Behavioral Foundations of Economic Theory." *Philosophy & Public Affairs* 6(4): 317–44.
Sen, Amartya. 1985. "Well-Being, Agency and Freedom: The Dewey Lectures 1984." *Journal of Philosophy* 82(4): 169–221.
Silvers, Anita. 1994. "'Defective' Agents: Equality, Difference and the Tyranny of the Normal." *Journal of Social Philosophy* 25(1): 154–75.

Smith, Matthew Noah. 2008. "Rethinking Sovereignty, Rethinking Revolution." *Philosophy & Public Affairs* 36(4): 405–40.
Skorupski, John, ed. 1998. *The Cambridge Companion to Mill.* Cambridge, UK: Cambridge University Press.
Street, Sharon. 2006."A Darwinian Dilemma for Realist Theories of Value." *Philosophical Studies* 127(1): 109–66.
Villa, Dana, ed. 2001. *The Cambridge Companion to Hannah Arendt.* Cambridge, UK: Cambridge University Press.
Werth, Lee F. 1998. "The Anthropocentric Predicament and the Search for Extra-Terrestrial Intelligence (the Universe as Seen Through Our Eyes Darkly)." *Journal of Applied Philosophy* 15(1): 83–88.
Wolff, Jonathan. 2002. *Why Read Marx Today?* Oxford: Oxford University Press.

PART I

Classic Questions

CHAPTER 1

AUTHORITY

A. JOHN SIMMONS

1. THE CONCEPT OF AUTHORITY

Thomas Hobbes, writing in the middle of the seventeenth century, offered this definition of authority: "the right of doing any action is called AUTHORITY" (Hobbes 1968, 218; xvi, para. 4). Hobbes was in this passage exploring the concept of authority at work in his account of the *political* authority of the sovereign person (or body) in a society. In another, slightly later work, Hobbes wrote, "I call authorities anyone in any subject whose precept or example is followed, because one hath been led thereto by a belief in their wisdom" (Hobbes 1972, 67; [*De Homine*, XIII, 7]). Here Hobbes was enumerating the six sources of "men's inclinations," one of which is our disposition to conform our conduct to the teachings of those we regard as wise. The two quite different notions of authority utilized by Hobbes in these two passages correspond to what contemporary theorists call *practical authority* and *theoretical* [or *epistemic*] authority.

Practical authorities are those whose commands or pronouncements give us distinctive kinds of reasons to act in accordance with them. Theoretical authorities are experts on their subjects. In both cases, our recognition of a pronouncement as issued from an authority provides us with reasons to act or to believe that are both *peremptory* and *content independent* (Hart 1982, 261). When accepted authorities tell us what to do or believe, we have reason to simply comply. Their status as authorities gives us reasons to do what they say even when we cannot ourselves discern, confirm, or appreciate the reasons they have for what they tell us. Similarly, pronouncements by authorities give us reasons that are independent of the actual content of the pronouncement. We have reason to believe an expert even when what he or she has asserted turns out to be false. Again, it is the mere status of the pronouncement as authoritative that establishes its reason-giving force.

The distinction between theoretical and practical authority is usually drawn in terms of the kinds of reasons given to us by exercises of those two kinds of authority: "Expert advice gives reason for belief, not action" (Green 1988, 27). It is only exercises of practical authority that give us reasons to act. Some theorists have tried to minimize this difference, characterizing practical authority as really just a complicated kind of theoretical authority (see the discussions in Green 1988, 27–28, and Raz 1986, 28–31). While that is mistaken (since practical authorities, such as political authorities, need not be experts on any subjects at all), the connection between theoretical and practical authority is actually stronger than it might at first seem. Most of us believe that those who have practical authority over us—our political or religious leaders, our military commanders, our judges or police officers—ought also to be experts or to possess genuine wisdom in their relevant domains, and reasons for belief regularly provide us with reasons for action, especially when they are reasons for believing that something is best done in a recommended fashion. What theoretical authority alone cannot give the expert, it seems, is a right that we act on those reasons. No expert has any special *right* that we act in one way or another merely in virtue of their expert pronouncements or could claim to be wronged by someone's utterly disregarding their expert "precepts or examples" (Green 1988, 27).

If practical authority—our primary concern here—does in fact consist of having a *special* right with respect to the actions of others, how should we understand that right? First, the right in question must indeed be some kind of special right, not a right shared by all or most people. While I, along with all of my fellow citizens, have a legal right to practice my preferred religion—and, in consequence, a right that others refrain from interfering with that practice—it would be deeply odd to say that this amounts to my possessing legal authority in that domain. But even when we focus on special, not generally shared rights, not all such rights seem to constitute authority. Suppose that I have made a promise to lend you my car on Friday. While we would then say that you have a special right to use my car on that day (and I have a special obligation to permit you to use it), we would be unlikely to say that you, as a result, "have authority over me (or over my car)" for the day. We might at most say that I had "authorized" your use of the car.

Suppose, by contrast, that I promise to spend the weekend helping you in whatever ways (within reason) you say would be most useful to you. While we might still simply say that you had a right to my help, it would in this case be more natural (than in the previous case) to say that you had acquired a kind of authority over me—particularly if the promise was not a friendly or gratuitous promise but rather was made (for example) in payment of a debt. While the "authority" in question is plainly severely limited in both duration and content, what makes it natural to call it authority in the first place is that it consists of a right to *specify* what the precise content of the promissory obligation will be (by specifying what kinds of help will be most useful). While the authority arises from or is grounded in the promise, the precise content of the promise is left open for specification by the one to whom that authority is granted. When I authorize my financial adviser to use her judgment in making investments for me, I make myself responsible for the financial consequences of her decisions. She acquires through my consent the authority to specify what the precise contents of my financial obligations will be.

While practical authority is often characterized as the right to create new obligations for others, it is better characterized as the right to specify the content of their already-created but unspecific obligations. The authority of a state or government to impose on me a specific (and likely changing) set of legal obligations would most naturally be said to be grounded in some fact about its relationship to me (e.g., that I consented to its authority or that it benefitted me in ways requiring reciprocation) or in some fact about its virtues (e.g., that it was just or democratic). My generic obligation to the state would have its source in such performances or facts. The state's correlative authority would consist in its right to dictate (no doubt, within limits) what the precise content of my unspecific obligation—my generic obligation to obey the law or to support and comply with my government—shall be.

However, even agreement on this—on the concept of practical authority as a special right to specify the content of the unspecific or generic obligations of others—leaves ample room for substantive disagreement about the concept of authority, because the term "right" can be used in a variety of ways. Following Hohfeld (1964, 35–64)—whose well-known analysis of legal rights is applicable as well to the analysis of *moral* rights—"right" can refer either simply to the absence of an obligation or duty (on the rightholder) to refrain from doing something—a "privilege" or "liberty right" to act—or to a claim for the rightholder that correlates with the obligations of others not to interfere, called a "claim right." The right in question could also be what Hohfeld called a "power"—namely, a right to alter existing normative relations by changing others' (or one's own) rights or duties. So practical authority could simply be a liberty right to command and coerce others, which others are free to resist if able; or it might be a claim right to command, which others have a duty to permit the authority to exercise but with those commanded having no duty to comply with the commands; or, more plausibly, it might be a power to specify binding duties that also includes a right not to be interfered with (or competed with) in that task. Political authority, for instance, is most often thought of as the state's (or government's, or society's) moral power to specify citizens' legal and political duties (which citizens are morally bound to discharge), free from interfering or competing efforts by other nations (or their citizens) or by rival individuals or groups within the state. This moral power is commonly referred to as the state's or government's "right to rule."

We must draw one final distinction to identify precisely the concept of political authority with which we deal here. The term "authority" can refer either to de jure authority—where those with authority actually *possess* the rights of which we have said practical authority consists—or only de facto authority, where possessing authority consists merely in claiming, exercising, or being generally *believed* (by those subject to the authority or by suitable officials) to possess those rights. When we refer to "the authorities" (in speaking of "the [political and legal] powers that be"), we are usually referring to those who (or those bodies that) possess de facto practical authority, usually without our making any implicit commitment as to their de jure status. Indeed, "the authorities" may refer only to those assigned authority by the prevailing structure of institutional rules, even when few believe that the institutional structure itself is legitimate (or, worse, only to those who merely wield physical power while claiming to possess the authority to do so). De facto authority is nonetheless distinguishable from the mere exercise of physical power, in which a right to specify duties is neither claimed nor acknowledged.

It is not difficult to find treatments of political and legal authority that focus on de facto authority. For instance, Max Weber's famous discussion of "the three pure types of legitimate authority"—rational/legal authority, traditional authority, and charismatic authority (Weber 1947, 328)—is a discussion of the unmixed forms of de facto practical authority acknowledged in modern societies. The three types of authority are distinguished according to the kinds of claims to legitimacy each makes and by the kinds of beliefs of those who regard themselves as subject to the authority. "Authority" here is simply power accepted as legitimate by those subject to it (and "legitimacy" is correspondingly equated with a general belief in legitimacy).[1] If we are interested in issues of political stability, we will no doubt be interested in questions about de facto authority—that is, in understanding what kinds of claims to authority are regularly accepted by subjects.[2] But if we are interested in political *rights*—in the moral standing of states or governments and in the moral rights and duties of political life—then we will focus (as we do here) on the idea of de jure authority.

2. Varieties of Practical Authority: Hobbes and Locke

Instances of practical authority vary considerably in terms of duration, comprehensiveness, and inevitability. Employers, for instance, normally exercise practical authority over their employees, but the domains within which they have authority and the duration of that authority seem almost infinitely variable—compare, for example, servants, day-laborers, federal judges, and so on. Practical authority can be isolated or part of an elaborate and rigid hierarchical structure, as in the hierarchies of legal, military, or religious authority.[3] Our subjection to some kinds of authority is easy to avoid, while subjection to, for example, parental or political authority seems virtually inevitable (and subjection to God's authority would be absolutely inevitable). Some philosophers have tried to impose order on this apparent chaos by advancing unified accounts of practical authority—accounts that purport to explain the sources of all of these instances of authority in the same way. And because so many of these kinds of practical authority have been taken to flow from the *consent* of those subjected to them, a consent-based account of authority is a natural candidate for such unification.

Hobbes's theory of (practical) authority is a good example of such a unified, consent-based view. Hobbes writes that "by authority is always understood a right of doing any act; and *done by authority*, done by commission or license from him whose right it is" (Hobbes 1968, 218; xvi, para. 4, emphasis in original; see also Hobbes, 1972, 84; *De Homine*, XV, 2). When persons act "with authority," Hobbes suggests, they exercise rights that were originally held by others—rights conferred by those others on the person(s) they authorize to act on their behalf. Once authorities are thus created, their actions (in their authorized capacities) should be understood as in fact the actions of those who authorized them: The "words and actions [of authorities are] owned by those whom they represent" (Hobbes 1968, 218; xvi, para. 4). Authorization makes us the authors of others' actions, as if those other persons were our puppets or were performing parts we had written for them in a play. But in this case, unlike a real play or a puppet show, "authoring" another's actions instead amounts to our acting as if that other's acts were our own by taking responsibility for them in advance: "he is called the author, that hath declared himself responsible for the action done by another according to his will" (Hobbes 1972, 84; *De Homine* XV, 2). So we can hardly complain when our authorities act (or decline to act) within the terms of their "commissions"; their acts (or omissions) are "owned" by us. In the political case, for example, "every subject is . . . author of all the actions and judgments of the sovereign instituted," so that whatever the sovereign chooses to do "can be no injury to any of his subjects" (Hobbes 1968, 232; xviii, para. 6).

That authority is created by "license" or "commission," of course, suggests that all authority is grounded in the consent of those for whom authorities act. This "authorization" view of authority, however, surely seems an odd view to be embraced by Hobbes, the champion of absolute, unlimited monarchy and an apparent proponent of the view that "might makes right." This odd conjunction of views in Hobbes's philosophy is explained by another oddity—by his peculiar ideas about when consent may be "presumed" to have been given to the actions of an authority. Consent for Hobbes must, of course, be given freely. Otherwise, it is not an act by an agent at all but only behavior of that agent's body. So "unfree consent" is unintelligible. But freedom, for Hobbes, is the "absence of *external* . . . impediments of motion" (Hobbes 1968, 261; xxi, para. 1 [my emphasis]). *Internal* impediments—such as fear, even if caused by external agents—do not limit freedom. But this means, of course, that consent given to another's authority, even if given at sword-point and only out of fear for one's life, is nonetheless free, and hence binding, consent (Hobbes 1968, 262–63; xxi, paras. 2–4).

Further, Hobbes's (in)famous mechanistic materialism commits him, he thinks, to a broadly egoistic psychological theory according to which each person is motivated (either always or "predominantly") by his or her own perceived best interest (Kavka 1986, 50–51). For Hobbes, this implies especially that each person, unless confused by religious (or other) claptrap, seeks above all to stay alive. Finally, we are, Hobbes thinks, entitled to infer that, because each always seeks his or her own continued existence, each may be *presumed* to consent to any arrangement that is necessary to staying alive. If others seek authority over us and are able to kill us, we may therefore be presumed to consent to their authority over us: "Every man is supposed to promise obedience to him in whose power it is to save or destroy him" (Hobbes 1968, 254; xx, para. 5). And such presumed consent to the authority of the powerful still counts as free and binding, because the only "impediment" to our will is the internal (even if supremely influential) impediment of our fear of death. Thus, Hobbes's reputation as a defender of the doctrine that "might makes right" turns out to be a half-truth. Another's might (i.e., his power to dispose of us at will) in fact "makes" our binding (even if only presumed) consent to his authority, and that authority, in turn, renders his actions toward us rightful. All political consent, Hobbes claims, "proceed[s] from fear of death," whether the society begins in a "free" contract (by "institution") or in conquest (by "acquisition"; Hobbes 1968, 252; xx, para. 2).

Hobbes applies this same authorization account of authority to all varieties of practical authority, not just political authority. But as a political philosopher, Hobbes is primarily interested in instances of practical authority that—like political authority—are quite comprehensive and largely inevitable. Thus, the central cases he considers (other than political authority) are the practical authority possessed by conquerors, parents, and God. The "despotical" authority (or "dominion") of the conqueror over the conquered derives from the conquered person's agreement to accept servitude "to avoid the present stroke of death": "It is not . . . the victory that giveth the right of dominion over the vanquished, but his own covenant" (Hobbes 1968, 255–56; xx, paras. 10–11; Hobbes 1972, 205–8; *De Cive*, VIII, 1–5). The parental authority of mother over child is based on the child's presumed promise "to obey her, rather than any other" in response to the fact that "the infant is first in the power of the mother, so as she may either nourish or expose it" (Hobbes 1968, 254; xx, para. 5; Hobbes 1972, 211–13; *De Cive*, IX, 1–3). Even the authority of God is derived by Hobbes from God's "irresistible power," to which "the dominion of all men adhereth naturally" (Hobbes 1968, 397; xxxi, para. 5; Hobbes 1972, 292; *De Cive*, XV, 5).

One of the principal aims of John Locke's *Two Treatises of Government* is precisely to distinguish these varieties of de jure practical authority[4] (or moral power) from one another, both in terms of their sources or grounds and in terms of their contents and limits. In doing so, Locke rejects Hobbes's unified authorization account of authority, accepting that legitimate practical authority can flow from sources other than an authorizer's explicit or presumed consent. He resists in the process the temptation—to which both Hobbes and Robert Filmer (1991) succumbed—to conflate the salient categories of practical authority. Hobbes and Filmer had, in Locke's view, confused both parental and political authority with despotical authority. Hobbes supposed that both parental and political authority must be absolute (like despotical authority), because both arise from a presumed choice of absolute subjection over death. Filmer likewise viewed both as absolute, with both deriving from God's grant to Adam of absolute (despotical) dominion over the earth (with all subsequent political authority, including that of the Stuart monarchs, understood as the inherited political and paternal authority of Adam's descendants). But in fact, Locke argues, parental authority "comes as far short of" political authority as despotical authority "exceeds it" (Locke 1960, 384: II, 174).

For Locke, God's authority over humankind is perfectly *sui generis*, God being the only one with a creator's authority over (or property in) human beings. But the other important kinds of practical authority are different not only from God's but from each other. Parental authority is that of parents over their children "to govern over them for the children's good, till they come to the use of reason," and it is thus a nonabsolute, severely limited right. God entrusts children to their parents' care, giving parents only those rights over their children that they need to do the "duty which is incumbent on them to take care of their offspring during the imperfect state of childhood" (Locke 1960, 381, 306–7; II, 170, 58). Despotical authority, by contrast, actually is "an absolute, arbitrary power . . . over another," but it derives from neither superior power nor "from compact" with a powerful conqueror. Rather, "it is the effect only of forfeiture," whereby an aggressor who makes war on the innocent forfeits all moral standing and makes himself "liable to be destroyed," like "any other wild beast or noxious brute" (Locke 1960, 383; II, 172). It is only political authority that "has its original only from compact and agreement, and the mutual consent of those who make up the community," and that consensual authority is limited (by the "voluntary agreement" that creates it) to use "by governors for the benefit of their subjects [and] to secure them in the possession and use of their properties" (Locke 1960, 381–84; II, 171, 173).

Locke's position on practical authority is in part a response to natural worries about the authorizing force of consent once one's account of practical authority is no longer conjoined with Hobbes's peculiar conception of freedom. Even if (with Hobbes) we presume consent to one-sided terms by those vanquished in war or by vulnerable children, when we more reasonably (with Locke) take coerced consent or consent by prerational beings to be unfree, and so not morally binding (or perhaps not even to be consent at all, properly understood), any plausible analysis of despotical or parental authority that we give will have to abandon the idea of authority as authorization. If all de jure practical authority derived from the consent of those subject to it, we would need to accept the conclusion that parents have no such authority over their minor children—a conclusion that Locke, with most of his audience, finds unacceptable. Only in the case of political authority does Locke preserve the authorization account favored by Hobbes.

3. Political Authority and Its Grounds

We should not exaggerate, however, the extent to which Locke abandoned Hobbes's authorization account of practical authority. While he offered nonconsensual accounts of divine, despotical, and parental authority, Locke was very much committed to the authorization view—as are most contemporary persons—with respect to the many more mundane instances of practical authority in our lives, such as the authority of employers over their employees, teachers over their students, or military superiors over those of inferior rank. Locke's foundational assertion of our "natural freedom," of our natural moral right to govern ourselves within the bounds of morality, implies that consent-based authority is the most "natural" sort. For while authority always in one way limits our freedom (by making the specification of our duties subject to the will of another), authority that has been authorized by those subject to it can be characterized as "freedom freely surrendered" and so as a use of freedom rather than simply an abridgement of it. Indeed, Locke's accounts of divine, despotical, and parental authority are in fact exceptions to this general rule that are similarly motivated by Locke's focus on individual freedom. Parental authority must be nonconsensual, because children are incapable of genuinely free (rational) choice and can only become capable of it by their subjection to parental rule (Locke 1960, 308–9; II, 61). Despotical authority is the consequence of persons freely abandoning the life of freedom and reason, and their personhood along with it, and the exercise of divine authority over us is what gives us our rights to freedom in the first place.

The consent-based accounts of political authority that drive much of the social contract tradition thus flow from a concern to reconcile a strong presumption in favor of individual freedom with a reasonably comprehensive and inevitable state authority. Consent to authority allows unfreedom to nonetheless flow from the exercise of freedom. The primary question for early-modern theorists of authority was not whether freely undertaken restrictions on freedom were binding (or adequately respected individual liberty) but rather just how much freedom could be legitimately surrendered by free consent: whether, for example, slavery or absolute political authority could be legitimated by free consent. But if we assume (with Locke) that there are limits to what free consent can legitimate, the ideal of a voluntary political association yields a natural and compelling account of political authority, along with a correlative account of the political obligations of citizens[5]—understood as obligations to accept the state's (government's, society's) specifications of the general, consensually (or contractually) undertaken moral obligation to support and comply with the state.

Many rival, nonconsent-based theories of political obligation have either attempted to extend the idea of "freely undertaken unfreedom" that motivates consent theories or to identify uncontroversial limits to individuals' rights to freely govern themselves—limits within whose range the state's authority might then be taken to fall. Thus, for instance, accounts of political obligation that base it on the principle of fairness (or fair play) originally did so by emphasizing that free cooperative activity, even without any consent or promises, can produce obligations to do one's fair share within the cooperative scheme. Reciprocation and associative theories of political obligation argue that individual liberty does not extend so far that it allows us (in the first case) to take the benefits that flow to us from the efforts of others without responding to this benefaction in kind or (in the second case) to ignore the moral requirements of relationships like those with family or friends. These kinds of theories have been discussed extensively, and I do not explore their relative strengths and weaknesses here.[6] Let us focus instead on another, different way in which political authority might be thought to be potentially in conflict with individual freedom.

Suppose we think of individual freedom as not only a right, which persons may retain or freely transfer (or lay down) as they please—thus creating freely undertaken unfreedom—but also as a responsibility belonging to all persons. Since "taking responsibility involves attempting to determine what one ought to do" (Wolff 1998, 12), the price of real freedom—or *autonomy*—is an obligation to ourselves examine and weigh the reasons that bear on our actions and to follow where the balance of reasons leads. This more robust idea of freedom appears to be suggested in Rousseau and utilized centrally in Kant. If we think we have an obligation to be autonomous, though, we may well think that the demands of practical authority—and, in particular, of political authority—are in direct conflict with this obligation of autonomy: "The defining mark of the state is authority, the right to rule. The primary obligation of man is autonomy, the refusal to be ruled" (Wolff 1998, 18). The Lockean idea that political consent can "preserve and enlarge freedom"—by a free acceptance of general restrictions on freedom (Locke 1960, 305–6; II, 57)—appears suspect if by "freedom" we now mean "autonomy" of the Kantian sort. Political authorities require us to act as we are commanded and because we have been so commanded, which we cannot do while judging for ourselves how best to act.

The central question of political philosophy now becomes: Can the exercise of genuine political and legal authority be consistent with lives in which each citizen can still "obey only himself and remain as free as before"? (Rousseau 1997, 49–50; I, vi, para. 4). Wolff defends a negative answer to this question. There is no "viable form of political association which will harmonize the moral autonomy of the individual with the legitimate authority of the state." Given our primary obligation, we should "embrace philosophical anarchism and treat *all* governments as nonlegitimate bodies whose commands must be judged and evaluated in each instance before they are obeyed" (Wolff 1998, 69, 71, emphasis in original).

This conclusion, of course, rests on our being bound by an exceptionally strong moral obligation of autonomy. As even Wolff admits, an ideal of perfect autonomy might well seem a dubious goal, given that our ability to live our lives well would then be dependent on our acquiring a personal mastery of the myriad practical disciplines within whose domains we all now regularly rely on the testimony of experts. Worse, even making a simple promise in everyday life appears to violate such an obligation to remain perfectly autonomous, for it gives another the right to determine how we shall act, thus preempting our own judgment about how it is best to act. But neither Rousseau nor Kant, of course—nor the vast majority of moral or political philosophers—thinks that we breach a basic moral obligation by making a promise or contract. Indeed, neither Rousseau nor Kant thought that even mutual promises that create a political society (to which all in consequence owe obligations of support and compliance) necessarily involve any moral wrongdoing. This suggests that Wolff's conception of our obligation of autonomy is too strong to be plausible and that many voluntary sacrifices of autonomy—and the authority for others that these sacrifices may create—are perfectly innocent and uncontroversial.[7]

The defender of one of the most influential contemporary accounts of practical authority accordingly concludes that what is most problematic about authority is not that it seems irreconcilable with autonomy. Rather, Raz argues, the real problem about authority that needs to be addressed is a distinct though closely related one. The claims of authority appear, on their face, to require of us a kind of *practical irrationality*. Joseph Raz suggests that what is troubling about authority is that we take authoritative pronouncements as reasons for action of a special sort—a sort that preempts our own judgments about where the balance of reasons lies. We should obey authorities even when we think them mistaken in their commands, thus acting contrary to the perceived balance of reasons that apply to us (Raz 1990, 5). Authority seems to require individual irrationality.

Raz responds that this appearance rests on an impoverished (and mistaken) conception of practical reason. Some valid reasons for action are "second-order" and "exclusionary"; that is, we sometimes have reasons to act contrary to the "balance of first-order reasons"—to exclude their weight in determining what to do (Raz 1979, 27). This can be true, for example, when authoritative directives are at issue. Such directives claim to replace and exclude the ordinary reasons for action that should otherwise govern our deliberations. When there are good grounds for believing that we will do better by complying with an authority's directives than we would do by relying on the balance of reasons as we perceive it, it is rational to comply with authority rather than doing what seems best independent of its directives. Authority is then justified or legitimate. In this we see the strongest similarity between practical and theoretical authority. In both cases, we can have exclusionary reasons (to act or to believe), because someone's being an authority attests to the existence of such reasons even when we cannot perceive or weigh those reasons.

In the case of political authority, of course, we are likely to do better by complying with its directives only when the authorities are in fact aiming to "serve" those subject to authority (Raz's "service conception" of authority) by designing their commands and rules to help their subjects conform their conduct to the reasons that independently apply to them. When this is the case, treating the government's directives as binding may be the best way to conform to those reasons. Authoritative political/legal directives can then supply reasons that preempt and replace subjects' ordinary reasons for action. Compliance with authority is then practically rational (and obligatory); indeed, it is practically rational even when governmental directives are mistaken and fail to achieve their service-oriented aim[8]; the authority claimed by government is then justified or legitimate (de jure).

Raz argues that political authority can in fact be justified in this "normal" fashion in several kinds of cases, including cases in which the authority is "wiser" than the subject (possessing special expertise the subject lacks); the authority has a "steadier will" (one less prone to weakness, bias, etc.) than the subject; the authority can establish solutions to coordination problems that subjects have difficulty solving for themselves; self-direction by subjects is very costly or time-consuming (and guidance by the authority has few drawbacks); and the authority can solve prisoners' dilemma style problems, in which no individually rational paths to collectively rational solutions are possible (Raz 1986, 75).

One obvious consequence of this Razian position on de jure political authority, of course, is that claims to authority, even by apparently similar states or governments, may vary dramatically in terms of their justifiability. Different governments (or the same governments at different times) may have very different ranges of expertise, and their success at generating salient solutions to coordination problems may vary as well. Similarly, different citizens will have both different levels of personal expertise (in various domains) and different kinds of reasons that apply to them independent of authoritative pronouncements. This means, as Raz concedes, that we will have to think about the justification of authority rather differently than we are used to doing (Raz 1986, 73–78, 100, 104). We can no longer think that political authority is either justified or not *simpliciter*. Various aspects of the authority claimed by states may be justified where others are not, and authority may be justified with respect to some subjects but not others. Perhaps, though, Raz is correct that the all-or-nothing approach in our thinking about political authority needs to be abandoned in any event.

What is less easy to abandon, however, is the idea of a tight connection between justified or legitimate authority and our ordinary understanding of *moral obligation or duty*. For Raz, justified (de jure) authority is (de facto) authority whose directives it is individually rational to treat as authoritative.[9] But simple practical rationality is in many cases not regarded by us as mandatory. We regularly make and act on choices that are not maximally rational, and we are often taken to be perfectly entitled to do so. Unless we think that independent obligations or duties owed to others are thereby breached, we do not normally think that any wrong is done in so acting. But the Razian "normal justification" of authority makes no distinction between other-regarding and self-regarding reasons for compliance with authority. As a result, in some cases whereby we would normally think an action only the one most rational for us—but in no way mandatory for us—Raz's theory implies that we are morally required to act and that authorities are justified in "imposing duties" to act.

One way to try to recapture this tight connection with duty or obligation might be to focus on Raz's apparent neglect of the connection between democracy and authority and to try to link authority's binding force to its democratic origins (and thus more firmly to reasons of collective good). Scott Shapiro, for instance, argues that "Raz's theory of authority is flawed because of the inadequate justificatory role that it accords to democratic decision making" (Shapiro 2002, 431). He rejects Razian "mediation models" of authority (according to which authorities are justified in virtue of serving effectively as "the mediation between reasons and persons") in favor of an "arbitration model," according to which "authorities are legitimate for a given subject just in case acceptance of the process as binding by some of the parties generates a moral obligation for the subject to abide by the outcome." Democratic procedures can produce legitimate, authoritative results because the majority's acceptance of those results gives all parties "reason to accept the outcome of the process" (Shapiro 2002, 433). That reason is that democratic procedures "represent power-sharing arrangements that are fair" (Shapiro 2002, 432). This arbitration model of political authority, Shapiro claims, "has surely been the dominant account of authority in modern liberal theory," including in its ranks the "social contract theorists" ("such as Hobbes, Locke, and Kant") and "fair play theorists" (Shapiro 2002, 432–33).

While both traditions of thought may involve some notion of "arbitration," there is nonetheless something initially odd about grouping together the theories of political authority at work in the classical social contract theories and those from theories of democracy, for there is surely an important difference between grounding authority in subjects' actual acceptance of a process and grounding it in their having reason to accept that process (which is Shapiro's real position on the subject). Further, of course, neither Hobbes nor Locke nor Kant thought that there was anything *naturally* authoritative about democratic decision procedures. Hobbes and Locke both viewed such procedures as producing binding results only for those who had given prior *consent* to membership in a democratically governed group; even Rousseau, that great champion of democracy, never suggested that democratic procedures produce binding results prior to the social contract that creates political society.

Shapiro's grouping of social contract and democratic theories looks less odd, however, when we consider some contemporary offspring of social contract theory—and, in particular, the political philosophy of John Rawls. Rawls describes his theory of justice as one "which generalizes and carries to a higher level of abstraction the familiar theory of the social contract" (Rawls 1971, 11). But while he finds the contractarian ideal of a fully voluntary political association attractive, Rawls claims that no political society can be a voluntary scheme "in a literal sense" (Rawls 1971, 13). Indeed, Rawls's theory proceeds on the assumption that "political society is closed: we come to be within it and we do not, and indeed cannot, enter or leave it voluntarily" (Rawls 1993, 136). But a society that is just—that offers its members fair terms of cooperation—"comes as close as a society can to being a voluntary scheme" (Rawls, 1971, 13). So "power-sharing arrangements that are fair" will generate results that are binding on everyone in the society, since each of us has a "natural duty . . . to support and to comply with just institutions that exist and apply to us" (Rawls 1971, 115). The "fundamental organizing idea" of Rawls's theory thus becomes that of "society as a fair system of cooperation between free and equal persons viewed as fully cooperating members of society over a complete life" (Rawls 1993, 9).

Rawls extends here not the Lockean but the Kantian branch of social contract theory. In Kant's view, we have a basic obligation to join with others to support—or to create where none exist—the political institutions that alone make justice possible and that allow each person "to enjoy his rights" (Kant 1991, 120). Because the tasks of making justice possible and of resolving basic social disagreements are "urgent" or "necessary"[10]—and because democratic procedures are the best way for a social group to perform those tasks—democracy seems to produce legitimate political authority and binding duties of compliance even without individual (or even general) consent to democratic arrangements. Indeed, refusal to consent to such arrangements may itself be morally wrong, as Kant (1991, 122) argued. David Estlund, agreeing, writes that in cases where consent is "wrongly withheld" from authority (where there is what he calls "normative consent" to authority), "authority can simply befall us" (Estlund 2008, 117). So "existing democratic arrangements" can have "authority over each citizen just as if they had established its authority by actual consent" (Estlund 2008, 157).

In a similar spirit, Shapiro writes that "deference to democratically elected authority under conditions of meaningful freedom is deference to a power-sharing arrangement that is *socially necessary, empowering,* and *fair*" (Shapiro 2002, 435, emphasis in original). We need a procedure for the resolution of conflict in societies; thus, society has the right to impose a fair procedure of that sort, at least provided that this is done within "conditions of meaningful freedom" (which would involve, e.g., guarantees of rights of franchise and free expression). Under such conditions "disobedience to the democratic will . . . amounts to an unreasonable arrogation of power" (Shapiro 2002, 437). Thomas Christiano agrees that "when there are disagreements among persons about how to structure their shared world together and it is important to structure that world together, the way to choose the shared aspects of society is by means of a decision making process that is fair to the interests and opinions of each of the members" (Christiano 2004, 15).

But it is important to see how heavily such democratic authority arguments rely on the idea that persons come prepackaged in political groupings ("shared worlds"), ready to be subjected together to their groups' procedures for resolving internal conflicts. Furthermore, these groupings must be regarded as morally legitimate for the arguments to work. Democratic procedures are not naturally authoritative with respect to just any kind of group (such as the group of "all people over six feet tall"). That my students—outnumbering me—vote to eliminate the final exam requirement in my class does not make their decision binding on me. Democratic decisions have no authority at all over people who are not legitimately subject together to the same collective decision procedure.

But the history of actual political life makes it extremely difficult to see how the world's de facto political groupings of persons and territories could be plausibly described as legitimate, even where authority is wielded democratically. In the United States, for instance, such democratic authority is wielded over the descendants of decimated and enslaved groups and over territories illegitimately annexed or seized. Many other classes of citizens may also be able to make reasonable claims of wrongful subjection to political power. Even were we now to perfect our democracy, this would be insufficient to render legitimate the claims to territories and subjects made by the government of a political group so unjustly formed.

Granted, democratic decision making is a fair procedure for resolving disagreement, and it may even be the fairest possible procedure or, among the various fair procedures, the one that is most likely to generate good/correct results (Estlund 2008, 8, 12). No one believes that it follows from this that the results of democratic decision making are always binding on all those within any group that disagrees about important matters. The results of U.S. elections could not suddenly be made binding on the citizens of British Columbia because the United States chose to annex that territory, even if in doing so it extended to these residents full U.S. citizenship rights (including franchise and free expression rights). How the members of a group became a part of the group makes all the difference as to whether democratic decision making has any authority with respect to them. History does matter morally.

However, if an illegitimate annexation cannot today make the democratic authority of our laws binding on the residents of that wrongfully annexed territory, presumably waiting until next week, or next year will not do the job either. It is not enough to say that we must take our systems of justice where we find them or that we must support those that are fair and stable and happen to claim authority over us. While it may be true that "the best solution [to the important social problems that political authority is meant to address] is a districted one" (Estlund 2008, 150), the difficulty remains that the boundaries of existing "districts" tend simply to be illegitimate. Even if the annexation of British Columbia were not resisted by the Canadian government and if U.S. institutions were to become stable and reliable dispensers of justice in that region, surely no one would deny that the residents of that illegitimately seized territory would nonetheless be entitled to complain of their wrongful subjection to this political authority. It is not "unreasonable" or "arrogant" or "dictatorial" (as Shapiro and Christiano claim) for us to refuse to accept even fair terms of cooperation imposed by those whose subjection of us to any terms at all is morally wrong. To deny this is to deny that individual liberty has any moral value worth considering.

One might try to respond by claiming "that personal liberty has value only when schemes of social cooperation are already in place" (Shapiro 2002, 437). While that claim seems to me false, it is certainly possible to overstate the importance of many kinds of personal liberty (as we saw in the case of Wolff's philosophical anarchism). But it hardly overstates the value of individual liberty to insist that it is possible for wrongs of subjection to be done *within* or *by* active "schemes of social cooperation" or that authority can be wrongly claimed and illegitimately imposed on innocents by those who represent cooperative political schemes. No "reasonable" person could deny this. It may well be, of course, that in certain kinds of social emergencies, the best course of action is to temporarily ignore such wrongs of subjection and to treat all as if they had been legitimately incorporated into a democratically governed body. But most of our shared political life lacks this "emergency" character. Remedies that take seriously and that rectify wrongs of subjection, for both groups and individuals, are routinely possible (even if politically difficult). Even in genuine emergency situations, it is doubtful that those best positioned to act as "authorities" either thereby acquire any right to so act (beyond a mere moral liberty) or acquire any other kind of status that is sufficiently enduring to count as political authority, properly so-called.

If we ask how the residents of an illegitimately annexed territory *can* come to be legitimately subject to their new government's authority, the most natural answer does not seem to appeal to the presence of an enduring emergency, to the mere passage of time, to the death of the wronged generation, or to the kind or quality of the government (the "terms of cooperation") to which those residents have been wrongly subjected. In the paradigm cases of illegitimate subjection—such as those involving "pacified" aboriginal peoples or recently conquered territories—what we tend to look for as a sign of genuinely de jure subjection to authority is some indication of acceptance of their new condition. Such acceptance might be facilitated by using various forms of redress of the relevant wrongs (such as the granting of partial group autonomy or payment of compensation), or it might be accomplished simply through gradual assimilation and identification. But absent such acceptance, it is hard to see how any "authority" over wrongly subjected peoples that is more extensive or enduring than "emergency powers" could possibly be justified in terms that they could (or should) accept.

It is, I think, a mistake to suppose that the moral boundaries of enduring groups that are (legitimately) collectively subject to a single conflict-resolution procedure can be determined in any way other than by identifying the individuals who freely accept group membership. To deny this is, I believe, either to sanctify merely conventional (and morally arbitrary) distinctions between persons—such as distinctions of legal nationality—or to mistakenly suppose that there are "natural" boundaries between the "groups" that must collectively address urgent tasks. If we refuse to take one of those false paths, however, we will find ourselves unable to fully explain the authority of democratically produced laws and government in terms of the intrinsic value of democracy or the ideal fairness (or epistemic superiority) of democratic procedures, for those arguments can gain traction only when applied to persons who have already jointly consented to be members of one political society, all subject to the same procedure for conflict resolution.

This, of course, returns us to Locke's view: that the authority of democracy is ultimately parasitic on the foundational political authority generated by free consent, a foundation that also tightly reconnects authority to our normal views of moral obligation. The authorization account of political authority thus looks as if it may be the (unstated) premise that is necessary for the plausibility of those rival theories of political authority that claim to have moved beyond it. That conclusion, however, should provide small comfort to those eager to justify the claims to political authority made by actual states. For so little free consent to political authority is in evidence in our political lives that evaluating actual states' claims in the terms of the authorization account seems bound to yield for actual states at best only very partial and severely limited de jure political authority (Simmons 2008, section 3.3).

NOTES

1. On the idea of (de jure) political legitimacy, see Simmons 2001. I do not discuss legitimacy further in this chapter. Some contemporary authors identify political legitimacy with political authority (e.g., Wolff 1998, 4–12), while others try to sharply distinguish the two (e.g., Buchanan 2004, 234–38). Where legitimacy and authority are taken to be identical, of course, accounts of de jure legitimacy vary in the same ways as the accounts of authority discussed here.

2. Theories of de jure authority and legitimacy also need to consider the stability of the various possible forms and structures of political society. We may, for instance, refuse to count inherently unstable arrangements as legitimate or as yielding genuine practical authority, but here authority and legitimacy are not simply equated with general belief in claims to authority or legitimacy.

3. In most political societies, practical authority is hierarchical, with political/legal authority establishing the set of duties and rights within whose constraints lower-order practical authorities (such as church leaders, employers, or parents) may permissibly exercise their authority. Genuinely rival practical authorities within the same domains—for instance, lord, king, and pope in medieval society—become unintelligible without some (at least implicit) priority rules or domain rules to preclude rival specifications of the same persons' duties.

4. Locke does not routinely use the word "authority" in the *Second Treatise*; he mostly prefers to use the word "power" to convey the idea of practical authority. He uses the word "authority" often in its theoretical (or epistemic) sense in *An Essay Concerning Human Understanding* and in his writings on religion. The *First Treatise* often contrasts "regal (kingly, royal) authority" and "fatherly (paternal) authority" (e.g., Locke 1960, 144–45; I, 6), while the *Second Treatise* uses "authority" primarily in defining the state of nature and in characterizing our "natural freedom" in terms of the absence of authority.

5. It is possible, of course, to try to defend an account of political authority that completely decouples it from citizens' political obligations. Robert Ladenson understands political authority (or "the right to rule") as a mere "justification right" (what we called a "liberty right" earlier) to use coercion against members of the society. As such, political authority implies no duties of allegiance or compliance for those members (Ladenson 1980, 138–41). This is the "thinnest" possible conception of de jure authority and one that actually challenges the distinction between de facto and de jure authority. Most who have commented on Ladenson's views find this conception too thin to count as a conception of authority at all (as opposed to simply the justified use of force; e.g., Raz 1986, 25–28).

6. For discussion of these and other theories of political obligation, see chapter 3 in Simmons 2008 and chapters 5 through 8 in Simmons 2005.

7. Indeed, Wolff seems himself unable to resist the apparent moral legitimacy of consensual arrangements, concluding that "a contractual democracy is legitimate, to be sure, for it is founded upon the citizens' promise to obey its commands. Indeed, any state is legitimate which is founded upon such a promise" (Wolff 1998, 69)—this despite his earlier insistence that "the concept of the de jure legitimate state would appear to be vacuous" (Wolff 1998, 19).

8. These remarks have briefly summarized what Raz calls "the dependence thesis," "the normal justification thesis," and "the pre-emptive [or "pre-emption"] thesis" (Raz 1986, 46–59).

9. Whether it can be rational to allow a generalization (that is, indirect reasoning) about compliance with reasons—such as the claim that obedience to an authority is likely to better secure such reason compliance than would individual efforts at compliance—to exclude deliberation about any particular act's direct compliance with those same reasons is a separate question that I do not attempt to address here. If it cannot, of course, Raz's views on authority must be rejected.

10. Anscombe appeals to "the necessity of a task" to try to explain both political and parental authority (Anscombe 1990). For doubts about such appeals, see Simmons 2005, 127–42.

REFERENCES

Anscombe, G. E. M. 1990. "On the Source of the Authority of the State." In *Authority*. Edited by J. Raz. New York: New York University Press.

Buchanan, A. 2004. *Justice, Legitimacy, and Self-Determination*. Oxford: Oxford University Press.

Christiano, T. 2004. "Political Authority." In *The Stanford Encyclopedia of Philosophy*. Stanford, CA: Stanford University Press.

Estlund, D. 2008. *Democratic Authority*. Princeton, NJ: Princeton University Press.

Filmer, R. 1991. *Patriarcha and Other Writings*. Cambridge, UK: Cambridge University Press.

Green, L. 1988. *The Authority of the State*. Oxford: Oxford University Press.

Hart, H. L. A. 1982. "Commands and Authoritative Legal Reasons." In *Essays on Bentham*. Oxford: Oxford University Press.

Hobbes, T. 1968. *Leviathan*. Harmondsworth, UK: Penguin.

Hobbes, T. 1972. *Man and Citizen*. Garden City, NY: Anchor.

Hohfeld, W. N. 1964. *Fundamental Legal Conceptions as Applied to Judicial Reasoning*. New Haven, CT: Yale University Press.

Kant, I. 1991. *The Metaphysics of Morals*. Cambridge, UK: Cambridge University Press.

Kavka, G. 1986. *Hobbesian Moral and Political Theory*. Princeton, NJ: Princeton University Press.

Ladenson, R. 1980. "In Defense of a Hobbesian Conception of Law." *Philosophy & Public Affairs* 9: 134–59.

Locke, J. 1960. *Two Treatises of Government*. Cambridge, UK: Cambridge University Press.

Rawls, J. 1971. *A Theory of Justice*. Cambridge, MA: Harvard University Press.

Rawls, J. 1993. *Political Liberalism*. New York: Columbia University Press.

Raz, J. 1979. *The Authority of Law*. Oxford: Oxford University Press.

Raz, J. 1986. *The Morality of Freedom*. Oxford: Oxford University Press.

Raz, J. 1990. "Introduction." In *Authority*. Edited by J. Raz. New York: New York University Press.

Rousseau, J. J. 1997. *The Social Contract and Other Later Political Writings*. Cambridge, UK: Cambridge University Press.

Shapiro, S. 2002. "Authority." In *The Oxford Handbook of Jurisprudence and Philosophy of Law*. Edited by J. Coleman and S. Shapiro. Oxford: Oxford University Press.

Simmons, A. J. 2001. "Justification and Legitimacy." In *Justification and Legitimacy*. Cambridge, UK: Cambridge University Press.

Simmons, A. J. 2008. *Political Philosophy*. Oxford: Oxford University Press.

Simmons, A. J., with C. H. Wellman. 2005. *Is There a Duty to Obey the Law?* Cambridge, UK: Cambridge University Press.

Weber, M. 1947. *The Theory of Social and Economic Organization*. New York: The Free Press.

Wolff, R. P. 1998. *In Defense of Anarchism*. Berkeley: University of California Press.

CHAPTER 2

EQUALITY

ELIZABETH ANDERSON

1. Equality: A Distributive Principle or an Ideal of Social Relations?

"Equality" in contemporary analytic philosophy is usually taken to refer to an equal distribution of goods. Post-Rawlsian debates over equality have started from the assumption that some kind of distributive equality is required and focused on *which* goods (resources, primary goods, advantages, capabilities, welfare, or opportunities for these) should be equally distributed and what kinds of considerations (such as desert, responsibility for the consequences of one's voluntary choices, and incentives that induce people to improve the lot of the least advantaged) can justify deviations from equality (Sen 1980; Arneson 2000b; Cohen 1989; Dworkin 1981; Pogge 2000).[1]

This chapter proposes a broader conception of equality that aims to recover the rich insights of the history of egalitarian thought and contemporary egalitarian social movements. On this view, "equality" refers to egalitarian ideals of social relations. Egalitarians aim to replace social hierarchies with relations of social equality on the ground that individuals are fundamentally moral equals. Historically, egalitarians have aimed their critiques at many different types of social hierarchy, including slavery, serfdom, debt peonage, feudalism, monarchy, oligarchy, caste and class inequality, racism, patriarchy, colonialism, and stigmatization based on sexuality, disability, and bodily appearance. They have envisioned a wide variety of models of equality in social relations, including communes, state communism, anarchism and syndicalism, companionate marriage, multiculturalism (in some guises), republicanism, democracy, socialism, and social democracy. Each of these conceptions includes some concern for distributive outcomes. However, egalitarianism has a much wider social agenda than is captured by distributive demands

(Young 1990). Feminists seek reproductive autonomy for women. There is no good that is being distributed equally when this egalitarian demand is met. In other cases, the equal distribution of a good does not satisfy the demand for equality. "Separate but equal" bathroom facilities for members of different racial groups would still be unequal even if the quality of facilities were equal, because their function is to constitute despised racial groups as untouchables—as an inferior caste. Egalitarian social movements have focused primarily on equality in social relations and tended to treat egalitarian distributions as conditions for or consequences of relational equality.

Against this relational conception of equality, one might object that the concept of equality is essentially quantitative: For two people to be equal, they must possess or enjoy equal amounts of some good. To be sure, we can describe relational egalitarian goals in terms that suggest such a picture: We can say that egalitarians seek a society in which people enjoy equal authority, status, or standing. However, authority, status, and standing essentially refer to types of interpersonal relations. To enjoy these goods is precisely to stand in certain social relations to others. There is nothing more to enjoying equal "amounts" of these goods than standing in certain types of symmetrical social relations with others. By contrast, within the distributive conception of equality, the good to be distributed equally—resources, welfare, capabilities, and so on—is such that the amount that one person has is typically logically independent of the amount of the good that the others in the comparison class have and also often logically independent of that person's social relations to the others in the comparison class. Equality in the distributive conception consists in the mere coincidence of what one person has with what others in the comparison class independently have and need not entail that the persons being compared stand in any social relations with one another. They might even live on different planets and have no interactions with each other. On the relational view, the only comparisons that fundamentally matter are among those who stand in social relations with one another and in which the goods of equality are essentially relations of equal (symmetrical and reciprocal) authority, recognition, and standing.

Egalitarians begin by analyzing the particular social hierarchy they oppose and offering grounds for objecting to it. They then propose various remedies—institutions and norms embodying particular ideals of social equality in the domain in question. Historically, these ideals have suffered from several limitations. Most egalitarians have tended to focus on just one ground of hierarchy at a time, neglecting other equally objectionable grounds. For example, socialists in the Marxist tradition tended to focus on class inequality while repeatedly putting off the quest for gender equality (Eley 2002).[2] Egalitarian remedies have also tended to start with a limited diagnosis of the underlying structures supporting objectionable social hierarchies, failing to anticipate how privileged groups invent new ways to maintain their superior positions once old ways are blocked. For example, liberal feminists such as John Stuart Mill (1975) argued against laws forbidding women from entering trades and professions. But Mill didn't anticipate that women would still be excluded by systematic private discrimination once they achieved legal equality. Finally, conceptions of social equality have often been utopian.[3] They have failed to anticipate unintended bad consequences of their proposed social arrangements. Socialist ideals based on comprehensive centralized state control of the economy failed to devise an adequate substitute for market prices in determining how to efficiently allocate resources.[4]

These limitations, far from undermining egalitarian thought, have spurred its development in light of experiences in putting various ideals of equality into practice. The lessons egalitarians have thereby learned have led to three broad trends over time. First, egalitarianism has become more inclusive and cosmopolitan: No longer focused on the parochial demands of this or that subordinated group, it is sensitive to the normative demands arising from the newfound consciousness of objectionable inequalities based on age, sexuality, disability, and membership in less developed states (Eley 2002). Second, it has become more sophisticated in its understanding of needed egalitarian remedies: No longer focused on legal formalisms (such as civic equality, careers open to talents, and group-blind antidiscrimination laws), it has advanced more complex conceptions of egalitarian social policies—notably with respect to the distribution of educational opportunities, income, wealth, and public goods such as environmental quality—and also ranged well beyond state- and law-centered remedies to conceptions of a more egalitarian *civil society* and *culture*—notably in advancing ideals of differentiated civil societies, respectful representation of subordinated groups, and an egalitarian politics of epistemic authority and civil discourse (Young 2000; Fraser 1997). Third, egalitarianism has largely set aside failed ideals such as centralized planning and utopian socialism (communes) while putting greater store in varied forms of democratic organization and cultural transformation and leaving room for regulated market orderings.

2. Types of Social Hierarchy

Because ideals of equality have emerged from critiques of existing social hierarchies, to understand equality we first need to grasp the varieties of social inequality. By "social hierarchy," I refer to durable group inequalities that are systematically sustained by laws, norms, or habits. The inequalities are durable in that they are reproduced over time by the social arrangements that embody them. They are also group based: They create *classes* of people who relate to one another as superiors to inferiors. *Isolated* individual inequalities detached from systematic social arrangements—for example, a single arbitrary act of discrimination against an individual for having green eyes—may be unfair but do not amount to social hierarchy. Social hierarchies are typically based on ascriptive group identities such as race, ethnicity, caste, class, gender, religion, language, citizenship status, marital status, age, and sexuality.

Three broad types of social hierarchy have been subject to egalitarian critique. First are hierarchies of domination or command. In these systems, those occupying inferior positions are subject to the arbitrary, unaccountable authority of social superiors and thereby made powerless. They must obey the commands of their superiors and ask their permission to exercise various liberties. To be subordinate in such a social relationship is to be unfree in the republican sense (Pettit 1997). This is the source of the egalitarian equation of freedom with equality. Freedom is achieved by liberating the oppressed from subordination in a dominance hierarchy and enabling them to govern themselves—either individually, under a system of common laws guaranteeing everyone's liberty rights, or collectively, in democratic forms of government whereby each has an equal voice in determining the laws to which all are subject, or in deciding who shall enact the laws. The paradigm case of a hierarchy of domination is slavery. Republicans, feminists, and socialists have applied the concept of slavery and its critique to undermine monarchy, patriarchal marriage, and capitalist wage relations ("wage slavery").

The second type of objectionable social inequality is hierarchies of esteem. In these systems, those occupying inferior positions are stigmatized—subject to publicly authoritative stereotypes that represent them as proper objects of dishonor, contempt, disgust, fear, or hatred on the basis of their group identities and hence properly subject to ridicule, shaming, shunning, segregation, discrimination, persecution, and even violence. In some cases, subordinate group members may be allowed to participate in mainstream organizations and benefits but only on the condition that they repress, hide, or abandon their stigmatized identities—for example, their sexual orientation, religion, language, customary dress, or ethnically distinctive name. Because esteem is positional, public representations of socially stigmatized groups are always shaped in invidious contrast to the stereotypes ascribed to those possessing honored group identities.

The third type of objectionable social inequality is hierarchies of standing. In these systems, the interests of those occupying superior social positions are given special weight in the deliberations of others and in the normal (habitual, unconscious, often automatic) operation of social institutions. As a result, those of higher rank enjoy greater rights, privileges, opportunities, or benefits than their social inferiors. They often have special standing to make claims on others and special influence over decisions in which their interests are at stake, especially when their interests conflict with others'. The interests of those occupying inferior positions are neglected or carry little weight in the deliberations of others and in the normal operation of social institutions. As a result, social inferiors are marginalized: They lack the rights, privileges, opportunities, or benefits that their superiors enjoy. They typically lack standing to make claims on others or have access only to inferior channels through which to make claims and have little influence over decisions in which their interests are at stake, especially in conflict cases.

Hierarchies of esteem, domination, and standing are often joined. The same groups that enjoy high esteem also exercise command over the actions of inferiors, enjoy greater access to resources and opportunities, and have special influence over decisions and the operation of institutions affecting their interests. The same groups that are stigmatized are confined to subordinate positions in command hierarchies, lack access to opportunities and resources, and are neglected or actively oppressed in the decisions and operation of institutions affecting their interests. However, as Nancy Fraser (1997) has argued, this is not always so. Gay men suffer stigmatization but do not appear to suffer from a relative overall lack of access to resources and opportunities, even if they are victims of discrimination in particular organizations such as the military. Middle- and upper-class married white women under the common law of coverture were legally subordinate to their husbands but often enjoyed considerable access to resources. Members of the "respectable" lower middle class of England were often poorer than their working-class neighbors but enjoyed higher esteem (Orwell 1937).

For analytical purposes it is useful to distinguish these three types of hierarchy even if they always coincided. Fraser (1997) distinguishes between "recognition" and "redistribution" and argues that egalitarian programs addressing one type of inequality sometimes reinforce inequality in the other. "Recognition" corresponds to esteem hierarchies and "redistribution" roughly to hierarchies of standing. We must add "command" hierarchies to offer a complete account of the objects of egalitarian critique.

3. Egalitarian Critiques of Social Hierarchy

The realm of values is divided into three great domains: the good, the right, and the virtuous (Dewey 1981). Each is defined in relation to the perspective from which people make judgments about each type. Judgments of goodness are made from a first-person perspective—that is, from the perspective of one enjoying, remembering, or anticipating the enjoyment of some object, individually or in concert with others ("us"). The experience of goodness—the sign or evidence of goodness—is one's felt attraction to an appealing object. Judgments of moral rightness are made from a second-person perspective, in which one person asserts the authority (in his or her own person or on behalf of another) to make claims on another—to demand that the other respect the rights or pay due regard to the interests of the claimant and to hold the other accountable for doing so. Judgments of moral wrongness, therefore, are essentially expressible as complaints by or on behalf of a victim that are addressed to agents who are held responsible for wrongdoing (Darwall 2006). The experience of encountering a valid claim of rightness is that of feeling *required* to do something, of being commanded by a legitimate authority. Judgments of virtue are made from the third-person perspective of an observer and judge of people's conduct and underlying dispositions. The experience of virtue is one's felt approval or admiration of people's character or powers as expressed in their conduct.

Egalitarians evaluate social inequality from all three perspectives. They condemn it as morally wrong, in the specific sense that it is *unjust* to those placed in inferior positions; they argue that it is *bad* for people—not just for those occupying inferior ranks but also for those in superior positions and for society as a whole; and they argue that it is *vicious*: It corrupts the characters of superiors and subordinates alike while the ideologies that rationalize hierarchy pass off vices as virtues and condemn virtues as if they were vices. Of these three types of egalitarian critique, judgments of justice dominate. This is apt, because it is with respect to judgments of justice that the specifically *egalitarian* assumption of the moral equality of persons plays the most critical role. However, the proper formulation of the egalitarian assumption of moral equality depends on the type of social hierarchy being criticized.

With respect to esteem hierarchies, egalitarians argue that all human beings have a basal claim to human dignity that does not need to be earned. With respect to hierarchies of standing, egalitarians argue that all human beings have a basal claim to equal moral considerability. With respect to command hierarchies, the argument shifts from how we relate to others as the objects of their regard and actions to how we relate to each other as agents. Rational adults, rather than all human beings, figure in this egalitarian argument. The foundational justification of command hierarchy depends on the idea that some adults are fit to rule and others only to follow, because they are incapable of self-government but instead must follow the reason of others. Against this, egalitarians argue that nearly all adults possess a threshold capacity of self-government sufficient to entitle them to autonomy and hence to entitle them to reject systems in which others wield unaccountable power over them. This is an empirical claim. If Aristotle had been right to suppose that significant classes of people were natural slaves, a stable egalitarian social order would be impossible. Even in the egalitarian view, there may be isolated cases of individuals who are so severely mentally incapacitated that they cannot govern themselves. They must be the wards of others. This concession does not justify the sorts of command hierarchy that egalitarians oppose, however. No durable command hierarchy could be based on a subject population barely able to comprehend or follow orders. In addition, while the fact that some adults suffer from such disabilities justifies paternalistic authority in their cases, such authority is never unaccountable or arbitrary.

The egalitarian assumptions of moral equality are more plausible when they are deployed dialectically against defenders of social hierarchy than when they are taken as foundational philosophical claims on the basis of which a theory of a just social order can be built a priori. The sorts of social hierarchies that human societies have constructed or have ever been able to construct have all been along the lines of ascriptive identity—such as race, caste, class, ethnicity, nationality, gender, sexuality, language, and religion—that cannot in any empirically adequate theory be thought to delineate social groups whose members generally lack capacities for self-government or possess any feature on the basis of which moral considerability or basal dignity could credibly be denied or derogated. Moreover, at least in cases of extreme social inequality, such as slavery and subjection of individuals to routinized public humiliation and violence, it is hard to advance any plausible justifications for inflicting such subordination and stigmatization on anyone. This argument addresses the worst kinds of social hierarchy, forcing advocates of social inequality to retreat to milder forms.

In response, advocates of social hierarchy typically make three claims. First, with respect to command hierarchies, they claim that certain social problems—notably but not exclusively, securing social order—can be solved only under a division of labor in which those competent to rule issue commands and others obey. Second, with respect to hierarchies of esteem and standing, inequalities of virtue—considerations of desert—can justify granting some individuals more esteem and giving their interests more weight than others. Third, such inequalities in esteem and consideration function as important incentives to productive activity. In all three cases, hierarchy is justified so long as it is grounded on genuine inequalities of merit or productivity (Kekes 2007).

Egalitarians within analytic philosophy have tended to respond to these arguments in a partially concessive spirit. Taking the object of evaluation to be a pattern in the distribution of goods, they tend to argue that equality constitutes a default baseline against which certain deviations may be justified. Thus, Rawls (1971) rejects inequalities based on desert but accepts inequalities needed to provide incentives to the more able to work in ways that improve the prospects of the least advantaged. G. A. Cohen (2008) rejects inequalities based on incentives but accepts them as rewards for differential desert. Both theories remain egalitarian in that they are founded on an assumption of the moral equality of persons, a default presumption of distributive equality, and a rejection of most of the bases on which inequality has ever been constructed.

Egalitarians in the history of political theory and those engaged in theorizing the grounds of egalitarian social movements offer a more complex response to inegalitarian claims, because they take the object of evaluation to be not simply a pattern of distribution but a system of social relations that, among its other effects, results in a distributive pattern. This enables a sociologically more sophisticated range of critiques of inequality as well as richer conceptions of what a society of equals could look like.

Consider, in this light, the first inegalitarian claim, that only command hierarchies can secure social order and other public goods. Against this claim, egalitarians divide into anarchist and democratic camps. Anarchists hold that there are no important public goods, the provision of which requires the coercive direction of some people's conduct by others. By exercising their powers of self-government, people are capable of fashioning spontaneous voluntary cooperative orders at a sufficient scale and possessing sufficient resilience to solve all the important problems that people confront (Godwin 1793; Kropotkin 1917). Hence, there is no reason why normal adults should not be entitled to make decisions for themselves in all cases. Because no adult is entitled to issue authoritative coercive commands to anyone else, every adult stands as an equal in relation to every other in an ideal anarchist society.

Democrats allow that there are some important problems, the solution to which requires the coercive coordination of individual conduct. Some coercive commands are necessary and therefore so are some commanders. Yet this does not justify setting up a hierarchy in which those in command wield *unaccountable* power over those commanded. This invariably invites corruption and abuse. Nor is it possible to devise a system of unaccountable power that can continuously select the most able to rule. The temptations of such power are too great: Rulers will either try to pass on their power to their offspring by the hereditary principle or the powers of command will be seized by the most ruthless. Neither selection method yields anything resembling meritocracy.

Democrats reconcile the necessity of command with the ideal of equality by conditioning the power of commanders and the legitimacy of their commands on the authorization of those to whom commands are issued. The point of this condition is to ensure the accountability of officeholders to those over whom they exercise the powers of office. Once this condition is effectively institutionalized (in part, for example, through periodic competitive elections of officeholders under a universal franchise), the ruler/subject relation is transformed into the relation of agent to principle, in which commanders are the servants of the people rather than their sovereigns. Lines of authority run from the people to officeholders before they can run back to the people.

The resulting hierarchy is of offices, not of persons. Individuals hold authority only in virtue of their office. Once out of office, or in contexts irrelevant to exercising the responsibilities of office, they have no authority over others. Their authority is limited to what they need to fulfill the function of office, to solve certain coordination problems and secure particular public goods. Democratically accountable officeholders, in holding only a mediating position between the people regarded as self-governing (as the source of the authority of laws) and the people regarded as subject to the laws, do not thereby constitute a social hierarchy in the sense of distinct classes of rulers and ruled. Of course, the temptations are ever present for officeholders to turn themselves into such a hierarchy. Democratic egalitarians therefore focus on such matters as strengthening the mechanisms of accountability, limiting the powers of office, and blocking the moves officeholders tend to take to entrench their power and constitute themselves as a self-perpetuating ruling class.

Consider now the second inegalitarian claim: defending inequalities in esteem on the basis of virtue. Again, such a claim, if interpreted as a bare distributive pattern, seems destined to require concessions from egalitarians. One who takes this claim to vindicate social inequality would therefore wonder at the fact that many egalitarians, including Rousseau (1761), Godwin (1793), Wollstonecraft (1792), and Paine (1792), took regard for virtue as a ground for the *critique* of esteem hierarchies. They argued that social hierarchies are invariably based not on genuine inequalities of virtue but on morally arbitrary differences such as aristocratic birth, economic class, and gender. More important, they argued that the erection of social hierarchy on the basis of competition for unequal esteem undermines the very virtues it claims to uphold. According to Rousseau (1761), as soon as people begin to seek superior esteem from others, virtue *ceases*. For people, in fact, offer their esteem to counterfeits of virtue—conspicuous displays of wealth and power, superficial beauty, derisive wit, sophisticated manners. Vanity, not virtue, becomes the dominant motive in society. It drives the quest for superior income, wealth, and power over others.

When society seeks to reward virtue with superior *standing*—that is, not just with esteem but with material benefits, special privileges, or exemptions from the constraints binding on others—these inducements or supposedly deserved rewards for virtue only drive it further from the scene. When wealth is taken as the deserved reward and hence a mark of estimability, people seek it directly rather than by cultivating virtue. Once attained, riches, privileges, and exemptions swell people's heads and make them feel entitled to mistreat others. In the competition to attain them, people try to prove their own superiority by abusing, enslaving, and humiliating others.

Rousseau's (1988) (partial) solution to the problem of competition for unequal esteem and standing is to provide an alternative ground of esteem and standing that is universalizable, nonpositional, and positive-sum. Equal citizenship status in a republic provides such a ground. When fellow citizens meet in the public square, they meet as co-sovereigns—as co-creators and guarantors of the republic that makes them free and independent. Each can stand erect before everyone else; no one has to bow and scrape before another. Everyone basks in the glory of the republic they jointly sustain. This basal equality of esteem, expressed in the upright bearing of the free citizen and the recognition of that status with all its rights and dignity by fellow citizens, constitutes the essential background condition for the practice of republican virtue. Thus, genuine virtue requires an underlying equality of esteem. Kant (2002) translates Rousseau's political vision to the universal moral realm of a notional kingdom of ends, turning the equal and reciprocal recognition citizens of a republic grant each other qua citizens into the dignity justly claimed by all persons as such, regardless of nationality or citizenship status. Importantly, this dignity entails a basal level of not only esteem but also of standing as a morally considerable being and a bearer of rights.

Defenders of social hierarchy might concede the importance of this basic human dignity and its implications for moral standing while still insisting on the ineliminability and importance of earned or merited esteem based on the realization of objective human excellences, such as outstanding scientific, artistic, and athletic achievement. It is possible that once social arrangements secure this equality of basic human dignity and standing, Rousseau's objections to esteem competition can be handled by additional arrangements. If so, egalitarians need not object to inequalities of achievement-based esteem, provided that the economy of esteem is configured in such a way as to prevent the reproduction of *group* hierarchy over time. What matters for social equality is not so much the unequal distribution of esteem in itself as its grounds, along with the structure of opportunities for attaining it. Egalitarians above all seek to end esteem hierarchies based on social group identities. Stigmatizing or honoring persons on the basis of their race, class, caste, gender, or similar identity is unjust and morally arbitrary. Such identities are neither meritorious in themselves nor a just proxy for genuine merits, opportunities for the acquisition and display of which must be open to all. Thus, titles of nobility, privileges of race and gender, and other official markers of unequal esteem accorded to identity groups should be abolished. Norms that entitle everyone to be treated civilly should be promulgated.

Egalitarians do not rest content with a laissez-faire system of competition for achievement esteem, even when the grounds for esteem are genuine human excellences and not counterfeits such as ethnicity and wealth. The temptation of those who earn esteem on the basis of superior achievement is to organize as a group so as to convert esteem into privilege, exclude outsiders, and monopolize access to the means of achievement to perpetuate the ingroup's intergenerational access. Alumni of elite schools, even if they were admitted on academic achievement alone, want their children to enjoy preferential admission. Moreover, they want their school or league to monopolize the power to define the terms of the prestige hierarchy so that their school or league stays on top. This involves such moves as defining exclusion as intrinsically meritorious (for example, taking selective admissions as a criterion of quality in itself) and downplaying service to the lower orders as a measure of institutional quality (for example, excluding from quality measures the degree to which a school opens up opportunities for achievement to the less advantaged).

Egalitarians support opposing strategies. With respect to individual opportunities to achieve excellence, egalitarians seek to eliminate barriers to entry (for example, alumni preferences), multiply criteria of merit beyond those monopolized by the advantaged (for example, to count overcoming adversity as a merit), and open up opportunities to develop merits to members of all social groups, especially the less advantaged, by enhancing their access to quality education and training. In general, this involves opening up access to means of developing merit that are independent of the status of their parents or identity group.

With respect to defining what counts as estimable achievement, egalitarians seek to count service to the less advantaged as estimable, because it helps to realize the society of equals that is a good for all. More generally, egalitarians seek to multiply and divide the arenas for competition so as to enable the widest possible diversity of individuals to compete. This explains part of the logic behind dividing athletic competitors by age, weight, and gender and creating competitive opportunities for the disabled, such as wheelchair basketball and the Special Olympics. The multiplication and division of domains of competitive achievement, plus wide access to means of development, help diverse people find some domain in which they can realistically compete for earned esteem (LaVaque-Manty 2009). The more *individual* competition is—the less high achievers function as groups to perpetuate their advantage by monopolizing access to the means of developing merit and the criteria for defining it—the less unequal patterns of esteem reflect and constitute an esteem *hierarchy*. Moreover, the more equal are opportunities for development, the more estimable is superior achievement. Winning a race loses some of its luster if part of the reason for victory is that potentially superior competitors were denied a meaningful opportunity to compete. Finally, egalitarians resist attempts to convert esteem into inequalities of material standing. True virtue may earn esteem, but privilege invites the abuse and neglect of inferiors.

Here the egalitarian critiques of social hierarchy on grounds of justice and virtue are united. Unlike contemporary analytic political philosophy, which tends to ask only what goods society offers individuals to enjoy, the egalitarian tradition regards human beings as the most important product of social arrangements. Social hierarchies undermine virtue up and down the ladder. Unaccountable power leads superiors to mistreat inferiors. Superior esteem inflames their vanity. Special privileges and influence promote egoism and short-circuit the bases of esteem competition, reducing them to vain displays of power, wealth, and advantage. People strive to accumulate superiority in such worldly goods to spite others. This has corrupting effects on social inferiors. Spite from the top inflames envy from the bottom. Subordination also makes people weak, dependent, groveling, sycophantic, and fearful. Powerlessness leads people to take a narrow, selfish view of public affairs. Instead of taking pleasure in the good of others, everyone in the social hierarchy, from top to bottom, enjoys bringing someone low.

Wollstonecraft (1792) sharpened the virtue critique of hierarchy by pointing to a different corrupting effect. If a trait is a genuine virtue, it should be regarded as a virtue regardless of who has it. Yet the reproduction of social hierarchy requires that some people be socialized for inferior roles. This process misrepresents vices as virtues befitting the inferior. Because it would not befit the inferior position imposed on them for women to be serious, strong, or courageous, women are praised for being frivolous, weak, and fearful. Such socialization may induce these vices in women, which in turn inflames a vain sense of superiority in men. Social hierarchy corrupts by systematically training subordinate groups for vice.

Finally, consider the egalitarian critique of social hierarchy on grounds of goodness. Nearly all egalitarians in the English tradition have been utilitarians who assessed the goodness of social arrangements in terms of human welfare. It is evident that social hierarchy is bad for those consigned to inferior ranks. Their fate—poverty, deprivation, unemployment or employment in grueling, dangerous, boring, servile tasks, powerlessness, humiliation, vulnerability to violence, insecurity—is obviously bad for them. Egalitarians also point to the ways in which inequality is bad for those at the top. This is an important feature of the nineteenth-century feminist critique of marriage, from Anna Doyle Wheeler and William Thompson (1996) to Harriet Taylor and John Stuart Mill (1975). The legal subordination of wives to their husbands, their exclusion from education, public affairs, and numerous public activities, the gendered division of labor, and the denial of the franchise to women drove men and women apart by ensuring that they share few interests and pleasures. Wives' subordination undermined the possibilities for true companionship and thus made marriage an emotionally and intellectually barren relationship for men—at least for intelligent and virtuous men.

On a society-wide scale, social hierarchy has additional ill effects. When occupants of superior ranks stake their sense of well-being in wielding unaccountable power over others, subjecting others to the humiliations of a stigmatized identity, or arranging institutions so that the interests of subordinate classes are systematically neglected or undermined, this undermines cooperation and eats away at the bases of social trust and solidarity. As Richard Wilkinson (2005) has documented, societies with more inequality have higher rates of violence, crime, depression, and other diseases and lower longevity, social capital, and overall happiness. More equal societies serve their members better. The question then is what kinds of institutional arrangements best embody social equality?

4. COMPETING VISIONS OF AN EGALITARIAN SOCIETY

Egalitarians have always been better at criticizing inequality than at devising a coherent and successful conception of a society of equals. This is to be expected. Although hunter-gatherer societies tend to be highly egalitarian, social hierarchy has been the rule since the rise of herding and agriculture. Ideals of equality for societies with an advanced division of labor have therefore had few models to work from; almost everything has been necessarily left to imagination and experiment. The great era of egalitarian experimentation for modern societies began with the French Revolution and flourished during the nineteenth century. Its enduring, large-scale achievements—democracy and social democracy—were not realized until after World War II.

During the nineteenth century, egalitarians focused on political and economic organization. They offered up rival visions of equality, exposing deep rifts among egalitarians along the following lines: (a) anarchism versus statism; (b) democracy versus revolutionary communism; (c) within democracy, representative versus participatory forms; (d) nation-state centered versus communal organization (utopian socialism, syndicalism); (e) state versus local worker control of productive enterprises; and (f) rejection versus use of markets to set commodity prices. Each of these visions of equality has been tested to some degree.

Anarchists never managed to win a wide following because they repudiated parliamentary politics, favoring revolution by violent insurrection without consulting the people. Their deeply undemocratic model of social transformation contradicted their professed desire to create a society of individuals living on terms of freedom and equality. Egalitarians have periodically experimented with communal forms of life, most significantly in the Israeli kibbutzim. However, these modes of organization have never enjoyed widespread appeal and have been mostly short-lived. The greatest failures were communism and state socialism, based on centralized planning of the economy and state ownership of productive enterprises. Two significant lessons were learned from these failures—the importance of democracy and the value of using competitive markets to efficiently allocate resources and promote economic growth. Social democracy incorporated these lessons while protecting people from exploitation, poverty, and excessive market risks through comprehensive social insurance and other policies to decommodify labor, from dignitary wages to labor unions to worker participation in corporate governance (Esping-Anderson 1990).

Three large questions remain open regarding egalitarian political and economic organization. (a) What is the proper scope of participatory democracy? While representative forms dominate modern democracies, experiments in participatory democracy continue to offer intriguing alternative possibilities (Bobbio 2003; Fung and Wright 2003). (b) What is the potential for extending democracy to the workplace? While democracy has triumphed for the governance of states, the governance of most workplaces remains autocratic. Bureaucratic forms of corporate authority (Anderson 2008), labor unions, and labor regulations can help tame social hierarchy within the firm. Yet from an egalitarian point of view there is no evident reason why workers should spend their productive lives under autocracy when citizens have repudiated autocratic governance at the state level (Walzer 1983; Bowles, Gintis, and Gustafsson 1993). In Germany, social democrats secured worker participation on corporate boards and lower levels of management in large corporations while achieving one of the most advanced and competitive economies in the world. Efficiency concerns thus do not justify workplace autocracy. Smaller-scale experiments with more democratic forms of worker-controlled enterprise continue in capitalist economies, but the results of such experiments are yet to be fully understood. (c) What is the potential for devising egalitarian political and economic institutions to transnational and even global scales? Thus far, cosmopolitan egalitarians have been long on theorizing global principles of justice (Caney 2005; Moellendorf 2002) but short on envisioning workable transnational institutional frameworks to implement such principles.[5]

This highly compressed summary of egalitarian debates in political economy illustrates two points. First, the fundamental egalitarian disagreements have been resolved not through a priori argument but through experiments in living. Ideals of social equality have been tested by putting them into practice and seeing whether people found them acceptable and appealing. Second, specifically distributive concerns have occupied only a modest part of the egalitarian agenda. Most of the work of egalitarianism has focused on transforming relations among people.

The latter point has become even more evident since the 1960s. Egalitarian social movements from the 1960s to the present have focused on overcoming bases of inequality that were largely neglected by the great egalitarian achievements of democracy and social democracy—inequalities of gender, race, sexuality, disability, and most recently, transnational inequality. Except with respect to the last issue, these new foci have led to a relative shift away from concerns of political economy toward a focus on issues of culture, representation, discourse, and the organization of civil society (Fraser 1997). The relational conception of equality I have advocated here can explain the logic of these cultural agendas better than the distributive conception can. Consider, for example, egalitarian concerns about speech. Feminist critiques of pornography and critical race theorists' critiques of hate speech are grounded in concerns about how denigrating and hateful speech can reproduce the subordination of oppressed groups. Feminist work on epistemic injustice (Fricker

2007)—on failures to listen to people, or grant them epistemic authority, on account of their subordinate social identity—also centrally concerns social hierarchy among speakers and listeners. Gays, lesbians, and transsexuals campaign against the wider culture's pathologizing of their sexual identities. These are campaigns against intergroup stigmatization. Egalitarians have divided over the relative merits of integration and segregation of subordinated racial and ethnic minorities. Some hold that the maintenance of distinctive identities and cultures requires accommodation of group self-segregation (Young 2000). Others argue that segregation is a linchpin of socioeconomic inequality and that integration is required to create a more democratic and tolerant culture (Anderson 2010). All of these debates focus on how members of different groups should relate to one another. It would be artificial and unilluminating to translate such issues into a distributive framework because, as noted above, the goods being "distributed" in such cases are *social relations* of equal authority, esteem, and standing. They are not such that the "amount" that one person "has" is logically independent of what others "have" or of the social relations in which each stands to the others. To put it another way, the goods of equal social relations are not "distributed" separately to individuals because they are essentially *shared* by those who stand in such relations.

5. The Distributive Implications of Relational Equality

I have argued that the relational conception of equality is superior to the distributive conception in part because it offers a better framework for understanding the history of egalitarian political theory and the concerns of egalitarian social movements. The latter, in turn, provide compelling normative reasons for adopting the relational conception. How are the two conceptions of equality related? Within the relational view, distributive concerns appear as but one part of the egalitarian agenda. Distributions matter as causes, consequences, or constituents of social relations. In general, a distribution is objectionable from an egalitarian point of view if it causes, embodies, or is a specific consequence of unjust social hierarchy. In some cases, social hierarchy is directly embodied in the unequal distribution of a good—for example, if some groups but not others have the right to vote, or some groups enjoy privileges and exemptions from general laws due to their superior standing or esteem. The case in which the state distributes nonuniversalizable special privileges and exemptions to its favorites represents the prime case in which "leveling down" is justified, due to the obligation of the state to treat all of its citizens as equals. In such cases an equal distribution of benefits and burdens is required. All adult citizens are entitled to vote and to have their vote count equally with all others. All should be equally subject to the criminal laws.

Where distributions are causally connected to social relations, one should not expect any simple distributive formula focused on a single core good to encapsulate the demands of relational equality. This is because the causes of different types of social hierarchy are various, and various distributive strategies can be employed to undermine or remedy the effect of any given cause. This fact helps explain Scanlon's (2009) claim that the sources of egalitarian concern are diverse. Among those he lists as egalitarian are the demand that the state treat everyone impartially by providing the same benefits to all and objections to caste and status inequality, to the domination of some people by others, and to the undue influence of the wealthy on political institutions. These seemingly diverse concerns are unified by the relational conception of equality. They amount to conceptions of the prerequisites for a society of equals and objections to the different forms of social hierarchy. They yield a variety of distributive requirements. A sufficientarian floor on income—a dignitary wage beyond bare subsistence—is needed to secure the least economically advantaged the ability to appear in public without shame and thereby to avoid stigmatization. The distribution of public educational services should be adjusted to individual need to ensure that students with physical and learning disabilities are able to acquire skills commensurate with their underlying potentials and thus enjoy equal standing with their peers. Constraints at the top of the income distribution may be needed to prevent the rich from exercising undue influence on political affairs, if, as is often the case, there are no effective alternative means to block the conversion of money into political influence. In these three examples, diverse goods—income, capabilities, and the primary good of the social bases of self-respect—appear in egalitarian distributive rules. The standard each rule sets—sufficientarianism, distribution in accordance with need, pressure toward equality (reducing the gap between the top and the bottom)—also varies with the problem to be solved.

Hence, on the relational view of equality, there is no single good that, were it to be distributed equally, would comprehend the distributive goals of egalitarianism. Distributions of various goods—income, wealth, capabilities, rights, opportunities, social esteem, state-provided goods—play different causal or constitutive roles in securing a society of equals; nor is strict equality in the distribution of goods always required to secure a society of equals. Consistently with relational equality, variation within constraints may be justified to serve other compelling societal interests, such as enabling market prices to signal to people where their efforts and other resources are best directed.

It follows that a great deal of discussion of egalitarianism within contemporary analytic philosophy is misguided. So-called "telic" egalitarianism holds that the state in which people are equally well off is good, even if they have no social or causal relation to each other. They could live on different planets, not interact in any way, and not even know of each other's existence (Parfit 2000; Temkin 2003).[6] Since the existence of the other party cannot make any difference to their lives, this state of affairs cannot be good or bad for anyone. It cannot have any implications for their virtues. Because no one is in a position to affect distributions across worlds, there is no one who can be held responsible for correcting inequalities between these people. It follows that this kind of equality cannot be cast as a second-person claim and so cannot be a demand of justice. It is detached from *all* of the normative concerns expressed in the history of egalitarian thought and by egalitarian social movements. As yet we have no explanation of what the goodness of this distributive equality consists in and no reason to care about it. It is irrelevant to any political concerns with equality.

More generally, the background conceptual framework of the "equality of what?" debates in contemporary political philosophy is misguided. It was launched on the assumption that there exists a single good that egalitarians should want to see equally distributed. Debates ensued as to what this good is—resources, primary goods, capabilities, welfare, and so on—and what grounds there could be—desert, responsibility, incentives, and so on—that could justify deviations from equality. On the view advanced here, the concern for equality cannot be reduced to concern about the distribution of a single good or expressed in a single simple formula (equality or equality adjusted for permissible grounds of deviation) for its distribution. Social relations of equality are complex and require a complex response.

If the relational conception of equality better embodies the full range of normative concerns of egalitarians than the distributive conception, then two methodological implications follow for those who want to advance egalitarian thought within analytical political philosophy. First, political philosophers need to become sociologically more sophisticated. Because the object of egalitarian concern consists of systems of social relations, we need to understand how these systems work to have any hope of arriving at normatively adequate ideas. Second, we need to take seriously the pragmatist point that the value of normative ideals cannot be tested in a priori argument alone. The critical testing ground for ideals of equality is in experiments in living. We need to try living within actual social embodiments of our ideals to see whether they meet, exceed, or fail our expectations of them, whether modifications would do better, and whether certain concrete conceptions of equality should be abandoned altogether. The answers to our normative questions will not be found in texts or armchair reasoning but in life.

NOTES

1. See Arneson's chapter on justice in this volume.
2. See Levine's chapter on Marxism in this volume.
3. See Stemplowska and Swift's chapter on ideal theory in this volume.
4. See Tomasi and Brenann's chapter on classical liberalism in this volume.
5. Pogge (2002) offers an important exception to this claim, although the normative assumptions on which he bases his institutional designs are weaker than full egalitarianism.
6. Arneson's (2000a, 340) formula, that "it is morally bad if some are worse off than others through no fault or choice of their own," is subject to the same objections posed here against Parfit and Temkin.

REFERENCES

Anderson, Elizabeth. 2008. "Expanding the Egalitarian Toolbox: Equality and Bureaucracy." *Proceedings of the Aristotelian Society Supplementary Volume* 82:139–60.

Anderson, Elizabeth. 2010. *The Imperative of Integration*. Princeton, NJ: Princeton University Press.

Arneson, Richard. 2000a. "Luck Egalitarianism and Prioritarianism." *Ethics* 110:339–49.

Arneson, Richard. 2000b. "Welfare Should be the Currency of Justice." *Canadian Journal of Philosophy* 30(4): 497–524.

Bobbio, Luigi. 2003. "Building Social Capital through Democratic Deliberation: The Rise of Deliberative Arenas." *Social Epistemology* 17(4): 343–57.

Bowles, Samuel, Herbert Gintis, and Bo Gustafsson, eds. 1993. *Markets and Democracy: Participation, Accountability, and Efficiency*. New York: Cambridge University Press.

Caney, Simon. 2005. *Justice Beyond Borders: A Global Political Theory*. New York: Oxford University Press.

Cohen, G. A. 1989. "On the Currency of Egalitarian Justice." *Ethics* 99:906–44.

Cohen, G. A. 2008. *Rescuing Justice and Equality*. Cambridge, MA: Harvard University Press.

Darwall, Stephen. 2006. *The Second-Person Standpoint: Morality, Respect, and Accountability*. Cambridge, MA: Harvard University Press.

Dewey, John. 1981. "Three Independent Factors in Morals." In *The Later Works, 1925–1953*. Edited by Jo Ann Boydston. Carbondale: Southern Illinois University Press. (Originally published 1930)

Dworkin, Ronald. 1981. "What Is Equality? Part 2: Equality of Resources." *Philosophy and Public Affairs* 10(4): 283–345.

Eley, Geoff. 2002. *Forging Democracy: The History of the Left in Europe, 1850–2000*. New York: Oxford University Press.

Esping-Anderson, Gøsta. 1990. *The Three Worlds of Welfare Capitalism*. Princeton, NJ: Princeton University Press.

Fraser, Nancy. 1997. "From Redistribution to Recognition? Dilemmas of Justice in a 'Postsocialist' Age." In *Justice Interruptus*. By Nancy Fraser. New York: Routledge.

Fricker, Miranda. 2007. *Epistemic Injustice: Power and the Ethics of Knowing*. Oxford: Oxford University Press.

Fung, Archon, and Eric Olin Wright. 2003. *Deepening Democracy: Institutional Innovation in Empowered Participatory Governance*. London: Verso.

Godwin, William. 1793. *An Enquiry Concerning Political Justice, and Its Influence on General Virtue and Happiness*. London: G. G. J. and J. Robinson.

Kant, Immanuel. 2002. *Groundwork for the Metaphysics of Morals*. New Haven, CT: Yale University Press.

Kekes, John. 2007. *The Illusions of Egalitarianism*. Ithaca, NY: Cornell University Press.

Kropotkin, Peter. 1917. *Mutual Aid: A Factor of Evolution*. New York: Knopf.

LaVaque-Manty, Mika. 2009. *The Playing Fields of Eton: Equality and Excellence in Modern Meritocracy*. Ann Arbor: University of Michigan Press.

Mill, John Stuart. 1975. *The Subjection of Women*. Indianapolis: Hackett. (Originally published 1869)

Moellendorf, Darrel. 2002. *Cosmopolitan Justice*. Boulder, CO: Westview Press.

Orwell, George. 1937. *The Road to Wigan Pier*. London: V. Gollancz.

Paine, Thomas. 1792. *Rights of Man. Part the Second. Combining Principle and Practice*. London: H. D. Symonds.

Parfit, Derek. 2000. "Equality or Priority?" In *The Ideal of Equality*. Edited by Matthew Clayton and Andrew Williams. New York: St. Martin's Press.

Pettit, Philip. 1997. *Republicanism: A Theory of Freedom and Government*. New York: Oxford University Press.

Pogge, Thomas. 2000. "On the Site of Distributive Justice: Reflections on Cohen and Murphy." *Philosophy and Public Affairs* 29(2): 137–69.

Pogge, Thomas. 2002. *World Poverty and Human Rights: Cosmopolitan Responsibilities and Reforms*. Cambridge, UK: Polity Press.

Rawls, John. 1971. *A Theory of Justice*. Cambridge. MA: Harvard University Press.

Rousseau, Jean-Jacques. 1761. *A Discourse upon the Origin and Foundation of the Inequality Among Mankind*. London: R. and J. Dodsley.

Rousseau, Jean-Jacques. 1988. *The Social Contract*. Translated by G. D. H. Cole. Amherst, NY: Prometheus Books. Available from http://www.constitution.org/jjr/socon.htm. (Originally published 1762)

Scanlon, Thomas. 2009. "When Does Equality Matter?" Unpublished paper, Harvard University, Cambridge, MA.

Sen, Amartya. 1980. "Equality of What?" In *Tanner Lectures in Human Values*. Edited by S. M. McMurrin. Salt Lake City: University of Utah Press.

Temkin, Larry. 2003. "Egalitarianism Defended." *Ethics* 113: 764–82.

Thompson, William. 1996. *Appeal of One Half of the Human Race, Women, Against the Pretensions of the Other Half, Men to Retain Them in Political and Thence in Civil and Domestic Slavery*. Edited by Dolores Dooley. Cork, Ireland: Cork University Press. (Originally published 1825)

Walzer, Michael. 1983. *Spheres of Justice*. New York: Basic Books.

Wilkinson, Richard. 2005. *The Impact of Inequality: How to Make Sick Societies Healthier*. New York: The New Press.

Wollstonecraft, Mary. 1792. *A Vindication of the Rights of Women*. Boston: Peter Edes.

Young, Iris Marion. 1990. *Justice and the Politics of Difference*. Princeton, NJ: Princeton University Press.

Young, Iris Marion. 2000. *Inclusion and Democracy*. New York: Oxford University Press.

CHAPTER 3

JUSTICE

RICHARD J. ARNESON

Just about everything concerning the topic of justice is contested. Even the name is controversial (Nozick 1974). In this chapter, the term *justice* refers to fairness in the distribution of benefits and burdens to persons in society.[1] There are at least four ideas at work here, each one variously interpretable: (a) what counts as a "fair" distribution, (b) how to conceive of benefits and burdens, (c) what the necessary and sufficient conditions for being a person (a being whose condition matters for purposes of justice) are, and (d) what the relevant individuation conditions for a society are, or, alternatively put, what the spatial and temporal scope of justice principles is. The latter two are important issues, but the discussion here concentrates on the first and second.[2]

I follow John Rawls (1999) and assume that judgments of justice have priority over other normative judgments. If a society is unjust, it ought to be changed to eliminate the injustice, whatever other nice features the society might have, even if those nice features would be threatened by moves toward justice. Like the other terminological decisions discussed so far, this one has controversial implications, and, in particular, it exerts pressure toward adoption of an expansive and inclusive account of justice, so that it can be plausible to deny that a society that is unjust might nonetheless (all things considered) be worth preserving as it is in order to preserve its desirable nonjustice attributes. Viewed this way, justice assessment is fundamental moral assessment and the principles of justice are the fundamental moral principles. The treatment of the topic of justice that follows is not comprehensive but merely examines some recent prominent proposals.

1. Utilitarianism

Utilitarianism comes in many versions and forms. For our purposes two are relevant. The utilitarian principle of right action is that one should morally always do whatever act, among those available, that would bring about the largest aggregate utility. The aggregate utility of a choice is the sum of its impacts, positive or negative, on each affected person. The maximization of utility can also be embraced as a standard of justice—institutions, laws, social practices, social norms, individual acts, and anything else that have a causal impact on aggregate utility can be regarded as more or less just, depending on their degree of utility maximization.

Utility here is individual good or welfare—what makes a person's life better or worse for that very person. Different accounts of individual good yield different versions of utilitarianism. Two prominent accounts are hedonism and desire satisfaction. According to the former, utility is pleasure and the absence of pain; according to the latter, utility is satisfaction of noninstrumental desire, with each desire weighted by its intensity.

Internal to utilitarianism is an arithmetical egalitarianism. Everyone's identical welfare gains and losses count exactly the same in the determination of right action and policy choice. In this respect, utilitarianism opposes aristocratic and other elitist views that accord extra moral value to achieving welfare gains and avoiding welfare losses for the aristocrats or people who count as elite by high placement on some favored dimension of assessment.

Utilitarianism is proposed as a theoretical criterion of right action and policy. Acceptance of it in this role does not commit one to acceptance of it as a practical decision-making guide. Given that when human individuals choose how to act they tend to be ill-informed, favor themselves and those near and dear to them, and are not very good at rationally incorporating information they do have into calculations of what to do, utilitarianism would be a poor decision-making guide for most people in most circumstances. Hence, the utilitarian should favor establishing laws, institutions, social practices, social norms, and even public and private moralities that will operate to produce the best possible results as assessed by the utilitarian standard. In terms made familiar by R. M. Hare, the utilitarian needs to distinguish different levels of moral thinking (Hare 1981; see also Railton 1984). At the theoretical level, the utilitarian standard of justice is that policies should maximize aggregate utility, but at the practical level, the norms that guide lawmakers, policy planners, and ordinary citizens should be whatever would best advance the theoretical aim. What these should be depends on the empirical facts.

2. John Rawls and the Critique of Utilitarianism

John Rawls's *A Theory of Justice*, perhaps the most profound contribution to its subject since the writings of Hobbes, aims to provide a substantial alternative to utilitarianism, which Rawls takes to be the dominant way of thinking about social justice within the broadly liberal tradition of political philosophy. Rawls objects that utilitarianism is not at its root a liberal theory; utilitarianism does not safeguard the rights of individuals. The objection is that utilitarianism ignores the separateness of persons or what Rawls calls the "distinction between persons" (Rawls 1999, 24). The problem (in part) is aggregation. Affirming that we should always do what maximizes the sum total of utility implies that if in peculiar circumstances entirely crushing one person's life prospects would bring about small gains for many people, perhaps already very well-off people, the numbers might yield the result that sacrificing one person for the sake of gaining benefits for many is what we should do. By the same token, eliminating the basic liberties of some for the sake of welfare gains for others might in principle be the right policy according to utilitarianism, depending on the amounts of utility gains and losses that alternative policies would bring about.

Denying these claims, Rawls identifies the substance of justice with what would be chosen by free and equal rational persons in a setting that is designed to be fair for the purpose of choosing principles of social regulation. The philosophically favored interpretation of that choice problem Rawls calls the "original position." Its decisive feature is the veil of ignorance, which stipulates that the imagined parties choosing principles are to be ignorant of all particular facts about themselves and aware only of general facts of physical science and social science. Rawls argues that the principles of justice that would be chosen in the original position are a principle requiring equal civil liberties for all and a principle to the effect that social and economic inequalities are acceptable just in case they (a) are attached to positions and offices open to all under fair equality of opportunity (FEO) and (b) maximize the benefits going to the worst-off social group. (For more on these ideas, see the chapter on Rawls by Leif Wenar in this volume.)

Civil liberties such as free speech are important for justice as defined in a broad way of this chapter, but I ignore them and simply assume that we are arguing among positions that agree about free speech and other basic democratic rights. Rawls's view on justice then encompasses FEO and the difference principle. FEO obtains in a society when (a) all may apply for positions of advantage, applications are assessed on their merits, and those who submit the most meritorious applications are selected and (b) all have a fair opportunity to become qualified for such competitions, so that any members of society with the same native endowments of talent and the same ambition and diligence have exactly the same prospects of competitive success. FEO holds that if there are to be social inequalities, the superior positions must be open to all on a basis of FEO. The difference principle determines when there should be such inequalities and how large they should be. Institutions should be arranged so that social inequalities work to make the position of the worst-off social group as favorable as possible. The inequalities that are just are those that are functional in this sense.

The Rawlsian principles measure the benefit levels that individuals achieve in terms of their holdings of primary social goods. These are resources and opportunities, distributable by society, that every rational person wants more of rather than less or, in a later formulation, that individuals would want if they give priority to developing and exercising their moral powers to cooperate with others on fair terms and to form, pursue, and revise as appropriate a conception of the good.

The idea that what we owe to one another is a fair share of primary social goods involves a division of responsibility between society and the individual. Given a fair share of resources, liberties, and opportunities, each of us has his or her own life to lead and is responsible for his or her choice of life aims, life strategies, or evolving plans of life meant to fulfill those aims.

Proposing a rights-based doctrine that emphasizes individual liberty in several ways, Rawls offers a version of philosophical liberalism that is a distinct alternative to utilitarianism, in which rights and liberties are regarded as means to a more ultimate moral goal.

3. Lockean Libertarianism

A take-no-prisoners assault on philosophical liberalism appeared in 1974, just three years after the publication of Rawls's book. Robert Nozick's *Anarchy, State, and Utopia* weaves together the natural rights doctrine of John Locke and Ayn Rand style libertarianism (see Nozick 1974; Locke 1690; Rand and Branden 1964). In Nozick's synthesis, individuals have absolute, exceptionless moral rights to live as they choose and do as they wish with whatever they legitimately own, provided they do not harm others in certain wrongful ways, especially through force, fraud, theft, assault, or causation of physical damage to the property of others. On this view, if one has a moral right to X, one is at liberty to do X and others are under an enforceable moral duty not to interfere (in certain ways). Moral rights are waivable, transferable, and forfeitable. One may always allow another person to do to one what one has a right that the other not do. Any right one has one may give to or trade with another person, and by violating rights of others one may come to forfeit some of one's own rights.

The core of the libertarian doctrine of rights is the affirmation of self-ownership. Each person is deemed to be the full rightful owner of him- or herself, which means that the entire bundle of rights standardly associated with ownership of material things is held by each individual person. Being the full owner of oneself, others have no property rights at all over one's body and no enforceable rights to use one's body to benefit others or behave as they wish. No one, then, has any positive rights to aid from others, absent voluntary contract or promise of such aid, and not even aid in the protection of one's Lockean rights. Moral rights according to the libertarian are agent-relative side constraints to be respected and not goals to be promoted.[3] In deciding what to do, within the limits of libertarian rights, one subtracts from the set of options any that would violate the rights of others and is morally free to choose any action from the remaining set of possible actions.

The distinctive character of Nozick's libertarianism reveals itself in his account of justice. People's holdings of private property in various parts of the earth are morally legitimate, just in case each person gets property by voluntary transfer from someone who is entitled to it, who in turn received it from someone who was entitled to it, and so on, all the way back to an initial legitimate appropriation of unowned material stuff. Legitimate appropriation of private property occurs against a background in which all people provisionally have rights to use freely any part of the earth. One may eat the fruit that grows on trees and cut down the trees to build fires, but any improvements one makes on unowned land would be available for free use by others. In this setting, one may appropriate unowned moveable pieces of the earth or tracts of land as one's private property provided that doing so does not make anyone's condition worse than it would have been under a regime of continued free use. Continued ownership remains subject to this Proviso, so one's property right in an object diminishes or lapses if one's ownership comes to render others worse off than they would have been under free use, but apart from that condition, Nozick envisages self-owning persons acquiring full, permanent, transferable, and bequeathable private property rights over material things. (The story about intellectual property would presumably also incorporate a version of the Proviso.) Nozick develops a right-wing libertarianism in contrast to the left-wing versions that start with the claim that whereas each individual person owns him- or herself, the earth belongs to all people in common, generation after generation (Vallentyne and Steiner 2000).

This entire edifice appears to rest on a flat denial of the claim that anyone owes anyone anything except to refrain from harming in specified ways and to keep one's voluntary contracts and promises. Why accept this denial that morality includes any requirements of beneficence? Nozick sketches an argument on this point. He suggests that the ideal that morality consists of absolute, exceptionless side constraints is best explained by the "separateness of persons" idea—the idea that each is the full, rightful owner of him- or herself and no one is properly a resource for any other person—and from this separateness of persons claim (along with some uncontroversial further premises) one can derive the full doctrine that the side constraints that bind us are the Lockean libertarian rights. If the argument could be filled out successfully, one could not deny that the substance of morality is Lockean libertarianism without denying that morality consists in absolute, exceptionless side constraints of any sort.

Nozick himself does not work out this argument sketch in detail, and it is hard to see how this might be done, so assessing the argument is difficult. I make two tentative remarks. One is that the starting point is eminently contestable. That there are some moral principles that are fundamental, and thus hold necessarily and universally, is plausible. But that such principles take the form of side constraints such as "Never steal anyone's property for any purpose" or "Never assault an innocent, nonthreatening person" is doubtful (Sen 1982). One can imagine an unending series of scenarios in which the consequences of not acting contrary to such rights become worse and worse and, at some point in the progression, a reasonable person will judge that the right gives way. A second remark is that it is radically unclear why a morality of absolute side constraints must assume the shape of Lockean libertarian rights as Nozick construes them. The absolute side constraints on one's choice of options might for all that has been said include a constraint not to be a free rider on fair cooperative schemes for delivering public goods and a constraint that one provide easy rescue to those in peril. The second-mentioned "constraint" is a positive duty to aid, but so far we have not been given reason to accept that constraints are limited to duties not to harm and do not extend to duties to aid.

One might object that positing a moral duty to help others or to promote the fulfillment of everyone's moral rights cannot be squeezed into the framework of an absolute side constraint view because one would have to draw arbitrary lines across continuous curves charting how much one might be obligated to provide for others by way of benefit at what cost to oneself. However, if line-drawing of this sort poses a problem for a morality of absolute side constraints, this is a problem that is in any case one the doctrine faces, whether or not duties to aid are included. Does the absolute side constraint against harming others forbid me from inflicting even a jot of damage on the persons or property of others as side effects of pursuing my own projects, and does it forbid me from inflicting even a tiny risk of causing such harm on others? (See Railton 2003.) I conjecture that if the absolute side constraint advocate can develop plausible nonarbitrary proposals for drawing moral lines marking reasonable tradeoffs among conflicting values, the person will have the theoretical resources to include duties not to free ride and duties to aid—duties that are anathema to the Lockean—in the array of side constraints to be respected.

Even if the idea of regarding natural moral rights as conceived by Nozick as absolute and exceptionless turns out to be a dead end, this would not dispose of Nozick's claims regarding what rights we have and what we owe each other. Lockean libertarian rights could be reinterpreted as allowing exceptions and as coexisting with duties of beneficence. How plausible such a moderate Lockeanism would prove to be is a further issue (on which, see Simmons 1992).

4. The Capabilities Approach and Luck Egalitarianism

Imagine two persons who have equal holdings of primary social goods such as income and wealth. One is legless, and one has fully functioning legs; otherwise they are similar. The former must spend most of her income to gain mobility, which the latter receives naturally and for free. Amartya Sen points out that according to the primary social goods standard, the condition of the two is the same, but for justice purposes, this is not right: The legless person is clearly seriously disadvantaged. More generally, individuals vary widely in the quality of their personal traits that bear on their ability to achieve worthwhile aims, and the relevant measure of a person's condition for purposes of justice is accordingly not her resource share but what she is enabled to be and do that she has reason to value, given her resources, personal traits, and other circumstances. In Sen's terms, the relevant basis of interpersonal comparison for justice is each person's set of capabilities to achieve functionings he has reason to value (Sen 1992). Martha Nussbaum amends Sen's proposal by specifying that justice requires that each person should be enabled to achieve an adequate or decent level of functioning in each of the several varieties of functioning that taken together constitute a decent or good enough human life (Nussbaum 1992, 2006).

Will Kymlicka (2002, 73–74) writes, "When inequalities in income are the result of choices, not circumstances, the difference principle creates, rather than removes, unfairness." To appreciate this worry, imagine a society that is regulated by Rawls's principles and in which those who end up worst off in social primary goods are all slackers—people who avoid remunerative hard work as much as possible—and many of those better off in terms of primary social goods are not favorably endowed in personal traits but simply engage diligently and steadily at remunerative hard work. It does not seem just that in these circumstances society is arranged for the maximal benefit of the slackers. This thought is the nub of the doctrine that has come to be called "luck egalitarianism" and that is most thoroughly articulated in some writings by Ronald Dworkin.

5. Ronald Dworkin's Equality of Resources Doctrine

Ronald Dworkin writes that his theory of justice aims to make people's personal resources sensitive to their choices but insensitive to their circumstances (Dworkin 2000, 89). This seems to dispose of the slackers. Dworkin explicitly works to develop an account of social justice, including an account of justice that incorporates an adequate view of personal responsibility into the view of what we owe one another insofar as we are resolved that when acting through the state we shall treat each other as equals (see also Cohen 1989).

According to Dworkin, justice requires equality of resources. This ideal is met when external resources are initially distributed via an auction in which all persons have equal bidding power and variability in people's endowments of personal resources is offset by a hypothetical insurance market in which individuals have the opportunity to insure against having low marketable talent and another hypothetical insurance market in which individuals can insure against being afflicted by handicaps. These markets are hypothetical because we assume counterfactually that all individuals lack any knowledge of the market price their talents might fetch and lack any knowledge of their particular likelihood of being struck by a genetic or early childhood disability. By extending the domain of advantages and disadvantages that individuals incur, all of which are to be balanced in the calculation that determines fair distribution, Dworkin's construction accommodates the worry about the narrowness of primary social goods calculation described three paragraphs above.

If we add to this picture the supposition that, after receiving a fair share of resources as dictated by the ideal auction and insurance markets, individuals interact in a fair framework for interaction and have the opportunity to insure at market rates against any misfortune they dread, we now have in mind a pure starting gate theory of justice. After an initial fair (equal) allocation that ideally compensates for bad brute luck, individuals thereafter experience luck only as mediated by their choices—option luck. So there should be a once a lifetime or once a generation initial distribution of resources to secure that all are treated as equals in the justice domain.

Matters are more complicated, however. Dworkin affirms that when ordinary insurance for future contingencies is unavailable, and when people have not received an equal start in life and then come to experience good and bad luck as they live their lives, justice requires that social arrangements such as a tax and transfer scheme be put in place that allocate to people what they would have been entitled to according to the insurance choices that the average member of the community would have made if she had had the opportunity to purchase insurance at competitive market rates in a fair initial situation (with everyone being fully informed of all information relevant to choice and commanding equal resources according to the equality of resources ideal).

The average member of the community, fully informed, might well choose to insure against misfortunes that she could avoid by her choices, because she knows that although she could, she likely won't, and the consequences would be bad, and helpful remedies are available. Perhaps the already-discussed slackers should get some compensation, in Dworkin's ramified view.

Leaving the exegesis of Dworkin to the side, it is not so clear that, at the level of theoretical moral principle at least, the theory of justice ought to hold individuals responsible for their choices in the sense of denying that predicaments that they fall into as a consequence of their choices trigger any obligation on the part of others to rescue the choosers from these predicaments or to compensate them for resulting losses. One's poor choices and the low-quality preferences that motivate them may simply reflect one's poor genetic and early childhood socialization endowments of preference forming and choice-making and choice-executing ability. Even if the individual is properly held responsible for his choices, to some degree, the task of sorting out what one is and is not responsible for begins to look tricky and might turn out to be intractable.

6. Interpersonal Comparisons, Welfare, and Equality versus Sufficiency versus Priority

Suppose there is a correct objective measure of the good quality of an individual's life, assessed from a prudential standpoint (for discussion, see Parfit 1984). Just suppose. How well a person's life goes for that very person can be decomposed into several components—for example, pleasurable experience, achievement, systematic knowledge, and love and friendship. How well a person does on each of these dimensions can be assigned a score, and there is an index or formula that enables us to compute, for any combination of scores on the several dimensions, the individual person's positive well-being score, and there is a similar measure of bads, the difference between positive and negative yielding the person's overall well-being level. This measure is cardinally interpersonally comparable. (The idea of a numerically precise measure is dubious, but we might hope for partial comparability and inexact, rough cardinal interpersonal comparisons.)

Let us say that a *welfarist* approach to justice holds that there is an interpersonal measure as just described and that this is the appropriate measure of people's condition for determining what we morally owe to one another. Both of these claims are controversial. Still, I assume that welfarism has an appeal.

Welfarism might consort with a wide variety of types of moral principle that might serve to regulate the distribution of social benefits and burdens. Some would be frankly elitist—steak and ale for the aristocrats; hamburgers and water for the common folk. Let us focus on principles that are egalitarian just in holding that a welfare gain or loss of a certain size has the same moral value, no matter whether it goes to you or me or anyone else, and no matter whether it goes to any member of any ascriptive group such as aristocrat or peasant or Croat or Serb or the like. We can distinguish several broad principles a broadly egalitarian theorist might adopt. A *sufficiency* principle holds that society should be arranged so that everyone attains a good enough or sufficient level of well-being—a well-being number that indicates a decent quality of life. A principle of *equality* holds that society should be arranged to that everyone attains the same level of well-being. A *maximin* principle holds that society should be arranged so as to maximize the level of well-being of whoever is worst-off in this respect.

Sufficiency notions play a useful role in public policy, as when we define a poverty line and seek policies that bring as many as possible to that line. However, at the level of fundamental principle, the objection arises that there is no nonarbitrary way to determine where to draw the line of sufficiency, so wherever we draw the line, it cannot have the importance for just policy that the sufficientarian takes it to have. Equality doctrines prompt the objection that it does not matter morally how one person's condition compares to that of another, so a fortiori it does not matter morally (except perhaps instrumentally) that everyone has the same or is treated the same in any respect. Equality is a more plausible idea when construed as an affirmation that all individuals have equal basic moral worth and dignity or that each person's interests should count the same as any other's in determinations of what we owe to one another. But equal worth does not imply equal shares. (See the chapter by Anderson on "Equality" in this volume.) Maximin looks to be an extreme doctrine, as it were, a dictatorship of the worst off. Why should a jot of extra well-benefit for the worst off take precedence over any amount of well-being gain for any number of better-off persons?

Prioritarianism names a family of doctrines that deny that it is intrinsically morally important how one person's condition compares to that of another yet affirm a version of the maximin idea that justice requires giving priority to improving the condition of the worst off (Parfit 1991). Priority holds that one ought to choose actions and policies that maximize moral value, which accrues only from benefit to persons (or avoidance of loss). The moral value of gaining a benefit for a person is larger the greater the well-being increase the person obtains from it, and larger the worse off the person would otherwise be in lifetime well-being.[4]

Prioritarianism is a close cousin of utilitarianism and will attract some of the same objections. The entire extended family of welfarist approaches to justice is also vulnerable to attack and has been attacked vigorously, from a range of viewpoints including those of Rawls and Dworkin, whose views we have already canvassed.

Equality, sufficiency, and priority are principles of distribution that can just as well be formulated in terms that do not assume interpersonal comparisons of welfare. Broadly speaking, an egalitarian distributive principle stipulates that better-off people have a special obligation to make sacrifices to improve the condition of those worse off. "Better off" and "worse off" need not be defined in terms of welfare or well-being.[5] The assumption of the welfarist is that, at least at the level of fundamental principle, what we should be concerned about is the overall quality of each person's life, assessed in terms of what fundamentally makes a life go better or worse for the one who lives it. The most straightforward objection to welfarism denies the possibility of cardinal interpersonal welfare comparisons. One can always concoct a measure of welfare, but one can concoct any number of them, and there is no basis for nonarbitrary choice of any one. Addressing the objective list advocate, one can ask, what warrants placing *these* items on the list and not others, and no good answer will be forthcoming. So goes the skeptical response. If it is on the right track, any attempt to incorporate interpersonal welfare comparisons in a theory of what we fundamentally owe each other is bound to be incorporating false claims at the heart of the theory.

A second line of objection does not deny the possibility of a welfarist measure but denies it could be fair to establish an enforceable system of justice on its basis, given that in modern diverse societies ordinary fairly reasonable people fan out into allegiance to many conflicting conceptions or morality and human good. It is deemed to be disrespectful and unfair to impose social obligations on people on the basis of a public ranking system that conflicts with their own fairly reasonable (reasonable enough) views of their own good.

A third line of objection affirms a division of moral responsibility between the individual and society that is said to conflict with any welfarist approach. Society—all of us taken together—is responsible for providing a fair share of opportunities and resources and liberties to all, and what people then do with their own lives is up to them and not the proper business of society. Given a fair distribution in the context of fair social arrangements, each individual is responsible for the quality of her life. This does not mean that she is obligated to aim prudently at the maximization of the quality of her life but rather that sheer shortfalls in well-being do not trigger justice obligations in others to make good the shortfall.

Welfarists have responses to these three lines of argument, which might or might not be adequate (Arneson 2004). At this point I leave this debate and inquire what options remain for justice if cardinal interpersonal welfare comparisons are eschewed.

One option is to base interpersonal comparison for purposes of justice on people's holdings of, or access to, a limited set of uncontroversial external goods, especially goods that are useful for carrying out a wide array of life plans. This is roughly the idea of Rawlsian social primary goods. This idea is afflicted by a difficulty already mentioned. People differ greatly in their talents and in their circumstances, and these greatly affect what any individual is enabled to be and do with a given set of external resources.

Another option involves comparing people's situations without reliance on interpersonal welfare comparisons. This project has been worked out in considerable detail under the heading of what economists call the "theory of fairness" (Varian 1974). The core idea is that of an envy-free distribution—one in which no one would prefer the situation of any other person to one's own. Initially the thought is that each person compares the consumption and leisure bundle she gets with the consumption and leisure bundle of every other person. The comparisons are then extended, for example, to situations involving production of goods. In the most general case, one compares the total set of external resources and circumstances plus talents and personal traits that any other individual has to those one has. When people differ in both internal and external resources and have different preferences, bringing about an envy-free distribution is not generally possible. Several conceptions of fair distribution have been identified that are satisfiable across the generality of cases without relying on interpersonal comparisons (see Fleurbaey 2008). To get a sense of the character of this approach, consider the egalitarian-equivalent distribution. Suppose there are a number of individuals. Each one has personal traits for which he is deemed personally responsible, along with circumstances (these will include some of his personal traits) for which he is deemed to be not personally responsible. There are external transferable resources, either just given to the justice agency or possessed by individuals, but such that they can be taken from present possessors and redistributed. To obtain the egalitarian equivalent distribution, we set a reference level of internal resources (traits and circumstances) and give maximin priority "to individuals whose current level of well-being would be obtained with the least resources if their circumstances were of the reference type" and if their traits for which they are responsible remained as they actually are (Fleurbaey 2008, 63).

The fairness approach just sketched holds that if the individual satisfies her preferences, she lives well in her own terms (though one cannot say she lives better than others who fail to satisfy their preferences). The welfarist disputes both taking preference satisfaction to be the ultimate desideratum and denying the coherence of individual comparisons.

A test case for assessing these approaches to justice is their response to the willing addict (righteous dope fiend). This person prefers above all to use heroin frequently, is glad to have this preference, and cares little or nothing for anything else. He prefers more years of life as an addict to fewer, but prefers a shorter life expectancy as an addict to a longer life expectancy as a nonaddict. He is neither cognitively impaired nor mentally ill, and his preference for heroin was not formed in debilitating circumstances. To sharpen the case, suppose that by some intervention one could alter the wiling addict's preferences so that he comes to lead a fulfilling life by the objective list standard, but in that event the person remains wistful for the life of the addict and never comes to prefer or endorse the course his life has taken. The welfarist and the fairness approach advocate will be, in theory, utterly opposed as to the right moral response here, though practical considerations might soften the conflict at the level of policy proposals.

7. Democratic Equality and Equality of Social Relations

Luck egalitarian doctrines have attracted estimable critics, including Elizabeth Anderson (1999) and Samuel Scheffler (2003). Consider a simple, strong version of this doctrine: Unchosen and uncourted inequalities should be eliminated, and chosen and courted inequalities should be left standing. One concern is that voluntariness of choice varies by degree along several independent dimensions, and it is not so clear how to integrate these dimensions into a single measure of voluntariness or how to respond to the range of partially voluntary choices.

Another criticism is that voluntary choice does not have the make-or-break significance for justice that luck egalitarianism assigns it. This criticism echoes a criticism of the Lockean libertarian treatment of voluntary choice, which, it is objected, the luck egalitarian swallows in a misguided attempt to accommodate conservative criticisms of left-wing theories of social justice. Common sense rejects the rigid position that if someone has become entangled in an unfortunate predicament through her own fault or choice, those who enjoy good fortune have no moral obligation of justice to lend a helping hand. By the same token, many would hold that when someone attains wealth and privilege that she would not have gained but for the sheer good brute luck of having received a favorable genetic endowment or early upbringing, there is no imperative of justice that requires eliminating this inequality, brought about by unchosen luck.

One possible response to this criticism is to point out that the personal responsibility factors that the luck egalitarian emphasizes might be considerations that affect what we owe to one another by way of justice even if these considerations do not entirely rule the roost. That one is badly off, or worse off than others, might generate a reason to help one, a reason that is dampened though not entirely eliminated the more it is the case that one has arrived in this unfortunate situation through one's own choice or negligence. In forming a considered judgment on this issue, it is hard to make further progress in the absence of a specific proposal that says what other factors are important for justice and how weighty a consideration personal responsibility is by comparison with these other factors.

This issue is further complicated by the obvious fact that, on any account of justice, factors that are standardly bundled under the category of personal responsibility will have instrumental significance. Holding people responsible for their choices can simply mean establishing carrot and stick incentives, so one gains an advantage for oneself if one behaves in a way that is deemed socially desirable and suffers a disadvantage if one behaves in a way that is deemed socially undesirable. For example, the difference principle might be better fulfilled by social policies that promote full employment than by direct cash grants to the group of people that is worst off in terms of primary social good holdings. Private voluntary associations will also deploy responsibility practices in pursuit of their own aims. If one wants to build a successful stamp-collecting club, one will do best to set up practices that will reward those who are assiduous in promoting the club's aims. For the assessment of luck egalitarianism, the question is whether or not, setting aside instrumental uses, some notions of personal responsibility have intrinsic moral importance.

The democratic equality theorist does not so much deny that responsibility has intrinsic moral significance but rather urges that the luck egalitarian misconceives its character. Elizabeth Anderson (1999) proposes that the egalitarian should affirm equality in social relations, equality of status. In a just society, democratic equality prevails. What justice requires is that every member of society is enabled throughout her adult life to participate as a fully functioning member of a democratic society. Each should be continuously enabled to function in all of the ways that together constitute full membership in a democratic society. This is a version of a sufficientarian doctrine: Each individual must be sustained at a "good enough" threshold level of capability to function as a full equal participant in a democratic society.

A conception of individual and collective responsibility is implicit in the democratic equality ideal. All of us together are responsible for bringing it about that each person is sustained at the decent threshold level of capability. If one falls below some threshold, no matter how this comes about, one is entitled to the help that restores one to the good enough level. Because the entitlement is to capabilities or real freedom to gain the relevant functioning achievements, responsibility rests on each individual to behave in ways that will transform the capabilities into achieved functionings at the good enough level. (To say that I am responsible for sustaining my own good health provided circumstances are arranged so I have the real freedom to do that is to say that if I fail to act to sustain my own good health, no one is morally obligated to make good the shortfall in my good health functioning.) Beyond the good enough level, provided there is a fair framework for interaction in place, individuals are on their own, in the sense that others are not responsible for helping them gain or sustain levels of advantage past the minimum needed for full participation.

From the democratic equality standpoint, luck egalitarianism appears to be both too harsh and unforgiving in its treatment of those who end up below the good enough capability level via their own choices and too intrusive in demanding redistributions of resources involving people who are above the good enough level but to varying degrees. Consider first those who end up below the democratic equality good enough level. According to the luck egalitarian, these people merit help only if their predicament is not of their own making, so procedures must be installed that attempt to sort the deserving from the undeserving needy and channel aid only to the deserving. This is unfair to those who are denied aid on the basis of moralistic judgments regarding their conduct and also unfair to those who receive aid only after being subjected to what has been called "shameful revelation"—being required to provide evidence that one lacks normal abilities and opportunities and hence should not be deemed personally responsible for being needy in a way that absolves others of obligations to help. In either case, the needy are not being treated with the respect that every person is owed.

Consider next the worry that luck egalitarianism is too intrusive. According to the simple luck egalitarianism under review, unchosen and uncourted inequalities should be undone whether or not the people who get the short end of the stick are below the good enough threshold or above it. The inequality in life prospects between Bill Gates and Donald Trump, if it is brought about by brute luck factors, merits redress, in just the same way and for just the same reason that the inequality between Bill Gates and a needy homeless person (who has not chosen or courted his needy homeless state) does. The democratic equality theorist surmises that something is awry here. The luck egalitarian justice conception illicitly extends the domain of egalitarian concern.

The root of the difficulty, according to the democratic equality critic, is that according to luck egalitarianism, sheer unchosen bad luck suffices to trigger justice demands for compensation and redistribution. But the mere facts that you were born with greater native talent potential and are more physically attractive are not plausibly understood as triggering egalitarian justice demands, nor does the sheer brute luck that an uninsurable meteor shower damages my crops and not yours generate a demand on my part for compensation from you and other lucky persons. As Anderson puts it, the proper concern of egalitarianism is oppression, which is always socially caused.

There are two components to luck egalitarianism—"luckism" and egalitarianism. Both come in different versions. The democratic equality critique attacks both components. The components function in tandem, so the best response to the democratic equality critique identifies the most plausible and promising combinations of them.

Regarding egalitarianism, the democratic equality critique revisits the disagreement among equality, sufficiency, and priority views that we have already discussed. The sufficiency doctrine faces the objection that there is no nonarbitrary line of sufficiency; there are simply different dimensions of human well-being, each of which varies by degree. The democratic equality theorist has a response: that the significant line marks the threshold level of capability which one must be above to be a fully participating member of a democratic society. This standard is vague and somewhat unspecific, but maybe that is not an objection. Maybe the line that morally matters is a vague, blurry line. The standard presupposes a commitment to the idea that a just society must be a democratic society, but perhaps that too is acceptable. If the society is ruled by dictatorship, or divided by caste hierarchy, the democratic equality ideal says one ought to shift to democracy and eliminate the castes.

What level of access to resources one needs to be a full participating member of a democratic society is surely to some considerable extent relative to the wealth of the society one inhabits. A level of wealth that would render me an excluded outsider in contemporary Europe or the United States might be sufficient for full participatory status in India or an even poorer democratic society. The democratic equality justice perspective thus seems to have somewhat conservative implications regarding global justice. A world could consist of fully democratic societies, each meeting the democratic equality standard even though the level of wealth differs enormously from society to society. In fact, one could face grim life prospects, a life of utter squalor, but still have the capability to be a full functioning member of a democratic society provided most others also face squalid life conditions. From the luck egalitarian perspective, something is askew in the democratic equality view. That people are living avoidably squalid lives through no fault or choice of their own does not register as a consideration at all, much less a decisive consideration, in the democratic equality perspective in the determination of what we owe to one another.

Samuel Scheffler (2003) offers another interpretation of the democratic equality ideal, or perhaps another aspect of it. He characterizes the egalitarian society as one in which relationships among people are unmarred by inequalities of status, power, rank, and authority. An egalitarian society is a society of equals. Justice is ancillary to social equality: The distribution of resources and opportunities is just, at least in part, to the degree that it promotes rather than undermines relations of equality. This is an attractive idea, but, as he notes, it is also somewhat elusive and hard to interpret. Inequalities of status, power, rank, and authority are widespread in existing democratic societies. Employers have power and authority over employees, physicians over patients, professors over adult students, and so on. In the public and private sector, many people work in large bureaucracies organized as top-down hierarchies. These inequalities are part of the fabric of modern society, not alien to it, many of us suppose. Widespread acceptance of great inequality in relationships challenges the idea that the fundamental egalitarian ideal is social equality understood as equality in relations among people.

One line that might be pursued allows that equality in relationships is one value among others and is often overridden by other values. So, perhaps, a lot of social inequality is acceptable all things considered in a society that adheres to democratic equality ideals. One might also distinguish constrained and unconstrained social inequality and interpret democratic equality as opposing only the latter or mainly the latter. Relationships of inequality in status, power, authority, and rank are constrained to the degree that subordinates in these relationships have acceptable exit options and to the degree that those on top are checked by effective accountability practices. An accountability procedure in an organization gives superior officials incentives to use their power and institutional privileges in ways that advance morally legitimate organization goals rather than the private aims of the officials.

From the luck egalitarian perspective, the ideal of equality in relationships looks to be an unlikely candidate for the role of fundamental organizing value for justice. From the social equality or democratic equality perspective, if I suffer bad life prospects and am looking forward to grim quality of life, I have no valid moral complaint if the overall distribution of benefits and burdens that includes giving me the short end of the stick promotes overall achievement of the appropriate level of equality of power, authority, rank, and status across society.

The luck egalitarian flips this perspective on social equality. For the luck egalitarian, power, authority, rank, and status are tools for promoting justice values, and society should be arranged so that the formation and distribution of these tools efficiently serves justice values—luck egalitarian aims. Here there is a rock-bottom disagreement.

8. Conclusion

In this essay I have identified some fault lines in current discussions about what we owe one another. Lockean libertarians think we owe each other nothing except not to harm or interfere in certain ways. Other theorists hold that every human being, just in virtue of being a human being, is owed help toward being enabled to lead a decent-quality life, and owes everyone else in turn. From that starting point, disagreements proliferate. Who owes help to whom, and on what occasions, and on what basis? Recent discussions make progress on all of these questions, but definitive answers seem to be, so far, elusive.

NOTES

1. The term *distribution* here allows a process/product ambiguity. *Fair distribution* can refer to a fair process of distributing or to a fair pattern that results from the process.

2. Notice that (c) is too narrowly framed. A full treatment of distributive justice should specify a fair distribution of benefits and burdens across persons and human individuals that are not persons and nonhuman animals that are also not persons.

3. To see this distinction, consider this example: Suppose you could prevent two people from breaking promises they have made but only by yourself breaking a comparably important promise you have made to some other person. The ordinary norm of promise-keeping is agent relative: It says to the agent that she should not break the promises *she* has made, so this ordinary norm implies one ought not to break one's own promises even to reduce the overall amount of promise-breaking generally, at least up to a point.

4. Why *lifetime* well-being? One could also apply the doctrine to individuals at a time, priority being given to those who are worse off now (see Mckerlie 2001).

5. Equality of wealth would require redistribution toward me if I have far less money than the average. My life might be going splendidly despite my lack of cash.

REFERENCES

Anderson, E. 1999. "What Is the Point of Equality?" *Ethics* 109(2): 287–337.
Arneson, R. 2004. "Luck Egalitarianism Interpreted and Defended." *Philosophical Topics* 32(1/2): 1–20.
Cohen, G. A. 1989. "On the Currency of Egalitarian Justice." *Ethics* 99(4): 906–44.
Dworkin, R. 2000. *Sovereign Virtue: The Theory and Practice of Equality*. Cambridge, MA: Harvard University Press.
Fleurbaey, M. 2008. *Fairness, Responsibility, and Welfare*. Oxford: Oxford University Press.
Hare, R. M. 1981. *Moral Thinking: Its Levels, Method, and Point*. Oxford: Oxford University Press.
Kymlicka, W. 2002. *Contemporary Political Philosophy: An Introduction*. 2d ed. Oxford: Oxford University Press.
Locke, J. 1980. *Second Treatise of Government*. Edited by C.B. Macpherson. Indianapolis, IN: Hackett. (Originally published 1690)
McKerlie, D. 2001. "Justice between the Young and the Old." *Philosophy and Public Affairs* 30: 152–77.

Nagel. T. 1991. *Equality and Partiality*. Oxford: Oxford University Press.
Nozick, R. 1974. *Anarchy, State, and Utopia*. New York: Basic Books.
Nussbaum, M. C. 1992. "Human Functioning and Social Justice: In Defense of Aristotelian Essentialism." *Political Theory* 20: 202–46.
Nussbaum, M. C. 2006. *Frontiers of Justice: Disability, Nationality, Species Membership*. Cambridge, MA: Harvard University Press.
Parfit, D. 1984. "What Makes Someone's Life Go Best?" In *Reasons and Persons*. Edited by D. Parfit, 493–502. Oxford: Oxford University Press.
Parfit, D. 1991. *Equality or Priority? The Lindley Lecture*. Lawrence: Department of Philosophy, University of Kansas.
Rand, A., and Branden, N. 1964. *The Virtue of Selfishness*. New York: Signet.
Railton, P. 1984. "Alienation, Consequentialism, and the Demands of Morality." *Philosophy and Public Affairs* 13(2): 134–71.
Railton, P. 2003."Locke, Stock, and Peril: Natural Property Rights, Pollution, and Risk." In *Facts, Values, and Norms: Essays Toward a Morality of Consequence*. Edited by P. Railton, 187–225. Cambridge, UK: Cambridge University Press.
Rawls, J. 1999. *A Theory of Justice*. Rev. ed. Cambridge, MA: Harvard University Press. (Originally published 1971)
Scheffler, S. 2003. "What Is Egalitarianism?" *Philosophy and Public Affairs* 31(1): 5–39.
Sen, A. 1982. "Rights and Agency." *Philosophy and Public Affairs* 11(1): 3–32.
Sen, A. 1992. *Inequality Reexamined*. Cambridge, MA: Harvard University Press.
Simmons, A. J. 1992. *The Lockean Theory of Rights*. Princeton, NJ: Princeton University Press.
Vallentyne, P., and H. Steiner. 2000. *Left-Libertarianism and Its Critics: The Contemporary Debate*. New York: St. Martin's Press.
Varian, H. 1974. "Equity, Efficiency, and Envy." *Journal of Economic Theory* 9: 63–91.

CHAPTER 4

FREEDOM

PHILIP PETTIT

The idea of freedom is relevant to political philosophy on three main fronts: in determining what it is for a choice to be free, what it is for a citizen to be free, and what it is for a state to be free. The issue of freedom in relation to choice divides in two, however, because one question concerns freedom in the exercise of choice, to rework a distinction of Charles Taylor's (1985, ch. 8), and another freedom in the opportunity for choice. Our discussion falls naturally, then, into four main sections: freedom in the exercise of choice, freedom in the opportunity for choice, freedom and the citizen, and freedom and the state. I discuss these topics in a manner that abstracts from practical difficulties; thus, I do not address the hard question of how to make trade-offs in cases in which not all the preconditions for freedom can be realized at once (Pettit 2007; Waldron 2007).

In this discussion I assume that in every choice there are at least two options, if only the options of doing something, x, or doing nothing. I make the following set of assumptions about such options:

- An option is a possibility that you can realize or not; given how things stand in the environment, it is up to you whether or not to realize it.
- There are many ways in which a given option, x, may be realized in action, if only because it may involve different bodily movements; it may take shape as x' or x''.
- What makes x' and x'' one option, x, is that they and their consequences are indiscernible in the independent features that make them attractive.
- An option need not vary in such features as it appears, now in one set of alternatives, now in another, even though its relational, opportunity costs vary.
- An option may change identity in some such cases: Taking a big apple is impolite when the alternative is a small apple but not when it is an orange.

- The attractive features used to individuate options should be taken to be common across individuals so that different individuals can face the same options and choices (Broome 1991; Pettit 1991).

1. Freedom in the Exercise of Choice

Given this understanding of options, let us consider a case where you face three options, *x*, *y*, and *z*. What factors might reduce your freedom to exercise choice? Or, more positively, what is required for you to enjoy the freedom to exercise choice? That is the question we address in this section.

This question breaks down into two more particular issues. The first is whether the reducers of freedom all have to emanate from the will of another or whether, more broadly, they can also originate in purely natural sources. I call this the "nature versus will" issue. The other issue arises on the assumption that the answer to the first favors "will". The question is whether the reducers of freedom all have to involve the active imposition of will by another—in a word, interference—or any form of dependency on the will of that other (any form of domination by that other). I call this the "interference versus domination issue."

The Nature versus Will Issue

How we decide the first issue is determined by how we choose to keep the books on issues of freedom. In particular, it depends on how we choose to draw the line between matters of social/political freedom on the one side and matters of psychological/physical freedom on the other.

Whether or not you can make a certain choice is likely to be affected by three types of factors, deriving respectively from mind, nature, and society. You must have the mental capacity required for making that sort of choice, escaping the counter-agential effects, for example, of obsession, compulsion, paranoia, confusion, and ignorance. You must have the natural capacity—the inherent, corporal ability and the physical, contextual opportunity—to realize the options by which the choice is characterized. Finally, given those options, you must not suffer the socially sourced pressure that would impact negatively on the choice: You must have relations to others of a kind that allow you to exercise choice—to choose as you will and only as you will.

A socially sourced form of pressure, plausibly, must be mediated by the attitudes of others toward you, in particular by the state of their will in your regard. Thus, it is distinct from the pressure that another might unintentionally impose as a result of accidentally falling into your path or of doing something that just happens to get in your way. Pressure might be social as a result of being sourced in the will of another, of course, and yet impose on your choice in psychological or physical ways. It is social by virtue of its origin in the will of another, not by virtue of the way in which it impacts your choice.

I propose that in discussions of social or political freedom we should limit the reducers of freedom to social factors. Given that our topic is the social capacity to exercise freedom, it does not seem right to say that purely psychological and physical hurdles—hurdles without a social origin—can reduce freedom in a choice. All that they can do, strictly speaking, is to ensure that there is no choice available in which you have the chance of enjoying social freedom. Here I follow Isaiah Berlin (1969) and perhaps the bulk of contemporary thinkers. But I break with Hobbes, for whom any sort of hindrance counts as reducing an agent's freedom, and I break with a recent school of thinkers who have followed Hobbes in this aspect of his views (Taylor 1982; Steiner 1994; Van Parijs 1995; Carter 1999; Kramer 2003). This rupture need not concern us greatly, however, because the break does not require a neglect of that work, as we shall see in section 2, but merely a reconstrual. Again, the issue is basically one of how best to keep the books.

Still, my reason for proposing to keep the books in a way that prioritizes will over nature is not purely methodological in character. There is a long tradition, explicitly opposed by Hobbes, in which the distinctive distress associated with suffering the impositions of another's will is contrasted with the inconvenience imposed by nature and is hailed as an evil that only freedom relieves. Freedom, as Algernon Sidney put it in the century before Hobbes, is "independency upon the will of another" (Sidney 1990). The idea was nicely summed up in *Cato's Letters*, a radical eighteenth-century tract: "Liberty is, to live upon one's own terms; slavery is, to live at the mere mercy of another" (Trenchard and Gordon 1971, Vol. 2, 249–50). Kant sounds the theme with brio in notes written in 1765 after reading Rousseau's *Social Contract*. "Find himself in what condition he will, the human being is dependent on many external things . . . But what is harder and more unnatural than this yoke of necessity is the subjection of one human being under the will of another. No misfortune can be more terrifying to one who is accustomed to freedom" (Kant 2005, 11).

The Interference versus Domination Issue

The second issue is whether the social freedom to exercise choice is reduced only by the active imposition of will—that is, interference—or by the wider category that I describe as domination.

There are a number of different ways in which I might interfere in your choice between x, y, and z. I might remove one of those options, perhaps by agenda-fixing or perhaps by obstructing you in some way. Or, given our way of individuating options, I might replace the option by an alternative that carries a penalty or the chance of a penalty: This is what happens, for example, when I make a credible, coercive threat. In either of these cases, I will have reduced your ability to choose by operating on the objects of choice. But I might also work on another front, denying you agential access to those options. I might deceive you about the options available, to take the most obvious case. Or I might induce confusion by manipulating you, say, by mesmerizing you, by overloading you with information, or by resorting to rhetorical persuasion.

This account of the different modes of interference has a high degree of plausibility. To ensure your freedom to exercise a choice between x, y, and z, the options first must be there to be accessed by you, just as they are; and second, you must have reasoned and informed access to them. When an option is removed or replaced, the same options will not be present or accessible. Likewise, when you are subject to deception or manipulation, you will not be able to enjoy access to them. Some thinkers hold that only a form of interference that prevents the choice of a certain option should count as an affront to freedom; they generally coincide with those who think that nature is as hostile to social freedom as will. On our way of individuating options, that approach would allow removing and replacing an option to reduce freedom but not deception or manipulation. Without adding more in defense of the line taken, I continue to assume that all four forms of interference are relevant. Those who take the narrower view can read what follows in light of their perspective.

However broad our notion of interference, we should notice that it still contrasts with the influence I may seek over the exercise of your choice between x, y, and z when I offer you a refusable reward for a choice, say, of x. Such an offer may offend on other grounds, but it will not remove or replace any option, and, assuming it is not deceptive or mesmerizing, it will not affect your access to the options either. It will, however, add a further option to x, y, and z: option, $x+$, that of taking x and then accepting rather than refusing the reward. Making the offer will increase the opportunity costs of taking x, y, or z, but it will not replace any of those options—certainly it need not do so—on the basis of our way of individuating options.

If interference is meant to be inimical to freedom in the exercise of choice, then it may be thought to impact on freedom only when it affects the option actually preferred by the agent—only when it frustrates the agent—or also when it affects any of the other, unpreferred options in the choice. Isaiah Berlin (1969, xlviii; see also xxxix) catches the difference between these two approaches in a nice metaphor that casts the relevant options as doors. The question is whether freedom requires only that the door you push on should be open or that all the doors you might choose to push on should be open. Does it require only that among the options on offer you should be able to do what you happen to like: that you are not frustrated? Or does it require, more strongly, that you should be able to do whatever you might happen to like: that you are not in any way interfered with?

Thomas Hobbes embraces the first of these approaches, when in *Leviathan* he suggests that someone is free in a choice to the extent that he "is not hindered to do *what he has a will to*" (1994, 22.2). He is followed, wittingly or unwittingly, by contemporary theorists who think that in promoting freedom the point is to minimize the expectation of actual interference—to minimize expected frustration—not to minimize the expectation of actual or counterfactual interference (Goodin and Jackson 2007; for critique see Pettit 2008a).

Nowadays most philosophers reject this equation of interference with frustration, probably because of an argument put forward by Berlin (1969, xxxix). He pointed out that if you can be free in virtue of happening to want an option that is open, despite the fact that other options are closed, then in any choice where there is one open option you can make yourself free by adapting your preferences so as to prefer that option. If you are in prison and suffer the unfreedom of someone who wants to live outside, you can remedy the situation just by some personal therapy: Make yourself want to live in the prison, say by reflecting on whatever good points there are in favor of the condition, and you will thereby ensure your freedom. For Berlin, and for most of us, this is absurd. Therapy may make you happier—it may give you greater preference-satisfaction—but it will not make you free. Freedom requires that all the doors in a choice be unlocked, not just those you choose to push on.

According to now-standard ways of thinking, the social freedom to exercise choice consists in noninterference: It is reduced by interference alone and by interference always. This view was first formulated properly by Jeremy Bentham, who described it as the "cornerstone" of his new system (Long 1977, 54). The interference-always thesis serves to bolster Bentham's claim that coercive law, even when it is imposed on terms that people universally endorse, takes the freedom to make their own choices from those on whom it is imposed: "All coercive laws . . . and in particular all laws creative of liberty, are, as far as they go, abrogative of liberty" (Bentham 1843, 503). The interference-alone thesis enables Bentham to hold that you do not suffer any loss of freedom in the exercise of choice by having to live under my power, dependent on my goodwill, provided that I do not actually interfere with you (see too Paley 1825; Pettit 1997a, ch. 1).

Both of these theses are highly questionable, at least on the assumption that it is the imposition of another's will that affects your freedom to exercise choice. The interference-always thesis looks to be false, because I may obstruct or coerce you, even deceive or manipulate you, and yet be subject to your control. I may not have a power of interfering with you at will and with impunity—in that sense I may not dominate you—but only a power of interfering with you on terms that you lay down. My interference may be nondominating or nonarbitrary, perpetrated under an arrangement that you set up.

Suppose you worry about drinking too much in the evenings and give me the key to the alcohol cabinet, making me promise to hand it back to you at twenty-four hours' notice and only at such notice. If I thwart your wishes on a given evening by refusing to return the key, I do not thereby impose my will on your choice, because what I do is subject to your control. The lesson is classically illustrated by the case of Ulysses, who establishes the terms on which his sailors are to keep him bound and guard him from the siren voices. This sort of interference ought not to count as an affront to freedom if, plausibly, we think of the instructing, controlling agent—you in the first case, Ulysses in the second—as one and the same person with the agent who suffers interference. Thus, the interference-always thesis is surely false.

The interference-alone thesis also appears to be false. Even assuming that I interfere with you when I act to affect an option other than the one you prefer—even on a broad construal of interference—it is quite implausible to think that I impose my will on your choice only by means of interference. If I have a power of interfering with you at will and with impunity—if I dominate you—then that in itself means that I can have a measure of control over your choice. Without actually interfering with you I can exercise a controlling form of invigilation or intimidation (Pettit 2008b).

I invigilate your choice among x, y, and z when I, aware of what you choose, am happy to let you choose as you will—thus I do not interfere with you—but I retain a power of interference and am of course disposed to exercise that power, should I no longer be content to let you choose as you will. In such a case you are assured of acting as you will, enjoying freedom to exercise choice, only to the extent that I remain good-willed; you depend on my continuing goodwill for the ability to choose as you want. But this means that whatever you do, you do it by my leave. You are more or less constrained to satisfy my will; it just happens, fortunately for you, that I am good-willed and that the constraint does not impose any actual restrictions.

I may invigilate you and subject you to my will without your being aware of it, though the exercise of my power (should it ever be exercised against you) would certainly make you aware. But if you ascribe invigilating power to me, then I may intimidate you and impose my will—or at least my will as you understand it—in a second manner. Indeed, I may intimidate you in this way even if you are wrong to ascribe an independent invigilating power; your very ignorance will provide me with a derived variety of power. Intimidation occurs, then, just insofar as you believe in my power of interference, rightly or wrongly; you shrink from the prospect of interference; and this aversion has the rational effect of priming you to keep me good-willed. If I appear to be good-willed, you may censor your choice of option to make sure that my goodwill remains in place. If I appear to be ill-willed, you may go out of your way to ingratiate yourself with me, acknowledging the rule of my will and, without in any way constraining it, trying to sway that will in your favor.

The fact that my will may impose on your choice via invigilation or intimidation means that not only does the interference-always thesis fail, so does the interference-alone thesis; the standard view on these matters is quite untenable. As we should opt for will in the nature-versus-will issue, then, so we should opt for domination on the interference-versus-domination question. The fact that my interference does not reduce your freedom unless it is dominating or arbitrary shows that domination is necessary for reducing freedom. The fact that my having a power of interference is enough in itself to reduce your freedom, as with invigilation and intimidation, shows that domination is sufficient for reducing freedom. Freedom should be equated with nothing more or less than nondomination (Pettit 2008b; Skinner 2008).

Adopting this view is of enormous significance, because it means that people's social freedom to exercise choice is under much more severe pressure than anyone committed to freedom as noninterference is likely to recognize. I may intimidate you without wanting to do so and without even being aware of doing so. Equally,

I may invigilate you without any general wish or consciousness of doing so. It may be that I cannot deny myself knowledge of your choice and that I cannot abjure the power of interference that I enjoy. I will exercise such unwitting, involuntary invigilation if you are my spouse and I have the asymmetrical power of interference that husbands held over wives in premodern society, or if you are my employee in a low-employment economy and I have the power to dismiss employees at will and with impunity.

Given that freedom is reduced only by the imposition of will—not, for example, by my accidentally getting in your way—it may seem strange to say that I can exercise unwanted and unwilled domination, thereby reducing your freedom. But there is no inconsistency here. While it is true that I do not want you to be dominated, the domination that you suffer still comes via my will; it consists in your depending on my will remaining a good will for your capacity to exercise certain choices.

To opt for will over nature and domination over interference is to take a line on the exercise of freedom of choice that is often now described as republican or neo-republican. This is because, arguably, freedom was conceptualized as nondomination in the long tradition from republican Rome through the Renaissance and the English civil war down to the time of the American war of independence and the French revolution (Pettit 1997a; Skinner 1998). One of the most active contemporary debates centers on the divide between the republican conception of freedom as nondomination and the alternative conception—sometimes loosely described as a liberal conception—of freedom as noninterference (Laborde and Maynor 2007).

Freedom as noninterference in a choice requires that you should not be exposed to interference, no matter what option you choose to take. Each door should be open, in the sense in which this requires an absence of obstruction or coercion and also an absence of deception or manipulative obfuscation. Freedom as nondomination goes one step further and argues that the openness of no door should be dependent on the goodwill of a would-be doorkeeper. The open-doors view can be defended, as we saw, on the grounds that if not all doors have to be open, then you can make yourself free by adapting so as to prefer the door that happens to be open. The republican view might be defended on parallel grounds. If depending on the goodwill of some door-keepers is not a problem for freedom, then you can make yourself free—again, counterintuitively—by ingratiating yourself with any door-keepers who happen to get in your way, inducing them to keep the doors open for you. Berlin (1969) argues for freedom as noninterference on the grounds that, absurdly, anything less would allow liberation by means of adaptation of preference. We might argue for freedom as nondomination on the grounds that, equally absurdly, anything less would allow liberation by means of the ingratiation of enemies (Pettit 2011).

The discussion in this section leaves one question hanging. We have spoken of freedom requiring you not to be exposed to another's interference or even to another's power of interference, real or assumed. But what is required to eliminate or, more realistically, reduce such exposure? Specifically, what is required to achieve a reduction, given that you do not reduce your exposure to me just by ingratiating yourself with me or just by giving me incentives not to impose my will on you? What measures would defend you against my will and not serve, like such incentives, to recognize and even reinforce the control of my will?

The quick answer to this question is that you will be protected against my will by being able to counter any interference by deploying against me the very resources of interference, invigilation, or intimidation that I might impose on you; by having an independent, protective agency use such resources against me on your behalf; or by having nature come to your assistance, imposing natural burdens or obstacles—the counterparts of interference—on the option of interfering. When I speak in what follows of your being protected against domination, where protection may be partial or complete, it is this sort of defense that I have in mind.

2. Freedom in the Opportunity for Choice

We saw in the last section that if I make you an offer, increasing your options from x, y, and z to x, y, z, and $x+$, then I do not reduce your freedom to exercise choice; I do not remove or replace an existing option, nor do I deny you access to information or reduce your capacity to reason. But, in another sense of freedom, I increase your freedom of choice by adding this improved option. The freedom I increase in such a case is not your freedom to exercise choice—this is merely preserved—but rather freedom in the sense in which it is synonymous with opportunity.

To the extent that choice was a focus of discussion about freedom down to the rise of economics—we shall see in the next section that it was not a main focus—the question addressed related to the freedom to exercise choice between given options, not the opportunity freedom that increases with an improvement in options. It was entirely natural, however, that this question should become a topic after the rise of economics. The science of economics is designed to show how the market—the "free" market—can serve to provide existing commodities and services at lower prices and can facilitate the production and provision of quite novel goods. If the market is to be justified, as economics seeks to justify it, then one obvious strategy is to argue that it generates greater opportunity and in that sense greater freedom of choice.

The dominant approach among economists is utilitarian in character, starting from the fact that with falling prices and increasing goods, people are positioned to achieve greater preference-satisfaction in the space of such options. They are likely to find either that what they already want is available at a lower cost or that there is something new that they want even more. Let us call this the "efficiency argument." It hails expanding people's opportunities for the incidental, instrumental reason that doing so improves the prospects for preference-satisfaction. But this argument, as it turns out, does not make a case for improving people's freedom as opportunity as such—only a case for giving people what attracts them most, whether or not they have a choice in the matter.

Imagine a choice where the market makes a new option, w, available side by side with the existing options, x, y, and z, and suppose that all people come to prefer w to the other options. Will it be important that all four options remain open, as freedom strictly requires? From the point of view of efficiency and preference-satisfaction, the answer has to be, no. From that viewpoint, the importance of an option's remaining accessible in a given choice will decline with the decreasing probability of its being chosen. The efficiency argument does not put an independent value on people's enjoying freedom in the improved choice that the market might make possible. It does not ascribe any intrinsic value to that freedom, or any value that derives from something other than the satisfaction of preferences. Thus, it might not register any fault in a development whereby the availability of x, y, and z declines in proportion to the probability of their being chosen and only w remains on ready offer.

Consider a policy that would provide a basic income for anyone who chose not to take a job, even in a full-employment society, thereby keeping open for everyone both the option of entering paid employment and the option of not doing so. Now imagine that most people actually prefer to enter paid employment. For someone who values freedom in the exercise of such a choice—whether freedom as noninterference or freedom as nondomination—the policy might remain attractive even in the scenario where most people seek paid employment; it would thereby enhance their freedom as opportunity. For someone who values expected preference-satisfaction in the space of options, however, the policy need not be very attractive in such a scenario. It will not be important to cater for how a person would fare, did he or she prefer not to take employed work, given that the person actually prefers to work.

Probably as a result of dissatisfaction with the standard utilitarian focus on the satisfaction of option-preferences, economists have tended recently to ascribe an independent value to freedom as opportunity, not just an efficiency-based value. Amartya Sen (1982; 2002) has been a leading figure in this development, arguing for the independent value of freedom as opportunity. This argument does not entail the rejection of the rational-choice, expectational approach that characterizes economic ways of thinking. It requires merely the recognition that people often have preferences, not just among the options in an available set but also among the different sets of options that might replace that set. They are each likely to have a preference between entering paid employment, working without pay, and enjoying full-time leisure. But they are equally likely to have a preference between the higher-order alternatives of a menu of options that includes full-time leisure and one that does not: a wider set of open doors, to revert to Berlin's metaphor, or a narrower set.

This recent development has generated a large literature among both economists and philosophers on the question of how different ways of changing a menu of options, or different ways of changing opportunities, compare in the account books of freedom: that is, freedom as opportunity (Pattanaik and Xu 1990; Sugden 1998; Carter 1999).

Any increase in the number of options available to an agent always seems to make for an improvement in such freedom (Pattanaik and Xu 1990). But are there other dimensions that are also relevant to determining the magnitude of the improvement? Suppose that the expansion consists of adding a tenth, fairly similar beer to an existing set of options over nine beers. Will that do as much for freedom as opportunity as would the addition of a tenth option of drinking wine? Intuitively not. An increase in the diversity of options available is as relevant as an increase in the number of options to the quality of opportunity that the agent enjoys. There are different ways in which diversity might be conceptualized and measured, but, however it is represented, diversity clearly matters.

There are other aspects of the options accessible to an agent that may also matter (Sugden 1998). One is the extent to which the options are objectively significant, as we might put it, in representing ways of changing the world. A second is the extent to which they are subjectively significant in representing options that matter within the local culture or according to the agent's own value system.

Imagine that two agents are each able to choose between pressing buttons A and B but that in one case the buttons are hooked up to the world so as to make various extensive changes likely, while in the other pressing the buttons has no extra effect whatsoever. It seems natural to think that the agent with a capacity to effect objective changes enjoys greater freedom as opportunity than the agent who has no such capacity. Or imagine, introducing subjective as distinct from objective significance, that a choice between options A and B is of great import within one agent's social or personal value system, while it is of no import whatsoever within the other's (Taylor 1985, ch. 8). Again, it seems natural to think that the first agent's freedom as opportunity gains more from the availability of the choice between A and B than does the freedom of the second.

Many other issues are raised by freedom as opportunity. One particularly difficult one is how we should interpret and weight opportunity freedom when it appears to conflict with exercise freedom. Suppose that by adding another option $x+$—that is, x with a reward—to existing options, x, y, and z, I make it harder for you to access x or y or z, thereby reducing your freedom as exercise. Or suppose that by adding $x+$, I change the character of x or y or z and thereby replace it with another closely related option. Or suppose, at the outside limit, that instead of offering you $x+$ in addition to x, y, and z, I offer you just the choice between $x+$, y, and z: I make you a nonrefusable offer. Are we to say that there is an increase in opportunity freedom in such cases? And, if we take that line, are we to think that that increase might compensate for the accompanying reduction in exercise freedom? I put those issues aside, though any comprehensive theory would have to adopt some line on them.

Even with those issues put aside, we can reasonably conclude that number, diversity, and significance are relevant dimensions, perhaps even the main criteria, in determining how far a given expansion of options makes for an improvement in freedom as opportunity. Where your exercise freedom is a function of how far you are protected against interference, invigilation, and intimidation, your opportunity freedom is likely to be a function of how numerous, diverse, and significant are the options available. Both sorts of freedom are relevant, as we shall now see, to the notion of freedom that applies to citizens or persons.

3. Freedom and the Citizen

Freedom in the long republican tradition is ascribed in the first place to persons and only in the second place to choices. The focus is on the freeman or free citizen, as it was put in English, the *liber* or *civis*, as it was put in Latin. To be a free person or citizen in this sense was, in the words of the Justinian's *Digest of Roman Law*, to be *sui juris*: someone who lives, in the phrase quoted above from *Cato's Letters*, on his or her own terms; someone, in particular, who does not live in *potestate domini*, in the power of a master.

Among the many ways in which Thomas Hobbes sought to revise the republican way of thinking, he may have been most successful in shifting the discussion from citizen to choice. The quotation in *Leviathan* on which we have already drawn pretends to define the freedom of a citizen but has the effect of putting the emphasis squarely on choice: on the things that an agent is left in a position to do. "A free-man is he that in those things which by his strength and wit he is able to do is not hindered to do what he has a will to" (Hobbes 1994, 21.2). On this approach, you will be a free citizen because and to the extent that you enjoy free choices. Your freedom as a person will have no significance as an independent object of normative concern; it will materialize as a side effect of the degree of exercise and opportunity freedom that you manage to achieve in your choices.

Is there any other way of relating your freedom as a person or citizen and your freedom in choice? In particular, is there any way of doing so that makes the category of personal or civic freedom more interesting and important?

The image of the free citizen is distinct from the ideal of having as much free exercise or opportunity as possible. You might enjoy such freedom because of your strength or cunning or good luck in getting others to let you act on your own will. You might not just live, but also thrive, on your wits. Consistently with achieving this level of freedom in choice, then, you might be in a subordinate position in relation to others in your society. Being in such a subordinate position, you would not intuitively enjoy the status of the free person or citizen. In a traditional image, you might be the court jester—Rigoletto perhaps—whose jibes are so feared by those around you that you get away with almost anything. In that case there would be a large range of choices in which you were protected against the domination of others, but as a mere jester you would not have the status that the ideal of the free person implies.

There is a floor constraint and a ceiling constraint on what freedom as a person or citizen ought to give you. It should give you a sufficient power of exercising choice, and a sufficient range of opportunities in which to exercise it, for you to be able, by local, historical standards, to achieve a familiar, almost clichéd ideal: to make your own way in life, to stand on your own two feet, to be able to function properly in your society (Sen 1985; Nussbaum 2006). Yet it ought not to give you more than can be given at the same time to other citizens—presumptively, all other people—in that society. If what you enjoy is not sufficient on the first score, then you will not enjoy *freedom* as a citizen, only something less; if it is not satisfactory on the second, then you will not enjoy freedom as a *citizen* or *person*: What you enjoy will not accrue to you in virtue of the fact of being a citizen like others in your society, only as a result of enjoying a special, privileged status.

These constraints suggest that to enjoy freedom as a citizen is to enjoy a certain freedom both as exercise and opportunity. On the exercise front, it would be nice to prescribe that you should have the same protections against domination as others in your society, but this is not realistic, because some people in any society are bound to have special sources of protection, say, as a result of greater-than-average intelligence or flexibility or strength. What we can and must prescribe, however, is that you should have culturally adequate protections on a common and equal basis with others. On the opportunity front, it would be nice to prescribe that you should have the freedom to do as you wish, but this, of course, is also impossible because it is bound to conflict with the freedom of others. What we can and must prescribe here is that you should be protected in the same range of choices as others, where those choices are sufficient to enable you to lead what counts intuitively as an independent life. Those choices may be hard to define and may vary from culture to culture, but they will presumably include the basic liberties of thought, speech, association, movement, residence, and occupation (Pettit 2008c).

On this way of reclaiming the old notion of the freedom of a citizen, such freedom consists in incorporation within a system that gives you protection against domination on the same basis and in the same range of choices as fellow citizens: others in your society. What basis might serve to support your freedom as a citizen? It cannot be the basis that a benevolent despot would provide, because you and others would live in dependency on the goodwill of that despot. The only plausible basis is a system of law and norm by which you and others are each protected and in which you are each therefore invested. This general investment is important, because it means that no one has to depend for protection on the goodwill of others; everyone has a personal interest in supporting the system by which each, in common with others, is protected.

For all we have said, your freedom as a citizen may look like a second-best ideal: a mix of exercise and opportunity freedom that is cut to the demands of living on equal terms with others. But this would be a mistake, for while your freedom as a citizen may be restricted to a set of choices like the basic liberties, the freedom in choice that a system of law and norm would provide gives freedom a new, normative character. Think of how possession becomes property under a law that gives you the right to be protected against would-be thieves and the right to be vindicated against successful ones: that is, to have the offense rectified. In the same way the freedom of choice that you might have been able to win by your self-protective efforts becomes a matter of right as it modulates into your freedom as a citizen: It consists of a right, guaranteed by general practices, to be protected against would-be offenders and, insofar as possible, to be vindicated against those who are successful. Your freedom becomes a form of legally and normatively supported property, as Rousseau and others have emphasized (Spitz 1995; Richardson 2002), not just a benefit that you happen to have the strength to secure. The importance of this normative, institutional grounding for the freedom of the citizen was marked in the Roman saying that the *servus sine domino*—the slave without a master—was not yet a *liber or civis*, not yet a free person or citizen (Wirszubski 1968).

The normative recasting that freedom undergoes with the appearance of the notion of the free person or citizen may support a rethinking of what the freedom to exercise choice requires. Someone who enjoys free choice in virtue of personal self-assertion, not social status, can be cast as enjoying something less than the full institutional freedom of choice that a citizen can access. And someone whose freedom of choice is restricted improperly—someone who is waylaid by a robber, for example—may yet have his or her institutional freedom of choice vindicated in the determination of the community to pursue the offender and seek a rectification—however that is understood (Braithwaite and Pettit 1990; Pettit 1997b)—of the offense.

The ideal of the freedom of the citizen has tended to get lost in contemporary discussion. The standard framework in which freedom to exercise choice is conceived suggests that it is always the freedom of a certain agent from a certain obstacle to perform a certain action (MacCallum 1967). But this neglects the factor that naturally becomes salient when we think of the freedom to exercise choice that a well-protected citizen enjoys: the laws and norms in virtue of which the freedom of choice is enjoyed. Your freedom as a citizen is not only a freedom from certain obstacles to perform certain actions but a freedom that you enjoy in virtue of incorporation with others in a system of law and norm.

While the ideal of the free citizen has often been lost to sight, however, it has never disappeared completely. Thus, it is noteworthy that it surfaces at various points in the work of Isaiah Berlin. In stating his ultimate ideal, he emphasizes the need to ensure that in relevant choices a person who is free "is not obliged to account for his activities to any man" (Berlin 1969, lx). If I am to be free in his preferred sense, as he puts it in his 1958 lecture, there must be "room within which I am legally accountable to no one for my movements" (Berlin 1969, 155). These comments are not given much elaboration, but they surely gesture at just the sort of ideal we have been discussing in this section.

4. Freedom and the State

Apart from choices and citizens, the property of freedom is also readily predicated of the state. This appears in the seventeenth century, republican way of speaking, in which the free state is a state that provides for the freedom of its citizens, not just a state that operates freely (Skinner 1998). It continues in the common assumption that the democratic state is a distinctively free state, serving freedom in a manner in which it cannot be served by any other regime (Habermas 1995; Holmes 1995).

No account of social freedom, whether it be interference based or domination based, can deny that the state may serve the cause of its citizens' freedom well by the laws and policies adopted. If freedom is noninterference, then all laws are themselves invasions of freedom, as Bentham insisted, but at least those laws may prevent more freedom than they perpetrate. If freedom is nondomination, then things may be better again. If it is possible for the laws not to be dominating (more on this later), then they will not take from the freedom of citizens as such; they will be more like the restraints that his sailors impose on Ulysses. Finally, if they are well designed, they may do much to protect people against the domination of other agents, providing resources, defenses, and options that reduce the possibilities of arbitrary interference, invigilation, and intimidation. More than that, indeed, they may serve to establish citizens in the enjoyment of a normatively recognized form of freedom, something that no amount of personal power can achieve for individuals.

The core issue in debates on the free state is whether there are ways of constituting the state that are inherently freedom-friendly. This is essentially the question whether democratization involves liberation, as is often assumed: Whether there is a more-than-contingent connection between democracy and freedom.

We have already noted that freedom of choice has tended to eclipse freedom as ascribed to citizens in contemporary usage and that the emphasis in the literature of economics and cognate disciplines has been on opportunity freedom rather than exercise freedom. Consistently with those tendencies, there has been a rupture in the connection between the notion of freedom and the notion of democracy. As with other shifts, the disconnection may have begun with Thomas Hobbes. He insisted in *Leviathan* (1994, 21.8) that the only sense in which a commonwealth or state could be free was when it operated in relation to other states as an agent free of the sorts of obligations that subjects owe to their sovereign. He gave no countenance to the suggestion that there is a sense in which a state is free just to the extent that it is democratic.

The idea that freedom in the state had nothing to do with democracy assumed particular salience with Bentham and his school. William Paley, one of Bentham's most clear-headed and influential followers, argued as early as 1785 that the cause of liberty might be as well served, in some circumstances, by "the edicts of a despotic prince, as by the resolutions of popular assembly"; in such conditions "would an absolute form of government be no less free than the purest democracy" (Paley 1825). The point was taken up by Isaiah Berlin, who maintained in 1958: "The connection between democracy and individual liberty is a good deal more tenuous than it seemed to many advocates of both" (1969, 130–31).

The disconnection between freedom and democracy that these thinkers champion derives from their view that freedom is always reduced by coercive law. Under that view, the best that the state can do in the annals of freedom is to prevent more interference than it perpetrates. In that case it is always going to be a contingent, empirical question as to whether democracy will do better than despotism in minimizing interference overall. There will be no particularly intimate connection between freedom and democracy or between freedom and any particular state constitution.

Does this change under the rival, republican view that freedom is reduced only by domination? In principle, it may. That view raises the question as to whether the state might be constituted in such a way that its laws and policies are not dominating. Can they be made subject to the control of those on whom they are imposed in such a way that, like the restrictions imposed by his sailors on Ulysses, they do not represent the imposition of an alien will (Pettit 2009)?

This question opens up a research program in constitutional and democratic theory (Lovett and Pettit 2009). The issue is whether there are any arrangements that might be put in place by the state such that, under those arrangements, citizens could rightly view the state as subject to their own control, not the organ of an alien will. The research program is challenging, because it will not be enough that the state implements a majority will, for example, or even a majority will formed in the ideal conditions envisaged by Rousseau in his *Social Contract*. You as an individual might be dominated by such a will just as much as by the will of another individual. The fact is so salient that it is hard to take seriously the supposedly ancient view of freedom, as Constant (1988) described it in 1819, according to which being free just means being a participating member of a majoritarian, self-determining assembly; even Rousseau never understood freedom in that sense (Spitz 1995).

But this is not the place to explore the research program further (Pettit 2013); it is enough to register that the program is there to be explored. The study of freedom is a continuing enterprise, not an investigation that can be declared to be either at a close or at a stalemate.

NOTE

I am most grateful to David Estlund for his helpful comments on an earlier version of this piece.

REFERENCES

Bentham, J. 1843. "Anarchical Fallacies." *The Works of Jeremy Bentham*. Vol. 2. Edited by J. Bowring. Edinburgh, UK: W. Tait.
Berlin, I. 1969. *Four Essays on Liberty*. Oxford: Oxford University Press.
Braithwaite, J., and P. Pettit. 1990. *Not Just Deserts: A Republican Theory of Criminal Justice*. Oxford: Oxford University Press.
Broome, J. 1991. *Weighing Goods*. Oxford: Blackwell.
Carter, I. 1999. *A Measure of Freedom*. Oxford: Oxford University Press.

Constant, B. 1988. *Constant: Political Writings*. Cambridge, UK: Cambridge University Press.
Goodin, R. E., and F. Jackson. 2007. "Freedom from Fear." *Philosophy and Public Affairs* 35: 249–65.
Habermas, J. 1995. *Between Facts and Norms: Contributions to a Discourse Theory of Law and Democracy*. Cambridge, MA, MIT Press.
Hobbes, T. 1994. *Leviathan*. Edited by E. Curley. Indianapolis, IN: Hackett.
Holmes, S. 1995. *Passions and Constraint: On the Theory of Liberal Democracy*. Chicago: University of Chicago Press.
Kant, I. 2005. *Notes and Fragments*. Edited by Paul Guyer. Cambridge, UK: Cambridge University Press.
Kramer, M. H. 2003. *The Quality of Freedom*. Oxford: Oxford University Press.
Laborde, C., and J. Maynor, eds. 2007. *Republicanism and Political Theory*. Oxford: Blackwell.
Long, D. C. 1977. *Bentham on Liberty*. Toronto: University of Toronto Press.
Lovett, F., and P. Pettit. 2009. "Neo-Republicanism: A Normative and Institutional Research Program." *Annual Review of Political Science* 12: 11–29.
MacCallum, G. C. 1967. "Negative and Positive Freedom." *Philosophical Review* 74: 312–34.
Nussbaum, M. 2006. *Frontiers of Justice*. Cambridge, MA: Harvard University Press.
Paley, W. 1825. *The Principles of Moral and Political Philosophy*. Vol. 4 of *Collected Works*. London: C. and J. Rivington.
Pattanaik, P. K., and Y. Xu. 1990. "On Ranking Opportunity Sets in Terms of Freedom of Choice." *Recherches Economiques de Louvain* 56: 383–90.
Pettit, P. 1991. *Decision Theory and Folk Psychology. Essays in the Foundations of Decision Theory*. Edited by M. Bacharach and S. Hurley. Oxford: Blackwell. Reprinted in P. Pettit (2002) *Rules, Reasons, and Norms*. Oxford: Oxford University Press.
Pettit, P. 1997a. *Republicanism: A Theory of Freedom and Government*. Oxford: Oxford University Press.
Pettit, P. 1997b. "Republican Theory and Criminal Punishment." *Utilitas* 9: 59–79.
Pettit, P. 2007. "Joining the Dots." In *Common Minds: Themes from the Philosophy of Philip Pettit*. Edited by H. G. Brennan, R. E. Goodin, F. C. Jackson, and M. Smith, 215–344. Oxford: Oxford University Press:.
Pettit, P. 2008a. "Freedom and Probability: A Comment on Goodin and Jackson." *Philosophy & Public Affairs* 36: 206–20.
Pettit, P. 2008b. "Republican Liberty: Three Axioms, Four Theorems." In *Republicanism and Political Theory*. Edited by C. Laborde and J. Manor. Oxford: Blackwell.
Pettit, P. 2008c. "The Basic Liberties." In *Essays on H. L. A. Hart*. Edited by M. Kramer. Oxford: Oxford University Press.
Pettit, P. 2009." Law and Liberty." In *Law and Republicanism*. Edited by S. Besson and J. L. Marti. Oxford: Oxford University Press.
Pettit, P. 2011. "The Instability of Freedom as Non-Interference: The Case of Isaiah Berlin." *Ethics* 121: 693–716.
Pettit, P. 2013. *On the People's Terms*. Cambridge, UK: Cambridge University Press.
Richardson, H. 2002. *Democratic Autonomy*. New York: Oxford University Press.
Sen, A. 1982. *Choice, Welfare and Measurement*. Oxford: Blackwell.
Sen, A. 1985. *Commodities and Capabilities*. Amsterdam: North-Holland.
Sen, A. 2002. *Rationality and Freedom*. Cambridge, MA: Harvard University Press.
Sidney, A. 1990. *Discourses Concerning Government*. Indianapolis, IN: Liberty Classics.
Skinner, Q. 1998. *Liberty before Liberalism*. Cambridge, UK: Cambridge University Press.
Skinner, Q. 2008. "Freedom as the Absence of Arbitrary Power." In *Republicanism and Political Theory*. Edited by J. Maynor and C. Laborde. Oxford: Blackwell.

Spitz, J.-F. 1995. *La Liberte Politique*. Paris: Presses Universitaires de France.
Steiner, H. 1994. *An Essay on Rights*. Oxford: Blackwell.
Sugden, R. 1998. "The Metric of Opportunity." *Economics and Philosophy* 14: 307–37.
Taylor, M. 1982. *Community, Anarchy and Liberty*. Cambridge, UK: Cambridge University Press.
Taylor, C. 1985. *Philosophy and the Human Sciences: Philosophical Papers 2*. Cambridge, UK: Cambridge University Press.
Trenchard, J., and T. Gordon. 1971. *Cato's Letters*. New York: Da Capo Press.
Van Parijs, P. 1995. *Real Freedom for All*. Oxford: Oxford University Press.
Waldron, J. 2007. "Pettit's Molecule." In *Common Minds: Themes from the Philosophy of Philip Pettit*. Edited by G. Brennan, R. E. Goodin, F. Jackson, and M. Smith, 143–60. Oxford: Oxford University Press.
Wirszubski, C. 1968. *Libertas as a Political Ideal at Rome*. Oxford: Oxford University Press.

CHAPTER 5

PROPERTY

GERALD GAUS

1. Private Property: Fundamental or Passé?

For the past half century, thinking within political philosophy about private property and ownership has had something of a schizophrenic quality. The classical liberal tradition has always stressed an intimate connection between a free society and the right to private property (Gray 1986). As Ludwig von Mises put it, "The program of liberalism ... if condensed to a single word, would have to read: *property*, that is, private ownership" (2005, 2, emphasis in original). Robert Nozick's (1974) *Anarchy, State and Utopia*, drawing extensively on Locke, gave new life to this idea; subsequently a great deal of political philosophy has focused on the justification (or lack of it) of natural rights to private property. Classical liberals such as Eric Mack—also drawing extensively on Locke's theory of property—have argued that "the signature right of any rights-oriented classical liberalism is the right of self-ownership" (2010, 53).[1] In addition, Mack argues that "we have the same good reasons for ascribing to each person a natural right of property" in "extrapersonal objects" (2010, 53). Each individual, Mack contends, has "an original, nonacquired right ... to engage in the acquisition of extrapersonal objects and in the disposition of those acquired objects as one sees fit in the service of one's ends" (2010, 53). Essentially, one has a natural right to become an owner of external property. Not all contemporary classical liberals hold that property rights are natural, but all insist that strong rights to private property are essential for a free society (see, e.g., Schmidtz 2010; Lomasky 1987). Jan Narveson has recently defended the necessity in a free society of property understood as "a unitary concept, explicable as a right over a thing owned, against others who are precluded from the free use of it to which ownership entitles the owner" (2010, 101).

The "new liberal" project of showing that a free society requires robust protection of civil and political rights, but *not* extensive rights of private property (beyond personal property) has persistently attacked this older, classical liberal position. L. T. Hobhouse (1964), one of the first new liberals, insisted that "we must not assume any of the rights of property as axiomatic"; we must replace the individualistic, "laissez-faire," older conception of property with a new, more social conception that recognizes that production is essentially a social enterprise, and so its fruits must be shared by all producers—most important, the workers.[2] Recent defenses of the new (or, as it is sometimes now called, "egalitarian") liberalism have continued to attack strong, classical liberal rights of private property, often by trying to distinguish the importance of private property as personal property from (far less important and highly qualified) property rights as the basis of market exchange (see, e.g., Fried 1995; Christman 1994, Part III; Waldron 1988, ch. 12), or else by seeking to show that, properly conceived, a defense of private property requires a state that ensures certain sorts of egalitarian distributions (see, e.g., Otsuka 2003; Vallentyne 2007).

The debate between classical liberals and new (or egalitarian) liberals in the last part of the twentieth century (and the beginning of the twenty-first) has been a continuation of the debate that commenced at the end of the nineteenth century, with the former upholding the central importance of the right to private property in a liberal society and the latter disputing or qualifying this. The apparent schizophrenic quality of this current debate is perceived once we recognize that the latter part of the twentieth century witnessed a fundamental reconceptualization of the concept of property. In his now classic essay, Thomas C. Grey announced the "disintegration of property." Grey acknowledged that in the less complex days of Locke and Blackstone—what he called the "high point of classical liberal thought"—property could be described in terms of a person's fairly unqualified ownership of a thing. To Blackstone, ownership was "that sole and despotic dominion which one man claims and exercises over the external things of the world, in total exclusion of the right of any other individual in the universe" (Grey 1980, 75). But, Grey pointed out, the law no longer deals with property as a unified authority over objects. For one, property is now seen as a bundle of various rights, liberties, and powers that can be divided among many parties in numerous ways, thus making the very idea of unified ownership passé. When an "owner of a thing begins to cede various rights over it—the right to use for this purpose tomorrow, for that purpose next year, and so on—at what point does he cease to be the owner, and who then owns the thing? You can say that each one of many right holders owns it to the extent of the right, or you can say that no one owns it" (Grey 1980, 70), and it doesn't seem to matter which. Second, Grey stressed that to even see property as primarily about rights over things or objects is largely anachronistic. "Consider the common forms of wealth: shares of stock in corporations, bonds, various kinds of commercial paper, bank accounts, insurance policies—not to mention more arcane intangibles such as trademarks, patents, copyrights, franchises, and business goodwill" (1980, 70). If, as Jeremy Waldron stated, private "[o]wnership . . . expresses the abstract idea of an object being correlated with the name of some individual, in relation to a rule which says that society will uphold that individual's decision as final when there is any dispute about how the object should be used," we are often left searching for the object of ownership (1988, 47). For Grey, once we understand that property as the classical liberal knew it has disintegrated, the debates between capitalism and socialism are really beside the point: We have a complex of dispersed rights held by different persons and organizations, including the state. Thus, according to Grey, "the substitution of a bundle-of-rights for a thing-ownership conception of property has the ultimate consequence that property ceases to be an important category in legal and political theory" (1980, 81).

If most philosophers rejected the bundle-of-rights view, or if most thought that property rights are important only when exercised over real property (objects such as land, resources, and so on), it would not be puzzling that so much of the debate about the place private property in the late twentieth century was a continuation of the nineteenth-century debate. But, oddly, the bundle-of-rights view is widely embraced, and philosophers know that many property rights are more akin to contractual rights (in which the core rights are to certain performances by other persons) than to a right to a parcel of land. Yet the debate has run on, often in terms of rights to things in the obvious sense, such as natural resources. When political philosophers debate substantive issues, it seems that we live in Locke's world; when they engage in conceptual analysis, they think in terms of the fragmented property rights of the twenty-first century.

In this chapter I seek to defend this charge while avoiding Grey's radical conclusion that the status of property no longer matters to political theory. I argue that political philosophers (and here I include some earlier essays of mine) for the most part have not successfully come to terms with the implications of the modern concept of property. I try to show that the fragmentation of property is real and is not easily overcome. I begin in Section 2 by reviewing the bundle-of-rights approach; Section 3 examines several attempts to identify a normative or logical structure to these rights that preserves the classic conception of ownership. In Section 4 I present an alternative conception of a regime of strong property rights that should be attractive to classical liberals yet avoids an appeal to the classic idea of ownership, accepting both Grey's fragmentation and the "no things" theses. However, even given the fragmentation of property, I hope to show that questions of the proper strength and scope of property rights remain at the core of political philosophy.

2. The Fragmentation of Ownership

Drawing on the classic analysis of A. M. Honoré (1961), let us say that a person (Alf) has full ownership of X if Alf has the following:

1. *Right of use*: Alf has a right to use X, that is,
    (a) Alf has a liberty to use X, and
    (b) Alf has a claim on others to refrain from use of X.

2. *Right of exclusion* (or possession): Others may use X if and only if Alf consents, that is,
   (a) if Alf consents others have a liberty to use X, and
   (b) if Alf does not consent others have a duty not to use X.
3. *Right to compensation*: If someone damages or uses X without Alf's consent, then Alf has a right to compensation from that person.
4. *Rights to destroy, waste, or modify*: Alf has a liberty to destroy X, waste it, or change it.
5. *Right to income*: Alf has a claim to the financial benefits of forgoing his own use of X and letting someone else use it.
6. *Absence of term*: Alf's rights over X are of indefinite duration.
7. *Liability to execution*: X may be taken away from Alf for repayment of a debt.
8. *Power of transfer*: Alf may permanently transfer (1) through (7) above to specific persons by consent.[3]

To have a property right is to have some bundle of these rights. Conceptually there is no problem with reconciling the bundle of rights view with full ownership: If one holds all these rights in an unlimited way, one is the owner of X in the classic sense.[4] However, in any advanced economy many (indeed, most) of these rights, liberties, and powers are often fragmented in some way. For any X, these rights (or, as they are called, "incidents") can be, and very often are, divided up among many different parties in complex ways. Suppose X is a case of real property, such as a house. One may sell his right to live in the house (rent it), put it in trust (in which case the trustee does not have the right to use it uneconomically), sign over to a historic commission the right to change the exterior, agree to a covenant with one's neighbors about acceptable exterior colors, and agree not to sell it to parties not approved by one's neighborhood association. On the other hand, there may be a law that does not allow the owner to refuse transfer on the basis of race; it may be mortgaged, in which case it may not be taken in payment of debt owed to third parties, and one may not have the right to destroy the house. If there are zoning laws, there are many uses that are precluded; if it used as a business, it may be illegal to exclude some persons on the grounds of race or ethnic origin. If there are building codes, many changes may be illegal. And many of these dispersions of rights may occur at the same time. Thus, the question of "Who is the owner?" may be answered by saying there is no owner, saying that there are many owners, or picking out some crucial incident such as the right to exclude (see Section 3) and saying whoever has *that* incident is the owner (but even this incident can be fragmented: for example, in a case of a business that has the right to exclude on some grounds but not on race or ethnicity). But nothing seems to turn on this: Whatever decision one makes about how to identify the "owner," the rights will be divided in whatever way they are: Who holds what rights, powers, and liberties is what is important, not who gets the honorific title of "owner."

3. Rescuing Ownership: Finding a Structure in the Bundle

The Justificatory Instability of Full Ownership

The most ambitious, and obvious, way to reconcile the traditional notion of ownership with the bundle of rights view is to argue that there is a compelling normative case for combining all these incidents (I discuss the problem of property over "no things" later, in Section 4.) In the present context we cannot review all the arguments seeking to demonstrate a normative basis for full ownership: In some sense this would constitute nothing less than a review of the classical liberal project.[5] I review here two of the most important approaches; I believe that the basic justificatory instability we uncover characterizes all defenses of full ownership.

The Problem of Restricted Justification. The most famous contemporary argument for ownership adapts Locke's argument from original acquisition. According to Locke,

> Though the Earth, and all inferior Creatures, be common to all Men, yet every Man has a *Property* in his own *Person*: this no Body has any right to but himself. The *Labour* of his Body, and the *Work* of his Hands, we may say, are properly his. Whatsoever then he removes out of the State that Nature hath provided, and left it in, he hath mixed his labour with, and joined to it something that is his own, and thereby makes it his *Property*. It being by him removed from the common state Nature hath placed it in, it hath by this *labour* something annexed to it, that excludes the common right of other men. For this *Labour* being the unquestionable property of the *Labourer*, no Man but he can have a right to what that is once joined to, at least where there is enough, and as good, left in common for others. (1960, sect. 27, emphasis in original)

The general form of an original acquisition argument for ownership is:

> Under conditions C, Alf's action ϕ in relation to any unowned object X makes Alf the (full) owner of X.

Thus, for Locke, if there is some unowned parcel of land (X), Alf's mixing his labor with the land (ϕ), under certain conditions C (such as enough and as good is left for others) renders Alf the owner of that land.

Two core challenges confront such arguments. First, and most obviously, it must be shown why ϕ-ing has an ownership-bestowing quality. As Nozick famously remarked, it is not clear why simply mixing your labor with an unowned thing makes the unowned thing yours rather than losing your labor. If you mix your tomato juice with the ocean, you lose your tomato juice; you do not gain the ocean (Nozick 1974, 174ff). I pass over this problem here, as it has been thoroughly explored in the literature (see, e.g., Becker 1977; Mack 2010; Russell 2004; Simmons 1992, ch. 5; Waldron 1988, ch. 6).

The second problem is our real concern: Even if it can be shown that some ϕ action grants one rights over an unowned object, it also must be shown that the justification of ϕ's ownership-bestowing qualities is such that a ϕ-er gets the full bundle of property rights over X. In regard to Locke's own theory, Steven Buckle has argued that since Locke justifies the necessity of property in terms of what is needed for humanity's survival and flourishing, uses of property that undermine this aim are not justified. Thus, Buckle argues that the Lockean justification of property involves limits of transfer: Trades that undermine the end of property (alienating food to obtain cocaine, for example) would not be justified (1991, 80; also see Gaus 1994, 222–24). In a similar vein, Locke explicitly excludes the right to destroy: If the world is given to humans by God to use, one cannot gain a right to simply destroy it. "Nothing was made by God for Man to spoil or destroy" (Locke 1960, sect. 31).

Jan Narveson recently advanced another original acquisition defense of private property:

> In the course of action, we use things, and if nobody else is already doing so, then the way is clear for us to use them, and to insist on the right to continue to use them. We do not need to justify our acquisition of *x* by demonstrating that it will best serve the public good if *we* are allowed to use it rather than someone else—even if that is quite often true. The point is that people being able to use what was previously unused, at will, enables a better off society. Indeed, it enables a better off society even in the (presumably numerous cases) in which there is someone out there who might make better use of it than the person who becomes the owner. (2010, 116)

Accepting that first possession justifies rights of use and, let us say, exclusion, we still do not have an obvious case for rights of transfer. Narveson seeks to expand the set of rights to include transfer by appealing to the Pareto criterion: If Alf and Betty can exchange their property, each will be better off. However, it is not clear that the Pareto criterion is really so hospitable to full ownership. Suppose we accept:

1. Original acquisition divides resources between Alf and Betty; and
2. Property rights must be mutually beneficial.

From (1) and (2), it seems easy to infer:

3. Alf's property right over some resource must benefit Betty and certainly must not be an overall cost to her.

In his original and insightful book *The Right to Exploit*, Gijs van Donselaar implicitly invokes this trinity of claims to argue against "parasitism" and thus fixed property rights in resources. Natural resources, van Donselaar argues, are scarce, and so we compete for them; property rights divide these resources, and if the property system is to be mutually beneficial, this division must work to the advantage of society. Consequently, if someone appropriates a natural resource but does not employ it in a way that improves the lot of others (and, of course, more strongly, if she employs it in a way that worsens others' lots), her claim to the scare resource cannot be justified through appeal to mutual benefit. Compared to the world in which the unproductive appropriator did not exist, others are worse off: The appropriator denies the use of the scarce resource to others by claiming property over it but does nothing with it. Thus, justified property is limited by whether one is productive (and, again, it seems difficult to justify rights to destroy). Indeed, we might question Narveson's insistence that the appropriator need not be the most efficient user of the resource. In a world where a less efficient producer has control of a scare resource, the opportunity costs of allowing her to control the resource (the gains society forgoes by not placing it in the hands of a more efficient producer) exceed the benefits (the gains from the resource being in the hands of the present, less efficient producer). This looks straightforwardly inefficient; there is a sense in which we are all worse off because the less efficient producer has gained control of the resource and so there are fewer of its fruits available to society. Thus, according to van Donselaar:

> The entrepreneur's duty is not just to produce as efficiently as he can, but to produce at least as efficiently as any of his competitors would have done in his position (as far as that position is defined by control over resources). That implies that he may be required to produce more efficiently than he can. Where he fails to do so, he has no right to be in his position. Where he fails, his factor endowments ought to be adjusted. (2009, 54)

As interpreted by van Donselaar, our trinity of claims makes each the steward of external resources over which one has property rights, a stewardship that requires the most efficient use for its continuance. Fixed rights in resources, von Donselaar argues, license parasitism: some gaining at the expense of others.[6] Again, we see that once we closely examine a supposed case for acquisition, it is exceedingly difficult to see how it grounds the full panoply of unfettered property rights. Let us call this the problem of *restricted justification*.

Liberty Upsets Ownership. It would seem that a far more promising approach to justifying full ownership would be to appeal to what Eric Mack calls the "ur-claim" of each to live her own life in her own way (2010, 55). As Loren Lomasky puts it, a liberal order that adequately accommodates our fundamental interest in pursuing our own projects in our own way must give an important place to robust property rights, which carve out a domain in which an individual has morally secure possession (1987, 111ff). Of special interest to our inquiry is that neither Mack nor Lomasky holds that there is a natural right to a certain bundle of property rights (Lomasky explicitly acknowledges the bundle-of-rights analysis). Both do, however, believe that we have a basic right to an adequate scheme of property rights that gives each the ability to appropriate and possess property, allowing one to live one's own life as one sees fit.

Some have argued that if (broadly speaking) the justification of property is to promote the autonomy or sphere of decision making for each, all that is required is the right to use and the right to exclude but not, say, the right to gain income (see, e.g., Christman 1994, 127ff). After all, Lomasky himself stresses possession: "The creation of social institutions that recognize and define principles of noninterference with a person's holdings transform *having* into rightful *possession*" (1987, 121, emphasis in original). But this seems too narrow: If the aim is to secure domains that are maximally responsive to a person's projects and desire to lead her own life in her own way, rights to engage in a wide variety of trades, investment, and commerce must be acknowledged (see Kershnar 2002, 247–49). One understanding of the human good is productive work. The work to be valued is varied, from the self-employed artisan to participation in team work, but it also involves organization, personal initiative, and innovation in production. One of the basic themes of Ayn Rand's *Atlas Shrugged* is that entrepreneurship is itself a form of human flourishing. Start-ups, innovation, risk-taking, organizing groups to solve problems and implement new ideas—all are basic to the projects, plans, and ideals of many.[7] To exclude all of these personal ideals about what is worth doing on the grounds that the right of use without the right of income is sufficient to live one's own life in one's own way unacceptably constrains the ability of many to lead lives in which they can fully realize their fundamental values.

But while the crux of the project-pursuit case for property seems to endorse a wide array of property rights (not just use but transfer, income, and even destruction), it also justifies the very fragmentation of property that poses the challenge to liberal ownership. Suppose we commence at "time zero" with a system in which all owners are full owners. Even so, it very often will be in the interests of individuals to fragment their property. Recall that many of our examples of fragmentation of house ownership (Section 2) were voluntarily made by the owner. Thus, even if we start out with a system of full ownership, if people make a series of free choices it is almost certain that ownership will end up fragmented. Nozick is famous for arguing that liberty upsets any pattern of holdings: If individuals start with some pattern of property holdings (P) but are able to freely choose what to do with their property, it is almost certain they will act in such a way as to bring about a non-P pattern (Nozick 1974, 160ff). What we now see is that, for the same reason, liberty upsets full ownership. If we start off with full ownership (which, after all, is simply a certain pattern of the incidents of the bundle), the free choice of individuals to trade and give away some incidents will result in a fragmentation of property rights. Thus, not only is the fragmentation of property a fact about the modern world, it seems an inevitable result of a system in which people are free to form bundles according to their own choosing. Let us call this the problem that *liberty upsets ownership*.

We now can see the problem of justifying full ownership. Many justifications are characterized by the problem of restricted justification: We can justify a stable right to property, but it seems unlikely that the justification will include the full range of incidents included in the ideal of full ownership. I have presented a sketch of the difficulties for original acquisition theories; the literature indicates that the same problem applies, for example, to the sort of self-expressive theory of ownership advanced by Kant and Hegel. For Kant, property is based on the necessity of a will acting in the world to go beyond mere possession of things with which it is involved and to claim a continuing juridical relation to its objects—to make them its property (see Kant 1999, 43ff). But while this may ground rights of use and exclusion, it is unclear that full rights to income and transfer follow (Westphal 1997; see also Ryan 1984, ch. 3). Much the same has been said of Hegel's related account (Waldron 1988, 432ff). Utilitarian or consequentialist arguments for property seem obviously open to a wide variety of possible restrictions on the rights of ownership; under nonideal conditions such as information asymmetry and other sorts of imperfect information, bargaining inequalities, and so on, there may be compelling grounds to limit the rights of owners (Ryan 1984, 106ff). Even Stephen Munzer's pluralist theory—drawing on utilitarianism but adding Kantian considerations and notions of desert—does not justify "unfettered private ownership" but rather "a constrained system of private ownership"(1990, 7). So most of the justifications that have been advanced for ownership seem, even if successful, to yield only restricted bundles. On the other hand, it does seem possible to justify all elements of the bundle by stressing the fundamental importance of giving individuals maximum ability to possess domains that suit their aims and projects, whatever they may be, but then we face the problem that liberty upsets ownership: Such a system allows individuals to fragment their ownership. And of course subsequent generations are born into a world of fragmented property, such as the one in which we find ourselves now.

It is hard to see how a full bundle of rights immune to fragmentation can be justified on autonomy/project-pursuit grounds. One possibility is to draw on Mill's argument that a defense of liberty should not defend the liberty to permanently alienate liberty (1977, 299). In a similar way, it might be argued that a defense of full ownership based on the pursuit of autonomy should not defend the ability to alienate full ownership. But this clearly will not do, for a defense of the right to alienate is essential to full ownership. It seems most odd to hold that on autonomy grounds we have the right to alienate all of the incidents (as in transfer) but not some short of all of them. If we take this (paternalistic?) line of reasoning seriously, the right to transfer and give away property is itself called into question. Alternatively, it might be argued that the fragmentation of property is a sort of negative externality: It creates an environment in which future generations of project pursuers enter a world not neatly divided up via full property rights. So the idea might be that we must limit the ability of the present generation to pursue their goals (by preventing fragmentation) in the interests of the autonomy of the future. Not only does this line of reasoning depend on highly controversial weighting of the autonomy interests of different generations, but once again it opens a Pandora's box for the classical liberal. If we now are limiting the property rights of the present to enhance the autonomy of the future, then the right to destroy or waste certainly looks susceptible to being limited on similar grounds. Whatever argument we employ to limit the right to fragment seems sure to ground a case for a less than full bundle.

Retreating to a Core

In the face of the difficulties of justifying the full set of property rights involved in liberal ownership, we might retreat to a core set of rights that characterizes ownership. For example, we might hold that one is the owner if one has the rights of use, exclusion, transfer, compensation, and income (see Gaus 1994, 213–4; see also Snare 1972, 200–6). But this is already a sufficiently large enough bundle that the problem of restricted justification is apt to arise again: We would need a justification that points to this, specific, entire bundle of rights. More important, each of these incidents itself fragments. For example, zoning and historic district laws regulate *some* uses; consumer protection and laws against fraud limit *some* transfers of rights; right-of-way provisions as well as racial discrimination laws prohibit *some* exclusions; banking and financial regulations prohibit *some* ways of earning income from a variety of financial instruments; limited liability companies restrict *some* rights of compensation. We should not think of the fragmentation thesis as holding that there are, say, eight discrete rights that may break apart: Each of these rights itself fragments into a variety of rights, liberties, and powers in particular contexts.

David Schmidtz, while acknowledging that "today the term 'property rights' generally is understood to refer to a bundle of rights that could include rights to sell, lend, bequeath, use as collateral, or even destroy," nevertheless insists that "at the heart of any property right is a right to say no: a right to exclude non-owners. In other words, a right to exclude is not just a stick in a bundle. Rather, property is a tree. Other sticks are branches, the right to exclude is the trunk" (2010, 80).[8] This is because, Schmidtz argues, "without the right to say no, other rights in the bundle are reduced to mere liberties rather than genuine rights" (2010, 80). More strictly, if one does not have the right to exclude but does have the right to transfer, income, and compensation, one can be said to have a *liability right*: Others can use X without one's consent, but they must compensate one for doing so, and one can transfer this right to others and earn income from it (Schmidtz 2010, 80–81).[9] Like most distinctions, this one becomes less clear when we look at it closely. Consider the classic case presented by Joel Feinberg:

> Suppose that you are on a backpacking trip in the high mountain country when an unanticipated blizzard strikes the area with such ferocity that your life is imperiled. Fortunately, you stumble onto an unoccupied cabin, locked and boarded up for the winter, clearly someone else's private property. You smash a window, enter, and huddle in the corner for three days until the storm abates. During this period you help yourself to your unknown benefactor's food supply and burn his wooden furniture in the fireplace you keep warm. Surely you are justified in doing all these things, and yet you have infringed the clear rights of another person. (1978, 102)

It looks very much like circumstances have transformed the cabin owner's property right into a liability right: The stranded hiker can use it provided she pays compensation. Even if the owner erected a large sign saying, "Can you use this cabin in case of emergency? No!" it would not be wrong for the hiker to use it provided she compensated afterward. Lomasky (1991) argues that in such cases the justification for property in the first place—that it facilitates projects—fails to justify the right to say "no": We cannot expect a person to accede to our project-based demands at an extraordinarily high cost to his own. In this case, while it seems unreasonable to insist on a property right, a liability right is justifiable.[10] (Note that this is a version of the problem of restricted justification, here about the scope of the right to exclude.) In this case we would not want to say that the owner of the cabin is not "really the owner," since he does not have a core right of exclusion in this case.

Thus, there are important rights to property that are, strictly speaking, liability rights, and only because they are liability rights rather than pure exclusionary rights (with the power to say "no") are they justifiable. Suppose, though, it is claimed that these are marginal and exceptional cases. Wouldn't we say that real and important property rights always involve the core power to say "no," and if one has that core right protected, one is the owner? I do not think so. Certainly exclusion (and, say, the ability to refuse transfer, part of the Schmidtz's [2010] general right to say "no") is an important incident, but so is the right to transfer. We cannot, I think, say that one who has the right to exclude and manage but not transfer is unambiguously the owner while someone who has a transferable liability right with right to income is not. Consider the principle of entail in the common law: An owner of an entailed property (such as a family estate) could exclude others at will and determine the use to which the land was put and earn income from its use but was without the right of transfer. Is she the owner? Not without reason is such a person often described as the "the holder" of the property. As Mrs. Bennett remarked of the Collinses in *Pride and Prejudice*, "Well, if they can be easy with an estate that is not lawfully their own, so much the better. I should be ashamed of having one that was only entailed on me" (Austin 1906, 202). Certainly in many contexts a transferable liability right may better allow one to advance one's ends than a nontransferable right to say "no." As the much-maligned Mrs. Bennett also sensibly remarked, "There is no knowing how estates will go when once they come to be entailed" (Austin 1906, 57).

Defragmenting Property: The Logical Structure of Ownership

Daniel Attas recently advanced a sophisticated analysis with the aim of showing "that ownership exhibits an internal coherence such that which incidents can subsist independently of others is not an entirely contingent matter.... the incidents of ownership cannot be divided coherently in just any odd way" (2006, 141). Attas disputes Grey's (1980) disintegration thesis, arguing that there is a *conceptual* structure of ownership, such that holding some incidents implies that one must hold others. First, Attas argues, we must distinguish the content from the form of the property right:

> If a property right can be said to reside in a person (P) with respect to a thing (X), then the content of the right is those features of it that have the thing owned as their subject (the right to use X, possess X and so on), and the form of the right is those features of it that have the right itself as their subject (the right is continuous, the right is transferable and so on). In other words, the content incidents are first order moral positions and the form incidents are second order moral positions. (2006, 141)

Attas divides the content incidents into two subgroups: control and income. The former includes, among other incidents, (a) possession, (b) use (e.g., consumption and modification), and (c) management. Importantly, Attas claims, "There is a certain progression in the scope of the control incidents, such that each incident presupposes or includes within it those that precede it" (2006, 141–42). One cannot have the right of use without the right of possession, and one cannot have the right to manage without the right to use. Thus, for Attas, "using the asset oneself is therefore simply one exercise of the right to manage" (2006, 142). Much depends here on just how we interpret these rights, but it is quite clear that one can have a right to manage that includes the right to allow others to use the property in broader ways than one can use it oneself (thus one has less than full use rights). A trustee may possess the right to manage a property without having the right to consume it. Interestingly, the trustee could sell the right to consume the property for enjoyment to a third party if this trade benefited the trustor, though the trustee herself has no right to use the property in uneconomic ways (see Section 2). In such cases, one who has the power to manage a property does not have the right to use it (certainly not to consume it) herself but would have the power to allow others to use it. But then her right is a power to allow others to consume it if they provide sufficient compensation (to the trustor), not itself a right of use.[11] Note that Attas says that "management includes the right to decide how a thing shall be used, to allow others to use the thing, or to impose certain conditions on its use"—neither of which need be the rights that Attas considers crucial for use—"consumption and modification" But then it is hard to see how "the right to manage must include all the control rights" (2006, 142).

"It also follows," Attas argues, "that control rights cannot be split among several partial owners since any control right by one person will exclude the possibility of any other control right held by any other" (2006, 142). We might interpret this in three ways: Given some property X, at some time t, (*i*) Alf and Betty cannot exercise joint control over some aspect of it, a; (*ii*) Alf cannot control aspect a of X while Betty controls aspect b; (*iii*) Alf and Betty cannot both independently control aspect a. Attas explicitly allows joint ownership as in (*i*) (Attas 2006, 142n) and (*ii*) cannot be correct. The city of New Orleans closely controlled modification of the front of my house facing the street (a), while I had wide control over the back (b). The city controlled some aspects of my property while I controlled others. So the worry must be about (*iii*): Two agents cannot independently exercise the same control over the same aspect. A coherent system of rights cannot recognize two, potentially conflicting property rights over the same aspect of the same thing. Whereas it might seem that this implies, to use Hillel Steiner's term, that a necessary condition for genuine control rights is that they must be "compossible"—if Alf and Betty have bona fide control rights over some aspect *a* of X, it must be possible for them to simultaneously exercise their rights (Steiner 1994).[12] A conflict of control rights as interpreted by (*iii*) would grant Alf a right to use aspect *a* of X in a way that is inconsistent with Betty's use, to which she also has a right, and so compossibility is violated. However, we do not require anything as strong as compossibility: A consistent set of rights requires that in situations of conflict, there are priority rules that determine under what conditions Alf's right gives way to Betty's. Again, we come to the complicated play of property and liability rules (see Section 3). One possibility is that Alf's right to use his cabin furniture may give way to Betty's right to build a fire out of it *if* Betty compensates Alf for her use and so overrides his right to use. We certainly require that conflicts of rights be sorted out, but this is consistent with a complex crisscrossing of control rights.

4. Property as Jurisdictions

Rethinking the Ideal of Strong and Extensive Property Rights

Most defenders (interestingly, not Attas)[13] of the classic view of ownership advance a case for "full liberal ownership"—that ownership is justified and consists of essentially of the entire bundle of incidents—because they wish to defend *strong and extensive property rights*. Classic liberals, holding that a free society must be based on private ownership, seek to justify extensive and strong property rights, and full ownership obviously seems to fit the bill.[14] But we have seen that liberty upsets full ownership (Section 3); it is hard not to wonder whether full ownership is really the ideal of strong and extensive property rights consistent with the aims of classical liberals. Thinking more broadly about what constitutes a strong regime of extensive property rights, we might distinguish two other senses of extensive and strong ownership.

A private property regime can be said to be *strong* if, whatever elements of the bundle one has, only weighty moral reasons, or reasons of great and pressing social utility, could justifiably override one's rights. Although some libertarians have held that these rights are absolute—they are of such weight that no considerations could justify overriding them—this seems an extreme view (think again of Feinberg's classic cabin case). Most classical liberals have held that taxation for public goods, poor provision, and taking land for critical public uses is justifiable; so too are some zoning laws. But while the classical liberal need not insist on anything like rights of absolute weight, it is certainly inconsistent with an ideal of strong rights to say, for example, that since property rights are created by the state, one's property rights cannot, conceptually, be infringed by any state taxation (see, e.g., Murphy and Nagel 2002; cf. Gaus 2010). Whatever part of the bundle one holds, he or she must provide weighty reasons justifying one's continued rights to control, transfer, and so on.

Property rights are *extensive* insofar as, for any given asset X, it is the case that there exists some nongovernmental agents or agencies that hold each of the incidents of the property rights bundle. This is not to say that there is any single agent, group, or corporation that holds all the incidents in relation to X but that each of the incidents is held by some such agent. Thus, the incidents over X may be highly fragmented: I might have sold my right to mine my land but not farm it; I might sell the water rights, the right to develop it, and so on. All these rights may be held by different individuals and corporations, but insofar as none are controlled by public decision making, we would still have a regime of extensive private property rights.

Conceptually, the strongest and most extensive system of private property rights would be one in which all the incidents over every asset are privately held, and each of these rights, liberties, and powers are maximally weighty. This may be a logical ideal, but it is unappealing as a normative ideal. There is, for example, a strong case for governmental control of public spaces and urban areas.[15] There is also good reason to laud the fact that the private ownership of land no longer includes the ownership of the airspace above it, which is now regulated by the state (Schmidtz 2010, 82–84). In contemporary American society, property rights are quite extensive, though certainly not maximal (think of the absence of transfer and income rights over heroin, certain sexual services, and kidneys) and certainly property rights are often overridden (think of licensing regulations, environmental regulations, health and safety rules, and so on). Nevertheless, we can still identify dimensions of strength and extensiveness: The classical liberal argues that, along both dimensions, a society should tend toward the stronger and more extensive ends of the continuums.

Liberalism, Jurisdictions, and Property in the Wide and Narrow Senses

Revisiting the argument for property based on project pursuit and one's desire to live one's own life in one's own way (Section 3), we can see that, while this argument seems to support the idea that each person has an extensive domain in which to lead her life in her own way, based on her own values, projects, and ends, it does not lead to the ideal of full ownership. To be maximally responsive to a person's ends and values, it would seem a system of property must allow people to devise domains that best suit their ends and purposes, and this very ideal leads to fragmenting property. However, while this ideal does not lead to the classic idea of full ownership, it does, I think, endorse a system of strong and extensive property rights. It requires a system of strong property rights insofar as, whatever incidents are part of one's domain, unless these rights are weighty, they do not provide a secure basis for living one's life as one sees fit. To grant property rights but allow that these are easily overridden by other moral and policy considerations hardly makes the rights a crucial tool in living one's own life in one's own way. Of course, in a more nuanced account of strength, we would have to consider the vexed issue of the relation of property and liability rights. Strict property rights are clearly a stronger (though in a somewhat different sense) form of property than liability rights, so a regime of strong property rights would certainly not be a regime in which people generally hold liability rights, as Schmidtz (2010) rightly maintains.

It may seem more obscure why these rights should also be extensive. There are two ways in which rights can fail to be extensive. First, there may be no right assigned over some aspect of some asset, and so people are at liberty to possess, use, or destroy it as they see fit, though others may compete and seek to interfere with this. Sometimes this is perfectly acceptable: We compete for space on the sidewalk without too many ill effects. But, typically, leaving assets in the "common" not only leads to their waste as people compete to consume them first, but the prospect of conflict undermines secure expectations of how one can go about fulfilling one's projects and living according to one's values and aims (Hardin 1968; Schmidtz 1991, ch. 2).

The other way in which private property fails to be extensive is, of course, when incidents are controlled by government. As I have argued throughout, classical liberals have always recognized that there is a considerable role for government, but there is always the problem that, because we do not agree on values, ends, and projects, government decisions typically advance the values of some over those of others. In this way government decision is at best a compromise and at worst a case of mere conflict. John Gray once noted how private property rights economize on collective justification:

> The importance of several [i.e., private] property for civil society is that it acts as an enabling device whereby rival and possibly incommensurable conceptions of the good may be implemented and realized without any recourse to any collective decision-procedure.... One may even say of civil society that it is a device for securing peace by reducing to a minimum the decisions on which recourse to collective choice—the political or public choice that is binding on all—is unavoidable. (1993, 314)

In public deliberation about political decisions, a person has simply one controversial set of values, ends, and projects, which may or may not be reflected in collective decisions; over her property a person's decisions—based on her controversial values and projects—have weighty, publicly recognized authority over others (Gaus 2009a). Thus, property is so important to the rights of the moderns because it allows each a jurisdiction in which his values and ends hold sway and so minimizes appeal to collective choices among those who disagree on the ends of life (Gaus 2007).

Once we see that property is crucially about securing a domain or jurisdiction in which one's values, ends, and aims hold sway, we can see that reference to things, objects, or even assets in our understanding of property (though we may employ it for ease of exposition) is not necessary. A shortcoming of Attas's otherwise impressive analysis is his reliance on the classic idea (taken from the analysis of real property) that "property assigns things (rights over things) to individuals"(2006, 134). The idea that property is about "using bits of things in the world" remains critical to the classic view of ownership.[16] Recall that, in addition to advancing the disintegration thesis, Grey's (1980) second challenge to the traditional conception of property was to deny that in most cases it makes sense to even talk of "things." As Grey stressed, when we think of complex financial instruments and intellectual property, the line between contract and property fades.[17]

This does not affect the jurisdictional view. Property rights define domains or jurisdictions, and these always are defined in terms of rights, claims, and powers relating to other agents. Sometimes these rights and claims clearly involve objects, while other times the property right is solely explicated in terms of rights, claims, and powers concerning the actions of others. Property merges into contract, but it also merges into the basic rights of the person—which is why the claim that we are self-owners is so plausible. Indeed, as Buckle (1991) shows in his study of natural law theories of property, the idea that one's property can be understood broadly to include all the rights in one's domain goes back to natural law theorists, who insisted on an intimate connection between a person's rights and what "belongs" to that person. This idea of what belongs to a person—her *suum*—concerns a set of "essential possessions": life, limbs, and liberty. Thus understood, says Buckle, the *suum* is "what naturally belongs to a person because none of these things can be taken away without injustice" (1991, 29). This is not to say that in most contexts we cannot distinguish, say, a right to free speech from the property right to one's Subaru Outback, but we should not expect a deep and clear distinction in principle between the rights, powers, and claims that comprise one's domain (Buchanan 1975, 10).[18]

5. Conclusion

Grey (1980) held that, given the disintegration of property rights, the old battle between liberalism and socialism was over: There was no unequivocal ownership to be granted to private parties or the state. Instead, we are faced with a disintegrated bundle of rights, some held by governments, some by individuals, some by corporations. There could be changes at the margin, but it seemed there was no longer any great dispute in principle. The typical response of those in the classical liberal tradition has been to seek to defend full liberal ownership against this disintegration or fragmentation thesis. I have argued that the disintegration thesis is powerful: It is not only what we are faced with in our contemporary world, it is the inevitable result of freedom under conditions of diversity of values and ends. But this does not mean that the question of whether a free society must have strong and extensive private property is passé. Socialists and new liberals argue that core human values require that many of the incidents be controlled by public, collective decision making, while the classical liberal insists on the importance of strong and extensive private property to protect freedom and promote efficient economic transactions. These disputes do not go away simply because the incidents are fragmented. The idea that, further, a regime of private property rights must grant full ownership is largely a distraction. The classic liberal who upholds such a bundle often believes she is defending the basis of a free society, but the very freedom she cherishes upsets the pattern of full ownership.

NOTES

1. See also the chapters in this volume on classical liberalism and on Nozick.
2. The "new liberalism" arose at the end of the nineteenth century in England, seeking to distance liberalism from capitalism. For an excellent account, see Freeden (1978). Very similar ideas were at the heart of the political philosophy of John Dewey (1980) and the American progressive movement.
3. See also Becker (1977, ch. 2) and Gruenbaum (1987, ch. 1).
4. An issue arises here concerning the legal power of the state to alter these incidents. If the state has such a power, it might be held that it, not Alf, is in some sense *really* the owner. Classical liberals thus typically hold that the state does not have the legal power to alter these incidents without consent (for Locke the consent of the people as represented in the legislature was required). Scott Arnold (2011) argues that in contemporary legal systems the state is the residue owner of everything.
5. I provide some brief sketches of common approaches and their difficulties in Gaus (2009b). See also the chapter on classical liberalism in this volume. For a useful general survey of accounts of property, see Reeve (1993). For a thorough but critical survey of attempts to justify liberal ownership, see Christman (1994).
6. This is a claim with which Gauthier appears to concur in his endorsement on the back of van Donselaar's book. In his *Morals by Agreement*, Gauthier (1986, 293) advocated a weak requirement of efficient use as necessary for rightful possession.
7. An investor in the "Impossible Project," a firm seeking to bring Polaroid film back into production, said to the founder: "I have looked all your team in the eye and none of them is in here for the money. They are in here to make it happen" (*Financial Times* 2009, 15).
8. Schmidtz attributes the metaphor of property as a "bundle of sticks" to John Lewis, *Law of Eminent Domain* (Chicago: Callaghan, 1888).
9. The classic analysis of this distinction is Guido Calabresi and A. Douglas Melamed (1972).
10. Schmidtz (2010, 82) acknowledges that "the right to say no is stringent but not absolute."
11. Attas seeks to avoid this conclusion by distinguishing content rights (rights directly relating to control of the thing) from formal incidents, such as powers of transfer. But the core point here is that a manager may not have full rights of use but powers to grant full rights of use; because it obscures this point we have grounds to question the utility of the content/form distinction.
12. In Steiner's terms, these rights are not "categorically composible" though, of course, they may be composible in some circumstances (i.e., where Alf and Betty happen to agree).

13. Attas's inclination is to hold that "property rights should be abandoned" (2006, 122).

14. Of course, classical liberals and libertarians exhibit great diversity on the nature of this case and how strong property rights must be. For an overview of the varieties, see Mack and Gaus (2003).

15. Liberal society has thrived in urban areas with extensive public space, not gated communities where all space is privatized. I make this point in Gaus (2000).

16. Advocates of this view sometime speak of "intangible things," which rather reminds one of "incorporeal body"—which Hobbes called "a mere sound" without sense (see Hobbes 1994, 21).

17. Attas seeks to erect a clear line: "A contractual right not only originates in a voluntarily initiated state of affairs (a transaction or a relationship), but also persists only so long as the state of affairs persists. In this sense it has no independent existence of its own" (2006, 144). But consider trusts set up by a contract that holds in perpetuity: These may far outlast any property right, which would revert to another at death. "The law requires trustees of a charitable trust to adhere to the donor's stated charitable purpose for the stated period, even if forever" (Brody 1997, 877).

18. I did not appreciate this point in Gaus (1994, 221n).

REFERENCES

Arnold, Scott. 2011. "Are Modern Liberals Socialists or Social Democrats?" *Social Philosophy & Policy* 28(2): 262–82.
Attas, Daniel. 2006. "The Fragmentation of Property." *Law and Philosophy* 25: 119–49.
Austin, Jane. 1906. *Pride and Prejudice*. London: Thomas Nelson and Sons.
Becker, Lawrence C. *Property Rights: Philosophical Foundations*. London: Routledge & Kegan Paul.
Brody, Evelyn. 1997. "Charitable Endowments and the Democratization of Dynasty." *Arizona Law Review* 39: 873–948.
Buchanan, James. 1975. *The Limits of Liberty*. Chicago: University of Chicago Press.
Buckle, Stephen. 1991. *Natural Law and the Theory of Property*. Oxford: Clarendon Press.
Calabresi, Guido, and A. Douglas Melamed. 1972. "Property Rules, Liability Rules, and Inalienability: One View of the Cathedral." *Harvard Law Review* 85: 1089–128.
Christman, John. 1994. *The Myth of Property: Toward an Egalitarian Theory of Ownership*. New York: Oxford University Press.
Dewey, John. 1980. *Liberalism and Social Action*. New York: Perigee.
Feinberg, Joel. 1978. "Voluntary Euthanasia and the Inalienable Right to Life." *Philosophy & Public Affairs* 7: 93–123.
Financial Times. 2009. (August 15–16): 15.
Freeden, Michael. 1978. *The New Liberalism*. Oxford: Oxford University Press.
Fried, Barbara. 1995. "Wilt Chamberlain Revisited: Nozick's 'Justice in Transfer' and the Problem of Market-Based Distribution." *Philosophy & Public Affairs* 24: 226–45.
Gaus, Gerald. 1994. "Property, Rights, and Freedom." *Social Philosophy & Policy* 11: 209–40.
Gaus, Gerald. 2000. "A Libertarian Alternative to Liberal Justice." *Criminal Justice Ethics* 19: 32–43.
Gaus, Gerald. 2007. "On Justifying the Moral Rights of the Moderns: A Case of Old Wine in New Bottles." *Social Philosophy & Policy* 25: 84–119.

Gaus, Gerald. 2009a. "Recognized Rights as Devices of Public Reason." *Philosophical Perspectives: Ethics* 23: 111–36.
Gaus, Gerald. 2009b. "The Idea and Ideal of Capitalism." In *The Oxford Handbook of Business Ethics*. Edited by George G. Brenkert and Tom L. Beauchamp, 73–99. Oxford: Oxford University Press.
Gaus, Gerald. 2010. "Coercion, Ownership, and the Redistributive State: Justificatory Liberalism's Classical Tilt." *Social Philosophy & Policy* 27: 233–75.
Gauthier, David. 1986. *Morals by Agreement*. Oxford: Oxford University Press.
Gray, John. 1986. *Liberalism*. Milton Keynes, UK: Open University Press.
Gray, John. 1993. *Post-Enlightenment Liberalism*. London: Routledge.
Grey, Thomas C. 1980. "The Disintegration of Property." In *NOMOS XXII: Property*. Edited by J. Roland Pennock and John W. Chapman, 69–85. New York: New York University Press.
Gruenbaum, James O. 1987. *Private Ownership*. London: Routledge & Kegan Paul.
Hardin, Garrett. 1968. "The Tragedy of the Commons." *Science* 162: 1243–48.
Hobbes, Thomas. 1994. *Leviathan*. Edited by Edwin Curley. Indianapolis, IN: Hackett.
Hobhouse, L. T. 1964. *Liberalism*. New York: Oxford University Press.
Honoré, A. M. 1961. "Ownership." In *Oxford Essays in Jurisprudence*. Edited by A. G. Guest, 107–47. Oxford: Clarendon Press.
Kant, Immanuel. 1999. *The Metaphysical Elements of Justice*, 2d ed. Edited and translated by John Ladd. Indianapolis, IN: Hackett.
Kershnar, Stephen. 2002. "Private Property Rights and Autonomy." *Public Affairs Quarterly* 16: 231–58.
Locke, John. 1960. "The Second Treatise of Government." In *Two Treatises of Government*. Edited by Peter Laslett. Cambridge, UK: Cambridge University Press.
Lomasky, Loren. 1987. *Persons, Rights, and the Moral Community*. New York: Oxford University Press.
Lomasky, Loren E. 1991. "Compensation and the Bounds of Rights." In *NOMOS XXXIII: Compensatory Justice*. Edited by J. Roland Pennock and John W. Chapman, 13–44. New York: New York University Press.
Mack, Eric. 2010. "The Natural Right of Property." *Social Philosophy & Policy* 27: 53–78.
Mack, Eric, and Gerald Gaus. 2003. "Classical Liberalism and Libertarianism: The Liberty Tradition." In *Handbook of Political Theory*. Edited by G. Gaus and C. Kukathas, 115–30. London: SAGE Publications.
Mill, John Stuart. 1977. "On Liberty." In *The Collected Works of John Stuart Mill*. Vol. 18. Edited by John M. Robson. Toronto: University of Toronto Press.
Munzer, Stephen R. 1990. *A Theory of Property*. Cambridge, UK: Cambridge University Press.
Murphy, Liam, and Thomas Nagel. 2002. *The Myth of Ownership: Taxes and Justice*. New York: Oxford University Press.
Narveson, Jan. 2010. "Property and Rights," *Social Philosophy & Policy* 27: 101–34.
Nozick, Robert. 1974. *Anarchy, State and Utopia*. New York: Basic Books.
Otsuka, Michael. 2003. *Libertarianism without Inequality*. New York: Oxford University Press.
Reeve, Andrew. 1993. "Property." In *A Companion to Contemporary Political Philosophy*. Edited by Robert Goodin and Philip Pettit, 558–67. Oxford: Blackwell.
Russell, Daniel. 2004. "Locke on Land and Labor." *Philosophical Studies* 117: 303–25.
Ryan, Alan. 1984. *Property and Political Theory*. Oxford: Basil Blackwell.
Schmidtz, David. 1991. *The Limits of Government*. Boulder, CO: Westview Press.

Schmidtz, David. 2010. "Property and Justice." *Social Philosophy & Policy* 27: 79–100.
Simmons, A. John. 1992. *The Lockean Theory of Rights*. Princeton, NJ: Princeton University Press.
Snare, Frank. 1972. "The Concept of Property." *American Philosophical Quarterly* 9:200–6.
Steiner, Hillel. 1994. *An Essay on Rights*. Oxford: Blackwell.
Vallentyne, Peter. 2007. "Libertarianism and the State." *Social Philosophy & Policy* 24: 187–205.
van Donselaar, Gijs. 2009. *The Right to Exploit: Parasitism, Scarcity, Basic Income*. Oxford: Oxford University Press.
von Mises, Ludwig. 2005. *Liberalism: The Classic Tradition*. Indianapolis, IN: Liberty Fund.
Waldron, Jeremy. 1988. *The Right to Private Property*. Oxford: Clarendon Press.
Westphal, Kenneth R. 1997. "Do Kant's Principles Justify Property or Usufruct?" *Jahrbuch fuer Recht und Ethik* 5: 141–94.

PART II

Approaches

CHAPTER 6

CLASSICAL LIBERALISM

JASON BRENNAN AND JOHN TOMASI

THE central question animating liberal thought is: How can people live together as free and equal? This question is being reinvigorated by the emergence of what we call *neoclassical liberalism*. Neoclassical liberals, such as David Schmidtz, Gerald Gaus, Charles Griswold, Jacob Levy, Matt Zwolinski, Will Wilkinson, and ourselves, share classical liberalism's commitment to robust economic liberties and property rights as well as modern or "high" liberalism's commitment to social justice. On the neoclassical liberal view, part of the justification for a society's basic structure is that it produces conditions whereby citizens have substantive liberty and can thus confront each other as free and equal. The basic structure of society is evaluable on the kinds of outcomes produced for citizens. Neoclassical liberals combine a robust commitment to social justice—a commitment as robust as that of high liberals—with a commitment to a more extensive set of basic liberties than that advocated by high liberals. Neoclassical liberalism thus stakes out a claim to be the morally ambitious form of liberalism.

To locate the distinct conceptual space being carved out by neoclassical liberals, we begin with a map of the ideological terrain. First we distinguish classical liberalism (and libertarianism) from high liberalism. Then we explain how neoclassical liberalism emerges in distinction from these other views.

By "classical liberalism" we mean a broad school that includes Adam Smith, David Hume, F. A. Hayek, and libertarians such as Robert Nozick.[1] High liberalism, by contrast, is the liberalism of, for example, T. H. Green, John Rawls, Ronald Dworkin, Samuel Freeman, Martha Nussbaum, and Will Kymlicka.[2] One way to distinguish between kinds of liberalism is by their differing conceptions of economic liberty. Classical liberals affirm what we call a *thick* conception of economic liberty; high liberals have a *thin* conception.

Most liberals agree that some liberties are more important than others. These basic liberties merit a high degree of political protection. On their lists of basic liberties, most liberals include not only some civil and political liberties but some economic liberties as well, such as the right to own property. But liberals differ about the *scope* of the basic economic liberties. Classical liberals interpret economic liberty as having the same wide scope accorded to the civil liberties. Just as recognizing religious liberty requires the general protection of independent activity in the religious realm, economic liberty requires the general protection of independent activity in economic matters.

A crucial junction point within the liberal tradition occurs with Mill's treatment of economic liberty (Freeman 2011). Mill suggests that economic liberties should be treated differently from freedom of thought, association, and religion. Decisions people make regarding labor and ownership have no intrinsic connection to liberty in Mill's sense. Economic activity is not an expression of liberty, and so rights and powers of ownership and labor should be defined mainly by the requirements of utility (Mill 2004, 209–23; Jacobson 2000, 293–95).

John Rawls likewise adopts a platform of economic exceptionalism. He gives the economic liberties a lower level of protection. He claims wide economic rights are not "necessary for the development and exercise of the moral powers" (Rawls 1993, 298). Regarding freedom of labor, Rawls recognizes the right to occupational choice but not the freedom to engage in self-organized economic activity and/or to hire others for productive purposes. Regarding ownership, Rawls recognizes only a basic right to personal property, severing any rights protecting the ownership of productive property (family farms, businesses, and other "means of production"). Rights to private productive property and contract are not basic, and so any laws recognizing such rights should be crafted to realize justice. This thin conception of economic liberty is a hallmark of the high liberal tradition.[3]

"Libertarianism" falls within the classical liberal tradition.[4] As classical liberals, libertarians affirm a thick conception of economic liberty. Traditional classical liberals hold that the economic liberties are on par with the civil liberties, but libertarians hold that economic liberties are the weightiest of all rights, possibly even moral absolutes. Some libertarians believe that all rights—such as free speech, free association, and sexual freedom—are simply instances of property rights. Some libertarians see economic liberties as so weighty that the state must enforce any contract that citizens voluntarily enter into—even slave contracts.

Left-libertarianism is a species of libertarianism that departs from standard libertarianism in its understanding of original appropriation.[5] On the standard libertarian view, natural resources begin in an unowned state. In contrast, left-libertarians hold that the world, or at least the economic value of the world's resources, begins as commonly owned by all. Left-libertarians, unlike neoclassical liberals, do not endorse a conception of social justice. They affirm thick economic liberty as a requirement of self-ownership, not of social justice.[6]

Figure 6.1 illustrates the conceptual space occupied by neoclassical liberalism, mapping it against rival liberal views.

Affirms Social Justice in Evaluation of Basic Structure?

		Yes	No
Understanding Of Economic Liberty	Thick	Neoclassical Liberalism	Traditional Classical Liberalism Standard Libertarianism Left Libertarianism
	Thin	High Liberalism	Civil Liberalism[i]

[i] We use the label "civic liberal" to refer to a possible view that might occupy the lower right quadrant. Imagine a possible view in which a person affirmed Rawls's first principle of justice, exactly as Rawls formulates it, but then stops there and does not affirm his second principle or any other principle of distribution justice. Such a civic liberal affirms the same view of civil, political, and (thin conception of) economic liberties as high liberals, but does not affirm social justice.

Figure 6.1 Varieties of Liberalism

Note that Figure 6.1 distinguishes liberal views from one another but does not distinguish liberal from nonliberal views.[7] For instance, Marxian socialism affirms social justice and a thin understanding of economic liberty, but it does not fall anywhere on the table. Certain conservative theories affirm a thick understanding of economic liberty and reject social justice but also do not fall anywhere on the table.

We distinguish classical and high liberalism by focusing on whether a view affirms a thick or a thin conception of basic economic liberties. In contrast, Samuel Freeman demarcates those two schools not by their substantive moral commitments but by their justificatory foundations. Freeman claims that most classical liberals emphasize private economic liberties because they believe such liberties are conducive to overall happiness. High liberals, he argues, deemphasize capitalist economic liberties because they are concerned with respecting citizens as free and equal. Thus, Freeman, following Rawls, calls classical liberalism the "liberalism of happiness" and high liberalism the "liberalism of freedom" (Freeman 2007, 45). High liberals are committed to substantive equality, substantive liberty, and social justice; classical liberals care only about formal equality and negative freedom.

This may accurately distinguish between high liberalism and many traditional forms of classical liberalism. However, this way of demarcating the classical and high liberal traditions closes precisely the questions that neoclassical liberals seek to open. Must defenses of thick economic liberty rely only on efficiency, happiness, or self-ownership? Do we fully respect people as free and equal self-governing agents by restricting their private economic liberty? Is a defense of the intrinsic worth of economic liberty compatible with a justice-based commitment to advancing the interests of the poor? Might a thick conception of economic liberty be a *requirement* of social justice?

1. The Status of Economic Liberty

In debates with classical liberals, high liberals believe they occupy the moral high ground. The term *high liberal* suggests a fulfillment or culmination of a movement. High liberals describe their ideal of substantive equality—with its manifest concern for the material well-being of the poor—as an evolutionary advance over the merely formal ideals traditionally defended by classical liberals (Nagel 2003, 63). For classical liberals and libertarians, this suggestion of evolutionary supremacy is suspect. Regardless of the concern high liberals show for the material well-being of citizens, they propose to *limit* the liberty of all citizens in what was traditionally considered one of freedom's most important realms: that of independent activity and decision making regarding the economic aspects of one's life.

Given the importance to high liberals of reducing the traditional scope and weight accorded to economic liberty, it is surprising that their defenses of these reductions tend to be brief and unsustained. Mill says property rights do not protect individuality because trade is a social act (1978, 94). But speech and association are no less social in nature. Rawls, as we have seen, simply states that citizens do not need thick economic liberties to develop their moral powers. But the moral powers of citizens include their capacity to develop and pursue a life plan for themselves. Rawls's argument for the importance of occupational freedom appears to support wider freedoms of labor as well. After all, one is defined not only by what profession one chooses but also by the terms that one accepts for one's work, the number of hours one decides to devote to work, and much more. So, too, reasons for protecting personal property would seem to apply to many forms of productive property (Nickel 2000). Some high liberals seek to justify economic exceptionalism by arguing that property rights are socially elaborated notions (Murphy and Nagel 2002). They say the arrangement and extent of property holdings we see in society are possible only in virtue of social structures. They claim that "everyday libertarian" beliefs—that property rights can constrain state activities and have an independent moral force prior to state—are confused. Yet high liberals hold many basic rights requiring social elaboration—such as the right not to be murdered—carry moral force prior to the state (G. Brennan 2005). Even if it is true that people could not possess and enjoy much property in a Hobbesian state of nature, they could also not exercise and enjoy many other basic liberties. Without some more persuasive distinction between property rights and these other rights, the high liberals' differential treatment of property rights seems unjustified.

Neoclassical liberals join with traditional classical liberals and libertarians in their skepticism about the high liberal platform of economic exceptionalism. However, neoclassical liberals offer positive arguments for thick economic liberty that distinguish them from classical liberals and libertarians alike.

Consider the libertarians: On Nozick's orthodox interpretation, he grounds this account of property in the concept of self-ownership. Property rights emerge as a relation of persons to objects in the world, by the process of self-owners mixing their labor with unowned things. Property rights are strongly prior to the state. The state exists to protect preexisting rights and so is bound by those rights.[8]

Instead of starting with the idea of self-ownership, some neoclassical liberals seek to ground property rights (and other economic liberties) in the same moral ideas affirmed by high liberals (Gaus 2007; Tomasi 2012a). For example, some neoclassical liberals focus on the moral ideal of citizens living together as responsible self-authors. This approach owes more to Kant than to Locke. By it, neoclassical liberals can affirm a wide range of individual freedom regarding economic questions for the same reasons they affirm general liberties with respect to religious and associational questions: A thick conception of economic liberty is a necessary condition of responsible self-authorship. Ownership rights are not so much relations among persons and objects as they are relations among persons as moral agents.[9] Rights emerge as a social recognition that honoring the capacity of one's fellow citizens to be self-authors requires that one respects their capacity to make choices of their own regarding economic matters. To restrict the capacity of people to make economic choices or, worse, to treat their economic activities merely as means to the social ends of others, would violate the dignity of such persons and so would be to treat them unjustly. Wide rights to economic liberty, while recognizable without the state, are validated and made fully binding by the political community. On this approach, the requirements of economic liberty help define the shape and limits of the state, even without being radically prior to it.

This approach to economic liberty helps highlight another important difference between neo- and traditional classical liberal views. While classical liberals such as F. A. Hayek and Milton Friedman advocate a social safety net, their advocacy seems ad hoc given their strong claims about the sanctity of property rights.[10] By contrast, neoclassical liberals advocate what we might call a "thoroughly principled" rationale for the safety net. A rationale for a policy is thoroughly principled if the same reasoning that supports the wider features of a view also support that particular policy. On the neoclassical approach described above, citizens' status as responsible self-authors may be threatened by conditions of extreme need. The neoclassical state must be empowered to define and interpret the set of basic rights so as to protect people's moral status as self-authors. Unlike many traditional classical liberals, therefore, neoclassical liberals can defend a safety net in a thoroughly principled way. The same grounds neoclassical liberals use to justify the social safety net also explain their objections to the pervasive encroachments on economic liberty endorsed by high liberals. Without constitutional guarantees protecting independent economic decision making, people cannot fully exercise their moral powers of self-authorship. Neoclassical liberals affirm the importance of economic liberty, and thus reject the high liberal platform of economic exceptionalism, for all these reasons.

High liberals think of themselves as occupying the moral high ground in their debate with classical liberals. They believe that by limiting the economic liberty of citizens, they thereby enable the state to pursue the distributive requirements of social justice. Here again, though, neoclassical liberalism is confounding the old lines of debate.

2. The Concept of Liberty and Guarantees

We often equate being free with an absence of constraints, impediments, or interference. For instance, a person has free speech when no one stops her from speaking her mind. We call this idea of liberty *negative liberty*.[11]

Marxists complained that negative liberties, by themselves, have little worth. Marxists state that liberty is valuable only if people have the financial and social means to exercise it. No one interferes with the homeless beggar, but he is not free in any meaningful sense. Thus, some Marxists say, real liberty is the effective power, capacity, or ability to do what one wills. We call this conception of liberty *positive liberty*. For example, a bird has the positive liberty to fly, but human beings do not.

High liberals agree with Marxists that, without proper resources, citizens will be unable to regard their negative liberties as valuable. Everyone, rich and poor, has the negative liberty to buy a yacht, but only the rich can *exercise* or *enjoy* this liberty. High liberals conclude that to guarantee people will enjoy their liberties and have positive liberty, they need legal guarantees that they will be supplied with adequate resources.

In response to the Marxist critique, classical liberals traditionally have argued that negative liberty exhausts the concept of liberty. Any other use of the terms *liberty* or *freedom* were confused and illegitimate. They pounded the table and insisted that liberty is liberty, not power. Isaiah Berlin and F. A. Hayek believed that identifying positive liberty as a genuine species of liberty would automatically license an extensive welfare state, a (possibly intrusive) social democracy, or even socialism, because such regimes offer legal guarantees that citizens would enjoy positive liberty (Berlin 2000; Hayek 1960, 16–19). Marxists and high liberals of course agree that anyone who believes positive liberty is important is thus committed to some sort of social democratic or socialist basic structure.

Neoclassical liberalism holds that all sides to this debate are mistaken. Classical liberals are mistaken for rejecting positive liberty as a genuine species of liberty. In addition, classical liberals, Marxists, and high liberals are mistaken for believing that a commitment to positive liberty automatically entails a commitment to an extensive welfare state, social democracy, or socialist economy.

Neoclassical liberalism concurs with Marxism that citizens should have the effective means to exercise their wills, to do as they please (provided they do not violate other citizens' rights), and to lead their conceptions of the good life. Neoclassical liberals agree with high liberals that citizens should have the effective means to face each other as free and equal.

Neoclassical liberals also argue that negative liberty matters in part because, historically, protecting negative liberties has been and will continue to be the most important and effective way of promoting positive liberty (Schmidtz and Brennan 2010; Brennan and Schmidtz 2010). Thanks to economic, cultural, and scientific growth, a typical citizen of a Western nation today enjoys far more positive liberty than a medieval king. This growth did not occur because a government declared or legally guaranteed that it would occur. It occurred because Western countries adopted functional background institutions that, over time, gave citizens the incentives and means to promote positive liberty through their commercial, literary, scientific, and cultural activities (Rosenberg and Birdzell 1986; North and Thomas 1976; Cameron and Neal 2003; Maddison 2007). In practice, promoting positive liberty does not come at the expense of negative liberty, as Berlin worried. Instead, positive liberty is promoted by respecting negative liberty.

Do we want government to issue legal guarantees that all citizens will enjoy positive liberty? It depends on what happens when the government does this. There is a difference between guaranteeing as rendering inevitable (as when an economist says setting the price of milk at a penny would guarantee shortages) versus guaranteeing as issuing legal declarations, whereby the government intends to produce a result.

Clearly, guaranteeing something in the latter sense is no real guarantee (for example, the No Child Left Behind Act legally guaranteed no child would be left behind, but some children have been left behind nevertheless). If we want to know whether governments should issue legal guarantees, we need to know how well such guarantees will work. If we give government the power to promote some valuable end, there is no guarantee that government will use that power competently (and thus succeed in promoting that end). There's also no guarantee that the people in government will use that power for the intended end rather than some private purpose of their own. According to neoclassical liberals, legal guarantees are instruments to be judged in context by their effectiveness at promoting social justice. A commitment to substantive outcome does not automatically commit one to any particular legal instruments.

Neoclassical liberals contend that classical liberals had no good reason for disavowing positive liberty. Classical liberal's real opposition was to socialism, not to positive liberty. Hayek rejected socialism in part because he believed it would tend to be tyrannical. Yet Hayek's main argument against socialism is that it would not actually make people richer, happier, healthier, and better able to live out their conceptions of the good life. Though Hayek thought that calling power "positive liberty" was a mistake, the main thrust of his work is this: Given human fallibility, if one cares about positive liberty, one should prefer classical liberal institutions to the other feasible alternatives.

Neoclassical liberals embrace positive liberty. They hold that it is important that citizens be positioned to make effective use of and enjoy their liberties. Compared to high liberals, neoclassical liberals are skeptical of the real-world capacity of extensive welfare states, social democracy, and especially liberal socialism to promote positive liberty.[12] Neoclassical liberals argue that the historically best means of promoting positive liberty has been to protect negative liberties. Neoclassical liberals tend to argue that if citizens' political, civil, and economic rights are protected, then over time there will be scientific, cultural, and economic progress that will benefit everyone and promote everyone's positive liberties (Schmidtz and Brennan

2010, 30–207; Brennan and Schmidtz 2010). Protecting negative liberties does not render such progress inevitable, but then nothing else does either.

3. Equality versus What Actually Matters

Material egalitarianism is the doctrine that all members of a society should have approximately the same income or wealth. High liberals have come to recognize the dangers of material egalitarianism—in particular, that it leads to the "leveling down objection" or that it might valorize the morally dubious sentiment of envy.[13] Thus, in light of such worries, high liberals have become skeptical of egalitarianism, and most will insist that they are not egalitarians per se. Nonetheless, they continue to recognize some pull toward material egalitarianism, in particular because they tend to regard material egalitarianism as a moral baseline from which departures must be justified.

Neoclassical liberals are unambiguous in their rejection of material egalitarianism. On the neoclassical view, material egalitarianism has no moral pull in itself. For example, imagine two societies, A and B. In both societies, the civil, political, and economic liberties are fully protected; everyone enjoys fair equality of opportunity; everyone has enough; and everyone has high levels of welfare. However, B is more egalitarian than A in its distribution of basic goods. Many high liberals would regard this as presumptive grounds for favoring B over A, but neoclassical liberals would not (Schmidtz 2006a, 114–19; Schmidtz 2006b). We might say that neoclassical liberals believe there is no moral *remainder* to material egalitarianism: It is not (normally[14]) a baseline from which departures must be justified, nor is it morally desirable, all things being equal. Instead, neoclassical liberals see material egalitarianism as beside the point.

A material egalitarian might say, "Some are rich and some are poor, so we should try to be more equal." A neoclassical liberal would claim, "The problem isn't that some people have *more*; it's that some people don't have *enough*. The poor of the Third World die of starvation, not inequality." Neoclassical liberals are not material egalitarians but instead *welfarists, sufficientarians*, and/or *prioritarians*.[15]

Welfarism is the thesis that part of what justifies social institutions is that they promote most people's welfare. For instance, David Schmidtz argues that prima facie, social institutions are good when they promote the welfare of most members of society without exploiting members whose welfare is not promoted (Schmidtz 1995, 158–66).[16] (Neoclassical liberals would add here that whether a commitment to welfarism in turn suggests a commitment to a welfare state depends in part on what degree a welfare state, as compared to the alternatives, actually succeeds in promoting welfare.) Sufficientarianism is the thesis that all people should have *enough* to lead minimally decent lives. Neoclassical liberals advocate market democratic institutions in part because they believe these institutions will tend to satisfy this condition of material adequacy. Prioritarianism is the doctrine that when considering changes to current institutions, all things being equal, we are required to give more weight to the worst-off members of society than the better-off members.

Neoclassical liberalism holds that welfarism, sufficientarianism, and prioritarianism capture all the moral force of egalitarianism. If welfarist, sufficientarian, and prioritarian goals have been met, from the standpoint of social justice, egalitarianism has no remaining attraction. Neoclassical liberals agree that a fair and just society gives everyone a stake in that society. A just society has institutions that ensure, as much as possible, that everyone has the resources needed to be a free person. (Recall that to ensure an outcome means to find institutions that produce the outcome, not necessarily to issue a legal guarantee of that outcome.) Still, the goal of society is to make everyone well off, not to make them equal. On this view, at best, material equality matters only when it is liberating or tends to make people's lives better.

Some (though not all) high liberals and others argue that equality of resources is necessary to make sure everyone has equal opportunity to exercise political influence (Rawls 2001, 139; Christiano 1996). They worry that unequal resources will lead to the rich seizing too much political power for themselves. High liberals contend that to guarantee that all citizens enjoy the fair value of their political liberties, they must have approximately equal resources. (High liberals hold that citizens enjoy the fair value of political liberty only when they each has strongly equal power and influence over the political process.) We call this the *political liberty argument for material equality*.

Gerald Gaus responds that the political liberty argument for material equality relies on empirical claims, claims that high liberals have not supported with empirical evidence and that, Gaus (2010) argues, the evidence actually speaks against. Using several different data sources and rankings of material inequality, political inequality, political openness, and political participation, Gaus argues that there is no correlation between material equality and the low value of political liberty.[17]

High liberals hope to prevent domination by empowering political bodies to design programs aimed to equalize the holdings of citizens. But this solution itself exposes citizens to dangers of political domination.[18] Neoclassical liberals share the high liberal concern that citizens be protected from political domination. As a matter of constitutional design, neoclassical liberals remove many divisive economic issues from the legislative agenda and thus limit the attractiveness of buying power. The approach of the neoclassical liberals, we might say, is ex ante; that of the high liberals is ex post.[19]

4. Methods of Social Construction

Classical and neoclassical liberals believe many social goals are best pursued indirectly, in particular, through spontaneous orders (Schmidtz and Brennan 2010; Hayek 1960; Hayek 1973; Hayek 1976). A commercial market is a paradigm of a spontaneous order. The production of the most ordinary commercial good—a lowly pencil—requires the mobilization of a staggeringly complex system of actors: foresters, miners, sailors, metallurgists, chemists, gluers, accountants, and more. Literally "*not a single person on the face of this earth*" knows how to make a pencil from scratch, yet pencils are produced (Read 1958, 372). The market mobilizes the army of people who make the pencil, but no one plays the role of general. The cooperative system that produces pencils is a product of human action but not of human design. Most people involved in making pencils have no idea they are doing so. Classical liberals have long been enthusiastic defenders of markets because of their productive capacities.

Recently, forward-looking thinkers of the left have expressed a greater openness to market society. As Jeremy Waldon puts it, "nobody today seriously imagines an economy either at the national or international level in which private property and markets do not loom large" (2011, 4). Even when accepting a role for markets, however, most high liberals remain "reluctant capitalists" (Dworkin 1985, 196).

Some high liberals are skeptical of markets not because they think markets are *ineffective* means to producing desired ends but because they think they are the *wrong* way to produce desired ends. High liberals say that it is not enough that good outcomes occur. Such outcomes must occur intentionally, an expression of our will as a group with a common aim. Markets, according to both their friends and their foes, are paradigmatically places where no one person or group of people has deliberate control over the outcomes. For example, F. A. Hayek claims that markets are a type of human order that produces ends but without any act of human will directed toward that end. Hayek says that markets thus cannot be said to serve any particular end or purpose (1976, 14–15).

Neoclassical liberals, however, need not accept Hayek's claim that markets lack a purpose. Human beings create markets, and in particular they create the background institutions that sustain and enable well-functioning markets. For instance, people can create (through deliberate political means) the rule of law, open access law courts, and properly designed property rights, on the expectation that when these institutions are in place, the market will then achieve social justice. In this case, a deliberate order creates and/or sustains a nondeliberate, spontaneous, emergent order for the purposes of producing social justice (Tomasi 2012a). Indeed, neoclassical liberals think that markets are a morally superior method of social construction. They see private economic liberties as among the basic liberal rights, essential preconditions for the exercise and development of the moral powers of liberal citizens. Neoclassical liberals embrace capitalism not reluctantly but with moral enthusiasm.

5. Social Justice

Opposition to social justice has long been a fixed premise of the classical liberal and libertarian traditions (Hume 1983, 27–29). F. A. Hayek (1976, 34) argues that "justice" applies only to the products of deliberate human will. But a free society is a spontaneous order rather than a made thing: The overall distributions emerge as a product of human action but not of human design. Nozick rejects the whole "redistributive" approach to justice: "There is no more a distributing or distribution of shares than there is a distributing of mates in a society in which persons choose whom they shall marry" (Nozick 1974, 149–50).

Still, we find *ingredients* of social justice within the views of many classical liberals. Adam Smith's critique of mercantilism is founded on a concern for the working poor. Smith measures the wealth of a nation not in terms of aggregate product but in terms of the substantive opportunities for success enjoyed by all (see Smith 1983, 567; Smith 1982a, 83, 343; Smith 1982b, 91). Recent classical liberals, such as Richard Epstein and Milton Friedman, likewise allow a variety of limitations on strict economic liberty as a response to social concerns: tax-funded assistance for the orphaned, the homeless, and the unemployed; tax-funded supplement in pursuit of the goal of quality education for all; and so on.

Even Hayek's attitude toward social justice is ambiguous. Hayek claims that differences between his and Rawls's views of justice are "more verbal than substantial" (1976, xiii). Hayek says that there exists "a genuine problem of justice in connection with the deliberate design of political institutions" (1976, 100). While regretting that Rawls uses the term "social justice" to refer to that problem, Hayek states that he has no basic disagreement with Rawls's idea that justice could serve as an (process-independent) standard of evaluation of a society's basic social institutions (Hayek 1976).

Neoclassical liberalism emerges against this background. Neoclassical liberals seek to provide a philosophically rigorous account of the traditional classical liberalism platform: thick economic liberty for all, limited government, a range of basic social service programs funded by taxation, and a foundational concern for the material well-being of the poor. Neoclassical liberals embrace social justice, seeing it as a standard that enables them to capture and clarify the moral ideals that have long undergirded classical liberalism.

While committed to thick economic liberty, neoclassical liberals positively affirm social justice (or social justice-like concerns). For example, using many of Rawls's own economic premises, Jason Brennan suggests that market-based societies are more likely to achieve social justice than Rawls's preferred regimes (such as liberal socialism, especially in its no-growth formulations). For Brennan, however, this is not a *reductio* or taunt: Brennan's worries spring from a concern about how best to exposit (and realize) values that he shares with high liberals. Thus, "Modern egalitarian liberals often correctly identify the test of a flourishing society: the end or minimizing of domination, poverty, and medical want, and the spread of education, opportunity, peace, and full political autonomy" (J. Brennan 2007, 288).

David Schmidtz is among the most prominent contemporary defenders of limited government and thick economic liberty. Schmidtz affirms core ideas within Rawls's conception of justice. Central among these is the idea that social institutions must benefit all classes of contributors, including the worst off. Schmidtz writes: "Rawls's most central, most luminously undeniable point is that a free society is not a zero-sum game. It is a mutually advantageous cooperative venture" (Schmidtz 2006a, 196). In Schmidtz's view, one of the principal ways of deciding among competing conceptions of justice, as well as competing conceptions of social morality more broadly, is by asking how those conceptions would facilitate people living well in conditions of peace, prosperity, and opportunity (Schmidtz 2006a, 9–12; Schmidtz 1995, 155–211). Schmidtz calls justice as fairness "a vision with grandeur" and urges readers to focus positively on the insights in the Rawlsian account (Schmidtz 2006a, 195–96).[20]

Gerald Gaus's work primarily concerns what it takes for institutions and principles to be publicly justified. Because there is reasonable disagreement over what human welfare is, and over welfare goals a government should pursue, Gaus (1998) rejects straightforward appeals to welfare as public justifications of principles of justice or of social institutions. Still, Gaus holds that for a set of institutions, including property rights, to be publically justified, all bound by the norms must have a stake in them. Gaus (2010) argues that property rights meet this test. Simultaneously, for Gaus, it is this concern for public justifiability—not efficiency or beneficence—that justifies a social minimum (Gaus 2010, 237; Gaus 1999, 117–96).

John Tomasi (2012a) proposes a hybrid view he calls "market democracy." Market democracy combines a classical liberal commitment to economic liberty with a high liberal commitment to fair shares. Rather than grounding economic liberty in a principle of efficiency, self-ownership, or liberty, market democracy defends thick economic liberty as a requirement of democratic legitimacy. If citizens are to be capable of endorsing the basic rules governing their political life, they need the protection of certain rights and liberties that allow them to develop their evaluative horizons. Thick economic liberties enable citizens most fully to develop the moral powers they have as responsible self-authors (Tomasi 2012b). The ideal of responsible self-authorship also leads market democracy to affirm a prioritarian account of justice. Unlike traditional forms of classical liberalism, market democracy is enthusiastic about ideal theory. Market democracy identifies a range of ideal market-based regime-types—most notably a regime called "democratic limited government"—that realize social justice. Market democracy is a challenge to the high liberal claim of evolutionary primacy. Compared to traditional high liberal views, Tomasi argues, market democracy offers a more complete realization of the liberal commitment to treat citizens as free and equal self-governing agents. Neoclassical liberalism is a *higher* form of liberalism.

6. Ideal Theory and the Facts

Many high liberals think political philosophers who study institutions should employ what Rawls calls "ideal theory"[21] (Rawls 2001, 135–40). The best way to characterize ideal theory is disputed.[22] Still, on one prominent interpretation, ideal theory concerns asking which institutions would best realize justice under these four conditions:

1. People have as strong a sense of justice as humanly possible.
2. Everyone is competent to play his or her role.
3. The basic institutions of society achieve their announced public aim (Rawls 2001, 137, sect. 41.3).
4. There are favorable background conditions (e.g., not too much scarcity to make society impossible).

Classical liberals typically balk at ideal theory (e.g., Schmidtz 1995, 183), saying that because the first three conditions of ideal theory are unrealistic, ideal theory provides no moral guidance. There is no point in asking what dinners Utopia's kitchens will serve.

However, many high liberals contend that the classical liberal rejection of ideal theory is mistaken. Political philosophers are concerned with identifying and characterizing just political regimes. The goal of political philosophy is to describe how a society ought to function, not to describe how it in fact functions. Philosophers are thus allowed to imagine societies in which no one free-rides on or takes advantage of social institutions (Rawls 2001, 137). Expanding on Rawls's idea of a "realistic utopia," David Estlund argues that the proper domain of normative thinking about politics lies between what Estlund calls "complacent realism" and "moral utopianism" (Estlund 2008, 258–75). Complacently realist views concede too much to the way things currently happen to be; moral utopian views ask for things that fall outside the domain of the possible. Even if the conditions of ideal theory are unattainable due to human moral or cognitive limitations, this does not make the institutions selected at the ideal level of theorizing any less intrinsically desirable. As G. A. Cohen has said, grapes are not rendered any less tasty just because they are out of reach (Cohen 1995, 256).

Neoclassical liberals ask: What if we apply these same standards to classical liberal institutional forms? Many worries about capitalism vanish under ideal circumstances, just as worries about democracy do. After all, neoclassical liberals positively affirm social justice as the ultimate standard of institutional evaluation. Thus, neoclassical liberals advocate capitalist institutional arrangements as requirements of social justice. If, when advocating enthusiastically capitalistic forms, neoclassical liberals aim at social justice, and if those capitalistic forms can satisfy the same ideal theoretic standards of feasibility that high liberals apply when evaluating their own preferred institutional forms, then the enthusiastically capitalistic institutions of neoclassical liberalism satisfy the ideal theoretic requirements of social justice.[23] Those capitalistic institutions must be recognized as socially just or—as some neoclassical liberals argue—as *more* socially just than the institutions favored by traditional high liberals.

Notice that the neoclassical affirmation of social justice, especially when combined with an acceptance of ideal theoretic forms of institutional analysis, disrupts the traditional high liberal arguments against laissez-faire capitalism or the "system of natural liberty." For example, a familiar argument against capitalist regimes is that, lacking the host of institutional guarantees of left-liberal regimes, they allow unjust inequalities to arise. Rawls, for example, deems laissez-faire capitalism unjust because it "secures only formal equality" and "aims for economic efficiency and growth constrained only by a rather low social minimum" (Rawls 2001, 137).

Whatever force this objection may have had against the traditional defenses of classical liberalism, it immediately becomes ambiguous when directed at neoclassical liberalism. Neoclassical liberalism, after all, can share many of the same moral ambitions as high liberalism. Thus, morally speaking, neoclassical liberalism "allows" only distributions that satisfy some externally generated standard, just as the high liberals do. As a practical empirical matter, of course, every regime can fail to generate the social conditions for which they were designed (and the presence or absence of formal institutional "guarantees" do not change this practical fact; Schmidtz 1997). Indeed, on that practical level, some neoclassical liberals argue that high liberal regimes such as market socialism have a history of "allowing" greater injustices—most notably with respect to civil liberties favored by all liberals—than do more enthusiastically capitalistically ones (Gaus 2010, 251–58, 274–75). But the more important point is the moral one. If property-owning democracy and liberal socialism constitute "realistic utopias," then so do the laissez-faire forms advocated by neoclassical liberals. Indeed, compared to the regimes advocated by high liberals, the enthusiastically capitalistic institutions advocated by neoclassical liberals are simultaneously more utopian *and* more realistic.

7. Conclusion

Twenty-five years ago, high liberal scholars could discharge their responsibility to allow students to consider market-affirming alternatives by including a unit on Nozick on their syllabi. After all, libertarianism was widely accepted as the cutting-edge exposition of pro-market liberalism. The emergence of neoclassical liberalism has changed this state of affairs. Unlike traditional libertarians, neoclassical liberals do not set up camp across a conceptual river that high liberals can approach only by leaving behind their own cherished political intuitions. Instead, neoclassical liberals have themselves crossed the river. They seek to engage high liberals in foundational debates on the basis of shared moral premises.

The stakes are high. Is liberalism a doctrine of limited governmental power and wide individual economic freedom or a doctrine that calls for expansive government involvement in the daily lives of citizens, most notably in economic affairs? To adjudicate this dispute, neoclassical liberals do not ask high liberals to abandon their own premises and convert to those of their political rivals. Rather, neoclassical liberals invite high liberals to join them in looking more deeply into the meaning and nature of premises they share.

As we see it, there are three philosophical issues that might be clarified through discussions between neoclassical liberals and high liberals. First, high liberals have a tendency to believe that material and social equality matters for its own sake, whereas neoclassical liberals are more likely to believe that equality is a distraction from the real ends of social justice. Second, many high liberals view the political liberties as especially important and thus believe it is morally imperative to have a strongly participatory democracy with a wide scope of power. Some neoclassical liberals view this position as contamination from Rousseau (or from what Benjamin Constant called "the liberty of the ancients") rather than a part of a genuinely liberal theory (Brennan 2007, 288–89). Third, neoclassical liberals hold that economic liberties have the same weight and wide scope as the civil liberties, whereas high liberals advocate a platform of economic exceptionalism. In every case, what generates these divergent tendencies? What deeper (subterranean) moral commitments lead high liberals to answer in one way and neoclassical liberals in the other? Which way of adjudicating each dispute might best fulfill the common liberal commitment to respect citizens as free and equal self-governing agents? These are questions neoclassical liberals have placed on the philosophical agenda.

NOTES

1. See the chapter "Nozick" by David Schmidtz and Christopher Freiman in this volume.
2. See the chapter "Rawls" by Leif Wenar in this volume.
3. See the chapter "Property" by Gerald Gaus in this volume.
4. Libertarian political philosophers include Robert Nozick, Eric Mack, and Jan Narveson. For a sophisticated survey of the varieties of libertarian thought, see Zwolinski (2008). Nozick revised portions of his libertarian theory but never rejected it. See Nozick (1989, 287) and Nozick (2001, 281–82).
5. See the chapter "Left-Libertarianism" by Peter Vallentyne in this volume.
6. Left-libertarians often affirm welfare state provisions. They do so not out of a commitment to social justice but out of a view of what it takes to render private property ownership consistent with the starting point of common world ownership (or common ownership of the economic value of the world's resources).
7. We leave open here what demarcates liberal from nonliberal views.
8. In the opening lines of *Anarchy, State, and Utopia*, Nozick states: "Individuals have rights, and there are things that no other person or group may do to them (without violating their rights). So strong and far-reaching are these rights that they raise the question of what, if anything, the state and its officials may do" (1974, ix).
9. We are indebted to Jason Swadley for this formulation.
10. Milton and Rose Friedman, for example, advocate a social safety out of beneficence rather than as a positive requirement springing from the moral foundations of their view (Friedman and Friedman 1979, 110–17).
11. See the chapter "Freedom" by Philip Pettit in this volume.
12. Note that "social democracy" is not all one thing. We might distinguish between the social insurance state and the regulatory state. Denmark, for example, has significantly

less constrained and regulated markets than the United States but provides more social insurance. See, for example, the Heritage Foundation's ranking of countries by levels of economic freedom, available at http://www.heritage.org/index/Ranking. Note that Denmark ranks higher (often greatly) than the United States on business freedom, trade freedom, monetary freedom, investment freedom, financial freedom, property rights, and freedom from corruption. It is approximately equal on labor freedom. If the Heritage Foundation did not count government share of GDP (which is high in Denmark due to welfare spending) as counting against economic freedom, then Denmark would rank as having much more economic freedom than the United States overall.

13. Freiman summarizes the leveling down objections as follows: "Insofar as justice demands equality, we have reason to favor policy that worsens the better off and betters none" (2011, 2).

14. Schmidtz (2006, 109–13), argues that some cases (such as when two people arrive simultaneously at a resource on which neither has a prior claim) call for equal shares.

15. See the chapters "Justice" by Richard Arneson and "Equality" by Elizabeth Anderson in this volume.

16. See also Schmidtz and Freiman's (apparent) endorsement, in this volume, of what they call the "precursor" to Rawls's difference principle.

17. See the chapter "Money and Politics" by Tom Christiano in this volume. Note also that the political argument for material equality is in tension with public choice theory. Public choice holds that rent-seeking and power buying occurs not because citizens have unequal resources but because they have unequal potential to receive concentrated benefits from government. See Mueller (2003, 333–58).

18. The middle-class savings programs of property-owning democracy, for example, require that some political body decides precisely who qualifies for those programs, what benefits they offer, and who pays.

19. Note that the different approaches here result more from differing empirical beliefs than from differing moral commitments.

20. In particular, Schmidtz agrees that "we judge a society [in part] by asking whether it is good for all of us, whether it truly is a land of opportunity, and by looking at the quality of life obtained by its nonprivileged members" (2006a, 195–96).

21. We do not mean to say that all high liberals work exclusively or even mostly at the level of ideal theory. In fact, some of the most prominent critiques of ideal theory come from high liberals, such as Amartya Sen and David Miller. Whether some libertarians, such as Nozick, should be seen as working at the level of ideal theory is a question we leave open.

22. See the chapter "Ideal and Nonideal Theory" by Stemplowska and Swift in this volume.

23. For an argument about the feasibility of capitalist arrangements with respect to the requirements of distributive justice, see Shapiro (1995).

REFERENCES

Berlin, Isaiah. 2000. "Two Concepts of Liberty." In *The Proper Study of Mankind*. New York: Farrar, Strauss, Giroux.

Brennan, Geoffrey. 2005. "The Myth of Ownership; Liam Murphy and Thomas Nagel." *Constitutional Political Economy* 16: 207–19.

Brennan, Jason. 2007. "Rawls's Paradox." *Constitutional Political Economy* 18: 287–99.
Brennan, Jason, and David Schmidtz. 2010. "Conceptions of Freedom." *Cato Unbound* (March 10). Available from http://www.cato-unbound.org/2010/03/10/david-schmidtz-and-jason-brennan/conceptions-of-freedom/.
Cameron, Rondo, and Larry Neal. 2003. *A Concise Economic History of the World*. New York: Oxford University Press.
Christiano, Thomas, 1996. *The Rule of the Many*. Boulder, CO: Westview Press.
Cohen, G. A. 1995. *Self-Ownership, Freedom, and Equality*. New York: Oxford University Press.
Dworkin, Ronald. 1985. "Liberalism." In *A Matter of Principle*. Cambridge, MA: Harvard University Press.
Estlund, David. 2008. *Democratic Authority*. Princeton, NJ: Princeton University Press.
Freeman, Samuel. 2007. *Rawls*. New York: Routledge.
Freeman, Samuel. 2011. "Capitalism in the Classical and High Liberal Traditions." *Social Philosophy & Policy* 28: 19–55.
Freiman, Christopher. 2011. "Prioritarian Justice and Positional Goods." Unpublished manuscript, College of William and Mary, Williamsburg, VA.
Friedman, Milton, and Rose Friedman. 1979. *Free to Choose*. New York: Avon Books.
Gaus, Gerald. 1998. "Why All Welfare States (Even Laissez Faire Ones) Are Unreasonable." *Social Philosophy & Policy* 15: 1–33.
Gaus, Gerald. 1999. *Social Philosophy*. Armonk, NY: M.E. Sharpe.
Gaus, Gerald. 2007. "On Justifying the Moral Rights of the Moderns: A Case of Old Wine in New Bottles." *Social Philosophy & Policy* 24: 84–119.
Gaus, Gerald. 2010. "Coercion, Ownership, and the Redistributive State: Justificatory Liberalism's Classical Tilt." *Social Philosophy & Policy* 27: 233–75.
Hayek, F. A. 1960. *The Constitution of Liberty*. Chicago: University of Chicago Press.
Hayek, F. A. 1973. *Law, Legislation, and Liberty*. Vol. I. Chicago: University of Chicago Press.
Hayek, F. A. 1976. *Law, Legislation, and Liberty*. Vol. II. Chicago: University of Chicago Press.
Hume, David. 1983. *An Enquiry Concerning the Principles of Morals*. Indianapolis, IN: Hackett.
Jacobson, Daniel. 2000. "Mill on Liberty, Speech, and the Free Society." *Philosophy & Public Affairs* 29: 276–309.
Maddison, Angus. 2007. *Contours of the World Economy, 1–2030 ad: Essays in Macro-Economic History*. New York: Oxford University Press.
Mill, J. S. 1978. *On Liberty*. Indianapolis, IN: Hackett.
Mill, J. S. 2004. "Of Property." In *Principles of Political Economy*. New York: Prometheus Books.
Mueller, Dennis. 2003. *Public Choice III*. New York: Cambridge University Press.
Murphy, Liam, and Thomas Nagel. 2002. *The Myth of Ownership*. New York: Oxford University Press.
Nagel, Thomas. 2003. "Rawls and Liberalism." In *The Cambridge Companion to Rawls*. Edited by Samuel Freeman. New York: Cambridge University Press.
Nickel, James. 2000. "Economic Liberties." In *The Idea of a Political Liberalism: Essays on Rawls*. Edited by Victoria Davion. Lanham, MD: Rowman & Littlefield, 2000.
North, Douglas, and Robert Paul Thomas. 1976. *The Rise of the Western World: A New Economic History*. New York: Cambridge University Press.
Nozick, Robert. 1974. *Anarchy, State, and Utopia*. New York: Basic Books.

Nozick, Robert. 1989. *The Examined Life*. New York: Basic Books.
Nozick, Robert. 2001. *Invariances*. Cambridge, MA: Harvard University Press.
Rawls, John. 1993. *Political Liberalism*. New York: Columbia University Press.
Rawls, John. 2001. *Justice as Fairness: A Restatement*. Cambridge, MA: Harvard University Press.
Read, Leonard. 1958. "I, Pencil." *The Freeman* 3: 371–79.
Rosenberg, Nathan, and L. E. Birdzell Jr. 1986. *How the West Grew Rich*. New York: Basic Books.
Schmidtz, David. 1995. *Rational Choice and Moral Agency*. Princeton, NJ: Princeton University Press.
Schmidtz, David. 1997. "Guarantees." *Social Philosophy & Policy* 14: 1–19.
Schmidtz, David. 2006a. *Elements of Justice*. New York: Cambridge University Press.
Schmidtz, David. 2006b. "When Inequality Matters." *Cato Unbound* (March 6). Available from http://www.cato-unbound.org/2006/03/06/david-schmidtz/when-equality-matters/.
Schmidtz, David, and Jason Brennan. 2010. *A Brief History of Liberty*. Oxford: Wiley-Blackwell.
Shapiro, Daniel. 1995. "Why Rawlsian Liberals Should Support Free-Market Capitalism." *The Journal of Political Philosophy*, 3: 58–85.
Smith, Adam. 1982a. *Lectures on Jurisprudence*. Indianapolis, IN: Liberty Fund.
Smith, Adam. 1982b. *The Wealth of Nations*. Indianapolis, IN: Liberty Fund.
Smith, Adam. 1983. *Essays on Philosophical Subjects*. Indianapolis, IN: Liberty Fund.
Tomasi, John. 2012a. *Free Market Fairness*. Princeton, NJ: Princeton University Press.
Tomasi, John. 2012b. "Political Legitimacy and Economic Liberty." *Social Philosophy & Policy* 29: 50–80.
Waldron, Jeremy. 2011. "Socioeconomic Rights and Theories of Justice." Public Law Research Paper 10-79. New York: New York University School of Law. Available from http://ssrn.com/abstract=1699898.
Zwolinski, Matt. 2008. "Libertarianism." In *The Internet Encyclopedia of Philosophy*. Available from http://www.iep.utm.edu/libertar/.

CHAPTER 7

SOCIAL CONTRACT APPROACHES

SAMUEL FREEMAN

1. GENERAL FEATURES

The idea that a political constitution, or society itself, is grounded in a social contract among society's members is a recurring feature of modern political thought. Since Thomas Hobbes's *Leviathan* (1651) many social and political theorists have regarded society as a cooperative undertaking for mutual benefit. The intuitive idea behind this understanding of the social contract is that if society's members are expected to recognize and comply with social norms (laws, conventions, etc.), then they should also be in a position to accept these norms and government's enforcement authority. Social cooperation is of course nonvoluntary—we have no choice but to be subject to the laws of some society, and few are able to choose the society they live in. The metaphor of a social contract is nonetheless invoked to emphasize that there are alternative ways to organize mutually beneficial cooperation and that societies should be organized according to those terms of cooperation that are generally acceptable to all rational members.

Another source for the idea of a social contract is the tradition of liberal and democratic thought that stems (respectively) from John Locke and Jean-Jacques Rousseau. Here, the social contract metaphor finds its support in the widely held conviction in democratic societies that freedom and equality are fundamental political values. Democratic societies reject inherited class privilege and legally enforced class boundaries. Their members generally regard themselves as civic equals and as free to decide their ends, activities, and conscientious convictions. Personal freedom gives rise to differences in aims, attitudes, and religious and moral convictions. One appealing response to demands to justify the source and purposes of political authority is to say that the constitution and exercise of coercive political power should be generally acceptable to free and equal persons. It is precisely because social cooperation is nonvoluntary that the specific terms of cooperation among free and equal persons should be grounded in their consent and agreement.

Locke and Rousseau argue that the *only* way that political authority legitimately can be exercised over free and equal persons is by their consent. But why insist on a *social* contract, a general agreement by everyone with everyone else? Why wouldn't each person's private contract with existing political powers suffice? One reason is that rational persons, before giving their consent, want to be assured that everyone else also consents to political authority and that all are committed to one another to obeying its laws—consent to political authority is then made conditional on mutual commitment. Another reason is that political power should not be regarded as a private power that originates in specially tailored bargains for mutual private benefit. It is rather a public power that is to be impartially exercised for public benefit and the common good (Locke 1988, 268). This is one significant way that social contract views differ from Robert Nozick's libertarianism, which regards political power as based in private economic contracts, not as a public power to be impartially administered for the public good, as the liberal democratic idea holds.[1]

The fact that social contracts are agreements by everyone with everyone else distinguishes them from a "contracts of government," wherein political subjects, individually or as a group, enter into an agreement with an existing political authority (e.g., the Magna Carta). Contracts of government are not social contracts among equals but instead take existing political power relations as given. They do not address the justice of existing regimes or their ex ante legitimacy. The point of a *social* contract—an agreement by everyone subject to political authority with everyone else—is to "authorize" government itself by establishing its right to rule and its political legitimacy.

David Hume argued, against Locke, that no government could ever achieve legitimacy if everyone had to agree to its authority. But none of the major figures within the social contract tradition—Hobbes, Locke, Rousseau, Kant, Rawls, and others—seriously contemplated actual social agreement as a condition for the governments' legitimacy. Kant was the first to make explicit that the social contract is an "idea of reason," not an actual event. It is a kind of thought experiment that conjectures what actual persons who are rational and properly informed would or could agree to if they were placed in hypothetical conditions that situate them as equals who are free to impose political constraints on themselves. The point of conjecturing a hypothetical social contract is not to create any actual obligations people do not already have; it is rather to discover and/or justify the implications of certain substantive assumptions regarding the freedom and equality of persons who are rationally and/or morally motivated to cooperate with others. Whether or not some or all members of society actually ever agree to these terms is of no consequence for this exercise (Rawls 1999a, 167). For, on the assumption that all relevant moral and evaluative assumptions and other reasons have been incorporated into the hypothetical social contract, the principles and institutions that would or could be agreed to therein are authoritative and binding on governments and their citizens, irrespective of any actual agreements they might make.

The social contract is then a method of philosophical explication and argument, of discovery and justification; it is not a method for creating duties and obligations that governments or their members do not already have. If the method is successful—and it has had different and competing applications—then we can understand more about the conditions of legitimate political authority; the justice of constitutions, economies, and societies; and our social and political rights, duties, and obligations. Social contract theorists might then say that the frequent criticism of social contract doctrine—that we cannot create obligations by a hypothetical contract but only by an actual one—is beside the point. We shall see below how they hope to vindicate this reply.

For clarification's sake, three different social contract traditions can be distinguished, each of which is connected with one or more major philosophers: (a) *interest-based views* originated with Thomas Hobbes's *Leviathan*; (b) *right-based conceptions* originated with Locke and Rousseau and underpin the liberal and democratic traditions of social contract theory; and (c) *convention-based conceptions* are contracts as conventions, traceable to David Hume. The first two are primarily normative; the third is ostensibly explanatory but inevitably comes with normative implications.

Social contract views of all three kinds rely on some conception of a person's good, which is advanced by the principles agreed to in the social contract. Contract views also reject the idea that there is some ultimate good to which everyone's good is subordinate and which is to be promoted or maximized, irrespective of individuals' good. This is one way social contract doctrines significantly differ from utilitarianism and other forms of consequentialism. Social contract theorists normally assume that there are a plurality of (intrinsic) goods or values, often incommensurable, and that the values that are rational for individuals to pursue depends on their capacities, desires, and circumstances. Individuals' good then differs and potentially conflicts.

Contract conceptions further assume that individuals are *equals* in some important respect, whether naturally or morally, and that they are *free* (again naturally or morally) in important respects. The focus on freedom, equality, and individual good supports the idea that social and political principles or relations should be mutually beneficial and generally acceptable to persons in light of their essential good—general acceptability being the intuitive idea encompassed by the metaphor of a social contract.

Both interest-based and right-based contract conceptions thus endorse the assumptions that (a) moral and political principles (of justice, etc.) are to be justified on the basis of a conception of a person's good, normally characterized by reference to certain fundamental interests (e.g., self-preservation in Hobbes, or "life, liberty, and estates" in Locke). Interest-based contract conceptions further contend that (b) these fundamental interests are specified without reference to moral concepts, and (c) moral assumptions, including individual rights and other principles of justice, are not otherwise invoked or incorporated into the social contract in the effort to justify political principles of justice. Instead, the normative principles relied on include only rational principles (e.g., principles of rational choice)—that is, principles that specify the concept of, or otherwise relate to, a person's good. Thus, (d) political principles of justice are conceived as rational instrumental means to realizing the fundamental interests of individuals engaged in social cooperation. In this regard, principles of justice are "reduced to" nonmoral interests and rational principles (of choice, etc.). The distinctive feature, then, of interest-based views is their aspiration to ground moral conclusions about justice and political authority in entirely nonmoral premises about people's interests and what they would choose if they were instrumentally rational and had true beliefs about their circumstances.

By contrast, right-based contract conceptions, while they normally endorse (a)—some statement of individuals' good and fundamental interests—reject (b) through (d) and instead rely on antecedent principles of right, moral interests, or other moral assumptions (e.g., moral equality or the equal right to natural freedom) in the justification of political principles. What makes a conception right-based then is that it incorporates concepts of right and justice (which may or may not include individual rights) into the social contract itself, along with assumptions regarding individuals' good and their fundamental interests. Political principles of justice are not then reduced to only nonmoral interests and principles of rational choice but instead incorporate some prior idea of what is right or reasonable. Critics say that such arguments are circular or question-begging and that the distinct advantage of interest-based views is that they avoid this problem. Right-based advocates reply that interest-based explications address only the morality-related concerns of amoralists or skeptics and are not relevant to ascertaining what justice requires of us (more on this in Section 3).

Thus, social contract views differ in multiple ways: Who are the parties to the agreement and how are their capacities and interests described? What rights and powers do they have? What are the circumstances of the social contract (state of nature, existing status quo, or strict equality)? What kinds of knowledge do the parties have? What are the rational and/or moral constraints on agreement? What is the purpose or object of the agreement (to authorize a sovereign, choose a political constitution, or choose principles of political and/or economic justice)? Because these parameters can be set differently, there is not one but several different social contract conceptions.

In the next three sections I explain the distinguishing features of three kinds of social contract approaches (interest-based, right-based, and convention-based views) focusing on works by the major historical and some leading contemporary figures from each tradition.

2. HOBBESIAN AND INTEREST-BASED CONTRACT VIEWS

In Plato's *Republic*, the Sophist Glaucon argues that justice is a pact among individuals, each of whom is concerned only with furthering his or her own interests. Interest-based social contract views develop this general idea. They seek to reduce justice to nonmoral terms in the following sense: Justice is explicated as the cooperative norms that are mutually beneficial and in each person's rational, enlightened interest to observe, on the condition that others do too. The fundamental interests of individuals furthered by cooperative norms are specified without reference to any moral notions (such as an interest in justice or doing what is right) and often are phrased in self-referential terms. However, purely self-interested motives are not necessary for an interest-based view. Hobbes recognized that people are often motivated by their religious convictions and other-regarding motives such as the welfare of their mates and families (called "conjugal affections") or by a sense of family honor, patriotism, and so on. But it is essential to an interest-based view that individuals' fundamental interests not be shared concerns for common purposes. Instead, individuals are regarded as having different interests that put them in potential conflict. When such conflicts arise, each individual prefers that his or her own fundamental interests be realized instead of the interests of others. This puts individuals into competition for scarce resources and other benefits that are means to achieving their fundamental goals. The social contract is a rational compromise or bargain among persons with conflicting interests, whereby each party is willing to moderate the direct pursuit of his or her interests and comply with cooperative norms on the condition that others do too. An essential feature of interest-based views is that each party to the social contract is made better off by the norms and conditions agreed to than he or she would have been in the absence of the contract. Pareto-improvements are then necessary and often sufficient conditions of interest-based contract views.[2]

Another characteristic of interest-based contracts is that the parties are historically situated in the sense that they know their present and historical situations; they have knowledge of their particular desires, interests, and circumstances; and they generally know as much about themselves and each other as you and I know about ourselves. In *Hobbesian* interest-based views, the parties' initial situation is defined in terms of a presocial and noncooperative state of nature without any political authority. The purpose of agreement from this noncooperative baseline is to establish and assure compliance with norms that specify conditions of (peaceable and efficient) social cooperation, on the assumption that humans are primarily concerned with advancing their own interests, are largely indifferent to the welfare of strangers, and have no concern for morality and justice for their own sake. In *conventional* interest-based views, the parties are seen as similarly motivated, but their historical circumstances are defined by the current status quo, including whatever cooperative norms are already in place. Because conventional views take the status quo as given, they do not seek to justify or critically assess prevailing norms of social cooperation; rather they presuppose them as a baseline from which to justify additional or alternative norms that are mutually beneficial (see, e.g., Buchanan and Tullock 1965). Conventional views thus resemble utilitarianism in this respect: They focus only on the future, and their attitude toward the past is to let bygones be bygones. Because of its predominant influence, primary attention here is given to the Hobbesian view.

Hobbes's *Leviathan*

Hobbes's own view relies on the idea of a social contract for two purposes: First, it is an analytical device designed to clarify the nature of political power and the necessary conditions of society and social cooperation. Its second purpose is normative and is not shared with contemporary contract views, that is, to justify the exercise of absolute political power as among the essential conditions of society and social cooperation.

Hobbes states that we have philosophical knowledge (versus that "knowledge called Experience") of something when we understand how its properties as we now know them could be generated from its parts (Hobbes 1991, 458). The social contract and the state of nature are analytical tools Hobbes uses to provide philosophical knowledge of the conditions of civil society. Hobbes theoretically dissolves civil society into its constituent parts—an aggregate of individuals not subject to civil laws or political power to enforce them. He imagines what circumstances would be like in this "state of nature" and asks how political society could result from this initial situation. A social contract is one way that a stable society could come about from a state of nature. By focusing attention on rational individuals in a state of nature, what fundamentally motivates them, and each of the properties that are necessary to constitute civil society from a state of nature, the social contract provides philosophical knowledge of the conditions that are necessary to establish and sustain civil society.

Hobbes sees human nature as predominantly self-focused (or, at best, family focused). The three most important motivations are, in order of priority, self-preservation, "conjugal affections," and acquiring the means for commodious living (Hobbes 1991, 235–36). Because resources are scarce, humans are put into a natural state of competition. They are roughly equal in strength of body and mind, so the weakest pose a threat to the strongest. Given these and other facts, Hobbes contends that in the absence of effective political power in a state of nature, it is irrational to trust others to observe cooperative norms (the "Laws of Nature"). Each person's rational response is to be in a "state of anticipation" and attack others first whenever circumstances seem propitious. The result is collectively irrational, a "war of all against all."

Hobbes's state of nature seems to be the first recognition of the structure of prisoner's dilemma situations. These are situations in which each person acts rationally to do what is best for him or herself, but all end up worse off than if they (jointly) had acted differently. Prisoner's dilemmas often arise when people do not trust one another to comply with cooperative norms. Hobbes's solution to the prisoner's dilemma of the state of nature is the social contract. What is required to lift inhabitants out of a state of nature—and thus, Hobbes contends, for us to avoid falling back into that situation—is (a) that everyone recognize and obey certain cooperative norms or laws of nature and (b) an effective sovereign with powers sufficient to enforce them. Hobbes's social contract is in effect a *contract of authorization*, or an agreement by everyone to authorize one person to exercise political powers necessary to enforce the "articles of Peace." The social contract is an agreement by everyone with everyone else; it is not an agreement with the sovereign itself (a contract of government). For Hobbes, any agreement with the sovereign is void because there can be no one with effective power to enforce it.

The sovereign's role is to stabilize civil society by providing all with the assurance that its cooperative norms are being enforced and that others will abide by them. Assurance that others will observe the laws of nature is necessary to make it rational for each of us to abide by them. Without political authority, it is irrational to observe cooperative norms, for we have no assurance that others will obey them too. Thus, Hobbes says, there is no "Right and Wrong, Justice and Injustice" in a state of nature (Hobbes 1991, 90). This means that moral duties are conditional on our having the assurance that others will observe them. Justice for Hobbes cannot demand that we act irrationally, contrary to our fundamental interests.

Hobbes argues that for the sovereign to fulfill its role of enforcing the laws of nature, there can be no limits on sovereign political power. To this any rational person would agree if given the opportunity. Locke and Rousseau object that it is irrational to give anyone absolute political power over oneself. Hobbes contests the stability of constitutional regimes that limit or divide political power on the grounds that they are unstable and degenerate into a state of war. History has decided the argument against Hobbes. Hobbes's lasting influence lies more in his account of justice and society as based in general agreement on mutually beneficial cooperative norms, rather than in his enthusiasm for unlimited powers of governments.

Contemporary Interest-Based Contract Views

Hobbes's legacy is well represented among contemporary game theorists, economists, and public choice theorists who see social cooperation as a response to prisoners' dilemma situations. Among philosophers, David Gauthier is a major contemporary representative of a Hobbesian interest-based contract view. Gauthier's primary aims are (a) to give a "rational reconstruction" of morality and (b) to show how capitalism is grounded in reason (Gauthier 1986, 339, 353). Gauthier regards rationality as individual utility maximization. Morality constrains individuals' choices and pursuits of their interests. Once we demythologize morality, it can be construed as an extension of principles of rational choice. Thus, morality is the rules and constraints that are rational to observe if people are to maximize their individual utility in social interaction. It is the restrictions on the pursuit of utility that rational individuals would mutually agree to in order to secure and best promote their long-term interests. Morality is then "reduced" to enlightened self-interest, for moral ideas are explained in terms of presumedly more basic nonmoral ideas alone.

Gauthier exhibits this basically Hobbesian theme via his defense of the "system of natural liberty" of the classical economists. For Gauthier (and Buchanan too), the model of Economic Man best characterizes human relationships outside families. "Economic Man is a radical contractarian in that all his free or noncoercive interpersonal relationships are contractual" (Gauthier 1986, 319). Contractual bargains are the basis of market behavior. Markets are "an ideal of human interaction" because (a) we act therein free of moral and other constraints on direct utility-maximizing behavior and (b) under perfect competition markets are efficient (Gauthier 1986, 100). However, because of externalities afflicting imperfect markets, real-world markets often fail; each person acts to maximize individual utility, and the outcome is an inefficient equilibrium (represented by the prisoner's dilemma). "Morality arises from market failure" (Gauthier 1986, 84). Its role is to approximate the efficient equilibrium that would result under perfect competition; but this requires cooperation, a joint strategy of mutual adherence to constraints on individual utility maximization. This is the role of Gauthier's social contract. It supplies the moral terms of cooperation needed to approximate the ideal of perfect market interaction.

Hobbes contends that markets and property are not possible in the absence of effective political power and that one of the roles of the sovereign is to specify and enforce property rules. Gauthier claims that the rational utility-maximizing inhabitants in a state of nature would realize that the benefits of market interactions outweigh the costs of predation and strife, and thus markets and natural property would arise by convention even in the absence of political power or an explicit social contract. Market behavior and private property are then conceived as presocial, and Gauthier's social contract is not an agreement either to political power or to the institution of property, or to markets as the primary mechanism for property's distribution. Instead, Gauthier's social contract is a bargaining process resulting in a bargaining solution ("minimax relative concession") that addresses the externalities of market failures and distributes the fruits of cooperation (the "cooperative surplus") that arise outside market relations. This bargaining solution mimics the perfect market by distributing the benefits and burdens of cooperation according to each person's marginal contribution. Gauthier's social contract has a limited function, but a necessary one, he believes, if peaceable and efficient social cooperation are to be possible.

Rawls objects to Hobbesian views like Gauthier's, which employ bargaining theory to explicate and devise solutions to the social contract, on the grounds that they rely on preexisting distributions of resources as well as differences in bargaining power that the parties bring to the social contract. "To each according to his threat advantage is hardly a principle of fairness" (Rawls 1999b, 58n). Simply because people agree to something does not mean that the terms of their agreement are morally justifiable, especially if the circumstances of their agreement are grossly unequal. Hobbesians reply that the only way to avoid taking some preexisting distribution of power and resources as given is to beg the question—as Rawls and other moral contractarians seemingly do—by importing moral standards that

Hobbesians regard as in need of a nonmoral rational foundation. Accordingly, Hobbesians generally do not question the morality of the status quo ante under which hypothetical bargaining and the social contract transpire. They regard Pareto-improvements to any situation as collectively rational and prima facie fair and just, because everyone benefits. To the objection that many contracts are unfair or unconscionable, Hobbesians may reply that there is a lot of superstition built into common-sense beliefs about morality and justice. Even if their views do not capture many of our considered moral convictions and are revisionary, Hobbesians contend that if we are to regard justice as anchored in reason and compatible with a scientific view of the world, then their interest-based contractarianism is the best "rational reconstruction" that can be given for morality and justice (Gauthier 1986, 339).

The appeal of Hobbesian views thus lies not in their fitting with our considered moral convictions but in their showing how moral norms can be grounded in a nonmoral conception of rationality (e.g., utility maximization) and our essential good. Hobbesians collapse questions of moral justification into questions of (rational) motivation: To justify norms is to show that they are responsive to each person's desires and interests (hence the emphasis on Pareto-improvements). Suppose we accept the general Hobbesian thesis that moral norms are mutually advantageous and in everyone's interest. A wide range of conceptions of justice could satisfy this condition when the alternative is a state of nature. The problem is to give a Hobbesian justification for a specific conception of justice by showing that everyone now will benefit and have sufficient reason to endorse and comply with its terms. Thus, Hobbes argued (to no avail), royal absolutism is in everyone's interest. Similarly, Gauthier and Buchanan both argue for the rationality of laissez-faire economic principles. However, many persons who now benefit from the status quo would be greatly disadvantaged if laissez-faire were to be enacted (e.g., beneficiaries of government regulation and subsidies, including minimum wage laws and people on public assistance). Why should they accept laissez-faire principles? Can it seriously be argued that it is irrational in mixed Western economies for anyone to refuse to endorse laissez-faire? Without resolving this motivational problem, it may be that the justificatory task of modern Hobbesian views cannot be carried through on their own terms.

3. Right-Based Social Contract Views and the Liberal and Democratic Traditions

Right-based contracts incorporate moral assumptions from the outset; they do not try to explicate justice or justify political principles purely in terms of a nonmoral conception of a person's good and rational principles of choice. Locke, Rousseau, and Kant—the major representatives of the natural rights theory of the social contract tradition—assume that individuals are born with a moral right of equal freedom; similarly Rawls assumes moral ideals of "free and equal moral persons" and of society as "well-ordered" by principles justifiable to all citizens.[3] These and other moral rights, principles, and ideals impose moral constraints on the political principles to which the parties to the social contract can rationally agree. As Rawls says, "the reasonable has priority over the rational and subordinates it absolutely" (Rawls 2001, 82).

Of course, the moral assumptions of right-based views need justification and cannot be justified (simply) by the social contract itself. Hobbesians contend that right-based views beg the question, for the only justification for morality as a whole is rational choice and interest. But right-based theorists regard Hobbesian reductions of morality to rational choice as futile exercises, for morality as a whole stands no more in need of justification than does the pursuit of one's rational interests. Morality and justice are seen as independent domains of practical reasoning, related but not reducible to rational interest. Accordingly, Locke said that the natural right of equal freedom is self-evident, whereas Kant said it is deducible from principles of pure practical reason (Kant 1999), and Rawls contends that his basic assumptions are our "considered moral convictions" whose justification depends on their being brought into "wide reflective equilibrium" with principles of justice via the social contract itself. These are complex and controversial debates that can be only mentioned here.

Locke's Consent Thesis and Social Contract Doctrine

Locke says that it is "evident in itself" to Reason that all men are born free, equal, and independent and that they have a duty to preserve themselves and the rest of humankind (Locke 1988, 269–71). This is a "Fundamental Law of Nature and Government" (Locke 1988, 375). Given our "Equal Right to Natural Freedom" (Locke 1988, 304), no person can be obligated to become a member of any political society and subject to another's political authority except by his or her own consent (Locke 1988, 330). We have reason to enter political society with others to protect our fundamental interests in our "lives, liberty, and estates," including our property. But to join political society as a permanent member, we must actually give our "express consent." Whether or not we join political society, our natural duty to preserve all humankind implies a duty to obey civil laws that are compatible with the laws of nature. This natural duty does not depend on our consent. Moreover, by residing within a society and enjoying its benefits, we give our "tacit consent" to obey its laws and not undermine it. However, Locke rejects the idea that we are under a political obligation to give a regime our allegiance simply because we are born within its territory. Instead, we must give our actual express joining consent to become a member of political society (Locke 1988, 347).

Locke's account of political obligation presupposes his social contract. For anyone to be under a political obligation or owe allegiance to a political regime, it must be legitimate. Locke's social contract provides the standard for the legitimacy of political regimes. Unlike Hobbes, for Locke a legitimate regime is not one that effectively exercises political power, even when generally accepted by most subjects; instead, a legitimate regime has a right to rule. No government is legitimate or has a claim to political authority and allegiance of its members unless it *could have been contracted into*, starting from a position of equal right and equal political jurisdiction in a state of nature, (a) without anyone violating his or her duties to God and the rest of humankind and (b) without doing anything irrational or that would make him or herself worse off than in a state of nature.

Locke contends that it is rational for each person to grant to government the authority to make and enforce laws that regulate exercise of his or her equal right to natural freedom and other moral rights and duties. But it would be irrational to agree to alienate entirely our freedom and the rights it includes and become subservient to another's arbitrary will; for the point of entering political society is to protect our fundamental interests in life, liberty, and property. To grant anyone absolute political power is to alienate the liberties necessary to achieve those interests. Thus, absolute monarchy is illegitimate (Locke 1988, 382). No government is legitimate unless it respects constitutional limits that incorporate our inalienable rights and liberties. Even if we have sworn allegiance to a political regime that now claims absolute political authority, our consent and political obligations are void, and we have the right, with other citizens, to depose an illegitimate government.

Hume famously argued that Locke's consent thesis implies that any existing government's legitimacy requires that it originated in the past in a social contract. This implies the absurd consequence that virtually no government is legitimate (Hume 1963). If Locke believed this, it would not be for the reasons Hume attributes to him. Locke's social contract thesis is not an historical test of political legitimacy, but rather a hypothetical one. He explicitly says we cannot be bound by the promises of our ancestors, suggesting that past agreements (e.g., in 1688 or 1789) are neither necessary nor sufficient for existing governments' legitimacy (Locke 1988, 347). However a government initially might have acquired political power in the distant past, its legitimacy *now* depends on the hypothetical condition, whether it *could have been* contracted into from a position of equal right without violating specific conditions.

Hume's argument may still suggest a problem with Locke's requirement of express consent for political obligation: Few of us (except as minors under duress) have formally sworn allegiance to the political constitution. Still our government, assuming it is just or nearly so, reasonably can claim legitimate authority not only to enforce laws against us but also demand our allegiance and special obligations (e.g., for jury duty and military service in national defense). These problems of individuals' political obligations aside, the core of Locke's social contract is its test of a government's political legitimacy. Locke's social contract provides the justification for a liberal constitution. Its main ideas—the people are sovereign, government originates in their consent, government has limited and fiduciary powers that are exercisable only for the public good, citizens have inalienable rights and a right of resistance when these rights are violated—supplied the conceptual framework for the American Declaration of Independence and the U.S. Constitution. But Locke did not argue for a democratic constitution or government in the modern sense; he envisioned instead a constitutional monarchy, in which people give up their own political authority and instead transfer it to a constitutional monarchy with a representative parliament. The idea that citizens retain legislative power and rule themselves was mainly Rousseau's contribution.

Rousseau and the General Will

The idea that political power is a *public power*, to be exercised impartially and only for the common good, is central to the liberal and democratic social contract traditions. Rousseau especially emphasizes the common good of democratic citizens and their role in establishing it. His social contract draws on Locke; his main innovations are the ideas that the people themselves should retain democratic authority to make ordinary laws and that they should legislate for the common good according to the "general will." The general will is an extension of the social contract. For Rousseau and Locke, free and equal persons are envisioned as joining together to form a "body politic," which establishes political society; the body politic then makes a political constitution. For Rousseau, ideally this constitution is radically democratic: Legislative power is retained by the people. In making laws, citizens are impartially to deliberate on and then vote based on their conscientious convictions regarding justice and the common good, or those measures that promote the fundamental interests of all citizens. If they do this correctly, their judgments should express the general will.

The general will is best understood as a form of deliberative reasoning exercised by citizens as members of the body politic. Rousseau distinguishes the general will from each person's "private will" and from the "will of all" or the "sum of private wills" (Rousseau 1987, 155). The will of all is the judgment that the majority or unanimity make when they vote for their particular interests as individuals or as members of some interest group (e.g., a religious association or business corporation). The general will is the judgments and decisions that the body of sincere, conscientious, and fully informed citizens *would jointly make* regarding the laws required by justice and the common good and in which they abstract from all particular interests and reflect only on their fundamental interests in the rational and moral good that they share in common as free and equal citizens.[4]

Rousseau's general will is an impartial point of view that legislators/citizens adopt in their deliberations and voting. Actual legislators/citizens should set aside their own and others' particular desires and interests and mimic as best they can the deliberations and decisions of the ideal legislators/citizens whose judgments express the general will. Rousseau argued for a direct democracy because he believed that the body of conscientious citizens, when adequately informed and presented with the right questions, is more likely to ascertain and vote the general will than any other legislative body.

Rousseau states that "moral liberty . . . alone makes man truly master of himself" and consists in "obedience to the law one has prescribed for oneself" (Rousseau 1987, 151). This law is the fundamental law of the society of the social contract—the laws enacted from the point of view of the general will, properly based on citizens' shared fundamental interests (Rawls 2007, 235). Rousseau's ideas of moral freedom and the general will later supplied the foundations for Kant's moral and political philosophy, including his seminal idea of moral autonomy and also the "original contract."

Rawls's Justice as Fairness

Rawls develops and transforms the natural rights theory of the social contract of Locke, Rousseau, and Kant. Rawls posits a social contract whose parties agree to substantive principles of justice. The role of these principles is to assess the justice of laws, the political constitution, and other "basic social institutions," including economic markets and property, that make possible the creation and distribution of income, wealth, social and economic powers and positions of responsibility, and the opportunities to occupy these positions. Rawls aims to provide, as an alternative to utilitarianism, a conception of justice that serves as "the most appropriate moral basis for a democratic society" (Rawls 1999a, viii).

Rawls's hypothetical social contract transpires not in a state of nature but in an "original position," where the parties are ignorant of their personal, social, and historical circumstances. Consider Locke's state of nature: Though formally equals, his parties know their historical situation and relative differences in talents and resources. Consequently, those less advantaged by nature and fortune agree to alienate their equal political jurisdiction to gain the benefits of political society. Locke envisions restricting the franchise to the class of amply propertied men. Though Locke's starting position might be politically egalitarian, he does not require a democratic constitution.

Rawls repudiates the moral relevance of the state of nature: "It is a historical surd . . . of no significance (Rawls, 2001, 55). Like the current status quo, the state of nature is beset with arbitrary contingencies (e.g., prevailing distributions of property, natural talents, skills, and other personal differences). If the purpose of the social contract is to justify principles of justice that assess political, social, and economic institutions and prevailing distributions of rights, powers, wealth, then, Rawls contends, we cannot assume beforehand any particular historical distribution of these and other social goods. Knowledge of particular facts about persons and social institutions are morally irrelevant to agreement on principles of justice for the political constitution, the economy, property, and other basic social institutions.

Thus, the parties to Rawls's social contract are situated behind a "veil of ignorance" regarding knowledge of any particular facts about themselves or others, or about their society and its history. They are then deprived of awareness of their own and others' social circumstances, particular talents and skills, aims and desires, and even their conscientious religious, moral, and philosophical convictions. Rawls's thought is that, in deliberation and agreement on principles of justice, none should be in a position to take unfair advantage of their knowledge of particular or historical circumstances. The parties to Rawls's social contract are symmetrically situated, strictly as equals.

Rawls calls his conception "justice as fairness" because its principles originate in an initial situation that is fair. Rawls's principles of justice are, first, the principle of equal basic liberties and second, fair equality of opportunity and the difference principle. The first principle guarantees equally to all persons in society abstract rights protecting liberty of conscience, freedom of thought and expression, freedom of association, political participation, the rule of law, and the integrity and freedom of the person (including the right to hold sufficient personal property for personal independence). Rawls's second principle says (a) offices and positions of responsibility are to be open to all to compete for on grounds of "fair equality of opportunity" and (b) laws and conventions that permit inequalities in income, wealth, and economic powers and responsibilities are to be designed to maximize the share that goes to the least-advantaged members of society.

Rawls states, "It is characteristic of contract theories to stress the public nature of political principles" (1999a, 16). Social contract theories generally incorporate the moral requirement that free and equal persons know the principles governing their social relations and do not have any illusions about them. Rawls emphasizes the "publicity" of principles of justice and their essential role in a democracy in providing a basis for public justification and criticism of social institutions. These principles supply the bases for democratic deliberation on grounds of "public reason"—an idea Rawls says originates in Rousseau's general will (Rawls 2007, 231; Rawls 1999b, 219). Similar to Rousseau and Kant, Rawls contends that in acting from principles of justice we are morally autonomous, for we act on a law we give to ourselves out of our rational and moral powers as free and equal moral persons (1999a, 252–57, 515).

Important Contrasts

There are important differences between interest-based and right-based social contracts. One common objection to right-based democratic views, especially nonhistorical ones, is that there is little or no bargaining; consequently there is not a genuine contract. Because of the moral constraints imposed on the agreement and the focus on principles that promote the common good, there is no need to invoke a general agreement by everyone. The same results purportedly can be achieved by impartial decision by a single individual.

This is an excessively legal interpretation that assimilates all contracts to economic bargains. It implies that none of the major figures in the social contract tradition—Locke, Rousseau, Kant, Rawls, even Hobbes—are contractarians. (For Hobbes, the social contract is not a negotiated bargain but a mutual authorization of an effective sovereign.) Not all contracts or agreements involve economic bargaining or compromises among opposing interests. People with diverse ends often jointly commit themselves to principles and causes to achieve shared ends (as in religious associations, marital vows, or the Mayflower Compact). The point of these "compacts" is not to resolve fundamental differences, for there may be none. It is rather to secure the future and keep the parties from later deviating from the shared purposes and norms of their association. Right-based social contract views normally involve contracts in this broader sense: The agreement is a joint precommitment among citizens to relations that maintain their freedom and equality and that promote their shared fundamental interests. Their precommitment settles principles and establishes institutions that bind citizens perpetually into political relations as equals and prevents them from later giving in to temptations that undermine the common good (Freeman 2007, 32–36). A problem with the forgoing objection—that in the absence of bargain, one person might as well choose for everyone—is that free and equal persons cannot be bound by the impartial choice of a single individual, who at most can decide for and commit only himself. Hence, the fact that God or another impartial chooser would select the same principles of justice as the parties in Rawls's social contract is irrelevant to the parties' self-imposition of reciprocal obligations to recognize and support those principles and comply with just institutions.

In the nature of bargains, interest-based views proceed from an idea of *mutual advantage*. A mutually advantageous contract is one in which each person gains as compared with his or her starting position. Right-based views, in the nature of shared precommitments, involve a different idea—that of *reciprocity*. A reciprocal agreement starts from an equal or fair baseline: Everyone benefits in relation to a starting position of equality of right, status, and situation. For example, interest-based agreements between serfs and landlords are mutually advantageous but not reciprocal, for the starting position is unjust. In the reciprocal agreements of the democratic contract tradition, there is no assurance that each person will benefit compared to his or her actual starting position—indeed, it is unlikely that all will, because the purpose is not to Pareto-improve the status quo while preserving its injustices but to provide standards for assessing current injustices and correcting them.

How, then, can actual people who benefit from current injustice accept the standards of right-based views? Many will not; if their sense of justice is weak, it may even be irrational for them to do so. But for democratic theorists, this is not an argument against the *reasonableness* or validity of right-based views. It is rather a motivational problem belonging to the process of transition from an unjust to a just society. Unlike Hobbesians, for right-based view proponents, justice is not defined as a rational compromise among conflicting interests, nor does the justification of a conception of justice require showing each person, regardless of his or her ends, that justice is rationally advantageous given that person's actual position in the world. Rather, right-based views contend that a conception is justified when it conforms to our reasoned judgments of justice. Hobbesian views might seem immune to this motivational problem, but we have seen how Gauthier and others confront a similar difficulty, namely persuading those advantaged by the current status quo that it is to their rational advantage to accept norms that would be agreed to by self-interested utility maximizers in a hypothetical state of nature. Unlike those who hold right-based views, Hobbesians cannot appeal to moral intuitions to address this issue. A motivation problem of some kind is confronted by any contract view that does not assume the justice of the prevailing status quo and take it as the basis for agreement. In the history of social contract thought, there are no *normative* doctrines of lasting significance that specify justice in terms of agreement from any prevailing status quo.

Finally, we should consider Hume's objection that social contracts are redundant and unnecessary because the real justification for principles is the reasons the parties rely on when coming to an agreement (for Hume, only reasons of utility are relevant). One reply is to concede that the social contract does not provide independent reasons, or at least not any more than rules of inference do. Obviously this does not show that either is unnecessary or redundant. On the contrary, the social contract is a method of analysis, argumentation, and justification appropriate for political philosophy. As a method of analysis, it enables us to clarify and explicate the fundamental political values of freedom and equality. As a method of argumentation and justification, it enables us to organize and combine the multiplicity of reasons relevant to social cooperation among free and equal rational (and reasonable) persons and then surmise the fair principles of social cooperation most suitable to them. Asking the question of whether contractarian methods of analysis, argument, and justification are unnecessary or redundant presupposes that there is some alternative systematic method that, for the *same* multiplicity of reasons, arrives at the *same* principles and applications and does so in a simpler yet more perspicuous and convincing way. The burden of proof here lies with those raising the redundancy objection.

4. Contracts by Convention

Hobbes, as we have seen, uses the idea of a social contract not only normatively but also analytically, to provide "philosophical knowledge" of the State and the conditions necessary for society. Hume also employed the idea of general agreement analytically, to give an empirical explanation for existing social institutions and norms. Hume takes (Western) societies and governments as they are and explains their psychological and social preconditions. Ostensibly he rejects the idea of a social contract. No such contracts ever occurred, he contends, and in any case cannot account for people's allegiance to governments and their laws, which is based on awareness of their "usefulness" or utility (Hume 1963). Nonetheless, Hume appeals to a tacit general agreement to account for political and economic norms and practices. He argues that "justice"—by which he means rules of property; consensual transfers; and promising, contracts, and other agreements—is required for society, for these institutions are necessary for economic production, exchange, and consumption. The "rules of justice" and governments that enforce them come about and are sustained by "convention or agreement betwixt us," whereby we all tacitly agree to comply with mutually beneficial rules on the condition that others do too (Hume 1960, 490, 498). Although the rules of justice originate in self-interest, once socially established they are maintained by our "sense of justice," a psychological disposition that causes us to approve of existing conventions so long as others do too and to disapprove of people violating them. Crucially, Hume argues that people's sense of justice is normally guided by their "concern for the public interest," or "public utility" (Hume 1960, 496, 499–500; Hume 1975, 201, 303–11).

Hume's naturalized contract by convention suggests normative consequences. Habitual compliance with conventions of justice, Hume contends, normally are in everyone's interest. Because approval of the "usefulness" of these rules is allegedly built into our "moral sense" and "sentiments of justice," public utility presumably should be our guide in applying and revising these rules and deciding disputes under them. Otherwise we act contrary to human nature and the role of existing laws and conventions in making society possible, risking social instability.

Contemporary rational choice theorists in philosophy, economics, political science, and psychology similarly contend that social norms can be explained as a kind of social contract or contract by convention. In evolutionary game theory it is argued that, even when people do not consciously act as rational utility maximizers, what explains their fitness capacity—to survive, reproduce, and achieve satisfaction of their preferences—is the subconscious adoption of certain conventional cooperative strategies of conduct ("tit-for-tat," etc.) that are more successful than other strategies in achieving cooperation. These inquiries often build on Hobbesian contractarianism, explaining cooperative norms as solutions to prisoner's dilemma type situations (see Axelrod 2006). Other theorists follow Hume and explain the evolution and stability of social norms in terms of conventions and coordination games (see Harman 1977; Skyrms 1996, 2004; Binmore 2005; Gibbard 2008; Gaus 2010). Like Hume, some of these theorists also appeal to social utility, contending that a tendency to approve of arrangements causing greater overall utility is among our innate natural predispositions. For example, Binmore (2005) and Gibbard (2008) both contend that humans are biologically predisposed to adopt an impartial position (an "original position," according to Binmore) in moral deliberations and approve of patterns of conduct that promotes greater overall utility. As did their forebear Hume, many utilitarians have appropriated the social contract for their own purposes.

5. Conclusion

Unlike utilitarianism, social contract doctrines are not a family of substantive moral and political conceptions; rather, they are a family of methods of justification that support different conceptions of justice: democratic egalitarianism (Rousseau 1987;

Rawls 1999a; Barry 1995); classical liberalism (Locke 1960; Kant 1999; Gauthier 1986; Buchanan and Tullock 1965); political absolutism (Hobbes 1991); utilitarianism (Binmore 2005; Gibbard 2008); and even libertarianism (Narveson 2001). Critics argue that the idea of a social contract is empty because it is used to argue for so many conceptions of justice, and appears to justify none of them. Advocates, however, regard it as a positive feature of contractarianism that it can encompass a diversity of substantive positions and provide a method of analysis and argumentation that permits the discernment and assessment of assumptions implicit in political conceptions of justice and of the conditions under which they would or could be acceptable to free and equal rational and reasonable persons (Rawls 1999a, 105). The question whether contractarian analysis and argumentation can *justify* any of these substantive conceptions depends on whether a contract theory incorporates an appropriate conception of freedom, equality, and all other reasons relevant to social and political justice.

NOTES

1. See the chapter on Nozick in this volume.
2. A Pareto-improvement is any change in people's circumstances that makes some or all of them better off without making anyone else worse off. A situation is Pareto-efficient when no further Pareto-improvements can be made given the current distribution of goods.
3. T. M. Scanlon's "contractualism" (1998) is also right-based, but because it is a general moral and not a political conception, it is not discussed here. Brian Barry (1995) builds a conception of justice, which he contrasts with Rawls, based on Scanlon's contractualism.
4. Rawls says that fundamental interests for Rousseau are *amour de soi* and proper *amour propre*; our capacities for exercising "free will" and acting on valid reasons; our capacities for self-improvement through developing our faculties, including intellect; our capacities for identification with others, including pity and compassion; and our capacities for moral attitudes and emotions. See Rawls (2007, 217–18).

REFERENCES

Axelrod, Robert, 2006, *The Evolution of Cooperation*. New York: Basic Books.
Barry, Brian. 1995. *Justice as Impartiality*. New York: Oxford University Press.
Binmore, Ken. 2005. *Natural Justice*. New York: Oxford University Press.
Buchanan, James, and Gordon Tullock. 1965. *The Calculus of Consent*. Ann Arbor: University of Michigan Press.
Freeman, Samuel. 2007. *Justice and the Social Contract*. New York: Oxford University Press.
Gaus, Gerald. 2010. *The Order of Public Reason*. Cambridge, UK: Cambridge University Press.

Gauthier, David. 1986. *Morals by Agreement*. Oxford: Clarendon Press.
Gibbard, Allen. 2008. *Reconciling Our Aims*. New York: Oxford University Press.
Hampton, Jean. 1988, *Hobbes and the Social Contract Tradition*, Cambridge, UK: Cambridge University Press.
Harman, Gilbert. 1977. *The Nature of Morality*. New York: Oxford University Press.
Hobbes, Thomas. 1991. *Leviathan*. Cambridge, UK: Cambridge University Press. (Originally published in 1651)
Hume, David. 1960. *Treatise of Human Nature*. Book III. Oxford: Oxford University Press. (Originally published in 1739)
Hume, David. 1963. "Of the Original Contract." In *Essays Moral, Political, and Literary*, 452–73. New York: Oxford University Press. (Originally published in 1741)
Hume, David. 1975. *Enquiries Concerning Human Understanding and Concerning the Principles of Morals*, 3d ed. Oxford: Oxford University Press. (Originally published in 1777)
Kant, Immanuel. 1999. *Metaphysical Elements of Justice*. Indianapolis, IN: Hackett. (Originally published in 1797)
Locke, John. 1988. *The Second Treatise of Government in Two Treatises of Government*. Edited by Peter Laslett, 265-428. Cambridge, UK: Cambridge University Press. (Originally published in 1689)
Narveson, Jan. 2001. *The Libertarian Idea*. Peterborough, Ontario: Broadview Press.
Nozick, Robert. 1974. *Anarchy, State, and Utopia*. New York: Basic Books.
Rawls, John. 1996. *Political Liberalism*. New York: Columbia University Press.
Rawls, John. 1999a. *A Theory of Justice*. Cambridge, MA: Harvard University Press. (Originally published in 1971)
Rawls, John. 1999b. *Collected Papers*. Edited by Samuel Freeman. Cambridge, MA: Harvard University Press.
Rawls, John, 2001. *Justice as Fairness: A Restatement*, Edited by Erin Kelly, Cambridge, MA: Harvard University Press
Rawls, John, 2007. *Lectures in the History of Political Philosophy*. Edited by Samuel Freeman. Cambridge, MA: Harvard University Press.
Rousseau, Jean-Jacques.1987. *The Basic Political Writings*. Indianapolis, IN: Hackett.
Scanlon, Thomas. 1998. *What We Owe to Each Other*. Cambridge, MA: Harvard University Press.
Skyrms, Brian. 1996. *Evolution of the Social Contract*. Cambridge, UK: Cambridge University Press.
Skyrms, Brian. 2004. *The Stage Hunt and the Evolution of Social Structure*. Cambridge, UK: Cambridge University Press.

CHAPTER 8

LEFT-LIBERTARIANISM

PETER VALLENTYNE

LIBERTARIANISM is a family of theories of justice, each member of which is committed to full self-ownership and certain moral powers to acquire property rights in natural resources and other unowned resources. Right libertarianism imposes no or very weak distributive constraints on the moral powers of appropriation, whereas left-libertarianism imposes certain egalitarian constraints on these powers. Here I articulate and briefly defend left-libertarianism.[1] Throughout, my goal is merely to motivate left-libertarianism rather than to attempt a conclusive argument for it.

1. JUSTICE

Libertarian theories are normally understood as theories of justice, but what is justice? The term *justice* is used in many different ways (e.g., permissible social structures, fairness), but libertarians generally understand their theories to be about either the *moral duties that we owe each other* or about our *enforceable duties*. We therefore limit our attention to these two concepts of justice. On both views, justice is not a matter of what it is morally desirable to do; it is only concerned with what morality *requires* us to do or not do. It may be morally desirable to help one's neighbor, but justice may nonetheless permit one not to do so. Moreover, as we shall see, each concept of justice is concerned with only a certain subset of moral requirements.

Justice as the moral duties that we owe each other is concerned only with avoiding *interpersonal wrongs* (i.e., actions that infringe a duty owed to someone). This can be understood narrowly to concern only duties owed to others or broadly to include duties, if any, owed to oneself. Either way, it does not address *impersonal wrongs* (i.e., actions that are wrong whether or not they wrong anyone; e.g., destroying cultural relics when no one is harmed and everyone consents). Justice in this sense is a matter of respecting rights, where rights correspond to duties owed to individuals.[2] As long as rights are understood broadly as perhaps pro tanto and highly conditional constraints protecting the holder's interest or will, justice, in this sense, is a large topic. It is sensitive to all moral issues affecting the moral permissibility of actions, except those issues that are relevant only to impersonal duties (which, by definition, are not sensitive to the interests or wills of individuals) and perhaps duties to self. Because I believe that there are no impersonal duties (a controversial claim), I believe that justice exhausts our moral duties, but I do not pursue this point here.

The second concept of justice sometimes addressed by libertarians is justice as our enforceable duties. These are our moral duties that others are permitted to enforce (use force to ensure compliance). Some of our duties (such as keeping a promise to join someone for dinner), for example, may not be permissibly enforceable. Moreover, justice in this sense includes enforceable impersonal duties, if there are any. Libertarians, however, all hold that the only enforceable duties are interpersonal duties. Thus, for libertarianism, justice as our enforceable duties is a strictly narrower topic than justice as the duties we owe each other.

For simplicity, I focus on libertarianism as theory of the duties that we owe each other. This makes it a bolder, and hence more difficult to defend, theory.

2. Libertarianism

Libertarianism is sometimes advocated as a derivative set of rules (e.g., on the basis of rule utilitarianism or contractarianism). Here, however, I reserve the term for the natural rights doctrine that agents initially *fully own themselves* in a sense that I clarify below. All forms of libertarianism endorse full self-ownership. They differ, however, with respect to the moral powers that individuals have to acquire ownership of natural resources and other unowned resources. The best-known versions of libertarianism are *right-libertarian* theories (e.g., that of Nozick 1974), which hold that agents have a robust moral power to acquire full private property in natural resources (e.g., space, land, minerals, air, and water) without the consent of, or any significant payment to, other members of society. *Left-libertarianism*, by contrast, holds that the value of natural resources belongs to everyone in some egalitarian manner, and thus that appropriation is subject to stronger constraints.

3. Full Self-Ownership

Libertarianism is committed to the thesis of full self-ownership (for agents), which holds that each agent, at least initially (e.g., prior to any wrongdoings or contractual agreements), morally fully owns herself. The rough idea of moral full self-ownership is that of having all the moral rights over oneself that an owner of an inanimate thing (e.g., a car) has over that thing under the strongest form of private ownership of inanimate things. The rough idea is also that a full self-owner *morally* has all the rights over herself that a slave-owner *legally* has over a slave under the strongest possible legal form of private slave ownership.[3]

Throughout, we are concerned with moral self-ownership as opposed to legal self-ownership. We are concerned, that is, with a particular set of moral rights independently of whether these are recognized by any legal system. The slaves of the antebellum United States were legal slaves, but, morally speaking, on the libertarian view, they fully owned themselves. Indeed, it is because they morally fully owned themselves that legal involuntary slavery was such a great injustice.

An agent has full self-ownership just in case she fully owns herself. This is simply the special case of full ownership, where the owner and the entity owned are the same. Assuming that one's body is part of oneself, this entails that one fully owns one's body. Assuming that one's mind is also part of oneself, full self-ownership also entails full ownership of one's mind—although exactly what this means is unclear and I do not pursue this matter here.

What, then, is it to own fully a thing? Ownership of a thing is a set of rights over that thing, and the core right is the right to control *use* of that thing. For these purposes, *use* of a thing is understood broadly to include all the ways that agents can physically impact upon it.[4] Possession, occupation, intrusion, disposition, alteration, and destruction are forms of use in this stipulative sense.[5]

Full ownership of an entity consists of a full set of (roughly) the following ownership rights:

1. *control rights* over the use of the entity (a liberty right to use, a power to authorize use by others, and a claim right that others not use without one's authorization);
2. *rights to compensation* (when someone uses the entity without one's permission);
3. *enforcement rights* (e.g., rights of prior restraint and punishment);
4. *rights to transfer* these rights to others (by sale, rental, gift, or loan);
5. *immunities to the nonconsensual loss* of these rights; and
6. *immunities to the loss* of *other rights* merely for the possession or exercise of these rights (e.g., no rental payment or user fee is owed).

Full ownership is a logically strongest set of ownership rights that one can have over a thing that is compatible with others having the same kind of ownership rights over everything else in the world (except for the space occupied by the first person and the thing in question). There is, however, a tension between one person's compensation and enforcement rights and the immunities to loss of others. For example, if I have a right, against you, to compensation for damage to my property, then your immunity to loss of your rights over your property is less than it would be if I did not have this right. As a result, there is no uniquely strongest set of compensation rights, enforcement rights, and immunities to loss. Everyone could have very strong compensation and enforcement rights against those who violate their rights, but this would entail that everyone has a less than maximal immunity to loss of their ownership rights. Alternatively (at the other extreme), everyone could have very weak compensation and enforcement rights while having a relatively strong immunity to loss. Neither set of rights is unequivocally stronger than the other. Different versions of libertarianism are thus free to defend different conceptions of compensation and enforcement rights (and corresponding immunities to loss).

Although the notion of full ownership is indeterminate with respect to compensation rights, enforcement rights, and immunity to loss, it is perfectly determinate with respect to rights to control use and rights to transfer. Strengthening these rights for one person does not weaken anyone else's ownership rights.[6] Thus, there is a determinate core to full ownership in general and full self-ownership in particular.

These statements require qualification. Just as libertarianism sometimes addresses the topic of justice in the sense of the duties that we owe each other and sometimes addresses the topic of justice in the sense of our enforceable duties, there are two notions of ownership that libertarians invoke. In the previous paragraphs I focused on what can be called *interpersonal ethical ownership*. It requires a full interpersonal liberty to use the object as such. Although full interpersonal ethical ownership of a thing is compatible with one having an impersonal duty with respect to the use of that thing as such, it is incompatible with any interpersonal duty (owed to someone) with respect to such use. If I owe you a duty not to drive my car on Fridays, then I do not fully own my car in the interpersonal ethical sense. My liberty to use it is not full, because it is restricted by the duty that I owe you concerning its use as such.

Libertarians who address the topic of justice in the sense of our enforceable duties do not invoke interpersonal ethical ownership. Instead, they invoke what can be called *political ownership*. This notion of ownership does not require any interpersonal liberty to use the object (i.e., absence of any duty owed to others concerning its use as such). It merely requires the absence of any enforceable duty owed to others with respect to the use of the object. Thus, I may fully own my car in the political sense, even if I owe you a nonenforceable duty not to drive it on Fridays. Although my liberty to use it is not full, my claim right against forcible interference is full, and that is what matters for the political ownership. Others are not permitted to forcibly interfere with my use of the car except to protect their enforceable rights. The relevance of the distinction between interpersonal ethical and political full self-ownership will become clear later as we examine objections to self-ownership.

So far, we have considered the concept of full self-ownership. We now consider its plausibility. Note that my goal is very modest: to provide a reasonably plausible rationale for endorsing full self-ownership. As with all fundamental moral principles, it is impossible to provide a compelling justification. My goal is simply to provide enough defense of full self-ownership to establish that it needs to be taken seriously as a moral principle.

Most people accept some form of partial self-ownership. It can be partial in the sense that only some of the above types of rights are present (e.g., no right to transfer one's rights to others). It can also be partial in the sense that the force of the rights, for a given element, is less than full. The right might be a merely pro tanto (all else being equal) as opposed to a conclusive right, or it might be conditional in various ways (e.g., on there being no social catastrophe at issue). I provide a partial defense of full self-ownership: conclusive and unconditional rights for each of the above elements. A fallback position is to defend some form of partial self-ownership. This, however, would be a departure from libertarianism in the strict sense.

Here we consider the security rights, the liberty rights, the power to authorize use by others, and the transfer rights that are part of full self-ownership. We leave aside the compensation rights, enforcement rights, and immunities to loss, because the concept of full ownership is indeterminate with respect to those rights.

Security Rights

Consider first the *security rights* that are part of the control rights of self-ownership. These are claim rights against interference with one's person. One's consent is necessary for permissible use of one's person. The security rights of self-ownership are, I claim, a plausible constraint on how agents may be treated by others. Agents are not merely objects in the world; they have moral standing and are capable of autonomous choices. As a result, they have a kind of moral protection against interference that limits how they may be used. For example, it is unjust to kill or torture innocent people against their will—no matter how much it promotes other important moral goals (equality, total utility, or whatever). The security rights of full self-ownership reflect this special status that agents have.

Of course, some deny—as act consequentialists do—that there are any non-goal-based constraints on how individuals may be treated. Even if one agrees that there are some such constraints, however, one might still deny that individuals have any rights against being so treated. Instead, one might hold that there is simply an *impersonal duty* (owed to no one) not to treat people in certain ways. It is certainly possible (indeed held by some) to claim that all constraints are impersonal constraints, but it is a very illiberal view. First, it does not recognize that certain forms of treatment (such as killing or assault) are not merely wrong—they wrong the individuals so treated. For example, an apology and compensation are typically owed when an individual is so treated. Moreover, the individual is not wronged if he or she has validly consented to the treatment. Although there may be some impersonal constraints protecting individuals, there are, I claim, at least the interpersonal constraints that the security rights of full self-ownership provide.

Even if one agrees that individuals have the certain rights of self-ownership, one might still insist that the rights have only a pro tanto (all else being equal) force and/or are only conditional (e.g., when no social catastrophe is involved). Libertarianism (of the pure sort considered here), however, holds that the rights are conclusive and unconditional.[7] So understood, the thesis of full self-ownership is subject to the powerful objection that it entails that it is unjust to slightly injure a person to save millions of lives. This is indeed an implication of the view, and it is admittedly very difficult to swallow. Clearly, reasonable and decent people would typically infringe the security rights of self-ownership in such cases. This does not, however, establish that it is just to do so. It may simply be that it is reasonable to behave unjustly in such extreme circumstances; this is my position. For in such cases, all the usual concomitants of injustice are still present. Guilt is appropriate for what one did to the sacrificed individuals, compensation is owed to them, and so on. As long as we recognize, as I think we should, that reasonable and decent people sometimes act unjustly when the stakes are sufficiently great, the admitted counterintuitiveness of recognizing conclusive and unconditional security rights of self-ownership need not be a conclusive objection.

Of course, the absoluteness of the security rights of self-ownership remains a significant counterintuitive implication, but all fully specified theories have some such implications. The real test of a theory is its overall plausibility—both in the abstract and in application over a broad range of cases. Sometimes intuitive judgments about concrete cases must be rejected in light of plausible abstract principled considerations. If one holds, as I do, that theoretical completeness and simplicity are important theoretical desiderata, then one will be suspicious of merely pro tanto principles and seemingly ad hoc conditionalizations. One may thus be willing to reject those intuitions that conflict with absolute security rights of self-ownership. This, of course, is a controversial claim, and indeed it is rejected by most. I merely mention it to indicate how the absolute security rights are likely to be defended. (As stated earlier, my aim is to provide motivating reasons for left-libertarianism, not an argument that all will find compelling.)

Liberty Rights and Powers to Authorize Use by Others

So far, we have considered the security rights that are part of the control rights of full self-ownership. We now turn to the *liberty rights* and the associated powers to authorize use by others that are the other part of these control rights.

If you fully own yourself, then you have a full liberty right to use your person. This does not mean that justice permits you to do anything that you want with your person. Clearly, using your fist to punch me in the nose is not permitted. Having a full liberty right to use your person means only that no one else has any claim right on your use of your person as such. Any action you perform may be wrong because it impermissibly uses other objects (such as my nose). The wrongness of your hitting my nose with your fist, for example, is the wrongness of using my nose without my permission. You have nonetheless a full liberty respect to the use of your fist in the sense that no one's permission is needed for your use of your fist *as such* to be permissible.

The liberty rights of initial full self-ownership reflect the view that others initially have no claim against us concerning the use of our person. Initially, we do not require their permission, nor are their interests relevant, for us to justly use our person as such—although, of course, we need their permission to use resources that they own.

Having full liberty rights to use one's person has the counterintuitive implication that we have no (initial) duty to provide personal assistance to others. Unlike the security rights issue discussed above, the issue here concerns the *duties of the agent* to provide personal services, whereas the security rights issue concerns *the permissibility of others* using the agent's person. The most problematic case is where we could avert a social catastrophe (e.g., the death of millions of people) at only a small personal cost (e.g., pushing a button so that a terrorist bomb does not go off). A very significant but somewhat less dramatic case is one in which one could provide a great benefit to a single person (e.g., save her life) with only a small personal sacrifice. Less significant, but still troublesome, are cases in which one could provide a small benefit to others at a smaller cost to oneself as part of a cooperative enterprise that generally benefits all. Again, in the extreme cases, these are indeed powerful objections. Nonetheless, I believe that their force can be weakened enough to make them palatable—given the general plausibility of the view that we are initially at liberty to use our person as we please.

To start, note that the above objection does not apply to political full self-ownership, as opposed to the stronger interpersonal ethical self-ownership. As noted previously, those who defend libertarianism as a theory of our enforceable duties, as opposed to a more general theory of our interpersonal duties, endorse full political self-ownership but not necessarily the stronger full interpersonal ethical self-ownership. Full political self-ownership does not entail that individuals have the full liberty to use their person. It allows that they may indeed have various duties to provide personal services to others. It merely insists that such duties are not enforceable duties. Thus, political libertarianism does not face this objection. Interpersonal ethical libertarianism, however, does, and I focus on it in what follows.

There are several well-known ways of softening the objection that we initially owe no personal service to others. One is to agree that it is highly morally desirable that one help in these cases but to insist that one has no obligation to do so. We all agree that there is something morally flawed about not providing personal services when this would greatly benefit others and impose only a small cost on oneself. Not all moral flaws, however, involve wrongdoing. Failing to help an elderly neighbor carry her groceries when she is having difficulty and we could help her is not morally ideal, but it may not be morally wrong.

A second way of softening the objection is to grant that it may be wrong to fail to provide personal services to others in need but deny that they have any *right* to such help. If they have no right—and no one else does either—then there is no injustice in failing to provide the services in question. It is an impersonal duty but not a duty owed to anyone. Given that we are concerned here only with the theory of justice—the duties we owe each other—failure to recognize impersonal duties is not a defect. The topic of impersonal duties is simply a topic that is not being addressed. Because I believe (but do not argue here) that there are no impersonal duties, this reply does not seem promising to me. Nonetheless, it is open to those who believe that there are impersonal duties.

Yet another way to soften the objection against full liberties to use one's person is to point out the radical implications of recognizing an obligation to others to help even in the special cases where the benefit to them is great and the cost to one is small. Typically, a great number of people (poor people, severely disabled people, orphans, etc.) would greatly benefit from an hour's personal service each week. Many of us deny that we have a duty to provide such service.

A final and important way to soften the objection against having full liberties to use one's person is to note that the claim is that individuals have this full liberty only initially (e.g., at the start of adult life). It can be weakened or lost by our choices over time. For example, if, as I suggest later, the use or appropriation of more than one's share of natural resources generates a limited duty to promote equality of effective opportunity, then some of the full liberty rights of self-ownership will be lost when one uses or appropriates more than one's share. The more general point here is that the implications of full self-ownership cannot be determined without knowing how other things are owned.

We have addressed the full liberty to use one's person that is included in full interpersonal ethical self-ownership. Also included is a full power to authorize use by others. This is like the full liberty to use except that it concerns use by others with the owner's authorization (as opposed to use by the owner). One has a full power to authorize use of one's person (as such) by others just in case others have no claim rights concerning such use. The consent of the owner is not only necessary for the just use of his or her person (as entailed by the full security right discussed earlier); it is also sufficient. No one else's consent (individual or group) is necessary for the just use of his person (as such).[8] Because the issues here are effectively the same as those addressed previously for the full liberty to use, I do not rehearse the relevant objections and replies here.

The security rights, liberty rights, and powers to authorize use of full control self-ownership do have some significant counterintuitive implications. On the other hand, all theories have some such implications, and the normative separateness of persons reflected in full security rights (and associated authorizing power) and full liberty rights has great theoretical appeal. Although it is highly controversial, I claim that, on balance, the thesis of full control self-ownership is sufficiently plausible to be taken seriously.

Even if agents have full *control* self-ownership, it does not follow that agents fully own themselves. The determinate core of full self-ownership includes one additional right that must be defended: the full power to transfer those rights to others. (Recall that full ownership is indeterminate with respect to compensation rights, enforcement rights, and immunities to loss. Hence, they are not addressed here.)

Full Transfer Rights

The claim that agents have the full power to transfer their rights of self-ownership to others generates two main possible objections. One is that this entails that there are no morally valid restrictions of gifts of one's person even when this upsets equality of opportunity (or related concerns). The other is that voluntary enslavement is mistakenly deemed morally valid. We consider these in turn.

If one has the full powers to transfer to someone else the control (and other) rights over one's person, then no restrictions on gifts of one's person are morally permissible. For example, one might give another one's kidney or a commitment of personal services (e.g., to paint someone's house or provide financial advice). In such cases, one transfers rights over one's person to another. If the transfer is a market transaction, this need not upset equality of opportunity. One transfers rights to someone else, but that person transfers back the market value (e.g., cash) of the transferred rights. If, however, the transfer is a gift, it may promote inequalities of opportunity. For example, when a privileged parent transfers certain valuable rights over their person to their privileged children, they may be decreasing equality of opportunity in society. Of course, not all gift transfers are like this. A gift to a disadvantaged person promotes, rather than upsets, equality of opportunity. Still, the objection is that full powers to transfer rights over one's person rule out the possibility of taxing all or part of gifts of one's person when they upset equality of opportunity.

I agree that full ownership includes a full power to transfer the rights to others and that this rules out restrictions on (e.g., taxation of) equality-disrupting gifts. I also agree that that is unfortunate, because I take equality of opportunity very seriously. Two points, however, should be noted. First, we are here discussing only full *self*-ownership. As we shall see later, the ownership of natural resources and artifacts (as opposed to rights over one's person) may not be full and transfers of such resources may be subject to taxation when they upset equality of opportunity. Second, those who benefit from gifts of self from others may be eligible for only a lower share of the value of natural resources.

We now turn to the second objection to the full transfer powers: the moral powers to sell, rent, loan, or give away one's rights over oneself. This includes, as an extreme case, the right to sell, rent, loan, or donate oneself into slavery. *Involuntary* enslavement, of course, is a gross violation of full self-ownership, but *voluntary* enslavement is something that full self-ownership allows. Intuitively, of course, this seems problematic.

If one thinks that a main concern of justice is to protect the *having* of effective autonomy, or to *promote* the having, or exercising, of effective autonomy, then voluntary enslavement will indeed be problematic. On the other hand, if one thinks that a main concern of justice is to protect the *exercise* of autonomy, it is not. A well-informed decision to sell oneself into slavery (e.g., for a large sum of money to help one's needy family) is an exercise of autonomy. Indeed, under desperate conditions it may even represent an extremely important way of exercising one's autonomy. The parallel with suicide is relevant here. In both cases, an agent makes a decision that has the result that he or she ceases to have any moral autonomy and thus ceases to exercise any. In both cases it will typically be one of the most important choices in the agent's life. I would argue that, assuming no conflicting commitments, protecting the agent's exercise of his or her autonomy in such a case overrides any concern for protecting or promoting her continued possession of moral autonomy. One has the right to choose to cease to be autonomous (by dying or losing rights of control). Thus, genuine voluntary enslavement is arguably not problematic; it is simply the limiting case of the sorts of partial voluntary enslavement that occurs when we make binding commitments and agreements (e.g., to join the military).[9]

In sum, the thesis that agents initially fully own themselves is, I claim, sufficiently plausible to be taken seriously. All forms of libertarianism are committed to full self-ownership. They differ with respect to the moral powers that agents have to use and appropriate natural resources. Next, I motivate a form of left-libertarianism, which holds that natural resources are to be used to promote effective equality of opportunity for a good life.

4. Rights to Use and Appropriate Natural Resources

Full self-ownership gives agents certain rights over themselves. This leaves open, however, what rights agents have to use or appropriate natural resources and other unowned resources. *Natural resources* are those things that have no moral standing (e.g., are not sentient) and have not been transformed by any (nondivine) agent. Thus, land, seas, air, minerals, and so on in their original (humanly unimproved) states are natural resources, whereas such things as chairs, buildings, and land cleared for farming are *artifacts* (composed partly of natural resources). All left-libertarians agree that the ownership of natural resources is governed by an egalitarian principle, but there are different views about the form of this egalitarianism.

We focus here on natural resources, but the issues apply to all unowned resources. For example, almost all libertarians would treat abandoned artifacts in the same manner as natural resources. They have ceased to be privately owned and revert to the commons along with unowned natural resources.

One (crazy) possible view holds that initially no one has any liberty right to use, or any moral power to appropriate, natural resources. A radical version of *joint-ownership left-libertarianism*, for example, holds that individuals may use natural resources only with the collective (e.g., majority or unanimous) consent of the members of society. Given that all action requires the use of some natural resources (land, air, etc.), this leaves agents no freedom of action (except with the permission of others), and this is clearly implausible. A less radical version of joint-ownership left-libertarianism allows that agents are at liberty to *use* natural resources but holds that they have no moral power to *appropriate* natural resources without the collective consent of the members of society (e.g., Grunebaum 1987). Although this leaves agents a significant range of freedom of action, it leaves them inadequate security in their plans of action. They have the security that others are not permitted to use their person (e.g., assault them) without their consent, but they have only limited security in their possessions of external things (except with the consent of others).

Agents are permitted to cultivate and gather apples, but others are permitted to take them when this violates no rights of self-ownership (e.g., when they can simply take them from the collected pile).

Given the central importance of security with respect to some external resources, it is implausible that agents have no power to appropriate without the consent of others. More specifically, it is most implausible to hold that the consent of others is required for appropriation when communication with others is impossible, extremely difficult, or expensive (as it almost always is). Even when communication is relatively easy and costless, there is no need for the consent of others as long as one appropriates no more than one's fair share.[10] Joint-ownership left-libertarianism is thus implausible.

A plausible account of liberty rights and powers of appropriation over natural resources must, I claim, be *unilateralist* in the sense that, under a broad range of circumstances (although perhaps subject to various conditions), (a) agents are initially permitted to *use* natural resources without anyone's consent and (b) agents initially have the power to *appropriate* (acquire rights over) natural resources without anyone's consent. This is just to say that initially natural resources are not protected by a property rule (requiring consent for permissible use or appropriation).

According to a unilateralist conception of the power to appropriate, agents who first claim rights over a natural resource acquire those rights—perhaps provided that certain other conditions are met. These additional conditions may include some kind of an interaction constraint (such as that the agent "mixed her labor" with the resource or that she was the first to discover the resource) and some kind of "fair share" constraint. In what follows, for simplicity, I ignore the interaction constraint and focus on the fair share constraint.[11]

Several unilateralist versions of libertarianism exist. *Radical right libertarianism*—such as that of Rothbard (1978, 1982), Narveson (1988, ch. 7; 1999), and Feser (2005)—hold that that there are no fair share constraints on use or appropriation.[12] Agents may destroy whatever natural resources they want (as long as they violate no one's self-ownership), and they have the power to appropriate whatever natural resources they first claim. On this view, natural resources are initially not merely unprotected by a property rule; they are also unprotected by a compensation liability rule (requiring compensation to others for the liberty rights they lose). This view, however, is implausible. No human agent created natural resources, and there is no reason that the lucky person who first claims rights over a natural resource should reap all the benefits that the resource provides, nor is there any reason to think the individuals are morally permitted to ruin or monopolize natural resources as they please. Some sort of fair share condition restricts use and appropriation.

The standard fair share condition on appropriation is the *Lockean proviso*, which requires that "enough and as good be left for others."[13] Indeed, as long as this clause is allowed to be interpreted loosely (as we do here), the Lockean proviso is simply the requirement that some kind of fair share condition be satisfied. Throughout, we interpret the Lockean proviso (following Nozick) to allow that individuals may appropriate more than their fair share of natural resources as long as they compensate others for their loss from the excess appropriation. The Lockean proviso, that is, is a requirement that a fair share of the *value* of natural resources be left for others.

The Lockean proviso is often interpreted as applying only to acts of appropriation (and not to mere use) and as imposing a condition that needs to be met only at the time of appropriation. I, however, interpret it more broadly. A fair share requirement is, I claim, just as plausible when applied to mere use. One is not at liberty to use natural resources any way that one wants. Others have some claims to enough and as good being left for them. One is not permitted, for example, to destroy, ruin, or monopolize more than one's fair share of natural resources—even if one makes no claims of ownership. Moreover, with respect to appropriation, it is not sufficient to satisfy the fair share condition merely at the time of appropriation. The fair share condition is an ongoing requirement for continued ownership. Suppose, for example, that there are just two people in the world and they divide natural resources between themselves in a fair way. Ten years later, two more people pop into existence (but not as a result of any choices the first two people made). It is implausible to think that the division of rights over natural resources remains fair just because it was initially fair. Instead, the Lockean proviso (or fair share test) should be understood as an ongoing requirement that can be satisfied initially but can fail to be satisfied due to later brute luck changes in the total value of natural resources (e.g., discovery of oil) or the number of agents in the world.[14]

Lockean libertarianism allows unilateral use and appropriation but requires that some version of the Lockean proviso be satisfied. It views natural resources as initially unprotected by any property rule (no consent is needed for use or appropriation) but protected by a compensation liability rule. Those who use natural resources, or claim rights over them, owe compensation to others for any costs (relative to a specified baseline) imposed but such use or appropriation.

Nozickean right-libertarianism interprets the Lockean proviso as requiring that no individual be made worse off by the use or appropriation compared with non-use or nonappropriation. This, I would argue, sets the compensation payment too low. It bases compensation on each person's *reservation price*, which is the *lowest* payment that would leave the individual indifferent with non-use or nonappropriation. Use or appropriation of natural resources typically brings significant benefits even after providing such compensation. There is little reason to hold that those who first use or claim rights over a natural resource should reap all the excess benefits that the resource provides.

Sufficientarian (centrist) libertarianism interprets the Lockean proviso as requiring that others be left an *adequate* share of natural resources (on some conception of adequacy).[15] Adequacy might, for example, require enough for basic subsistence or perhaps enough for "minimally decent" life prospects. Depending on the nature of the world and the conception of adequacy, the sufficientarian proviso may be more, or less, demanding than the Nozickean proviso.

Although sufficientarian libertarianism is an improvement over Nozickean libertarianism by being sensitive to the quality of life prospects left to others by the use or appropriation, it nevertheless fails, I would argue, to recognize the extent to which natural resources belong to all of us in some egalitarian manner. Suppose that there are enough natural resources to give everyone fabulous life prospects, and someone appropriates (or uses) natural resources, leaving others only minimally adequate life prospects and generating ultra-fabulous life prospects for herself. It is implausible to hold that those who use or first claim a natural resource are entitled to reap all the benefits in excess of what is needed to leave others adequate life prospects. Natural resources were not created by any human agent, and their value belongs to each of us in some egalitarian manner.

Left-libertarianism[16] holds that natural resources initially belong to everyone in some egalitarian manner. We have already rejected one version—joint-ownership left-libertarianism—for failing to be unilateralist (i.e., because it requires the permission of others for use or appropriation of unowned natural resources). We now focus on Lockean (and hence unilateralist) versions of left-libertarianism.

Equal share left-libertarianism—such as the views of Henry George (1879) and Hillel Steiner (1994)—interprets the Lockean proviso as requiring that one leave an equally valuable per capita share of the value of natural resources for others. Individuals are morally free to use or appropriate natural resources, but those who use or appropriate more than their per capita share—based on the *competitive value* (based on demand and supply; e.g., market clearing price or auction price) under morally relevant conditions—owe others compensation for their excess share.

Equal share libertarianism is, I would argue, not sufficiently egalitarian. Although it requires that the competitive value of natural resources be distributed equally, it does nothing to offset disadvantages in unchosen internal endowments (e.g., the effects of genes or childhood environment). Equal share libertarianism is thus compatible with radically unequal life prospects. Indeed, it is compatible with some having fabulous life prospects and others miserable ones. I claim that justice requires a more robust kind of egalitarianism.

Consider, then, *equal opportunity left-libertarianism*, such as that of Otsuka (2003).[17] It interprets the Lockean proviso as requiring that one leave enough for others to have an opportunity for well-being that is at least as good as the opportunity for well-being that one obtained in using or appropriating natural resources. Individuals who leave less than this are required to pay the full competitive value of their excess share to those deprived of their fair share.[18] Unlike the equal share view, those whose initial internal endowments provide less favorable effective opportunities for well-being are entitled to larger shares of natural resources.

Obviously, the importance of equality in general, and equality of life prospects (effective opportunity for well-being) in particular, are highly controversial, and I do not attempt a defense here. However, I claim that equal opportunity left-libertarian is the most plausible version of libertarianism. All versions of libertarianism give agents a significant amount of liberty and security. The main issue at hand concerns requirements for some kind of material equality of agents (equality of life prospects). According to equal opportunity left-libertarianism, one has the power to use or appropriate natural resources as long as one pays for the competitive value of the use or rights in excess of one's equality of opportunity for well-being share. The payment is owed to those who have been left with less than equal opportunity for well-being. Thus, equal opportunity left-libertarianism holds that there is a *limited* duty to promote equality. One does not need to do everything possible to promote equality. One has no duty at all to promote equality if one has not used or appropriated more than one's equality of opportunity share of natural resources. If one uses or appropriates more, then one acquires a duty to promote equality of effective opportunity for well-being, but that duty is limited to what can be efficiently achieved with the payment that one owes.

5. Conclusion

There are many important questions and aspects of left-libertarianism that I have not addressed, including the following: (a) Is the value of natural resources in a given country to be divided among those in that country or among all those in the world? I see no reason to think that the value belongs just to the residents of the country and I favor a globalist distribution. This, of course, is a very general issue in the theory of justice. (b) What is the status of children and animals in libertarian theory? I would argue that children, and even animals, are self-owners in an interest-protecting (rather than a choice-protecting) sense (see, e.g., Vallentyne 2002, 2003). (c) What is the status of future people? I would argue that *definite* future people (those who will exist with certainty) have the same rights as those currently existing (see, e.g., Steiner and Vallentyne 2009). The case of merely possible future people is much more complex and a general problem for population ethics. (d) What is the status of the state in libertarian theory? Although Nozick (1974) attempts to defend the justice of a minimal state on libertarian grounds, I believe that he fails. Although many of the state activities are just on libertarian grounds, the monopoly on the use of force is not (see, e.g., Simmons 1993; Vallentyne 2007). (e) What compensation rights and enforcement rights do individuals have? As I suggested above, full ownership leaves these indeterminate. One of my current projects is to articulate and defend a specific set of such rights whereby the use of force is limited to minimizing uncompensated harm for rights intrusions (e.g., no role for punishment). All of these issues are very controversial, and I merely flag them here for further investigation.

Full self-ownership, I have suggested, captures important aspects of liberty and security in the theory of justice. To make this liberty and security effective (and not merely formal), a plausible version of libertarianism must be unilateralist and permit the use and appropriation of natural resources without the consent of others. If one also grants the importance of equality of life prospects, then equal opportunity left-libertarianism is, I believe, the most plausible version of libertarianism.[19]

NOTES

1. This chapter draws heavily from Vallentyne (2009).
2. Some authors understand rights as the *enforceable* duties owed to an individual. However, I understand rights in the broader sense of a duty owed to an individual.
3. For insightful analysis of the notion of ownership, see Christman (1994). For a superb analysis of the concept of self-ownership, on which I build, see Cohen (1995), especially chapter 9.
4. For simplicity, I ignore the possibility that, for the ownership of mental beings (e.g., self-ownership) there may be ways of using a person that primarily involve a mental, rather than a physical, impact. This is an important but underexplored issue.
5. Rights can be construed as protecting choices or as protecting interests. For simplicity, I assume here that they protect only choices. My own view is that rights protect both choices and interests with the former being lexically prior. It would, however, introduce needless complexities for the purposes of this chapter.
6. For a defense of the view that full ownership is indeterminate with respect to rights to compensation, enforcement rights, and immunity to loss but determinate with respect to control rights, see Vallentyne, Steiner, and Otsuka (2005). For criticism, see Fried (2004, 2005).
7. It is worth noting, however, that the most influential contemporary libertarian theorist, Nozick, allows in a note (1974, 30) that perhaps it may be permissible to infringe rights in order to avoid moral catastrophe. He does not, however, endorse this exception.
8. Suppose, for example, that others are permitted to kiss you if and only if everyone consents to it. You have a full security right against being kissed (since your consent is necessary for permissible kissing), but you have only a weak power to authorize being kissed (since everyone else's consent is needed in additional to yours). In this case, the right to control kissing you is held jointly by all and not merely by you.
9. For further defense for the right of voluntary enslavement see Nozick (1974, 331), Feinberg (1986, ch. 19), Steiner (1994, 232–34), and Vallentyne (1998, 2000).
10. For elaborations of this criticism, see, for example, Fressola (1981) and Cohen (1995).
11. Given greater space, I would argue that no interaction constraint is needed. All the agent needs to do is to *claim* rights over unowned resources and satisfy the fair share constraint.
12. Kirzner (1978) also argues against any fair share condition. He does so, however, on the grounds that those who discover a resource are actually creating it and that creators are entitled to their creations. I believe that this argument fails but cannot here argue the point.
13. Locke (1689) was not a Lockean libertarian in a strict sense. He disallowed appropriation that would lead to spoilage, he rejected the right of voluntary self-enslavement, and he held that one had a duty to provide the means of subsistence to those unable to provide for themselves.
14. The need for an ongoing proviso that also applies to mere use is forcefully and insightfully defended by Mack (1995)—although he defends a very weak proviso. Roark (2008) defends the need for a proviso on use and not merely on appropriation.
15. Simmons (1992, 1993) defends a position roughly of this sort—although his position is not strictly libertarian in a few respects.
16. Left-libertarian theories have been propounded for over three centuries. For selections of the writings of historical and contemporary writings, see Vallentyne and Steiner (2001a, 2001b).

17. Van Parijs (1995) is in the same spirit as equal opportunity left-libertarianism—although with significant twists on gifts and job rents.

18. I simplify here. Otuska's (2003) view does not invoke the requirement to pay competitive rent. Although I would defend this version of the equal opportunity view, I do not attempt to do so here.

19. For helpful comments, I thank David Estlund.

REFERENCES

Christman, John. 1994. *The Myth of Property*. New York: Oxford University Press.
Cohen, G. A. 1995. *Self-Ownership, Freedom, and Equality*. Cambridge, UK: Cambridge University Press.
Feinberg, Joel. 1986. *Harm to Self*. New York: Oxford University Press.
Feser, Edward. 2005. "There Is No Such Thing as an Unjust Initial Acquisition." *Social Philosophy and Policy* 22: 56–80.
Fressola, Anthony. 1981. "Liberty and Property." *American Philosophical Quarterly* 18:315–22.
Fried, Barbara. 2004. "Left-Libertarianism: A Review Essay." *Philosophy & Public Affairs* 32: 66–92.
Fried, Barbara. 2005."Left-Libertarianism, Once More: A Rejoinder to Vallentyne, Steiner, and Otsuka." *Philosophy & Public Affairs* 33: 216–22.
George, Henry. 1879. *Progress and Poverty*. New York: Robert Schalkenbach Foundation.
Grunebaum, James. 1987. *Private Ownership*. New York: Routledge & Kegan Paul.
Kirzner, Israel. 1978. "Entrepreneurship, Entitlement, and Economic Justice." *Eastern Economic Journal* 4:9–25. Reprinted in *Reading Nozick*, ed. J. Paul (Oxford: Basil Blackwell, 1981), 383-401.
Locke, John. *Two Treatises of Government*. Edited by P. Laslett. New York: Cambridge University Press, 1963. (Originally published in 1689)
Mack, Eric. 1995. "The Self-Ownership Proviso: A New and Improved Lockean Proviso." *Social Philosophy and Policy* 12: 186–218.
Narveson, Jan. 1988. *The Libertarian Idea*. Philadelphia: Temple University Press.
Narveson, Jan. 1999. "Original Appropriation and Lockean Provisos." *Public Affairs Quarterly* 13:205–27. Reprinted in *Respecting Persons in Theory and Practice* (Lanham, MD: Rowman & Littlefield, 2002), 111–31.
Nozick, Robert. 1974. *Anarchy, State, and Utopia*. New York: Basic Books.
Otsuka, Michael. 2003. *Libertarianism without Inequality*. Oxford: Clarendon Press.
Roark, Eric. 2008. "Using and Coming to Own: A Left-Proprietarian Treatment of the Just Use and Appropriation of Common Resources." PhD dissertation, University of Missouri, Columbia.
Rothbard, Murray. 1978. *For a New Liberty: The Libertarian Manifesto*, rev. ed. New York: Libertarian Review Foundation.
Rothbard, Murray. 1982. *The Ethics of Liberty*. Atlantic Highlands, NJ: Humanities Press.
Simmons, A. John. 1992. *The Lockean Theory of Rights*. Princeton, NJ: Princeton University Press.
Simmons, A. John. 1993. *On the Edge of Anarchy*. Princeton, NJ: Princeton University Press.
Steiner, Hillel. 1994. *An Essay on Rights*. Cambridge, MA: Blackwell.

Steiner, Hillel, and Peter Vallentyne. 2009. "Libertarian Theories of Intergenerational Justice." In *Justice Between Generations*. Edited by Axel Gosseries and Lukas Meyer, 50–76. Oxford: Oxford University Press.

Vallentyne, Peter. 1998. "Critical Notice of G. A. Cohen's *Self-Ownership, Freedom, and Equality*." *Canadian Journal of Philosophy* 28: 609–26.

Vallentyne, Peter. 2000. "Left-Libertarianism: A Primer." In *Left Libertarianism and Its Critics: The Contemporary Debate*. Edited by Peter Vallentyne and Hillel Steiner, 1–20. New York: Palgrave.

Vallentyne, Peter. 2002. "Equality and the Duties of Procreators." In *Children and Political Theory*. Edited by David Archard and Colin MacLeod, 195–211. Oxford: Oxford University Press.

Vallentyne, Peter. 2003. "The Rights and Duties of Childrearing." *William and Mary Bill of Rights Journal* 11: 991–1010.

Vallentyne, Peter. 2007. "Libertarianism and the State." *Social Philosophy and Policy*, 24: 187–205.

Vallentyne, Peter. 2009. "Left-Libertarianism and Liberty." In *Contemporary Debates in Political Philosophy*. Edited by Thomas Christiano and John Christman. Oxford: Wiley-Blackwell.

Vallentyne, Peter, and Hillel Steiner, eds. 2000a. *Left Libertarianism and Its Critics: The Contemporary Debate*. New York: Palgrave Publishers.

Vallentyne, Peter, and Hillel Steiner, eds. 2000b. *The Origins of Left Libertarianism: An Anthology of Historical Writings*. New York: Palgrave Publishers.

Vallentyne, Peter, Hillel Steiner, and Michael Otsuka. 2005. "Why Left-Libertarianism Isn't Incoherent, Indeterminate, or Irrelevant: A Reply to Fried." *Philosophy & Public Affairs* 33: 201–15.

van Parijs, Philippe. 1995. *Real Freedom for All*. New York: Oxford University Press.

CHAPTER 9

MARXIST AND SOCIALIST APPROACHES

ANDREW LEVINE

From the 1920s through the 1970s, leading Marxist philosophers seldom subjected Marx's positions to intensive scrutiny, even as they invoked his authority in behalf of their own contentions. Because their views were fraught with political significance in circumstances in which Marx's authority mattered, and because they gravitated toward "continental" styles of argument that were grandiose and programmatic, they approached Marxism, as it were, from the outside—without engaging Marx's arguments the way philosophers characteristically do, from within. Marx's writings were points of political, historical, and theoretical reference; not points of departure for engaging in a "conversation" with Marx himself. Analytical Marxism, which emerged in the 1970s and flourished for about a decade and a half, was cut from a different cloth. As a largely Anglophone and university-based intellectual current, it was accountable to academic, not political, constituencies. Analytical Marxists were therefore freer to reconstruct, defend, and, where appropriate, criticize Marxist positions than were other Marxists; freer to go where their arguments led. Their approach to Marx and Marxism was almost entirely from within.

However, at this historical moment, when increasingly frequent and severe capitalist crises are creating conditions favorable for putting socialism and perhaps Marxism back on the agenda, it is important that we view the situation from the outside so as to better assess where we are and where it is still possible to go. Indeed, it is impossible to say much about the most promising strains of Marxist theory without taking account of their histories and trajectories. The story I relate has mainly to do with analytical Marxism, a movement that is now in eclipse and that may never come back. But it is a story worth telling because, in several key respects, any revival of socialist or Marxist theory in the years ahead will have to resume where analytical Marxism left off.

Fifty years ago, there was a socialist bloc—divided and not very socialist—comprised of states that were officially Marxist, and there were significant self-identified Marxist movements in many First and Third World countries. Where Marxist politics flourished, a Marxist theoretical culture followed en suite. In Great Britain, North America, and Australasia, where Marxism did not flourish, the facts on the ground elsewhere did little to promote Marxist philosophy at home, especially in academic precincts where political philosophy is produced. Thus, a distinctively Anglophone Marxism had yet to emerge. Ironically, by the time it did, Marxism had become nearly as much a dead letter in countries where it had only recently dominated the prevailing intellectual culture as it had been, until then, in the English-speaking world.

For anyone who has lived through these transformations, the changes are remarkable. In the United States in the early 1960s, if Marxism was taught at all in universities, it was only to show how wrong it was. It is different today. Thanks to analytical Marxism, it has become clear that what people used to think was wrong is not wrong at all, at least not for the reasons they supposed, and, while Marxism has passed out of fashion, it is no longer unrespectable. Not unrelatedly, and thanks also to analytical Marxism, it has become less clear what, if anything, Marxism is. I return to this question presently.

For militants in the generation of 1968, there was a palpable need for "revolutionary theory." But, in the English-speaking world, there was also a lack of anything that might fill that need—first because orthodox Communism was discredited, then because indigenous (pre–World War I) left traditions had been largely forgotten, and finally because imported (mainly French and German) noncommunist Marxism resisted easy assimilation into the intellectual culture. However, in short order, the need overwhelmed the last two of these difficulties; research on American radicalism (including socialism) abounded and continental Marxisms flourished. It soon became apparent, however, that the American radicalism of the late nineteenth and early twentieth centuries was a non-starter, and that neo-Hegelian, existentialist and structuralist Marxisms were of more interest to apolitical academics in fields remote from political philosophy than to philosophers with a lively interest in real-world politics. Viewed from without, it had been a flash in the pan. I would venture, nevertheless, that there is at least one continental strain of Marxist theorizing, associated with the work of Louis Althusser, that philosophers intent on reviving Marxism should not ignore (Levine 2003). I resume this thought after recounting aspects of analytical Marxism's history. My point is that, whatever leading analytical Marxists—G. A. Cohen, Jon Elster, John Roemer, and others—came to believe, it is plain, in light of the work they did, that there is a defensible and distinctively Marxist core theory that other intellectual traditions cannot accommodate, and that recognizing this is potentially of monumental importance in its own right and also indispensable for reviving theoretical departures anchored in nonanalytic currents of Marxist thought. That this is so is ironic inasmuch as analytical Marxists were, from the beginning, indifferent to or hostile towards non- or rather *pre*-analytic strains of twentieth-century Marxist theory.

At first especially, they were more friendly toward positions associated with the classical Marxism of the years before the First World War and the Bolshevik Revolution. This led to a certain awkwardness for Marxists ensconced in a university culture committed in principle (though of course not always in practice) to liberal norms, for even classical Marxism was not an open ideology. Indeed, from the time Marxism crystallized into a significant tendency in European labor movements, the specter of dogmatism was never far away. As Marxism became an increasingly hegemonic ideology, the situation became even worse. It became worse still in the aftermath of the Bolshevik Revolution. After the consolidation of Soviet power, official Communism became the orthodoxy of the new regime and later of the "peoples' democracies" established on the Soviet model after World War II. Dissident Marxisms abounded, of course, but even they had a dogmatic tinge. In short, for nearly all self-identified Marxists, "revisionism" was a sin to be avoided. Thus, when they altered or abandoned Marx's positions, Marxists seldom acknowledged doing so. They expended considerable ingenuity instead on pouring new wine into old bottles.

Analytical Marxists also wanted, at first, to defend Marx's (or classical Marxist) positions. However, it was clear from the outset that the positions they hoped to sustain had to be reconstructed (revised) before they could be defended. It became clear too that there was much that could not be defended at all. This was inevitable. It would have been astonishing, and unprecedented outside religious circles, if very much that Marx or any other thinker maintained could survive unscathed when subjected to the kind of scrutiny analytical philosophy and empirical social science bring to bear.

Analytical Marxism coalesced at a time when mainstream political philosophy was already focused on notions of justice and equality, as conceived in the work of John Rawls and his close followers (Rawls 1971). Working in milieus in which interest in Rawls's work raged, it was inevitable that they too would engage it—topically and substantively. This transpired in ways that facilitated the incorporation of Marxism, or rather the Marxism of the analytical Marxists, into the fold of mainstream liberal political philosophy.

Classical Marxism was insistent on three points: that Marxism is "scientific," not "utopian"—in other words, that its case for socialism is based on the discovery of real historical processes, not moral arguments; that justice is not a transhistorical "critical" concept, but one whose content is relative to particular "modes of production"; and that, unlike most utopian socialists, Marxists are not committed, at least directly, to equality. On each count, analytical Marxists took exception—at first implicitly, then expressly.

It was justice, not equality, that drew attention first, probably because questions about the relation between these concepts had not yet come sharply into view. For philosophers who identified with Marxism or who "worked on" Marx, the first and, for a long while, the only issue was whether there is a Marxist conception of justice at all (Lukes 1985; Buchanan 1982; Wood 2009, part 3). The orthodox view is "no." The analytical Marxist consensus, however, was that Marxism can and will accommodate a notion of justice, though it was never entirely clear what that notion was—and, in particular, how, if at all, it differed from Rawls's understanding. In retrospect, justice was the proverbial foot in the door; it led first to analytical Marxism's identification with "utopian socialism" (Cohen 2001)—with efforts to moralize the case for socialism—and ultimately to the absorption of ostensibly Marxist views into the Rawlsian fold where, for all practical purposes, they have disappeared without a trace.

Marxist "insurgencies" in economics and other social sciences underwent a similar fate: Marxists won respect but at the price of giving up on the idea that there are distinctively Marxist positions or methodologies. Analytical Marxist economists were not the first to bridge the supposedly unbridgeable gap between Marxist and "bourgeois" economics, but they were more determined than their predecessors to do so explicitly. Thus, the fate of Marxist economics was sealed in the 1970s when a handful of young, mathematically adept Marxist economists showed how the conceptual foundations of Marxist economic theory could be recast in neo-classical terms (Roemer 1986a). Because this work was also a creature of the academy, beholden to the disciplinary standards of mainstream economics, and because mainstream economics was the dominant paradigm, there was never any doubt which idiom would prevail, even allowing that Marxist and neo-classical economics are in relevant respects formally equivalent. Marxists might still focus on topics that traditional Marxist economists investigated, topics of little interest to their colleagues. But, apart from the issues they studied and the phenomena they modeled, there was no longer any pretense of anything distinctively "Marxist" in what they did.

Similarly, in sociology, as research became increasingly empirical and quantitative, there was no alternative but to employ standard methodologies (see Wright 1998, 2005). Marxists remained more interested than other sociologists in issues pertaining to class, and they were interested too in the explanatory uses of that concept. Moreover, they deployed a conception of class, derived from Marx, that differed in important respects from mainstream accounts of systemic status and income differentials or established cultural divides. In this sense, there is a distinctively Marxist social science. But there is nothing distinctively Marxist about the methodological approaches investigators employ. Traditional Marxism had long maintained a contrary view: Marxists, it was said, deployed a "dialectical" methodology unknown, or at least unused, in bourgeois social science. As this claim also came under increasing scrutiny, it became apparent that it had never been entirely clear what this method was and that, to the extent that there was something distinctive, dialectical methodologies fail to pass muster (see Wright, Levine, and Sober 1992). At the same time, it was argued that the defensible explanations Marxists provided—in either their actual or "reconstructed" versions—were of a piece with those of bourgeois social science. This finding has resonated in erstwhile Marxist quarters. By now, it has become all but impossible even to use the adjective *bourgeois* derisively—except in an ironic sense. But if Marxist political philosophy is just left liberalism and if there is nothing distinctive about Marxist social science except the topics it investigates, what's left? The idea that nothing or almost nothing is left motivated, or rationalized, the diminution if not the outright abandonment of what had formerly comprised Marxism in analytical Marxism's latter days.

With varying degrees of virulence, disillusioned Marxists of decades past would sometimes turn into apostates. Analytical Marxists avoided that fate. Nearly everyone who worked on Marx analytically has remained sympathetic to the moral and political imperatives that had drawn them into the Marxist ambit. Ironically, analytical Marxism's apolitical tenor contributed to its benign denouement. It would have been different had its practitioners been part of a political current that went sour, leaving them feeling betrayed. But once it emerged that Marxist positions were found wanting or not fundamentally different from their bourgeois rivals, it instead was just that there was nothing there, and therefore nothing to inveigh against. However, the situation is more complicated than this because, no matter how the analytical turn turned out for its practitioners, analytical Marxism's legacy is not nearly as destructive of Marxism as it may appear. Indeed, thanks to the work analytical Marxists did, we can now say with greater assurance that there is something fundamental in Marxist theory that is distinctively Marxist—something that transcends the conceptual frontiers of liberal political philosophy and mainstream social science.

For most of the 1970s, analytical philosophers working on Marxist themes focused mainly on morality and justice not on explanatory strategies or other methodological issues. Neither was much attention paid to *explananda*, objects of explanation, that non-Marxist historians and social scientists ignore. With the publication of G. A. Cohen's *Karl Marx's Theory of History: A Defense*, this changed (Cohen 1978). From that point on, Marx's theory of history, historical materialism, assumed center stage. That change made Marxist explanations and, more important, Marxist objects of explanation Topic A.

Noncommunist twentieth-century Marxists had nearly abandoned historical materialism, usually without acknowledgment. However, for Marx (implicitly) and the classical Marxists (explicitly), historical materialism was central to virtually all other theoretical concerns, including the one that occupied Marx's attention more than any other in the later decades of his life: his investigation of "the laws of motion" of the capitalist mode of production. What Marx had to say about capitalism's trajectory and its future cannot be understood except in relation to his theory of history. Even the concepts Marx deployed for making sense of capitalism—among others, forces of production, relations of production, modes of production—arise in and are integral to that theory.

Historical materialism provides an account of history's structure and direction. Mainstream historiography is not opposed to Marx's account; rather, it regards the very idea of a theory of history, Marxist or otherwise, as outside its ken. In the mainstream view, every event (no matter how it is identified) is explainable. But there is no explanation for history itself and therefore no theoretically motivated way to categorize historical epochs or to conceptualize history's directionality. Even a trivial account of history's structure and direction—formed by conjoining all particular explanations—would be out of the question because, in the mainstream view, there is no theoretically defensible way to identify discrete events and therefore no principled way to conjoin their (potential) explanations (Wright, Levine, and Sober 1992).

There is, however, a tradition of thought that identifies real historical divisions and movement from one to another. The preeminent exponent of this tradition was Hegel (2010, originally published posthumously 1837). Hegel's philosophy of history, like the philosophies of history that preceded it, was *teleological*: It explained history by concocting a narrative told from the vantage point of history's end—its *telos*. In this way, Hegel discerned a structure and directionality in what had come before—a tiny fraction of the past but a part replete with philosophical significance. Marx's account of history's structure and directionality was formed in a milieu in the sway of Hegelian thought, but his was not a teleological theory. Since the seventeenth century, scientists investigating the physical universe had rejected teleological explanations, as did Marx. As Cohen discerned, the explanatory strategy he deployed is similar to one that is commonplace in modern science, especially biology. Wittingly or not, Marx advanced functional explanations.

When Marxists claim, for example, that the "economic base" explains the legal system that superintends it, they maintain that the economy and the law causally interact but that there is an explanatory asymmetry—that the economy explains the law (not vice versa) because the law is as it is in order to reproduce the economic base (not vice versa). Reproducing the economic base is the law's function. Within the analytical fold, Cohen's—and, if Cohen was right, Marx's—use of functional explanations was challenged by advocates of "rational choice" explanations, proponents of the idea that the beliefs and desires of instrumentally (means-ends) rational individuals suffice to explain the phenomena historical materialism investigates (see Elster 1985). The crux of the debate had to do with "mechanisms" (or rather, their absence) in the theory Cohen reconstructed. Those who advocated for rational choice explanations argued that functional explanations only made sense in conjunction with accounts of how the functional relations they identified were achieved. Thus, we can explain why giraffes have long necks by appealing to their function (enabling giraffes to reach the high-growing leaves of trees in their environmental niche) because we know the mechanism, natural selection, through which that functional relation is achieved. Thus, it was claimed, we ought not to say, for example, that forms of consciousness are functional for reproducing the economic base unless we can specify how this relation comes about, something Marx and Cohen after him failed to do. It is fair to say nevertheless that Cohen won the debate (Roemer 1986b). However, rational choice proponents won in the sense that they established the *bona fides* of rational choice explanations within Marxism. Indeed, in the years before it extinguished itself, "analytical Marxism" and "rational choice

Marxism" became virtually synonymous. Not everyone fell into line, but those who did not were peripheral to the main thrust of the movement.

Imputing rational choice explanations to Marx was an improbable turn. Rational choice explanations had long been the stock and trade of economists, but their importation into the other social sciences was largely the work of anti-Marxists. What Jon Elster and other critics of functional explanations in Marxism proposed was linked, historically and conceptually, with a particularly influential case in point—the "methodological individualism" of Karl Popper (1957). How ironic that, having begun with the aim of defending Marxist orthodoxy, analytical Marxism ended by reconstructing Marxism in terms that its enemies advanced, but this is where the arguments seemed to lead.

In the period when analytical Marxism arose and flourished, political movements that identified with Marx and Marxism were still alive around the world. Whether or not to identify with Marxism therefore had political significance. That will probably never be the case again, no matter how far the pendulum swings back. I am confident that, before long, Marxist themes will again receive the attention they deserve. However, after so many years without political points of reference, it is unlikely that those who advance Marxist positions will identify with Marxism even to the extent of analytical Marxists. However, it's the ideas that matter, not the name. I conclude by sketching what I have in mind—with reference both to analytical Marxism's legacy and to some of Marx's views about the state, which analytical Marxists largely ignored.

First, though, I would reiterate that, in light of this last (and perhaps final) moment in the history of Marxist theorizing, there is only one way forward: to begin where analytical Marxism left off. There is no turning back to more orthodox views on the importance of normative concepts such as justice and equality, the differences between Marxist and bourgeois economics, or claims for a distinctively Marxist methodology. Nor will it do to rule out rational choice explanations solely because opponents of Marxism developed this explanatory strategy. Analytical Marxism undid venerable convictions for compelling, though not always incontrovertible, reasons. One must either go on from there or else explain why, against the framework of the conclusions they reached, a different, less heterodox point of embarkation is feasible and appropriate.

Notwithstanding the reconsiderations of some of its former defenders, historical materialism has not been undone—if anything, its core contentions have been strengthened. What have been undone or rather diminished are historical materialism's explanatory pretensions. It is now clear that it need not, and almost certainly does not, explain actual epochal transformations—it only specifies what *would* happen in the absence of countervailing factors. Because historical materialism makes no claims about the prevalence or potency of other factors, it would be consistent with its contentions if the best explanation for, say, the transition from European feudalism to capitalism does not involve contradictions between forces and relations of production, as it would if no other factors obtained. Nor does the theory predict a communist future by showing that socialism and eventually communism are literally inevitable. Historical materialism only explains how capitalism became historically possible and how socialism and then communism become possible too as productive forces develop. As for the inevitability of these epochal economic structures, the theory claims only that the trajectory it depicts *would* be realized *ceteris absentibus*, other things being absent. Because other factors are never absent, the theory does not imply that these outcomes are literally inevitable. Capitalism might never have come into being; similarly, a socialist and then a communist future, though on the historical agenda, might never come to pass.

The general point is plain: It is one thing to claim that there is a "logic" inherent in historical change and something else to determine how this logic applies to the past, present, and future. This point holds for causal theories, like historical materialism, and for teleological philosophies too. For Hegel, the "end" (*telos*) is immanent from the outset. However, the end can be blocked by extra-historical factors. Thus, history would not have reached the "end" Hegel identified had the human race died out before its course had fully unfolded. This could have happened—if, say, disease wiped out the entire human population or if the earth had collided catastrophically with a meteor or asteroid. It is only in the absence of interferences like these that the end determines everything historical that precedes it.

There is, nevertheless, an important difference, even in this respect, between theories like Marx's and Hegel's. This difference was not generally recognized because historical materialists were characteristically vague about what their theory claimed regarding the trajectories of precapitalist economic structures. Cohen's account, on the other hand, was clear: Marx's theory, as Cohen reconstructed it, recognizes only three epochal divisions (or four, if "primitive communism" is included) and therefore only two epochal transformations: from precapitalism to capitalism, and from capitalism to socialism. These terms—*precapitalism, capitalism*, and *socialism*—denote sets of property relations. They differ qualitatively because the ownership rights their respective property relations entail differ: In precapitalist economies, there is (private) ownership of both persons and things; under capitalism, no one owns anyone else but external "means of production"—things, not persons—are privately owned. Then, under socialism, there is private ownership of neither persons nor things; means of production are owned socially. These are meaningful but general descriptions. To own something is to have rights to control it and to benefit from it. Throughout history, there have been many, different forms of ownership of persons, ranging from chattel slavery to the various obligations that burden direct producers in feudal societies. There have also been and still are many forms of private ownership of external means of production. And there are, in principle, many forms of social or public ownership; state ownership is not the only kind. Therefore, within an historical materialist framework, there are many possible futures, and there were alternative possible pasts. In short, historical materialism is open in a way that teleological philosophies of history can never be. A celebrated metaphor of Hegel's underscores the difference: When, at the setting of the sun, the owl of Minerva takes flight, the philosopher, looking back on the day that has passed, discerns inevitability in what came before. Historical materialists, looking back, see paths not taken alongside those that were; they see a future replete with possibilities, some wondrous, some catastrophic, and some distressingly continuous with our changeable, but indefinitely sustainable, present.

Because preanalytic Marxists were less clear about what Marx's theory of history maintained than analytical Marxists were, and because at a high enough level of abstraction the theory does indeed assert an all but "inevitable" sequencing of modes of production, historical materialism's openness was not generally acknowledged. It was therefore natural for Marxists of a traditional bent to lapse into Hegelian understandings of historical inevitability. From an ethical and political point of view, this misunderstanding was disabling. It encouraged what Cohen would later call an "obstetric" model of politics, according to which Marxists are like midwives, facilitating—but not causing—outcomes that are all but preordained (Cohen 2001, 58–78). On the obstetric model, the Revolution can be delayed or even blocked by outside factors, and an "incorrect" line can impede its coming indefinitely. However, in the "normal" course of events, it is likely to occur. Revolutionaries can make the process better or worse, but they do not make revolutions—history does that.

Cohen argued that its implicit commitment to obstetric politics speaks against the scientific socialism Marxists have traditionally defended and for its long-standing rival, utopian socialism, which Marxists have traditionally reviled. He argued that the time has come for socialists to appeal to values like freedom, justice, and equality—not to invoke inexorable historical laws. This is also dismissive of the theory Cohen formerly defended. No doubt, Marxists were wrong to dismiss normative arguments categorically; no doubt too, Marxist politics suffered as a result. Historical materialism's central contentions remain defensible; it is a mistake, albeit one easily made, to think that they are politically disabling. For historical materialists, the future is open—anything is possible, subject only to material constraints. Marxists need not relegate themselves to the role of midwives, awaiting the Revolution in the way that believers await the coming (or second coming) of the Messiah. If they understood Marx right, they would know that it is up to them to make actual what historical development only makes materially possible.

If historical materialism only shows that socialism and communism are possible at high levels of development, one might think the theory otiose. This too would be a mistake. Even with its explanatory pretensions deflated, historical materialism has implications for political philosophy that mainstream liberalism does not and probably cannot accommodate.

In its diminished state, the theory still accords explanatory preeminence to sets of property relations, which can only take certain determinate forms. Thus, it provides something like a table of elements. In much the way that the periodic table shows the forms matter must take (at a certain level of organization), historical materialism shows the forms economic structures must take. But unlike the periodic table, it also predicts (irreversible) movement from one structure to another, *ceteris absentibus*, in the absence of other causally pertinent factors. And, in light of concerns evinced in current discussions of politics and society, it does something even more timely. Inasmuch as property relations are the basis for Marx's accounts of class formation and class struggle, the theory also maintains that division and conflict, not consensus, is key to understanding social order and that class divisions are the most fundamental divisions of all. Experientially, societies may be relatively harmonious or divided along any number of dimensions—including gender, race, and ethnicity. These non-class divisions may be of great ethical and political importance. But, if Marx was right, class structure and conflict is not on par with them. Whatever its degree of saliency, class is the most basic societal division, the one in relation to which all others gain their explanatory, political, and ethical bearing.

It has become fashionable, in academic circles that represent themselves as "left" or even "Marxist," to invoke race and gender divisions and others as well, along with class, as if they all stand on more or less the same plane. In practice, other social divisions often take precedence over class. Thus, class analysis is widely discounted, and, even when it is not, it is thought to be just one research agenda among others. I would venture that this ungrounded pluralism will be among the first casualties if and when Marxist approaches revive.

There is another respect in which historical materialism's explanatory pretensions must be retracted. This has to do with its account of the relation between the economic "base" and legal and political "superstructures" and "forms of consciousness." As remarked, historical materialism holds that an economic base—a set of production relations—(functionally) explains legal systems, political institutions, and the ideas through which persons and societies make sense of themselves, and that superstructural phenomena and forms of consciousness are as they are because they are functional for reproducing the social relations that comprise the underlying economic order. However, it had always been unclear precisely what was supposed to be explained. The view toward which Marxists gravitated was *everything* superstructural or having to do with consciousness. But once this thought was subjected to serious scrutiny, its implausibility became manifest (Cohen 1998). To explain a phenomenon is to account for it in contrast to relevant alternatives. This is why, for example, the answer the celebrated bank robber of the Depression era, Willy "the Actor" Sutton, gave when asked why he robbed banks continues to amuse. He said, "That's where the money is." For the questioner, the issue was, "Why do you rob banks as opposed, say, to working in a store?" Sutton's answer assumed a different "contrastive set." For him, the question was, "Why banks as opposed, say, to newsstands?" But economic explanations seldom figure in the contrastive sets implicit in explanations for most phenomena involving laws, institutions, and ideas. To take just one example: Why is marriage a sacrament in the Roman Catholic Church but not in most Protestant denominations? Because the question is about religion, it has to do with forms of consciousness, but the best explanation is almost certainly theological, not economic.

By reflecting on examples of this kind, it becomes clear that there is no economic explanation for everything, or even for everything *important*, so long as "important" is understood subjectively. For Catholics and Protestants, the maintenance or not of a sacramental system can be of such overwhelming importance that nothing less than individuals' prospects for eternal salvation depend on it. If these phenomena and others like them have no economic explanation, it can hardly be that the economy explains all important things. However, it is plausible to say that there are economic explanations for legal and superstructural phenomena and forms of consciousness *insofar as they affect the underlying historical materialist dynamic* and that even points of religious doctrine can be explained economically, when and insofar as they encourage or impede the reproducibility of the economic base. This is not a trivial contention, and it is far from obvious that it is true. The economy explains legal and superstructural phenomena and forms of consciousness insofar as they have consequences for sustaining (or undermining) production relations. Whatever else they do falls outside the theory's explanatory range.

Liberalism acknowledges no fundamental connection between the state and the economy. This is not to say that liberals deny the obvious or that what economic elites and their subordinates do affect the workings of political institutions. But the institutions themselves are thought to comprise a separate sphere altogether; the state is one thing, and civil society, where the economy is lodged, is something else.

Marxists traditionally assumed a tighter connection but without the benefit of developed political theories. Instead, they gestured toward a vague "economic determinism." Analytical Marxists did almost nothing to rectify this theoretical deficit. When their aim was still to defend a semblance of orthodoxy, they had little to say about political institutions as such. As their thinking evolved in a Rawlsian direction, this did not change. But Marx had a great deal to say that bears on political theory and so did Marxist revolutionaries, especially V. I. Lenin. Analytical Marxists were not much interested in this strain of theorizing, but Althusserians were (Balibar 1976). Implicitly, they laid the groundwork for a distinctively Marxist political theory that transcends the conceptual horizons of Rawlsian liberalism.

Rawlsian liberalism, along with the rest of bourgeois political philosophy, is committed to the state form of political organization—that is, to the kind of political system that emerged at the dawn of the capitalist era, where political authority was concentrated into a unitary institutional nexus. Hobbes was the preeminent philosopher of this development; and, to this day, two Hobbesian doctrines remain central to modern understandings of the state (Levine 2001). The first is that the state exists to "solve" or at least mitigate what amounts to a generalized prisoners' dilemma, where the pursuit of individuals' interests in the absence of reliable authority relations leads to outcomes that realize those interests less well than need be. A "sovereign" capable of monopolizing the means of coercion makes outcomes better for everyone—by making individuals unable to be free to do what is individually best, when and to the extent that restrictions are expedient for order's sake. The other Hobbesian idea is that the state is created by individuals for the sake of their own well-being and therefore that neither God nor Natural Law has anything to do with its origin or justification. States are of, by, and for individuals. Group identifications that mediate between the individual and the state may be beneficial or not, and they may or may not affect the workings of political entities. But they play a subsidiary role in the political sphere. The state is a state of the whole people; if there are politically consequential societal divisions, their locus is in civil society—outside the political arena.

Marx rejected this individualistic approach to political theory—he regarded class struggle, not individuals' interests, as the point of departure for thinking about institutional arrangements up to and including the state itself. Thus, as Marx and Engels declared in *The Communist Manifesto*, the state is "the executive committee of the ruling class," and its function is to reproduce the prevailing system of class domination. Class struggle takes myriad forms in many arenas, but it is ultimately waged in and over the state. This is why Marxists have always insisted that the establishment of a new form of civilization, resting on a new mode of production, must be preceded by a political revolution in which coercive power is taken away from the old ruling class and placed in the hands of the new. For socialism and then communism to come into being, the bourgeois state, run by functionaries of capital, must give way to a *dictatorship of the proletariat*. I remark presently on what Marx and his closest followers had in mind by that politically unfortunate, but philosophically fecund, expression.

For Marx, the state exists to organize ruling class domination and to disorganize subordinate classes. To succeed, revolutionary struggles must counter this disorganizing effect by establishing unity among subordinate classes, a process that is only completed after political power is seized and the state's coercive apparatus is securely in the hands of a new ruling class. This is tantamount to saying that states exist to solve intraruling class coordination problems. Under capitalism, there are competing capitals, with conflicting interests. But capitalists share an overriding interest in maintaining the economic structure, the basis of their power and wealth. The bourgeois state, the *class dictatorship* of the bourgeoisie, is the means through which they realize this end; it coordinates competition in ways that assure the continuation of the system in place. This contention is similar to the Hobbesian claim that states exist to solve interindividual coordination problems that would otherwise lead to a devastating war of all against all. For Hobbes and his successors, a stateless condition is detrimental to everyone's interests. People therefore have a stake in avoiding it, even if to do so, their own liberty must be restricted. For Marx, members of the ruling class have a similar stake in maintaining the existing order. This is why a state is indispensable for enabling ruling classes to discharge the missions historical materialism imputes to them. Without a state, capitalists would not be able to exploit direct producers; they would therefore be unable to develop productive forces to the point where capitalist production relations "fetter" further development, making a socialist revolution both possible and necessary. And without a state, the proletariat would not be able finally to overcome its own internal divisions and, in so doing, capacitate itself for the work ahead: executing the transition from socialism to communism.

On these points, all Marxists agree. However, the Marxist tradition is bereft of political theories built on this understanding. Marx's reflections on the Paris Commune (Marx and Lenin 1989), and Lenin's elaboration of his ideas in *The State and Revolution* were exceptions (Lenin 1917). The implications of this work are far-reaching. But, notwithstanding the efforts of Balibar and other Althusserians, they have so far remained largely undeveloped.

Marx and Lenin used, and overused, *dictatorship*—an unfortunate and misleading word that nevertheless denotes an important facet of their thinking. In ordinary speech and in mainstream political theory, dictatorship is a form of government—one in which a dictator rules without legal constraints. To enhance their legitimacy, dictatorships often make a pretense of respecting legalistic forms, but dictators are ultimately free to do as they please. This is not what Marx and Lenin had in mind in their philosophical reflections on politics. In that context, the term refers not to governments but to the state. Their contention was that states are dictatorships in the sense that their ability to compel compliance rests ultimately on force, not laws. This is not an unusual claim. From the time that Hobbes and other early theorists of sovereignty turned political philosophy into a philosophy of the state, the consensus view was that political power rests on force; because they too are Hobbesian statists—even liberals agree. Of course, they favor forms of governance that are not dictatorial, but they too regard states as dictatorships in Marx's and Lenin's sense. What is uniquely Marxist is the idea that states are *class* dictatorships. It is historical materialism that underlies this conviction. The genuine novelty in Marx's position therefore follows from his account of history's structure and direction, not from any unusual theory of governance or from a misguided valorization of dictatorial institutions.

Bourgeois class dictatorships need not and typically do not assume dictatorial forms of governance. Parliamentary democracies are bourgeois class dictatorships, as is the regime established by the U.S. Constitution, Bill of Rights and all. Similarly, proletarian class dictatorships need not be dictatorships in the colloquial sense—though, once in power, exigent historical reasons forced Lenin and his followers to concoct a dictatorial government, much to the detriment of Marxist political theory and ultimately also to the revolution itself. But in principle a dictatorship of the proletariat can be even more democratic in its forms of governance than any bourgeois class dictatorship—if only because control rights over productive assets, once socialized, would no longer be immune from political, and therefore democratic, control. The implications of this position are, as of now, obscure. Rectifying this situation should be a prime concern.

Marx and Lenin led the way, reflecting on the distinctive institutional forms bourgeois and proletarian class dictatorships characteristically support. For the dictatorship of the proletariat, the Paris Commune was the model. With its example in mind, Marx and later Lenin prescribed popular militias in place of standing armies, popular tribunals instead of independent judiciaries, and direct democracy, implemented through popular and workers' councils, in place of the governing institutions of parliamentary regimes.

Marx's and especially Lenin's reflections on these matters imply that, at a level of generality that abstracts away from historical details and contingencies, different class dictatorships have their own distinctive institutional forms. The problem with their accounts, Lenin's especially, was that in their enthusiasm for the institutions that emerged spontaneously when the communards controlled Paris, they lost sight of the merits of liberal constraints on state, even proletarian state, powers (Levine 1993). The results of their indifference are well known, inasmuch as "Marxist-Leninists" adopted their illiberalism at the same time that they overlooked their commitment to democracy. Now that Marxism-Leninism is defunct, and Marxists have made peace with liberal theory and practice, it should be less difficult than in decades past to bring liberal concerns back in.

There is however a potential conflict between Rawls's "political liberalism," his account of political legitimacy, and a revived Marxist political theory (Rawls 1993). Political liberalism is a second-order theory—an account of how first-order liberal protections should be justified. Its main contention is that constraints on state and societal interferences with individuals' lives and behaviors are best defended from within the framework of an "overlapping" consensus of "reasonable" comprehensive doctrines—not, as has long been the norm, by appealing to moral philosophical commitments or conceptions of the good society that persons could "reasonably reject." Rawlsians believe that Rawls's theory of justice can be defended this way; and, in principle, it is an open question whether Marxian communism can, but the prospect is unlikely. However appealing Marx's vision of the good society may be, "reasonable" people, committed to "reasonable" comprehensive doctrines, can and do reject it. It is even less likely that the coercive imposition of this vision can be conceived in ways that accord with political liberal—or, indeed, ordinary liberal—strictures. For while the regime established under Lenin's aegis was needlessly illiberal, it is far from clear that proletarian class dictatorships can discharge their historical mission in ways that are entirely in accord with first-order liberal constraints. To establish communism, it is necessary to transform institutions and persons in ways that almost certainly violate liberal understandings of legitimate uses of state power.

Unlike genuinely liberal states, proletarian class dictatorships cannot be "fair" to competing conceptions of the good, for it is their task to transform the atomized and acquisitive denizens of capitalist societies into socialist (and eventually communist) men and women with communal and solidaristic dispositions, a project that involves the deployment of state power to implement a particular and contentious conception of the good. Marx's and Lenin's reflections on the Paris Commune focused on the transformative effects of democratic participation and on dismantling ("smashing") bourgeois state institutions, replacing them with functional counterparts of a different, more democratic type. But the ideas they developed lent themselves to other applications as well. Thus, the state's role in transforming consciousness became a major theme in the work of some of the most creative Marxist political thinkers of the twentieth century: Antonio Gramsci (1971) especially and also, as noted, Louis Althusser (2008). Althusser's contention is that the institutions that shape "subjectivity," even when they are not juridically part of the state because they operate outside its "repressive apparatus," are state institutions—that in addition to a "repressive state apparatus" there is also an "ideological state apparatus" (ISA). They work in tandem to reproduce particular kinds of class dictatorships (states). Thus, the family and the church, to the extent they shape "opinion" or otherwise facilitate social control, count as state institutions as much as the courts or the police. In short, Althusser defined the state functionally and then reconstructed the concept in a way that incorporates not just some but all the mechanisms of social control that are functionally integral to reproducing the existing regime.

One motivation for this reconceptualization of the state was to lend support, from within an ostensibly "orthodox" (Leninist) framework, to notions of "cultural revolution." The idea, though not the term, was a theme of Gramsci's, and there is no doubt that Althusser's account of the ISA owes much to Gramsci's work. He also had a more directly political motivation. Althusser wanted to lend support to what he and others in the West at the time saw as vital in the Chinese Cultural Revolution. As a Communist, he was officially anti-Maoist. But it was an open secret that Althusserian Marxism represented Chinese positions from within a framework that the French Communist Party could at least tolerate. Looking back on this barely hidden political agenda from a vantage point several decades later reinforces the point made earlier: that it is far from clear that a revival of a Marxist approach in political philosophy would or should represent itself as Marxist. The term is so weighted down with historical baggage that the description could be a needless and unproductive distraction. It is the ideas that matter—not the name they go by.

However that may be, circumstances do seem to be bringing Marxist themes back onto the agenda. As the crisis of contemporary capitalism intensifies, the time may soon come when capitalist property relations are again no longer assumed. Socialism, if not Marxism per se, is therefore likely again to become a focus of attention. One can only hope that, if and when it does, Marx's work and the work of those who built on it will be accorded their due. It would be a dreadful waste were future theorists to find themselves, as it were, reinventing the wheel.

I would suggest, finally, that Rawlsian and, more generally, liberal egalitarian political philosophy may finally be reaching a point of exhaustion where there is little left to add. This "internal" development could also help refocus attention on themes drawn from Marx's theory of history and from the strain of political theory that Marx, Lenin, Gramsci, and Althusser developed. Thanks, ironically, to the interest analytical Marxists have shown in mainstream liberal philosophy, it should be easier than it was in decades past to address Marxist themes in a way that incorporates liberalism. It should be easier too to avoid even indirect justifications for the illiberalism of the Marxisms that ended badly and that continue to make an unequivocal resumption of the Marxist project problematic.

REFERENCES

Althusser, Louis. 2008. *On Ideology*. Translated by Ben Brewster. London: Verso.
Balibar, Étienne. 1976. *Sur la Dictature du Prolétariat*. Paris: Maspero.
Buchanan, Allen E. 1982. *Marx and Justice: The Radical Critique of Liberalism*. Totowa, NJ: Rowman & Littlefield.
Cohen, G. A. 1978. *Karl Marx's Theory of History: A Defence*. Oxford: Oxford University Press.
Cohen, G. A. 1998. *History, Labour and Freedom: Themes from Marx*. Oxford: Oxford University Press.
Cohen, G. A. 2001. *If You're an Egalitarian, How Come You're So Rich?* Cambridge, MA: Harvard University Press.
Elster, Jon. 1985. *Making Sense of Marx*. Cambridge, UK: Cambridge University Press.
Gramsci, Antonio. 1971. *Selections from the "Prison Notebooks."* New York: International Publishers.
Hegel, G. F. W. 2010. *The Philosophy of History*. Ithaca, NY: Cornell University Press. (Originally published posthumously 1837)
Lenin, V. I. 1917. *The State and Revolution*. London: Allen & Unwin.
Levine, Andrew. 1993. *The General Will: Rousseau, Marx, Communism*. New York: Cambridge University Press.
Levine, Andrew. 2001. *Engaging Political Philosophy: Hobbes to Rawls*. Malden, MA: Blackwell.
Levine, Andrew. 2003. *A Future for Marxism? Althusser, the Analytical Turn and the Revival of Socialist Theory*. London: Pluto.
Lukes, Steven. 1985. *Marxism and Morality*. Oxford: Oxford University Press.
Marx, Karl, and Lenin, V. I. 1989. *The Civil War in France: The Paris Commune*. New York: International Publishers.
Popper, Karl. 1957. *The Poverty of Historicism*. London: Routledge & Kegan Paul.
Rawls, John. 1971. *A Theory of Justice*. Cambridge, MA: Harvard University Press.
Rawls, John. 1993. *Political Liberalism*. New York: Columbia University Press.
Roemer, John E. 1986a. *Analytical Foundations of Marxian Economic Theory*. Cambridge, UK: Cambridge University Press.
Roemer, John E., ed. 1986b. *Analytical Marxism*. Cambridge, UK: Cambridge University Press.
Wood, Allen W. 2009. *Karl Marx*. New York: Routledge.
Wright, Erik O. 1998. *Classes*. London: Verso.
Wright, Erik O. 2005. *Approaches to Class Analysis*. Cambridge, UK: Cambridge University Press.
Wright, Erik O., Andrew Levine, and Elliott R. Sober. 1992. *Reconstructing Marxism: Essays on Explanation and the Theory of History*. London: Verso.

PART III
Democracy

CHAPTER 10

DEMOCRACY

JEREMY WALDRON

A philosophical essay on democracy should be more than a simple recitation of normative arguments for and against the kind of electoral and representative processes that we are familiar with in modern "democratic" polities. It should go the heart of questions such as "What is democracy?"; "What sort of social ontology does it presuppose (for example, in its ostensible commitment to rule by the people)?"; and "What principles does it purport to embody?" Until these questions are answered, we are not really in a position to evaluate the normative claims that are made on behalf of actually existing democratic systems.

1. THE TERM *DEMOCRACY*

Although it can refer to a general equality of status (e.g., Tocqueville 1994) or a rough equality of economic condition (Archer 1995), the term *democracy* is most often used in a political sense. It conveys an ideal for a political system, one that regulates the formal allocation of political authority. We call a country a democracy in virtue of certain features of the procedures by which rulers are chosen, laws enacted, and policies implemented in that country.

In this political sense, democracy is usually taken to mean "rule by the people," and it is opposed to oligarchic, dictatorial, and monarchical characterizations of authority. In an oligarchy, a society is ruled by an élite few, and those few choose the policies and make the laws. An example is modern China, which is ruled by a cadre of the Communist Party. In a dictatorship or a monarchy, rule is vested in one person and exercised by him on his own, with recourse to whatever advisors and subordinates he may choose. Examples include Saudi Arabia and the Vatican, both of which are monarchies, one hereditary and the other elective. North Korea is an example of a dictatorship. Of course, these are very rough distinctions. The few in an oligarchy can vary from a small handful to a privileged party with thousands of members. Also, it may be difficult to distinguish an extensive oligarchy from an imperfect democracy. Apartheid South Africa could not be described as a true democracy, because it excluded the majority of the country's population from the franchise, but it was democrat-ish in the sense that it enfranchised millions of ordinary members of the white minority—including women and poor people. Like ancient Athens (which did not enfranchise women and slaves and so excluded almost two-thirds of the adult population), "democracy" in apartheid South Africa gave political power to common people. Both systems were discriminatory, but both had already abandoned the principle that political issues were too important to be entrusted to anyone other than a privileged élite.

Democracy is rule by the people—but rule by the people over whom? Was the British Empire democratic after the establishment of full adult suffrage in Britain in 1928? Was India ruled democratically between 1928 and 1948 because the country that ruled it was a democratic country, with ordinary people in Britain having the right (through Parliamentary elections) to govern the way the Empire was administered? Obviously not: A country is ruled democratically only if the people who are ruled are the very people who participate in ruling. Democracy, as Abraham Lincoln (1991) put it, is government of the people by the people—and the people in each mention must be the same. Just as democracy in Britain requires that the people of Britain be ruled by the people of Britain, so democracy in India requires that the people of India be ruled by the people of India. This reflexiveness is always rough around the edges. Inevitably some of the people who are ruled are not among the rulers. Children, for example, may not vote, and resident aliens and felons are sometimes disenfranchised. But the general principle is that any adult citizen, however lowly, over whom authority is exercised is to be enfranchised as a voter in a system that allows the mass of voters to choose their rulers and determine directly or indirectly which laws are enacted and which policies are followed.

2. People or Persons?

The ontology of democracy is not easy to figure out. The etymology of the term suggests that it means "rule by the people," and that formulation seems to presuppose the existence of some collective entity called "the people"—the demos—in any political system to which the term *democracy* is applied. Yet most political systems that call themselves democratic are organized on an individualistic basis. Democratic decisions are made as the upshot of millions of decisions made by particular men and women, each voting on his or her own, usually in secret, isolated from others. The individual decisions are registered and counted, and great care is taken to ensure that the count is fair; however, the fairness in question seems best understood as fairness to the individual participants, not to something called "the people." Individuals vote, and a ruling result for the society is determined on the basis of those individual votes. As for "the people"—it seems that we have no need for that hypothesis. We may talk about "the will of the people," but all we really mean are the wills of the persons (millions of them) and a political outcome determined on the basis of those millions of individual wills. Indeed, the way we use the phrase "the people" reflects this. At the end of an election when the result is known, we say "The people have spoken," not "The people has spoken." The syntax indicates that "people" is being used as the plural of "person" rather than as a singular entity in its own right.

In other words, we should not assume that the idea of rule by the people commits us to anything other than methodological or normative individualism. Democracy is an ideal of persons working together in in the context of political procedures that treat them as equals. The fact that there may be tens or hundreds of millions of them involved in these processes does not alter the fact that democracy is a way of respecting individuals (equally) and taking their interests seriously.

Much the same can be said about phrases like "the will of the majority" and "the general interest." As to the former, we should be very careful with any inference that commits us to the existence of some entity called "the majority," which rules in this kind of political system. Sometimes in democratic decision making, people who are bound together by class, cultural, or religious interests may prevail politically, and others may complain about "the tyranny of the majority" because their interests are being subordinated to the interests of members of this larger and therefore more powerful group. But we should not assume that such a class exists (or that such a complaint is justified) every time an issue is decided by majority voting. In many cases, there is no more to be said about "the majority" than that it comprises a certain number of individuals (or a certain proportion of individuals in the polity) who happen to have voted the same way on a given issue.

G. E. M. Anscombe (1976) once observed that the majority in a polity may be frustrated by the polity's following the principle of majority decision (MD). Simplifying from the illustration she gave,[1] we can imagine that three issues are up for decision and five voters (constituting the entire population of a very small state) vote on each of them. Each issue is to be determined by MD. After the votes are cast, the situation is as follows:

	On Issue 1	On Issue 2	On Issue 3
Voter A	in majority	in majority	in majority
Voter B	in majority	in majority	in majority
Voter C	in majority	in minority	in minority
Voter D	in minority	in majority	in minority
Voter E	in minority	in minority	in majority

Voters A and B are in the fortunate situation of being in the majority on all three of the issues up for consideration, but for most of the voters (three out of five), that is not the case. Voters C, D, and E are each in the minority on most of the issues (two out of three). Thus, the majority is in the minority on a majority of issues even though the issues are decided by majority rule. This seems like a paradox—and the configuration of votes may or may not be of concern, depending on how the issues are related to one another—but it is paradoxical only if we assume that there is supposed to be some entity called "the majority" that gets its way in a system of democratic voting. We need not make any such assumption. All we need to assume is that everyone affected by the issues under consideration should be entitled to vote, and each of the issues should be settled on the basis that the view (on that issue) that receives the greatest number of votes should prevail.

As for the general interest, we should not think of this as anything separate from the interests of individuals. Talk of the general interest (like talk of the common good) is a way of considering the interests of individuals taken together. If we adopt a social welfare function—such as the principle of average utility or Rawlsian maximin—to determine what shall count for us as the general interest in circumstances where our interests as individuals diverge, we are still not attributing an interest to a thing called "the people." A social welfare function is justified by some account of what is appropriate in circumstances where the interest of large numbers of individuals point in different directions. It is not justified by any principle of moral consideration for something called "society." I do not mean these comments to sound conservative or libertarian (though they have the ring of Margaret Thatcher's famous dictum that "there is no such thing as society").[2] They are not meant to preclude altruism or social justice or solidarity within a society, but they involve the frank acknowledgement that these are ways of considering the interests of persons (large numbers of them); they do not shift us away from either methodological or ethical individualism.[3]

Also, we should not torment ourselves in democratic theory worrying about the correspondence or lack of correspondence between the will of the people and the general interest. These are just *façons de parler* concerning different ways of aggregating (respectively) individual decisions or individual interests. The moral considerations that lead us to adopt a certain social welfare function (for the purposes, say, of policy science) may or may not be the same as the moral considerations that lead us to adopt a certain political decision procedure in the constitution of our polity; and the results of the two may or may not be congruent. In fact, it is quite unlikely that they will fit together given that the function of a political decision procedure is to allow decisions to be made in a polity among those who disagree about the appropriate social welfare function.[4]

So far these are just analytical points in defense of the individualism that I think is characteristic of the democratic ideal. More substantively, however, it is sometimes said that democracy cannot exist or flourish except as an attribute of a people whose members are bound together by strong bonds of fraternity, common history, or a shared way of life. (Political theorists have used this claim, for example, to cast doubt on the prospects for democracy in the context of the European Union: Because there is no European demos, there can be no European democracy.)[5] Some think democracy is necessarily an exercise in self-determination and that self-determination is generally attributed as a right to nations or to peoples understood as reasonably homogenous entities.[6] A second view is that democracy cannot flourish without a public realm in which people feel comfortable arguing with each other and deliberating together about matters of common concern. Without a common language—indeed, without common media of communication such as newspapers and such—this may be very difficult (Anderson 1991). These attributes—a public realm, a common language, and common media—are not characteristic of every collection of persons in a given territory; they presuppose that the persons have constituted themselves as a people among whom deliberative politics is possible. Finally, some claim that there cannot be a democracy without some feeling of sympathy and mutual solidarity among the citizens greater than that felt among any random collection of human beings. This is partly a matter of the decisions that need to be made—for example, redistributive decisions that may require some sections of the polity to give up certain advantages or wealth in favor of others. It is also partly a matter of the trust that democracy presupposes: In a democracy, individuals and parties are putting themselves in one another's hands or making themselves vulnerable by being willing to give up power to their political opponents in circumstances under which they are not physically compelled to do so. Some of these arguments are no doubt exaggerated, and they sell short the experience of democracies like the United States in the late nineteenth and early twentieth century that did not presuppose, but managed rather to forge, a civic identity among the most disparate of populations. Yet even if they contain a grain of truth, these claims need not commit us to the idea that democracy is the rule of an entity—the people, or the majority—with its own will and its own resolutions. We can still adopt an individualist view of what democracy is, even if we concede that its success presupposes a certain social background.

3. Political Equality

So what is the individualist principle embodied in the democratic ideal? The most important is the principle of political equality, which commands equal respect in the political realm and equal consideration of interests.

Regarding equal consideration of interests, we find that, these days, no one will deny that in public policy and the enactment of law, the well-being of all members of the community should be taken into account. In principle this might occur under any political system, and philosophers, when they imagine a political system with people like themselves in charge, may convince themselves that democratic representation is not necessary to persuade them to take seriously and consider justly the interests of all. The impartial benevolence of the philosopher-kings may be sufficient. Yet for most of history and for most political systems, the interests of most people—particularly the common people (workers and the poor)—have been ignored by the powerful or, worse, treated as subjects for exploitation. Experience has shown that these interests will be taken seriously only when the common people are empowered politically to engage in public decision making themselves or to choose and hold accountable those who engage in public decision making.[7] Admittedly, this is not a sufficient condition: Experience has not shown that democratic institutions always take seriously the interests of the common people; sometimes their capacity to do so is corrupted by various factors, including the social and economic power of those who seek to neglect or subordinate them. But however much people talk of benign monarchs or an elite of philosopher-kings devoted to justice and the common good, the enfranchisement and representation of ordinary people appears to be necessary for the proper consideration of their interests.

Of course, people disagree about what it means for the interests of all to be properly considered. Most philosophers accept that people's interests should be considered equally—that people are entitled to equal concern—by those who exercise political power over them.[8] But equal concern is not the same as aiming at equality (of outcome, opportunity, resources, primary goods, or anything else). There is much more work to be done in the wake of general acceptance of a principle of equal concern. So even when they dedicate themselves to equal consideration of the interests of all, people may still disagree about what the social welfare function ought to be. Interests pull in different directions, and we must not assume there is any greater univocality among the interests of the common people than among the interests of the rich. However, for most of history and invariably in all nondemocratic systems, "the neglect of the interests of the common people" is not a matter of the powerful adopting a social welfare function with which some of us disagree: It is a matter of their not adopting any credible social welfare function at all, so far as the interests of their powerless subjects are concerned.

Well-being can be understood in terms of interests or in terms of preferences. In the previous paragraph, I spoke of interests that can be understood in objective terms. I did this in order to be fair to the opponents of democracy, conceding at least the theoretical possibility that the well-being of the common people might be properly considered by others. But the principle of equal concern may also be understood to require that rulers pay attention to the interests of each ordinary person as he or she sees them and to the impact of public measures of law and policy on the life of each ordinary person as that life is actually lived or experienced. Of course in a country of tens or hundreds of millions, detailed attention to the circumstances and lived experience of each person's life may be impossible. Still, democratic input or democratic representation may be indispensable for conveying effectively to the centers of power a sense of the typical impact (or the typical range of impacts) of proposed measures on ordinary people's lives. Academic political theorists sometimes talk about "deliberative democracy," in which abstract issues of justice are addressed in political debate (Elster 1998). That is no doubt important, but we also must not neglect the informational dimension of democracy—conveying to the centers of power information about people's lives of which the rulers may otherwise be ignorant or to which they may be indifferent or worse.

John Stuart Mill went further in *Considerations on Representative Government.* Speaking of a political system in which "the working classes may be considered as excluded from all direct participation in government," he conceded that it may no longer be the policy of those who are represented in Parliament to neglect or sacrifice the interest of the working classes to their own. But, he went on,

> Does Parliament, or almost any of the members composing it, ever for an instant look at any question with the eyes of a working man? When a subject arises in which the labourers as such have an interest, is it regarded from any point of view but that of the employers of labour? I do not say that the working men's view of these questions is in general nearer to the truth than the other: but it is sometimes quite as near; and in any case it ought to be respectfully listened to, instead of being, as it is, not merely turned away from, but ignored. (1991, 67)

This view that attention must be paid not only to the interests of ordinary people but to their own perspective on any situation in which their interests are involved leads us in the direction of the second aspect of the principle of political equality: equality of respect in the political realm.

Respect is something that is accorded to people as recognition of their personhood and dignity (Darwall 1977). In moral theory (especially in Kantian moral theory), it is associated with a recognition of people's capacity for moral judgment and practical reason—their ability to form a judgment on the morality of a matter and act on it. Of course, people differ in their moral character and in the sophistication of their judgments, and there is a dimension of respect that addresses this as well: We may respect one person as a person of sound judgment or reliable moral disposition but not another. However, we have no doubt that people generally, barring some catastrophic mental impairment, are capable of moral judgment. We imagine that this capacity is directed, in the first instance, to the governance of each person's own actions. Each person, even the poorest or the most ordinary, has a life to live, and each uses his or her rational capacities to organize their lives in accordance with judgments they make about values (i.e., about what makes a life worth living). It is widely accepted that people are entitled to recognition and respect in regard to the exercise of these capacities, and individual rights such as personal autonomy and religious freedom are founded on this respect.

People's moral capacities also include a sense of justice and the common good—an ability to reflect on and determine a reasonable relation between their values and activities and the similar values and activities of others (Rawls 1999, 441–49; Rawls 1996, 48–54). This capacity may be directed to personal relations with others, in families, for example, or in the workplace, or it may be directed to broader questions about appropriate relations among millions of people living in a given society. This capacity commands respect, but its exercise cannot be given the same decisive authority as an individual's autonomous direction of his or her own life. The reason—obviously enough—is that many people will be directing a similar capacity to the same situation, and people may well differ in the judgments they make in the exercise of this capacity. If my sense of justice yields results that are different from yours, then its application to a given situation (in which we are both involved) may not be compossible with the application of your sense of justice. This prospect of disagreement is crucial to our thinking about democracy. Even if we think there are objective, right answers to the questions of justice and the common good that people direct their senses of justice toward, we know that the issues are complicated and that with the best will in the world people will come up with different answers, reflecting perhaps their differing perspectives and experiences.[9]

Questions of justice and the common good are, of course, the fundamental questions of politics. They are questions about property, economy, what aid we owe to one another personally and collectively, and the basic terms of social and economic coexistence. They include questions about what social welfare function should direct public policy, but they are also questions about fundamental duties and rights, responsibilities, and entitlements that must be embodied in law. These questions have to be answered—usually in a single answer that can stand in the name of the whole society. But the objectively right answer to any of these questions, if there is one, does not disclose itself authoritatively from the skies: All we have on earth are humans' best attempts to identify the right answer.

At this point, then, there is a choice to be made in the organization of a political community. Should the answer to these questions of justice and the common good be entrusted to some expert or committee of experts who, there is reason to suppose, are more likely than any ordinary person to reach the right answer? Or should we proceed to decisions about them on the basis of respect for the sense of justice of everyone in the community?

A commitment to democracy represents a choice in favor of the second of these options. When decisions about justice or the common good need to be made in a given society, all the members of that society are empowered to form a view and contribute to the process of public decision. Two lines of reasoning support this option. The first is simple respect for the capacity of ordinary men and women to form reasonable and considered views on matters of public importance. To assign decisions to an expert or committee of experts would be to act as though individuals' views did not matter; it would insult them, and it would mean slighting rather than respecting the capacities involved in their formation. Of course, empowering ordinary individuals might involve a greater risk of wrong or inappropriate answers than empowering a committee of experts, but the case for democracy is that it is worth accepting this risk for the sake of respect for the opinions of ordinary people.

Also, the democratic option is bolstered by the difficulty of identifying experts whose decisions would be superior to those of ordinary people working through some democratic mechanism. These include difficulties of determining the criteria for expertise, which are likely to be as controversial as the first-order questions the experts must address. Even if the criteria can be agreed on, there are difficulties in identifying the persons who satisfy the criteria. Thus, it is important to remember that expertise cannot be thrust on a people as an alternative to democracy. The rule of the experts must be made legitimate if it is to work politically, and that means it must have popular consent or popular appeal at some level (Estlund 1993).

A second line of argument for the democratic option is based on autonomy. It draws on the principle that justifies our empowerment of people in regard to decisions about their own lives. In a self-regarding case, where an individual's own interests are at stake, we believe that that person should have a say in any decision; his attention to his own interests and his opinion about his own conduct should be respected. A principle of autonomy explains why we privilege individual self-determination in these cases.

It is true that we should not give decisive weight to P's autonomous determination in cases where the decision involves Q's interests and conduct. But it is mistake to think that our concern for autonomy simply evaporates when other people's interests enter the picture. What happens instead is that we keep hold of the principle of autonomy but apply it in a modified way. In simple two-person cases, we may say that the individual self-determination of each person must be respected in the mode of decision making that is used to settle some question involving them both. We privilege, for example, anything the two of them agree to (when no one else's interest are involved), and, on the basis of respect for the autonomy of the two of them, we say that their decision—taken in a way that respects them both—is no one else's business. We certainly do not say that because there are now two of them, rather than just one, the value of autonomy goes out the window and the decision might as well be taken by a third party—more expert in moral matters than either of them.

None of this changes when we are talking about decisions that must be made among millions of people rather than just one or two individuals. It remains the case that the decision in question is to be made by them, in a way that respects each and every one of them. The importance of the autonomy principle that requires the involvement of each person in a social decision affecting him or her does not evaporate simply because the decision also affects the interests and conduct of millions of other members of the group. However, autonomy now has a bearing on the question of the decision procedure that is much more complicated and indirect than what it had in the one-person case. Given that many people are involved, no one person's view can be made decisive in and of itself simply based on the fact that his interest and his conduct are affected. But notice that we do not swerve away from autonomy as a general principle. Nothing is allowed to qualify respect for any one person's view except respect for the view of some other person who is involved, and even then only on terms that treat their autonomy equally. Just because many people are involved does not mean that individual autonomy gives way to the independent claims of expertise. We look instead for a decision procedure that gives each person's view as much weight as possible in determining the social choice, provided that no less weight is accorded to the views of each of the others.

One such procedure might be the principle of unanimity, which we imagined operating in the two-person case. However, using only this decision procedure might be impracticable in cases involving social decision making by millions. In the two-person case, failure to secure the consent of both leaves them in a default position of inaction (at least as far as joint action or action concerning them both is concerned). Each is thrown back on his or her own resources to pursue purely self-regarding action or to try and work something out with someone else. That may or may not be satisfactory in the two-person case. It is almost certainly unsatisfactory in the million-person case, where it may be a matter of material or moral necessity that some decision be made in the name of the whole group and where leaving things as they are—in a default position absent unanimity—may itself wreak serious injustice. So we look for alternatives to the unanimity rule, and once again we look for alternatives that represent complicated ways of continuing to respect individual autonomy.

Whether it is motivated by the value of autonomy in each person's governance of his or her own life or a by principle that respects the political views that individuals have formed, the choice of a democratic decision procedure will be imbued by a concern for equality. On both lines of argument, we will attempt to accord as much weight as possible to each person's views (on some matter of public decision), but we will subject that attempt to a constraint of equality: No greater weight is to be accorded to any one person's views than to those of any other.

Defending the equality constraint is easier when the case for democracy is based on the autonomy argument than when it is based on the equal respect for political opinions argument. In the case of the autonomy argument, we may say that each person has an equal stake because each must make a life under the conditions that the political decision determines. Colonel Rainsborough summed it up in 1649 in the Putney Debates when he said, "[T]he poorest he that is in England has a life to live as the greatest he; and therefore truly, sir, I think it's clear that every man that is to live under a government ought first by his own consent to put himself under that government" (Sharp 1998, 103). Of course, on any given measure, some may be affected more than others. We respond to this in some cases with a principle of subsidiarity in an attempt to match the decision-making constituency to the interest most affected. But if we accept that democratic decision making determines a whole range of political, social, and economic issues—indeed, the broad shape of the basic structure of a society—then a case can be made that each person who has a life to lead within that structure should have an equal say.

With the equal respect argument, the situation is more controversial. John Stuart Mill is famous for proposing a system of plural voting, giving greater weight to the opinions of those who were better educated:

> [T]hough every one ought to have a voice—that every one should have an equal voice is a totally different proposition. . . . If, with equal virtue, one is superior to [another] in knowledge and intelligence—or if, with equal intelligence, one excels the other in virtue—the opinion, the judgment, of the higher moral or intellectual being is worth more than that of the inferior: and if the institutions of the country virtually assert that they are of the same value, they assert a thing which is not. (1991, 179–80)

The difficulty, however, which Mill acknowledges, is discerning who is superior along any of these dimensions. Political theorists and statesmen have not found Mill's proposals relative to educational qualifications convincing. Certainly the legitimacy conditions for such extra weightings will be very difficult to satisfy in a polity where people disagree about the value of education and about what it is to be more or less expert or more or less responsible in the exercise of the franchise.[10] The problem is likely to be particularly intractable in societies where high education qualifications are correlated with distinctive class interests.[11] In the face of these difficulties, equality might be defended as a default position.

4. Majority Decision

So far we have said nothing about which decision procedure should be used against the background of these concerns and constraints. A unanimity principle seems to give great weight to each person's view, and in a way it satisfies the constraint of political equality (provided we ignore the greater interest that some may have in preserving the status quo, which is almost inevitably the outcome of the use of such a principle). But it is unsatisfactory for the reasons given earlier.

One principle that does promise a way of making social and political decisions, that breaks the impasse generated by the unanimity requirement while continuing to offer respect for the participation of each person affected, is the principle of majority decision MD.[12] Decision theorists have shown that, at least for straightforward cases, MD uniquely satisfies constraints of decisiveness, equality, maximal weight for each person's input, and impartiality among outcomes (May 1952). As already argued, MD should not be valued in a democratic context because it empowers some entity called "the majority" or because it is a way of getting at "the will of the people." The entities that it empowers are ordinary individuals, and its virtue is simply that it treats them as equals, it accords the views of each as much weight as is consistent with equality, and it is not biased ex ante in favor of any one of the options under consideration.

I believe this defense of MD is a compelling one, though in the next couple of sections we will identify some complexities and qualifications. MD has also been defended on epistemic grounds. James Mill (1992) famously argued that MD's form creates outcomes that may represent an application of the utilitarian greatest happiness principle, but this is a highly unstable result, hostage as it is to certain assumptions about what motivates people to vote. If they are voting their ideals or their own view of the general interest, or if there are great differences in the intensity of preference represented by each vote, then there is no guarantee whatever that a majority result will represent the greatest happiness of the greatest number.

Even less convincing is the argument for MD based on Condorcet's "Jury Theorem." The Marquis de Condorcet (1976, 33–70) proved that, if voters are facing a simple binary question and if the average voter is more likely to get the answer right than wrong, then the likelihood that the right answer will be chosen by a majority increases to certainty as group size increases. The trouble with this argument is partly in its premise—Condorcet himself believed that "a very numerous assembly cannot be composed of very enlightened men" (Condorcet 1976, 49)—and partly in applying some of the assumptions it makes about the independence of individual votes. Political philosophers continue to be attracted to the Jury Theorem due to its formal character. However, we need to remember that it is an utterly mechanical result and that its workings have no epistemological dimension whatsoever: The Jury Theorem works best when we are explaining the enhanced likelihood that a majority of balls chosen at random from a shaken jar will be white when the jar contains fifty-one white balls and forty-nine black balls.

We are familiar with MD in all sorts of areas other than democratic decision making. Judges use it in supreme courts; tenure committees use it in universities; juntas may use it in administering oligarchies. Its main advantages are its decisiveness (at least for simple cases), its neutrality, and the way it treats voters as equals. In some contexts the latter feature may be less important. However, in the theory of democracy it is of paramount importance, and that explains why the idea of democracy is so often associated with majoritarianism.

5. Procedures and Outcomes

In the arguments just considered, the principle of political equality is applied to questions about the empowerment of persons so far as their inputs into the process of arriving at collective decisions are concerned and it is applied also to the decision procedure itself. Some philosophers argue that our use of political equality is incomplete if it is not also deployed to evaluate the outcomes of the decision procedure and that where these outcomes seriously offend or violate the principle of political equality, some adjustment to its application to the decision procedure and to the inputs may be required. So, for example, Charles Beitz (1989, 64) argues that applying the principle of political equality simply to legitimize majority decision as a procedure narrows its meaning unacceptably. Political equality might also be called up to justify institutional arrangements dedicated specifically to scrutinizing the content of majoritarian outputs and screening out egregious violations. (Judicial review of legislation is often defended as such a mechanism.)

The difficulty with such arrangements arises when the members of a community are divided as to which outcomes (in their content) offend the principle of political equality. Disagreement about this quickly opens up into disagreement about the essentials of justice, which is of course one of the issues that political equality commands us to settle by a procedure that respects the disparate views of all citizens. The institutional arrangements that are envisaged for scrutinizing outcomes do not normally satisfy this criterion. Even if some citizens judge them effective in screening out outcomes that they believe are unjust, others will protest that their views about justice are slighted in the matter. So, if the outcome-scrutinizing arrangement is a court, some will complain that the court is using inegalitarian decision procedures to settle important matters for the polity. For example, whether affirmative action to remedy past discrimination treats members of the political community as equals will now be settled, one way or the other, by majority voting among a handful of judges, and the outcome of that vote among the judges will determine whether or not the resulting legislation prescribing affirmative action is treated as an acceptable outcome of majority voting among all the citizens. That is bound to seem like a procedural affront to political equality.[13]

This leaves us at something of an impasse. The defender of majoritarian procedures cannot deny that the principle that justifies them also has implications for evaluating the output of majority decisions, and the defender of output scrutiny cannot but be troubled by the use of what is essentially an aristocratic method (rule by a wise and trustworthy elite) to resolve major issues of contention in what purports to be a democratic society. This issue is not going to be settled any time soon.

6. Complexity and Representation

It is important to grasp all these features of the fundamental relation between majority decision and political equality (and all the difficulties as well) before going on to consider further complexities in actually existing polities. In a number of regards, the account of majority decision considered in the previous two sections is quite simplistic. Some of the complexities that we must consider relate to formal decision theory, and some are institutional.

Simple majority decision may be fine for binary decisions, but as Arrow (1950) and others have shown, more complex procedures may be necessary to avoid circularity or impasse for decisions among multiple options. This is certainly an important result. However, we should not lose sight of the fact that Arrow's paradox does not specifically discredit democracy. It points to difficulties that may afflict any decision procedure (including voting on a court or among the members of a junta of philosopher-kings in case they disagree with one another); and its "impossibility" implication is not the impossibility of making decisions by fair procedures but the apparent impossibility of guaranteeing that a procedure is available to yield a fair and determinate result under all of the circumstances of decision that may arise. The challenge posed by Arrow's paradox is to devise various arrangements that might preempt or resolve democratically the difficulties that it poses. Possible candidates include arrangements for legislative leadership and other forms of agenda-setting, as well as the bundling of issues through the commitments of political parties. These are almost certainly imperfect solutions, but they may be adequate for the purposes of real-world polities. Certainly, they can be judged better and worse from a democratic point of view—better, for example, if they represent plausible elaborations and applications of the very principles of political equality that underpin the primary argument for the enfranchisement of ordinary people.

In general, we should bear in mind that whatever the vicissitudes of formal decision theory, in the real world, decision procedures will be established in the context of complex institutional arrangements. These include not just political parties and legislative agenda setting but also government through representative assemblies and the organization of an electoral system.

It is sometimes said that modern representative democracy is a distant second-best to the Athenian ideal of direct democracy, where decisions were taken in a plenary assembly of all enfranchised citizens.[14] We adopt it as second-best either because we are fearful of the outcomes of direct democratic decision making or because we think that direct democracy is impracticable. The first of these reasons takes us back to the concerns about expertise discussed in Section IV. If representative government is justified as a way of empowering (and legitimating the rule of) a class of persons whose expertise is somewhat greater than that of ordinary people, then we shall have to concede that Jean-Jacques Rousseau (1968, 141–42) was correct in saying that it rests in the last analysis on a fundamentally nondemocratic approach.

The second justification for representative as opposed to direct democracy—the practicability justification—needs careful unpacking. At one level it is about crude considerations of time and place: Our modern polities comprise tens (sometimes hundreds) of millions of citizens, and there is not the remotest possibility of assembling them in one place as the Athenians could do (just) with their plenary assemblies of eight or ten thousand (Hansen 1999, 125ff). At another level, it is about the possibility of dialogue and deliberation: How can there be real deliberation among millions of people? Of course there are various media like newspapers and the Internet that do enable thousands of people's views to be brought into relation with one another in some sort of rough deliberative struggle. But responsible political deliberation requires a more structured forum, not as an alternative to the rough process of society-wide debate but as a way by which rough, society-wide deliberation can be brought into focus for the specific purposes of policy-making and legislation. To the extent that representative structures make this possible, they have a justification that is not necessarily at odds with the political equality. Like political parties (with whose work they interact), representative arrangements frame and channel deliberation and decision making among the people, so that it takes on a character appropriate for formal tasks such as legislation. Indeed, a case can be made that representative structures are superior to direct democracy so far as legislation is concerned because they present both the interests and the opinions of ordinary people in an abstract form that matches the abstract generality required in legislation by the principle of the rule of law.[15] (Much the same too can be said about structures like bicameralism in a democracy and the formalities of parliamentary deliberation.)

Much depends, of course, on how the system of representation is set up. We are familiar with the abstract idea of a legislature being a microcosm of the nation—geographically, for example, if representatives are elected on a constituency basis, and ideologically in terms of party-political affiliations. It is often thought important that legislatures also represent a country's mix of gender, ethnic, and perhaps class identities; this can be achieved both through choices that are made about districting and electoral boundaries and through parties' responsiveness to informal norms of diversity in the candidates they sponsor. These matters are intensely controversial, but for the most part the hard choices they represent are not choices that cut across the fundamentals of political equality. They are choices about the appropriate way to ensure the equal representation of interests and perspectives and about the appropriate way to relate the egalitarian foundations of democracy to the specific framing of policy and legislative debates.

It is important to ensure that the organization of the electoral system in a representative democracy does not undermine the basic premise of political equality. If, for example, legislative choices are made by majority voting among representatives, efforts must be made to ensure that the empowerment of particular legislators does not amount to the privileging of some electors over others. An example might be a system that treated the vote of legislator A as the equal of the vote of legislator B, even though legislator A's constituency comprised ten times as many voters as legislator B's constituency.[16] I do not mean that we should think necessarily in terms of a simple arithmetic function for mapping political equality among voters onto districting and onto the status and empowerment of representatives.[17] But it is important that the foundational principle of political equality be kept in mind when we are considering and evaluating representative arrangements. Political equality does important work in the foundations of democratic theory, but it must not be confined to the foundations.

NOTES

1. I am indebted to Gorman (1978) for this simplification. Anscombe's own paradigm is more elaborate.
2. This well-known quotation can be traced to Keay (1987).
3. For different forms of individualism, see Lukes (1973).
4. In Section V, I briefly consider the utilitarian theory of democracy, espoused by thinkers such as James Mill (1992), who thought that the use of MD among individuals with each voting on his or her own interests makes it likely that democratic outputs will conform to the greatest happiness principle.
5. See, e.g., Rosanvallon and Moyn (2006, 229).
6. See the discussion in Waldron (2010).
7. See the excellent discussion in Mill (1991, ch. III).
8. But see Dworkin (1986, 295–96) for the view that the principle of equal concern is incumbent only on organizations that exercise coercive authority, such as states.

9. See Rawls (1996, 54–58) on what he calls "the burdens of judgment." See also Waldron (1999, 111–13 and 151–52).

10. For a fine discussion see Christiano (2008, 116–28).

11. See Beitz (1989, 35) and Estlund (2008, 215–16).

12. I use the term "majority decision" rather than "majority rule" because the latter has inaccurate connotations of rule by an entity called the majority. See also the discussion in Arendt (1973, 164).

13. For an argument to this effect, see Waldron (2006).

14. Indeed, some have argued that the two kinds of system are so radically different that it is misleading to use the same word—"democracy"—to cover them both (see Dunn 2005, 19–20).

15. See the discussion in Waldron (2009, 345–54) and Urbinati (2006).

16. This happens in the U.S. Senate between, say, a senator from New York and a senator from Delaware, but in that context it is a historical reflection of the coming together of quasi-independent states; it is rather like the equal representation of demographically disparate nation-states in the U.N. General Assembly.

17. For a helpful discussion of the issues here, see Buchanan and Tullock (1962, ch. 16).

REFERENCES

Anderson, Benedict. 1991. *Imagined Communities: Reflections on the Origin and Spread of Nationalism*. London: Verso.

Anscombe, G. E. M. 1976. "On Frustration of the Majority by Fulfillment of the Majority's Will." *Analysis* 36: 161–68.

Archer, Robin. 1995. *Economic Democracy: The Politics of Feasible Socialism*. Oxford: Oxford University Press.

Arendt, Hannah. 1973. *On Revolution*. New York: Penguin Books.

Arrow, K. J. 1950. "A Difficulty in the Concept of Social Welfare." *Journal of Political Economy* 58: 328–46.

Beitz, Charles. 1989. *Political Equality*. Princeton, NJ: Princeton University Press.

Buchanan, James, and Tullock, Gordon. 1962. *The Calculus of Consent: Logical Foundations of Constitutional Democracy*. Ann Arbor: University of Michigan Press.

Christiano, Thomas. 2008. *The Constitution of Equality: Democratic Authority and Its Limits*. Oxford: Oxford University Press.

Condorcet, Marquis de. 1976. "Essay on the Application of Mathematics to the Theory of Decision-Making." In *Condorcet: Selected Writings*. Edited by Keith Michael Baker. Indianapolis, IN: Bobbs-Merrill.

Darwall, Stephen. 1977. "Two Kinds of Respect." *Ethics* 88: 36–49.

Dunn, John. 2005. *Democracy: A History*. New York: Atlantic Monthly Press.

Dworkin, Ronald. 1986. *Law's Empire*. Cambridge, MA: Harvard University Press.

Elster, John. 1998. *Deliberative Democracy*. Cambridge, UK: Cambridge University Press.

Estlund, David. 1993. "Making Truth Safe for Democracy." In *The Idea of Democracy*. Edited by David Copp. Jean Hampton, and John Roemer. Cambridge, UK: Cambridge University Press.

Estlund, David. 2008. *Democratic Authority: A Philosophical Framework*. Princeton, NJ: Princeton University Press.

Gorman, J. L. 1978. "A Problem in the Justification of Democracy." *Analysis* 38: 46–50.
Hansen, Mogens Herman. 1999. *The Athenian Democracy in the Age of Demosthenes: Structure, Principles, and Ideology*. Norman: University Of Oklahoma Press.
Keay, Douglas. 1987. "Interview with Margaret Thatcher." *Woman's Own*, September 23.
Lincoln, Abraham. "Address Delivered at the Dedication of the Cemetery at Gettysburg, November 19, 1863." In *Great Speeches*. New York: Dover Publications.
Lukes, Steven. 1973. *Individualism*. Oxford: Basil Blackwell.
May, Kenneth O. 1952. "A Set of Independent Necessary and Sufficient Conditions for Simple Majority Decisions." *Econometrica* 20: 680–84.
Mill, John Stuart. 1991. *Considerations on Representative Government*. Amherst, NY: Prometheus Books.
Mill, James. 1992. "Government." In *James Mill: Political Writings*. Edited by Terence Ball. Cambridge, UK: Cambridge University Press.
Rawls, John. 1996. *Political Liberalism*. New York: Columbia University Press.
Rawls, John. 1999. *A Theory of Justice*, rev. ed. Cambridge, MA: Harvard University Press.
Rosanvallon, Pierre, and Moyn, Samuel. 2006. *Democracy Past and Future*. New York: Columbia University Press.
Rousseau, Jean-Jacques. 1968. *The Social Contract*. New York: Penguin Books.
Sharp, Andrew. 1998. *The English Levellers*. Cambridge, MA: Cambridge University Press.
Tocqueville, Alexis de. 1994. *Democracy in America*. New York: Alfred A. Knopf.
Urbinati, Nadia. 2006. *Representative Democracy: Principles and Genealogy*. Chicago: University of Chicago Press.
Waldron, Jeremy. 1999. *Law and Disagreement*. Oxford: Oxford University Press.
Waldron, Jeremy. 2006. "The Core of the Case against Judicial Review." *Yale Law Journal* 115:1346–406.
Waldron, Jeremy. 2009. "Representative Lawmaking." *Boston University Law Review* 89: 335–56.
Waldron, Jeremy. 2010. "Two Conceptions of Self-Determination." In *The Philosophy of International Law*. Edited by Samantha Besson and John Tasioulas. Oxford: Oxford University Press.

CHAPTER 11

DELIBERATION

ROBERT B. TALISSE

1. Deliberation in General

Deliberation denotes any activity aimed at bringing rational considerations to bear on a decision. Of course, philosophers disagree about what a *rational consideration* is and what it is to make a *decision*, and there is debate over what it means for rational considerations to be *brought to bear on* a decision. But we can sidestep these complications by considering a simple case: Abby must decide whether to go to a movie or to the library. How shall she choose? If she flips a coin, she has not deliberated about what to do. If, on the other hand, she weighs her options by taking into account, say, that she promised to meet a friend at the movies, or that she has a term paper due tomorrow, or that the movie has received markedly negative reviews, Abby deliberates. In the former case, Abby selects a course of action on the basis of nonrational considerations. The coin flip does not engage the question of what she *should do*; it is insensitive to the *reasons* she has to perform one or the other act. In the latter case, her choice is based in some attempt to discern the relative merits of her options; she attempts to determine what she *has reason* to do. Accordingly, when deliberation culminates in a decision to act, Abby can provide *reasons why* she acts as she does; she can, in this sense, *explain* herself. We may say, then, that deliberation lies behind acts that are properly described as being *deliberate*.

Not all deliberation aims at action. We deliberate also to find out what is the case. Hence, we distinguish theoretical from practical deliberation. Theoretical deliberation is aimed at figuring out what to believe, and practical deliberation is aimed at figuring out what to do. One way of conceptualizing the difference between these two modes of deliberation is to consider their different "direction of fit" (Platts 1979; Anscombe 1957). When we practically deliberate, we do so with the aim of bringing the world into conformity with our ends; when we engage in theoretical deliberation, we aspire to bring our beliefs into conformity with the world. Our theoretical deliberations, then, invoke a standard of correctness; they *answer to* the facts. Our practical deliberations, by contrast, are evaluable only in terms of effectiveness. However, that we distinguish between the two kinds of deliberation does not suggest that our practical and theoretical concerns are wholly distinct. A detective gathers clues and assesses the evidence to decide who to arrest; he attempts to get a clear view of the facts so that he can act appropriately. In conducting an experiment, scientists act in ways which help them to discern what the facts are in the case; they perform the experiment to figure out what to believe.

It may seem that whenever we deliberate, we are seeking for effective means to our ends. In theoretical deliberation, we want to arrive at true belief, and so we attend to our evidence and try to believe accordingly; in practical deliberation, there is something we want to bring about by means of our action, so we try to find out which of the acts available to us is likely to achieve the desired result. Indeed, in one prominent sense of the term, we act *rationally* when we perform actions that can be plausibly regarded as suitable means to our ends.

Hence, many have held that deliberation is always *instrumental*, always about means rather than ends. The instrumentalist holds that we find ourselves with the ends that we have, and the task of deliberation is to discern appropriate means. Aristotle is sometimes interpreted as holding this position, and instrumentalism remains a popular view among philosophers.

The popularity of instrumentalism is unsurprising, given its intuitive appeal. Whether I should raise the glass of water to my mouth is a question that in large part turns on whether I aim to quench my thirst, and whether I should read the newspaper is largely a matter of whether I aspire to be well-informed about current events. When asked why I read the paper, it seems perfectly reasonable to answer that I want to be informed. Similarly, that *you* want me to drink does not by itself provide for me a reason to raise the glass; I must also have an aim *of my own* that would be satisfied by doing as you say. The instrumentalist picture thus comports well with the popular view, often ascribed to Hume, among others, according to which only desires, and never reasons, can motivate action. Indeed, there is a straightforward sense in which the question of what I have reason to do turns on what I desire; for example, I have *reason* to raise the glass to my mouth because I desire to drink. In the absence of the relevant desire, what reason could I have to raise the glass?

Yet we often take ourselves to be engaged in rational reflection about the appropriateness of our ends. We sometimes ask ourselves whether the things that we want are *worth wanting*, that is, whether achieving our ends is, indeed, valuable, and sometimes we seem to be deliberating about what our ends are, that is, what we *really* want. Instrumentalists contend that when we seem to be deliberating about our ends, we are really deliberating about the appropriateness of a proximate end in light of a more distant or higher-order aim. However, there are compelling lines of argument that hold that it is possible to deliberate about our ends as such. Elijah Millgram (1997), for example, argues forcefully for the view that our ability to revise our ends in light of experience shows that deliberation about ends is possible, and

Christine Korsgaard (2008, ch. 1) argues that instrumental reasoning presupposes the possibility of deliberation about our ends. If deliberation about ends is possible, instrumentalism is false.

The debate over instrumentalism resides for the most part in the area of philosophy known as meta-ethics, a crossroads at which normative questions about human behavior meet with concerns in epistemology, metaphysics, philosophy of language, philosophy of mind, and psychology. I cannot pursue this debate further. I mention it mainly because instrumentalism has an analogue in political philosophy that until quite recently has been at the core of democratic theory.

2. Deliberation in Democratic Theory

For most of the twentieth century, democratic theory was dominated by a family of views that may be generally characterized as *aggregative*. Aggregative views conceptualize political behavior along roughly instrumentalist lines. Rational political actors behave in ways that they judge will best satisfy their political interests or preferences. Political action hence is not aimed at the production of or reflection on those interests; they are regarded as simply given. The task of the political agent, then, is to discern the most effective means to achieving his political ends; accordingly, political deliberation is understood as primarily strategic. Because different political agents often have competing political ends, the task of democracy is to coordinate competing interests in a way that produces definite outcomes while sustaining civic peace. Democracy, on aggregative views, is in large measure a matter of conflict management, where bullets are replaced by ballots (Bobbio 1984, 156).

The aggregative view is, in essence, the schoolyard view of democracy. Each actor gets exactly one vote, each actor votes in accordance with his or her preference, each vote is given equal weight, and the majority rules. The principle guiding the schoolyard view is that when interests collide and yet a collective decision must be made, we should follow a procedure that affords to each actor equal input and aggregates the inputs into a collective decision. Insofar as this decision is produced by aggregating the preferences of all, it can be said to represent the majority will or common good.

Of course, the schoolyard view is too simplistic to qualify as a theory of democracy. Modern democracies are too populous, and the decisions they need to make are too complex to be captured in the schoolyard view. But once we attempt to introduce the requisite complexity, we confront a range of difficulties concerning, roughly, "how to do the relevant math" (Shapiro 2003, 10), how to aggregate inputs so that the result could be regarded as an expression of a popular will. Famous results associated with the social choice theorist Kenneth Arrow (1950) show that there is no way to transform expressions of individual preference into a rational collective decision that could plausibly claim to represent the popular will.[1]

From these developments, many concluded that the very idea of a popular will is nonsensical or "empty" (Riker 1982, 239). Hence, a range of *minimalist* views developed that retained the aggregative view's conception of the political agent while jettisoning the idea that collective decision should represent the popular will. One such view is the "Madisonian" view proposed by William Riker (1982).[2] Riker has it that democratic elections exist solely for the purposes of "restraining officials" (1982, 12) and enabling people to "get rid of rulers" (1982, 244) who have "offended" them (1982, 242). In Riker's view, then, democracy is "not popular rule, but rather an intermittent, sometimes random, even perverse, popular veto" (1982, 244). The closely-related *elitist* conception associated with Joseph Schumpeter (1962)—and, more recently, Richard Posner (2003)—holds that democracy is "that institutional arrangement for arriving at political decisions in which individuals acquire the power to decide by means of a competitive struggle for the peoples' vote" (Schumpeter 1962, 269). The elitist hence sees democracy as means for *producing* government by means of elections; citizens select "bosses" (1962, 269) who, in turn, must maintain a sufficient level of popularity or else face the "punishment" of losing the next election (Posner 2003, 182). A third kind of minimalist view, *interest-group pluralism*, holds with the elitist view that democracy is a market-like arrangement by which aspiring officials compete for votes (Dahl 1956, 3). The pluralist, however, introduces a view of power that is more nuanced than that of the elitist. The elitist sees political power as fundamentally residing in the offices of government; the pluralist, by contrast, sees power as distributed throughout society, especially in the various kinds of groups formed by individuals with shared interests. On the pluralist view, democracy is a constant negotiation among multiple interest groups, with competing groups exerting pressure on elected officials well beyond Election Day. The pluralist, that is, rejects the view that democracy is rule by elected elites, holding instead that democracy is rule by competing minorities (Dahl 1956, 133).

Despite their differences, the aggregative and minimalist views share an instrumentalist conception of deliberation according to which political agents act rationally when they select efficient means to their ends. Again, the instrumentalist view takes ends as given and not subject to rational evaluation, except insofar as proximate ends serve as means to more distant ones. Thus, democracy's value is instrumentalized; it is the best means for maintaining social stability amidst masses of people with conflicting interests. For the minimalist, then, the task of democratic theory is descriptive, not normative. Consequently, these views do not speak to familiar normative questions of political theory concerning the justification of democracy or the basis for the collective bindingness of democratic outcomes. Indeed, some minimalist views deny that such questions even make sense.

The normative questions that the descriptive views had abandoned were revived in light of the political and social movements of the 1960s. Must one obey racist laws? Must one risk one's life in an unjust war if drafted? Is democracy best understood as the "dictatorship of the proletariat"? Why should one submit to rulers at all? That a leading democratic theorist could assert at the time that "political apathy may reflect the health of a democracy" (Lipset 1963, 32) is indicative of one of minimalism's principal shortcomings; minimalism's strictly descriptive aspiration left it unable to speak to the political activity of the day, much of which was couched in the normative language of justice, freedom, and equality. Furthermore, the claim that minimalism was nonnormative became increasingly suspect. For the minimalists indeed adopt certain minimal normative commitments, such as that the rulers who "offend" the people do not deserve nonetheless to rule and that stability is a good. Lastly, minimalist views seem self-defeating. They ultimately rely on popular voting to select who shall become "boss" and who shall be "punished"; however, if the social choice results show that there is no "popular will," then there is no sense in which a vote could reveal popular dissatisfaction with a given official or policy. Put otherwise, if the social choice results are taken to show that the aspiration to discern a "popular will" and "common good" by means of the aggregation of individual votes is nonsense, then the idea that voting expresses a meaningful "veto" must also be discarded (Coleman and Ferejohn 1986; Cohen 1986, 30; Miller 1992).

These dissatisfactions led in the 1970s and 1980s to a resurgence of normative democratic theory, at first in the form of *participatory democracy* (Pateman 1970; Macpherson 1977; Mansbridge 1983; Barber 1984) and then later as *deliberative democracy*. Both of these developments can be seen as extensions of the more general revival of normative theory that was stimulated in large part by John Rawls's *A Theory of Justice* (1971), although I cannot rehearse this story here.[3] Although there is much to say about participatory democracy, the remainder of this essay will focus on deliberative democracy.

3. Deliberation in Deliberative Democracy

Beginning in the 1980s, democratic theory took what is aptly characterized as a "deliberative turn" (Dryzek 2000, 1; Goodin 2008, 2). At present, there is a wide variety of views that claim the label *deliberative democracy*, and almost all conceptions of democracy in currency involve some aspect of deliberation.[4] Although the term may suggest that nondeliberativist views do not employ a conception of deliberation, this is not correct. The difference between deliberative conceptions of democracy and their nondeliberativist counterparts is not that the former embrace, while the latter reject, the idea that deliberation is central to democratic politics (cf. Freeman 2000, 377); rather, the difference lies in their respective conceptions of deliberation and, hence, of rational political agency.[5]

One of the defining commitments of deliberative democracy is the idea that in deliberation, one's aims can be rationally transformed (Elster 1997, 11). The contrast with instrumentalism is instructive. Instrumentalists hold that deliberation always proceeds against the backdrop of a fixed conception of our ends; deliberation is not supposed to result in their *revision*. In fact, instrumentalism contends that a change in ends is never the result of a rational process because reason cannot evaluate ends; an act of deliberation that results in a change of ends is an act of deliberation gone awry. Deliberative democrats reject this picture. On their view, deliberation makes possible a rationally broadened sense of one's ends, a more coherent picture of one's preferences, and an enhanced sense of the public good (Manin 1987, 351; Cohen 2009, 26). Some claim that deliberative democrats hold that it is the *aim* of deliberation to effect such changes of interest and preference (Elster 1997, 10; Przeworski 1998, 140; Stokes 1998, 123); however, most deliberativists wisely deny this, arguing instead for the weaker view that deliberation requires an *openness* to such changes but does not aim at them (Cohen 2009, 333–34; Gutmann and Thompson 2004, 20).[6]

That properly conducted deliberation could have this effect is explained by a related contrast between deliberativists and instrumentalists. Instrumentalists tend to see deliberation as primarily *individual* or internal to the agent. To be clear, the instrumentalist could allow that under certain conditions it would be prudent for deliberators to consult with others; such engagements might be necessary to gather pertinent facts or establish terms of cooperation. But the instrumentalist holds that there is nothing *intrinsic* to deliberation that requires the input of others. By contrast, deliberative democrats employ a conception of deliberation that is *interpersonal* and *dialogical* (Bohman 1996, 27) or "external-collective" (Goodin 2000, 81). On the deliberativist view, deliberation involves the *exchange of reasons* rather than merely the sharing of information or the expression of opinions (Gutmann and Thompson 2004, 3). Similarly, *exchanging* reasons amounts to more than simply announcing or asserting one's reasons; exchanging reasons involves engaging in reasoned discussion with others who may raise objections, criticisms, questions, and challenges to one's reasons, in addition to advancing their own reasons. This is not to say that deliberativists must deny the internal and self-reflective aspects of deliberation[7]; rather, for the deliberative democrat, deliberation must always involve some degree of engagement with others. Hence, deliberation is a process in which one's antecedent aims and objectives could change as new information and reasons are considered.[8]

This dialogical feature of deliberation brings into view a further crucial element of deliberativism. As deliberation is in the first instance an affair of reasoning together, it involves a *justificatory* element. As a process of exchanging reasons, deliberation is aimed at providing *justification* for political proposals; the task of deliberation is to articulate and examine *reasons why* some given proposal or course of action should be favored. Hence, insofar as persuasion or agreement is an aim at all, it must always be understood as *rational* persuasion or agreement *for the right reasons*. In Jürgen Habermas's oft-quoted phrase, the only force that operates in deliberation is "the unforced force of the better argument" (1998, 306). Accordingly, deliberative democrats draw a sharp distinction between deliberation and strategic behavior, such as bargaining. According to the deliberativists, bargaining might be useful in securing compliance, but, as it does not aim at justification, it is not deliberation.

The combination of the interpersonal and justificatory features of deliberation introduces constraints on *what can count* as a reason in deliberation. Because the aim of deliberation is ultimately to reason together with a view toward justifying political proposals, deliberation requires actors to advance considerations *that could be recognized by others as reasons* (Cohen 2009, 224; Freeman 2000, 379). To say simply "I prefer option P" is not to provide a reason in favor of P, nor does saying "I do not want P" count as a reason against P; indeed, Habermas and others influenced by him have argued that there is something performatively contradictory about assertions of this kind in a deliberative context (Habermas 1990, 88–89; Benhabib 1996, 71–72; Elster 1997, 12).[9] According to the deliberative democrat, deliberation is not simply a matter of expressing or revealing one's preferences, nor is it merely a matter of discussing with others why one holds the views one holds; it is rather the attempt to determine with others what we have reason to do, and this requires that deliberators trade in considerations that are accessible to others as reasons (Gutmann and Thompson 2004, 4), or reason "from the standpoint of all involved" (Benhabib 1996, 72). Thus, the reasoning involved in deliberation has a distinctively *public* component. In addition to being an interpersonal exchange of reasons, it also involves an attempt to *reason together* by means of considerations which could be shared.[10] In this sense, deliberation is said to be focused on the common good rather than the private advantage of individual citizens.

To summarize, deliberative democrats advance a conception of deliberation which is (a) noninstrumentalist, (b) interpersonal, (c) justificatory, and (d) public. But how does this conception of deliberation figure into a conception of democracy? We turn now to three broad styles of deliberative democratic theory.

4. Three Styles of Deliberative Democracy

All versions of deliberative democracy hold that deliberation contributes to democratic legitimacy, that deliberation is a central element of the collective bindingness of democratic decisions (Cohen 2009, 21; Benhabib 1996, 69; Gutmann and Thompson 2004, 10; Dryzek 2000, 1). Unsurprisingly, this core commitment is interpreted differently among deliberative theorists, depending on their more general orientation within democratic theory. One way to get a handle on the various versions of deliberative democracy, then, is to categorize them according to the three broad programs within contemporary democratic theory: liberalism, civic republicanism, and radical democracy.[11] It should be stressed that these categories are loose and nonexclusive.[12] They should be taken as different *approaches*; the point is to convey the flavor of the views in currency.

Liberal deliberativism follows principally from the later work of John Rawls (2005), and among its main exponents are Joshua Cohen (2009) and Amy Gutmann and Dennis Thompson (1996, 2004). As it is a variety of liberal democratic theory, liberal deliberativism shares with nondeliberative liberal views the idea that a liberal society is a "fair system of cooperation among free and equal citizens" (Rawls 2005, 22). Given this, a question arises about how the exercise of political power could be legitimate. To explain: As the individual liberties secured in modern liberal societies result in a *pluralism* of moral doctrines and conceptions of the good life, citizens will often disagree deeply about how the state should act. Consequently, when the state enacts laws and policies, some will be forced to do what they would not otherwise do (indeed, some will be forced to do what they want not to do). How could coercion be consistent with the freedom and equality of each? Democracy is believed to provide the solution. The coercion of some by others can be consistent with a due recognition of the freedom and equality of all, provided that the coercion in question is the result of a system of collective decision which treats all as equals. Prior to the deliberative turn, liberal views tended to regard free and open elections in which each citizen was afforded exactly one vote as such a system. The bindingness of democratic outcomes was taken to derive from the fact that the democratic system gives each person bound by its outcomes *equal input* into the decision process. By giving each citizen equal input, the process accords to each *equal consideration*. Hence, "one man, one vote" suffices for collectively binding decisions.

According to liberal deliberativists, legitimacy "requires more than that the interest of all be given equal consideration in binding collective decisions" (Cohen 2009, 243). To be sure, it is not that liberal deliberativitsts deny that collective decisions must be reached by processes that respect the equality of all citizens; rather, their view is that "one man, one vote" elections are insufficient for respecting equality. For example, the equality ensured by "one man, one vote" is compatible with vast inequalities of social influence, opportunity, and privilege (Gutmann and Thompson 2004, 16). According to the liberal deliberativist, since deliberation involves the attempt to justify coercion to those who must endure it (Gutmann and Thompson 2004, 4), it is by deliberating together that citizens treat each other as equals (Cohen 2009, 224). To satisfy the requirement of treating all citizens as equals, democratic decisions must be in some way sensitive to the reasons citizens can advance in support of their favored policies. Accordingly, decision making must be preceded by episodes of open and inclusive public deliberation in which citizens attempt to justify to each other, by means of reasons accessible to all, their views concerning how political power should be exercised. In this way, those whose views lose out can still affirm the legitimacy of the outcome, because it was produced in a way that was receptive to their reasons.[13]

Of course, liberal deliberativists often propose this model of deliberative legitimation as an *ideal* of democratic politics. Cohen holds that democratic decisions are legitimate insofar as they would have been the outcome of an ideal deliberation among citizens; hence, actual democratic politics should "mirror" ideal deliberation "as far as possible" (2009, 23). This means that democratic governments must seek to "facilitate" and sustain "favorable conditions" for public deliberation among citizens (Cohen 2009, 224). Gutmann and Thompson claim that it is a "requirement" for legitimacy that "citizens or their representatives actually seek to give one another mutually acceptable reasons to justify the laws they adopt" (2004, 100). Some champion ambitious reconstructions of democracy, envisioning new institutions which aim to realize the deliberative ideal. Bruce Ackerman and James Fishkin (2003) propose a new national holiday for carefully structured nationwide deliberation events and "deliberative polls" designed to reveal how a well-informed populace would vote on a given issue (Fishkin 1997); others call for the formation of a fourth, "deliberative" branch of government (Leib 2004).

Although civic republicanism has its roots ultimately in premodern sources, contemporary civic republican deliberativists frequently draw inspiration from Rousseau, John Dewey, and Hannah Arendt.[14] At the core of civic republicanism is the view that political liberty consists in being a citizen in a self-governing community (Habermas 1996, 22). There are debates among civic republicans concerning what this commitment amounts to,[15] and not all republicans embrace deliberative democracy. Rather than review this material here, I will focus on Philip Pettit's (1995, 2003) deliberativist gloss on this fundamental republican commitment. According to Pettit, citizens are free when they are not *dominated*, that is, subject to arbitrary interference from others (2003, 152).[16] From this, the problem arises of how citizens can ward off the domination of the state. The state is, after all, a necessarily powerful entity that is charged with interfering with its citizens. How can its interference be kept nonarbitrary?

Note the difference between the civic republican problematic and the liberal one previously described. The republican question is not how political coercion could be made consistent with treating citizens as equals; it is rather how the exercise of the state's coercive power could be made consistent with the liberty of the citizens. Put differently, the liberal sees legitimate state actions as *justified* reductions of individual liberty; the civic republican holds, by contrast, that the interference of the state is not liberty-reducing when it is nonarbitrary, that is, forced to track the "avowed or avowable" interests of the citizens (Pettit 2003, 152) and thus the "public good" (Sunstein 1993, 26).

According to Pettit (2003), the key to effectively constraining the state is popular contestation. This requires political conditions in which citizens "have access to the reasons" which drive state action, and can reasonably "expect to be heard" when they advance objections to those reasons (Pettit 2003, 152). Republican liberty thus requires deliberative democracy. Pettit calls this the "contestability argument" for deliberative democracy (2003, 153). As Pettit notes, this argument dovetails nicely with considerations advanced by fellow republican, Cass Sunstein, who in a long list of related publications, has proposed the view that the U.S. Constitution "was designed to create a deliberative democracy" (1993, 19), a "republic of reasons" (1993, 20). According to Sunstein, democratic government acts legitimately when it can offer reasons "that can be intelligible to different people operating from different premises" (1993, 24), and thus be held publicly accountable.

An interesting further contrast between the republican and liberal deliberativists emerges. Whereas liberal deliberativists tend to see deliberation as providing indispensible *input* into democratic decision-making processes, the republicans focus on the contestability of decisions that have already been made. Simplifying a bit, we could say that for liberal deliberativists, the legitimacy of a democratic outcome resides in the past; it is a matter of how the decision came to be and whether that process was sufficiently deliberative. Republican views, by contrast, seem to hold that the legitimacy of a democratic decision lies in its ability to survive the scrutiny of citizens *after* its enactment; the question for the republican, especially those in Pettit's mode, is whether a given decision represents *arbitrary* interference. As we have seen, state interference is arbitrary on Pettit's view when it does not track the avowable interests of the citizens. This "tracking" element of the republican view seems to render republican deliberativism inherently consequentialist in its view of the legitimacy of state action; liberal views, by contrast, tend to reject this kind of consequentialism in that they locate the legitimation of collective decisions in the deliberative processes that occur *prior* to the decision process.

Thus far we have examined the ways in which deliberation has been incorporated into liberal and civic republican conceptions of democracy. But there is a range of views that sees deliberative democracy as an *alternative* to liberal and civic republican democratic theory, rather than a supplement to them. I gather these views under the category of *radical democracy*, although the label is admittedly somewhat artificial.

Drawing often from varied sources in critical theory, feminist philosophy, and environmentalism, radical democratic deliberativists often begin from a critique of both liberal and civic republican views. The critique begins with the charge that liberal and republican versions of deliberative democracy are focused exclusively on the state and its actions, and consequently can operate "only on the surface of the political economy" (Dryzek 2000, 21). On radical views, the state and its apparatus are not the main sites of democratic politics; democracy resides primarily in *civil society* or the *public sphere*, arenas of citizen interactions outside of the state (Behnabib 1996, 75; Habermas 1996, 26). The radical democrats' objection is that liberal and republican views are unfit to address concerns regarding the ideological, economic, and structural inequalities that flourish in the public sphere of contemporary democratic societies (Benhabib 1996, 75); continuing, they charge that encouraging public deliberation under such conditions tends simply to further entrench the status quo and provide further advantage to agents who are already disproportionately powerful (Young 2001, 670). This general line of criticism encourages a closely related charge that, by focusing on the state, liberal, and republican views abandon the aim of democratizing civil society, including especially the workplace and economic relations more generally (Dryzek 2000, 27).[17]

One way to capture the contrast between radical democratic deliberativism on the one hand and liberal and civic republican deliberativisms on the other is to say that the latter views appeal to deliberation for the purposes of legitimating state coercion and reaching consensus on state policy, whereas the former appeals to deliberation as a way of rendering society more *authentically* democratic (Dryzek 2000, 29). The authenticity of a democracy is measured by the degree to which the collective institutions of society are controlled by "autonomous and competent actors" (Dryzek 2000, 29), who are actively engaged in various forms of social "critique" of (Benhabib 1996, 87) and "struggle" (Young 2000, 50) against the status quo. Yet the aim of such activity is not the establishment of a new, perhaps more inclusive and just status quo but rather the continuation of the struggle by means of "democratic iterations," acts of challenge, resistance, criticism, and defiance designed to disrupt and transform the status quo (Benhabib 2006, 48). In this way, radical democratic deliberativists are often closely allied with post-Marxist agonists such as Chantal Mouffe, who see democratic politics as perpetual agitation and dissent against the very aspiration of reaching a reasoned consensus about the terms of political association (Mouffe 1996, 254ff; cf. Mouffe 2000, ch. 4). Consequently, radical democratic deliberativism often joins with various modes of political activism (Young 2001), green political theory (Dryzek 2005), and global democracy (Benhabib 2006; Bohman 2007).

Once again, these are only rough sketches of types of deliberative democratic theory. Within each category, there are many variants. However, these glosses are sufficient to help us to organize the variety of deliberativist views.

5. Looking Ahead: The Epistemology of Deliberative Democracy

To conclude, I return to the conception of deliberation at work in deliberative democratic theory. I begin by discussing a serious concern about deliberative democracy in general. I then consider two responses to this concern. This will enable us to take up broader questions concerning the epistemic dimension of deliberation and eventually to identify key issues that have not been given sufficient attention in the deliberativist literature as yet.

In any of its versions, deliberative democracy holds that proper democracy requires citizens to engage in collective deliberation with those with whom they disagree. This component of deliberative democracy raises concerns regarding the social dynamics of face-to-face disagreement. In a widely discussed essay, Lynn Sanders argues that, even though deliberative democrats frequently punctuate the need for deliberation to be inclusive, egalitarian, and respectful, evidence from actual deliberative forums—such as juries—shows that the same patterns of gender and racial privilege that prevail in the broader society tend to replicate themselves in the deliberative contexts (1997, 370).

Sanders notes, for example, the "basic finding" of multiple studies that in jury deliberations, "men talk more" and are more likely to be selected to lead juries; moreover, in interracial deliberative groups, the contributions of white men tend to be more influential (1997, 363). This is explained in large part by the fact that deliberation is "a certain kind of talk" that naturally puts a premium on speakers' rhetorical prowess, including the ability to speak in ways that seem calm, collected, reasonable, eloquent, and authoritative, characteristics culturally associated with being white and male (Sanders 1997, 370). The challenge, then, is that deliberative democracy prizes modes of social engagement that tend to systematically disenfranchise, exclude, or disadvantage persons of color, women, immigrants, the uneducated, the poor, and the working class. Deliberative democracy, the challenge runs, is simply the rule of political elites, because deliberation as understood by most deliberative democrats is the activity of political elites (Young 2001, 677).

To meet this challenge, some deliberativists have proposed broadened conceptions of deliberation that include modes of communication that do not focus on reason giving. Iris Young has moved the furthest in this direction; she contends that properly democratic communication aims primarily at "understanding" across differences of gender, class, race, and ethnicity rather than the justification of coercion (1996, 127). Accordingly, Young proposes a model of deliberation in which reason giving is joined by greeting, rhetoric, and storytelling (Young 1996, 129ff; 2000, ch. 2); she also holds that democratic deliberation must be understood to include acts that are "rowdy" and "disorderly" such as "street demonstrations and sit-ins, musical works and cartoons" (Young 2001, 688). She contends that a model of deliberation which includes these nonrational styles of communication is necessary to counteract exclusionary deliberative norms.

There are several difficulties with Young's proposal. First among these is that Young provides no reason for thinking that her additional components of deliberation—greeting, rhetoric, and storytelling—are free from the distorting influences of social privilege. Why should we think that Young's broadened conception of deliberation is any less prone to distortion than the more usual conceptions? Indeed, it seems likely that the same hierarchies will surface once reason giving is supplemented with nonrational modes of communication (Dryzek 2000, 67). But more important, the introduction of nonrational elements into the conception of deliberation threatens to dissolve the deliberativist view of deliberation into the instrumentalist view. Consider: As described by Young, storytelling, rhetoric, and greeting do not advance claims but rather "embody," "reveal," and "exhibit" (1996, 131ff) the perspectives and values of speakers. Young claims that these modes of disclosure are necessary, because "values ... often cannot be justified through argument" (1996, 131). This invokes an image of the citizen employed in the various minimalist views of democracy discussed above. Moreover, by introducing nonrational components into her conception of deliberation, Young dilutes the justificatory function of deliberation. When deliberation consists in part of communicative acts that do not advance reasons but reveal facts about the identities and experiences of speakers, it can no longer been seen as aiming at justifying coercion or legitimating state action. At best, storytelling can help me to understand *your* reasons for favoring some given policy option; it cannot by itself give *me* a reason. Young's expanded conception of deliberation, then, marks a departure from the public component of the deliberativist conception of deliberation as well.

Young concedes in later work that storytelling, rhetoric, and greeting may serve significant functions in helping to establish conditions favorable to mutually respectful and inclusive argument, but they cannot serve as substitutes for argument

(2000, 79). Yet if she holds that storytelling, rhetoric, and greeting are *supplements* to deliberation rather than deliberation itself, Young proposes nothing that deliberative democrats deny (Dryzek 2000, 68). More important, if Young is offering only a suggestion about ways in which deliberation could be enabled by these measures, she has not addressed the concern prompted by Sanders. Even when aided by the kinds of nonrational communication Young identifies, deliberation is still focused on reason giving, and, if Sanders is correct, deliberation is subject to systematic distortions. The lesson, then, is that deliberative democracy is still in need of a theory of political action, especially in real-world contexts in which the deliberativist ideal of egalitarian, respectful, and inclusive public reasoning will never be realized.

A different way forward has been suggested by David Estlund. Estlund begins by noting that the deliberativist image of free reason exchanging among equals includes norms of calmness, orderliness, and, in a word, civility because the point of deliberation is to block "power's interference with reason" (2008, 193). Accordingly, the idea of civil collective reasoning can be upheld as an *ideal* without being taken as a prescription for how citizens must act in real-world contexts where power does indeed interfere with reason. To explain: Estlund holds that as an *ideal* the deliberativist image of civil collective reasoning can be used to identify "breakdowns" in real-world contexts (2008, 200). After all, it is precisely by reference to such an ideal that Sanders is able to identify the ways in which real-world deliberative contexts manifest objectionable tendencies; recall that, according to Sanders, deliberative democracy is problematic because in real-world deliberative contexts (such as juries), forms of social power prevail over reason. However, in real-world contexts, where power is unequally distributed and allowed influence in deliberative contexts, the deliberativists' ideal of civility proposes inappropriate constraints on political action. Put otherwise, deliberativists propose the norms of civility because they are concerned with blocking power's interference with reason; so in contexts where power does interfere with reason, those norms are canceled.

This does not mean, however, that in real-world contexts, anything goes (Estlund 2008, 192). Rather, Estlund argues that in real-world contexts, a more permissive set of norms prevails; more specifically, real-world deliberation will often permit exercises of "countervailing power" designed to "remedy epistemic distortion wrought by the initial insertion of power" (2008, 193–94). These norms may allow "sharp, disruptive, and even suppressive" tactics (2008, 185), including "conscientious suppression of an overrepresented message . . . or the introduction, through sharp transgressive methods, of an underrepresented message" (2008, 194). It seems that these more permissive norms would also allow the various forms of political activism and public protest identified by Young (2001). Deliberative democracy hence can sustain its commitment to civil argumentation among free and equal citizens while recognizing the need in certain contexts for modes of political action that are disruptive and unruly; we need not abandon or reject the deliberative ideal to accommodate the concerns identified by Sanders.

It is worth emphasizing that, in Estlund's view, the more permissive real-world norms are justified by the same desideratum that gives rise to the ideal norm of civility, namely, that collective decision should be driven by reason and not power. The exercise of "countervailing power" in the real-world context, then, is understood as "remedial" (2008, 194), that is, aimed at counteracting the effects of the initial power's interference with reason (2008, 200). Yet the point is not simply to fight fire with fire but rather to use countervailing power in the service of the deliberative ideal, to help neutralize the epistemic distortions introduced into the deliberative situation by the original exercise of power.

That Estlund should propose this kind of view is unsurprising, given that he holds that the bindingness of democratic outcomes is due to the fact that deliberative democratic processes are epistemically best—most likely to produce correct results—among the morally permissible options for collective decision. To be sure, not all deliberativists share this strongly epistemic orientation, and many resist the idea that the bindingness of democratic outcomes is partly due to their epistemic merits. Nonetheless, nearly all deliberativists make some appeal to the epistemic benefits of deliberation. Deliberation is said to make collective decisions more "justifiable" (Gutmann and Thompson 2004, 21), "rational" (Benhabib 1996, 71; Dryzek 2000, 174), "wise" (Young 2000, 30), and "intelligent" (Anderson 2006, 13), and some argue for deliberative democracy on the broader grounds that it is the political instantiation of the epistemic norms that should govern our cognitive lives as such.[18]

But once it is admitted that democratic deliberation has among its aims the improvement of collective decisions, we must introduce additional epistemic elements into the deliberativist conception of deliberation.[19] For example, if deliberation involves the collective weighing of reasons for a collective decision, it necessarily invokes distinctions between *good*, *bad*, *sufficient*, and *insufficient* reasons; pooling these together, we may speak of the *epistemic merits* of the reasons offered in support of a decision. The deliberativist must hold that it is not enough for citizens to offer reasons *of the right kind* for their views; the reasons they offer must have, or at least be plausibly held to have, the right relation to the facts.

To put the matter differently, reasons offered for a given policy could satisfy the justificatory and publicity requirements as previously identified and yet be defective epistemically and thus likely to frustrate the project of producing better outcomes. Now, the most obvious way in which a reason could be defective is that its force is dependent on factual claims that are known to be false; another way would be for the force of the reason to be dependent on factual claims for which there is insufficient justification. It seems, then, that deliberativists need to introduce considerations about the *quality* of the reasons raised in deliberation—the strength of the evidence offered, the degree of epistemic justification speakers have in advancing their reasons, the truth of the factual claims referenced by the reasons, and so on. But this means that proper democratic deliberation proceeds not simply by reasons that are *acceptable* to all; the reasons must also be of a certain epistemic quality. And this suggests that the deliberators must be able to *evaluate* the epistemic merits of reasons advanced in deliberation. Moreover, deliberators must be able to draw proper inferences from the good reasons, avoid fallacies, correct for cognitive biases, and so on. To do these things, they must possess certain epistemic capacities or embody certain cognitive virtues (Talisse 2009, ch. 5). It seems, then, that deliberative democracy makes some pretty strong epistemic demands on citizens.

Despite the fact that there has been a lot of work focused on the practical tasks of implementing deliberative democracy, there has been relatively little attention paid to the epistemological issues that the deliberativist program raises. Perhaps this is due to the fact that when we turn to the empirical literature regarding the public's epistemic abilities, things begin to look bleak. This literature reveals that the average democratic citizen knows little about even the basic workings of government, misunderstands the division of powers among the different branches of government, has implausible views about the major policy decisions presently facing the country, and is subject to the full range of cognitive biases. As one may expect, deliberative groups consisting of average citizens are, epistemically, a mixed-bag.

This has led some to argue that deliberative democracy is a mere "pipe dream, barely worth the attention of a serious person" (Posner 2003, 163). But, as I have argued elsewhere (Talisse 2005, 2007, 2009, ch. 5), the inference from public ignorance to the rejection of deliberative democracy is too hasty because the public ignorance literature is generally insensitive to the fundamental distinction between truth and justification, and so treats all false belief as ignorance, and ignorance as a univocal phenomenon. As a moment's reflection will reveal, sometimes one is justified in holding a false belief, just as sometimes one can believe what is true for bad reasons; moreover, not all instances of false belief are instances of ignorance, and sometimes true belief is consistent with being ignorant.

Of course, the fact that the public ignorance data rely on coarse epistemic categories does not by itself vindicate deliberative democracy; all that follows is that the public ignorance critique is not sufficient to defeat deliberative democracy. Whether the epistemic burdens deliberativism places on citizens are overly demanding is still a concern. But what counts in addressing this concern is not the number of false beliefs the average citizen has about politics but the ways in which average citizens form and revise their beliefs given the information they have. In addressing this issue, deliberative democrats would do well to attend to recent work by social epistemologists examining the ways in which information is distributed and disseminated, how reliable epistemic institutions function, and how epistemic authority is conferred.[20] Closely related discussions in informal logic concerning the dynamics of real-world argumentation are also highly relevant, as are studies by cognitive psychologists of belief formation and revision in individuals and groups. Armed with conceptual tools gleaned from these areas, deliberative democrats would be well placed not only to address concerns about public ignorance and epistemic demandingness but also to devise critiques of our existing social epistemic practices, institutions, and norms.

In our present era of rapidly advancing communication technology, democracy has become more self-consciously epistemic. News outlets tout their epistemic reliability ("the no spine zone"), blogs fact-check and instantly reveal inconsistencies in statements made by political figures, popular political commentary claims to expose "lying liars" and "idiots," politicians engage in "straight talk," and political activists speak truth to power. If, as the deliberativists contend, democracy involves the exchange of *reasons*, rather than, say, *slogans* or *insults*, then it is irreducibly epistemic. Consequently, engagement between democratic theory and broader epistemological issues seems unavoidable. Yet, with a few notable exceptions (Gaus 1996; Sunstein 2006; Estlund 2008; Goodin 2008), deliberative democrats have not attended in a systematic way to the epistemology of deliberation. This, it seems to me, is the crucial next step that deliberative democrats must take.

NOTES

1. See also Downs 1957.
2. Riker most often uses the term *liberalism* to describe his view. But his use of the term is idiosyncratic, and I use *liberalism* in the following discussion in its standard sense. Thus, I describe his view as "Madisonian," as Riker sometimes does (1982, 9).
3. See the entries in this volume on Rawls and on Democracy. See also the essays collected in Freeman (2002).
4. Joseph Bessette (1980) is often credited with coining the term *deliberative democracy*. For a sense of the variety of views, see the essays collected in Bohman and Rehg (1997), Elster (1998), and Fishkin and Laslett (2003). See Bohman (1998) and Freeman (2000) for helpful if somewhat dated surveys of the literature.
5. Hence, Shapiro notes, "Underlying the normative literature on democracy is a series of debates about rationality" (2003, 10). See also Rawls (2005, 448), who states, "The definitive idea of deliberative democracy is the idea of deliberation itself."
6. Dryzek seems to modulate between the two views, claiming at one point that the "defining feature" of deliberative democracy is that "individuals that are participating in democratic processes are amenable to changing their minds and their preference as a result of reflection induced by deliberation" (2000, 31), but elsewhere he asserts that deliberative democracy's "defining feature" is "preference change through deliberation" (2000, 32). Benhabib suggests a still stronger view: "The formation of coherent preferences cannot precede deliberation; it can only succeed it" (1996, 71). See Rostboll (2008, ch. 2) for helpful discussion of this issue.
7. For example, Robert Goodin (2000) promotes a deliberativist view that emphasizes the role of internal reflection.
8. See Cohen (2009, 237–40) for elaboration.
9. Note the contrast with instrumentalism, where wanting P is most surely a reason for P, and wanting P, *all things considered*, is a *decisive* reason in favor of P.
10. According to some, the publicity of deliberation entails that citizens must refrain from invoking reasons that derive from or presuppose moral or religious commitments that others are free to reject (Rawls 2005, Part 4; Cohen 2009, 232ff); others see deliberation as requiring the introduction of sectarian moral commitments (Gutmann and Thompson 2004, ch. 2). This has led to an extensive literature concerning the position of religious citizens in deliberative democracy and whether religious reasons are welcome in public discussion. I cannot review this debate here, but see Audi and Wolterstorff (1996) and Eberle (2002).
11. I follow the rough categorization offered in Habermas (1996).

12. For example, Cohen's view is clearly liberal in the sense described below, but Cohen sees himself—rightly, in my view—as drawing on certain elements of radical democracy (2009, 326ff)

13. A fascinating liberal alternative called *epistemic proceduralism* has been developed by David Estlund. Estlund argues that the bindingness of democratic decisions derives in part from the epistemic merits of the process which produces them. I'll have occasion to say a little but more about this view in the following discussion. The view is intricately laid out in Estlund (2008).

14. See Skinner (1998) for a discussion of the premodern sources of current civic republicanism.

15. Some go so far as to hold that the actual *exercise* of citizenship—and not simply having the *status* of being a citizen—is intrinsic to freedom and, indeed, to the good life as such (Sandel 1998, 325).

16. Pettit's nondomination conception of freedom is supposed to occupy the middle ground between negative (freedom as noninterference) and positive (freedom as self-mastery) views of freedom, holding that freedom consists in the absence of mastery by others. The merits of his view cannot be examined here. See Pettit (1995) for a full elaboration.

17. But see Pettit (2003, 153).

18. Hence, Misak states, "Deliberative democracy in political philosophy is the right view, because deliberative democracy in epistemology is the right view" (2004, 15). See also Talisse (2009).

19. Cohen (2009, ch. 11) argues, compellingly in my view, that the very concept of deliberation requires the introduction of a conception of truth.

20. Goldman (1999) and Sunstein (2006) are especially instructive.

REFERENCES

Ackerman, Bruce, and James Fishkin. 2003. "Deliberation Day." In *Debating Deliberative Democracy*. Edited by James Fishkin and Peter Laslett. Oxford: Blackwell.
Anderson, Elizabeth. 2006. "The Epistemology of Democracy." *Episteme* 3: 9–23.
Anscombe, G. E. M. 1957. "Intention." *Proceedings of the Aristotelian Society*, New Series 57: 321–32.
Arrow, Kenneth. 1950. "A Difficulty in Social Welfare." *Journal of Political Economy* 68: 328–46.
Audi, Robert, and Nicholas Wolterstorff. 1996. *Religion in the Public Square*. Lanham, MD: Rowman & Littlefield.
Barber, Benjamin. 1984. *Strong Democracy*. Berkeley: University of California Press.
Benhabib, Seyla. 1996. "Toward a Deliberative Model of Democratic Legitimacy." In *Democracy and Difference*. Edited by Seyla Benhabib. Princeton, NJ: Princeton University Press.
Benhabib, Seyla. 2006. *Another Cosmopolitanism*. New York: Oxford University Press.
Bessette, Joseph. 1980. "Deliberative Democracy: The Majority Principle in Republican Government." In *How Democractic Is the Constitution?* Washington, DC: AEI Press.
Bobbio, Norberto. 1984. *The Future of Democracy*. Minneapolis: University of Minnesota Press.
Bohman, James. 1996. *Public Deliberation*. Cambridge, MA: MIT Press.

Bohman, James. 1998. "The Coming of Age of Deliberative Democracy." *Journal of Political Philosophy* 4: 418–43.
Bohman, James. 2007. *Democracy across Borders*. Cambridge, MA: MIT Press.
Bohman, James, and William Rehg, eds. 1997. *Deliberative Democracy*. Cambridge, MA: MIT Press.
Cohen, Joshua. 1986. "An Epistemic Conception of Democracy." *Ethics* 97: 26–38.
Cohen, Joshua. 2009. *Philosophy, Politics, Democracy*. Cambridge, MA: Harvard University Press.
Coleman, J., and J. Ferejohn. 1996. "Democracy and Social Choice." *Ethics* 97: 6–25.
Dahl, Robert. 1956. *A Preface to Democratic Theory*. Chicago: University of Chicago Press.
Downs, Anthony. 1957. *An Economic Theory of Democracy*. New York: Harper Books.
Dryzek, John. 2000. *Deliberative Democracy and Beyond*. New York: Oxford University Press.
Dryzek, John. 2005. *The Politics of the Earth*. New York: Oxford University Press.
Eberle, Christopher. 2002. *Religious Conviction in Liberal Politics*. Cambridge, UK: Cambridge University Press.
Elster, Jon, 1997. "The Market and the Forum." In *Deliberative Democracy*. Edited by James Bohman and William Rehg. Cambridge, MA: MIT Press.
Elster, Jon, ed. 1998. *Deliberative Democracy*. Cambridge, UK: Cambridge University Press.
Estlund, David. 2008. *Democratic Authority*. Princeton, NJ: Princeton University Press.
Fishkin, James. 1997. *The Voice of the People*. New Haven, CT: Yale University Press.
Fishkin, James, and Peter Laslett, eds. 2003. *Debating Deliberative Democracy*. Oxford: Blackwell.
Freeman, Samuel. 2000. "Deliberative Democracy: A Sympathetic Comment." *Philosophy & Public Affairs* 29: 371–418.
Freeman, Samuel, ed. 2002. *The Cambridge Companion to Rawls*. Cambridge, UK: Cambridge University Press.
Gaus, Gerald. 1996. *Justificatory Liberalism*. New York: Oxford University Press.
Goldman, Alvin. 1999. *Knowledge in a Social World*. New York: Oxford University Press.
Goodin, Robert. 2000. "Democratic Deliberation Within." *Philosophy & Public Affairs* 29: 81–109.
Goodin, Robert. 2008. *Innovating Democracy*. New York: Oxford University Press.
Gutmann, Amy, and Dennis Thompson. 1996. *Democracy and Deliberation*. Cambridge, MA: Harvard University Press.
Gutmann, Amy, and Dennis Thompson. 2004. *Why Deliberative Democracy?* Princeton, NJ: Princeton University Press.
Habermas, Jürgen. 1990. "Discourse Ethics." In *Moral Consciousness and Communicative Action*. Cambridge, MA: MIT Press.
Habermas, Jürgen. 1996. "Three Normative Models of Democracy." In *Democracy and Difference*. Edited by Seyla Benhabib. Princeton, NJ: Princeton University Press.
Habermas, Jürgen. 1998. *Between Facts and Norms*. Cambridge, MA: MIT Press.
Korsgaard, Christine. 2008. *The Constitution of Agency*. New York: Oxford University Press.
Leib, Ethan J. 2004. *Deliberative Democracy in America*. College Park, PA: Penn State University Press.
Lipset, S. M. 1963. *Political Man*. New York: Doubleday.
Macpherson, C. B. 1977. *The Life and Times of Liberal Democracy*. New York: Oxford University Press.
Manin, Bernard. 1987. "On Legitimacy and Political Deliberation." *Political Theory* 15:338–68.
Mansbridge, Jane. 1983. *Beyond Adversary Democracy*. Chicago: University of Chicago Press.

Miller, David. 1992. "Deliberative Democracy and Social Choice." *Political Studies* 40:54–67.
Milligram, Elijah. 1997. *Practical Induction*. Cambridge, MA: Harvard University Press.
Misak, Cheryl. 2004. "Making Disagreement Matter." *Journal of Speculative Philosophy*. 18(1): 9–22.
Mouffe, Chantal. 1996. "Democracy, Power, and 'The Political.'" In *Democracy and Difference*. Edited by Seyla Benhabib. Princeton, NJ: Princeton University Press.
Mouffe, Chantal. 2000. *The Democratic Paradox*. New York: Verso.
Pateman, Carol. 1970. *Participation and Democratic Theory*. Cambridge, UK: Cambridge University Press.
Pettit, Philip. 1995. *Republicanism*. New York: Oxford University Press.
Pettit, Philip. 2003. "Deliberative Democracy, the Discursive Dilemma, and Republican Theory." In *Debating Deliberative Democracy*. Edited by James Fishkin and Peter Laslett. Oxford: Blackwell.
Platts, M. 1979. *Ways of Meaning*. London: Routledge and Kegan Paul.
Posner, Richard. 2003. *Law, Pragmatism, and Democracy*. Cambridge, MA: Harvard University Press.
Przeworski, Adam. 1998. "Deliberation and Ideological Domination." In *Deliberative Democracy*. Edited by Jon Elster. Cambridge, UK: Cambridge University Press.
Rawls, John. 1971. *A Theory of Justice*. Cambridge, MA: Harvard University Press.
Rawls, John. 2005. *Political Liberalism*, expanded ed. New York: Columbia University Press. (Originally published 1993)
Riker, William. 1982. *Liberalism Against Populism*. New York: W.H. Freeman and Co.
Rostboll, Christian. 2008. *Deliberative Freedom*. Albany, NY: SUNY Press.
Sandel, Michael. 1998. "A Reply to my Critics." In *Debating Democracy's Discontent*. Edited by Anita Allen and Milton Regan. New York: Oxford University Press.
Sanders, Lynn. 1997. "Against Deliberation." *Political Theory* 25: 347–77.
Schumpeter, Joseph. 1962. *Capitalism, Socialism, and Democracy*. New York: Harper Books.
Shapiro, Ian. 2003. *The State of Democratic Theory*. Princeton, NJ: Princeton University Press.
Skinner, Quentin. 1998. *Liberty before Liberalism*. Cambridge, UK: Cambridge University Press.
Stokes, Susan. 1998. "Pathologies of Deliberation." In *Deliberative Democracy*. Edited by Jon Elster. Cambridge, UK: Cambridge University Press.
Sunstein, Cass. 1993. *The Partial Constitution*. Cambridge, MA: Harvard University Press.
Sunstein, Cass. 2006. *Infotopia*. New York: Oxford University Press.
Talisse, Robert B. 2005. "Does Public Ignorance Defeat Deliberative Democracy?" *Critical Review* 16: 455–63.
Talisse, Robert B. 2007. "Democracy and Ignorance." *Critical Review* 18:453–66.
Talisse, Robert B. 2009. *Democracy and Moral Conflict*. Cambridge, UK: Cambridge University Press.
Young, Iris Marion. 1996. "Communication and the Other: Beyond Deliberative Democracy." In *Democracy and Difference*. Edited by Seyla Benhabib. Princeton, NJ: Princeton University Press.
Young, Iris Marion. 2000. *Inclusion and Democracy*. New York: Oxford University Press.
Young, Iris Marion. 2001. "Activist Challenges to Deliberative Democracy." *Political Theory* 29: 670–90.

CHAPTER 12

RELIGION AND POLITICS

ROBERT AUDI

CONTEMPORARY democratic states tend to be highly secular, even as, in some of them, religious fundamentalism is growing. Let us take a secular state to be roughly one whose legal and institutional frameworks exhibit separation between the state and the church—meaning religious institutions. Religious citizens commonly see secular states as unfriendly toward religion. An important question for this essay is how secular governments can provide for the liberty of all in a way that observes a reasonable separation of church and state and minimizes alienation of religious citizens. Achieving the optimal balance between an appropriate secularity in the state—which in practice implies governmental neutrality toward religion—requires both institutional principles, such as those appropriate to a constitution, and principles of civic virtue that apply to individual conduct. Let us start with the former.

1. SEPARATION OF CHURCH AND STATE

An appropriate church–state separation is widely and plausibly considered a protection of both religious liberty and governmental autonomy. This separation is most commonly discussed in relation to restricting governmental activity toward religion. We may also take the separation more broadly, as requiring some restriction of the activities of churches toward government. That facet of separation will also be considered. As to governmental regulation and structure, three central principles are (a) a liberty principle, which requires government to protect religious liberty; (b) an equality principle, which requires its equal treatment of different religions; and (c) a neutrality principle, which requires governmental neutrality toward religion.

The liberty principle is implicit in the standards for freedom of action, conscience, and thought essential for a sound democracy. The appropriate scope of liberty has been extensively discussed. Here I simply record sympathy with the idea, defended in Mill's *On Liberty* (1859, 9–10) and in a multitude of writings following it, that justification of restrictions of liberty must come from adequate evidence that nonrestriction will be significantly harmful. Mill had in mind harm to persons; on my view, preventing harm to property or the environment may also justify some restrictions of liberty.

There are different kinds of establishment. *Formal establishment* occurs when (as in England) there is a statutory or broadly constitutional governmental role for a particular religion. Formal establishment may simply provide for representation of a particular religion in one or more governmental institutions: No governmental powers are conferred, as opposed to, say, membership in a parliamentary body. In any case, formal establishment does not imply *doctrinal establishment*, which occurs when certain substantive religious doctrines (say, about the meaning of marriage) are given a specific legal role. Doctrinal establishment may exist in degrees: Its extent is proportional to the power of the established church and the strength of the specifically religious doctrines built into that role. If, moreover, a specific denomination is established, this represents a higher degree of establishment than where only a much wider framework, say, Christianity, is established. If, by contrast, only "civil religion" is established, the degree is lower still.[1]

Formal establishment is possible where the religious officials in question are committed to exercising governmental influence only where it meets nonreligious criteria for benefiting the populace a whole. Doctrinal establishment may imply governmental support for special privileges, such as higher educational funding, for members of the established church, but its strength varies with the doctrines, especially those constituting a moral or political view, characteristic of the established religion. Formal establishment may, but need not, carry doctrinal establishment with it. Doctrinal establishment may, depending on the religion in question, have little or no effect on governmental policy. For these reasons, it is a contingent matter whether establishment necessarily results in unjustified restrictions of liberty or is simply a matter of special representation by one segment of the population. Even merely formal establishment, however, constitutes a liability to unjustified governmental restrictions of liberty and is at least unharmonious with the equal treatment of religions—and of citizens themselves—which is an ideal of democracy.[2]

The equality principle prohibits establishment as ordinarily understood: minimally, as implying that a particular religion has state endorsement and some statutory role in determining laws or public policies. If all religions had a common element and if establishing a religion could be built solely on this element, then a *limited* kind of establishment might be possible within the constraints of equal treatment of different religious (limited partly because the common element might be major in one religion and minor in another).[3] Even such limited establishment, however, would be inconsistent with governmental adherence to the neutrality principle. The neutrality principle is not entailed by even the other two together nor clearly required by the U.S. Constitution. In political philosophy, it is also more controversial.[4] Much more could be said about each, but here a few further clarifications must suffice.

Although liberty is the default position for a liberal democracy (a kind of democracy in which, as on Mill's conception, a commitment to preservation of a kind of maximal liberty is a basic structural element), it cannot be unlimited. The limitations are determined by moral considerations such as human rights.[5] The appropriate limitations would in any case prohibit certain extreme forms of religious conduct, any kind that, like ritual human sacrifice and ceremonial mutilation of children, violates clearly reasonable standards for protection of persons. Even nonviolent wrongful treatment of women and, especially, children may be justifiably prohibited by law, as where children are forced, under religiously protected parental powers, to marry in their teens, as the State of Texas has maintained occurred in a Mormon community raided by Texas authorities in the spring of 2008.

This limitation on protection of religious liberty has many kinds of manifestations. Proper protections of religious liberty provide for great diversity in styles of life but prohibit (non-self-defensive) harms to other persons. Even restrictions of religious liberty that involve only standards of dress may be warranted. Consider how certain garments would be dangerous in a factory in which they might be caught in machinery. The questions raised recently in France concerning dress codes for students and, in Turkey, concerning the propriety of head scarves for women are different and more controversial. We can say, however, that the mere fact that a mode of dress is not a direct harm to anyone does not imply that government can have no justification for restricting it in public. The case for governmental restraint should, other things equal, be stronger in proportion to the importance of the mode of dress for the religious citizens in question.

As these points indicate, equality must be understood to allow differential treatment provided its basis is nonreligious and otherwise justified. Consider having state holidays on Christian feast days. This may, in fact, advantage Christians but may be justifiably instituted as sufficiently serving a majority of the population, although not *on the ground that* this majority is Christian. The policy might equally have benefited some other religious group. Structural bias is not entailed by differential effect. But, as the equality principle implies, minority religious groups should, at least within the limits of practicability, be given comparable leave for their religious observances, particularly in government employment.

Even religious freedom and governmental neutrality toward religion, then, *may* be limited in some ways in a morally well-grounded liberal democracy that is *appropriately* neutral in matters of religion. This point may be uncontroversial, but there is disagreement concerning the degree to which a liberal democracy may *promote* the practice of religion as such, provided it does not favor any one religion.[6] Suppose a majority of the people want national interdenominational celebrations of certain religious holidays or, say, compulsory religious education in the schools. Why is this objectionable? After all, a government might (as in some European countries) provide for religious children to be instructed only in their own denominations and by people approved by authorities in those denominations, and, for the nonreligious, governments might provide religious education that, being simply *about* religion, is essentially secular. Such curricular requirements might, however, benefit the religious, if only by promoting understanding of the religions studied and thereby limiting prejudice or, sometimes, exposing secular students to some of their attractive elements that can be brought into the curriculum without endorsement. The requirements might, to be sure, also benefit secular students, say, by reducing dogmatism among religious students or even their religious identification itself.

Neutrality toward religion—the third standard of the partial theory of church–state separation that I am defending—presents a definition problem even apart from the difficulty of defining "religion."[7] Two points will add clarity. First, neutrality does not imply indifference. Indeed, religious liberty is an important kind and governments should solicitously preserve it. Second, as noted already, governmental neutrality toward religion does not prevent contingencies from adversely (or positively) affecting religious institutions through laws or public policies.[8] Consider science education. Government may require teaching evolutionary biology in public school science—even in required science courses—despite some religious parents' contending that this infringes their religious liberty to bring up their children believing in, say, creationism. To be sure, a liberal-democratic government may not properly sponsor hostility to religion, but that cannot be understood to preclude teaching, as true or highly confirmed, a theory that denies some scriptural claims. Teaching evolutionary theory as true does not (at least for all versions of that theory) imply any metaphysical claims, including any denial that the physical world was created by God.[9]

Given that for some political philosophers (notably Rawls), liberal democracy should be neutral toward "comprehensive" views of the good, it should be stressed that the governmental neutrality supported here is not *value*-neutrality. Such neutrality is not implied by every kind of neutrality toward comprehensive views of the good. There is no easy way to specify just what range of values government should be neutral toward, but that it need not be value-neutral overall is evident even in relation to the kinds of moral considerations that, for any sound democracy, figure in restricting liberty. As illustrated above, these involve a notion of harm. Thus, even on a negative conception of morality according to which its concern is only to prevent harm, we would still need an account of harms or of some still wider range of evils that can justify limitations on the freedom of citizens. For liberal democracy is clearly committed to supporting the maximal liberty that citizens can exercise without producing certain harms (or a substantial likelihood of them).[10] Thus, even if a liberal state could be neutral toward the good, it cannot be neutral toward the bad.

There is, however, no sharp distinction between a government's restricting liberty as a way to prevent harm and its doing so as a way of promoting some good. Consider education. Compulsory education is essential to prevent the harms attendant on ignorance. These include dangers to the physical or psychological health of the population due to ignorance or superstition (as where inoculations or hygienic measures are resisted), waste of resources, and liability to political manipulation by demagogues as well as. But education is surely one kind of good, and in practice it is impossible to provide education in a way that makes it effective in preventing harm yet is not, in the main, inherently good. This is illustrated by competent teaching of history, literature, and science, among other subjects. Moreover, at least where it is the liberty of children that is restricted, considerations of what is for their positive good, as opposed to preventing harms to them, may carry substantial weight. They may certainly carry such weight in choosing among different ways in which children's liberty may be restricted to avoid harm to them.

2. Freedom of Expression versus Coercive Conduct

The liberty, equality, and neutrality principles apply to conduct in general, but so far I have focused on principles of governmental conduct that are most needed for preserving a reasonable separation of church and state. These three principles apply to governmental laws and policies relating to free expression as well as to other kinds of behavior. Free expression, however, may have many purposes besides advocacy of laws or public policies, and most of it is nongovernmental in any case. In both instances—those of advocacy or other support of laws or public policies and those of free expression with no such purpose—liberal democracies recognize a moral right to "maximal" freedom of expression in public discourse. Here, as in other realms of conduct, liberty is the default position: Roughly, in regulatory activities, it is restrictions of liberty, especially of thought, expression, and free association, that governments must justify. Permitting "natural" and other liberties does not normally need justification.

Those engaging in free expression need not have any particular purpose in expressing themselves. More important here, they need not aim at coercion or even persuasion. By contrast, advocacy of laws or public policies normally is intended to persuade, and most of those are coercive. Moreover, supporting them by voting to institute them is commonly intended to require conformity on pain of legal penalty, which is a form of coercion. For coercion of others, as opposed to free expression, there are higher standards—both moral and legal. We are morally free, and should be legally free, to seek to *persuade* others to do things of kinds that we ought not to *coerce* them to do. The preferability of persuasion over coercion is especially prominent where a proposed law is one whose support depends on religious considerations.

Related to this distinction is another: In both ethics and politics, it is essential to distinguish *rights* from *oughts*. There are things many of us ought to do, such as give to charity, which we nonetheless have a moral right *not* to do. No one may coerce charitable contributions or even properly assert that financially able noncontributors violate the rights of charities. Much of what we ought to do lies in the realm of private conduct, say, between spouses or friends. Here as elsewhere having a right to do something, such as make a demand on a friend, does not imply having any reason to do it and is compatible with the wrongness of doing it.

Given our moral rights, free expression and advocacy should be *legally* limited only by a harm principle, *roughly* a principle to the effect that the liberty of competent adults should be restricted only to prevent harm to other people, animals, or the environment (in that order of priority). *Ethically*, however, both free expression and advocacy—and especially advocacy of coercive laws and public policies—should meet standards higher than this very permissive legal one. The next section proposes and defends some principles expressing such higher standards, and the concluding section will take up ethical standards concerning free expression with content that does not support coercion.

3. Ethical Standards for the Advocacy of Laws and Public Policies

Regarding the ethics of good citizenship, many principles have been proposed. The most plausible ones embody some notion of appropriate reasons for citizens in democracies to take as a basis of political decisions. The reasons may also be called public, secular, or evidentially adequate. Here is a well-known principle from Rawls:

> Public reason is the sole reason the court exercises. It is the only branch of government that is visibly on its face the creature of that reason . . . Citizens and legislators may properly vote their more comprehensive [e.g. religious] views when constitutional essentials and basic justice are not at stake. (1993, 235)

Rawls has qualified this principle in ways that complicate assessment of his view. In the same lecture he adds, "provided they do this in ways that strengthen the ideal of public reason itself" (1993, 247) and in the preface to a later version of the same work, he says that reasonable comprehensive doctrines "may be introduced in public reason at any time provided that in due course public reasons, given by a reasonable political conception, are presented sufficient to support whatever the comprehensive doctrines are introduced to support" (1993, li–lii).[11]

A different standard has been proposed by Kent Greenawalt:

> Legislation must be justified in terms of secular objectives, but when people reasonably think that shared premises of justice and criteria for determining truth cannot resolve critical questions of fact, fundamental questions of value, or the weighing of competing benefits and harms, they do properly rely on religious convictions that help them answer these questions. (1988, 12)[12]

Still more permissive toward the propriety of basing political decisions on religious reasons is Weithman's view that

> Citizens of a liberal democracy may base their votes on reasons drawn from their comprehensive moral views, including their religious views, without having other reasons which are sufficient for their vote—provided they sincerely believe that their government would be justified in adopting the measures they vote for. (2001, 3)[13]

I have defended a standard I have termed *the principle of secular rationale*:

> Citizens in a free democracy have a *prima facie* obligation not to advocate or support any law or public policy that restricts human conduct, unless they have, and are willing to offer, adequate secular reason for this advocacy or support (e.g. for a vote). (Audi 2000, 86)[14]

This principle is probably more restrictive than any of the above except for Rawls's principle cited first—on the assumption that the laws in question, which restrict human conduct, very commonly involve either "constitutional essentials" or basic justice and so would fall under his restrictions as well.[15] Here are some of the needed qualifications of secular rationale principle and an indication of its basis.

First, prima facie obligations are *defeasible* and may be overridden. Appeal to religious considerations could be necessary to muster support for laws that will prevent Nazis from coming to power. Then one *should* appeal to them. Emergencies may produce overriders of many prima facie obligations. Second, the prima facie obligation in question is compatible with a *right to act otherwise*. The secular rationale standard is an element in good citizenship; it need not be legally enforced nor taken to curtail liberty. It does not limit rights, legal or moral. Still, there are wrongs within rights—as with as with prosperous people's giving nothing to charity or a teacher's sharply criticizing a good student for a subtle though avoidable error in a paper—that we ought not to do even though we have a right to.[16] Third, a *secular reason* for an action (or a belief) is roughly one whose status as a justifier of action (or belief) does not evidentially depend on (but also does not deny) the existence of God, nor does it depend on theological considerations or on the pronouncements of a person or institution *as* a religious authority. This notion is epistemic, roughly a matter of evidential grounding. It is not a matter of the content of reasons: A secular reason may be that preserving governmental neutrality toward *religion* is desirable.

Not just any reason is appropriate to advocacy of law or public policy. My concern here is religious reasons, but there are other kinds, such as claims based on superstition, that are ethically unacceptable. Hence the requirement of an *adequate* reason: one that, in rough terms, evidentially justifies what it supports. Excusability is the fifth element needing comment. It can explain why a person who does not live up to the principle of secular rationale is not ipso facto a "bad citizen." Like other failures, this one may be fully excusable, as with someone brought up under conditions of scrupulously systematic religious domination that makes acting otherwise psychologically impossible. Any theory of obligation or responsibility should take excusability into account, but excusability is only a protection from blameworthiness, not a status to be sought. The sixth point needed here is that principle of secular rationale is *nonexclusive*: It does not rule out having *religious* reasons for legal coercion, nor imply that such reasons can have no justificatory power, nor rule out having *only* religious reasons for lifting oppression or expanding *liberty* (which is not to say that there are no ethical applicable to using such reasons). It concerns coercion, not behavior of just any kind, and it accords with the idea that freedom is the default position in a liberal democracy.

Defining religion is another problem for understanding secularity. Fortunately, we do not need a definition, as opposed to important criteria. Here are nine, each relevant to, although not strictly necessary for, a social institution's constituting a religion or (as applied to individuals) to an individual's having a religion: (a) appropriately internalized belief in one or more supernatural beings (gods); (b) observance of a distinction between sacred and profane objects; (c) ritual acts focused on those objects; (d) a moral code believed to be sanctioned by the god(s); (e) religious feelings (awe, mystery, etc.) that tend to be aroused by the sacred objects and during rituals; (f) prayer and other communicative forms concerning the god(s); (g) a worldview according the individual a significant place in the universe; (h) a more or less comprehensive organization of life based on the worldview; and (i) a social organization bound together by (a) through (h).[17] Some of these, say, (a), (d), (g), and (h), are more important than others for understanding religion and indeed for this essay; but the vagueness of the notion of a religion remains a problem for political philosophy.

Two further clarifications are needed. First, a person can be religious without belonging to an institutional religion, and these elements of a religion (at least the first seven) apply to individual conduct. Second, secularity is no easier to characterize than religion and shares the vagueness of "religion." It is clarifying, however, to note that secularity in individuals is compatible with their being *spiritual*, for instance, devoted to meditation, nonviolent, and sensitive to subtle apparent communications from nature or the apparently supernatural. We must therefore distinguish the spiritual from the religious. Spirituality is compatible with *secularism*, in the sense of a position calling for a strong separation of church and state and implying opposition to religious worldviews as, for instance, not rational. Secularity, then, is compatible with but does not entail, secularism. Endorsing the principle of secular rationale does not commit one to either of these.

4. Natural Reason, Secularity, and Religious Convictions

Regarding the basis of the principle of secular rationale, I will suggest only that, first, it supports liberal democracy and religious liberty; second, it helps to prevent religious strife; and, third, it is needed to observe the do-unto-others principle—a kind of universalizability standard—because clearly, rational citizens may properly resent coercion based essentially on someone *else's* religious convictions. Note that it might also be called *the principle of natural reason*.[18] This would highlight both its central stress on our natural rational endowment and its continuity with certain elements in the natural law tradition as expressed in Aquinas (among others). It would also indicate that the principle centers on what people have in common and is not antireligious. Clearly we can take our natural endowment as God-given even if we regard the *knowledge* it makes possible—notably including moral knowledge—as attainable independently of theology or religion. A religion can make moral claims and even "scientific" (factual) claims—understood roughly as claims having moral or scientific content and confirmable by moral or scientific methods. There is no good ground for holding either that such claims must be tied to the religion in question for their intelligibility or their justification or that a religion or theology's implying unreasonable positions in these moral or scientific matters has no bearing on assessing it, particularly in its bearing on sociopolitical life.[19]

Natural reason is a general human capacity for apprehending and responding to grounds for belief and for action.[20] It is customary to speak of human reason in relation to both the theoretical realm, in which we must regulate belief, and the practical realm, in which we must regulate action. Theoretical rationality is present given an appropriate responsiveness to the grounds for belief, which may be broadly conceived as truth indicators. Practical rationality is present given an appropriate responsiveness to grounds for action, grounds that may be broadly conceived as goodness indicators. A person rational in an overall way—globally rational—must have both kinds of rationality and a significant degree of integration between them.

Natural reason is plausibly considered an endowment of normal adults who have the kind of understanding of a natural language appropriate to functioning in civil society. Given this level, the prima facie obligation to have natural reasons is not in general unfulfillable. Certainly normal adults literate enough to understand even the narrative passages of the Bible can get at least a foothold in understanding such reasons and in seeing some of the benefits of having them where instituting coercive laws or public policies is in question.

5. Natural Reasons and Religious Identity

In the light of these examples, we can also address the idea that according natural reason the status suggested by the principle of secular rationale jeopardizes the sense of identity of religious citizens or at least imposes on them a kind of second-class citizenship. Why should this be so? The principle does not imply that religious reasons are not *good*, or even less truth conducive than secular ones. It also reflects the specific understanding that religious people can *view* the former as generally better reasons and can be motivated more (or wholly) by them. The principle posits a prima facie obligation to have adequate secular reasons for supporting institutional coercion; it does not preclude or disparage having religious reasons.

It should help to consider the power of the Golden Rule: Any normal adult can understand, through natural reason, the revulsion to being compelled to do something (such as kneel and recite prayers) on the basis of someone *else's* religious convictions. If we can rationally want others to abstain from coercing us on the basis of their religious reasons, we can understand religious reasons well enough to be guided by the principle of secular rationale.

It may also help to stress a complementary companion to the secular rationale principle:

> *The principle of religious rationale*: Religious citizens in a liberal democracy have a prima facie obligation not to advocate or support any law or public policy that restricts human conduct, unless they have, and are willing to offer, adequate religious reason for this advocacy or support.

The underlying idea is that the ethics of good citizenship calls on religious citizens to constrain their coercion of fellow citizens by seeking a rationale from their own religious perspective. They may do this quite compatibly with seeking a secular rationale, and each effort may aid the other. This is a perspective that, in such a weighty matter, it might be at best hypocritical for religious citizens to ignore. This point is defensible both on ethical grounds and from at least the majority of religious perspectives—including some from which the principle of secular rationale would be rejected. The point is one reason why the principle may be considered an element in the ethics of citizenship.

Given the common coincidence between religious reasons for legal constraints on freedom and natural (thus secular) reasons for the same constraints, the principle of religious rationale is an important complement to its secular counterpart. The same kind of coincidence might be expected regarding religious and secular reasons for supporting basic liberties. Freedom of religion is a central case, but the dignity of persons, which is supportable on both religious and secular grounds, is another basis of convergence between secular and religious reasons.

6. Toleration

The ethics of citizenship in a pluralistic democracy must take account not only of actual disagreement between citizens but of the possibility of *rational* disagreement between "epistemic peers": roughly, persons who are (in the matter in question) equally rational, possessed of the same relevant evidence, and equally conscientious in assessing that evidence. Rational disagreement between epistemic peers can occur not just interreligiously—between people who differ in religion (or one or more of whom is not religious at all) but also intrareligiously. There is, for instance, no one Christian position on abortion and no one Islamic position on the status of women.[21]

To be sure, if we think a disagreement is with an epistemic peer and we wish to retain our position, we should try to find new evidence for it or at least try to discover a basis for thinking the disputant is not as rational or as conscientious as we are in appraising the issue. But sometimes the most reasonable conclusion is that there is epistemic parity between us and hence the disagreement cannot be readily resolved in one's favor. This may seem to many conscientious citizens to be how things stand on the permissibility of assisted suicide, capital punishment, or abortion.

How should one respond to a situation of persisting disagreement with an apparent epistemic peer? One response is skepticism: Conclude that neither party has knowledge or even justification. Perhaps, however, there is a difference in the disputants' conflicting justifications that neither can discover. But we should not always suppose that this is so or that our own view is rationally preferable to that of an apparent epistemic peer. A better response here is humility: minimally, concluding that we might be mistaken or less justified than our peer is in holding a contrary position. Humility tends to prevent taking one's view as a basis for establishing coercive laws or public policies, and in that way it gives some support to the idea that for democracies liberty is the default position: the preferred position when there is not a cogent reason for coercion.

With all this in mind, we might endorse

> *The principle of toleration*: If it not reasonable for proponents of coercion in a given matter to consider themselves epistemically superior to supporters of the corresponding liberty, then in that matter the former have a prima facie obligation to tolerate rather than coerce.

In practice, this principle depends on the conscientiousness of those who would coerce. If unconscientious, they would readily think it reasonable to take defenders of the liberty in question to be less than epistemic peers. If conscientious, they would tend to resist taking this view. Indeed, highly conscientious government officials—or virtually any conscientious, rational, and tolerant person with coercive power over others—will, if unopposed by actual disputants, try to think of the best *hypothetical* defense they can construct in favor of the liberty they would restrict. They would then extend the principle to that case.

7. Privatization versus Activism: Religious Considerations in Public Discourse

It is appropriate to conclude with some comments on some of the standards for religious expression—whether argumentative or simply expressive—in public discourse. So far as religion is concerned, these standards are in effect standards for *non*privatization of religion.

We might begin with the point that the uses of religious language are unlimited: Think not just of advocacy and persuasion but of self-expression, self-description, and providing information. I may need to indicate my religious position to say, in any depth, who I am. I might also want to *persuade* an audience of theistic physicians not to violate our relation to God by facilitating assisted suicide, even though I have, despite religious opposition to it, *voted* to legalize it for natural reasons based on respect for the liberty of others with different religions or none.

The position presented here sharply contrasts with the view that "the 'principle of secular rationale' rests on a false distinction between generally accessible reasons and religious ideas ... there is no convincing constitutional or philosophical reason that democratic deliberation should be secular" (McConnell 2007, 161).[22] First, I make no claim that all religious ideas are inaccessible, on the basis of natural reason, to normal adults. But religious experience and sheer religious authority may, in the thinking of some people, figure as grounds of reasons, and there we either lack accessibility in a relevant sense or lack a basis in natural reason for either belief or action. Second, that a reason figures in deliberation, even importantly, is compatible with its being restricted in the moderate way the principle of secular rationale requires. The secular rationale principle does not preclude even overtly religious reasons playing a role in such deliberation; its force is instead to constrain that role in a way that is defensible from many religious perspectives as well as on secular grounds. Granted, the constraints appropriate to the discourse and deliberations of the judiciary and, perhaps to a lesser extent, to legislators and other governmental officials acting officially, are stronger than those appropriate to citizens as such. These differences in degree are consistent with the principle and indeed seem to support it. Given these points, there is no justification for speaking of epistemic "pre-screening devices like the principle of secular rationale" (McConnell 2007, 169).[23] Religious reasons are not implied to be admissible in political discourse, inappropriate as possible evidences, or epistemically deficient.

A further point is that the principle of secular rationale applies to coercion, not liberalizations. One reason why liberalization (as lifting restrictions of freedom) differs from coercion in the range of appropriate reasons supporting it is that freedom is the default position in liberal democracy and may properly be supported by a wider variety of reasons than those needed to justify coercion. Liberalization can be justified by simply showing the lack of adequate natural reasons for coercion and, arguably, may be properly supported by conscientiously held personal reasons that include religious ones. This is not to say that appeal to religious reasons favoring liberalization is always evidentially adequate; it may be not only unneeded but also intellectually weak, misleading, or even divisive. Still, where religious reasons for liberalization, say, for lifting oppression, are combined with secular ones, this may have the good effect of enhancing both justification and motivation to act accordingly and of indicating an important case in which the two kinds of reasons coincide in their implications for law or public policy.

A fourth point is that even where we seek to enhance liberty, we could still be injudicious in the *way* we appeal to religious considerations, even where doing so is in itself unobjectionable. Doing it in a sectarian way, as where we appeal to a controversial clerical authority, may invite those with competing religious views to enter the discussion in such a way that avoidable trouble and perhaps serious strife will ensue. To be sure, there are apparently "comprehensive reasons" (in Rawls's sense), such as the value of a Kantian kind of autonomy, that are shared by all the religious traditions likely to be represented in a political discussion in a democratic state. But, even where such commonality among religions exists, pointing it out may or may not lead to people's bringing into public discourse religious arguments that divide rather than unify them.

The points so far made are addressed to individual citizens but also bear on the conduct of religious institutions and, indeed, on that of clergy acting as such and not simply as citizens. This is an important dimension of the topic of the proper relation between religion and politics in a democracy. Church–state separation is often conceived unidirectionally. But separation is symmetrical. Moreover, institutional ethics overlaps political philosophy in a way that makes the following principle appropriate for churches:

> *The principle of ecclesiastical political neutrality*: in a free and democratic society, churches committed to being institutional citizens in such a society have a prima facie obligation to abstain from supporting candidates for public office or pressing for laws or public policies that restrict human conduct, particularly religious or other basic liberties.[24]

This principle applies not only to religious institutions as social entities but (where this is different) to their official representatives acting as such. Even for churches not committed to citizenship in a liberal democracy, a case can be made that it would be good for them to recognize such a prima facie obligation of neutrality. This may support their commitment to their own religious mission, and it tends to conduce to political stability insofar as that is threatened by tensions that would come from religious institutions vying in the political arena. To be sure, if churches do enter politics, adhering to the principle of secular rationale would be desirable; but this mitigatory role is consistent with the ecclesiastical neutrality principle, which remains plausible. Ecclesiastical neutrality is generally desirable even where departures from it would not support coercion of a kind that is not justifiable by secular reasons.

It may be objected that the ecclesiastical neutrality principle rules out churches and clergy taking *moral* positions. Granted the principle is no clearer than the distinction between the moral and the political. But making that distinction is intrinsic to any theory of clerical virtue. Three points will help. First, at least numerous kinds of moral propositions are secular in the sense in which the reasons have been said to be so above. Second, if some propositions are both moral and religious—say, that it is wrong to disobey God's command not to kill—either their behavioral directive (in this case, abstention from killing) can be justified by natural reason or they do not ground cogent objections to the principle. Third, a position need not be considered political simply because it is politically controversial, say, in contention between opposing political parties. Thus, stem cell research raises politically controversial moral issues, but its moral permissibility is not thereby a political question. Suppose, however, that clergy's taking public positions on its morality is consistent with the ecclesiastical neutrality principle. It does not follow that those positions may thereby be unobjectionably argued in public wholly on the basis of religious considerations. The principle of secular rationale makes advocacy wholly on this basis prima facie impermissible. Both principles imply that it is prima facie wrong to recommend *voting* for or against candidates on the basis of their positions on these issues, even if that basis is not political.

The points previously made about the conditions under which religious reasons may be brought into public discourse consistently with the principles of secular rationale and ecclesiastical neutrality leave open some matters of judgment that deserve brief comment. What are some of the general *standards* of good citizenship for the sociopolitical use of religious discourse? One is simply judiciousness. Will what we say be illuminating or alienating, consensus building or divisive, clarifying or obfuscating? There are myriad considerations here, of both ethical sensitivity and prudence. A second consideration is a spirit of reciprocity, based partly on a sense of universal standards available to all rational, minimally educated adult citizens. Consider the do-unto-others rule. The *wording* is Biblical; the *content* is a call for reciprocity, and it is expressible in nonreligious language and represents a standard that, in some form, is central in any plausible ethical view.

I close with the suggestion that public discourse in a liberal democracy is best served by citizens having an appropriate *civic voice*.[25] Such a voice is a matter of intonation and manifest respect for others' points of view and convictions. Our voice is not determined by the content of what we say but by *how* we say it. That, in turn, is partly a matter of *why* we say it. Our public voice may properly reflect religious elements, but in citizens adhering to the principle of secular rationale—of natural reason—it indicates respect for standards that, simply as rational persons, we do or can have in common and should take as a basis for setting proper limits on liberty. If these standards are not implicit in our religious commitments, they are at least likely to a reasonable basis on which we can conscientiously argue against coercive laws or policies based on someone else's religious convictions.

The relation between religion and politics is a topic of great importance in the current global climate. Religion is a powerful force in politics, a pervasive element in the culture of most nations, and influential in many other realms. In many Western societies where the influence of religion has tended to wane among the more educated citizens, its influence among immigrants is often growing, as it widely noted in press reports about Germany, the Netherlands, Italy, and other countries. Whatever its sociocultural role, as we strive to support democratic government, we must find a sound and credible theory of the standards that should structure governmental relations toward both institutional religion and religious individuals. The essay has defended three principles toward this end: one calling for governmental protection of religious liberty, the second requiring government to treat different religious elements equally, and the third requiring governmental neutrality toward religion. These standards do not, however, speak to the ethics of citizenship for individuals. For that case I have proposed a principle of secular rationale—of natural reason—aimed at enhancing cooperation in pluralistic societies while respecting the importance of religious perspectives and convictions that may often divide people. This principle is combinable with a counterpart principle of religious rationale, which calls on religious citizens to seek adequate religious reasons before supporting coercive laws or public policies. Both principles are supported by the principle of toleration, which requires abstaining from coercion where apparent epistemic peers argue for liberty, and by the principle of ecclesiastical neutrality. All of these principles support positing a prima facie obligation to respect liberty and to support its restriction only for the kinds of reasons that can be both respected and shared by rational, adequately informed citizens regardless of their religious position. The principles also make room for religious reasons to shape inquiry, to figure in deliberation, and to guide the discourse of religious citizens. The proper role of religious reasons in attempts to justify coercion is limited, but this is, in the long run, as much a protection of religious liberty as of the freedom rights of all citizens irrespective of their religious convictions.[26]

NOTES

1. On one view of nonestablishment in the United States, the weak form of doctrinal establishment implicit in, say, requiring the Pledge of Allegiance (which refers to one nation "under God") an element of what I call formal establishment would be constitutional in the United States. For a case that such elements of "civil religion" are not unconstitutional, see Perry (2009).

2. For critical discussion of the compatibility of various forms of establishment with democracy, see Laborde (2011).

3. Whether "civil religion" might be establishable within the limits of the equality and neutrality principles is considered in my prior work (Audi 2009).

4. See Wolterstorff's contribution to Audi and Wolterstorff (1997).

5. This is argued in the context of an account of moral rights in my prior work (Audi 2005). It presupposes that rights have major importance but not that they are morally basic. The limitations could be defended by appeal to other kinds of moral standards.

6. An extensive debate on the kind of religious neutrality appropriate to liberal democracy is provided by the contrasting views in Audi and Wolterstorff (1997).

7. For a legally informed analysis of governmental neutrality toward religion that defends neutrality in a way that supports this essay, see Koppelman (2006).

8. Vouchers that provide funds for parents to educate their children in schools of their choice—religious or secular—may also be viewed in relation to the three principles, especially the neutrality principle. They may differentially benefit the religious yet are not defined so as to favor religious over nonreligious citizens. Greene (1999) indicates special issues relating to the U.S. Constitution and some relevant legal literature.

9. For discussion of this issue see Greenawalt (2005) and my critical study (Audi 2007). One may be reminded here of the "Lemon test": "First, the statute must have a secular legislative purpose; second, its principal or primary effect must be one that neither advances nor inhibits religion; finally, the statute must not foster 'an excessive entanglement with religion'" (*Lemon v. Kurtzmann* 403 US602 1971).

10. Mill's famous harm principle (1859, 9-10) exemplifies the kind of view in question.

11. This proviso seems extremely permissive and raises serious difficulties that cannot be pursued here.

12. This view is refined and defended in Greenawalt's later work, but the kinds of comments I make here should not be affected by his further work on the topic. Some of the points I make I in the following discussion are extended or given a wider context in my prior work (Audi 1990).

13. This principle is close to one defended in Wolterstorff: "Let citizens use whatever reasons they find appropriate"—with the understanding that their goal is "political justice, not the achievement of one's own interests" (1997, 112-13).

14. This formulation is drawn from my work (Audi 2000, 86). The principle has been widely discussed for example by Wolterstorff (1997), Weithman (2001), and Eberle (2009).

15. My principle is in the main also less restrictive than one proposed by Habermas: He holds that "religious citizens must develop an epistemic stance toward the priority that secular reasons enjoy in the political arena" and that a "requirement of [secular] translation"—that "the truth content of religious contributions can only enter into the institutional practice of deliberation and decision-making if the necessary translation [of "convictions in a religious language"] already occurs in . . . the political public sphere" (2006, 10, 14). Even on a loose interpretation of "translation," this is a burdensome requirement that would likely keep many religious considerations from entering the decision making in question

16. This is defended in detail and by appeal to diverse examples in my previous work (Audi 2005).

17. These features are stressed by Alston (1964, 88). (I have abbreviated and slightly revised his list.) This characterization does not entail that religions must be theistic, but theistic religions are my main concern. It is noteworthy that in *United States v Seeger*, 380 US 163 (1965), the Supreme Court ruled that religious belief need not be theistic, but theistic religions raise the most important church–state issues at least for societies like those in the Western world. For discussion of the significance of *U.S. v. Seeger* in relation to church–state aspects of the foundations of liberalism, see Greene (1994). For discussion of the problem of defining "religion" constitutionally, see Greenawalt (2006), especially pages 498–511, which also discusses the notion of public reason.

18. One qualification is that there are secular reasons whose normative domain is not clearly encompassed by natural reason understood as an endowment of normal rational persons. Consider an aesthetic reason for believing that a line of poetry detracts from the value of the poem in which it occurs. If this requires sensitivity that a rational person need

not have, it is not a natural reason, at least of an "ordinary" kind. The kinds of secular reasons are that are apparently not also natural ones, however, can be separated from the kinds of concern in this essay, which clearly are natural in the relevant sense.

19. For an informative discussion of Thomistic natural law theory that confirms this (e.g., by countenancing self-evident moral principles) see Grisez, Boyle, and Finnis (1987).

20. Compare the idea, implicit in this conception of natural reason as crucial for understanding limitations of governmental power, that "procedure-independent normative standards for democratic decisions does not support the rule of the wiser citizens" (religious or other) and that political philosophy should recognize "a requirement that political authority be justifiable to those subject to it in ways they can accept" (Estlund 2008, 39).

21. In a treatment of religion and minority rights, J. A. van der Den notes a tension in Islam. Speaking of "rights in the Qu'ran itself," he lists "the right to life, respect, freedom, equality, education, remunerated employment, property, leaving their country in the event of oppression, and a good life" (2008, 178). But he immediately adds: "The Qu'ran also contains rules that trample roughshod over equal rights, such as Sura 4: 34, which offers the following three-phase model for dealing with insubordinate wives: talk to her, shun her in bed, and, if that proves unavailing, beat her" (2008, 178).

22. Note that McConnell's objection also applies to many other political philosophers, including Rawls, Greenawalt, and Habermas.

23. The term *prescreening* is misleading *both* in suggesting limitations on expression and in implying that religious reasons are disallowed, rather than (prima facie) prohibited from standing alone as a basis of coercion.

24. The principle of ecclesiastical neutrality and its counterpart for clergy acting as such in public (rather than simply as individual citizens) are drawn from my prior work (Audi 2000). I noted there that the notion of institutional citizenship needs explication, but it is sufficiently clear for its limited purpose here. Chapter 2 also clarified the political in contrast with the moral. I should add that I do not consider it self-evident that a church should want to be an institutional citizen. But even for a church that does not, the principle of ecclesiastical political neutrality expresses a desirable standard.

25. The concept of civic voice is clarified in Chapter 6 of my prior work (Audi 2000) with special reference to the importance of motivation as typically influencing one's voice: Our motivation for what we say commonly influences our voice every bit as much as its content, and (as explained there) this is one among other reasons why civic virtue calls for avoiding the giving of reasons for coercion that (even if one thinks them evidentially adequate) do not motivate one and hence serve only a kind of rationalization. Any given content may be voiced in importantly different ways, and some of the differences are highly significant for the quality and harmony of civic discourse and political conduct.

26. For many helpful comments on this essay, I thank David Estlund.

REFERENCES

Alston, William P. 1964. *Philosophy of Language*. Englewood Cliffs, NJ: Prentice-Hall.
Audi, Robert 1990. "Religion and the Ethics of Political Participation." *Ethics* 100(2): 386–97.
Audi, Robert. 2005. "Wrongs Within Rights." In *Philosophical Issues. Nous* suppl. 15: 121–39.

Audi, Robert. 2007. "Religion and Public Education in Constitutional Democracies." *Virginia Law Review* 93(4): 1175–95.
Audi, Robert. 2009. "Natural Reason, Natural Rights, and Governmental Neutrality Toward Religion." *Religion and Human Rights* 4: 1–20.
Audi, Robert, and Nicholas Wolterstorff. 1997. *Religion in the Public Square: The Place of Religious Convictions in Political Debate.* Lanham, MD: Rowman & Littlefield.
Eberle, Christopher J. 2009. "Basic Human Worth and Religious Restraint." *Philosophy and Social Criticism* 35(1/2): 151–81.
Estlund, David M. 2008. *Democratic Authority: A Philosophical Framework.* Princeton, NJ: Princeton University Press.
Greenawalt, Kent. 1988. *Religious Convictions and Political Choice.* Oxford: Oxford University Press.
Greenawalt, Kent. 2005. *Does God Belong in Public Schools?* Princeton, NJ: Princeton University Press.
Greenawalt, Kent. 2006. *Religion and the Constitution*, Vol. 2. Princeton, NJ: Princeton University Press.
Greene, Abner S. 1994. "Ronald Dworkin's *Life's Dominion*." *George Washington Law Review* 62(4): 646–73.
Greene, Abner S. 1999. "Why Vouchers Are Unconstitutional, and Why They're Not." *Notre Dame Journal of Law, Ethics, & Public Policy* 13(2): 397–408.
Grisez, Germain, Joseph Boyle, and John Finnis. 1987. "Practical Principles, Moral Truth, and Ultimate Ends." *American Journal of Jurisprudence* 32: 99–151.
Habermas, Jürgen. 2006. "Religion in the Public Square." *European Journal of Philosophy* 14(1): 1–25.
Koppelman, Andrew. 2006. "Is It Fair to Give Religion Special Treatment?" *University of Illinois Law Review* 3: 574–604.
Laborde, Cecile. 2011. "Political Liberalism, Republicanism and the Public Role of Religion." *Journal of Political Philosophy* 13
Mill, J. S. 1859. *On Liberty.* Indianapolis, IN: Hackett.
McConnell, Michael W. 2007. "Secular Reason and the Misguided Attempt to Exclude Religious Arguments from Democratic Deliberation." *Journal of Law, Ethics and Culture* 1(1): 159–74.
Perry, Michael J. 2009. "Religion as a Basis of Law-Making? Herein of the Non-Establishment of Religion." *Philosophy & Social Criticism* 35(1/2): 105–26.
Rawls, John. 1993. *Political Liberalism.* New York: Columbia University Press.
van der Den, Johannes. 2008. "Religious Rights for Minorities in a Policy of Recognition." *Religion and Human Rights* 3(2): 155–83.
Weithman, Paul. 2001. *Religion and the Obligations of Citizenship.* Cambridge, UK: Cambridge University Press.
Wolterstorff, Nicholas. 1997. "The Role of Religion in Decision and Discussion of Political Issues." In *Religion in the Public Square.* Edited by Robert Audi and Nicholas Wolterstorff, 67–120. Lanham, MD: Rowman & Littlefield.

CHAPTER 13

MONEY IN POLITICS

THOMAS CHRISTIANO

Money is necessary to politics as it is to most activities in modern liberal democracies. Money funds most of the activities of politics, such as campaigning and lobbying, persuasion, and the development of political ideas. Political activity would be massively less valuable without the use of money, just as economic activity would be a lot less valuable without the existence of money. Money funds most of what politics is about, and politics is often about the expenditure and distribution of money. People have interests in money at stake in politics, and those who have a lot of money have interests in keeping it or increasing their share of it as well as the capacity to influence the process through the expenditures necessary to politics. Those who do not have money have interests in increasing their wealth, but they have fewer means for achieving that increase.

However, in part because of the necessity of money to politics and in part because of the distinctive features of political activity for a democratic society, the necessity of money to politics can pose problems, normatively speaking, for the political system. For most people, the political system should be designed to make collective decisions that aim at the common good and justice and in a way that treats all citizens as free and equal participants. The influence of money on a political system can threaten these aims.

I discuss four basic mechanisms by which the expenditure of money can influence the political system: money for votes, money as gatekeeper, money as means for influencing public and legislative opinion, and money as independent political power. These four basic mechanisms correspond roughly to the four basic aspects of the democratic process. The first relates to the process of law and policymaking, the second to the setting of the agenda of this decision making, the third to the formation of opinion and preference, and the fourth to the independent social and economic constraints on successful policymaking. Most writers ignore two or more of these mechanisms, but they have very different structures and pose distinct normative questions. I discuss the basic normative issues that arise for each of these mechanisms: corruption, inefficiency, distortion of the deliberative process, and political inequality. I then address some questions about the importance of political equality in assessing these mechanisms and the conflicts between political equality and free expression.

1. Money for Votes

Because money is necessary to finance campaigns, in systems of private financing of campaigns sometimes those with a great deal of money can secure special treatment for themselves or their firms or even their favorite causes from those to whose election campaigns they give financial support. These favors can be in the form of support for public policy or legislation, pressure for lax execution of laws, or access to the politician when such public matters arise. Another mechanism along similar lines occurs when politicians operate what is in effect a protection racket for private firms. They ask for money from those firms in exchange for protecting those firms from interfering public policy and law; those who do not give money are not protected. One can imagine that the price extorted from the firm determines the level of protection by the government. In this way a private market arises of financial support for electoral competition in exchange for action on public law and policy. The motives for securing special treatment do not, strictly speaking, have to be self-interested, although most scholars of this phenomenon think they are. To be clear, I do not focus on the case of bribery in which a politician derives personal income from giving special favors; I discuss only mechanisms in which politicians receive money for funding campaigns.

The problem of money for votes is probably the most frequently discussed problem generated by the influence of money in politics. Virtually every campaign finance system in existence is focused on trying to eliminate this kind of money-for-votes exchange. It has been the principal preoccupation of campaign finance law since the middle of the nineteenth century in the kinds of proto-democratic states that existed then. It is also the one rationale for campaign finance restrictions that has been acceptable to the U.S. Supreme Court, though most other contemporary democratic states give weight now to mitigating the great inequalities in political influence that can arise from an unregulated process of campaign finance.[1]

There are really four possible and important wrongs that people have in mind when they think of corruption: (a) a deontological concern with very serious forms of dishonesty and theft, (b) inefficiency, (c) distortion of the deliberative process, and (d) inequality. Although I do not think that any of these forms of corruption are unique to democracies, I focus on their presence in democracies only.

Michael Walzer has argued that vote selling is impermissible on the grounds that the accepted social purposes of money and votes are quite different and that the spheres of money and votes ought to be kept quite autonomous. The acts of selling and buying votes subvert the socially accepted purposes of politics (Walzer 1983). There is some intuitive power behind this idea, but matters are muddied by the fact that money is an essential means of transaction for virtually every activity outside intimate relations in modern societies. Furthermore, one must ask why a system in which one exchanges money for votes is an undesirable one. I contend that the problems of inefficiency, deliberative distortion, and inequality supply the reasons.

The basic inefficiencies in selling legislative votes for money are the problems of cost spreading and diversion of money away from productive investment. Public policies and law are usually financed through the general revenue. If a public policy is tailored to suit the interest of a particular and limited group in society while being financed through general revenue, most of the benefit will go to that group even though it pays for only a small part of the cost. When money can buy votes, those who pay the rest of the full cost are not included in the decisions made later. So the system gives power to a small group that receives most of the benefit but pays only a small fraction of the costs. Because vote-buyers ignore the costs to others, the cost to the society as a whole of the legislation they favor may outweigh the benefits.

The processes of deliberation concerning the common good could be damaged by such an arrangement. A significant amount of discussion and deliberation is necessary for a democratic society to make reasonably good law and policy. Citizens and legislators learn from the presence of robust debate, at least over the long run. Now discussion and deliberation occur at a society-wide level only to the extent that citizens and legislators think seriously about how to advance the common good in a just and equitable manner. But if legislators must often vote for policies in exchange for campaign donations from particular interests, policies will not be chosen on the basis of the best reasons but rather on strategic considerations concerning how to advance the special interests or concerns of these groups. The role of good-faith discussion and learning correspondingly diminishes. Also, to the extent that discussion occurs, it will often be taken to be a mask for advancing special interests or seen as mere "cheap talk" (Beitz 1989).

To be sure, this result will normally occur only when the extent of selling votes represents a significant proportion of all legislative voting. If it occurs only slightly, it might not damage the process of deliberation very much. But note that even if vote selling is not occurring a lot, if most people think that it is, they may be unwilling to invest much in serious debate on law and policy. Here the need for empirical research that clearly studies this phenomenon becomes quite important to the health of a democratic society.

What about when citizens are paid to vote for a particular candidate in an election (Brennan 2011)? One problem is that this replaces an intentionally artificially created equality with an unintentionally created inequality. Because of the declining marginal utility of money, on average those with less money will generally sell their votes to those who have a lot of money. Because less well-off voters face a collective action problem, even if they are interested in retaining some kind of equality in the voting process, the system of voting, which is supposed to be egalitarian, could be replaced by a nonegalitarian scheme. People may have duties to avoid this, which they owe to the other members of the community and in particular to those members of the community whose equal status is particularly vulnerable. A simple enforceable prohibition on citizen vote selling may be sufficient to block this kind of activity.

This problem presumably also arises with legislative vote selling. The overall effect of such actions biases the process of policymaking quite strongly toward wealthy and well-organized economic interests and could pose a serious threat to political equality.

The empirical evidence is mostly against the thesis that money buys legislative votes in the United States. First, the amount of money in politics is relatively small compared to the value of the budgets of modern states. This suggests that the investments have a spectacularly high rate of profit, but then there would be a lot more money chasing legislative votes in politics, making the rate of profit closer to that seen in ordinary investments. Second, the amount of money spent by political action committees and corporate and union interests is only a fraction of the total amount that goes into elections, so these parties cannot really determine the outcomes of elections. Most money comes from relatively small donors. As a consequence, the large donors do not normally pose a serious threat to campaigns. Third, we see that many firms that have interests that could be protected by the government do not give any money. The contribution limits are rarely reached, and usually people and PACs fall far short of them. Finally, every effort to show that there is a correlation between contributions and votes has shown little significant effect of money on legislative votes when controlling for other factors such as party, constituency preferences, incumbency, and so on.[2]

There has been some pushback against this argument recently. Some have attempted to model threats to finance the opponents that need not be acted on, in addition to actual contributions and votes, and argue that this explains the data well. This research is still ongoing.[3] Moreover, there is a substantial amount of conviction among participants within the system that money does buy votes. That should make one pause, but it is technically compatible with the previously mentioned results to the extent that there is a small effect of contributions on votes. Furthermore, all this evidence comes from the United States. Some have argued that money can buy votes in other specific democracies (Samuels 2001).

Some argue that there is evidence that campaign contributions may influence the amount of effort a legislator is willing to put into a piece of legislation and what kind of information that legislator is willing to look at, which can have an indirect impact on the early crucial stages of the legislative process (Hall and Wayman 1990).

2. Money as Gatekeeper

A very distinct mechanism has money functioning as a gatekeeper and in effect as a kind of agenda setter for collective decision making. In systems of campaign finance in which people finance their own campaigns, those who are able to raise a great deal of money are more likely to run viable campaigns, whereas those who cannot generate as many funds for their campaigns often drop out of the competition. In this mechanism, the persons who pay serve as the gatekeepers of the system because they choose which candidates to support. Unlike the money for votes mechanism, there need be no suggestion here of quid pro quo, venality, or corruption in this phenomenon. The donors simply choose to give money to like-minded persons—those who seem to have the same values and beliefs. Donors need not ask for anything in return.

There are at least three problems that can arise from the fact that private money is a gatekeeper: inequality in agenda setting, distortion of the deliberative process, and inefficiency. This might matter a great deal, as the affluent (the upper middle class and the wealthy) are much more likely to participate in financing campaigns than those who are less well to do. Because political support here functions more like a consumption good, the money has declining marginal utility. So people must appeal to the affluent in order to run viable campaigns. If there are significant commonalities of opinion and interests among the broad mass of the affluent that distinguish them from the less well-off groups, then the interests and points of view of the affluent sectors of society will be better represented in political campaigns than those of the less well off. Disagreements may occur, but they will be limited primarily to those among the affluent. Other dissenting views, no matter how prominent in the population at large, will tend to be marginalized.

Some serious empirical evidence indicates that some of these relations hold in the United States. Larry Bartels has argued that there is solid evidence to the effect that the votes of senators in the U.S. Senate are not responsive at all to the members of the bottom one-third of the income scale and show little responsiveness to the middle third (Bartels 2008, ch. 9). Martin Gilens has argued that government policy is responsive to people's views when everyone agrees, but when the worst off and middle-income groups disagree with the better off, the affluent win out (Gilens 2005). Furthermore, there is substantial evidence that about 10 percent of the population gives money for political campaigns, and we know that these donors are concentrated at the upper echelons of the distribution of income in the United States.[4] Although I have not seen evidence one way or another for the causal link, the model linking these two phenomena makes sense.

One prominent account of the value of democracy is that it publicly treats citizens as equals by giving them an equal say in the process of collective decision making through which extensive and significant disagreements about substantive law and policy are resolved (Dahl 1989; Cohen 2001; Christiano 2008). However, we have a sense that the process fails to treat persons as equals when it gives them substantially unequal opportunities with which to shape collective decision making. This suggests that there is great inequality of opportunity for influencing the political agenda in the society that cuts along lines of economic class that are correlated with distinct interests and points of view. The effect is that the political society is responsive to the affluent but not to the nonaffluent. Here we have a publicly clear way in which the political system is not advancing the interests of persons equally and in which it seems to be giving less weight to the interests and viewpoints of the nonaffluent than those of the affluent. This strikes most as a profound injustice, and the essence of democracy is to avoid this injustice. We discuss the issue of political inequality in more depth later.

The distortion of the deliberative process occurs as a consequence of these same facts. Because politicians and political campaigns are important influences on the process of deliberation in society and they are recruited by the affluent, the interests and points of view of the nonaffluent will receive relatively little attention. The process of deliberation, which purports to be concerned with the common good, will systematically marginalize information about the interests of a large proportion of the population. Furthermore, the process of deliberation does not benefit from the infusion of the distinct points of view that the nonaffluent have to offer.

There may also be some inefficiency in the making of law and policy to the extent that the full costs of policies that are favored by the affluent will not be registered because the losses to the nonaffluent parts of society are not given a full hearing. The benefits of policies for the nonaffluent will also not be fully taken into account. Thus, we could have a kind of cost spreading by the affluent to the whole of society, while the benefits accrue primarily to the affluent class.

Some argue that money has only a small effect on the political process because incumbency has a massive effect on who wins (Smith 2000). Incumbency is very important, but this does not imply that money is not also important. Every incumbent had to be at one time a challenger, and the amount of money raised is known to make a large difference to the prospects of challengers. It should also be noted that the influence of the affluent could be mitigated by the presence of large associations that represent the interests of the nonaffluent. Trade unions sometimes serve this role, as in the case of labor unions in Great Britain (Ghaleigh 2006, 51).

One set of methods for limiting the effect of money on politics consists of capping private contributions to candidates or parties; another is limiting private expenditures of candidates, parties, or third parties.[5] A third method is to ban or severely curtail television and radio advertising. This could be combined with public slots devoted to examining the views of different candidates. Because advertising is the most expensive part of campaigning, this might limit the expense and make money a bit less of a gatekeeper.[6]

A common method for overcoming these problems is public financing of elections. Contemporary states that pay some or all campaign finances try to do so in a way that avoids any implication that the state plays favorites. Their choices piggyback on private choices. Either the state pays a candidate or party in proportion to the amount of private money raised by that party, or it may give a certain amount to every candidate on the condition that he or she has received a certain amount privately. When the state funds campaigns in these ways, the private gatekeeping function of money is modified but not extinguished, because the state's contribution still depends on previous private contributions. The method most independent of private funding apportions money to votes in previous election cycles. Some apportion money to the number of votes received in a previous election cycle, and others give the same funding to all parties or candidates that received a minimum amount in the previous cycle. These methods are biased in favor of parties that have been successful in the past and make it difficult for new parties or candidates to break into the electoral competition.[7]

A recent innovative proposal for state financing of elections requires that the state give equal vouchers to each person in an election cycle, which they can use only to support candidates or parties (Adamany and Agree 1975; Ackerman and Ayres 2004). When this method excludes other methods of financing, it supports a more egalitarian method of election, but it may be too restrictive, and this kind of proposal often is accompanied by private financing as well. The effects of such a system of election finance are unknown at the moment.

One further gatekeeping function of money is that affluent persons are most likely to be called on to be politicians, advisors to politicians, or bureaucrats. Positions of power and influence in the government tend to go to those with advanced degrees in various fields because these positions of power and influence require specialized knowledge and skills. In addition, positions of power in the bureaucracy often go to persons who are familiar with the areas that are being monitored and regulated by the bureaucracy, such as leaders in industry and business as well as lawyers. Wealthy persons also receive powerful positions as rewards for financial support (Miliband 1970). This must have a substantial effect on bureaucratic policymaking.

3. Money as a Means for Influencing Opinion

Money is an important tool for the cultivation of sophisticated opinion and the wide transmission and broadcast of opinions to the public. Because of the declining marginal utility of money in this context, those with a great deal of money can finance the broadcast of opinions. Those with little money are not likely to do so and as a consequence are not likely to be well heard. Those with a great deal of money can finance the production of ideas and arguments while those with little cannot. The dominance of the affluent holds over the general processes of dissemination of opinion and ideas and over the processes of discussion and debate in periods of election. This effect on the process may be of great importance to democratic ideals. If a certain sector of the society has a much greater influence on the process of opinion creation, modification, and dissemination than any other sector, the likelihood is that that sector will determine the conceptions of justice and its importance, the common good, and individual interests that are available for discussion and adoption in the society. This could create radically different opportunities for effective participation in the society and have a very significant effect on what interests are actually advanced.

In addition, money is necessary to finance the activities of lobbyists who influence legislative opinion. Lobbyists have an essential and deliberative function in a political society. They focus the attention of politicians on particular problems of policymaking and supply crucial information and ideas to those politicians. They make arguments for policies and law that sometimes persuade politicians, and they supply crucial arguments to them for persuading others. Those who pay the lobbyists could have a significant effect on what arguments, ideas, and information politicians receive as they attempt to make legislation and policy.

Scarcity

One of the vexing questions surrounding the issue of money in politics is the question of scarcity. Although I have been speaking as if the opportunities for expression in the media are scarce, many have questioned this. However, we need to distinguish among different kinds of scarcity. One possible form of scarcity is in space for messages. Many people have observed that the broadcast of opinion on television is not in any way incompatible with the broadcast of opinion on radio stations or other media. In addition, with the development of the Internet, the broadcast of opinion is significantly less expensive than it has ever been before. In some sense, everyone has opportunities to broadcast opinion. Thus, there is little scarcity in what we might call the message space of politics. The space is sufficiently large to broadcast all messages.

Another kind of scarcity may be more important than message space scarcity for our purposes. I call this *socially induced cognitive scarcity*. The basic idea here is that individual persons have limited cognitive space to consider many different messages. The nature of the limitation is complex. There are limits to what any brain can cognize, but the scarcity I have in mind is different. The problem relates to the division of labor in society. We do not expect or desire that most people spend as much time on political issues as, say, political scientists, political economists, politicians, political consultants, or even political activists. Society's proper operation requires specialization in very different tasks: Plumbing, medicine, teaching, building, science, manufacturing, farming, law, government, and other tasks are all full-time jobs, and there is a great deal of specialization in these tasks. Nearly all of these jobs essentially require eight or more hours a day, but they are exhausting and leave only just enough time and energy for most people to engage with their families, friends, and pleasurable hobbies. Of course, the family is an absolutely essential part of the whole structure of society to the extent that it involves the moral, physical, and intellectual raising of children, which is a time-consuming and tiring task. The family is also one of the central sources of well-being in people's lives. Once we account for all these essential tasks, we can see that most people spend almost all of their time and energy on them, and it is desirable that they do.

Politics is not an easy activity either. Political issues are usually quite complex, and the complexity of society ensures that there are many diverse interests and points of view. There is a lot of disagreement, which most people find unpleasant. Furthermore, because politics involves many moral issues, it creates heated emotions from those on different sides of the issues. Accusations of criminality, treachery, corruption, injustice, and stupidity are common in politics. Once we take into account the reality of the complexity of politics and its moral and emotional intensity, we can see that paying attention to politics for ordinary citizens is an energy- and time-consuming activity. People have some time and energy left over for politics—but not a lot. The most active of citizens who have families and day jobs have about an hour a day to consider politics, and most find it difficult to even get to this level. Of course, the political system is designed with an eye to this phenomenon. Political parties, interest groups, opinion leaders, newspapers, and news television are all designed to give ordinary citizens shortcuts to understanding political issues. Because the cognitive capabilities of ordinary citizens allows only a small number of new messages about politics to be considered seriously, every political entity in society must spend a huge amount of time deciding how to get noticed and be taken seriously by ordinary citizens.

Though I think it is impossible to dominate the message space now, it may be possible to dominate the socially limited cognitive space that ordinary individual citizens devote to politics. The main newspapers, magazines, and broadcast stations on network and the cable television are the main venues through which ordinary citizens receive their political information. To some significant extent, it is rational for citizens to receive their political information from these sources because they package the news so that it can be understood quickly and efficiently. Ordinary citizens already use network and cable TV stations as sources of entertainment and relaxation, so television is a relatively inexpensive source for news for them. These sources have also gained a (only partially justified) reputation for impartiality and thoroughness. This is partly because they have learned how not to offend large numbers of people, which would be disastrous for the station's ratings. Furthermore, it is rational for citizens to coordinate with others on their news sources by watching the same news programs so that they have a shared basis of discussion.

I want to emphasize here that this phenomenon of socially limited cognitive space is a natural by-product of a highly desirable structural property of society. It may be that citizens should devote more time to politics than they currently do, but we know that the amount of time we can demand from them for this aspect of their lives is quite limited, given the needs of a complex economic system. Because it is sufficiently limited, this space can be dominated by wealthy groups that can afford to buy or fund large parts of it.

To be sure, the large-scale media in many democratic societies are for-profit entities, and they compete with each other for an audience. Presumably people can have some kind of influence on the content of what is broadcast or written through media. If enough people do not like what they hear or read, they can influence what is said by threatening to "vote with their feet" (Entman 1990). Certainly the main motor driving the media is advertising, and that advertising may be most concerned with the relatively affluent, so extra weight will be accorded to the affluent even here. The advertisers also have interests in what is communicated. We need to discover what impacts these different pressures have on the content and broadcast of messages in a modern democratic society.

Another aspect of the mechanism of money as a means of influence on opinion is the financing of think tanks and intellectual activity generally. In most modern democratic societies, a significant amount of financing is private, and this may also have the effect of biasing the generation of opinion toward the points of view and interests of the better off. Again, these institutions need not speak with one voice; there may be substantial disagreement among them, but the concern is that the disagreement is limited by the commonalities of economic class and that this sets an agenda for thinking that is decidedly biased toward the interests and viewpoints of the better off. On the other hand, in modern liberal democracies, large public institutions such as universities may provide some counterbalance to these influences.

This mechanism of money as a means of influence on opinion, while potentially very powerful, is quite muddy. We need much more research on the impact of economic class on the generation and transmission of opinion.

4. Money as Independent Political Power

In this case money does not operate directly on the process of collective decision making; it operates as an independent constraint. If the government does something to pursue some democratically chosen aim and capitalists can either subvert the aim or subvert some other government aim (say, by decreasing investment and thereby increasing unemployment), then the activities of capitalists can amount to an independent exercise of political power. Governments must make decisions with an eye to what powerful economic entities do in response to those decisions. In some cases, the powerful groups respond to popular policies by subverting other popular aims. For example, a large company or group of companies can take their capital elsewhere (increasing unemployment) if the society imposes costly environmental regulation. In other cases, the government can anticipate the actions of the powerful group and decline to pursue an otherwise popular policy and aim. Money, in mixed economies and in capitalist economies, can confer a significant amount of power on very wealthy individuals and corporations, which enables them to undermine or deflect popular policies. To the extent the wealth that can exercise this power is disproportionately controlled by affluent groups, we have another mechanism by which political power can be unequally distributed as a consequence of the distribution of money.[8]

5. Money, Politics, and Equality

Here I discuss in more depth the threat that the money as gatekeeper and money as a tool for opinion formation pose to political equality and why it is important. The basic concern is that those who have more money to spend on politics will tend to have their voices or the voices of those who agree with them better heard than many others. This creates a deep inequality in the opportunity to influence the making of opinion and preference and the selection of candidates and thus the setting of the agenda for collective decision making.[9] The problem of money in politics is not intentional discrimination as, for example, property qualifications on the franchise in the past were. For instance, the U.S. Supreme Court ruled against a variety of campaign finance provisions as improper limits on free expression. The intention may be to protect free expression, and the unequal influence of money on politics the expected side effect.

Some might argue that inequality of opportunity for political influence gives persons unequal chances to engage in the kind of political self-realization that is a component of the good life. But we might feel that this particular kind of inequality is significant but not all that important. Political self-realization is one among many interests, and it is one that not all persons share, so that persons who have fewer opportunities for this type of engagement are not seriously damaged overall. This inequality does not carry as much weight, I think, as the concern for inequality in politics generally does.

A better explanation of the significance of wealth-induced inequalities of opportunity for influence on opinion can be seen if we accept the thesis that there are likely to be significant conflicts of interests between those who have less wealth and those who have more wealth. The most important of these concerns are over how to share the wealth and products of society. There are also conflicts that arise from the varied interests that people have when they live in very different sectors of society. Their background experiences, desires, and needs may be different. These differences are likely to have great significance for the interests of these persons. These differences in interest are likely to imply conflict of interests over how the society is organized. My sense is that differences in economic class are as important for the overall interests a person has in life as any differences that exist. Thus, differences of interests and points of view are not randomly associated with differences in wealth; they are on the contrary systematically and statistically connected with them. This is probably not so for differences in height or even differences in attractiveness. To be sure, not all wealthy people support the interests and viewpoints of the wealthy, although the general statistical tendency may be quite strong. These ideas must all be taken as working hypotheses in this chapter, but it is of the first importance that empirical research be conducted on these issues.

Now if there is some significant statistical tendency for the interests and points of view of persons to divide along lines of economic class, then this poses a problem for inequality of opportunity of influence on opinion and decision making. To the extent that we can expect the points of view of persons to reflect the circumstances of their lives and to be biased in various ways toward their own interests (and I think this is a fairly fundamental assumption to all democratic theory), and to the extent that economic class is a significant determinant of point of view and interests, we have reason to think that a system of communication that is financed primarily by the well-to-do will tend to reflect their distinctive interests. It will neglect discussion of the interests of the other economic sectors of society. I see two potentially worrisome implications of this situation. First, it suggests a publicly clear way in which the interests of the great majority of the population are not receiving significant attention in decision making. The interests of most people are not treated as worthy of much consideration. This seems to me to violate the most fundamental principle animating democracy as expressed by the remarks of Colonel Rainsborough in the Putney Debates: "I think that the poorest he that is in England hath a life to live, as the greatest he" (Woodhouse 1951, 52).

Second, a system with such large inequalities of influence over the process of communication presents to the public a distorted and truncated vision of the society that is being discussed. The interests of most members of society go ignored to a significant degree. The points of view of most of those members receive scant attention, which implies that an enormous amount of local knowledge fails to make an appearance in the public sphere. The damage to the deliberative process could be quite severe, and it is a consequence of the inegalitarian effect of money on politics.

David Estlund has objected to this political egalitarianism on the grounds that, first, it seems to invite leveling down of opportunities to influence the political system. Second, he argues that this concern for equality is not necessary for equal respect. The second concern can only be fully explained after the first is. Estlund's idea is that if one regards equality of opportunity for political influence as a basic ideal of democracy, then one must argue that systems in which there is very little discussion and deliberation are superior to systems in which there is a lot of discussion and deliberation as long as there is equal opportunity in the former but not the latter. Because political equality of the substantive variety explored here recommends leveling down, Estlund thinks so much for worse for political equality (Estlund 2000).

However, egalitarians have two responses to the leveling-down concern. First, they say that equality is one concern among many and that it does not always override other concerns such as quality of deliberation. It is not, for all that, an insignificant moral good. In this view, while the situation in which there is more deliberation may be better, all things considered, than the situation in which there is less deliberation, it may be that it is worse in one respect than the more equal state of affairs (Temkin 2009). This has not been argued against as far as I know.

A second response, which I favor, rejects the idea that equality implies leveling down at all. Very crudely, the principle of equality on this view identifies for any situation an ideal egalitarian distribution relative to which all other distributions are unjust. This ideal egalitarian distribution is Pareto-efficient. It takes the total amount of relevant good produced by the most productive action in the situation and distributes it equally. To be sure, this will not always be feasible, but it gives us a standard relative to which other distributions within the feasible set can be seen as approximations. The rule of approximation may allow that some, or even all, unequal distributions are closer approximations to the ideal distribution than the Pareto inferior equal distributions are. The reason for holding this Paretian egalitarian principle is that there is an internal connection between the rationale for equality and the importance of the thing distributed. If the item distributed were not such that more is better than less or less is better than more, no one would care about the equality.

The implication of the second conception of the principle of equality is that, while all inequalities are unjust, some equality may be even more unjust than Pareto superior inequalities. The principle of equality so understood would give us reason to regret inequalities but would not give us reason to level down. So if we had a choice between an egalitarian distribution of opportunities and a nonegalitarian distribution in which everyone had more opportunity, we would regret the inequality but not prefer the Pareto inferior equality (Christiano and Braynen 2008).

The system of political influence endorsed by the principle of political equality will admit some inequalities, because only a decentralized system can foster the diversity of positions so necessary for robust debate and give expression to the great variety of interests in the society. Decentralization also produces significant inequalities, because the decentralized process cannot be entirely controlled. As long as these inequalities arise from a system that promotes everyone's opportunity to participate in politics relative to other feasible arrangements, the principle of equality will favor such an arrangement.

Estlund argues that equality of opportunity for political influence is not necessary for equal respect. He argues that equal respect or disrespect can be the result only of arrangements that result from the condescension or ill will of persons. But I am not convinced of this. It seems to me that if a system is known to disadvantage certain persons systematically and is nevertheless maintained, that is sufficient for the relevant failure of respect. Consider a system of discussion in a classroom in which each person participates if he or she is loud enough to barge in. The quieter persons are de facto excluded, though this is in no way intended by the group. It is simply a known by-product of the arrangement. If nothing is done to mitigate the problem, disrespect has been shown to the quieter persons. Estlund is right to say that inequality need not show disrespect. To the extent that the society has done its best to approximate the ideal egalitarian distribution, it does not show disrespect to anyone even though they have less. There is something to regret because the interests of those who have less opportunity for influence are likely to suffer; however, if we cannot do better, then the system does not display disrespect. If we can get closer to the ideal egalitarian distribution but we do not, then this mere failure displays disrespect. I think that the political difference principle that Estlund articulates (which requires that the opportunities of those with the least opportunity be maximized) is often a reasonable approximation to the ideal egalitarian distribution, but it is not, I think, a principle of justice—rather it is a principle of least injustice, or so an egalitarian can argue.

Freedom of Expression

Some argue that limitations on expenditures in elections and contributions to candidates or parties both violate some core commitment of the principle of freedom of expression (Anderson 2000). Others argue that only limits on expenditures limit free expression. Still others believe that neither limits the right of free expression (Dworkin 1999).

Once we distinguish the first three mechanisms of the effects of money on politics, we can see that the relation of freedom of expression to campaign finance limits varies with the mechanism. Limits on contributions and perhaps expenditures do not seem particularly burdensome to the interest in free expression if the main target is expenditures by special interests to influence votes by legislators. These are simple exchanges, and generally the use of money to buy things (that are not expression) is not regarded as a core interest in the freedom of expression. This seems to be what the U.S. Supreme Court was saying when it accepted contribution limits with the aim of limiting quid pro quo arrangements. It may have erred by failing to include some expenditure limits under this umbrella, but the basic idea is fairly clear. However, when we think in terms of the gatekeeper and opinion-formation mechanisms, the issues become clouded. With the gatekeeper mechanism, the spending of money to support a candidate one approves of and without any assumption of quid pro quo seems a fairly straightforward realization of the interests in freedom of expression. One expresses one's approval of a candidate or party and the ideas and policies they advocate.

This suggests a problem with the Supreme Court's claim that there is a crucial distinction between contribution and expenditure limits. Contribution and expenditure limits that attempt to suppress the money-for-votes mechanism do not implicate free expression, while those that attack the gatekeeper mechanism do implicate a core exercise of the freedom of expression. When we focus on the money-for-votes mechanism, it makes sense to say that the limits are all unproblematic. With the gatekeeper and opinion-formation mechanisms, clearly all the limits frustrate core interests of the freedom of expression. Once we distinguish mechanisms, we can see the insights in each position.

Focusing on limits that regulate the gatekeeper and opinion-formation mechanisms, one might argue that the limits are like time/manner/place restrictions because they merely affect the frequency with which one can express one's views. Ronald Dworkin argues that "Citizen equality does require ... that different groups of citizens not be disadvantaged, in their effort to gain attention and respect for their views, by a circumstance as remote from the substance of opinion or argument, or from the legitimate sources of influence as wealth is" (Dworkin 1999, 81). But these limits are not entirely viewpoint neutral, because the underlying rationale is to limit the speech of the affluent on the grounds that the affluent are likely to share distinctive interests and points of view and so unduly dominate the agenda to the neglect of other views and interests. Indeed, if wealth had nothing to do with the substance of opinion and argument, and opinions were entirely randomly distributed across economic class, we would not be all that concerned with the dominance of wealth in democratic politics.

Limits on the gatekeeper mechanism through expenditure caps restrict a core exercise of the freedom of expression. This does not by any means imply that there should not be limitations, but these limitations can be justified only by balancing the interest in freedom of expression against the democratic purposes. To be sure, the limits are temporary and very specific and do not undermine the long-run ability to express ideas. But those with more absolutist tendencies regarding freedom of expression will not want to make the trade-off.

Even if the cost to free expression that results from restrictions on campaign finance are not prohibitive, the costs to free expression required to democratize the process of opinion and preference formation and dissemination are great, at least in an economy that allows a significant amount of private property. Some have argued that one need limit the process of opinion and preference formation and dissemination only during election campaigns and not elsewhere (Cohen 2001). The rationale for this is not clear, because the long-run development of opinion and preference is more important to the course of a democracy than the short-term developments in electoral campaigns. Perhaps the following compromise makes sense: Limit expression around electoral campaigns to make sure that all the different sectors of society receive a hearing during those periods. Supplement this with vouchers to all persons that they can spend on whatever groups they wish. The limits might be justified on the grounds that an egalitarian process of deliberation is of paramount importance during the campaigns and the limits to private expenditures are only temporary. For the long-term process of development of opinion and preference formation, the system of vouchers could be put on a permanent footing while imposing very few restrictions on free expression. This compromise attempts to satisfy the democratic concerns by making sure that potentially broadly held opinions at least have adequate resources to develop, and it satisfies our concern that free expression should not be limited in most contexts. It is not obvious that much more could be done to equalize opportunities to influence the long-run development of opinion anyway.

NOTES

1. See the essays in Ewing and Issacharoff (2006) and Posada-Carbo and Malamud (2005) for reviews of some different campaign finance systems.
2. These theses are widely defended by contemporary scholars of election financing and legislative process. See, for example, Sorauf (1994); Hall and Wayman (1990); and Ansolabehere, de Figueirido, and Snyder (2003).
3. This research is briefly described in Lessig (2010).
4. See any of the references in note 2 above.
5. For example, the United States permits contribution limits but rejects expenditure limits, whereas the United Kingdom has recently chosen to impose expenditure limits but has rejected contribution limits.
6. See Geddis (2006) for New Zealand's experience with this method.
7. See del Castillo (2005) for Spain's experience with this method.
8. See Lindblom (1977) for more on this idea. See also Przeworski and Wallerstein (1988). For the relationship between this phenomenon and equality, see Christiano (2010).
9. See Cohen (2001) for an articulation of this principle. See also Dworkin (1999).

REFERENCES

Ackerman, Bruce, and Ian Ayres. 2004. *Voting with Dollars: A New Paradigm for Campaign Finance*. New Haven, CT: Yale University Press.

Adamany, David, and George Agree. 1975. *Political Money: A Strategy for Campaign Financing in America*. Baltimore, MD: Johns Hopkins University Press.

Anderson, Annelise. 2000. "Political Money: The New Prohibition." In *Political Money: Deregulating American Politics—Selected Essays on Campaign Finance Reform*. Edited by Annelise Anderson, 171–85. Stanford, CA: Hoover Institution Press.

Ansolabehere, Stephen, John M. de Figueirido, and James M. Snyder. 2003. "Why Is There So Little Money in U.S. Politics?" *Journal of Economic Perspectives* 17: 105–30.

Bartels, Larry M. 2008. *Unequal Democracy: The Political Economy of the New Gilded Age*. Princeton, NJ: Princeton University Press.

Beitz, Charles. 1989. *Political Equality: An Essay in Democratic Theory*. Princeton, NJ: Princeton University Press.

Brennan, Jason. 2011. *The Ethics of Voting*. Princeton, NJ: Princeton University Press.

Christiano, Thomas. 2008. *The Constitution of Equality: Democratic Authority and Its Limits*. Oxford: Oxford University Press.

Christiano, Thomas. 2010. "The Uneasy Relationship between Democracy and Capital." *Social Philosophy & Policy* 27(1): 195–217.

Christiano, Thomas, and Will Braynen. 2008. "Inequality, Injustice and Leveling Down." *Ratio* XXL: 392–420.

Cohen, Joshua. 2001. "Money, Politics and Political Equality." In *Fact and Value: Essays on Ethics and Metaphysics for Judith Jarvis Thomson*. Edited by Alex Byrne, Robert Stalnaker, and Ralph Wedgwood, 47–80. Cambridge, MA: MIT Press.

Dahl, Robert. 1989. *Democracy and Its Critics*. New Haven, CT: Yale University Press.

del Castillo, Pilar. 2005. "Financing Political Parties in Spain." In *The Financing of Politics*, 93–103. London: Institute for the Study of the Americas.

Dworkin, Ronald. 1999. "Free Speech and the Dimensions of Democracy." In *If Buckley Fell: A First Amendment Blueprint for Regulating Money in Politics*. Edited by E. Joshua Rosenkranz, 63–101. New York: Century Foundation Press.

Entman, Robert. 1990. *Democracy without Citizens: Media and the Decay of American Politics*. New York: Oxford University Press.

Estlund, David. 2000. "Political Quality." *Social Philosophy & Policy* 17: 127–60.

Ewing, K. D., and Samuel Issacharoff, eds. 2006. *Party Funding and Campaign Financing in International Perspective*. Oxford: Hart Publishing.

Geddis, Andrew. 2006. "The Regulation of Campaign Funding in New Zealand: Practices, Problems and Prospects for Change." In *Party Funding and Campaign Financing in International Perspective*. Edited by K. D. Ewing and Samuel Issacharoff, 13–32. Oxford: Hart Publishing.

Ghaleigh, Navraj Singh. 2006. "Expenditure, Donations and Public Funding under the United Kingdom's Political Parties, Elections and Referendums Act 2000." In *Party Funding and Campaign Financing in International Perspective*. Edited by K. D. Ewing and Samuel Issacharoff, 35–56. Oxford: Hart Publishing

Gilens, Martin. 2005. "Inequality and Democratic Responsiveness." *Public Opinion Quarterly* 69(5): 778–96.

Hall, Richard, and Frank Wayman. 1990. "Buying Time: Moneyed Interests and the Mobilization of Bias in Congressional Committees." *American Political Science Review* 84:797–820.

Lessig, Lawrence. 2010. "Democracy after *Citizens United.*" *Boston Review* (September/October).
Lindblom, Charles. 1977. *Politics and Markets: The World's Political Economic Systems.* New York: Basic Books.
Miliband, Ralph. 1970. *The State in Capitalist Society.* New York: Basic Books.
Posada-Carbo, Eduardo, and Carlos Malamud, eds. 2005. *The Financing of Politics: Latin American and European Perspectives.* London: Institute for the Study of the Americas.
Przeworski, Adam, and Michael Wallerstein. 1988. "Structural Dependence of the State on Capital." *American Political Science Review* 82(1): 11–29.
Samuels, David. 2001. "Does Money Matter? Credible Commitments and Campaign Finance in New Democracies: Theory and Evidence from Brazil." *Comparative Politics* 34(1): 23–42.
Smith, Bradley A. 2000. "Campaign Finance Regulation: Faulty Assumptions and Undemocratic Consequences." In *Political Money: Deregulating American Politics—Selected Essays on Campaign Finance Reform.* Edited by Annelise Anderson, 36–72. Stanford, CA: Hoover Institution Press.
Sorauf, Frank. 1994. *Inside Campaign Finance: Myths and Realities.* New Haven, CT: Yale University Press.
Temkin, Larry. 2009. "Illuminating Egalitarianism." In *Contemporary Debates in Political Philosophy.* Edited by Thomas Christiano and John Christman, 155–78. Malden MA: Wiley-Blackwell.
Walzer, Michael. 1983. *Spheres of Justice: A Defense of Pluralism and Equality.* Boulder, CO: Basic Books.
Woodhouse, A. S. P., ed. 1951. *Puritanism and Liberty, Being the Army Debates (1647–9) from the Clarke Manuscripts with Supplementary Documents,* 2d ed. London: J.M. Dent & Sons.

PART IV

The Globe

CHAPTER 14

GLOBAL JUSTICE

MATHIAS RISSE

1. THINKING ABOUT JUSTICE IN A GLOBALIZING WORLD

Justice generates especially stringent claims.[1] In Shakespeare's *Merchant of Venice*, Shylock makes his demand to a pound of his delinquent debtor's flesh in terms of justice. Until the clever Portia finds a device for voiding the contract, the presumption is that it must be granted. Conceptually, demands of justice are the hardest to outweigh or suspend. Kant goes too far insisting that there is no point for us to continue to live on earth unless justice prevails (1996, 473). Still, justice plays a central role in human affairs precisely because it enables persons to present claims of such stringency. A theory of *justice* explains why certain individuals have particularly stringent claims to certain relative or absolute shares, quantities, or amounts of something whose distribution over certain people must be justifiable to them. Alongside justice there is also *rectificatory justice*, and perhaps other kinds. Yet because our concern in all but Sections 8 and 9 is with justice, *justice* here refers to justice unless otherwise noted.

Increasing political and economic interconnectedness draws much philosophical attention to the question of the conditions under which such stringent claims arise. Do claims of justice arise only among those who share membership in a state? Alternatively, do they arise among all those who are jointly subject to the global political and economic order? Or do they apply among all human beings simply because they are human? Inquiries into *global justice* differ from those into *international justice* precisely by not limiting inquiry to what states should do. They may also question the very moral acceptability of states and explore alternative arrangements.

When Hobbes devoted *De Cive* to exploring the rights of the state and the duties of its subjects, he did something fundamentally new. Focusing on the confrontation between individual and state, after all, meant *not* to focus on the relationship of the individual with particular rulers or multiple authorities. It meant to assess a person's relationship with an enduring institution that made exclusive claims to the exercise of certain powers within a domain. Centuries later, Kavka could write that "the relationship between the individual and the state forms the core of Western political philosophy," just as "the relationship between morality and prudence lies at the center of Western ethics" (1986, 21). Due to its focus on the state (a reflection of the political realities of the age), until recently, modern political philosophy has done comparatively little to theorize justice outside of states or to assess political and economic structures other than states in light of such inquiries.

Now, however, we must ask with some urgency about the conditions under which principles of justice apply. That inquiry is central to the burgeoning field of global justice. This question about the applicability of principles of justice also generates (renewed or new) interest in political structures such as a world state: a world with federative structures stronger than the United Nations, with a more comprehensive system of collective security, in which jurisdictions are disaggregated, or in which border control is collectively administered or abandoned entirely. Reflection on such structures is of great interest in an increasingly politically and economically interconnected world where enormous differences in life prospects nonetheless persist. Depending on what one thinks about the conditions under which demands of justice apply, one may favor one or other of these structures. Even if one thinks that subverting the state system is practically impossible, one may still explore *moral* objections to it, specifically from a standpoint of justice. Such inquiries naturally assume the shape of determining the conditions under which principles of justice apply.

Fleischacker (2004) shows that the modern conception of *domestic justice* incorporates several premises. First, each individual has a good that deserves respect, and individuals are due rights and protections to that end. Justice is not (merely) a matter of realizing, say, a divine order. Second, some share of material goods is among the rights and protections everyone deserves. Third, the fact that each person deserves such rights and protections is rationally and secularly justifiable. Fourth, the distribution of these goods is practical: It is neither a fool's project nor self-undermining, like attempts to enforce friendship. Fifth, it is for the state (and conceivably other political entities) to achieve justice. These commitments about how the fates of individuals are tied together are strikingly unusual by historical standards. It is such an understanding of domestic justice that also generates the debate about *global justice*. If each individual has a good that deserves respect, we must ask if corresponding duties expire at the borders; if shares of material goods are among the rights and protections everyone deserves, we must ask if this depends on where people live. If protections require rational justification, we must ask if such justification is available for (what I call) the normative peculiarity of the state. If the distribution of these goods is practical, we must note that today a network of organizations seeks to make this true globally. Plausibly, entities other than states should also strive for justice.

The "global (political and economic) order" and an "increasingly interconnected world" have particular meanings in this context. Our current global society has emerged from developments that began in the fifteenth century through the spread of European control, continuing with the formation of new states through independence or decolonization. While this order has no government, it comprises treaty- and convention-based norms regulating territorial sovereignty, security and trade, some property rights, human rights, and the environment. Politically, the United Nations Charter codifies the most significant rules governing this system. Economically, the Bretton Woods institutions (International Monetary Fund, World Bank, later also the General Agreement on Trade and Tariffs/World Trade Organization [WTO]) form a network intended to prevent war and foster worldwide betterment. Jointly with more powerful states, these institutions shape the economic order.

The term *globalization* describes processes that erode the political and economic importance of national boundaries and increasingly affect life chances through the system of rules that is constitutive of the global order. "Globalization" is not new. It traces back to the spread of European control, a process accompanied by the emergence of a state system whose central features were reflected in the doctrine of "sovereignty." Political philosophers of the seventeenth and eighteenth centuries, such as Grotius, Locke, Hobbes, Wolff, Vattel, and Kant, explored questions about that stage of globalization. They developed the doctrine of sovereignty, explored under what conditions one could acquire non-European territories, and considered what kind of ownership there could be of the seas. The spread of European control was complete by the end of the nineteenth century. By that time, political philosophers such as Tocqueville and Mill had already been busy justifying why non-Europeans should endure political dependence. A period of devising rules for the spread of an "empire" gave way to a period of justifying its persistence.

After World War II "global governance" came into its own, in the form of the international institutions mentioned previously. Political philosophers at this stage of globalization worry about normative issues that such governance raises. Among these issues is the question of whether principles of justice indeed apply only within states. Perhaps such principles apply to the global order as well. Or, again, they might apply independently of political and economic structures and instead hold because of common humanity and thus apply to all human beings. By "positions on global justice" I mean views about the conditions under which principles of justice hold.

2. The Grounds of Justice

We can formulate positions on global (distributive) justice in terms of the distinction between *relationism* and *nonrelationism*. That distinction captures some of the most important debates in contemporary political philosophy. "Relationists" think principles of justice hold only among persons who stand in some essentially practice-mediated relation to each other. "Nonrelationists" think such principles may apply among those who stand in no such relation.

A reference to practices keeps nonrelationism from collapsing into relationism. The relation of "being within 100,000 km of each other" is not essentially practice mediated, nor is, more relevantly, that of "being a fellow-human." I say "essentially" practice-mediated relations because there may be practices associated especially with this latter relation that are dispensable to understanding its content. Paradigmatic nonrelationists base the applicability of principles of justice on common humanity and relationists on shared political structures. Relationists and nonrelationists disagree about the *grounds* of justice, the norm-generating conditions or considerations that render demands of justice applicable among persons for whom these conditions and considerations hold. I use the term "grounds" to remain neutral between relationists and nonrelationists and thus arrive at a rather abstract formulation in terms of "conditions or considerations." I use the term "relationship" sufficiently broadly for relationists and nonrelationists to register as offering different accounts of what one might call the "justice relationship."

Relationists may hold a range of views about the nature of the relevant relation. They may disagree about the scope of justice, or the range of people in the justice relationship. *Globalists* think the relevant relation holds among all human beings in virtue of the existence of practices that relate all humans to each other within a single global order. *Statists* think the relevant relation holds (only) among individuals who share membership in a state.[2] They owe an account of what it is (exclusively) about shared membership in states that generates demands of justice. Globalists owe an account of what it is about involvement with, or subjection to, the global order that generates demands of justice. Those who accept duties of justice that hold (only) among people who share a state endorse "the normative peculiarity of the state"; those who do not, reject it. Statists endorse the normative peculiarity of the state; globalists and nonrelationists do not. So whereas globalists and statists are united by being relationists, globalists and nonrelationists are united by rejecting the normative peculiarity of the state.[3]

Relevant versions of nonrelationism take the scope of justice to be global, including all of (and only) humanity. Yet nonrelationists may determine the scope differently. One could limit justice to a subset of humanity by insisting on the normative importance of, say, sex or race. Or one may insist that justice must have all sentient beings in its scope, at least higher animals and conceivably rational Martians. Yet the former possibility is implausible, and the latter I set aside. Nonrelationists owe an account of how common humanity generates demands of justice.[4] Relationists think of principles of justice as regulating practices that some persons share with each other. This implies two things. First, for relationists, principles of justice apply only to those who respectively share the practices. Relationists are motivated by the moral relevance of practices in which certain individuals stand. Such practices may include not only those that individuals chose to adopt but also those of which they have never chosen to partake. Second, relationists think of principles of justice as regulating only those practices rather than every aspect of the lives of those who share them.

3. RAWLSIAN RELATIONISM

To illustrate what is at stake, note that John Rawls is a relationist. He famously calls justice "the first virtue of institutions, as truth is of systems of thought" and talks about "justice in social cooperation" (1999a, 3; also see the chapter on Rawls by Leif Wenar in this volume). Justice here is a characteristic of institutions, which are practices. Rawls's principles regulate the practices constitutive of the basic structure of society (the way in which the major social institutions fit together into one system and how they assign fundamental rights and duties and shape the division of advantages from cooperation). "Justice," says Freeman by way of expounding this approach, "poses the general problem of fairly designing the system of basic legal institutions and social norms that make production, exchange, distribution, and consumption possible among free and equal persons" (2007, 305). Many aspects of advantage and its distribution are natural facts, but "what is just and unjust," says Rawls are not these facts, but "the way that institutions deal with these facts" (1999a, 87).

Relationists can recognize duties to those with whom they do not stand in the justice relationship. Alas, those duties would either differ relevantly from duties of justice or else in some other way differ from those duties of justice that hold among individuals who share the relevant relation. Nagel (2005) adopts the former approach, insisting that justice only holds within states. Rawls (1999b) adopts the latter and implicitly acknowledges a distinction between duties of justice that hold within states and other duties of justice that may hold otherwise. The duty of assistance to "burdened societies" in *The Law of Peoples* is not one of justice (Rawls 1999b, 106, 113–20; see also Freeman 2007, ch. 9). Duties of justice are duties with regard to shares in a system of economic production and exchange, which Rawls thinks presuppose a basic structure.

Rawls is a statist. His main goal is to offer principles of domestic justice. *The Law of Peoples* adds an approach to international justice by way of sketching the foreign policy of a society within which his domestic principles of justice apply. Methodologically in the background is Rawls's political constructivism. Rawls begins with domestic justice and works "outward" from there to *The Law of Peoples*, and "inward" to local justice (2001, 11). These other subjects presuppose domestic justice. As Freeman says:

> The principles that appropriately regulate social and political relations depend upon the kinds of institutions or practices to be regulated, and these principles are to be "constructed" on the basis of ideas that are central to the functioning of those institutions or practices and people's awareness of them. (2007, 270)

Freeman sees this political constructivism—a view on justification—as integral to Rawls's rejection of global principles of justice. The convictions and intuitions that must be in reflective equilibrium to obtain a theory of justice concern the practices and institutions in which we lead our lives. These convictions are less developed outside of the domestic setting.

Wenar (2006) offers a plausible reading of Rawls that responds to critics, such as Caney (2002), who think *The Law of Peoples* is incoherent with Rawls's earlier work. Crucially, both in the domestic and in the global case, Rawls draws on ideas implicit in the public political culture. Rawls believes "that humans should be coerced only according to a self-image that is acceptable to them," which means that "[s]ince 'global citizens' cannot be presumed to view themselves as free and equal individuals who should relate fairly to each other across national boundaries, we cannot legitimately build coercive social institutions that assume that they do" (Wenar 2006, 103). Wenar rightly uses this observation to explain why Rawls did not advocate global egalitarian ideals of a sort that Beitz (1999) and Pogge (1989) found a natural extension of his principles. Global public political culture is of a different (much thinner) nature than that of a constitutional democracy.

4. The Grounds of Justice: Some Further Clarifications

Nonrelationists object that by making justice practice-mediated relationists either tie justice to properties of individuals that omit too much of moral importance (for practices individuals have not selected) or overemphasize some morally important aspects at the expense of others (for practices in which individuals chose to participate). Parallel to what I said about relationists, nonrelationism implies two things: Nonrelationists seek to avoid the alleged arbitrariness of restricting justice to the regulation of certain practices,[5] and because nonrelationists do not limit justice in this way, they will plausibly apply principles of justice to the whole range of advantageous and disadvantageous events in a life. (Regarding the use of "will plausibly": Recall that there is *logical* space for nonrelationists to proceed differently.) For nonrelationists, justice is a property of the distribution of advantage, broadly understood. Whereas for relationists individuals stand in the justice relationship if they have special claims within particular practices, for nonrelationists that relationship is distinguished by the absence of special claims.[6]

Two clarifications are important here. First, "grounds" differ from "circumstances" of justice. "[T]he circumstances of justice obtain," explains Rawls, following Hume, "whenever persons put forward conflicting claims to the division of social advantages under conditions of moderate scarcity" (1999a, 110). Both circumstances and grounds tell us "when demands of justice apply," but they do so in different senses. "Circumstances of justice" specify those living conditions of human beings under which *any* principles of justice apply *in the first place*. Unless we live under such circumstances, no principles of justice apply to begin with. If we live under these circumstances, the grounds specify *which* principles of justice apply to *which* people.

Second, consider Pogge's widely quoted definition of "cosmopolitanism":

> Three elements are shared by all cosmopolitan positions: First, *individualism*: the ultimate unit of concern are *human beings*, or *persons* . . . . Second, *universality*: the status of ultimate unit of concern attaches to *every* living human being *equally*—not merely to some sub-set, such as men, aristocrats, Aryans, whites, or Muslims. Third, *generality*: this special status has global force. (1994, 89)

None of the positions I discuss (statism, globalism, nonrelationism) denies the moral equality of persons. Each of these positions has capacities to makes sense of individualism, universality, and generality. A crucial issue for each of these positions is how rich a notion of moral equality its advocates wish to endorse and how the relevant notion of moral equality relates to ideas of political and distributive equality. In any event, one needs additional arguments to derive distributive equality of anything from ideas of moral or political equality. Statists deny a close link between moral and political equality: All human beings are morally equal, but it is only in the presence of certain practices (those of shared citizenship in a state) that ideas of political equality even apply. Statists may or may not find inequality among individuals in one country (in terms of outcomes, resources, or opportunities) morally problematic, but they do not find inequality among countries *as such* morally problematic. Globalists and nonrelationists may endorse a global maximin, sufficiency criterion, or other criteria. A range of views on inequality is open to them, but none depend on shared membership in states.

We have learned the basic cosmopolitan lesson: Moral equality is an essential part of any credible theory of global justice. In the domain of justice, the term *cosmopolitan* has become the victim of its own success. Therefore, we should conduct the philosophical debate in the terms discussed in this chapter rather than in a way that thinks of cosmopolitanism as a distinctive position on global justice. We live on a "cosmopolitan plateau" in the way in which Kymlicka (2002) (following a suggestion by Ronald Dworkin) claims that plausible political theories populate an "egalitarian plateau." All plausible theories of domestic justice define "the social, economic and political conditions under which the members of the community are treated as equals" (Kymlicka 2002, 4). Similarly, all plausible theories of global justice ascribe significance to moral equality.

5. Nonrelationism

Nonrelationists insist that relations in which particular individuals stand with each other cannot have the kind of moral importance that would imply that moral obligations (or a broad range of obligations) apply only among those who do so. Caney (2005) suggests a version of this approach. He offers the following thought regarding the relevance of economic interaction and a similar thought would apply to all practices:

Consider a world with two separate systems of interaction that have no contact but are aware of each other and suppose that one of them is prosperous whereas the other is extremely impoverished. Compare, now, two individuals—one from the prosperous system and the other from the impoverished system—who are identical in their abilities and needs. The member of the prosperous system receives more. But it is difficult to see why—concentrating on any possible and reasonable criteria for entitlement—this is fair. *Ex hypothesi*, she is not more hard-working or more gifted or more needy. In all respects they are identical (bar one, namely that one is lucky to live in the prosperous society and one is not) and yet an institutionalist approach confers on one more benefits. (2005, 110)[7]

To develop his case, Caney's strategy is to identify a moral argument of sorts and then to argue that that argument appeals to properties that everyone has. Limiting such arguments to particular groups means to commit what Caney, following Black (1991), calls the "fallacy of restricted universalism": "A distributive theory, that ascribes rights and claims on the basis of certain universal attributes of persons, cannot at the same time restrict the grounds for those claims to a person's membership or status within a given society" (2005, 357). Attempts to derive principles of justice from universal attributes that nevertheless are supposed to be limited to certain groups (e.g., compatriots) commit this fallacy. Consider the way in which Caney applies this strategy to civil and political liberties. He argues for the "scope$_1$ claim": "the standard justifications of rights to civil and political liberties entail that there are *human* rights to these same civil and political liberties" (2005, 66), according to the scope$_1$,

> because the standard arguments for civil and political rights invoke a universalist "moral personality." That is, the relevant aspect of persons is the right to be subject to principles to which they can reasonably consent (for contractarians), or their use of moral language (for Habermas), or their humanity and status as persons (for deontologists), or their ability to lead a fulfilling life (for perfectionists). As such, it would be incoherent to adopt any of these lines of reasoning for a particular right and then ascribe that right only to other members of one's community. (2005, 77)

Arguments of this sort at the very least pose a challenge for relationists to explain just what it is about their preferred relation that, in the case that interests us, generates demands of justice that would apply only among those who share that relation. Whether they succeed at this task and so can respond to nonrelationists such as Caney is the subject of the next section.

6. Statism and Globalism

Statists and globalists disagree about what relation is relevant for the applicability of principles of justice. Nonetheless, they are both relationists, resting claims of justice on nationally or globally shared practices, respectively, and thus to some extent use similar arguments to defend their views. Defenses of relationism may enlist two strategies.

The first strategy draws on the fact that it is (conceptually) difficult for us successfully to press demands on each other at all, especially the stringent demands of justice. Relationists are well equipped to deal with this difficulty. They can help themselves to considerations that arise from within the practices they consider central to the applicability of justice. They need not deny that there can be natural rights and duties of justice at all. But arguments in their support can enlist only features of shared humanity. Crucially, derivations of transactional and associational duties (the kind of arguments relationists offer) can enlist a larger set of considerations. They can use claims about persons having undergone certain transactions under specific conditions (e.g., promises, contracts) or about them living in certain human-made arrangements that often assume different shapes and that put demands on those involved in them. Claims of justice cannot succeed merely based on references to the significance of something for the claimant. We need reasons why others ought to provide what is significant. Nonrelationists can most readily meet that challenge if they restrict themselves to establishing rights and duties pertaining to elementary human concerns, such as basic-needs satisfaction. Relationists are better equipped to make such a case. In particular, duties pertaining to *relative*, rather than *absolute*, economic status are (at the very least) easier to establish, and are more demanding, if we can resort to shared practices to make that case.

To illustrate, consider Scanlon's (2003) influential discussion of objections to inequality and hence to differences in relative economic status. Scanlon identifies five reasons to pursue greater equality: (a) to relieve suffering or severe deprivation, (b) to prevent stigmatizing differences in status, (c) to avoid unacceptable forms of power or domination, (d) to preserve the equality of starting places that is required by procedural fairness, and (e) because procedural fairness sometimes supports a case for equality of outcomes. Statements (b) and (e) are the clearest expressions of egalitarianism; (d) is consistent with considerable inequalities and so is only weakly egalitarian, whereas (a) and (c) are not egalitarian at all. Scanlon argues that Rawls uses (b) through (e), and perhaps (a) as well, to argue in support of his principles of justice. So those principles are supported by reasons that are distinctly egalitarian but also by reasons that are distinctly not.

Crucially, however, even the force of (c) and (d) depends on the practices (if any) that the relevant individuals share. For instance, to explain what counts as unacceptable forms of power, it helps to explore how individuals respectively contribute to the maintenance of an economic system and hence also what the economic ties among them are to begin with. Undoubtedly, some exercises of power are unacceptable regardless of what relations individuals stand in. But the more ties there are among individuals, the more possibilities there will be for them to contribute to the maintenance of relations, which in turn generate rationales for them to complain about certain exercises of power. Similarly, to assess how much reason there is to preserve the equality of starting places on behalf of procedural fairness, it is essential to assess to what kinds, and range, of procedures the individuals are jointly subject. Thus, if we seek to argue for obligations pertaining to relative standing without making use of relations, there is little we can say. We can derive more demanding obligations if we can resort to relations.

The second strategy in defense of relationism appears in Scheffler's (2001) account of the link between special relations and responsibilities. Relations create responsibilities because having reason to value relations noninstrumentally just *is* to have reasons to see oneself under, and actually have, special obligations. As Scheffler puts it, to attach noninstrumental value to a relationship with someone means "to be disposed, in contexts which vary depending on the nature of the relationship, to see that person's needs, interests, and desires as, in themselves, providing me with presumptively decisive reasons for action, reasons that I would not have had in the absence of the relationship" (2001, 100;. note that to call reasons "presumptively decisive" means to grant that, in principle, they could be outweighed, although they present themselves as reasons on which agents must act). Skepticism about such responsibilities succeeds only if we have no reasons at all to value our relations noninstrumentally. The case is clearest for family ties and friendships but less clear for political relations, and presumably statists can more readily make the case than globalists. Beitz (1999, 212), for instance, does not use such reasoning to support his globalism but wonders instead about the relevance of such arguments *even* for shared membership in a state.

Statists must develop their version of relationism in a way that supports the normative peculiarity of the state. They could first use the two strategies in support of relationism to rebut nonrelationism and then offer an account of the normative peculiarity of the state to rebut globalists (and thus settle the intramural debate between relationists once relationism has been accepted). Two proposed accounts of the normative peculiarity of the state are *coercion-based statism* (i.e., what distinguishes membership in a state is its coerciveness) and *reciprocity-based statism* (i.e., what distinguishes membership in a state is its intense form of cooperation).[8]

These views, however, face the challenge that forms of coercion and cooperation also hold within the global order as such, which makes it problematic to argue that principles of justice govern *only* the relation among those who share a state. Statists can respond by arguing that the normative peculiarity of the state is based on its particular kind of coerciveness or cooperativeness. Risse (2006), for instance, accounts for the state's coerciveness in terms of legal and political immediacy. The legal aspect consists in the directness and pervasiveness of law enforcement. The political aspect consists in the crucial importance of the environment provided by the state for the realization of basic moral rights, capturing the profundity of this relationship.

However, assuming that Risse's (2006) account succeeds in explaining what is morally special about shared membership in states, one must still wonder whether this account matters *for justice*, that is, whether it can explain why principles of justice apply *only* among those who share a state. That is the point that globalists push. Capturing globalist resistance to statism, Beitz argues that global interdependence

> involves a pattern of transactions that produce substantial benefits and costs; their increased volume and significance have led to the development of a global regulative structure.... Taken together, these institutions and practices can be considered as the constitutional structure of the world economy: their activities have important distributional implications. (1999, 148)

It does not matter precisely what the nature of international economic interdependence is. The dispute between statists and globalists already arises for a loose sense of interconnectedness.

Beitz argues that in an interdependent world, limiting justice to domestic societies means taxing poor nations so that others may live in "just" regimes (1999, 149ff). Beitz's target is Rawls. He argues that if Rawls's case for his principles succeeds, their content should not change as a result of enlarging the scope of the original position to include the global order. Beitz considers two objections (1999, 154–61). The first insists that interdependence is necessary but insufficient for the applicability of justice. The global order lacks any effective decision-making mechanisms, as well as any real sense of community, and these, the objector says, are also necessary for an order's being subject to standards of justice. Beitz responds that these differences fail to show that principles of justice do not apply globally; instead, they show that it is harder to implement the principles.

According to the second objection, features of cooperation within states override requirements of global principles *even if* justice applies globally. Rich countries may deserve their advantages because of differences in organization or technology. Beitz responds that this entails basing entitlements on morally arbitrary factors such as those that, as Rawls insisted, ought not to affect one's share of social primary goods. Thus, he rejects this move much as Rawls rejects principles of justice drawing on undeserved social or genetic characteristics.

7. Pluralist Internationalism

One way of making progress in light of the debate among statists and globalists discussed in the previous section is to deny that there is a single justice relationship in which any two individuals either do or do not stand. One may use *principles of justice* as a collective term for different principles with their *respective* ground and scope. Let us call *nongraded* or *monist internationalism* the view that principles of justice either do or do not apply, that they do apply within states, and thus that they apply among people who share membership in a state and only then. Nongraded or monist internationalism is the same as statism. Introducing this additional terminology allows us to connect statism to other views that endorse the normative peculiarity of the state. Coercion-based and reciprocity-based statism are versions of monist or nongraded internationalism.

Graded internationalism holds that different principles of justice apply depending on the associational (i.e., social, legal, political, or economical) arrangements. Graded internationalism allows for associations such as the WTO, the European Union, or the global order as such to be governed by principles of justice but endorses the *normative peculiarity* of the state. Among the principles that apply within other associations we find weakened versions of principles that apply within states;

for this reason I talk about *graded internationalism*. I lack the space to motivate the graded view in detail, but suffice it to say that all those who live, say, under the WTO are tied to each other much more loosely than individuals who respectively share a state. It is therefore plausible to think that the principles of justice that hold within the WTO are weakened versions of those that hold within a state.

However, now that we have introduced a nonmonist view, we also must take seriously the idea that some grounds could be relational, whereas others would not be. We must consider the possibility that there is no deep conflict between relationism and nonrelationism. Perhaps advocates have respectively overemphasized facets of an overall plausible theory that recognizes both relationist and nonrelationist grounds. Integrating relationist grounds into a theory of justice pays homage to the idea that individuals find themselves in, or join, associations and that membership in some of them generates duties. Integrating nonrelationist grounds means taking seriously the idea that some duties of justice do not depend on the existence of associations. One obvious nonrelational ground is common humanity. One view that develops these ideas could be called *pluralist internationalism* or just *internationalism*. The use of the term *internationalism* for this position acknowledges the applicability of principles of justice outside of and among ("inter") states. This view endorses the state's normative peculiarity but recognizes multiple other grounds of justice, some relational (e.g., subjection to the global trade regime) and others not (e.g., common humanity). Respectively different principles are associated with these different grounds, all of which are binding, say, for states and international organizations. Internationalism transcends the distinction between relationism and nonrelationism.

Internationalism offers one way of preserving the plausible aspects of nonrelationism, globalism, and statism. Obviously making this view credible, and proving its fruitfulness, requires detailed discussions of its implications for a wide range of areas. The costs of making such a move are considerable, because one would give up on the uniqueness of the justice relationship. One would also have to meet the challenge that such a pluralist view does not, one way or another, collapse into one of the original views. Other ways of making progress in this debate are possible as well, including those that abandon the state's normative peculiarity. We have now reached the research frontier in this field.[9]

8. Does the Global Order Wrongfully Harm the Poor? Part 1

So far we have talked only about justice. However, perhaps the main theme in an assessment of global justice should be whether the global order wrongfully harms some people—presumably the weakest—the global poor. If so, we should think of global justice primarily in terms of moral obligations to rectify harms (where the harms are not simply defined by a conception of justice). There are different ways of articulating that thought. First, one may say the global order wrongfully harms human beings because of the sheer existence of borders. Perhaps frontiers are inconsistent especially with the value of freedom and with liberal justice. Second, perhaps the global order wrongfully harms the poor (i.e., individuals who are unable to meet basic needs) by imposing an institutional framework that is not as advantageous to them as some alternatives. Finally, one may argue that the extents of poverty and inequality themselves reveal that the global order wrongfully harms the poor.

One way of making the point that national borders can function as unjustified restrictions of freedom draws on Amartya Sen and Martha Nussbaum's approach to freedom in terms of "capabilities." [10] Nussbaum offers a list of capabilities central for a life with dignity. "Bodily integrity" is on her list, of which one instantiation is "being able to move freely from place to place" (2006, 76). The challenge is to explain why this capability can be limited by frontiers. However, appeals to the value of freedom to assess the legitimacy of borders cut both ways. It is true that frontiers limit choice, but so does any immigration policy. Permissive immigration policies in countries where many people wish to live are likely to constrain some who already live there.

Some have argued that immigration barriers are unjust owing to liberalism's commitment to moral equality. Liberalism, Carens (2003) notes, condemns the use of morally arbitrary facts about persons to justify inequalities. Examples include race, sex, and ethnicity. Political communities that treat people differently on the basis of such features are illiberal and unjust. Yet citizenship seems as arbitrary as any of those. Maintaining borders, to him, is as offensive as other perhaps more obvious cases of injustice because it differentiates rights based on origin. Carens is correct that moral equality and the value of common humanity cannot stop at borders, but it has been argued that this does not mean shared citizenship is as morally irrelevant as race or ethnicity. The fact that shared citizenship arises in a manner for which individuals deserve neither credit nor blame does not make it morally irrelevant. On this view, there is no inference from moral equality to political equality regardless of what structures persons share.[11]

In a related vein, one may argue that a system of states cannot properly consider all affected interests, and so they automatically wrongfully harm persons. The actions of states affect many who have no say in the design of policies. For instance, Mexicans who wish to enter the United States never consented to the existence of an American people that can unilaterally constrain immigration. Yet interests can be properly considered in domain-specific ways. To the extent that trade policies affect interests, for instance, we should ensure that such policies are fair, but that does not mean one must *enfranchise* everyone connected to a country by trade arrangements. We also need morally acceptable immigration policies that spell out how many people from country A have a claim to immigration to country B. But once these claims are met, no additional demands, especially to enfranchisement, arise. Moral acceptability here does not require consent.

The next question is whether the global order harms the poor because there is a feasible alternative under which the situation of the global poor is improved, as presented by Pogge (2002). Pogge seems to think "feasibility" is primarily a matter of allocating money. It would just take 1.2 percent of the income of rich economies, $312 billion annually, to bridge the aggregate shortfall of those living on less than $1 per day to the $2 line (2002, 7). Pogge's proposal for raising some of those funds is the Global Resource Dividend, which taxes extraction of resources. Yet while Pogge's calculations show that abject poverty could be surmounted *if* closing such a gap is a matter of transferring money, it is doubtful whether financial transfers are enough to seriously mitigate poverty. Suppose in situation S1 we have the funds to cover the financial shortfall. We still need reliable ways of distributing funds to individuals who do not simply have bank accounts that they can securely access. We would also need an environment in which individuals can actually spend the money on available goods and services. Both of these scenarios involve *institutional* improvements, especially if one wants the changes to be lasting. Similar points apply if one wishes to support medical and educational advancements. One cannot simply start to "work on AIDS" but instead must build and maintain medical infrastructure. One cannot improve education by building a few schoolhouses but must also invest in teacher training and provision of books, supplies, family support, and much else.

That *sustainable* measures for *enduring* changes require good institutions has become a guiding insight for many at the intersection between the social sciences of development and its practice. Having funds to close the aggregate *financial* shortfall between S1 and S2 is at best necessary but not sufficient for S2 to be feasible. Pogge may respond that while it is true that money does not automatically educate or cure anyone, the money would be used precisely to take care of these issues in appropriate ways. Money is not enough by itself, but the other necessary conditions normally require money. This is fair enough, but the relevant points now are these: We have found a sense in which the poor are wrongfully harmed, namely, if not enough effort goes into exploring possibilities for implementing appropriate institutional change. But while this is presumably a valid charge, it makes it much harder than it appears in Pogge's proposal to ascertain how to go about creating a feasible alternative and who is guilty of what failings in this regard.

9. Does the Global Order Wrongfully Harm the Poor? Part 2

Let us consider the import of poverty and inequality statistics. Statistics do not show in any obvious way that the global order harms (let alone *wrongfully* harms) the poor. For instance, while indeed 1.2 billion people in 1998 lived below the poverty line of $1.08 PPP 1993 per day (Pogge 2002, 98),[12] there is now less misery than ever before, as measured in terms of any standard development indicator. The progress made over the past 200 years is miraculous. In 1820, 75 percent of the world population lived on less than $1 a day (appropriately adjusted). Today, in Europe, almost no one does. In China, the figure is fewer than 20 percent; in South Asia, around 40 percent; and altogether slightly more than 20 percent. The share of people living on less than $1 a day fell from 42 percent in 1950 to 17 percent in 1992. Historically *almost everyone* was poor, but that is no longer true.

What conclusion such statistics warrant depends on (a) the period considered ("Sub-Saharan Africa has made progress over a 200-year horizon, but not for the last 20 years"); (b) whether one looks at absolute or relative quantities ("the number of abysmally poor has remained unchanged for 15 years, but their share of the world population decreased"); and (c) whether one looks at individuals or countries ("the median developing country has experienced zero growth over the last 20 years; still, inequality between two randomly chosen individuals has fallen"—because of growth in India and China). Still, what is remarkable is not that so many now live in poverty but that so many do not; not that so many die young but that so many do not; not that so many are illiterate but that so many are literate. If one looks at the past 200, 100, or even 50 years, things have improved dramatically for the poor. The 200-year and the 50-year horizon (roughly speaking) are especially significant. The former captures the period when the industrial revolution perfected the system of the division of labor, which led to technological advancements across the board, advancements originating largely in what are now industrialized countries but that have worked to everyone's benefit. The 50-year horizon captures the period when the global order came into its own. Historically speaking, the global order at least seems to have benefited the poor dramatically.

Surely, one may say, developing countries are better off than 200 years ago, but should we not assess if *wrongful harm* has occurred by asking what things would be like had European supremacists never invaded the rest of the globe? The trouble is that it is impossible to say anything about this benchmark. What are we to make of the idea that the world would be a better place if states had never emerged, or if colonialism had never happened? Such questions defy sensible answers. It is hard (if not impossible) to assess when agents came close to deciding differently, or natural events may readily have occurred in other ways. It is equally hard to assess what alternate course would then have emerged. Had Europeans not colonized Africa, alternate political structures may have allowed indigenous peoples to exploit their continent's wealth to build prosperous civilizations. It is also conceivable that war would have thwarted such efforts. According to Herbst (2000), physical geography in Africa impeded the emergence of powerful states.

There is yet another way of articulating the thought that developing countries are being harmed by the global order: a benchmark of fairness, the reference point being a state of nature where resources are distributed fairly. "'Worldwide 34,000 children under age five die daily from hunger and preventable diseases.' Try to conceive a state of nature that can match this amazing feat of our globalized civilization!" writes Pogge (2004, 274). Yet state-of-nature references cannot distinguish between the view that the global order does harm and any other view explaining how such poverty could arise. Such references show only that the situation is not as we would have hoped. Whatever else is true, among the three benchmarks we have considered, the historical benchmark is the only one of which we can make sense. In terms of that benchmark, the global order has brought tremendous advances.

10. Concluding Remarks

There are many questions about global justice that I have been unable to discuss here. For example, the philosophical foundations of human rights have attracted much attention recently. (See the chapter by Alan Buchanan in this volume.) Topics that are in need of much more, and are accessible to, philosophical analysis include immigration and fairness in trade. In need of but less accessible to philosophical analysis is the question of how to distribute the burdens from climate change. Deserving of more attention are also political and economic structures other than states. We must explore, for instance, what demands of justice, but also what types of accountability, apply to entities such as the WTO or the European Union.

Political philosophy would also benefit tremendously from systematic resurrection of the topic of humanity's collective ownership of the earth. (See the chapter by Peter Vallentyne, "Left-Libertarianism," in this volume.) To illustrate, suppose the population of the United States shrinks to two people, but these two people control access through border-surveillance mechanisms. Nothing changes elsewhere. Surely these two should permit immigration since they are grossly under-using their area. We can best explain this view by the fact that all of humanity has claims to the earth. Immigration is but one topic that such theorizing could illuminate. Humanity's ownership of the earth was the pivotal theme of seventeenth-century political philosophy. In an age in which global problems have become central, we have much to gain from reinvigorating that standpoint.

NOTES

1. Many thanks to Micha Glaeser, Gabriel Wollner, and David Estlund for helpful comments.
2. I disregard differences between citizenship and permanent residency and speak of shared membership.
3. Some of my terminology draws on Sangiovanni (2007), yet my usage deviates from his. For instance, globalism, on my account, is by definition a relationist view. To remember the relationist meaning of this term easily, the reader should connote it with *global order* rather than with *globe*.

4. Globalists and statists disagree about both grounds and scope but agree that grounds are relational. Relationists may also agree about the scope while disagreeing about the grounds. Later we encounter coercion-based and cooperation-based statists. Both think the people who respectively stand in the justice relationship are those who share a state. They agree about the scope of justice while disagreeing about the grounds in the sense that they disagree about what it is about shared citizenship that generates demands of justice. Distinctive of a ground is the account of the conditions and considerations that are norm-generating. The term *scope* does not do much independent work: It would be inappropriate to stipulate that grounds always be specified so precisely that the scope is uniquely fixed. Yet once the grounds are fixed, disagreement about the scope should be relatively minor and of the magnitude of a dispute about who exactly counts as a citizen given that this matter is largely fixed through legal rules. I define *globalism* as a view about *grounds*, not as one about the scope that is consistent with a nonrelationist ground.

5. Miller (2007, 32ff) reminds us that "arbitrary" sometimes means "undeserved" and sometimes "should make no difference." Differences in needs are undeserved but should make a difference. The manner in which I have introduced nonrelationism seeks to characterize this position in a way that avoids pitfalls from this ambiguity.

6. Tan captures the nonrelationist's concern with arbitrariness: "At the foundational level of deliberation about global justice, impartiality requires that we do not allow people's nationality to influence our views of what people's baseline entitlements are.... A person's nationality, a mere accident of birth, cannot by itself be a reason for giving her greater consideration at the foundational level" (2004, 158; see also 27ff and 159ff). See also Pogge (1989, 247); Moellendorf (2002, 55ff, 79).

7. See also Moellendorf (2002, 79) and Tan (2004, 158).

8. Nagel (2005) is a coercion-based statist. Blake (2001) is best understood as a kind of internationalist, as is Sangiovanni (2007). But their views can be enlisted to defend coercion-based or reciprocity-based statism, respectively.

9. I develop internationalism in my book *On Global Justice*, forthcoming from Princeton University Press in 2012.

10. See Sen (1985; 1999) and Nussbaum (2006; 2000).

11. For elaboration, see Blake (2001).

12. PPP means "purchasing power parity": the poverty line is fixed at what $1.08 bought in the United States in 1993.

REFERENCES

Beitz, Charles. 1999. *Political Theory and International Relations*, rev. ed. Princeton, NJ: Princeton University Press.

Black, Samuel. 1991. "Individualism at an Impasse." *Canadian Journal of Philosophy* 21(3): 347–77.

Blake, Michael. 2001. "Distributive Justice, State Coercion, and Autonomy." *Philosophy & Public Affairs* 30: 257–96.

Caney, Simon. 2002. "Cosmopolitanism and the Law of Peoples." *Journal of Political Philosophy* 10: 95–123.

Caney, Simon. 2005. *Justice Beyond Borders: A Global Political Theory*. Oxford: Oxford University Press.

Carens, Joseph. 2003. "Who Should Get In? The Ethics of Immigration Decisions." *Ethics and International Affairs* 17: 95–110.
Feinberg, Joel. 1973. *Social Philosophy*. Englewood Cliffs, NJ: Prentice Hall.
Fleischacker, Samuel. 2004. *A Short History of Distributive Justice*. Cambridge, MA: Harvard University Press.
Freeman, Samuel. 2007. *Justice and the Social Contract. Essays on Rawlsian Political Philosophy*. Oxford: Oxford University Press.
Herbst, Jeffrey. 2000. *States and Power in Africa*. Princeton, NJ: Princeton University Press.
Kant, Immanuel. 1996. "The Metaphysics of Morals." In *Immanuel Kant: Practical Philosophy*. Edited by Mary Gregor, 353–605. Cambridge, UK: Cambridge University Press.
Kavka, Gregory. 1986. *Hobbesian Moral and Political Theory*. Princeton, NJ: Princeton University Press.
Kymlicka, Will. 2002. *Contemporary Political Philosophy: An Introduction*. Oxford: Oxford University Press.
Miller, David. 2007. *National Responsibility and Global Justice*. Oxford: Oxford University Press.
Moellendorf, Darrel. 2002. *Cosmopolitan Justice*. Boulder, CO: Westview.
Nagel, Thomas. 2005. "The Problem of Global Justice." *Philosophy & Public Affairs* 33(2): 113–47.
Nussbaum, Martha. 2000. *Women and Human Development: The Capabilities Approach*. Cambridge, UK: Cambridge University Press.
Nussbaum, Martha. 2006. *Frontiers of Justice: Disability, Nationality, Species Membership*. Cambridge, MA: Harvard University Press.
Pogge, Thomas. 1989. *Realizing Rawls*. Ithaca, NY: Cornell University Press.
Pogge, Thomas. 1994. "Cosmopolitanism and Sovereignty." In *Political Restructuring in Europe: Ethical Perspectives*. Edited by Chris Brown, 89–122. London: Routledge,
Pogge, Thomas. 2002. *World Poverty and Human Rights*. Cambridge, UK: Polity.
Pogge, Thomas. 2004. "'Assisting' the Global Poor." In *The Ethics of Assistance: Morality and the Distant Needy*. Edited by Deen K. Chatterjee. Cambridge, UK: Cambridge University Press.
Rawls, John. 2001. *Justice as Fairness: A Restatement*. Edited by Erin Kelly. Cambridge, MA: Harvard University Press.
Rawls, John. 1999a. *A Theory of Justice*, rev. ed. Cambridge, MA: Harvard University Press.
Rawls, John. 1999b. *The Law of Peoples*. Cambridge, MA: Harvard University Press.
Risse, Mathias. 2006. "What to Say about the State." *Social Theory and Practice* 32(4): 671–98.
Sangiovanni, Andrea. 2007. "Global Justice, Reciprocity, and the State." *Philosophy & Public Affairs* 35(1): 3–39.
Scanlon, T.M. 2003. "The Diversity of Objections to Inequality." In *The Difficulty of Tolerance. Essays in Political Philosophy*. By Thomas Scanlon, 202–19. Cambridge, MA: Cambridge University Press.
Scheffler, Samuel. 2001. *Boundaries and Allegiances. Problems of Justice in Liberal Thought*. Oxford: Oxford University Press.
Sen, Amartya. 1985. *Commodities and Capabilities*. Amsterdam: North Holland.
Sen, Amartya. 1999. *Development as Freedom*. New York: Random House.
Tan, Kok-Chor. 2004. *Justice Without Borders. Cosmopolitanism, Nationalism, and Patriotism*. Cambridge, UK: Cambridge University Press.
Wenar, Leif. 2006. "Why Rawls is Not a Cosmopolitan Egalitarian." In *Rawls's Law of Peoples: A Realistic Utopia?* Edited by R. Martin and D. Reidy. Oxford: Blackwell.
Williams, Bernard. 2005. "In the Beginning Was the Deed." In *Realism and Moralism in Political Argument*. Edited by Geoffrey Hawthorn. Princeton, NJ: Princeton University Press.

CHAPTER 15

HUMAN RIGHTS

ALLEN BUCHANAN

1. What Is a Philosophical Theory of "Human Rights" About?

There is a long philosophical pedigree for the concept of human rights as moral rights that all people possess, regardless of whether these rights are recognized in law or social practice and independently of whether the individual has done anything to earn them, such as contribute to society. For brevity I will call such rights *moral human rights*. Nowadays the term *human rights* is often used differently to refer to the *international legal human rights* that are the focus of *international human rights practice* (hereafter, the practice). In the practice the term is also used to refer to rights that *should* be international legal human rights, as when new international human rights treaties are proposed.

The practice includes a consensus that there is a core set of documents that contain canonical statements of rights and indicate their moral foundations. These documents include, at minimum, the Universal Declaration of Human Rights (UDHR), the Covenant on Civil and Political Rights (ICCPR), and the Covenant on Economic, Social, and Cultural Rights (ICESCR). Because its highly developed jurisprudence influences the interpretation of international legal human rights worldwide, the European Convention on Human Rights (ECHR) may also be added to the list. Human rights practice is the totality of institutional and organizational efforts to promote international legal human rights, including the activities of treaty bodies and other international organizations such as the UN Human Rights Council; the judicial application of legal human rights in regional human rights regimes and in domestic courts; the activities of domestic and human rights nongovernmental organizations (NGOs); and policies that make foreign aid, access to loans and credits, and membership in multilateral institutions conditional on meeting international human rights standards.

Recently philosophers have developed theories that aim to shed critical light on international legal human rights. A key point of contention is whether international legal human rights are best understood, at least in significant part, as an attempt to realize moral human rights through international law.[1] If they are, then a satisfactory justification for having a system of international legal human rights, and for the inclusion of particular rights in it, depends on whether an adequate theory of moral human rights can be produced.

The Ambiguity of "Human Rights"

Philosophers invite confusion when they use the phrase *human rights* without specifying whether they mean international legal human rights or rights that should be international legal rights or moral human rights. For example, Beitz (2010, 109) argues that human rights practice is a global practice in which states have duties to respect and promote international legal human rights in the case of their own citizens and in which their failure to do so provides a pro tanto reason for other states to take corrective action. On this view, the practice, including the system of international legal human rights, presupposes a world of states. Given the centrality of international legal human rights in the practice, the most charitable interpretation of Beitz's use of the phrase *human rights* is that he is referring to rights that are or, according to the best interpretation of the practice, should be international legal human rights.

Tasioulas (2010, 114) takes himself to be providing an objection to theories such as Beitz's by pointing out that the concept of human rights would be applicable and useful even if there were no states—if there was a single world government or global anarchy. But Beitz need not deny that the concept of human rights understood as *moral* rights applies to situations where there are not states if his claim is about the concept of international legal human rights, understood as those rights that are or should be part of the system of international legal rights. Moreover, even if one thinks that international legal human rights are grounded in moral human rights (a view Beitz disputes but Tasioulas embraces), it is perfectly consistent to hold that the concept of international legal human rights, unlike that of moral human rights, presupposes the state system.

Like Nickel (2007), Griffin (2008), Altman and Wellman (2009), and myself (Buchanan 2003) in earlier writings, Tasioulas (2010) assumes, rather than argues for, the Grounding View (GV): *An adequate justification for international legal human rights requires appeals to moral human rights.* GV is weaker than the thesis that for every international legal human right one must show that it is either identical to, or derivable from, some moral human right. Instead, GV leaves open the possibility that some international legal human rights are justified by appeal to other moral reasons.[2]

GV needs defending for two reasons. First, there are a number of ways to justify creating an individual legal right; showing that it would help realize some moral right is only one of them. So why assume that any international legal human right presupposes the existence of moral human rights? Second, as I explain below, some versions of "political" theories of human rights, including Rawls's (1999) and Beitz's (2010), contend that grounding international legal human rights on moral human rights is neither necessary nor workable.

Regarding the first point, consider the legal right to health care in the domestic context. It is a mistake to assume that to justify having this legal right it is necessary first to show that there is moral right to health care and then argue that the best way to realize it is to create a corresponding legal right. There are other plausible grounds for having a legal right to health care. One can argue that such a legal right is the most efficient way for citizens to fulfill duties of beneficence, that it is necessary to avoid great disutility, that a decent society requires it, that it is necessary for the sake of solidarity or to promote equality of opportunity, that it is required by a proper recognition of individual dignity or the equal moral worth of individuals, or that it is needed if the country is to be economically competitive. A combination of such justifications is sufficient to ground the legal right, without any appeal to a moral right to health care.

Similarly, one should not assume that international legal human rights are justifiable only if there are corresponding moral human rights. Consider the legal human rights to physical security, democratic governance, and due process. One can argue that considerations of utility, decency, and respect for autonomy and dignity all converge on the conclusion that there should be an international legal right to physical security. One can then argue for having other international individual legal rights, including the right to democratic governance and due process rights, by citing evidence that these are generally needed to secure the right to physical security. At neither stage of the argument is it necessary to establish the existence of moral human rights.

Justifying the Grounding View

Nevertheless, there are two weighty reasons for holding the GV. First, although the language of the core documents is muddy, by far the clearest strand of justification is the idea of giving international legal effect to preexisting moral rights that all humans have in virtue of their inherent dignity or worth. The opening passage of the UN Charter, which preceded the UDHR, proclaims that the member states "reaffirm faith in fundamental human rights, in the dignity and worth of the human person" (Preamble to the Charter of the United Nations 1945). The UDHR's preamble appeals to "the inherent dignity and . . . equal and inalienable rights of all members of the human family," states that "human rights should be protected by law," and asserts that "all human beings are born free and equal in dignity and rights" (UDHR 1948). These are clearly references to moral, not legal, rights. The preambles of the ICCPR and ICESCR replicate this language almost verbatim. The most straightforward interpretation of this phrasing is that the project the UDHR begins is to establish a global practice that realizes moral rights of all human individuals that exist independently of that.[3] If this is the central goal of the practice, as articulated in the core documents, then the fact that *some* legal rights can be established without appeal to moral rights is irrelevant. International legal human rights are not just run-of-the-mill legal rights; they are legal rights designed chiefly to further the central goal of respecting the dignity or equal moral worth of individuals by realizing moral rights, and the nature of that goal imposes constraints on what counts as a justification for them.[4]

The assertions that there are rights we are "born with," that are grounded in the "inherent" dignity of the human person, and that apply to all individuals without further qualification imply that these moral rights are unearned in the sense that their ascription does not depend on the individual's contribution to society or other meritorious behavior and are independent of their recognition in any social practice. In brief, the moral rights that are to be realized through a system of international legal rights are possessed by individuals *on their own account, simply by virtue of their being human*.

Note, however, that "simply by virtue of being human" here means only that these moral rights are ascribed to all individuals independently of any further gender, racial, ethnic, or other qualifications, such as social contribution; it does *not* preclude the possibility that the ascription of some (or all) moral human rights depends on assumptions about institutional context. It also does not imply that these rights are to be deduced a priori from a concept of human nature or that they exist preinstitutionally in a state of nature. Thus, for example, one can say that the right to freedom of the press implies an institution that has not always existed in human society but it is still a right that people have simply by virtue of their humanity; this means that the right is ascribable to all of us, not just those who meet further qualifications beyond being human. To the extent that international legal human rights are created to help realize moral human rights, then, a necessary condition for justifying international legal human rights is showing that there are moral human rights.

Although the core documents appeal to moral human rights, they do not rely on a theory of them; hence, it is not surprising that they and subsequent human rights treaties sometimes make implausible claims about what should be included in a system of international legal human rights. For example, ICESCR notoriously includes the right to periodic holidays with pay. This putative right is too specific to be included in a list of legal rights intended to apply to all societies. In contrast, it is plausible to assert that, under modern conditions, there is a moral human right to respite from work without serious economic loss to the individual.[5] This more abstract right can be realized through a number of institutional mechanisms. Guaranteeing periodic holidays with pay is only one of them—and one that may not be appropriate or feasible in many societies. Those who hold the GV believe that a sound theory of moral human rights would provide resources for avoiding such errors. So the GV not only accords with the central idea of the practice as expressed in the core documents; it also promises to provide resources for critical revision of the system of international legal human rights.

Beitz (2010) suggests that there is a more basic goal of human rights practice and that a proper characterization of it need not employ the concept of moral human rights. He notes that the founding of human rights practice was a response to the widely held perception, in the ruins of World War II and the Holocaust, that it was necessary to devise a discourse and a set of institutions that would protect individuals from harm inflicted by their own states (Beitz 2010, 130–33). But Beitz's account is seriously incomplete: He fails to note that, very early on, indeed with the drafting of the UDHR, the dominant view was that achieving the needed protection required a clear affirmation of the principle that individuals were all *equally worthy* of serious protections *on their own account*, that is, independently of whatever value they derive from their membership in a national or ethnic or racial group and independently of their contribution to society. The UN Charter, the UDHR, and the two Covenants are scrupulous in avoiding any suggestion that the possession of these rights is conditional in any of those ways, instead insisting that all human individuals, without any further qualification, possess them. They, as well as subsequent conventions, use the language of inherent dignity to convey this fundamental idea.[6] They could just as well have used the language of equal moral worth (or basic moral equality). Beitz's characterization of human rights practice includes the idea that individuals are to be protected but not that they are worthy of protection on their own account, omitting the key idea of dignity. Strangely, it also ignores the clear references to moral human rights in the core documents.

Beitz is correct to emphasize that the practice began as a response to World War II and the Holocaust, but he does not explain why the need to protect against such horrors took the form of international legal rights of individuals rather than legal duties of states (with no correlative rights of any kind); rights of ethnic, racial, or religious groups (rather than individual rights); or simply a weakening of international legal strictures against intervention in domestic conflicts. What Beitz overlooks is the fact that the fascist ideologies that were generally thought to have been the root cause of the catastrophes to which the creation of a regime of international legal human rights was the response were both *radically collectivist* and *radically inegalitarian*. They explicitly repudiated both the idea of the *equal* dignity of all human beings and the idea that all people are deserving of stringent protections *on their own account*, independently of their group membership or contribution to society. As an extreme form of nationalism, fascism held that whatever value individuals have derives from their role in furthering the life of the collective, hence its radical collectivism. As an extreme variety of racial thought, fascism held that some humans lack significant moral worth, hence its radical inegalitarianism.

To the extent that human rights practice is a conscious reaction to the horrors wrought by fascism, it is not surprising that the core documents explicitly affirm what fascist ideology denied—hence the emphasis on the equal dignity of every human being and the notion that all individuals are entitled to stringent protections on their own account.

This central idea—the repudiation of radical inegalitarianism and radical collectivism—could perhaps be conveyed by the notion of equal moral worth or dignity, without reference to moral human rights. But unless such abstract notions can be cashed out in more determinate requirements for how individuals are to be treated, they provide little guidance for constructing a list of international legal human rights. The idea that a proper recognition of the dignity or equal moral worth of human individuals requires respect for their moral rights adds needed content.

Theories of moral human rights can be viewed as attempts to give content to the notion of respecting dignity or equal moral worth, and the insistence that these rights are possessed by all can be seen as a clear affirmation of equal dignity or moral worth. The language of rights is better suited to the task of providing content than the language of mere duties. One can have a duty regarding a person without owing that duty to her and hence without any suggestion that the person herself is worthy of serious moral consideration in her own right. If the central goal of the practice is not just to provide substantial protections to individuals against state power but to do so on the assumption that they are all equally worthy of these protections on their own account, then the widely held view that international legal human rights are attempts to give legal effect to moral human rights makes good sense. If that is the case, then a philosophical theory of legal human rights cannot avoid reliance on an account of moral human rights.

There is a second reason to affirm the GV: It is consonant with the most natural understanding of the historical relationship between the UDHR and subsequent treaties. The UDHR is not a legal document but rather an attempt to list moral rights of all human individuals that are suitable for being given international legal effect, in the expectation that this will be realized in subsequent treaties, which did indeed occur. The UDHR does not just identify some moral values or other as being worthy of international legalization; it focuses primarily on a particular kind of moral item "unearned" rights that all human individuals have independently of their being recognized in law or social practice.

These two considerations constitute a strong prima facie case for the GV; nonetheless, several prominent theorists reject it, embracing instead a radically different understanding of international legal human rights and therefore of the practice.

Political Theories

The label "political theories of human rights" is applied to the theories of Rawls and Beitz. Both of their theories can be reasonably interpreted as consisting of two main elements: a rejection of the GV and a positive view according to which the key to justifying international legal human rights is understanding their political function in the international order. For Rawls (1999, 79) the political function is that compliance with international legal human rights (properly pruned) renders a state immune from external interference. For Beitz (2010, 30–32), violation of international legal human rights within a given state supplies other states with a pro tanto reason for taking some sort of corrective action (not necessarily coercive intervention).

Rawls rejects theories that attempt to ground legal human rights in rights that all individuals have by virtue of their humanity/dignity or equal moral worth and instead contends that legal human rights are best conceived as specifying the conditions for intervention: If a state complies with legal human rights (or, rather, a subset of them, what Rawls calls "human rights proper"), then it is entitled to good standing in international society and should be regarded as immune to infringements of its sovereignty (Rawls 1999, 81).[7] Many critics, including Beitz, have pointed out that Rawls's characterization of the political function of international legal human rights does not fit the practice: These rights serve to do much more than mark the boundaries of immunity from intervention.

Rawls believes that the idea that all human beings have certain moral human rights simply by virtue of their humanity, dignity, or equal moral worth is inconsistent with the moral views exemplified in decent though hierarchical societies. A society qualifies as decent for Rawls if it is not aggressive toward other societies and exemplifies a common-good conception of justice; that is, the society's institutions reflect the belief that the good of each member of society counts (Rawls 1999, 68).

Rawls holds that international legal human rights, properly conceived, are the requirements that a society must meet to qualify as a form of cooperation (Rawls 1999, 65). Unfortunately, he says too little about what counts as cooperation, only contrasting it with slavery and stipulating that it includes the requirement that the good of all members of the society must be taken into account in the public order. Rawls does not say why it is so important that society be noncoercive and take every individual's good into account. One obvious answer would be that this is required by proper respect for equal moral worth or dignity. Rawls cannot avail himself of this answer, because he thinks doing so would be inconsistent with the moral views of decent hierarchical, that is, inegalitarian societies. Yet it is unclear that he can give any satisfactory answer that does not commit him to the fundamental equality of all individuals.

A society can be cooperative in Rawls's minimal sense and satisfy his criteria for decency and yet involve systematic discrimination on grounds of race or gender. Thus, his view is inconsistent with the egalitarian character of many international legal human rights (e.g., rights of equality before the law, equal rights to remedies for violations of rights, and rights against discrimination on grounds of race or gender). Quite apart from that, however, the question is this: Why should states be regarded as immune from intervention so long as they respect that minimal set of rights that is required for their society being decent and a form of cooperation in Rawls's undemanding sense? Rawls's answer is that requiring anything more substantial would violate liberalism's commitment to tolerance.

The understanding of tolerance that leads Rawls to this radically revisionist position on international legal human rights is implausible (Buchanan 2010a, 26–30). His conception of tolerance is too lax because his criteria for decency are too undemanding: They omit minimal epistemic standards. A society that is decent in Rawls's sense may deny equal rights for women or minorities because its dominant moral view is based on false factual assumptions. Thus, a morality that endorses systematic racial or gender discrimination would be worthy of toleration, according to Rawls, even if it relied on false beliefs about the natural inferiority (in intelligence, moral agency, etc.) of those relegated to an inferior status. In such a morality, the good of those subject to discrimination would count but would count less—perhaps much less—than the good of those that are wrongly regarded as naturally superior, *and the source of this deep inequality would be a patently false set of factual beliefs*. Rawls simply stipulates his undemanding criteria for decency. He offers no argument for them and does not address the issue of minimal epistemic standards. He suggests that the only alternatives are his notion of toleration or the unreflective, wholesale transfer of a liberal point of view to the international scene. But there is nothing peculiarly liberal about insisting on minimal epistemic standards when the stakes are extraordinarily high, as in the justification of the most basic features of society.

Beitz also rejects attempts to ground international legal human rights in moral human rights, declaring that the attempt to do so will lead the theorist to misunderstand the actual practice of human rights. But his skepticism is aimed only at the least plausible understandings of moral human rights. He assumes that moral human rights must be conceived as preinstitutional, that is, as natural rights traditionally understood (Beitz 2010, 51–53). He then notes that many international legal human rights presuppose modern institutions. As I have already noted, adherents of the GV can simply reject the assumption that moral human rights are preinstitutional. Instead, they can operate with a conception of the moral rights that all or most human beings now have, where this takes into account institutions and other social conditions, so long as these are widespread and likely to persist. Alternatively, they can conceive of moral human rights as preinstitutional but simply point out that an attempt to realize them in a system of international legal rights will need to take existing institutions into account. In either case, adherents to the GV can accommodate the fact that (at least some) legal human rights presuppose institutions. Beitz's criticism applies only to theories that *identify* legal human rights with moral rights understood as preinstitutional rights, not those that attempt to *ground* legal human rights in moral human rights. To my knowledge, no contemporary theorist holds the identity view, though many hold the GV. Once we distinguish between the grounding and the identify views, Beitz's central contention evaporates: There is nothing about the attempt to invoke moral human rights to justify international legal human rights that prejudices or distorts one's attempts to give an accurate characterization of the practice.

Although Beitz appears to reject attempts to ground international legal human rights in moral human rights, unlike Rawls, he nonetheless tries to ground them in general human interests. He says that legal human rights can be understood as protecting "urgent interests," defined as those that "would be recognizable as important in a wide range of typical lives that occur in contemporary societies" (Beitz 2010, 110). But urgent interests thus defined are incapable of generating duties, much less the directed duties, entailed by rights. To say that one has a moral right to everything that is recognized as important in a broad range of typical lives would be excessive, to say the least, nor would it be plausible to omit reference to moral human rights and say that every "urgent" interest thus defined deserves protection by a corresponding international legal human right.

Beitz provides no satisfactory alternative to GV—only the undeveloped notion of interests that are morally important enough to ground duties—a notion that, if fleshed out sufficiently, would presumably look rather like that of moral human rights. He admonishes theorists who subscribe to the GV to abandon it and focus on understanding human rights practice, but his own characterization of the practice indicates that it lacks the normative and conceptual resources to justify the system of international legal human rights.

My assessment of political conceptions is summarized as follows. Rawls's version is implausible because of its inaccurately narrow conception of the function of legal human rights and its defective notion of tolerance. Beitz's version is incompatible only with a version of the GV that no one seems to hold—one that asserts if international legal human rights are justified by appeal to moral human rights, then international legal human rights must not presuppose institutions.[8] Beitz's view is also normatively unsatisfying: His appeal to urgent interests falls far short of a justification for having a system of international legal rights.

2. The Inadequacy of Current Interest-Based Views

To his credit, Griffin (2008, 3) takes seriously the idea that dignity plays a central role in justifying international legal human rights. He offers a specific interpretation of dignity: It is the status of being a "normative agent." Normative agency, for Griffin, includes three elements: autonomy (the ability to have a conception of a worthwhile life), liberty (freedom from interference by others), and provision (adequate resources for implementing one's conception of a worthwhile life). Griffin contends that the best justification for international legal human rights is that they are needed to realize moral human rights (understood as protections for normative agency). Thus, he subscribes to the GV.[9]

Several philosophers argue that it is implausible to hold that normative agency is the only interest that grounds moral human rights (Raz 2010, 324–26). Consider the right against torture. It is true that being tortured can have a negative impact on one's normative agency, but it has other effects that also contribute to the justification saying that there is a right against it. Being tortured is terrifying and painful, and it tends to undermine one's capacity for trust and intimacy.

I agree that the interest in normative agency is too narrow a base for an account of moral human rights capable of grounding a plausible list of international legal human rights. There is, however, a more basic problem that broader interest-based theories such as those of Nickel (2007) and Tasioulas (2010), as well as needs-based accounts such as those of Miller and Altman (2009) and Wellman (2009), share with Griffin's account: The conception of interests (or needs) with which they operate is too limited to make sense of strong rights against discrimination on grounds of gender or race—a type of international legal human right that is arguably of considerable importance in the practice (Miller 2007).

Such rights, which appear in the Women's Convention and ICESCR, prohibit all forms of discrimination, not just those that are so severe that they undercut the opportunity for a minimally good life, or undermine normative agency, or thwart the satisfaction of their needs (General Assembly of the United Nations 1979, Preamble and Article 1; General Assembly of the United Nations 1976, Article 7.a.i). For example, a person might be doing exceptionally well in life but still be paid less because of her gender or color, or she might suffer discrimination of a more symbolic sort, such as being required to use separate drinking fountains or toilets. In a world with a long and shameful history of racism and sexism, such discrimination can be reasonably viewed as an affront to dignity or a denial of equal moral worth, even if it is not so damaging to a person's good as to qualify as a rights violation according to current interest-based or needs-based theories.[10]

Interest-based and needs-based theories purport to provide content for the notion of dignity or equal moral worth that figures so prominently in the discourse of human rights practice. It is plausible to hold, as they do, that respect for dignity or recognition of equal worth requires the protection of certain basic interests, including the satisfaction of needs. But the examples of "soft discrimination" noted above suggest that there is a social-comparative aspect of dignity or equal moral worth that such accounts neglect.[11]

The social-comparative aspect of dignity focuses not on whether an individual's life is minimally good (Nickel 2007), or whether she is living reasonably well as a normative agent (Griffin 2008), or whether her needs are being satisfied (Miller 2007; Altman and Wellman 2009) but rather on whether she is being treated as if she had a lower basic moral status by virtue of the fact that she is a woman or a person of color. Discriminatory treatment can be an affront to dignity in the social-comparative sense even when it does not prevent the individual from living a minimally good life, doing reasonably well as a normative agent, satisfying her needs or functioning well. The social-comparative aspect of dignity or equal worth has to do not with how well one is doing but with how one is being treated vis-á-vis others and the view of one's relative status that this treatment expresses. To capture the social-comparative aspect, it appears that current interest-based theories must either expand their conception of the interests to be protected or acknowledge that moral human rights and consequently the international legal human rights that are designed to realize them not only protect interests but also in some instances secure the individual against the threat of being relegated to an inferior status. Needs-based theories, in contrast, seem incapable of accommodating the social-comparative aspect of dignity. To the extent that they meaningfully distinguish needs from interests, they must construe needs either in a strictly biological fashion (something like Maslowian drives) or as what might be called core interests, those whose satisfaction only assures a minimally satisfactory human life. On either construal, needs-based theories offer an implausibly lean conception of what dignity or respect for equal moral worth requires and cannot begin to explain the presence of strong rights of discrimination in lists of legal human rights. Two crucial questions for future research are whether a theory of international legal human rights should include the idea that dignity or equal moral worth has a social-comparative aspect, and, if so, what sort of theory can capture it. One possibility worth considering is that a proper recognition of the equal moral worth of individuals has two components: protection of basic interests and protection against being relegated to an inferior status (even when this does not undermine basic interests).

3. Insufficient Attention to the Institutional Challenges to Human Rights Practice

Institutions and the Scope and Conflict Problems

Those who subscribe to the GV typically think that a theory of moral human rights is needed to resolve questions about the proper scope of international legal human rights and to address conflicts among them. But in the practice, international legal human rights are specified and conflicts among them are addressed through the attempts of treaty bodies to monitor compliance, the work of NGOs in translating treaty obligations into concrete behavioral standards and policies, domestic legislation and judicial decisions, and rulings by courts in regional human rights regimes.

If one looks only at the rights-norms as they appear in treaties, their abstractness and the lack of resources in the documents for specifying their scope and resolving conflicts among them will naturally lead one to conclude that the scope and conflict problems are of mammoth proportions. But this would make about as much sense as inspecting the formulation of civil and political rights in the U.S. Constitution's first ten amendments and concluding that they are so hopelessly abstract that there is no way of determining their scope or resolving conflicts among them in a principled way—ignoring the fact that their current embodiment in law is the result of a couple of centuries of legislation and adjudication.

Legal processes constitute a kind of *institutionalized practical reasoning*. This reasoning, whose quality depends on the nature of the institutions, can help specify legal norms and resolve conflicts among them in a morally plausible way. Before assuming that a philosophical theory is needed to answer questions concerning scope and conflict, one would first need to assess the effectiveness of existing legal processes in human rights practice in addressing these problems. One would also need to determine whether these processes are already implicitly relying on philosophical theories, perhaps underdeveloped ones. To my knowledge, no philosopher theorizing international legal human rights has addressed these questions.

An Enriched Conception of Philosophical Theory

Evaluating the resources of existing legal processes for solving scope and conflict problems will require a social moral epistemology of international legal human rights. By "social moral epistemology" I mean the systematic comparative study of the efficacy and efficiency of alternative institutions and practices so far as they facilitate the formation of justified norms and the beliefs needed for their appropriate application. A central task of social moral epistemology is to identify the features of institutions and practices that lend moral plausibility to the norms and beliefs they foster.

With respect to institutionalized norms, moral plausibility has two dimensions: procedural legitimacy and content credibility. Legitimate institutional processes can contribute to the legitimacy of the norms they produce. Procedurally legitimate norms are presumptively authoritative independently of their content. Institutional processes can also confer moral credibility on norms when they are considered from the standpoint of content, if those processes have epistemic virtues that provide assurance that the content will be appropriate, given the purpose or function of the norms. For example, if a norm is meant to protect a certain interest, then institutional processes that shape the content of the norm should be informed by accurate information about what threatens the interest and what measures will reliably counter those threats.

A social moral epistemology of international legal human rights would have to begin with an accurate characterization of the processes by which these rights are initially formulated, specified, contested, and revised and then go on to evaluate the contribution that these processes make to the moral plausibility of international legal human rights. Assuming that constitutional rights in well-developed liberal constitutional democracies have considerable moral plausibility and that this is due in part to the specific characteristics of that sort of polity, including not only its democratic character but also the quality of its legal system, one would first try to identify the relevant characteristics and make their contribution to the moral plausibility of the norms explicit. This would involve exhibiting the epistemic virtues of various institutional arrangements—for example, showing how democratic legislative processes help identify interests worthy of the exceptionally strong protection that constitutional rights provide, in part by ensuring that law making draws on reliable information about what is conducive to citizens' well-being. The next step would be to determine whether the practice contains processes that have these epistemic virtues. If the conclusion is that human rights practice is deficient in this regard, then the next task would be to devise proposals for institutional development that would remedy these defects by actions that are both feasible and consistent with the values that the practice is supposed to promote. Such an institutional approach to the normative challenges to the practice presupposes a much more ambitious role for philosophical reasoning than merely providing a theory of moral human rights. An account of which moral human rights should be realized in international law and an account of how well legal-institutional processes perform in addressing scope and conflict problems is also needed.

4. Normative Challenges to Human Rights Practice

A philosophical theory should respond to the full range of normative challenges to human rights practice. By "normative challenges" I mean objections to or problems with the practice that bear on what our practical stance toward it should be—whether we should support it, oppose it, seek to reform it, or try to dismantle it. So far, I have argued that the proper strategy for justifying international legal human rights, if the primary goal is to marshal the resources of international law to protect individuals from threats to their dignity or equal moral worth, is to ground these legal rights, at least in significant part, on moral human rights. At present, there is no satisfactory theory of moral human rights and no developed attempt to ground a system of international legal human rights in such a theory. *In fact, none of the theorists discussed in this article has even addressed the fundamental question of why international, as opposed to purely domestic, legalization of moral human rights is needed.*[12] Yet even if we had a satisfactory account of how *all* international legal human rights are grounded in moral human rights, three serious normative challenges would remain: (a) the questionable legitimacy of institutional efforts to implement legal human rights; (b) the questionable legitimacy of legal human rights norms themselves, given the apparent deficiencies of the processes by which they are created and specified; and (c) the supremacy problem (the controversial nature of the claim of international human rights law to override even the most fundamental domestic law).

The Questionable Legitimacy of Institutional Implementation of Legal Human Rights

The implementation of legal human rights appears to be morally arbitrary. For example, neither China nor the United States is likely to be excluded from favorable trade regimes because of their human rights violations. This unevenness in implementation is only one aspect of a larger problem philosophers have often neglected: the legitimacy of institutional efforts to implement legal human rights. The question is not whether institutional efforts to implement legal human rights are *regarded* as legitimate but whether they *are* legitimate—whether the institutions that wield power in the name of human rights do so with rightful authority.

Even if all states ratified all human rights treaties, the legitimacy of institutional efforts to promote compliance with international legal human rights would still be questionable because of doubts about the legitimacy-conferring power of the state consent that creates treaty-based obligations. First, on any reasonable account of legitimacy, many states themselves lack legitimacy, so it is hard to see how their consent could confer legitimacy on institutional efforts to achieve compliance with legal human rights. Second, the asymmetry of power in the international order is so great that it is doubtful that the consent of weaker states would be sufficiently voluntary to confer legitimacy. Third, even in the case of democratic states that satisfy reasonable standards for legitimacy and are powerful enough to give genuine consent, the chains of delegation between citizens and the actors who create legal human rights treaties are disturbingly attenuated.

At least from a broadly liberal perspective, it is now thought that democracy is a necessary condition of state legitimacy. The institutions of the practice, including those that create international legal human rights and wield power to promote compliance with them, are not democratic in anything like the way legitimate states are. If this is correct, then either these international institutions are illegitimate or the requirements of legitimacy for states and international institutions differ (Buchanan and Keohane 2006).

Remarkably, none of the following books that aim to shed critical light on the justification of international legal human rights addresses these issues of institutional legitimacy: Rawls's *The Law of Peoples* (1999), Nickel's *Making Sense of Human Rights* (2007), Griffin's *On Human Rights* (2008), Talbott's *Which Rights Should Be Universal?* (2005), Beitz's *The Idea of Human Rights* (2010), Pogge's *World Poverty and Human Rights* (2008), and Wellman's *The Moral Dimensions of Human Rights* (2011).

The Questionable Legitimacy of International Legal Human Rights Norms

The legitimacy of legal norms depends in part on the legitimacy of the processes by which they are created and their content is specified. In a liberal constitutional democracy with a developed legal system, a bill of rights is typically the outcome of processes that appear to possess considerable legitimacy, and the legitimacy of the processes lends legitimacy to the norms: These rights are usually embedded in constitutions that enjoy some sort of democratic authorization, both in their origins in representative constitutional conventions and, more important, in the option of constitutional amendment through representative processes. Further, the constitutions in which domestic bills of rights are embedded are supported by a broader democratic culture, by a legal culture and legal institutions that take the principles of the rule of law seriously, and by a structure of liberal social and political institutions, including a civil society that helps to stimulate and inform legal and political developments. Finally, the content of domestic constitutional rights is determined through the constitutionally structured interaction of a representative legislature and an independent judiciary. Taken together, these features give us reason to have some confidence that domestic constitutional rights enjoy both procedural legitimacy and content credibility.

Human rights treaties, in contrast, emerge from processes that inspire considerably less confidence. They are not embedded in a well-developed legal system, and at present there is neither a democratic global polity nor a global legal culture. So even if *some* system of international legal human rights could be grounded on a theory of moral human rights, this would give us little reason to think that the actual system we have is justified.

The Supremacy Issue

International human rights law claims authority over even the most legitimate states, even within what had previously been regarded as their exclusive domain, namely, the treatment of their own citizens. Among legal scholars there is an ongoing debate about the conflicting claims of legal supremacy of international human rights law on the one hand and the constitutional law of liberal-democratic states on the other. The central question is this: Why should a liberal democracy, with a well-developed constitutional law that already provides admirable legal rights for its citizens, acknowledge the supremacy of international legal human rights, so far as its treatment of its own citizens is concerned? Given the questionable legitimacy of international legal human rights norms already noted, their claim of supremacy seems all the more dubious.

When acknowledging the supremacy of international legal human rights amounts to changing the domestic constitution of a state, *how* this is accomplished may matter greatly. It can be argued, for instance, that the ordinary process for ratifying treaties is not sufficient for subordinating U.S. constitutional provisions to international legal human rights and that some more fundamental form of democratic authorization, such as a constitutional amendment or a special national legislative act, is required. None of the other philosophers mentioned engage the supremacy problem or the moral issues involved in alternative responses to it, yet these are among the most serious normative challenges to the practice.[13]

The Limits of Traditional Philosophical Theorizing

It should now be clear that attempts to provide moral justifications for international legal human rights that make no reference to the role of institutions cannot succeed in addressing the full range of normative challenges to human rights practice. Even if a convincing philosophical justification for every right listed in every human rights treaty were available, the institutional implementation of these rights would still be of questionable legitimacy. Further, such a philosophical justification would not show that states with well-developed, rights-protecting legal systems should acknowledge the supremacy of legal human rights within their borders.

The Greater Need: Theoretical Advances or Institutional Development?

I suggest that (a) the most serious institutional challenges can be met only by further institutional development and (b) that if such development occurs, the need for a philosophical justification for legal human rights norms will diminish. The cogency of the first part of this suggestion is clear enough: If the international institutions that create and implement international legal human rights suffer a legitimacy deficit, it will be remedied only through institutional changes. In particular, these institutions will have to become more democratic or at least more resistant to the distorting influences of the great disparities of power that now exist among states, and the states that participate in them will themselves have to become more democratic.

The second part is less obvious, but the key idea is simple: The right sort of institutional development in human rights practice would produce a situation analogous to that which now exists in well-developed domestic legal systems. In such systems, legal rights are morally plausible because they are the products of legitimate institutional processes and enjoy content credibility due to the epistemic virtues of the institutional processes that shape their content. It is true that content credibility is weaker than justification: The idea is that the epistemic virtues of the institutions provide reasonable, though defeasible, assurance that the content of the norms is appropriate, given their purpose. Nevertheless, where legal norms have procedural legitimacy and content credibility, the need for a deep philosophical justification for them seems less pressing.

There are two ways in which international legal human rights could gain moral plausibility through institutional development, independently of whether better philosophical justifications for them are developed. First, international institutions that create and implement international legal human rights could come to have virtues like those that confer procedural legitimacy and content credibility on legal rights in the best domestic legal systems. Second, legal human rights could become more thoroughly incorporated into domestic legal systems, with ever more domestic legal systems achieving the virtues that confer procedural legitimacy and content credibility on their laws. If this second development occurred, then the deficiencies of international institutions would not matter, because the moral plausibility of legal human rights would be assured at the domestic level. At present, much of the concern about the lack of justification for international legal human rights stems from the fact that they are regarded as external legal requirements, imposed through international institutions of dubious legitimacy and an even more doubtful ability to specify the content of laws in morally credible ways.

The claim is not that any legal right created in a commendable institutional context is beyond criticism. Instead, it is that, so long as it does not clearly violate some important moral principle, is compatible with the central idea of the practice, and originates and survives in an institutional context that confers procedural legitimacy and content credibility, an international legal human right does not need a deep philosophical justification to perform its proper functions in human rights practice. Even if I am wrong about this, however, a weaker though nonetheless interesting conclusion follows from my analysis: If there is sufficient institutional development in the practice, either through the emergence of better international institutions or through more thorough incorporation of international legal human rights into more developed domestic legal systems, then the need for a philosophical justification for international legal human rights will be no greater than the need for a justification of domestic civil and political rights.

5. Conclusion

My aim has been to assess recent attempts by philosophers to shed light on the justification of international legal human rights and, in the light of this assessment, to indicate the direction that fruitful theorizing should take. My main findings have been as follows:

1. Philosophical discourse that uses the phrase *human rights* to refer both to moral human rights and international legal human rights promotes confusion.
2. Philosophers tend to assume, rather than argue, for the GV, the thesis that to justify international legal human rights it is necessary to show that they are grounded, at least in significant part, in moral human rights. The GV requires a justification, however.
3. The assumption that legal human rights are best seen as attempts to help realize moral human rights fits well with the justificatory language of the core human rights documents and with the actual history of the development of international legal human rights through treaties following the ratification of the Universal Declaration of Human Rights. Moreover, the attempt of "political" theories to bypass the task of constructing a theory of moral human rights fails.
4. Current theories that attempt to ground international legal human rights in moral human rights have assumed that, when realized, moral human rights protect certain morally important interests or needs of individuals. It is not clear, however, that existing accounts of the relevant interests or needs can make sense of the prominence in the practice of strong rights against discrimination on grounds of gender or race.
5. Although philosophers have largely ignored them, the institutional dimension of human rights practice is subject to several serious normative challenges, and these would remain potent even if it were shown that all existing international legal human rights are grounded in moral human rights.
6. Some of the most serious normative challenges to the practice can be met only by institutional development, not better philosophical theories.[14]

NOTES

1. The qualifier "at least in significant part" is meant to leave open the possibility that some international legal human rights are grounded in other moral considerations.

2. Carl Wellman (2011, 71–84) endorses GV.

3. The preamble also includes the idea that respect for human rights is needed for international security, but it is the idea that human rights are grounded in the inherent dignity or equal worth of the human person that distinguishes the Charter, the UDHR, and the Covenants from traditional international legal discourse, marking the beginning of the modern human rights era. The language of inherent dignity or equal moral worth is also found in the Racism Convention, the Migrants Convention, the Vienna Declaration, the Children's Convention, and the Torture Convention.

4. Morsink's (1999) rigorous and widely acclaimed analysis of the intellectual origins of the UDHR and the processes by which it was drafted strongly supports this reading of the document. In particular, he provides impressive evidence that the dominant view among the drafters was that their task was to formulate a list of moral rights possessed by all people, on the assumption that these rights would in the future be given international legal effect, and that these rights were conceived as being possessed equally by individuals on their own account, independently of social or legal recognition or being bestowed by God (what he calls the "inherence idea").

5. I thank Tony Cole for this point.

6. See, for example, the Convention on Eliminating All Forms of Discrimination Against Women, para. 1 (General Assembly of the United Nations 1979).

7. For more on Rawls on human rights, see the chapter "Rawls" by Leif Wenar in this volume.

8. Beitz suggests briefly and tentatively that a theory that grounds legal human rights in a short list of natural rights would face a dilemma: either the natural rights will be sufficiently lean to be plausible, in which case it will be hard to generate the full list of international legal rights from them; or they will be rich enough to generate the full list but at the expense of plausibility. Apart from the fact that grounding views need not construe moral human rights as natural rights (i.e., as preinstitutional), Beitz does not support his surmise by examining any attempts (such as the work of Nickel 2007, Griffin 2008, and Tasioulas 2010) to execute the grounding strategy.

9. Griffin does not distinguish clearly between moral and international legal human rights. However, he does think that his theory of moral human rights provides a critical perspective on international legal human rights: He criticizes particular international legal human rights by arguing that they cannot be grounded in moral human rights properly understood.

10. I develop this point in detail, with further examples, in Buchanan (2010b).

11. The same is true for capability theories: Being relegated to an inferior status need not undermine one's capabilities: Being relegated to an inferior status need not undermine one's capabilities for "central functionings."

12. I take up this issue in Buchanan (in press).

13. For an investigation of the supremacy issue, see Buchanan and Powell (2008).

14. For their comments on earlier versions of this chapter, I thank Samantha Besson, Matthew Braddock, Tony Cole, David Estlund, Nicole Hakimi, Kristen Hessler, Whitney Kane, Steven Ratner, Gopal Sreenivasan, and John Tasioulas.

REFERENCES

Altman, A., and C. Wellman. 2009. *A Liberal Theory of International Justice*. Cambridge, UK: Cambridge University Press.

Beitz, C. 2010. *The Idea of Human Rights*. Oxford: Oxford University Press.

Buchanan, A. 2010a. "Justice, Legitimacy, and Human Rights." In *Human Rights, Legitimacy and the Use of Force*. Edited by A. Buchanan, 13–30. Oxford: Oxford University Press.

Buchanan, A. 2010b. "The Egalitarianism of Human Rights." *Ethics* 120(4): 679–710.

Buchanan, A. 2003. *Justice, Legitimacy, and Self-Determination: Moral Foundations for International Law*. Oxford: Oxford University Press.

Buchanan, A. In press. "Why *International* Human Rights?" In *Foundations of Human Rights*. Edited by Matthew Liao and Massimo Renzo. Oxford: Oxford University Press.

Buchanan, A., and R. O. Keohane. 2006. "The Legitimacy of Global Governance Institutions." *Ethics & International Affairs* 20(4): 405–37.

Buchanan, A., and R. Powell. 2008. "Recent Work: Constitutional Democracy and the Rule of International Law: Are They Compatible?" *The Journal of Political Philosophy* 16(3): 326–49.

General Assembly of the United Nations. 1945. *Preamble to the Charter of the United Nations* (October 24). Available from http://www.un.org/en/documents/charter/preamble.shtml.

General Assembly of the United Nations. 1948. *The Universal Declaration of Human Rights* (December 10). Available from http://www.un.org/en/documents/udhr/.

General Assembly of the United Nations. 1979. *International Covenant on Economic, Cultural, and Social Rights* (January 3). Available from http://www2.ohchr.org/english/law/cescr.htm.

General Assembly of the United Nations. 1981. *The Convention on Eliminating All Forms of Discrimination Against Women* (September 3). Available from http://www.un.org/womenwatch/daw/cedaw/cedaw.htm.

Griffin, J. 2008. *On Human Rights*. Oxford: Oxford University Press.

Miller, D. 2007. *National Responsibility and Global Justice*. Oxford: Oxford University Press.

Morsink, J. 1999. *The Universal Declaration of Human Rights: Origins, Drafting and Intent*. Philadelphia: University of Pennsylvania Press.

Nickel, J. 2007. *Making Sense of Human Rights*, rev. ed. Malden, MA: Blackwell.

Pogge, T. 2008. *World Poverty and Human Rights*. Cambridge, UK: Polity Press.

Rawls, J. 1999. *The Law of Peoples*. Cambridge, MA: Harvard University Press.

Raz, J. 2010. "Human Rights without Foundations." In *The Philosophy of International Law*. Edited by S. Besson and J. Tasioulas, 321–38. Oxford: Oxford University Press.

Talbott, W. J. 2005. *Which Rights Should Be Universal?* Oxford: Oxford University Press.

Tasioulas, J. 2010. "The Legitimacy of International Law. In *The Philosophy of International Law*. Edited by S. Besson and J. Tasioulas, 97–116. Oxford: Oxford University Press.

Wellman, C. 2011. *The Moral Dimensions of Human Rights*. Oxford: Oxford University Press.

CHAPTER 16

WAR

JEFF MCMAHAN

Much of what might be called the "classical" theory of the just war was formulated prior to the advent of modern states and the emergence of doctrines of state sovereignty. The classical writers understood the morality of war to be only one dimension of a unified body of natural law that governs individual human action in much the same way that the laws of nature govern the nonhuman world, except that the human subjects of natural law were thought to enjoy free will, which enabled them, unlike natural objects, to violate at least some of the laws to which they were subject. Natural law was thought to be addressed primarily to the conscience of the individual person and was only derivatively concerned with the formation, structure, and functioning of political and legal institutions. The doctrines of the classical just war theorists were therefore largely individualist in character—that is, they were focused on whether or when it was permissible for individuals to go to war and what it was permissible or impermissible for them to do in war.

Working within the natural law tradition, the classical just war theorists understood themselves to be discovering and articulating objective moral truths. In contrast to many later theorists in the just war tradition, they did not, at least for the most part, formulate moral principles by reference to what they believed the likely consequences would be if people were to accept and attempt to follow those principles; nor did they try to determine what principles potential adversaries might realistically be able to agree to, or could rationally accept, for governing their relations with one another. These ways of reasoning about the selection of principles for the governance of war had to await the development of institutional means of regulating relations among actual and potential adversaries. The principles of classical just war theory therefore made few concessions to purely pragmatic concerns.

Just war theory has traditionally been divided into two sets of principles: those governing the resort to war (*jus ad bellum*) and those governing the conduct of war (*jus in bello*). The classical theorists tended to regard *jus in bello* as dependent on *jus ad bellum*, in the sense that what it is permissible for an individual to do in war depends on whether his war is just and in particular on whether it is being fought for a "just cause"—that is, an aim that is sufficient to justify the resort to war. Writing in the first half of the sixteenth century, Francisco de Vitoria argued that soldiers "*must not go to war*" when "the war seems patently unjust," even when they are ordered to do so by a legitimate authority, for "one may not lawfully kill an innocent man on any authority, and in the case we are speaking of [when soldiers are confident that their war is unjust] the enemy must be innocent" (Vitoria 1991, 307–8). By "innocent" Vitoria meant "having done no wrong" (Vitoria 1991, 303). Francisco Suárez, writing roughly half a century later, reaffirmed Vitoria's view: "No one may be deprived of his life save for reason of his own guilt"; thus, it is impermissible in war to kill any of those who "have not shared in the crime nor in the unjust war" (Suárez 1944, 845–46). From this it seems to follow that it is impermissible to kill soldiers who fight in a just war.

The classical theorists did, however, grapple with the problem of uncertainty. How are soldiers to know whether their war is just or unjust when they typically have limited access to empirical information, limited opportunities for deliberation, and little or no education in just war theory, much less in moral theory generally? Some classical theorists concluded that in conditions of factual or normative uncertainty, the duties of soldiers to members of their community, together with their duty of obedience to their ruler, made it permissible or even obligatory for them to fight. Vitoria, for example, argued that "in cases of doubt . . . they had better fight," a view shared by most of his successors to the present day (Vitoria 1991, 311–12). Some of the classical theorists who held this view sought to bolster it with another claim that would also be adopted by later theorists who otherwise held a quite different view—namely, that moral responsibility for the participation of soldiers in an unjust war lies not with the soldiers themselves but with the rulers who order them to fight and that their lack of responsibility affects the permissibility of their fighting. The earliest classical theorist to advance this claim was Augustine, who contended that "he to whom authority is delegated, and who is but the sword in the hand of him who uses it, is not himself responsible for the death he deals" (Augustine 1950, 27). Hobbes, who wrote more than 1,200 years after Augustine, made the same point:

> What I beleeve to be another mans sin, I may sometimes doe that without any sin of mine. For if I be commanded to doe that which is a sin in him who commands me, if I doe it, and he that commands me be by Right, Lord over me, I sinne not; [thus,] if I wage warre at the Commandement of my Prince, conceiving the warre to be unjustly undertaken, I doe not therefore doe unjustly. (1651)

Although Hobbes shared this particular view with Augustine, his work was crucial in overthrowing the classical theory, with its emphasis on the individual, and in introducing many of the essential elements of what I refer to as the "traditional" theory of the just war, particularly its identification of the sovereign state as the principal agent in war. The canonical statement of this latter view was given later by Rousseau, who wrote that "war . . . is something that occurs not between man and man, but between States. The individuals who become involved in it are enemies only by accident . . . A State can have as its enemies only other States, not men at all" (Rousseau 1947, 249–50).

According to Hobbes, there can be no morality in the absence of a sovereign capable of enforcing the moral rules he imposes on his subjects. Because states are themselves sovereigns, they are not subject to any higher power that could coerce them to comply with a moral code imposed on them. On Hobbes's view, then, the idea that it could be *morally* impermissible for a state to go to war verges on incoherence. And states could not bind themselves to a contract that would restrict the occasions for the resort to war, for their self-interested reasons for compliance would be outweighed whenever they perceived an opportunity for an easy victory over another state, with all the rewards that would bring. All states would therefore know in advance that such a contract could not be effective. It could, however, be in the interest of each state to reach agreement with other states on a set of rules that, if generally observed, would limit the violence and destructiveness of war when it occurred. Provided that initial noncompliance with the rules by one state would not be fatal to its adversary, and given that no state would long endure noncompliance by an adversary without retaliating in kind, such a contract could be robustly self-enforcing. This is because violations of the *in bello* rules rarely offer a decisive advantage yet almost invariably provoke one's adversary to commit atrocities in return; therefore, in general, they increase both the costs of the war and the probability of vicious reprisals if one loses without substantially increasing the probability of victory. Thus, while compliance with *ad bellum* constraints would be against the interests of many individual states, so that there could be no reasonable expectation of reciprocity, compliance with *in bello* rules could be in the interest of each state, because it would normally have less to gain from violating the rules than it would from its adversary's continued compliance. Reciprocal restraint in matters of *jus in bello* can, therefore, often be rational for both parties.

Hobbesian moral and political theory, along with the pragmatic considerations to which it appealed, was instrumental in shifting the attention of just war theorists away from *jus ad bellum* to *jus in bello*. By the nineteenth century, less than two centuries after Hobbes wrote, it had come to be commonly accepted that the resort to war was a sovereign prerogative of states. States could legitimately go to war for any reason. This view was reflected in international law, which confined itself to the attempt to restrain the conduct of war. As one commentator wrote in 1906, "International Law . . . does not consider the justice or injustice of a war. From a purely legal standpoint, all wars . . . are neither just nor unjust. International Law merely takes cognizance of the existence of war as a fact, and prescribes certain rules and regulations which affect the rights and duties of neutrals and belligerents during that continuance" (Hershey 1906, 67). By this time, the classical view that the permissibility of participation in a war could depend on whether the war was just had largely been abandoned. When theorists had ceased to recognize moral or legal constraints on the resort to war, the *in bello* rules were necessarily held to be independent of *jus ad bellum*.

The principles of *jus in bello* were then formulated with practical considerations in mind. On the assumption that general observance of the rules must serve the interests of all, aggressors as well as victims, the guiding aim of the rules had to be one on which all could agree. That aim was to reduce the overall level of violence, particularly by insulating ordinary life among civilians to the greatest possible degree from the destructive effects of warfare. This led to the general acceptance, in principle if not always in practice, of the traditional interpretation of the requirement of discrimination. In its generic form, this is the requirement to discriminate between legitimate and illegitimate targets by directing intentional attacks against the former only. According to traditional just war theory, the distinction between legitimate and illegitimate targets coincides with the distinction between combatants and noncombatants. The traditional requirement of discrimination thus seeks to confine the effects of combat to the combatants themselves, shielding civilians and their collective life to the maximum extent possible, and it does this without reference to matters of *jus ad bellum*. It does not identify combatants on either side as wrongdoers or as innocent victims. The rules of *jus in bello* are neutral between the belligerents and are equally satisfiable by all. That the principles of *jus in bello* are independent of *ad bellum* considerations became a central pillar of the traditional theory of the just war. It is also a foundational assumption of the international law of war, which has often guided the development of our thought about the morality of war rather than being guided by it.

The neglect or even repudiation of *jus ad bellum* together with the development of moral and legal doctrines of *jus in bello* that were neutral between wrongdoers and innocent victims may well have had an unforeseen but tragic effect. In a world that recognizes no significant moral or legal constraints on the resort to war, doctrines of *jus in bello* that actually succeed in mitigating the terrible effects of war can also weaken whatever prudential or moral inhibitions political leaders may have about the initiation of war. The more the expected costs of war are reduced by the expectation of general conformity with the rules, the more attractive the option of war may seem. This is particularly dangerous when the rules are designed to limit the costs to wrongdoers no less than the costs to their victims.

It is arguable that these moral and legal doctrines and the expectations they created were among the conditions that facilitated the outbreak of the First World War and, to a lesser extent, the Second as well. After those two cataclysmic wars, it was no longer possible to think of the resort to war as a sovereign prerogative of states that cannot be restricted either morally or legally. Legal and moral doctrines of *jus ad bellum* were resurrected but in radically simplified forms. The response in international law was an extreme shift from the recognition during the nineteenth century of an unrestricted right of resort to war to a sweeping prohibition of war, with only two exceptions, both stated in the UN Charter. War could be legally permissible only if authorized by the Security Council or in "individual or collective self-defense if an armed attack occurs." Just war theorists tended to follow the international lawyers, arguing that the only just cause for war is defense against aggression. Both international law and the theory of the just war retained their state-centered and pragmatic character. What changed was that the aim of regulating and moderating the conduct of war no longer had priority over the aim of preventing war from occurring at all. The sovereign right of states to resort to war was replaced by the sovereign right of states against military aggression.

In the traditional theory of the just war, both the principles of *jus ad bellum* and those of *jus in bello* are grounded in doctrines of self-defense. Interestingly, however, the understanding of the morality of self-defense that informs the principles of *jus ad bellum* is quite different from that found in the traditional principles of *jus in bello*. In keeping with the traditional theory's collectivist or statist character, its doctrine of *jus ad bellum* is generally understood as deriving from what Michael Walzer, the theory's most eminent proponent for at least the last hundred years, calls the "domestic analogy." This is the claim that the principles governing the resort to war are the same as those that govern the morality of self- and other-defense among individual persons. One such principle is that if Attacker wrongfully and culpably attacks Victim, both Victim and Third Party have a right to take necessary and proportionate defensive action against Attacker, while Attacker has no right of self-defense against them. What the domestic analogy asserts is that this principle is equally true whether Attacker, Victim, and Third Party are individual persons or states (Walzer 1977).

This account of self-defense is *asymmetrical* between the wrongful attacker and the innocent victim. Yet the understanding of the morality of self-defense that informs the traditional principles of *jus in bello* is *symmetrical*, extending the same rights and liabilities to combatants on all sides in a war. Even after the emergence of a newly invigorated doctrine of *jus ad bellum* in the twentieth century, the independence and thus the moral neutrality of the principles of *jus in bello* were preserved. This was accomplished by restricting the application of the principles of *jus ad bellum* to states and their governments. No individual combatant—indeed, no individual at all other than those directly involved in decision making about the resort to war—could be held accountable for matters of *jus ad bellum*, according to the traditional theory. Combatants are answerable only for their conformity with the principles of *jus in bello*, which also constrain the commands that states may give their combatants. We see here the lingering influence of the view of Augustine and Hobbes, cited earlier, that it can be permissible for combatants to fight in an unjust war because responsibility for their mere participation lies solely with their rulers, whom they are bound to obey.

This is a curious inversion of the hierarchy of responsibility recognized by common sense morality and, to some extent, domestic criminal law. In these other domains, the perpetrators of wrongful acts are generally thought to bear at least equal and often greater responsibility for those acts than mere accessories, such as instigators. Thus, when John Stuart Mill considered a possible legal arrangement whereby pimps, but not the patrons of prostitutes, would be prosecuted, he observed that this would involve "the moral anomaly of punishing the accessory, when the principal is (and must be) allowed to go free" (Mill 1961, 301). Similarly in traditional just war theory and the law of war, the accessories, or instigators—that is, the officials who give the order to fight an unjust war—bear *all* the responsibility, whereas the perpetrators bear none at all.

Another peculiarity of the traditional theory's doctrine of *jus in bello* is, as noted previously, that the principles of permissible defense it presupposes are quite different from those that govern individual self- and other-defense outside the context of war and, according to the traditional theory, indirectly govern the conduct of states via the domestic analogy. In cases of individual self- and other-defense, the usual situation is that one party is a wrongful aggressor while the other is an innocent victim. According to the familiar understanding of the morality of defensive action, the aggressor acts wrongly and therefore forfeits both his right not to be attacked and his right of defense, while the victim retains both of these rights. According to the traditional doctrine of *jus in bello*, the situation is entirely different with the rights, permissions, and liabilities of combatants in war. Combatants on *both* sides act permissibly in fighting, yet *all* forfeit their right not to be attacked. But, although they forfeit their right against attack, they retain their right of self-defense. This defies the ordinary logic of self-defense. How can each party be morally justified in killing the other?

Most of the accounts of the morality of self-defense that find any support in the literature imply that it is impossible for each party in a conflict to be justified in killing, or trying to kill, the other. There do, however, seem to be such cases. Suppose, for example, that armed Roman guards drag two men into the Colosseum and tell them that unless they fight until one kills the other, both will be killed immediately. Neither, it seems, is obligated to sacrifice himself, because nothing distinguishes one from the other and it makes no sense to suppose that they could both be required to sacrifice themselves, for neither *could* sacrifice himself unless the other were to kill him. Because each would be required to sacrifice himself yet neither could actually do it, both would be killed by the guards. Because it is better for one to survive than for both to die, it seems that each is permitted to try to kill the other. One might call cases in which this is true "symmetrical defense cases."

The coerced gladiators' situations are symmetrical: both are morally innocent, and neither pursues any goal other than survival. In this, however, they are unlike combatants on opposing sides in a war. For the usual situation in war is that one side's aims are unjust—at least in the minimal sense that they are not aims that it is permissible to pursue by means of war—while the other side's aim, or at least its dominant aim, is just—namely, preventing the other side from achieving its unjust aims. How could it be that in these conditions combatants on both sides are morally permitted to kill combatants on the other side?

Defenders of the traditional theory typically offer one or more of three answers. Some defend the principle that all combatants may legitimately kill enemy combatants on the ground that the violence and destruction of war will be kept to a minimum if combatants on both sides believe that they may permissibly kill enemy combatants but not anyone else. According to this reasoning, which is congenial to rule consequentialists and contractualists, including Hobbesian contractualists, the principle is justified by the effects it would have if people were to act on it. A second justification is often paired with the first: namely, that all combatants are permitted to kill enemy combatants because all combatants *consent* to become legitimate targets when they become soldiers. By wearing a uniform and carrying their arms openly, combatants consciously *identify* themselves as legitimate targets for their enemies. The principle that all combatants may legitimately be killed by their enemies is therefore justified not merely because of its effects but also because combatants have waived their right not to be killed, at least vis-à-vis enemy combatants.

The third answer to the question of how it could be permissible for combatants on both sides to kill their adversaries is more salient in the traditional literature than the other two and is indeed implicit in the language of the traditional theory. When traditional theorists claim that it is impermissible intentionally to kill the innocent in war, they are using the term *innocent* in two ways. First, they use it in accordance with its etymology to mean "those who pose no threat"—that is, noncombatants. They also mean to imply that it is *permissible* to kill those who are in this sense *noninnocent*—that is, those who *do* pose a threat: namely, combatants. But they also use *innocent* to refer to those who, as Michael Walzer puts it, "have done nothing, and are doing nothing, that entails the loss of their rights" (Walzer 1977, 146). The innocent, in short, are those who are not morally liable to be attacked or killed because they pose no threat to others. The noninnocent, by contrast, *are* liable to military attack (that is, have lost their right not to be attacked) precisely because they do pose a threat to others. In Walzer's words, the "right not to be attacked . . . is lost by those who . . . pose a danger to other people" (Walzer 1977, 145). All combatants are assumed to pose a threat to others and are thus legitimate targets; noncombatants pose no threat and are not legitimate targets.

The second defense of the traditional doctrine of *jus in bello* is that all combatants waive their right not to be attacked; the third is that they forfeit it. These defenses may seem incompatible, for how can combatants waive a right they do not have because they have already forfeited it? Perhaps the waiving comes first, which would mean that the permissibility of killing combatants in war is overdetermined. According to this understanding, combatants first grant their adversaries permission to act against their right not to be attacked. Because they retain that right, they could presumably withdraw the permission. But because they then forfeit (that is, lose) the right, the prior waiving or granting of permission becomes irrelevant.

The first of these three defenses, which seeks to justify principles by reference to their utility, has little appeal as an account of the *morality* of *jus in bello* to those who are neither rule consequentialists nor contractualists, in particular those who believe that people have certain rights quite independently of utility or agreement. I cannot here settle the dispute between these different schools of thought about the nature of morality, but it is worth noting that those who believe that people have rights seem to have the option of maintaining their view *and* achieving the practical advantages that consequentialists and contractualists claim that their *in bello* rules provide. Defenders of rights can do this by acknowledging that the principles that consequentialists claim would have the best consequences and that contractualists claim people could rationally agree to accept can function effectively as *legal rules*. Morality, they can argue, addresses us as competent moral agents and demands that we not violate rights; but when we formulate laws, we must take into account that the people governed by them will often have false factual or moral beliefs, be motivated by self-interest rather than a desire to act rightly, or not know how best to achieve their aims. Because of this, it may be necessary for our legal principles to diverge from the moral principles governing the same area of conduct. If it is true that combatants who are told to follow the traditional *in bello* rules will in general act more morally than combatants who are told to respect people's rights, defenders of a rights-based morality can concede that the law of war ought to be based on the traditional rules.

The second claim—that combatants consent to be legitimate targets—seems false. If aggressors were to attack my country unjustly and I were to enlist in the military to defend my fellow citizens, I would not see myself as thereby consenting to be attacked by the aggressors. Those who claim that soldiers consent may respond that when I don the uniform and carry a weapon openly, I am identifying myself as a legitimate target for enemy combatants, which is the same as consenting to be attacked. To this I would reply that when I wear the uniform I am merely adhering to a convention that serves the useful purpose of drawing the aggressors' fire toward me and away from the people I am defending, which is quite different from giving the aggressors permission to attack me.

Those who claim that soldiers consent will argue that what is involved in my adopting the role of a soldier is not up to me, not a matter of my beliefs or intentions, but is instead determined by the nature of the role itself. Just as I cannot voluntarily become a firefighter and then say that I never consented to take risks to extinguish fires, so I cannot become a soldier and claim I never consented to be a legitimate target for enemy combatants. Just as the role of a firefighter involves a commitment to expose oneself to certain risks, so the role of a soldier involves becoming a legitimate target in conditions of war. It is doubtful, however, that there is any such determinacy about the features of the role of a soldier. No doubt many people, including many soldiers, do conceive of the role in this way. Those who enlist with this understanding of the role arguably do thereby consent to become legitimate targets. But many others do not see this as a necessary feature of the role. Even if it were a socially agreed feature of the role of a soldier that it involves being a legitimate target, a person who enlists without being aware of that would no more consent to be a legitimate target than I would consent to be a soldier if I signed an enlistment form believing that I was joining the Boy Scouts. Perhaps by signing the form I would have legally committed myself to be in the army. Signing might be a matter of strict liability, for it was my responsibility to know what I was signing. But if I did commit myself by signing, it was not because I *consented*.

The third defense of the traditional theory is the least plausible of the three. It is tantamount to the claim that defensive action in war is necessarily self-justifying. It concedes that the defending agent has no right not to be attacked and that his attacker is justified in attacking him but denies the principle that there can be no right of defense against an attack to which one is liable. Yet this principle is compelling. How could it be permissible to kill a person who acts with moral justification and will not violate one's rights?

Proponents of the traditional theory have not, to my knowledge, explained how merely posing a threat to another could cause a person to lose his rights—or, in particular, how posing a justified threat causes a soldier to lose his rights but does not cause other people (such as police officers or third-party defenders of innocent people) to lose theirs. Traditional just war theorists tend instead to appeal to facts about the defending soldier, such as that he acts under duress or in conditions of factual and moral uncertainty, to explain why he retains a right of defense against a justified threat. But facts of these kinds generally do not provide a moral justification for attacking or killing people but instead provide only an excuse—that is, a reason not to blame people even though they have acted wrongly. They are irrelevant to whether a justified attacker loses or retains his rights.

As these remarks indicate, the symmetrical account of defensive rights found in the traditional doctrine of *jus in bello* has no plausibility in any other context, except, perhaps, in violent games, such as boxing, in which the antagonists consent to be attacked in certain ways and their acts of violence neither wrong nor harm other people. Recognizing this, traditional just war theorists have generally claimed that conditions of war are so different from other conditions in human life that war must have its own special and quite different morality. According to this view, whenever a state of war arises, the familiar constraints on attacking and killing people cease to be binding on combatants in their relations with enemy combatants. Combatants whose acts of war are instrumental to the achievement of unjust goals do no wrong in killing enemy combatants, even though their victims may be doing nothing more than engaging in necessary and proportionate defense of themselves and other innocent people. This is a feature of the special morality of war that does not apply to other forms of conflict.

The traditional theory thus makes it critical to be able to distinguish with precision between war and other forms of conflict, because it is only in war that the familiar asymmetrical principles of defense are supplanted by their symmetrical counterparts. What is it, then, about war that differentiates it so radically from other forms of conflict that it must have its own distinctive morality? The answer, I think, is: *nothing*. Consider one way in which civil wars often arise. The government of a state oppresses a particular group of its citizens, perhaps an ethnic or religious minority (or majority), or the population of a particular region. The oppression provokes morally justified nonviolent protests that are violently suppressed, either by the police or the army. This provokes larger protests in which some of the protesters use force to try to defend themselves. These are suppressed even more bloodily, yet the protests continue, becoming larger, more widespread geographically, and more violent. As the resisters become more numerous, better organized, and better armed (perhaps by capturing weapons from soldiers who have been defeated or have defected), their aim gradually shifts from merely stopping the persecution to overthrowing the government—an aim that, we may assume, has now become legitimate. They establish hierarchies of political and military authority and begin to exercise control over certain territories, however limited. Eventually there is full-scale civil war, the conduct of which, according to traditional just war theorists, is now governed on both sides by the traditional principles of *jus in bello*. In the early stages, however, the ordinary asymmetrical principles applied. When soldiers attacked nonviolent protesters, they acted wrongly. Protesters then acted permissibly in defending themselves, and the soldiers were guilty of further wrongdoing when they responded with violence to the protesters' defensive action. At each point before the conflict became a civil war, the soldiers acted wrongly in using violence against those who, by hypothesis, acted with moral justification in opposing the government. Yet later, after the violence had escalated to the point of civil war, it became permissible, according to the traditional theory, for soldiers to kill rebel fighters. What happened that could account for this?

This is not a challenge to locate a precise point at which a conflict becomes a war, analogous to the challenge to identify a precise point at which day ends and night begins. The traditional theorist does not have to defend the view that there is some point at which a soldier's killing of a resister ceases to be murder and becomes permissible. The challenge is, rather, to identify any differences between the early stages of the conflict and the later stages that can justify the claim that the moral principles that apply in the later stages are different from those that applied in the earlier stages. But all that seems to have occurred is that the resisters have become more numerous, better coordinated in their action, and more powerful. These considerations seem insufficiently significant to summon wholly different moral principles into effect.

Suppose, however, that traditional just war theorists are able to identify some property of war that justifies their claim that the conduct of war is governed by moral principles different from those that govern other forms of violent conflict. One assumption they then seem committed to is that when one state militarily attacks another, a state of war exists. Only if that is so can it be certain that, as the traditional theory asserts, soldiers on the side that has been attacked will be acting permissibly if they participate in a military counterattack. Suppose, for example, that the government of state A is engaged in a campaign of domestic genocide. State B justifiably invades to stop the genocide. The traditional theory is committed to the view that as soon as B's invasion begins, a state of war exists, for it implies that A's soldiers act permissibly when they counterattack to thwart the justified humanitarian intervention (even though they have acted impermissibly if they have participated in the genocide). The reason they could not permissibly counterattack unless there were a state of war is that their action would be judged wrong by the asymmetrical principles that govern conflicts other than war. It can be permissible for them to counterattack only if the principles that apply in this situation are the symmetrical principles of the special morality of war. Hence, the traditional theory presupposes that any military attack by one state against another creates a state of war in which the symmetrical principles apply.

Notice what this means. When the symmetrical principles of the special *in bello* morality come into effect, soldiers on both sides lose their right against enemy soldiers not to be attacked or killed by them. That means that soldiers must be endowed with remarkable powers of moral alchemy. Merely by conducting a surprise military attack against unmobilized soldiers in another state, they can cause those other soldiers' moral rights to *vanish*. This is highly convenient for soldiers who engage in aggression. Their potential adversaries have a right not to be attacked or killed, but whenever they are attacked militarily by soldiers acting as agents of another state, a state of war exists in which their rights simply disappear. A soldier's right not to be attacked thus vanishes the moment he comes under military attack.

The defender of the traditional theory may deny that the theory implies that soldiers' rights against attack vanish when they are attacked in a way that initiates a state of war. Rather, soldiers retain the right, but it is violated not by the enemy soldiers but by those who command them—the enemy state or government. This response, however, does not solve the problem; it shows only that the objection can be stated in either of two ways. If the traditional theorist distinguishes between two rights—a soldier's right *against enemy soldiers* that they not attack him and his right *against the enemy government* that its soldiers not attack him—the objection is that the theory implies that the first of these rights vanishes though the second remains. If the traditional theorist says there is only one right—the right not to be attacked— then the objection is that the theory implies not that enemy soldiers can cause the right to vanish but that they can, merely by conducting an attack, substantially narrow the scope of their enemies' rights. They can make it so that their enemies' rights cease to constrain *them*, even if they continue to constrain their government. That is still a remarkable form of moral alchemy.

Either way, the implication is absurd. And if the government of a state can create a state of war through an official declaration of war, as most people, including most just war theorists, have assumed, then the traditional theory has the even more absurd implication that the government of one state can cause both its own soldiers and those in another state to lose their right not to be killed, or cause its scope to be narrowed, simply by uttering the magical incantation, "We hereby declare war. . . ." Traditional just war theorists will presumably want to disown this alleged implication. Because on their view war is so different from other forms of conflict that it is governed by its own special morality, what they ought to say is that a state of war cannot be conjured into existence by mere declaration. They are committed to defending a morally substantive concept of war.

Let us say that a soldier who fights in a just war is a "just combatant" while a soldier who fights in a war that lacks a just cause is an "unjust combatant." As I noted earlier, there is a different way in which traditional just war theorists might defend their claim that unjust combatants act permissibly when they attack and kill just combatants as a means of achieving their state's unjust aims. They can accept that just combatants retain their right not to be attacked and appeal instead to the claim of Augustine and Hobbes that all responsibility for the killing and wounding of just combatants by unjust combatants lies with the latter's rulers rather than with the combatants themselves. If the location of responsibility for an act of killing can affect the permissibility of the perpetrator's act, it could be permissible for unjust combatants to kill just combatants even when that would violate the latter's right not to be killed. For if all responsibility lies with the rulers, all the wrongdoing must be theirs as well.

This idea presupposes a different form of moral alchemy whereby a morally autonomous agent is converted by his role as a soldier in a state of war into a mere instrument: "the sword in the hand of him who uses it." This seems mistaken as well, for a variety of reasons. First, it denies the obvious by claiming that soldiers, at least in their role as soldiers, are not the ones who bear moral responsibility for what they themselves do. Second, even if it were true that they were wholly lacking in moral responsibility for their participation in an unjust war because all responsibility lay with their rulers, what would seem to follow is not that their participation was permissible but that it was neither permissible nor impermissible in the way that the action of a robot is neither permissible nor impermissible. Third, what if they had no rulers? Imagine a society in which decisions about the resort to war were made by a vote of all the soldiers in the armed forces. It seems arbitrary to suppose that soldiers from such a society could not permissibly fight in a certain war when soldiers from a different society acting under orders *could* permissibly fight in the exact same war. Fourth, the view that permissibility follows responsibility implies that if a soldier engages in moral deliberation in a time of war and asks whether a certain act or course of action is permissible, the first question he should ask is, "If I do it, who will be responsible?" If he consults the traditional theory of the just war and finds that his rulers will be responsible, he can then conclude that the act would be permissible. He can conclude that even though rights will be violated if he acts, he will not be the violator; rather, his government, acting through him, will be. It is, therefore, permissible for him to act. Yet this is no way to determine whether an act is morally permissible.

Finally, the suggestion that soldiers do not act wrongly because responsibility for their action transfers to their rulers seems incompatible with the view, which all traditional just war theorists accept, that soldiers do act impermissibly if they violate the rules of *jus in bello*, even when they are ordered to by a superior. For their view to be coherent, traditional just war theorists must explain why a combatant can never be morally responsible for his participation in an unjust war—no matter how obvious it is that the war is unjust and irrespective of what his motivating reasons are for participating—but *is* morally responsible for his violations of the rules of *jus in bello*.

In contrast with the traditional theory, the revisionist account of the just war asserts that war is morally continuous with other forms of conflict and is governed by the same principles that apply to other forms of violent conflict. According to revisionism, there is no special morality of war. Like the traditional theory, the revisionist account is based on principles of self- and other-defense. But it does not reason analogically from the principles that govern self-defense at the individual level; rather, it claims that those principles, which are asymmetrical between the wrongful aggressor and the innocent victim, apply uniformly to defensive action both outside war and in war. Just war is not the exercise by a state of its right of self-defense; it is the coordinated exercise by persons of their individual rights of self- and other-defense.

On this view, the limits of individual self- and other-defense are also the limits of national defense. Traditional theorists often assume otherwise. In accordance with the domestic analogy, they conceive of the state as an individual agent that has not only a right of self-defense but also a duty to defend its citizens. This duty, they assume, makes it permissible for the state to cause more harm to others, including innocent bystanders, in the course of defending its citizens than might otherwise be proportionate. Revisionists whose approach to the morality of war is individualist in character reject this. They argue that just as a third party may not defend an innocent person if doing so would, as a side effect, cause greater harm to innocent people than the person would be permitted to cause in his own defense, so the state and its agents may not cause harm to innocent people in defending its citizens that is greater than that which its citizens would be permitted to cause in their own defense. There is nothing in the relations that people establish among themselves within a state that can extend their permissions to harm people outside the state.

The revisionist account's rejection of the idea that there is a special morality of war that is distinct from the principles that apply outside the context of war is a corollary of what I identified earlier as the fundamental division between the traditional and revisionist accounts—namely, that the revisionist account rejects the traditional claim that the principles of *jus in bello* are independent of the principles of *jus ad bellum*. The special morality of war recognized by the traditional theory, which is different from the moral principles that govern conflicts other than war, is confined to the doctrine of *jus in bello*. It is only in the *in bello* principles that the morality of defensive action is held to be symmetrical between those whose action supports unjust ends and those who oppose that action. When the revisionist theory insists that the same asymmetrical principles of defense that apply at the *ad bellum* level also apply at the *in bello* level, it is rejecting the independence of the principles of *jus in bello* from those of *jus ad bellum*. It claims instead that the moral asymmetry that the traditional theory recognizes at the *ad bellum* level between the wrongful aggressor and the innocent defender extends to the *in bello* level as well. What it is permissible for combatants to do in war thus depends on whether their action supports a just cause. Those who fight without a just cause cannot have the same rights as those who fight for a just cause.

Even for the traditional theory, the requirement of just cause is pivotal. Unless a war satisfies the requirement of just cause, it cannot satisfy various of the other traditional principles of *jus ad bellum*. A war without a just cause cannot, for example, satisfy the principle of right intention, which requires that war be intended to achieve the just cause. Neither can it satisfy the principles of necessity and proportionality, which require, respectively, that war must have a higher probability of achieving the just cause than any less harmful course of action and that the expected bad effects of war not be excessive in relation to the importance of achieving the just cause. The revisionist account goes further, however, by claiming that, except in certain rare instances, none of the principles of *jus in bello* can be satisfied by combatants who fight without a just cause ("unjust combatants"). According to the revisionist account, if a war lacks a just cause, those against whom it is fought are in general not morally liable to military attack. But if no one is liable to attack by those who fight without a just cause, it follows that unjust combatants have no legitimate targets; therefore their action is necessarily indiscriminate. Neither can any act of war by unjust combatants be necessary in the sense that it has a higher probability than any alternative act of war of making the greatest contribution to the achievement of the just cause that is possible in the circumstances. Finally, acts of war by unjust combatants can very seldom be proportionate. This is because the ultimate aims of their action are unjust and their means of achieving them involve the infliction of wrongful harms on those who justifiably attempt to defend their rights and the rights of their innocent compatriots. Any good effects of acts of war by unjust combatants are therefore likely to be incidental and wholly insufficient to outweigh the combatants' intended ends and means, which are largely or entirely bad. One might summarize these claims of the revisionist account by saying that while it is implausible to suppose that it could be permissible to pursue aims that are unjust even by means that are benign, it is considerably more implausible to suppose that it could be permissible to pursue such aims by means of killing people who have done nothing to lose or compromise their right not to be killed.

It seems, however, to be a virtue of the traditional theory that because its principles of *jus in bello* must be independent of *jus ad bellum*, they are equally satisfiable by combatants on all sides in a war. This is a virtue because it is important to have *in bello* principles that function in practice to restrain the conduct not only of just combatants but of unjust combatants as well. Yet this apparent advantage comes at a cost, which is that such principles will generally be manifestly implausible as *moral* principles, however useful they might be as rules of *law*. Consider, for example, the requirement of discrimination as traditionally interpreted, which prohibits intentional attacks against noncombatants but permits attacks against combatants. As I have noted, the alleged permission is especially problematic, since combatants who fight for a just cause, and therefore against those who are liable to attack, have done nothing to forfeit their right not to be attacked. Nor in most cases can the justification for attacking them be a lesser evil justification, since their defeat would normally be the greater evil. While the prohibition of intentionally killing noncombatants may seem intuitively plausible, even traditional theorists do not understand it literally, as they concede that there are exceptions, such as workers in munitions factories and civilian officials in departments of defense (or departments of war, as they were more accurately called when governments were less sophisticated at "public relations"). But once these exceptions are admitted, it becomes impossible to hold a principled line against the expansion of civilian liability. If noncombatants who work in munitions factories and departments of defense are legitimate targets, why not also scientists in industry or academia whose work is instrumental to the production of improved weapons technologies, or academic strategists who serve as consultants to the military during war?

Next consider the *in bello* requirement of proportionality, which I suggested can seldom be satisfied by unjust combatants. What have the traditional theorists had in mind when they have asserted that this requirement is equally satisfiable by just and unjust combatants alike? When they have addressed this issue at all, they have typically said something similar to what Protocol I to the Geneva Conventions says: namely, that harms caused to noncombatants must not "be excessive in relation to the concrete and direct military advantage anticipated." Yet military advantage is not in itself a good; whether it is instrumentally good depends on the goals the military action serves. If those goals are unjust, military advantage is instrumentally bad and cannot counterbalance or compensate for harm caused to innocent people.

Traditional theorists thus face a dilemma. If the principles of *jus in bello* are formulated to be independent of those of *jus ad bellum* and so are equally satisfiable by just and unjust combatants alike, they will inevitably lack credibility as moral principles, even if they make good law. If, alternatively, the *in bello* principles state genuine moral constraints on action in war, they cannot be satisfied by the action of unjust combatants. Given that the satisfaction of these principles is regarded by the traditional theory as a necessary condition of permissible conduct in war, it follows that soldiers cannot permissibly fight in the absence of a just cause. Since this implication is incompatible with the traditional theory, the theory seems condemned to embrace principles of *jus in bello* that, though perhaps well suited for law and therefore of considerable practical significance, cannot plausibly be regarded as correct moral principles.

Practical considerations do not, however, uniformly favor the traditional theory. The widespread acceptance of the traditional theory's claim that soldiers are not responsible for matters of *jus ad bellum* has had one conspicuously regrettable effect: by reassuring soldiers that they do no wrong by fighting in war provided they obey the traditional *in bello* rules (which, as we have seen, permit action that is morally wrong and arguably prohibit action that is morally permissible), the traditional theory facilitated the participation in unjust wars of countless generations of soldiers. If, by contrast, a society were to teach that it is seriously morally wrong to kill people in pursuit of unjust aims, its soldiers would be more likely to resist the pressure to fight in an unjust war. It is therefore reasonable to believe that if people generally accepted the revisionist account rather than the traditional theory, unjust wars would be less likely to occur or to continue once they had begun.

A defender of the traditional theory might object that if soldiers are encouraged not to fight in wars they believe to be unjust, there will always be a risk that they will mistake a just war for an unjust war, refuse to fight, and thus prevent a just war from being fought or cause it to be lost. But the history of war is reassuring on this point. People have a strong tendency to believe that any war their country fights must be just. For this and other reasons, people are much more likely to believe that an unjust war fought by their country is just than to believe that a just war fought by their country is unjust. Thus, while there has been no shortage of unjust wars in which those who fought believed that they were in the right, it difficult to find even a single instance in which a government has sought to fight a just war but been impeded by the moral scruples of soldiers (or civilians) who have mistakenly believed it to be unjust.

There are other significant differences between the practical implications of the two approaches to just war. I conclude by briefly discussing two such differences. One concerns the permissibility of preventive war—that is, war that is initiated to address a threat that is neither present nor imminent but is anticipated at some future time. The traditional and revisionist accounts can agree that it may be desirable to prohibit preventive war in law and convention to prevent states from using the prevention of future aggression as a pretext for engaging in present aggression. But the traditional theory has stronger principled—as opposed to practical—reasons for condemning preventive war than the revisionist theory has. The reason usually given in the writings of traditional theorists appeals to the domestic analogy. Just as no individual may attack another merely in anticipation of a future attack, so no state may attack another in the absence of a present or at least imminent threat. There is, however, a deeper reason why the traditional theory must generally condemn preventive war. Recall that the traditional theory claims that the only people who are legitimate targets in war are combatants and that combatants are defined as those who pose a threat. But preventive war involves attacks on unmobilized soldiers on their home bases in what is, at least until the moment of the attack, a time of peace. At the time when they are attacked, these soldiers pose no threat and hence are not combatants in the relevant sense. They are illegitimate targets. Preventive war, therefore, is necessarily indiscriminate.

This does not mean that the traditional theory rules out preventive war absolutely. But it does mean that preventive war necessarily involves the intentional killing of people who are innocent in the sense identified as relevant by the traditional theory. This leaves it open for the theory to offer a necessity or lesser evil justification for the killing of innocent people in a preventive war. A successful justification of this sort would, however, have to show that the expected harm to innocent people that would be averted by preventive war would *greatly* exceed the harm that the war would cause. Because this is seldom the case, the traditional theory can seldom justify preventive war.

The revisionist account, by contrast, can in principle offer a liability-based justification for preventive war. It can take its cue from the fact that in domestic society we accept that people can sometimes make themselves liable to preventive action by actively planning and preparing to engage in serious wrongdoing. In law such people can be liable to arrest and criminal sanction under laws of conspiracy and attempt. The revisionist account—though not the traditional theory—can avail itself of this understanding of liability to argue that potential adversaries can make themselves liable to preventive attack by engaging in active planning and preparation for wrongful aggression. According to the revisionist account, therefore, the prevention of future aggression can in principle be a just cause for war.

The other issue on which the traditional and revisionist accounts diverge is humanitarian intervention—that is, war initiated to defend people in another state from threats originating within their own state, usually from their own government. The traditional theory is generally inhospitable to humanitarian intervention. This is because it bases its account of *ad bellum* defensive rights on the domestic analogy. A state that persecutes its own population is nonetheless a sovereign individual. To intervene against it to stop the persecution is therefore analogous to coercively harming a person to prevent her from harming herself. It is, according to the domestic analogy, an objectionable form of paternalism. The traditional theory holds that states have a sovereign right against intervention unless they forfeit it by engaging in aggression against another state.

Because the revisionist account is individualist rather than statist, it is more permissive with respect to humanitarian intervention. If individuals in another state are morally responsible for threats to the fundamental human rights of others, they may be liable to be attacked or killed to prevent them from violating those rights. That the violations would occur within a state that has not attacked any other state is morally relevant for various reasons, but it does not mean, as it does on the traditional theory, that intervention to prevent the violations would violate the rights of that state. What is most important according to the revisionist account is that the individuals against whom the humanitarian war would be fought would be liable to military attack to prevent them from violating the rights of others. The defense of fundamental human rights can therefore be a just cause for war according to the revisionist account. Because that account posits *in bello* defensive rights that are asymmetrical between just and unjust combatants, it implies further that soldiers in the offending state have no right of defense against a justified humanitarian intervention.

This review of the two approaches' implications for preventive war and humanitarian intervention may suggest that the traditional theory gives a more restrictive account of morally permissible war. But this is an illusion. It may recognize fewer just causes for war, but overall it is far more permissive than the revisionist account in that it permits soldiers to fight for *any* cause, whether just or unjust. Even if the revisionist account recognizes a greater range of just causes for war, its requirement of just cause applies to both political rulers and individual soldiers alike, so that no one may fight without a just cause. By contrast, the traditional theory's requirement of just cause constrains only political rulers, leaving individual soldiers morally free to fight and kill for whatever aims, just or unjust, their rulers may choose to pursue.

REFERENCES

Augustine. 1950. *The City of God*. New York: Modern Library.
Hershey, A. S. 1906. *The International Law and Diplomacy of the Russo-Japanese War*. New York: Macmillan.

Hobbes, T. 1651. *De Cive*. London: J.G. Available from http://www.constitution.org/th/decive.htm.
Mill, J. S. 1961. *On Liberty* in *The Philosophy of John Stuart Mill: Ethical, Political, and Religious*. New York: Random House.
Rousseau, J.-J. 1947. "The Social Contract." In *Social Contract: Essays by Locke, Hume, and Rousseau*. London: Oxford University Press.
Suárez, F. 1944. "De Triplici Virtute Theologica: Charitate." In *Selections from Three Works*. Oxford: Clarendon Press.
Vitoria, F. 1991. *Political Writings*. Cambridge, UK: Cambridge University Press.
Walzer, M. 1977. *Just and Unjust Wars*. New York: Basic Books.

PART V

Injustice

CHAPTER 17

HISTORICAL INJUSTICE

JEFF SPINNER-HALEV

In 1998 National Sorry Day emerged in Australia after the release of a government report titled "Bringing Them Home" about the stolen generations of aboriginal children in Australia. In 2008 the Australian prime minister apologized to aborigines for past injustices inflicted on them, including the "stolen generations." Shortly afterward, the Canadian prime minister apologized to indigenous peoples for past government actions that placed their children in Christian boarding schools with the intent to assimilate them. The U.S. House of Representatives passed a resolution apologizing for slavery and Jim Crow in the summer of 2008, while state legislatures in Alabama, Maryland, and North Carolina all issued apologies for slavery. In 1993 the U.S. Congress apologized for the overthrow of the Hawaiian monarchy 100 years previously, while in 2009 the California Parliament apologized for laws that discriminated against Chinese Americans in the nineteenth and twentieth centuries.

The academy and the politicians are moving in tandem on this issue, as political theorists and philosophers have increasingly addressed the issue of past injustices. While a few scattered articles on the topic appeared in the 1970s, since 2000 a spate of scholarly literature on historical injustice has emerged. Political communities need to take responsibility for their past, some charge, by which they mean that apologies, reparations, or compensation are due to the injured communities. These arguments typically suggest that if political communities are to be moral, then they must remember the past—and not just the past they are proud of but also the parts of the past that are shameful. Many of these arguments suggest, for example, that if the United States (or Australia, or Canada, and so on) is to successfully confront racism, it must confront its racist past. If we—the dominant political communities in the New World—are to treat indigenous peoples properly, then we must have a better understanding and accounting of the past. An apology is often part of the solution to past injustices, as are reparations and compensation.

Why, however, does the history of an injustice matter? All injustices have a past, after all. Nahshon Perez defines historical injustices as those in which all the original wrongdoers, and all the original victims, have passed away. The wrong is also noteworthy enough to merit our attention; it is not a minor case of John's stealing Jane's wallet in 1725 in London. It is an event (or events) that we know took place, so issues of information are not a major obstacle to understanding the injustice. Historical injustices concern people that were *not* involved in the wrong (Perez 2011). I would add that historical injustices are injuries done to groups; it is the harm done to many people that commands attention.

Still, many critics of taking past injustices into account say what should matter is current injustices, not past ones. If an injustice exists, the political community should be concerned, but why is the history of the injustice important? Arguments about past injustice rarely say much about this issue, perhaps because they are case driven—usually by one of two cases (indigenous peoples or black Americans). Driven by cases, these arguments rarely develop a theory of historical injustice. For example, Thomas McCarthy says his argument about memory and injustice applies only to African Americans: "The 'logics' and 'dynamics' of the constellations associated with the near extermination of Native Americans; the forceful subjection of the inhabitants of territories conquered from Mexico; the involuntary incorporation of Native Hawaiians, Puerto Ricans, and Alaskan Eskimos; and the exclusion or oppression of various groups of immigrants are sufficiently different to warrant separate treatment" (McCarthy 2002, 624). McCarthy's argument is atypical only in that he notices that other groups besides the one he discusses are victims of historical injustice. But in typical fashion, his argument applies to one group, begging a question about much of this literature: Does it present us with a principled argument or merely a complaint?

1. Memory

Some advocates of repairing historical injustice suggest that somehow the past calls us; in other words, we are obligated to remember its injustices. Pablo De Greiff says, "We have an obligation to remember what our fellow citizens cannot be expected to forget" (McCarthy 2002, 629). Similarly, W. James Booth argues that the "past wants to be remembered." The past is there for us to remember, which we are called to do: "In invoking it, and giving it voice and remembrance, we answer its call. We do not make, or construct, this past" (Booth 2006, 67). Others argue that nations are intergenerational communities; their institutions and moral relationships persist over time and through generations. Members of these nations rightfully think they made demands on their successors; the same is true for obligations. A political community reaches from the past to the future, so we as a political community are responsible for the past just as it affects the moral character of our society. In one typical argument, Farid Abdel-Nour argues that people who take pride in their nation's achievements are also responsible for unjust consequences of their nation's actions: "When she is actively proud of national achievements in a way that allows her to imagine herself as having brought them about, she renders herself responsible for the specific historical actions with which they were in fact brought about" (Abdel-Nour 2003, 713; see also Sparrow 2000; Ivison 2002; Thompson 2002; Kukathas 2003; Weiner 2005; McCarthy 2004). By being part of a community with a history, we become responsible for that history. Thus, if an injustice occurred in our political community's past, then we are responsible for that injustice, or so these arguments suggest on their surface.

When we are asked to take responsibility for the past, however, it is not clear which part of the past we are responsible for. We (by which I mean all people) cannot be expected to remember all historical injustices. The idea that the past calls us does not tell us which past is calling. The past cannot be there waiting to be remembered, because we forget most of it, as we must: "It is impossible to recover or recount more than a tiny fraction of what has taken place"; the content of the past is "virtually infinite" (Lowenthal 1999, 214). History is boundless; it is beyond the recall capacity of any person or people to remember even a tiny part of history. To remember the past is to choose to remember a particular past: *Remembering means choosing*. The idea that the nation is an intergenerational community and so in some sense is responsible for past injustices does not say much about which injustices we should remember or which past injustices need redress.

Arguments today that suggest that we are, somehow, called to remember the past overlook the fact that we forget most of history. How could it possibly be otherwise? Lawrie Balfour argues that the "story of reparations is centrally a story of memory's suppression"—meaning that most Americans are opposed to reparations, because they have suppressed the memory of slavery (Balfour 2003, 40; see also Hendrix 2005). But most of history is forgotten, as it must be. It's not that the past calls to us; it is that we call to the past—but not just any past, only particular pasts. Any account of remembering historical injustice, or of being responsible for the past, must give an account of which injustices (which pasts) we should recall.

Arguments about a political community's responsibility for the past also leaves many historical injustices without an agent to repair the injustice. The Crimea Tatars were expelled from the Crimea (in the Ukraine) by Stalin. But Stalin is dead, and the Soviet Union no longer exists. Does that mean that no one is responsible for addressing the injustices faced by the Tatars? Similarly, governments are sometimes radically transformed. Is the Japanese government today, drastically altered after World War II, responsible for injustices done to the Ainu (an indigenous people) before the war? One response is to say that sometimes no one is responsible to help end the injustice, because the causal agent no longer exists. As Janna Thompson and Chandran Kukathas state, if the communities that committed the injustices disappear, then there is no agent responsible to help fix the injustice, and there is nothing to be done (Thompson 2002, 76; Kukathas 2003). One might think that the skeptics of repairing historical injustice would use this argument—the number of governmental changes through time is one more reason to focus on current injustices, regardless of their historical roots. Why, however, should the vagaries of history be an excuse to allow an enduring injustice to fester?

It is not clear why a responsible agent for the injustice must be found to have a political community responsible to correct the injustice. A country such as Sweden may have refugees from Bosnia or Somalia, and Sweden may have little responsibility for causing their exile and impoverishment. But once they are part of the Swedish political community, isn't the political community responsible for helping the refugees live decent lives?[1] Justice does not mean that people or communities take responsibility for the past but rather that political communities take responsibility for the present and future. This does not mean that the history of an injustice is unimportant, but it does mean that using history to find the causal agent for the injustice is not particularly helpful.

2. Reparations

Arguments for reparations might seem more promising on this score, because reparations focus on particular injustices. We know that if the thief of a stolen bicycle is found, reparations would mean returning the bicycle in the condition it was taken, or the equivalent—money equal to what the bicycle, or a similar bicycle, was worth. Yet how can we determine the compensation or reparations for an injustice done decades or centuries ago to many people? The problem might be worse than it seems: Christopher Morris argues that it is likely that if the injustice in question did not occur, then the descendants of the victim of the past injustice would not exist (Morris 1984). If slavery did not exist, for example, the descendants of slaves would not exist. This is true for even less obvious examples, as any small injustice will affect the victims' procreation. Hundreds of millions of sperm cells are contained in a male's ejaculation so "any trivial difference affecting conception would . . . [bring] it about that a different individual is conceived" (Morris 1984, 177; see also Wheeler 1997; Kershnar 1999). Not only is the amount of reparations hard to determine, but the descendants of the victims of the past would not exist but for the injustice.

A rare response to this nonidentity problem dismisses it for leading to absurd conclusions. Daniel Butt agrees that it is unlikely that the exact children born shortly after the Bhopal or Chernobyl disasters would have been born if these disasters did not occur. Perhaps we can even say these children owe their existence to these disasters. Yet Butt poignantly asks, "Would anyone seriously argue that, in the event of their suffering health problems, they should not be compensated on account of the non-identity problem?" (Butt 2009, 106; see also Simmons 1995, 178–79). These children were harmed by an injustice, and so they are owed rectification for this harm. What we can say is this: If these unjust acts did not take place, then almost certainly fewer children in the area of Bhopal or Chernobyl would have health problems than currently do, which is sufficient reason for compensation to be owed to the victims.

A different response, pursued by Andrew I. Cohen and George Sher, is to argue that injustices are sometimes passed on to each generation anew. We can assume, Sher and Cohen suggest, that parents want to support their children and that in fact they have a duty to do so. An injustice done to parents that inhibits their ability to care for their children as well as they would have otherwise been able to is then also an injustice to the children. The injustice done to the parents also harms the children, and so the perpetrators must also compensate the children. This compensation is not endless; once the children have reached a certain level of welfare that is sustainable over time, the claims for redress fall away. A child whose welfare falls below a certain minimum because her parents are unable to provide sufficiently for her due to an injustice inflicted on them is also a victim of that injustice. If as an adult she suffers because of this welfare deficiency—which is due to an injustice done to her parents—then she is owed compensation from the perpetrator of the injustice; in this way compensable claims for injustice are passed down through the generations (Cohen 2009; see also Sher 2005).

How can we determine who deserves compensation? If the problem is that some people's ancestors suffered harm that may have been passed down, how are we to determine which people today deserve reparations? If it is just a few individuals, perhaps careful genealogical research may solve this problem—or it might complicate the matter, as victims of injustice may marry nonvictims. But none of the advocates of reparations suggest such a route. Rather, implicitly and often explicitly, they have certain social groups in mind, usually African Americans. Cohen suggests that if the descendants of victims are under some level of welfare ("W"), then we can assume they are due compensation. Cohen talks about Luke and Jill and others in his argument, so it is unclear how the argument transfers over to groups, which is clearly what he has in mind. Indeed, at the end of his article he discusses black Americans, as do nearly all arguments for reparations (Cohen 2009, 102). Yet how do we move from Luke and Jill to white and black Americans? If some Irish Americans are poor, do they have a claim for compensation? If they do, is the claim against the descendants of Irish landowners? the Irish government? the British government? the U.S. government? We could, of course, extend this query to all poor people, trying to determine how they arrived at their impoverishment. Trying to do so, though, would be nearly impossible in large societies with millions of poor people. This explains why the move to groups makes sense as a practical matter, but Cohen does not explain how his argument can work for groups. What if some members of a certain group seen as impoverished do not live in poverty? What if some members of a group generally seen as above baseline "W" are in fact below it?

Cohen notes these kinds of problems in reparations arguments: There are "determinacy problems," "counterveiling moral considerations," and so on to weigh (Cohen 2009, 102). It is hard to determine how an injustice done centuries ago affects one particular person today. Yet Cohen dismisses the difficulties in doing so, because in "most cases of plausible reparations claims, many generations of people have suffered needlessly under the yoke of subjugation and now languish in penury" (Cohen 2009, 102). This may be the case, but then why is the argument not that the American political community should focus on the injustices that black Americans face because they face them *now*? If the injustice that black Americans face now is enough to ignore the frustrating details in determining how people today are responsible for past injustices, why are the injustices that black Americans face today not enough to say that we should work to end this injustice? Cohen argues that compensation is due if the descendants of injustice fall below a certain baseline of "W." Yet once we revert to a baseline, why does the history of the injustice matter? Most reparation arguments suggests that anyone below a certain minimum deserves compensation if their low economic status is below "W." If that is the case, why does it matter if we can trace the reason for being below the minimum to an injustice that took place many years ago, if we can in fact do so. We can simply say that all people below this level "W" are owed assistance.

One possible way around this objection is to argue that those who benefit from an injustice should pay for it. This argument answers one common objection to repairing historical injustice: Some people argue that their ancestors were not living in the country when the injustice took place, so they are not responsible for any costs incurred. Some advocates note that members of the dominant community in the United States benefited (and benefit) from the forced labor of slaves: "Our national inheritance was to a large degree unjustly acquired at the expense of African Americans. The issue is not whether someone has personally benefited from slavery, but if they share in and benefit from an unjustly acquired and unfairly distributed national inheritance. This is not a matter of collective guilt but of collective responsibility" (McCarthy 2004, 758; see also Robinson 2001; Butt 2007). The symmetry between unjust acquisition and responsibility is attractive, but not all past injustices caused economic gain. It is not clear that the Ottoman Empire (or Turkey) gained economically from the Armenian genocide, or that the expulsion of the Tatars from the Crimea was economically beneficial. In other cases, it may simply be impossible to determine the economic gains or losses. It may also be the case that the ancestors of both the perpetrators and victims gained economically from the historical injustice. The economic gain argument also sidesteps the fundamental reason for the injustice. If African American slaves were found to have contributed little to the overall American economy, would that make slavery any less just? The radical injustice of slavery, of snatching people away from their families in Africa, of sending them on a journey to the United States, where many were killed, of selling people to others who had complete control of them—these radical injustices remain apart from whatever economic gains were received from slaves.

A different reparations argument focuses on the original injustice. Robert Nozick argues that if a holding is originally just, and is transferred by just means, then under most circumstances its current owner has a just claim to the property. If the original holding is unjust, or if a transfer is unjust, then reparations are called for. In Nozick's account, justice and agency are closely intertwined. If you have less than others—if you live under conditions of inequality—that in itself is not a matter of (in)justice. Only if someone wrongly took some of your or your ancestor's holding has an injustice occurred. A welfare baseline is usually not a concern for Nozick. Yet how reparations are calculated, or what to do when nearly all holdings in a country are unjust—as most are in nearly every country in the world—is not addressed by Nozick in his remarkably brief comments on the subject, given how little property is justly held in the world today according to his theory. Nozick does say that in the case of large injustices the principle of rectification might call for transfer payments from rich to poor, but then he leaves the issue dangling, calling it complex and the proper subject for a full principle of rectification, which he does not offer (Nozick 1974, 152, 231). One of the few interpretations of Nozick's rectification principles argues that given the ubiquity of injustice in the world, Nozickean rectification most likely leads to an egalitarian redistribution of entitlements (Litan 1977).

Other compensation arguments are more specific than Nozick's. In one of his arguments for reparations, Bernard Boxill states that compensation for the unpaid labor of slaves deserves to be repaid; if the original victims are now dead, the right to compensation is inherited by their descendants. It does not matter, Boxill argues, if the descendants are now well off: "The inheritance argument, however, would be unaffected if slavery's long reach had ended some time ago and it no longer harmed the black population. It relies on the assumption that the U.S. Government owes the present black population a debt for an unjust loss it helped to cause, and such a debt is not revoked just because the creditor has recovered from the loss and is prosperous" (Boxill 2003, 69; see also Westley 1998, 465; Hill 2002, 411–12). This argument is about unpaid labor; the labor stolen from slaves is owed to their descendants. If the slaves die with a debt owed to them, their descendants inherit that debt.

Yet the labor of many people other than African Americans was exploited during the nineteenth century. Many people were appalled at the working conditions in the industrializing world. With the backing of the American state, sweatshops thrived, and unions were treated harshly and sometimes violently (Foner 1977; Savage 1990; Papke 1999; Stowell 2008). This is not to compare the injustice inflicted on slaves to workers but to say the wealth of all developed countries was built on the backs of many different people and through many different kinds of oppression. The problem with the debt argument is similar to the problem that besets the argument about the importance of memory and taking responsibility for the past: No attempt is made to determine if the general principle of compensation for exploited labor is actually generalizable. In a world full of past injustices, any argument that suggests the importance of historical injustice must have an account of which injustices from the past should be of concern today. Given the scarcity of resources and the large numbers of past injustices, attempts to pay reparations for all past injustices could quickly detract from society's ability to address current injustices. Yet why should dead victims of injustice be given a priority over living victims of injustice (Perez 2011)? In fact, no advocate of repairing historical injustice actually makes such an argument, probably because it is present injustices that motivate much of their argument, as discussed below.

3. Time and Injustice

A common argument against rectifying historical injustices is that the passage of time changes how we should think of older injustices. These arguments suggest that the world changes over time in ways that either make the consequences of past injustices hard to determine or that undoing these injustices results in a new set of injustices. Land changes hands in the normal and just course of events, and for different reasons. David Lyons argues, for example, argues that the Lockean proviso invoked by Robert Nozick means that Native Americans would have had to share their land with the Europeans that came across the ocean (Lyons 1977). Lyons does not excuse the way Native Americans were expelled from their land, but he does argue that the need Europeans had for more space, and the considerable land used by the relatively small population of Native Americans, does suggest that justice means the latter had an obligation to share their land with Europeans. When Native Americans press claims for the loss of their land, however, some presume that they have a just claim to all of their land. Lyons's argument suggests that it is hard to determine what their just claims to land would be today. We cannot assume that a just holding centuries ago would be, absent an unjust taking in the interim, a just holding today. Intervening factors might mean that justice would compel the land to be distributed differently than the just holdings of centuries ago.

Similarly, Jeremy Waldron argues that there is no reason to think if certain historical injustices did not occur that we would now be living in conditions of justice: "Are we so sure that a smooth transition, untainted by particular injustice, from some early nineteenth-century status quo ante would leave us now where we actually want to be? Quite apart from particular frauds and expropriations, things were not marvelous in the nineteenth century.... Why take all that as the baseline for our present reconstruction?" (Waldron 1992, 14). Further, many indigenous peoples took land from one another in unjust ways. The Aztecs, for example, excelled in warfare, and they conquered many peoples and forced them to pay tribute. They did not rule with modern conceptions of justice in mind. Focusing on particular historical injustices overlooks the ubiquity of (past) injustice. Waldron also argues that there is no fact of the matter when it comes to land that was unjustly taken. We do not know what would have happened if land was not taken unjustly from indigenous people. We cannot know how free people will use (or would have used) their freedom: "Would they have hung on to the land and passed it on to future generations of the tribe? Or would they have sold it—but this time for a fair price—to the first honest settler who came along?" (Waldron 1992, 14). Also, who knows what the settler would have done with the land? In other words, we do not know what would have happened if this particular injustice did not occur. Similarly, George Sher argues that the case for compensation fades over time because the epistemological indeterminacy of the counterfactual becomes greater as time passes (Sher 1981). If an injustice occurs, the relevant comparison for compensation is not how well off the person would have been if the injustice did not occur compared to having nothing. Rather, just as we would expect that the person would work to make the most of his or her life without the injustice, we should expect the same with the injustice occurring. Although an injustice may be a setback, the effects of this setback may become smaller over time, to the point that it no longer exists. Sher is clear that his argument applies to ancient wrongs; he is more sympathetic to more recent claims—which apparently means three or four centuries —for compensation for historical injustice.[2]

Waldron also argues that some injustices cannot be reversed without committing another injustice. If people are forcibly expelled from their land, for example, those who immediately occupy it may be committing an injustice. Over time their children and grandchildren (and so on) may very well develop deep attachments to the land; their liberty and identity may be intertwined with this land. To take away someone's land because of an injustice committed decades or centuries earlier is to commit another injustice no more defensible than the first (Waldron 1992, 14–19). Daniel Butt responds to this argument by questioning why we should assume that the severity of a past injustice fades with time (Waldron 1992, 14–19). While Waldron argues that over time people's lives adjust to the circumstances created by an injustice, perhaps the injustice has lasting effects—so people have adjusted, but badly.

Still, these arguments point to the difficulty in determining how to repair past injustices. Given the ubiquity of past injustice, one could say that everyone has adjusted to living in a world affected by injustice. Given this, one can easily accept the idea that what should matter are current injustices; after all, there are plenty enough of those to worry about.

4. Enduring Injustice

The problem with arguments that focus on past injustices is that they do not explain why the history of the injustice matters. Unsurprisingly, many reparations arguments speak about the present as motivating their arguments. The typical reparations arguments begin with a list of the current inequalities between black and white Americans—the large differences in income, wealth, living conditions, and educational opportunities (Magee 1993; Westley 1998; Brophy 2008). The argument then moves to an explanation of these gaps, which is found in history: "It is impossible not to link the continuing economic disparity between the races to our history of race-based economic exploitation begun in slavery and continued through discrimination" (Magee 1993, 876). Another typical argument suggests that until the racial gaps on the measures of education, health, income, and wealth close, the debt from the past injustice of slavery and racism has not been paid (Valls 2007; see also Brooks 2004). If the racial gap did not exist, the implication is, then the past injustice would not matter. If black Americans did not suffer from current injustice, there would be little call for reparations. Reparations are called for because of *current* conditions, not because of the past, though this issue remains confused in many reparation arguments.[3]

As Leif Wener correctly points out, if there is not a current injustice, the advocates of reparations would not make their case (Wenar 2006). Wenar's observation may very well explain Lawrie Balfour's argument that "reparations could create a basis for attacking the deep economic inequality Du Bois understands to be incompatible with democracy" (Balfour 2003, 41; also see McCarthy 2002, 641). There are few calls for reparations for the Huguenots, who were alternatively massacred, left alone, and then drastically oppressed in France, until most fled to neighboring countries. There are few calls for reparations to Chinese Americans, who were also victims of great oppression: "No variety of anti-European sentiment has every approached the violent extremes to which Chinese agitation went in the 1870s and 1880s" (Higham 1963, 25). Lynchings, riots, massacres—Chinese Americans faced these and more. "Decades of anti-Chinese violence, segregation, and discrimination" culminated in the Chinese Exclusion Act of 1882, which outlawed most Chinese immigration and made it impossible for Chinese immigrants to become naturalized citizens (Chen 1980, 129; see also Pfaelzer 2007). Because these groups do not suffer from any injustice today, few think of them—or the many other groups that suffered from injustice in years past but no longer do—when the topic turns to historical injustice.

I have argued here that past injustices alone cannot be the reason why an historical injustice is a problem today, but it is also not right to say the history of an injustice never matters. Instead of using the past as a way to determine causality when thinking about historical injustice, we need to refocus the issue, in part by stitching together some assumptions made in the historical injustice literature as a springboard to reconceptualize the issue. There are no arguments that suggest *all* historical injustices are a challenge for a political community to solve; the historical injustice literature has focused on current injustices that have a long history that connects to the present. These arguments focus on groups that were victims of an injustice long ago and that still suffer from injustice. This suggests that the issue is not just past injustice but rather one of enduring injustice. Enduring injustice has an historical and a contemporary component. All enduring injustices are also historical injustices, but the reverse is not true, because some historical injustices no longer persist today. The Chinese Americans are victims of historical injustice but not enduring injustice. The reason why the examples of indigenous peoples and African Americans are so powerful is not only that they have suffered from injustice in the past but also that these historical injustices continue in the present.

Four criteria define an enduring injustice. First, there is good reason to think the present injustice is in important ways connected to past injustices. Causality arguments that stretch through decades or centuries are often hard to prove, but we can make reasonable suppositions. One could argue that the misery of Native Americans was caused by American policies that pushed indigenous peoples aside, shamelessly broke treaties with them, treated them harshly, and so on. Yet we do not know what would have happened if Americans treated indigenous peoples with more respect and decency; it is hard to imagine that the traditional indigenous way of life would have survived once whites took to industrialization. It is likely that if indigenous peoples were treated with more respect, they would have had more control (not complete control) of the transformative process they encountered, and they would have wrestled with modernity from a position of cultural coherence and not decimation. This almost surely would mean that their position today would be much different and better. Many indigenous peoples are suffering in many ways, and it seems likely that if they were treated better by the colonialists and then the Americans, they would be better off today.

Second, it seems that without a change of course of action, the injustice will persist. Nearly all the arguments on historical injustice share this assumption, although this does not mean this assumption is correct. There is no way to know the future with certainty—it is possible that imprisonment rates for black Americans will suddenly plummet, while their educational attainment and income will begin to rise, but given past patterns, this seems unlikely.

Third, the pattern of past and current injustice will typically lead, in some cases, to a problem of trust. Trust correctly looms large in the literature on historical injustice. Leif Wenar argues, perhaps with some exaggeration, "Justice, taken as relations of mutual recognition and trust, cannot now go forward in these contexts because of the lingering presence of the past in the minds" of groups that are victims of historical injustice (Wenar 2006, 403; see also Williams 1998; Ivison 2002; Thompson 2002). Mistrust may not be quite the barricade that Wenar suggests, but it surely makes it harder to achieve justice. Many black Americans are suspicious of government attempts to ensure that many children receive routine vaccinations because of their memories of the infamous Tuskegee experiment, in which black men with syphilis had treatment withheld by the U.S. government in order for researchers to follow the course of the disease (which they did even after penicillin, an effective treatment, became widely available). Similarly, the Tuskegee experiment has apparently led many blacks to believe that AIDS is actually a plot devised by the U.S. government to harm the black population. It may be that the government will have to work to overcome the mistrust. (Trust may be less of an issue when the current government is not recognizably the descendent of the past government that caused the injustice.)

Fourth, the problem of enduring injustice raises an important question: Why is the injustice enduring? We can locate this problem within liberal justice, or rather a failure of liberal justice. Most views of liberalism see justice (and injustice) through the lenses of fair procedures, individual rights, equal respect and regard, and the redistribution of wealth. While this last aspect is rather controversial, I use here the framework of egalitarian liberalism, which sees large gaps in income and wealth as violating liberal principles. Many liberals see one important solution to unjust inequities in terms of wealth and money, whereas trying to ensure a good education for all is often seen as another important way to improve the conditions of the poor (Kymlicka 2001, 83–84). Many forms of injustice are remedied with the protection of individual rights and a fair system of justice. Many immigrants, for example, face discrimination when they first arrive in the United States, but this discrimination typically lessens over time. Discrimination against women and many religious groups has, over time, faded in the Western democracies. One view is that, in the history of liberalism, the idea of religious toleration came to be seen as a right, and the idea of rights expanded beyond religious freedom with the rise of the idea of human rights (Zagorin 2003). What some of these examples show is that it is not just that the idea of individual rights has spread, but that many groups no longer face discrimination (or they face less discrimination than in the past) from their fellow citizens and from nonpublic institutions. Chinese Americans may still face some discrimination today, but few doubt their humanity—few think that they deserve less respect as others—and the discrimination they face is considerably less than that of their ancestors, while their economic achievement is much greater.

Yet in cases of enduring injustice, most observers do not think that the injustice will fade, at least not with the normal liberal remedies. It may be that the pattern of injustice that began decades or centuries ago feeds into injustice today. Perhaps the exact form of injustice is not the same, but one can recognize the injustice today as beginning some time ago. The origins of the poverty of many Native Americans can be traced back to pushing them onto reservations, but U.S. government policies affecting reservations impacted (and impact) Native American poverty. For example, the policy of ending communal ownership land worked out badly and probably did more to deepen than to alleviate Native American poverty.[4] Some people argue that the racism that was built into the American state long ago still exists and that many of these patterns of racial inequality persist not only as a vestige of the past but also because institutions perpetuate them, sometimes wittingly and sometimes unwittingly. More than forty-five years after the Civil Rights Act, many black Americans were still impoverished; the incarceration rate of black men is six times the rate for whites. The issue is not only the continuation of poverty and the alarmingly high rate of imprisonment but society's lack of good solutions to these problems.

In other, less frequent cases, one might say that the injustice against some groups is an effect of past injustice, even if no one is perpetuating the injustice today. The Tatars, who live in exile, may have their individual rights respected, and even if no one perpetuates an injustice against them now, they may still see exile as leaving them in a state of injustice. Similarly, some peoples view certain land as sacred. Hills, stones, and mountains are sometimes sacred ground to indigenous peoples, such as Ayers Rock in Australia or the Black Hills in the United States. The Black Hills, where special ceremonies were performed, are considered sacred to the Lakota Sioux. The U.S. Federal government agreed to the Sioux rights to the land in 1850s by treaty; however, after gold was discovered there, the United States broke the treaty to seize the land. This land was, and still is, mined. The Sioux eventually sued and won in the U.S. Supreme Court, which found the treaties that gave away the land fraudulent. The Sioux were awarded compensation ($700 million today, including interest) but not the return of the land. The Sioux have refused to accept the money, as they maintain that this sacred land cannot be bought.

Liberal courts have a hard time seeing why money is insufficient compensation for lost land, which is echoed in liberal theory. In his skeptical argument about historical injustice, Jeremy Waldron talks about tribal *owners* of land, wondering if they might have sold it if it had not been wrongly taken from them. His examples include his aunt's inheritance and a stolen car (Waldron 1992, 20). Lost land, in this view, can be compensated with either money or different land. What can be lost can be replaced: This is certainly true for money and cars. Waldron does say that his argument may not apply to cases "where the dispossessed subject is a tribe or a community, rather than an individual, where the holding of which it has been dispossessed is particularly important for its sense of identity as a community," but it is hard to put much stock in this caveat, because the main subjects of Waldron's essay are tribes (indigenous peoples) whose identity is very much tied to land (Waldron 1992, 19). Waldron's brief caveat is overwhelmed by the rest of the argument, which is devoted to showing that the land claims of indigenous peoples have faded over time.

The idea of sacred land also highlights why the history of an injustice can matter. This is not just about learning from past failures; the only way to make sense of a group's attachment to land that they no longer occupy is through an understanding of history (or, at least, the group's understanding of history). The Crimean Tatars want to return to their land. This normal-sounding sentence, however, is wrought with moral implications, because many of the people who want to return never lived in the Crimea. They look at the Crimea as their ancestral homeland. The idea of sacred land makes sense only if the idea of collective memory (or narrative) and historical attachments have meaning.[5] If the Lakota had no collective narrative, if the past did not matter to them, the Blacks Hills would be just another place, and there would be little problem about selling it. Standard accounts of egalitarian liberal justice would ask if the Tatars receive unequal treatment where they live or if their rights are violated. These questions, though, do not capture the injustice of exile or of separation from a sacred place. The Tatar homeland is kept alive in exile by connecting the past to the present (Uehling 2004).

One partial solution to the problem of enduring injustice is offered by Burke Hendrix, who agrees with Waldron that the land of indigenous peoples cannot simply be returned to them but then argues that indigenous peoples should be given the right of first refusal when their now-occupied lands go up for sale (Hendrix 2008, 49). This insightful idea makes sense only if injustices done long ago by and to people who are now dead have some moral weight today. Of course, one might say that all injustices have a past—if I stole your bicycle, it is now a matter of history. But if my grandfather stole your grandfather's bicycle, it is doubtful that I owe you compensation for the theft. Yet land stolen from a people has a different character, which highlights that victims of enduring injustice are groups (and their members) and not individuals apart from group attachments. The injustice to individual Tatars and families was their forcible eviction from their homes. An unjust eviction from one's home is an injustice but not a challenge to liberalism or even an enduring injustice. The collective eviction of a people, however, poses a more fundamental challenge to liberalism and begs for a group solution. The injustice to the Tatars as a people is their exile from their ancestral homeland, and so overcoming it means facilitating their return in a general way, in ways that do not cause another injustice.

If the state gives the right of first refusal to a particular tribe, it may do so without knowing if the ancestors of a particular Native American family lived on that land. If the past did not matter for current injustice, if justice is only about the redistribution of wealth and the protection of rights, then Hendrix's idea of the right of first refusal would not make sense. Similarly, when mistrust arises and becomes a political problem, it is because members of a particular group feel this mistrust.

The history of an enduring injustice is important because it can help inform us about the nature of the injustice, particularly when the issue lies outside the bounds of liberal justice. Mistrust between a government and a group that is a victim of injustice is often comprehensible only by taking the history of the injustice into account. The ideas of sacred land and exile also make sense only if the history and memory (or collective narrative) of a group matters. Still, the contemporary focus on injustice by those skeptical of repairing historical injustice supplies an important corrective to the idea of historical injustice. What should drive our concern about repairing injustice are today's injustices. Of course, there are many injustices today, and my argument does not insist that enduring injustices are more important to address than other kinds of contemporary injustices; how to prioritize the injustices a political community faces depends on many factors, and I cannot address that issue here. Yet certainly injustices that have endured for a long time should, *prima facia*, be of concern to the political community. To turn away from a group that has suffered for decades or centuries, or to tell them that the injustices they face are of low priority, is not something that should be done lightly. What the advocates of repairing historical injustice remind us is that while it may be easy to pass over long-standing injustices because many of us have become accustomed to them, it is cold-hearted and unjust for a responsible political community to do so without very good reason. None of this means that people alive today are responsible for the past. Some injustices may have their roots in the past, yet if they are present today, then the issue regards who can help alleviate them now, not who caused them at their origin. The idea of taking responsibility for the past too readily invites the response that people alive today are not responsible for the past; but they are responsible for the present, and that is reason enough for them to care about injustices that endure in their midst.[6]

NOTES

Much of my argument here is expanded upon in my contemporaneously published book, *Enduring Injustice* (Cambridge, UK: Cambridge University Press, 2012).

1. I leave aside here the possibility of global responsibility.

2. Sher does not explicitly state the time frame for an ancient wrong versus a compensable past injustice. The main example in his work justifying compensation for historical injustice is American slavery, which reaches back to the seventeenth century.

3. Other backward-looking arguments include Hendrix 2005, 775 and McCarthy 2004, 751.

4. The Dawes Act in the late nineteenth century forced most tribes to divide their communal land into individual plots, which was part of a policy to try to make Indians more like white citizens (Hoxie 1984; Parker 1989; Banner 2005). This policy ended in 1934, only to begin again with the unfortunately named Termination policy in the 1950s, which strove to break up ("terminate") indigenous tribes by ending their communal control of land; plots of land were given to some individuals, while others were given money and encouraged to move to urban areas. Like the Dawes Act, Termination was widely considered a failure (though it took the U.S. government less time to realize this the second time around), partly because the cultural structure of some tribes was destroyed (Prucha 1986, 344).

5. I prefer the term "collective narrative" to "collective memory." This is explained in Spinner-Halev 2007.

6. I do not have space here to pursue the argument about responsibility.

REFERENCES

Abdel-Nour, F. 2003. "National Responsibility." *Political Theory* 31(5): 693–719.
Balfour, L. 2003. "Unreconstructed Democracy: W.E.B. Du Bois and the Case for Reparations." *American Political Science Review* 97(1): 33–44.
Banner, S. 2005. *How the Indians Lost Their Land: Law and Power on the Frontier*. Cambridge, MA: Belknap Press of Harvard University Press.
Booth, W. J. 2006. *Communities of Memory: On Witness, Identity, and Justice*. Ithaca, NY: Cornell University Press.
Boxill, B. 2003. "A Lockean Argument for Black Reparations." *The Journal of Ethics* 7(1): 63–91.
Brooks, R. L. 2004. *Atonement and Forgiveness: A New Model for Black Reparations*. Berkeley: University of California Press.
Brophy, A. L. 2008. *Reparations: Pro and Con*. Oxford: Oxford University Press.
Butt, D. 2007. "On Benefiting from Injustice." *Canadian Journal of Philosophy* 37(1): 129–52.
Butt, D. 2009. *Rectifying International Injustice: Principles of Compensation and Restitution between Nations*. New York: Oxford University Press.
Chen, J. 1980. *The Chinese of America*. San Francisco, CA: Harper & Row.
Cohen, A. I. 2009. "Compensation for Historic Injustices: Completing the Boxill and Sher Argument." *Philosophy & Public Affairs* 37(1): 81–102.
Foner, P. S. 1977. *The Great Labor Uprising of 1877*. New York: Monad Press.
Hendrix, B. A. 2005. "Memory in Native American Land Claims." *Political Theory* 33(6): 763–85.
Hendrix, B. A. 2008. *Ownership, Authority, and Self-Determination: Moral Principles and Indigenous Rights Claim*. University Park, PA: Penn State University Press.
Higham, J. 1963. *Strangers in the Land: Patterns of American Nativism, 1860–1925*. New York: Atheneum.

Hill, R. A. 2002. "Compensatory Justice: Over Time and Between Groups." *Journal of Political Philosophy* 10(4): 392–415.

Hoxie, F. E. 1984. *A Final Promise: The Campaign to Assimilate the Indians, 1880–1920*. Lincoln: University of Nebraska Press.

Ivison, D. 2002. *Postcolonial Liberalism*. Cambridge, UK: Cambridge University Press.

Kershnar, S. 1999. "Are the Descendants of Slaves Owed Compensation for Slavery?" *Journal of Applied Philosophy* 16(1): 95–101.

Kukathas, C. 2003. "Responsibility for the Past: How to Shift the Burden." *Politics, Philosophy and Economics* 2(2): 165–90.

Kymlicka, W. 2001. *Contemporary Political Philosophy: An Introduction*. New York: Oxford University Press.

Litan, R. E. 1977. "On Rectification in Nozick's Minimal State." *Political Theory* 5(2): 233–46.

Lowenthal, D. 1999. *The Past Is a Foreign Country*. Cambridge, UK: Cambridge University Press.

Lyons, D. 1977. "The New Indian Claims and Original Rights to Land." *Social Theory and Practice* 4(3): 249–71.

Magee, R. V. 1993. "The Master's Tools, from the Bottom Up: Responses to African-American Reparations Theory in Mainstream and Outsider Remedies Discourse." *Virginia Law Review* 79: 863.

McCarthy, T. 2002. "*Vergangenheitsbewaltigung* in the USA: On the Politics of the Memory of Slavery." *Political Theory* 30(5): 623–48.

McCarthy, T. 2004. "Coming to Terms with Our Past, Part II: On the Morality and Politics of Reparations for Slavery." *Political Theory* 32(6): 750–72.

Morris, C. W. 1984. "Existential Limits to the Rectification of Past Wrongs." *American Philosophical Quarterly* 21(2): 175–82.

Nozick, R. 1974. *Anarchy, State, and Utopia*. New York: Basic Books.

Papke, D. R. 1999. *The Pullman Case: The Clash of Labor and Capital in Industrial America*. Lawrence: University Press of Kansas.

Parker, L. S. 1989. *Native American Estate: The Struggle over Indian and Hawaiian Lands*. Honolulu: University of Hawaii Press.

Perez, N. 2011. "On Compensation and Return: Can the 'Continuing Injustice Argument' for Compensating Historical Injustices Justify Compensation for Such Injustices or the Return of Property?" *Journal of Applied Philosophy* 28(2): 151–68.

Pfaelzer, J. 2007. *Driven Out: The Forgotten War against Chinese Americans*. New York: Random House.

Prucha, F. P. 1986. *The Great Father: The United States Government and the American Indians*, abridged ed. Lincoln: University of Nebraska Press.

Robinson, R. 2001. *The Debt: What America Owes to Blacks*. New York: Penguin.

Savage, L. 1990. *Thunder in the Mountains: The West Virginia Mine War, 1920–21*. Pittsburgh, PA: University of Pittsburgh Press.

Sher, G. 1981. "Ancient Wrongs and Modern Rights." *Philosophy & Public Affairs* 10(1): 3–17.

Sher, G. 2005. "Transgenerational Compensation." *Philosophy & Public Affairs* 33(2): 181–200.

Simmons, A. J. 1995. "Historical Rights and Fair Shares." *Law and Philosophy* 14(2): 149–84.

Sparrow, R. 2000. "History and Collective Responsibility." *Australasian Journal of Philosophy* 78(3): 346–59.

Spinner-Halev, J. 2007. "From Historical to Enduring Injustice." *Political Theory* 35(5): 550–73.

Stowell, D. O. 2008. *The Great Strikes of 1877*. Urbana: University of Illinois Press.

Thompson, J. 2002. *Taking Responsibility for the Past: Reparation and Historical Injustice*. Cambridge, UK: Polity Press.

Uehling, G. L. 2004. *Beyond Memory: The Crimean Tatars' Deportation and Return*, 1st ed. New York: Palgrave Macmillan.

Valls, A. 2007. "Reconsidering the Case for Black Reparations." In *Reparations: Interdisciplinary Inquiries*. Edited by J. Miller and R. Kumar, 114–29. Oxford: Oxford University Press.

Waldron, J. 1992. "Superseding Historic Injustice." *Ethics* 103(4): 4–28.

Weiner, B. A. 2005. *Sins of the Parents: The Politics of National Apologies in the United States*. Philadelphia, PA: Temple University Press.

Wenar, L. 2006. "Reparations for the Future." *Journal of Social Philosophy* 37(3): 396–405.

Westley, R. 1998. "Many Billions Gone: Is It Time to Reconsider the Case for Black Reparations?" *Boston College Third World Law Journal* 19: 429.

Wheeler, S. C. III. 1997. "Reparations Reconstructed." *American Philosophical Quarterly* 34(3): 301–18.

Williams, M. 1998. *Voice, Trust and Memory: Marginalized Groups and the Failings of Liberal Representation*. Princeton, NJ: Princeton University Press.

Zagorin, P. 2003. *How the Idea of Religious Toleration Came to the West*. Princeton, NJ: Princeton University Press.

CHAPTER 18

RACE

TOMMIE SHELBY

POLITICAL philosophers study the basic ideas and values that have played or should play a central role in the political sphere.[1] Reflecting on idea of "race" and the normative significance of race relations is therefore an essential part of the enterprise of political philosophy. The principal goal is to think systematically about whether, and if so how, race should figure in our evaluation of institutional arrangements and power relations, in our treatment of each other within civil society, and in our self-conceptions and group affiliations.

It is now a widely held conviction that a just society should embody the norms of "racial equality" and "antiracism." However, these values admit a wide range of conflicting interpretations. Thus, much of the philosophical work on race today strives to explain just what racial equality and antiracism mean. Do they simply mean that society should be (largely) free of racism and racial discrimination, and, if so, what constitutes "racism" and "racial discrimination"? Does being committed to these values mean that disadvantages caused by the history of racial domination and exploitation should be remedied, and if so, which ways of responding to this legacy are fair to all affected? Do racial equality and antiracism mean that society should be "colorblind," and, if so, what would this involve? Do they entail ultimately abandoning the very idea of race, or can the concept, despite its known problems, somehow be salvaged and put to legitimate political uses? These and related questions are what preoccupy political philosophers who think about race today.

1. The Idea of Race

It is well known that the race concept has been used to justify gross forms of injustice: slavery, genocide, colonial subjugation and exploitation, forced segregation and arbitrary civic exclusion, and land and resource expropriation.[2] Regarding the continuing currency of the notion as inherently dangerous, some philosophers have attempted to undermine the very idea of race (Appiah 1996; Zack 2002; Blum 2002, chs. 5–9). For them, antiracism involves debunking a widely held myth, an illusion that is the ideological lynchpin of racism—namely, that races are real.

These *racial skeptics* argue that the concept of race is intellectually bankrupt, for it necessarily entails several propositions that, given what biologists and anthropologists now know about human variation, are not true. In particular, they argue that the race concept, properly explicated, entails the following false claims: (a) There is an underlying essence or cluster of intrinsic properties, inherited through reproduction, that all members of a putative race share and that differentiates a race from all others (racial essentialism); (b) a person's race determines (to a significant degree) his or her aptitude, culture, or moral character (racial determinism); (c) there is a biological basis for rank ordering racial groupings from superior to inferior (natural racial hierarchy); and (d) interracial reproduction has deleterious biological consequences (miscegenation as pathological). There is consensus that these four claims (sometimes called "classical racialism") are false. Yet some philosophers do not believe that race is merely a myth. Despite its pernicious uses and the common confusions that surround it, they insist that "race" does identify a real, nontrivial, and valuable type of human variation.

The debate over the reality of race can take one deep into controversies in metaphysics, philosophy of language, and philosophy of science. Our concern here is with the race idea only insofar as it bears on basic political values and concepts. Still, it is useful to outline the main positions on this question.

As mentioned, the *skeptic* maintains that there is no meaningful sense in which races can be said to exist. "Race," according to the skeptic, is a spurious category, equivalent to "witch" or "phlogiston." Rejecting the skeptic's claim, the *naturalist*, typically relying on population genetics, argues that there are in fact sound biological reasons to divide the human species into subspecies units called "races" (Andreasen 1998; Kitcher 1999; Kitcher 2007). Naturalists maintain that racial classification has (at least potentially) taxonomic or explanatory significance in biology. Though there are no racial essences and races are not natural kinds, races are *biological kinds*. Naturalists do not believe that interracial procreation is harmful, but they do believe that, largely because of geographical barriers (e.g., distance, deserts, mountains, and oceans), some populations have been reproductively isolated from other populations for very long periods and that, as a result, some populations manifest certain phenotypic traits at a greater or lesser frequency than other such populations. We can therefore think of a race as a relatively inbred lineage of common geographical origin whose members are identifiable by their visible, inherited physical traits. One consequence of this approach is that "real races" do not correspond to, and in fact may undermine, our commonsense folk categories of racial classification (e.g., "black" and "white").

Social constructionists hold that "race," though perhaps lacking biological significance, is a meaningful *social* category that divides humans into subgroups for both illegitimate and legitimate social purposes (Goldberg 1993; Mills 1998, ch. 3; Haslanger 2000; Sundstrom 2002; P. C. Taylor 2004). On this view, "race" is not (or is no longer) fundamentally about biology but about social relations; races are (or have become) *social kinds*. The groups that we now call "races" were created by a set of historically specific and ever-changing social practices. Individuals now use familiar racial labels, such as "black" and "white," for ascription and self-identification, and there are formal and informal norms that regulate this labeling. Such systems of classification are rule-governed and sustained by convention (sometimes by law), not determined by biology. "Race" is therefore an institutional construct, a social fact. Thus, in this sense, races are as real as the police or money.

Some argue that such metaphysical disputes distract from or obscure a deeper, underlying concern, which is actually *normative* (Stubblefield 2005, ch. 2; Mallon 2006). Specifically, how should we deal with the troubling dimensions of the race idea while at the same time thinking cogently about and responding appropriately to matters of race? A number of philosophers have argued that we should not jettison the race idea but rather reconstruct it so that it no longer rests on falsehoods or morally suspect assumptions (Outlaw 1996; Haslanger 2000; Root 2001; Hardimon 2003; P. C. Taylor 2004; Glasgow 2009). This would free the race concept for use within antidiscrimination law, for identity construction and group affiliation, and for scientific and biomedical research. On this view, "race" has necessary uses, for there are vital goals, including public ends, we cannot achieve without it. Others doubt this revisionist project could be successful and thus insist that everyone should stop using the race idea, as it is inherently dangerous, cannot be reformed, and causes more harm than good; alternative concepts (e.g., "racial identities" or "racialized groups") should be used to designate the relevant social groups (Appiah 1996; Blum 2002).

2. RACISM

The contemporary debate about racism centers on two questions: What is racism, and what is it about racism that makes it wrong? A number of accounts treat racism as, broadly speaking, a state of mind. Some of these theories focus on certain *beliefs*, the specific content of which is said to make them racist (Appiah 1990; Skillen 1993; Shelby 2003). For example, Appiah (1990) has suggested that racism is the belief that race is a morally relevant distinction, a legitimate basis for treating people differently. He distinguishes between *extrinsic* racism and *intrinsic* racism. Extrinsic racists believe that race is morally relevant because they believe that a person's race determines traits and tendencies (e.g., honesty, laziness, or intelligence) that are morally acceptable bases for differential treatment. Intrinsic racists believe that the mere fact that two persons are of different races is (or at least can be) a legitimate reason for preferring one to the other, quite apart from any further morally relevant characteristics that their race might signify.

For Appiah (1990), both forms of racism rest on *cognitive errors*—the false belief that there are racial essences that determine morally relevant traits and the invalid inference that race, in itself, justifies partiality. However, he claims that most racists are not simply mistaken but *irrational*. Their judgment has been so deformed that they are incapable of seeing their errors, blindly resisting all evidence that contradicts their racist beliefs and thus demonstrating that these beliefs are mere *prejudice* and rooted in rationalization (sometimes called "false consciousness"). The source of this deformation, generally unrecognized by the subject, is typically the fact that the subject is personally invested in viewing the world in racist terms, because, for example, his sense of self-esteem depends on it or he is eager to secure advantages that racist beliefs seem to justify. This type of error-prone and irrational race-thinking arouses our moral concern primarily because, when such thinking is widespread, it so often leads to the oppression of the weak and vulnerable.

Another set of theories focuses less on belief and more on noncognitive mental states, such as desires, hopes, intentions, and fears (Gordon 1995; Garcia 1996; Schmid 1996; Blum 2002). For example, Garcia (1996) argues that racism is, fundamentally, vicious race-based disregard for the welfare of certain people. Its central and most troubling form is race-based hatred, ill will, or hostility. Milder forms of racism involve not quite malice but disrespect or insufficient concern for people assigned to certain racial groupings. On this view, racism is not primarily a problem of cognition or rationality. Racism, on Garcia's view, is inherently immoral, but holding a particular belief, no matter how wrongheaded or irrationally held, is not, in itself, immoral. A particular belief is racist, then, not because of its content but because it is rooted in or rationalizes racial hostility. What makes racism wrong is that it is a failure to give others the respect and goodwill they are owed.

Thinking of racism as a mental state—whether cognitive, affective, or conative—raises questions about the relation between racism and the unconscious mind (see Lawrence 1987; Krieger 1995; and Levine and Pataki 2004). We are susceptible to perceiving the world in ways of which we are unaware; our motives can be opaque to us; we sometimes harbor unacknowledged feelings; and self-deception is ubiquitous. So it is possible, indeed likely, that racist mental states are sometimes unconscious, which raises the difficult but understudied question of how to morally assess implicit racial bias and unconscious prejudice in subjects who sincerely and explicitly disavow racist attitudes (Kelly and Roedder 2008; Faucher and Machery 2009).

A natural way to think about racist *actions* is to view them as behavior animated by a racist state of mind, and so, one does something racist when the action stems from racist beliefs or sentiments (Garcia 1996; Blum 2002; Arthur 2007). Extending this idea, some argue that *institutional racism* occurs when racist beliefs or sentiments affect the decision making of individuals who craft and execute the policies of an institution (Wasserstrom 1976). Though the context of action is within an institution, the target of moral appraisal is still the individual.

But some question this focus on individuals and their mental states in accounts of institutional racism. These thinkers, sometimes operating within a consequentialist framework, insist that an institution's policies can be racist solely in virtue of their effects. For example, Ezorsky (1991) distinguishes between overt racism and institutional racism. Overt racism is a harmful action undertaken because of the agent's racial prejudice against the victim or because the agent is accommodating the racial prejudice of others. Institutional racism, on the other hand, occurs when an institution employs a policy that is race-neutral in content but nevertheless has a negative impact on an unfairly disadvantaged racial group. Those who make and apply the policies need not intend this result and may not themselves be racists. What is nonetheless wrong with the institution, according to Ezorsky, is that it perpetuates the effects of overt racism and encourages racist attitudes and stereotypes. The underlying idea is that some groups in society have already been disadvantaged by overt racism, and an institution that is not intrinsically racist may nevertheless effectively keep these groups in their disadvantaged condition, thus leading some to conclude that they occupy this low station because of the disadvantaged groups' culpable failings or inherent inferiority. Because the institution in question may not be responsible for the group's prior disadvantages, the racism with which it is implicated may be extrinsic to the institution itself. Nevertheless, considerations of basic fairness or corrective justice may justify seeking to mitigate these negative institutional effects by requiring particular institutions (e.g., schools or firms) to implement different policies.

While maintaining the focus on institutional failings rather than individual blameworthiness, a different approach to institutional racism focuses its appraisal on the *intrinsic* features of an institution rather than merely its external effects (Shelby 2004). We define an "institution" as a system of public roles and rules that enable and regulate cooperative action for some specified purpose. There are criteria for assigning persons to specific roles, and each role requires certain rules to be followed. An institution is not an abstract entity; it must be embodied by personnel that occupy official roles and make and administer policy. Given this conception of an institution, we can think of racism as attaching to at least three intrinsic features of institutions.

First, the *goals* of an institution might be racist—for example, to exterminate, subordinate, exploit, exclude, stigmatize, marginalize, or otherwise harm the members of a racial group. Such goals may be the purposes for which the institution was designed (though perhaps now long forgotten) or the aims of its current officials. These goals need not have been made explicit or public. The rules and role criteria may be (or appear to be) race-neutral in content but may nevertheless be designed to achieve or sustain the subjugation of some racial group. The institution need not be effective in achieving its goals yet be criticizable for its aims, and so institutional racism should not be evaluated solely in terms of the institution's actual effects.

Second, racism can be a matter of the *content* of the rules and role criteria of an institution, where these rules and criteria contain racial bias or are racially discriminatory, unjustifiably favoring some racial groups over others. Those who administer the rules and criteria need not themselves be racist for the institution to operate according to racist principles, and administrators need not perceive the racial bias inherent in the procedures they apply. (A more detailed discussion of racial discrimination appears in Section III.)

Finally, racism can be implicated in the *application* of institutional procedures. The goals of the institution may be legitimate; the content of the rules and role criteria, when viewed in the abstract, may be race-neutral and otherwise just. However, administrators may fail to impartially and consistently apply the institution's rules and criteria due to personal prejudice, whether conscious or unconscious. Whatever the substantive content of institutional procedures, formal justice demands evenhandedness in their application. Institutional racism occurs when this distorting effect of prejudice is pervasive, thus leading to the systematic violation of the formal requirements of justice.

Of course an institution can have all three of these features simultaneously—for example, the institutions that constituted the Jim Crow and Apartheid regimes. However, the point of the concept of institutional racism is to take account of the fact that racial hierarchy and inequality can be systematically reproduced in the absence of explicit racist rules and overt racial animus.

3. Racial Discrimination and Social Justice

As with racism, there is much disagreement about what racial discrimination is and what makes it unjust. Today most people use the label "discrimination" to criticize particular actions or policies on moral or legal grounds. It is analytically useful, however, to classify certain actions or policies as discrimination without thereby assuming or implying that everything that falls into this category is impermissible or wrong, only then to go on to ask which actions or policies in the category are objectionable (i.e., "wrongful discrimination") and why. Taking this approach, we should next note that discrimination necessarily involves but is more than judging two persons or two groups to be different (e.g., with respect to race, gender, or nationality) or valuing one type of person over another (e.g., the industrious over the lazy). The distinction or preference must also function (at least implicitly) as a basis for treating people differently (leaving aside, for the moment, whether the basis is sound). Discriminatory actions and policies favor some over others or benefit some while burdening others based on some distinction or preference. Not all such discrimination is morally wrong. Hiring as surgeons only those with steady hands is perfectly permissible even though it discriminates against those with shaky hands.

Moreover, there is wrongful discrimination that should not be prohibited by law. The refusal to befriend someone simply because of that person's race is wrongful discrimination, but it would be illegitimate to legally proscribe it. Political philosophers are largely concerned with identifying wrongful forms of discrimination that entail injustice or rights violations and thus are legitimately prohibited by government action. So when is discrimination based on race unjust and thus permissibly proscribed?

An influential view is that race-based discrimination is *always* unjust because it is a violation of the principle of *colorblindness*, which holds that race should never be a consideration in determining how government institutions treat persons regardless of the purpose or rationale behind such race-conscious measures. This principle is straightforward and easy to apply, but its validity is far from self-evident. What might justify it?

One argument is this: Race, as we have learned from history, is an invidious social distinction, so dangerous and divisive that the state, given its power, should be forbidden from using racial classification in policy and law and perhaps should be granted the authority to restrict the use of racial distinctions by private firms and institutions. Here, racial discrimination is considered unjust because of its propensity to produce negative social consequences (e.g., to sow social discord or to reduce human welfare). There is no doubt that treating people differently because of their race often causes great harm and can be a source of strife. For this reason some argue that it is legitimate to protect stigmatized and disadvantaged racial groups from further harm and abuse by restricting the use of race-based distinctions in certain contexts (e.g., in employment and policing), even when such use is not motivated by racial prejudice (Fiss 1976; Sunstein 1994).

But is the state's use of racial distinctions unjust no matter the purpose or context? As has been mentioned earlier and will be discussed further below, there are good reasons to doubt this. Yet, even if we were to grant that, on grounds of general welfare and administrative efficiency, the state should never treat people differently because of their race, there is still the popular idea that all racial discrimination is *intrinsically* unjust, that people have a *right* not to have their race considered in public decision making. Can the colorblind principle make sense of this idea?

One approach is to argue that persons are not to be treated as representatives of their race but rather as individual persons. There are no group rights—only rights of individuals to equal treatment. However, the use of classifications and generalizations in law and public policy is ubiquitous, absolutely necessary, and entirely legitimate. Imagine trying to make policy or laws without relying on broad categories such as "persons over the age of y" or "persons who scored at least z on the exam." These classifications treat persons "as individuals" no more than racial classifications; and they do not presuppose that groups rather than individuals have rights.

A different approach is to argue that public institutions should not advantage or disadvantage persons because of traits they possess for which they are not responsible. One's relative life prospects should depend solely on one's choices and effort. Because an individual's race, whether understood as a biological or social difference, is an immutable characteristic that the individual is not responsible for having, the state should not allow it to affect the person's relative life chances.

Boxill (1992, 12–18) has objected to this argument on the grounds that, while perhaps one's *overall* life prospects (measured by, say, resources or welfare) should not be hampered by traits one is not responsible for, many opportunities, goods, and services are legitimately given to some persons and denied to others because of traits for which they are not responsible. For example, some people are given certain desirable jobs because of their intelligence or height. If such traits allow those who possess them to provide important goods and services, then it is not unjust to prefer them for certain jobs despite the fact that they are not responsible for these traits. Thus, just because no one is responsible for his or her race, it does not follow that race should never be a consideration in how a person should be treated.[3]

A different account of wrongful racial discrimination, one that does not rely on or attempt to justify the colorblind principle, focuses on *moral status*. On this account, racial discrimination is unjust when it treats race as relevant to basic human worth or moral standing (Boxill 1992, 17; Piper 1993; Alexander 1992, 158–63; Hellman 2008, 34–58). Racial discrimination thus violates the principle that because all persons have inherent and equal moral worth, they should be treated with equal respect. A similar principle states that no one's interests should be treated as if they were less important than others' simply because of the person's race (Singer 1978).

No plausible political morality holds that the members of some particular race are moral inferiors or anything less than full moral persons. If public officials treat the members of a race differently because these officials regard them as due less than equal consideration on account of their race, this is surely unjust discrimination. The question is whether all unjust racially discriminatory treatment can be understood in this way.

Everyone is equal with respect to intrinsic worth or moral status. But individuals and groups do differ with respect to their needs and abilities, and such differences rightly bear on how they should be treated. From the fact that one is owed equal respect as a human being, it does not follow that one should in all contexts be treated the same as others (e.g., with respect to the distribution of scarce resources, social services, and valued positions). It is consistent to believe that blacks, as human beings, are owed equal respect and yet to believe that they are naturally less competent than whites when it comes to performing tasks that require high intelligence. That is, a person might think that though blacks are not morally inferior, they are intellectually inferior, just not to a degree that justifies second-class citizenship or strong forms of paternalism.[4] There is a difference between having a right to be *treated as an equal* and having a right to be *treated equally* (i.e., the same as others) in all contexts and with respect to all goods, services, and opportunities.

Some argue that because all persons are owed equal respect, there is a standing presumption in favor of treating everyone equally unless there is a relevant difference between persons that rationally justifies differential treatment (Williams 1962). It is rational to give medicine to only those who are sick and jobs to only those competent to perform them, and so such differential treatment is consistent with equal respect for the sick and the healthy, the competent and the incompetent. But to grant suffrage rights to only those who are left-handed is to treat right-handed citizens without due respect. Such treatment is arbitrary, irrational, and unfair. Armed with this idea, one might argue that since race, as a matter of scientific fact, does not determine a person's needs or abilities, race is *always* an irrelevant characteristic, an immaterial criterion, for benefiting or burdening someone (Baier 1978).

However, things are not that simple. We cannot determine the relevance of a selection criterion without identifying the particular purposes the criterion is supposed to serve. Also, because a selection criterion might serve a policy's or an institution's purposes well but these purposes might include such things as exploiting a vulnerable race, we must also assess whether these purposes are legitimate. Thus, a sound principle of differentiation must not only satisfy a condition of relevance— that is, the distinction must be rationally aligned with or likely to advance some policy or institutional goal—but the goal must be one that the discriminating agent is morally permitted or authorized to pursue.

Interestingly, this makes it an open question whether differential treatment based on race might sometimes be justified (e.g., if the goal is to increase racial diversity or integration in public schools), contrary to what some advocates of color-blindness suppose. In this connection, it is worth pointing out that the expression "discrimination on the basis on race" is often used ambiguously, and this ambiguity often obscures the morally relevant distinction between treating a person differently (e.g., denying her an important opportunity) on the grounds that she is a member of an inferior race and treating her differently (e.g., compensating her for an injustice she has suffered) on the grounds that she has been wronged because *others* believe she is a member of an inferior race. In both cases, the treatment differed "on the basis of race," but the race-based considerations are rather different and the differences are morally important.[5]

With this analytical machinery in place, we might say, then, that differential treatment based on race (i.e., racial discrimination) is unjust when (a) it is based on the presumption, perhaps implicit, that one race has inferior moral status to another or (b) it is not based on a relevant principle of differentiation that would further a legitimate end. Race-based discrimination that takes either of these forms is fundamentally unjust and intrinsically wrong (Alexander 1992; Blum 2002, 78–90).

Notice that this account of wrongful racial discrimination does not depend on the discriminator intentionally seeking to harm members of the disfavored racial group, nor, in the second form of discrimination, does it depend on the discriminator being a racist (i.e., having racist beliefs or sentiments). Yet when malicious intent or racial prejudice is the source of the unjust discrimination, this creates an additional wrong from which the law might seek to protect certain groups, particularly those socially salient groups who suffer because these attitudes are widespread. Some regard this wrong as an *expressive harm*, a form of stigmatizing, insulting, or demeaning others (Woodruff 1976; Blum 2002, 84–85). Some argue, however, that an expressive harm may occur even if the discriminator does not actually have malicious intent or prejudice toward those discriminated against; it is enough if a suitably informed and impartial observer, given who the discriminator is and the social context, would *interpret* the action as conveying such intentions, beliefs, or sentiments (Arthur 2007, 30–33; Hellman 2008, 59–85).

A final set of questions regarding racial discrimination involves three related issues. First, some discussions of racial discrimination invoke the idea of *meritocracy*. The main concern here is competition for jobs or job-related benefits (and perhaps admission to selective colleges). According to some, using racial distinctions in employment is a violation of meritocratic principles: It violates the right of the best qualified to be selected for employment or promotion, for a person's race is never a form of merit or a qualification (Goldman 1975). Some argue against this widely held belief on the grounds that "merit" is a matter of how ability affects productivity or efficiency; it is not a matter of moral desert or justice per se (Daniels 1978). Merit claims are based on the fact that certain job-related abilities enhance productivity; thus, claims to hire the *best* qualified are only as strong as the obligation to increase productivity. Considerations of justice can override considerations of productivity. A different response is to argue that "race" can indeed be merit or a legitimate qualification (Davis 1983; Dworkin 1985, ch. 14). There is no set of abilities or traits that constitute merit as such; a person's abilities or traits constitute merit only insofar as they enable that person to provide valuable goods and services. If being black enables a doctor or police officer to garner the trust of those she serves and thereby perform her job better, then race qualifies as merit.

A second issue concerns *reaction qualifications* (Singer 1978; Wertheimer 1983; Boxill 1992, 29–31; Alexander 1992, 173–76). Here race is treated as a basis for discrimination, not because the employer is racist, partial to members of her own race, or arbitrary in her selection criteria, but because of the reactions of *others* to the race of her employees (as in the examples of the doctor and police officer just mentioned). The difficult question here is when reliance on reaction qualifications is consistent with racial justice. If one's customers do not want to be served by blacks, then it might hurt the profitability of one's business to hire blacks, and if this racist preference is sufficiently widespread, then hiring blacks could threaten the life of the business itself and perhaps one's livelihood. One plausible response to this problem is to legally prohibit the use of reaction qualifications in employment when consumer reactions are based on racial animus or prejudice. Exclusion on grounds of race is insulting and unjust when it is the result of and communicates contempt for the one being excluded (Dworkin 1985, ch. 14). To be fair, effective enforcement of this principle would be necessary to prevent some businesses from gaining a competitive advantage through the covert use of illicit reaction qualifications.

Finally, there is the question of *statistical discrimination*. The issue here is not about whether race in itself is a legitimate basis for differential treatment. Those who defend statistical discrimination as sometimes rational and not unjust may accept that race as such is not a relevant basis for differential treatment. But they may nevertheless think that race may be used as a *proxy* for some other characteristic (the material trait) that race highly correlates with. The material trait (e.g., being a criminal, an illegal immigrant, or a terrorist) is a morally relevant basis for differential treatment but is more difficult or costly to detect. The use of proxies in law and public policy is unavoidable and often legitimate (e.g., consider the use of age as a proxy for responsible drivers). The question is whether it is ever permissible to use a suspect category like race as a proxy, and if so, under what circumstances.[6]

4. Responding to Racial Injustice

Some philosophers have sought to explain and justify measures they believe to be appropriate practical responses to racial injustice and its consequences. This might seem like a policy matter with little philosophical significance. However, the issues here are not just about which public policies for combating racial injustice are most cost-effective or politically feasible. The primary concern is with what is sometimes called *corrective justice*: the principles for determining how we should rectify injustices. Because corrective justice is a component of a full theory of justice, the question of which methods for rectifying racial injustices treat perpetrators and victims fittingly yet are fair to all concerned is a question of political philosophy.

As already noted, the modern world has seen and been shaped by the most ghastly and inhumane forms of racial domination imaginable, and despite the apparent consensus today that racism is wrong, some still suffer because of racial injustice and its historical consequences. So, in light of our discussion of racism and racial discrimination, we might say that the appropriate response to racial injustice is to abolish or reform any institution that operates on the basis of, or is otherwise distorted by, racism; to secure the civil rights and equal civic standing of all regardless of race; and to institute antidiscrimination measures, constitutional and legislative, that protect citizens from racism and unjust racial discrimination. But this is not the end of the story.

A long history of racial injustice has left the members of some racial groups severely disadvantaged with respect to wealth, income, employment, education, and political influence in their respective societies. Moreover, racist ideology has led some members of non-white groups to suffer from a sense of inferiority and self-doubt, which can negatively affect employment and educational performance and compromise self-respect. Where there are large and persistent racial disparities in socioeconomic status, these are arguably attributable, at least in part, to the legacy of racism and racial discrimination. Even if a society were to effectively protect citizens from racial discrimination in the present, there would still be the question of how to respond to the harmful effects of these historical injustices.[7] Philosophers have taken at least two distinct approaches to this question.

The first is to defend the need for *reparations*. Where a serious racial injustice is recent and the direct victims and perpetrators are alive and readily identifiable, the case for reparations is relatively straightforward: If the victims were seriously harmed (physically, materially, or psychologically) by the injustice, then, by the principle of rectification, they are entitled to reparations (to be made "whole" again) from those who wronged them.[8] Things get more complicated when neither those who have been made worse off because of an injustice nor those who have benefitted from the injustice were direct parties to the original injustice and, indeed, may not even have been born at the time. But some think the principle of rectification still applies.

There are three influential arguments. The *harm argument* says that a past racial injustice can initiate a causal chain of harms, perhaps over many generations, down to the present and that the state (here assumed to be a continuous corporate body down to the present) that perpetrated these injustices (or failed to protect its citizens from them) would then owe reparations for the *current* harms from which the victimized race suffers (Boxill 2003; Fullinwider 2000; McCarthy 2004). The *unjust enrichment* argument states that when a past racial injustice disadvantages some and advantages others, the beneficiaries of the historical injustice, having been unjustly enriched, owe reparations (or restitution) to those who have been disadvantaged by the injustice, even if these beneficiaries were not responsible for the harm caused by the injustice (Bedau 1972; McGary 1999, ch. 6). The *inheritance argument* says that an unrepaired past racial injustice creates a liability that attaches to the holdings of the initial perpetrators and thus to the relevant inherited portion of their heirs' holdings, regardless of whether those heirs committed any injustice themselves; and the descendants of the original victims therefore inherit their ancestors' rights to those unpaid reparations, regardless of whether these descendants have been harmed or disadvantaged by the original injustice (Boxill 1972, 2003; Thompson 2001). These arguments are sometimes used in combination.[9]

A somewhat different (though perhaps compatible) way of responding to the harmful effects of past racial injustice is to argue that the undeserved disadvantages of members of historically oppressed racial groups should be neutralized or ameliorated. The idea is not so much to compensate for past wrongs but rather to promote fairness in the present or future. Some versions of this argument focus on resource inequities, arguing that wealth should be redistributed to make members of historically oppressed racial groups more equal to whites or more economically self-sufficient. Other versions focus on inequality of opportunity, arguing that a long history of racial injustice has unfairly handicapped members of historically oppressed racial groups in the competition for valued positions and their extrinsic rewards (e.g., income and prestige). It is therefore argued that society should take measures to eliminate these unjust socioeconomic disadvantages (e.g., through the redistribution of wealth, income subsidies, or educational initiatives) to create a fairer (though not necessarily equal) playing field (Goldman 1975; Lyons 2004). More controversially, it is argued that the members of disadvantaged racial groups should be given preference in employment over equally, or perhaps more, qualified white applicants (Sher 1975; Jacobs 2004, chs. 4–5; Anderson 2010, ch. 7). This latter approach is often criticized on the grounds that it is a form of wrongful racial discrimination or that it violates meritocratic principles. The strength of these criticisms therefore depends on the validity of the conception of discrimination being invoked or on whether meritocratic principles are sound or inviolable. Others argue against this approach on the grounds that it unfairly imposes burdens and costs on whites not responsible for the injustices that continue to disadvantage historically oppressed racial groups.

But now let us suppose that the civil rights of all persons in society are secure, antidiscrimination measures have been enacted and are effectively enforced, reparations (if due) have been made to the victims of racial injustice, and the handicaps that reduce the competitiveness of historically oppressed racial groups have been remedied or neutralized. Still, racial stereotypes and racial prejudice may nevertheless find expression in civic and economic life, causing racial division and resentment. After all, antidiscrimination laws cannot extinguish racism; they can only deter individuals and organizations from acting on racist attitudes or provide a basis for legal remedy should one's rights be abridged because of racism. In light of this, some philosophers have argued that the state may have to take further measures to promote antiracist values and to foster racial conciliation (Wasserstrom 1976; Dworkin 1985, ch. 14). For instance, it may be necessary to increase the representation of historically oppressed racial groups in positions of authority and prestige to fight the negative stereotype that they are not competent to perform these roles (Gutmann 1996). To combat stereotypes and foster interracial contact and cooperation, the state may need to actively encourage, facilitate, and perhaps even mandate integration in schools and neighborhoods (Anderson 2010) to inculcate an ethos of tolerance and mutual understanding, it may be necessary to actively promote the value of racial diversity in all aspects of social life.[10]

5. Racial Identity and Community

It is common to hear people expressing a desire to live in a "colorblind" or "postracial" society. In one version of this vision, the good society is one in which not only has racial justice been fully realized, but an individual's race is generally regarded as having no social or political significance whatsoever (Wasserstrom 1976; Zack 1993). In this society, no one celebrates racial diversity or takes pride in racial identity. There are no institutions or private associations in which race figures in the selection of members. Race is not a consideration when forming bonds of allegiance or affection. Those who defend this vision generally view racial differences as an illusion, as unreal, or they think race, while perhaps real, is a trivial form of difference that, like hair or eye color, should be given no normative weight. We can call this vision *postracialism*. (See the article by Satz on "Gender" in this volume for discussion of Susan Okin's parallel position on the transcendence of gender.)

Some proponents of postracialism believe that the state should aggressively promote this ideal by, say, discouraging racial self-segregation and the formation of racial identities, disseminating the message of postracialism, and refusing to recognize or support race-based private organizations. Others think postracialism is an ethical ideal worth defending and striving for but (perhaps in opposition to political perfectionism) that the stance of the state should be *tolerance* toward race-based affiliation; that is, the state should not interfere with the formation of racial identities and associations.

Racial pluralists reject the ideal of postracialism. They believe that racial identity and affiliation can have intrinsic value and should have a place in a good society. Although some pluralists maintain that a just state should tolerate such racial ingroup fraternity, others regard tolerance of racial group affiliation in civil society as insufficient for a just society. These latter pluralists insist that some *public recognition* of racial difference is required.

To feel the force of the pluralist vision, it is necessary to understand the conception of racial identity and group affiliation that it presupposes.[11] Historical context and power dynamics loom large here. If there had not been centuries of Europeans dominating and exploiting non-European peoples using the race idea to legitimate such actions, postracialism might be an appropriate stance. This history cannot be erased, however, even were its many injustices fully rectified. The victims of white domination have often rejected the tenets of racial ideology that demean, misrepresent, and stigmatize them. Out of self-respect, they have publicly asserted their status as moral equals. But instead of discarding the race idea altogether, many have cultivated positive racial identities and racial solidarity that have enabled them to survive and to resist their oppression. Racially oppressed groups have forged and sustained distinctive traditions, values, and ideals, often refusing to assimilate fully to white norms and expectations. Historically oppressed racial groups are often proud of their collective identities and sometimes seek to celebrate them publicly. On the basis of these identities, they have formed race-based organizations and institutions for political, religious, economic, and educational purposes. Their ingroup affinity has sometimes expressed itself as a desire to live together in the same countries, regions, cities, or neighborhoods. Though "white" identity might be irredeemable and morally suspect (but see Stubblefield 2005, 144–77), these non-white racial identities need not reflect racial hostility toward other racial groups. Even if racial justice were achieved, many would still want to preserve their racial identity, some forms of racial affiliation, and some race-based organizations and institutions.

Some racial pluralists claim that historically oppressed racial groups who, like some ethnic groups or national minorities, have distinctive cultural practices are entitled to public recognition of these differences and the public support needed for these practices to survive (Young 1990; C. Taylor 1994; Outlaw 1996, ch. 6; Alcoff 2006).[12] Such recognition and support entail that the state must treat some racial groups differently. For instance, it may mean that some racial groups, and not others, should be accorded some group autonomy within the larger polity. It may mean that the state should affirm the value of these racial identities. It may mean that the state should fund the educational institutions and social organizations of some racial groups and not others. It certainly requires that the state not pressure historically oppressed racial groups to assimilate to the dominant culture and perhaps that it protect these groups from the intolerance of private individuals and organizations. It may also mean that the state should require that public educational institutions teach all citizens about the history and cultures of the nation's racial minorities.

Some racial pluralists still endorse the ideal of interracial community. They insist, however, that in a multiracial society, particularly one with a history of serious racial injustice, this ideal should be understood as realized, not when one unified yet racially undifferentiated community exists but when multiple overlapping and nested race-based communities cohere on the basis of mutual respect.

6. Conclusion

What we mean, or should mean, by "racial equality" and "antiracism" is far from obvious and a deeply contested matter. Philosophers have a crucial role to play here, not so much in settling these controversial questions once and for all but in offering compelling interpretations of these values, using careful reasoning to sort through common confusions, and debunking bogus ideas that might initially seem attractive or cogent. Moreover, philosophizing about race can deepen, and perhaps alter, our understanding of other fundamental political values, such as fairness, community, equality, and tolerance.

NOTES

1. I thank David Estlund and Lawrence Blum for helpful feedback on earlier drafts of this essay.

2. For helpful overviews of this history, see Mills (1997) and Fredrickson (2002).

3. For additional criticisms of the principle of colorblindness, see Gutmann (1996), Sundstrom (2008, ch. 2), and Anderson (2010, ch. 8).

4. Darby (2009, ch. 4) argues that widespread assumptions about black cognitive inferiority and moral deficiencies not only threaten to attenuate blacks' rights but can affect what rights blacks actually have.

5. For discussion of this point, see Nickel (1972) and P. W. Taylor (1973).

6. For general discussion of this issue, see Maitzen (1991) and Alexander (1992, 167–73). For defenses of statistical discrimination based on race, see Levin (1992) and Risse and Zeckhauser (2004); for critiques of race-based statistical discrimination, see Thomas (1992), McGary (1999, ch. 10), and Lever (2005).

7. For empirical examinations of the contemporary impact of historical racial injustice in the United States, see Brown et al. (2003).

8. Affirmative action programs are sometimes defended as reparations or compensation for *recent* injustices (see Thompson 1973; Ezorsky 1991, ch. 4; Boxill 1992, ch. 7; McGary 1999, ch. 6). For criticisms of the reparations approach to affirmative action, see Sher (1975) and Goldman (1975).

9. For criticisms of the idea of reparations for past racial injustice, see Waldron (1992), Kershnar (2002), and Arthur (2007, ch. 6).

10. For criticisms of racial diversity as a justification for differential treatment, see Sher (1999).

11. For detailed discussion, see Appiah (1996), Outlaw (1996), Gooding-Williams (1998), P. C. Taylor (2004), Shelby (2005), and Alcoff (2006).

12. For criticisms of this view, see Boxill (1992, ch. 8), Appiah (1996), and Shelby (2005, ch. 5.).

REFERENCES

Alcoff, L.M. 2006. *Visible Identities: Race, Gender, and the Self*. New York: Oxford University Press.

Alexander, L. 1992. "What Makes Wrongful Discrimination Wrong? Biases, Preferences, Stereotypes, and Proxies." *University of Pennsylvania Law Review* 141(1): 149–219.

Anderson, E. 2010. *The Imperative of Integration*. Princeton, NJ: Princeton University Press.

Andreasen, R. O. 1998. "A New Perspective on the Race Debate." *British Journal for the Philosophy of Science*, 49(2): 199–225.

Appiah, K. A. 1990. Racisms. In *Anatomy of Racism*. Edited by D. T. Goldberg. Minneapolis: University of Minnesota Press.

Appiah, K. A. 1996. Race, Culture, Identity: Misunderstood Connections. In *Color Conscious: The Political Morality of Race*. Edited by A. Appiah and A. Gutmann, 30–105. Princeton, NJ: Princeton University Press.

Arthur, J. 2007. *Race, Equality, and the Burdens of History*. Cambridge, UK: Cambridge University Press.

Baier, K. 1978. "Merit and Race." *Philosophia* 8: 121–51.

Bedau, H. 1972. "Compensatory Justice and the Black Manifesto." *Monist* 56: 20–42.

Blum, L. 2002. *"I'm Not a Racist, But . . .": The Moral Quandary of Race*. Ithaca, NY: Cornell University Press.

Boxill, B. 1972. "The Morality of Reparation." *Social Theory and Practice* 2: 113–23.

Boxill, B. 1992. *Blacks and Social Justice*, rev. ed. Lanham, MD: Rowman & Littlefield.

Boxill, B. 2003. "A Lockean Argument for Black Reparations." *Journal of Ethics*, 7(1): 63–91.

Brown, M. K., M. Carnoy, E. Currie, T. Duster, D. B. Oppenheimer, M. M. Shultz, D. Wellman. 2003. *Whitewashing Race: The Myth of a Color-Blind Society*. Berkeley: University of California Press.

Daniels, N. 1978. "Merit and Meritocracy." *Philosophy & Public Affairs* 7(3): 206–23.

Darby, D. 2009. *Rights, Race, and Recognition*. Cambridge, UK: Cambridge University Press.

Davis, M. 1983. "Race as Merit." *Mind* 92: 347–67.

Dworkin, R. 1985. *A Matter of Principle*. Cambridge, MA: Harvard University Press.

Ezorsky, G. 1991. *Racism and Justice: The Case for Affirmative Action*. Ithaca, NY: Cornell University Press.

Faucher, L., and Machery, E. 2009. "Racism: Against Jorge Garcia's Moral and Psychological Monism." *Philosophy of the Social Sciences* 39(1): 41–62.

Fiss, O. M. 1976. "Groups and the Equal Protection Clause." *Philosophy & Public Affairs* 5: 107–77.

Fredrickson, G. M. 2002. *Racism: A Short History*. Princeton, NJ: Princeton University Press.
Fullinwider, R. 2000. "The Case for Reparations." *Report from the Institute for Philosophy and Public Policy* 20.
Garcia, J. L. A. 1996. "The Heart of Racism." *Journal of Social Philosophy* 27(1): 5–46.
Glasgow, J. 2009. *A Theory of Race*. New York: Routledge.
Goldberg, D. T. 1993. *Racist Culture: Philosophy and the Politics of Meaning*. Oxford: Blackwell.
Goldman, A. 1975. "Limits to the Justification of Reverse Discrimination." *Social Theory and Practice* 3(3): 289–305.
Gooding-Williams, R. 1998. "Race, Multiculturalism and Democracy." *Constellations* 5(1): 18–41.
Gordon, L. R. 1995. *Bad Faith and Antiblack Racism*. Atlantic Highlands, NJ: Humanity Press.
Gutmann, A. 1996. "Responding to Racial Injustice." In *Color Conscious: The Political Morality of Race*. Edited by K. A. Appiah and A. Gutmann, 106–78. Princeton, NJ: Princeton University Press.
Hardimon, M. O. 2003. "The Ordinary Concept of Race." *The Journal of Philosophy* 100(9): 437–55.
Haslanger, S. 2000. "Gender and Race: (What) Are They? (What) Do We Want Them to Be? *Noûs* 34(1): 31–55.
Hellman, D. 2008. *When Is Discrimination Wrong?* Cambridge, MA: Harvard University Press.
Jacobs, L. A. 2004. *Pursuing Equal Opportunities: The Theory and Practice of Egalitarian Justice*. Cambridge, UK: Cambridge University Press.
Kelly, J., and Roedder, E. 2008. "Racial Cognition and the Ethics of Implicit Bias." *Philosophy Compass* 3(3): 522–40.
Kershnar, S. 2002. "The Inheritance-Based Claim to Reparations." *Legal Theory* 8(2): 243–67.
Kitcher, P. 1999. "Race, Ethnicity, Biology, Culture." In *Racism*. Edited by L. Harris, 87–117. Amherst, NY: Humanity Books.
Kitcher, P. 2007. "Does 'Race' Have a Future?" *Philosophy & Public Affairs* 35(4): 293–317.
Krieger, L. H. 1995. "The Content of our Categories: A Cognitive Bias Approach to Discrimination and Equal Employment Opportunity." *Stanford Law Review* 47: 1161–248.
Lawrence, C. R. 1987. "The Id, the Ego, and Equal Protection: Reckoning with Unconscious Racism." *Stanford Law Review* 39(2): 317–88.
Lever, A. 2005. "Why Racial Profiling Is Hard to Justify: A Response to Risse and Zeckhauser." *Philosophy & Public Affairs* 33(1): 94–110.
Levin, M. 1992. "Responses to Race Differences in Crime." *Journal of Social Philosophy* 23(1): 5–29.
Levine, M. P., and T. Pataki. 2004. *Racism in Mind*. Ithaca, NY: Cornell University Press.
Lyons, D. 2004. "Corrective Justice, Equal Opportunity, and the Legacy of Slavery and Jim Crow." *Boston University Law Review* 84: 1375–404.
Maitzen, S. 1991. "The Ethics of Statistical Discrimination." *Social Theory and Practice* 17: 23–45.
Mallon, R. 2006. "'Race': Normative, Not Metaphysical or Semantic." *Ethics* 116(3): 525–51.
McCarthy, T. 2004. "Coming to Terms with Our Past, Part II: On the Morality and Politics of Reparations for Slavery." *Political Theory* 32(6): 750–72.
McGary, H. 1999. *Race and Social Justice*. Malden, MA: Blackwell.

Miller, D. 1999. *Principles of Social Justice*. Cambridge, MA: Harvard University Press.
Mills, C. W. 1997. *The Racial Contract*. Ithaca, NY: Cornell University Press.
Mills, C. W. 1998. *Blackness Visible: Essays on Philosophy and Race*. Ithaca, NY: Cornell University Press.
Nickel, J. W. 1972. "Discrimination and Morally Relevant Characteristics." *Analysis* 32(4): 113–14.
Outlaw, L. T. 1996. *On Race and Philosophy*. New York: Routledge.
Piper, A. M. S. 1993. "Two Kinds of Discrimination." *Yale Journal of Criticism* 6: 25–74.
Risse, M., and R. Zeckhauser. 2004. "Racial Profiling." *Philosophy & Public Affairs* 32(2): 131–70.
Root, M. 2001. "The Problem of Race in Medicine." *Philosophy of the Social Sciences* 31(1): 20–39.
Schmid, W. T. 1996. "The Definition of Racism." *Journal of Applied Philosophy* 13(1): 31–40.
Shelby, T. 2003. "Ideology, Racism, and Critical Social Theory." *Philosophical Forum* 34(2): 153–88.
Shelby, T. 2004. "Race and Social Justice: Rawlsian Considerations." *Fordham Law Review* 72: 1697–714.
Shelby, T. 2005. *We Who Are Dark: The Philosophical Foundations of Black Solidarity*. Cambridge, MA: Harvard University Press.
Sher, G. 1975. "Justifying Reverse Discrimination in Employment." *Philosophy & Public Affairs* 4: 159–70.
Sher, G. 1999. "Diversity." *Philosophy & Public Affairs* 28(2): 85–104.
Singer, P. 1978. "Is Racial Discrimination Arbitrary?" *Philosophia* 8: 185–203.
Skillen, A. 1993. "Racism: Flew's Three Concepts of Racism." *Journal of Applied Philosophy* 10(1): 73–89.
Stubblefield, A. 2005. *Ethics along the Color Line*. Ithaca, NY: Cornell University Press.
Sundstrom, R. 2002. "'Racial' Nominalism." *Journal of Social Philosophy* 33(2): 193–210.
Sundstrom, R. 2008. *The Browning of America and the Evasion of Social Justice*. Albany, NY: SUNY Press.
Sunstein, C. R. 1994. "The Anticaste Principle." *Michigan Law Review* 92(8): 2410–455.
Taylor, C. 1994. "The Politics of Recognition." In *Multiculturalism: Examining the Politics of Recognition*. Edited by A. Gutmann, 25–73. Princeton, NJ: Princeton University Press.
Taylor, P. C. 2004. *Race: A Philosophical Introduction*. Cambridge, UK: Polity Press.
Taylor, P. W. 1973. Reverse Discrimination and Compensatory Justice. *Analysis* 33(6): 177–82.
Thomas, L. 1992. "Statistical Badness." *Journal of Social Philosophy* 23(1): 30–41.
Thompson, J. J. 1973. "Preferential Hiring." *Philosophy & Public Affairs* 2(4): 364–84.
Thompson, J. 2001. "Historical Injustice and Reparation: Justifying Claims of Descendants." *Ethics* 112(1): 114–35.
Waldron, J. 1992. "Superseding Historic Injustice." *Ethics* 103(1): 4–28.
Wasserstrom, R. 1976. "Racism, Sexism, and Preferential Treatment: An Approach to the Topics." *UCLA Law Review* 24(3): 581–622.
Wertheimer, A. 1983. "Jobs, Qualifications, and Preferences." *Ethics* 94: 99–112.
Williams, B. 1962. "The Idea of Equality." In *Philosophy, Politics, and Society*. Edited by P. Laslett and W. G. Runciman, 110–31. Oxford: Basil Blackwell.
Woodruff, P. 1976. "What's Wrong with Discrimination?" *Analysis* 36(3): 158–60.
Young, I. M. 1990. *Justice and the Politics of Difference*. Princeton, NJ: Princeton University Press.
Zack, N. 1993. *Race and Mixed Race*. Philadelphia: Temple University Press.
Zack, N. 2002. *Philosophy of Science and Race*. New York: Routledge.

CHAPTER 19

GENDER

DEBRA SATZ

THE subordination of women characterizes virtually every society in the world. Facts about this subordination differ from place to place: In some countries, there are extensive inequalities in the mortality and morbidity rates for men and women, women cannot hold political office, women are brutalized by rape and violence, and girls are last on the list to get an education or even food (Joshi 1998, 169–77; Nussbaum 2000). Even in the most gender-equal societies, while matters are less extreme, men and women still face very different life prospects. In the United States, for example, working women still face a "second shift" in the home, are paid less than men for comparable work, are more likely than men to be poor, and have substantially lower prospects of being selected for top levels of employment or political leadership. In 2010, only fifteen CEOs of Fortune 500 companies were women ("Top Women CEOs," 2010).

Political philosophies offer different theoretical tools that we can use to evaluate women's unequal position. It is important to note, however, that for the majority of its long and venerable tradition, much of political philosophy simply took gender inequality as a *given*, either ascribing it to nature or simply ignoring it. This was especially true with respect to the family: The gendered division of labor in the family was justified by an appeal to brute biological differences, or theorists failed to notice women's subordination in the home at all. Some theorists who did notice such subordination viewed the family as outside the concerns of political philosophy or as a private domain inappropriate for public intervention. A number of influential philosophical accounts of social justice explicitly legitimated men's rule over women by appeal to patriarchal norms.

John Stuart Mill (1988 [1869]) was an important exception, arguing in *The Subjection of Women* that the unequal position of women in the family could not be justified by appeal to "women's nature," about which he insisted on complete agnosticism.

Such appeal could be fairly evaluated, he contended, only *after* the constraints on women's opportunities had been fully lifted and we had the chance to see what men and women who were equally free were really like.

Moreover, Mill argued that inequality in the family has damaging effects on men and women's equality in the wider social world. Consider, he asks, the consequences of "the self-worship, the unjust self preference" nourished in boys growing up in male-dominated households in which "by the mere fact of being born male he is by right the superior of all and every one of an entire half of the human race" (Mill 1988 [1869], 86–87). How will such boys grow up into men who treat women as equals?

Feminist scholarship has continued, extended, and deepened Mill's attack on the conception of the family as a private personal realm off limits to those concerned with promoting justice. Attention to gender has revealed the complex interpenetration of "public" and "private." Indeed, the idea that "the personal is political" is a core thesis that has been brought to the fore of political philosophy by feminism. Another central claim, now widely acknowledged in political philosophy, is that the status of women does in fact raise significant issues of justice. Because of pioneering feminist scholarship, it is no longer possible to judge a theory of social justice as satisfactory if it ignores the gendered family and its implications for the division of labor and the structure of opportunity in the wider society. This means that many contemporary theories of justice are in need of reform. Some liberal egalitarians betray their own principles of commitment to autonomy and equal opportunity by their failure to explicitly question the traditional gendered division of labor, both within the family and within the society as a whole (Okin 1989; Kymlicka 2002, 386).

The prevalence of gender inequality gives rise to a number of distinct questions. Some of these questions are normative: What, if anything, makes the inequalities that obtain between men and women unjust? Are all such gender-based inequalities unjust? What role is there for gender differences in a just society; that is, what would count as (full) justice for women? What are legitimate means for combating gender injustice? What framework(s) should we use to think about these issues?

There are also perplexing empirical questions. While feminists agree that gender hierarchy is unjust, they offer very different analyses of its sources and main features. Is the "linchpin" of women's subordination their role in the domestic division of labor within the family (Okin 1989)? Is it the structure of the labor market (Bergmann 2002; Folbre 1994)? Is it the product of males' tendencies to sexual violence and domination (MacKinnon 1989)? Or is it a consequence of women's biological role in reproduction (Firestone 1970)? Arguably, all of these factors are important contributors to gender inequality, and it is doubtful that any one of them can be fully reduced to the others. Nonetheless, some factors may be more causally important than others. Deepening our understanding of the influence and interplay of these multiple factors and also the ways that gender interacts with other axes of social disadvantage, such as race, disability, and class, is clearly important to the project of advancing gender justice.

Answers to these empirical and normative questions are often connected insofar as those who think that differences between men and women reflect only differences in their biology will be less likely to condemn those differences as unjust than others who think those differences are a legacy of workplace discrimination, sexist laws, and constrained opportunities. Nevertheless, the relationship between these two domains is not one of entailment: It is possible to think that socially caused gender inequalities are justified and that biological differences between men and women can raise questions of justice. For example, as I explain below, some people think socially caused gender inequalities are justified if they are freely chosen. Additionally, the fact that a disadvantage has a biological origin says nothing in itself about whether or not society has an obligation to accommodate it or redress it.

Feminist and nonfeminist political philosophers give different answers to both the normative and the empirical questions. Some feminists have questioned whether standard philosophical accounts of social justice actually have the resources to address woman's subordination, arguing that we need an explicitly feminist philosophy.[1] But there are as many differences *within* feminism as *between* feminist and nonfeminist accounts of social justice. In this chapter I critically survey some of the most prominent issues of justice raised by gender and the main debates about how to address them. Before doing so, however, it is important to examine the concept of gender itself.

1. What Is Gender?

Starting in the 1960s, a standard way of understanding gender referred to the socially constructed roles, behaviors, and characteristics that a given society considered appropriate for men and women (see World Health Organization 2012). On this conception, while sex is biologically determined, gender is solely a function of culture and social structures. Underlying this distinction has usually been the premise, implicit or explicit, that the most significant differences between men and women are a function of culture, can be changed, and are subject to moral criticism. Simone de Beauvoir (1973/1949) captured this assumption in her pithy remark that one is not born but rather *becomes* a woman. In other words, being a "woman" is not a physical destiny produced by female reproductive organs: Social causes are needed to bring "men" and "women" with different characteristic identities into being. Moreover, only once these characteristic identities are socially created does subordination on the basis of gender becomes possible. Physical differences alone, some contend, cannot explain this subordination (see Haslanger 2000). Feminism's rejection of biological determinism as the basis for gender inequality has been supported by work in history and anthropology that has shown the historical and cultural variability of gender (Scott 1986) as well as laboratory and clinical research that has documented the dismal history of exaggerated or imaginary physiological differences (Fausto-Sterling 1992).

By the late 1970s, a number of scholars were pointing to difficulties with the sharp divide between sex and gender, stressing the mutual interaction between biology and social forces. For example, they pointed out that we could not even understand sex-based differences in height, weight, and physical strength without taking into account diet and the social division of labor (Jaggar 1983, 106–13). Thus, in societies where neither men nor women perform hard physical labor, the gender gap in strength and size is smaller than in those in which men alone perform such labor. It has also been argued that the causal arrow can go the other way: Biological differences can influence men and women's social behaviors.

This blurring of the divide between sex and gender resurrected the debate about the extent to which women are fundamentally the same as or different from men. On the one hand, many feminists continue to argue that there is nothing of great importance—and certainly nothing that can explain women's social subordination—to presocially distinguish men from women (Okin 1989; Haslanger 2000; MacKinnon 1989). They maintain that it is not biology but the cultural significance given to biological difference that is the problem. They argue that the fact that so many biological differences are socially influenced only strengthens their position.

Alternatively, some feminist scholarship has argued that there are indeed significant essential differences between men and women—whether nature, nurture, or both best explain these differences—but that these differences are in need of revaluation. This viewpoint accepts that men and women's differences may lead them to take up different roles in life but insist that the set of their respective opportunities must be equally good. These "difference" feminists have sought recognition for, and appreciation of, the characteristics historically associated with women, stressing the positive value of care, empathy, and nurture (Gilligan 1982; Noddings 1984; Ruddick 1990). They have argued, for example, that, given its evident importance, the caring labor that goes on in the family should be given greater public recognition (Kittay 1999). The fact that such work is currently denigrated does not show the real value of such work; rather, these feminists argue that the denigration itself is due to the fact that childcare is seen as "women's work" and thereby accorded less importance. They have also pointed out that there are undesirable consequences of modeling women's opportunities on those of men's: For example, it is a bad thing to be unable to spend time with one's children.

Despite the undistinguished history of the attempt to locate significant gender differences in biology as an explanation of women's inequality, the search continues. The issue continues to be whether characteristic differences in men and women's traits are best explained by biological differences between men and women. Consider the question of why there are far fewer women mathematicians then men. Some argue that women are innately predisposed against being good at mathematics or abstract reasoning; others argue that the causal story is crucially about social causes such as gender stereotyping, lack of role models, and so on. This debate is fueled by recent fMRI studies that purport to show significant processing differences in male and female brains, leading to different cognitive strengths and weaknesses, as well as by, on the other hand, a slew of studies showing the effects of gender stereotyping on K–12 math education. Unfortunately, it is all too easy to overemphasize the influence of biological factors. Women are a diverse category, as are men, and what commonalities the genders share across time and place might be largely the result of an unfortunate history of unfairness and constraint and not biology.

In the end, however, the critical issues are normative. Even when there appear to be biological differences between men and women that explain some gender choices and gender patterning—such as the fact that men cannot give birth to or nurse children—it is a different thing altogether as to whether—and to what extent—such differences justify inequalities in social circumstances. Nothing about women's economic prospects or social roles *logically follows* from the fact that gender may have some biological underpinning in sex. Indeed, one of the great innovations of modern liberal thought is the idea that differences between people—on the basis of religion, sex, race, or social class—cannot by themselves *justify* unequal political, civil, and social rights and opportunities. For the most part, current debates in philosophy about gender do not question liberalism's "egalitarian plateau," which affirms that justice requires treating people as equals (Kymlicka 1990). Rather, they concern the means and ends of gender justice, including the legitimacy of arrangements that, while seemingly arising on this egalitarian plateau, instantiate inequalities and the appropriate means for rectifying those inequalities that are deemed to be unjust.

2. Justice and Gender

Ends

Which gender inequalities, if any, are just? Is there anything unjust about the gender inequalities that attach to family roles? Is there anything unjust about the gender inequalities that attach to social roles outside the family? While it seems obvious to some people that gender inequalities are unjust, others see the issue differently. The latter advocate evaluating gendered practices in terms of their relationship to individual choice and decision. On this view, what matters is whether men and women *choose* to lead different kinds of lives: Gender differences that result from their different choices are justified; those that issue from coercion are not. However, we can quickly see that it is not obvious how to extrapolate from this view to gender. Coercion is a contested concept in political philosophy (Wertheimer 1987). Rarely does a coerced individual face a situation in which there are literally no choices. Even the decision to surrender one's money to a robber rather than forfeit one's life has a voluntary aspect. Given that even under constraints we make choices, and that in fact all choices are constrained, how do we determine which constraints are legitimate? What makes a constraint an instance of illegitimate coercion?

Consider how the choice/coercion dichotomy plays out with respect to the assumption of gender roles within the family. First, we need to place this question in context: Despite the advances prompted by the feminist movement during the last quarter of the twentieth century, most families remain based on an unequal division of labor. Around the globe, women do the vast majority of domestic labor—not only tending the house but also raising and caring for children. Feminist economists and sociologists have further shown how women's role in parenting constrains their ability to pursue careers and compete for demanding jobs (Folbre 1994). Many women therefore remain economically dependent on their male partners and vulnerable to poverty in the event of divorce. Women's economic dependency in turn gives their husbands/male partners considerably more power and bargaining advantage within marriage (Sen 1990a).

Nevertheless, could it not be argued that these discrepancies issue from women's own choices? Childrearing may be an expensive lifestyle choice in terms of its opportunity costs, but it is usually a choice nonetheless. Men and women have different aspirations that lead women to value caring for children over the additional income that is available in the market economy. Many people make choices that disadvantage them on the labor market or have otherwise high opportunity costs, but philosophers have argued that we have no obligations of justice to beach-bum surfers or to lovers of very fine claret. We are not obligated, on grounds of justice, to subsidize the expensive tastes of others (Dworkin 2000). If women freely choose to spend their time caring for their children, then they must take responsibility for assuming the costs, including the opportunity costs, of their choices.

Those emphasizing the choice dimension of contemporary gender differences point out that the traditional family has already seen many changes in the last seventy years, changes that make it more plausible to see women's current employment and family situations, at least in the developed world, as freely chosen.[2] In the decades following World War II, increasing numbers of women entered the labor force. The development of the birth control pill made it easier for women to avoid unwanted pregnancies and to plan when to have children, and there are a growing number of single-parent families, gay families, and extended families. Economic, technological, and social factors have together made the full-time stay-at-home housewife and mother with a working husband a statistical minority.

Laws governing families have also changed. In almost all developed nations, legal restrictions on marriage, divorce, and abortion were relaxed in a relatively short time, between the mid-1960s and the mid-1980s (Glendon 1987). In *Loving v. Virginia*, for example, the U.S. Supreme Court struck down state laws preventing people from different races from marrying; *Roe v. Wade* legalized abortion. Of course, many of these changes have been contested, and there remain serious constraints on a woman's reproductive choices, including her choice about whether to end her pregnancy, nor can gay people usually marry. But it is nevertheless true that the family has increasingly evolved from a hierarchical institution based on fixed-status assignments to a set of relationships among individuals based on their own consent.

Those who emphasize the role of choice in explaining and justifying gender inequalities might acknowledge that legal constraints on choice remain but argue that this simply means that we should further extend the domain of choice and fully allow individuals themselves to determine what kinds of families they want to create. Thus, those advocating a choice perspective would allow people to make their own agreements about procreation, work, and family without state restriction. These arrangements could include not only rights to abortion and contraception but also rights to contract away parental bonds and to sell and buy gametes and reproductive labor; choices in favor of polygamy and polyandry, gender hierarchical families, and workplaces side by side with more egalitarian ones; and families in which women do all domestic labor and those in which it is shared. As long as such arrangements are chosen, then there is no objection to any person participating in them.

However, these recommendations for the future do not show that women in current circumstances have freely chosen their own life trajectories. In many parts of the globe, girls and women enjoy a second-class status: Within the family, they are the last to be fed, last to be educated, and last to receive medical care. They face other obstacles outside the family: They do not have the same property rights as men, there are restrictions on their participation in political life, and they are vulnerable to violence and sexual abuse.

The idea that most women currently choose their gender roles, even within the developed democracies, has been disputed in three ways. First, some feminists have argued that key aspects of women's roles and paths in life are largely set *before* they have developed the capacities of choice. We can call this the "there is no choice" objection. In *The Reproduction of Mothering*, Nancy Chodorow (1978) argued that the fact that children's primary nurturers are today mothers itself leads to a sexually differentiated developmental path for boys and girls. Girls identify with the same-sex nurturing parent and feel more connected to others; boys, by identifying with the absent parent, feel themselves to be more "individuated." Girls are primed to care for others, while boys are primed to attend to themselves. Chodorow argued that mothering is thereby reproduced across generations by a largely *unconscious* mechanism that, in turn, perpetuates the inequality of women at home and at work.[3] Moreover, not only is the mechanism unconscious, but it traces back to a past in which women's choices to mother were not free, a time when women were excluded by law from many professional opportunities.

Chodorow's work has been the subject of much controversy, but it is undeniable that girls and boys grow up facing different expectations of how they will behave. Children receive strong cultural messages—from parents, teachers, peers, and the media—about sex-appropriate traits and behaviors. Girls are supposed to be nurturing, self-sacrificing, nonaggressive, and attractive; boys should be rambunctious, self-confident, and capable of taking charge. "Caring" is largely seen as a feminine characteristic to be promoted in girls and discouraged in boys. Such signals about appropriate gender behavior are everywhere—beginning at birth—often implicit and subtle and largely unconscious but in other cases quite overt. If we bring the observation that boys and girls respond to different expectations to bear on the fact that capability and even talent are shaped by environment and culture, then it becomes less plausible to see "choice" as the driving factor in the assumption of unequal gender roles.

Some critics of choice-based perspectives on family and reproduction further argue that some choices are not and cannot be fully informed. Marriage and childbearing have implications that are not easily known in advance. Can a woman who has never been pregnant accurately predict the effects of ceding her parental rights to a child? Can an eighteen-year-old woman who agrees to a traditional gendered division of labor in her marriage know what she will feel like as a fifty-year-old woman without market-valued skills suddenly left by her husband?

Note that this line of argument has the implication not only that girls' choices are shaped by patterns of childrearing and weak information but also so are boys.' The fact that many of our choices are shaped in childhood or made with uncertain information does not by itself tell us what is objectionable about those choices: At most, it leads us to be cautious about fully basing our views of what people deserve in life on what they choose. To show that some ways of shaping or making choices are objectionable we have to say more about either the ways these choices are shaped—by arguing, for example, that women face greater constraints on their choices than men do—or that some choices are actually morally problematic or otherwise inferior to others. Thus, the "there is no choice" argument that proceeds on the basis of unconscious gender socialization and diverse psychological paths in life does not by itself establish the wrong of gender inequality; but it does block one possible line of defense of that inequality: that it was freely chosen.

A second response stresses the ways that women's choices with respect to family and children interact with unjust social structures *outside* the family, in particular, with the sex segregated division of labor in the economy, where women still earn only about 75 percent of what men earn for comparable work. We can call this the "unfairly constrained choice" objection. Given women's lower wages, it is *rational* for families who must provide for their own childcare to choose to withdraw women and not men from the workforce. Once these women withdraw, they find themselves falling further behind their male counterparts in skill development and earning power. Childcare is an immensely time-consuming activity, and those who do it single-handedly are unlikely to be able to pursue other goals such as education, political office, or demanding careers. The structures of work and family thus form a "cycle of vulnerability" that conditions the lives and choices of women (Okin 1989).

Even those who do somehow manage to combine work and family face serious obstacles, including the lack of good-quality subsidized day care for children; jobs with little flexibility for those who need to care for a sick child; school schedules that seem to be premised on having a parent at home; and the social expectation that working women will continue to work a "second shift" (Hochschild 1989), assuming the responsibility for the bulk of household labor. Statistical analysis shows that motherhood tends to lower a woman's earnings, even if she does not take any time off from paid work (Folbre 1994; Correll, Benard, and Paik 2007). Why should mothers pay an economic price simply for giving birth to a child when fathers do not pay any comparable economic cost? Why should the opportunity sets of men and women be so different with respect to the possibilities of combining work and family?

If the constrained set of choices facing a woman is unfair, then even a choice that is the best one available within this set might nevertheless not be legitimate. To take an extreme example: Even if slavery is a slave's best choice when faced with the alternative of death, this does not make slavery justified. Thus, the second response allows for choice but argues that choice does not justify in this particular context. Rather, it is the context of choice—and the fact of unequal choice sets and unequal opportunities for men and women—on which we need to focus.

Over a century ago, Mill pointed out that women's decision to marry could scarcely be called "free," given women's low wages and dim employment and educational prospects. Although the situation of women in many parts of the world has dramatically improved, marriage remains an economic necessity for many women today as well. For example, the odds of being poor in the United States are greatest for single women with children.

Women's choices are constrained by the fact that most jobs and most men assume that women will be the primary caretakers of children and perform the majority of the domestic labor. Additionally, empirical research shows that the jobs done by women are undervalued *because* women do them. This suggests that, at least to some extent, women's diminished opportunities are the result of conscious or unconscious bias. In countless controlled studies, individuals give lower ratings to the same resumes, scholarly articles, or artistic works when they carry a female rather than a male name (Paludi and Strayer 1985; Martell 1996). Discrimination takes many forms, including stereotyping and statistical discrimination (Valian 1998). The choice perspective obscures the social context in which choice takes place and is particularly inattentive to the background inequalities that give rise to differential constraints on men's and women's choices. It is insensitive to the fact that gender discrimination—whether intentional or not—is still a fact of life in many employment contexts.

This is not to say that all men have it easy or are not also disadvantaged by the current gender division of labor. Men who try to depart from their gender norms face social costs in terms of stigmatization and diminished opportunities, and there are social costs for adhering to those norms: Men have shorter life spans, less extensive social networks, and less time with their children than do women.[4] The assumption that women are better nurturers of children than men has, until fairly recently, meant that women and not men were overwhelmingly granted custody of their children in the event of divorce. But the "unfairly constrained choice" objection rests on the evidence that, on the whole, women have a less desirable set of opportunities than men do. If this evidence is weak, then the "unfairly constrained choice" argument will not be well supported. But is the evidence weak?

Ultimately this depends on which opportunities we think are most valuable. As I suggested, on many significant measures of social well-being women fare worse than men: income and wealth; vulnerability in the face of divorce; access to prestigious social positions; and, for those women who work, less leisure time. In much of the world the consequences of disparities in opportunities are stark: Amartya Sen (1990b) estimated that over 100 million women are missing due to premature morality and morbidity in the developing world. Trafficking, violence, and abuse are also parts of the lives of far too many women.

One other piece of prima facie evidence for unequal opportunities comes from the fact that women have organized themselves into a movement to contest gender norms and expectations while men, by and large, have not done so. Qualitative research also suggests that many women do try to get their male partners to do more household work and childcare but encounter resistance (Hochschild 1989). Finally, recent data has pointed to a decline in women's happiness in relation to men's as women both enter a gender structured workforce (which assumes that the worker is not also a primary caretaker) and attempt to care for their children. Although there is now broad subscription to the values of gender equality, in reality most couples do not live up to these principles even when they espouse them, and working women are continuing to bear an extra burden.

A third response to the choice justification of gender inequality argues that, because children are "public goods," assets that contribute to the wealth and well-being of an entire society, the fact that women care for children without financial compensation is wrong. We can call this the "unfair compensation" objection. When women engage in mothering, they perform socially needed work: They raise the next generation of productive workers and citizens. Rather than a lifestyle choice, by providing for a stable population base, women contribute to social well-being (Folbre 1994). Given that less than 1 percent of private-sector employers provide childcare assistance, and that most child care is inadequate or too expensive for most families, some theorists have argued that the work women do in caring for children should be compensated according to its fair market value. On this view, the problem is not the gendered division of labor per se—not the structure of opportunities—but the unfair compensation for the labor of childrearing and other domestic work.

Would the gendered division of labor cease to be objectionable if women were simply paid to stay at home? If income and wealth were more equally distributed across men and women, would that remove the objections to gendered families and activities? Are all the choices that women and men might in the future make with respect to gender and family roles unproblematic?

These are questions with disputed answers. Although it has been argued that paying women for childcare is an improvement over the status quo, and while the arguments of some philosophers would suggest that if men and women's opportunities were similar then having characteristic gender roles would be no problem (van Parijs 2001), it is likely that women (and men) would have more opportunities and more freedoms if work schedules and expectations were restructured to accommodate the need for dependent care on the parts of both men and women. The current division of labor in the larger society and in the home arguably imposes greater costs on both men and women than would be the case in a world where labor markets were structured to allow for more flexibility for both genders.

Beyond these objections to the choice-based defense of gender inequality, a number of philosophers have raised concerns about deferring to gendered individual choices even in more equal contexts and even in the absence of such factors as unconscious psychology, exploitation, and coercion. Elizabeth Anderson (1993) and Michael Sandel (1998) have argued that some choices represent the *corruption* of important goods. They suggest, for example, that gendered practices such as female prostitution and commercial surrogacy are degraded forms of intimacy and human relationship. They argue that when women sell sex to men or sell their capacity to bear a child to others, they are alienating themselves from their own capacities and normal emotions, alienating themselves from their children, and alienating themselves from other people. If markets distort the appropriate bonds between mothers and children, or alienate women from their own sexuality, or objectify them as objects in the eyes of men, then choices that make use of the market can be problematic even if they take place against a background of equality and freedom. Of course, such arguments are controversial because views about sexuality and even motherhood differ. Some would contend that there is nothing wrong with prostitution per se but only with its criminalization and the desperate circumstances that may prompt some women to choose it (Nussbaum 1998).

There is also no consensus on whether the use of markets does degrade such goods. Markets are largely instrumental mechanisms that allow people with different values to engage in mutually beneficial trade. Two people do not have to agree on the proper way of valuing the Bible in order to exchange it (Satz 2010b). Nonetheless, these critics do have a point when they insist that a world in which all human relationships take the form of contractual relationships does not seem especially attractive. There is an evident difference between two people caring for each other out of love and concern and the same two people engaging in such care on a contractual basis.

Other theorists have pointed out that an individual's choices about his or her gender and family roles can have negative consequences for third parties, for example, for children or other adults. Ann Cudd (2006) argues that women who choose to be stay-at-home moms support a system of patriarchal domination that makes it more difficult for other women to make other kinds of choices. This is because the gendered division of the labor supports statistical discrimination, a form of indirect discrimination based on the fact that a person belongs to a group that has certain average characteristics. It is rational for these characteristics to be used by employers as proxies for the productivity of the members of that group. If the average woman bears greater responsibility for the household than her male counterpart, then she will also be more likely to be absent from the workplace. Even after entering the workforce, some women quit their jobs and stay at home to take care of their children (Gornick and Meyers 2003). All of these individual choices, when aggregated together, might make women as a group less attractive employees for demanding jobs.

Others have argued that contractual practices like prostitution and commercial surrogacy can have third-party effects as well, promoting a view of women as baby machines or as sexual servants to male desires (Satz 2010b). These practices might themselves have some effects on women's employment prospects in conventional labor settings, promoting stereotypes of women catering to men at work. Catherine MacKinnon (1994) has argued that practices like prostitution along with pornography silence women in other social settings: They make it harder for a woman's "no" to be heard as anything other than a "yes."

For egalitarians, while women and men's individual choices are a part of the story of what maintains gender inequality, the larger part is institutional. They point to the role of social structures that accommodate some identities and ways of life while excluding others. If the workplace and the social division of labor are structured in ways that systematically disadvantage women, or at least disadvantage mothers, then these structures need to be changed. Similarly, because gender identity is shaped at an early age, and because families powerfully shape the aspirations of children and thus play an important role in determining what children grow up to do and be, then the free choices of adult family members can have problematic consequences for children. Egalitarians argue that if gendered families encourage the subordination and deference of girls, then a just society must seek to redress those effects in some way, regardless of what the parents prefer.

Choice-based arguments and arguments concerned with ensuring equal opportunities or consequences for men and women likely differ on the nature of the families that they would allow. For example, while a choice-based contractual view favors plural marriages, arguments that look at egalitarian consequences do not straightforwardly imply a right to legalized polygamy. The crucial question would be whether polygamy is possible without the subordination of women. Similarly, a choice-based view might have no objection to traditional marriages as long as these were freely entered into, while egalitarians would worry about the effects on children, other women, and social norms. There is serious disagreement among political philosophers as to how to balance freedom, equality,[5] and, more specifically, values based on freedom of association and freedom of religion with the value of gender equality. This disagreement has implications, as we shall see, for the scope of legitimate state intervention in family life.

Some argue that gender itself would not exist in a just society. If gender is defined as a hierarchical institution that allows men to exercise power over women, then, as Susan Okin put it, "a just future would be one without gender. In its social structures and practices, one's sex would have no more relevance than one's eye color or the length of one's toes" (Okin 1989, 171; see also Shanley 2009). Okin and others have argued that the gender system is actually a caste system that locks women into disadvantaged social positions. The end of this caste system requires the end of gender—the end of the dichotomous roles assigned to men and women simply on account of their sex. On this view, a just society would break the link between childbearing and the raising of children and between having female reproductive organs and being a "woman."

As I noted previously, however, some advocates of gender justice believe that women's differences from men should be acknowledged and valued. These theorists believe that gender injustice has consisted in not adequately valuing the practices and attributes associated with women: caring, altruism, and a sense of obligation to others. Of course, there is no logical inconsistency with valuing characteristics such as these and wanting to abolish gender. It can surely be argued that these are valuable characteristics but that they should not be viewed as the property of any one gender, or as defining a gendered identity. There is nevertheless a tension between these two positions. Those who celebrate women's differences from men may be skeptical as to whether the ideal of gender equality understood in terms of sameness is the best way to capture feminism's aspirations (Jaggar 1990). Many people reject the idea that justice requires the doing away with men's and women's different ways of being in the world, arguing that the problem is not gender difference but gender hierarchy.

Means

Different theories disagree as to what counts as achieving justice for women. As we have seen, some view justice through the lens of choice, others through the lens of opportunities, and still others through the lens of exploitation. Even among those who agree on a given conception of justice for men and women, there is still the question of means. When is it legitimate for the state to interfere with the choices of individuals in the family? in the workplace? in religious institutions?[6] How we view the legitimacy of state action in these realms will depend on our views of the scope and importance of different freedoms, such as religious freedom, and the extent to which individual choices in these realms have important causal effects on women's equality, opportunity, and well-being.

Is the state even the best means for advancing gender justice as opposed to informal social sanctions, consciousness-raising, and nongovernmental organizations? If it is, how should the state act? Is gender justice best advanced through gender-neutral or gender-conscious policies and laws? In its treatment of individuals, to what extent should the state abstract from, accommodate, or seek to abolish gender differences? At the heart of these questions is the issue of how we should define and respond to sexual difference. On one hand, stressing the differences between men and women reinforces cultural stereotypes about femininity that some argue sustain gender inequalities (Williams 1998). On the other hand, treating women the same as men runs the risk of excluding women who do not conform to male norms, for example, those who engage in childbearing and childrearing as their primary activity.

Consider how this debate about means plays out with respect to laws about divorce and workplaces. Starting in the late 1960s, American divorce laws were reformed to be consistent with gender neutrality in family law. Alimony became available to husbands as well as wives; what had been previously viewed as separate property within marriage became viewed in many states as joint assets; and either party on a "no-fault" basis could initiate divorce. By the 1970s, the Supreme Court was insisting that women workers have the same social security, welfare, and workers' compensation benefits for their families as did men and that women and men in divorce be viewed in a way that abstracted from their sex-based classifications.

Nevertheless, these changes did not issue equal outcomes for men and women following divorce and instead gave rise to different views about the acceptability and meaning of gender neutrality in law. Postreform divorce still leaves women in an economically more vulnerable position than men. Some of the reasons for this relate to what has been excluded from the division of assets: the intangible assets of professional degrees and qualifications, pensions, insurance, and related benefits of which, given women's unequal responsibilities in the family, men have had a disproportionate share. Another problem has been that spouses have been expected to become self-sufficient as quickly as possible, and so alimony was meant to be limited. For women who spent their entire working lives raising children, ensuring their future earnings has been a daunting task, nor is child support always paid, even when it is court mandated.

The cumulative effect of these factors is that after divorce men's discretionary income rises while women's steeply declines. For example, in the United States, women's standards of living have been found to decline between 13 percent and 35 percent after divorce, while men's standard of living increases by 11 percent to 13 percent (Peterson 1996). In Britain, the mean net income after divorce increases slightly for men, whereas it decreases 14 percent for women (Jarvis and Jenkins 1999). While many of these problems can be addressed within a gender-neutral framework, some have argued that the needs of displaced homemakers warrant special recognition given the disadvantages they face in the workforce stemming from their previous disproportionate responsibility for raising their children. Theorists have argued that gender neutrality in law, understood as equal formal rights and standards, cannot bring about gender justice and so should be rejected as a means.

The workplace is another domain in which philosophers have argued about the application of gender-neutral laws. Consider the status of laws protecting pregnant persons from workplace discrimination. Some states passed laws to protect women from being fired if they became pregnant and requiring employers to give such women reasonable maternity leave. If we assess these laws from a gender-neutral perspective, they look like a special privilege accorded to women, because only women can become pregnant. Such laws emphasize sex differences and not sex similarities. Those who advocate a gender-neutral standard argue that by basing what people are entitled to on their differences, the law tacitly reinforces cultural stereotypes about pregnancy and motherhood. Against this, theorists have argued that a formulaic insistence of gender neutrality is unable to counteract women's actual disadvantages. They insist that the focus must be on gender disadvantage and not gender difference.

The workplace also raises the question of why sex-segregated employment continues, despite the removal of legal discrimination. Interestingly, although women have been moving into some male-dominated occupations such as bus driving and bartending, there has been no corresponding increase of interest by men in female-dominated job sectors such as housecleaning, day care, and secretarial work. Respecting choice and enacting antidiscrimination laws have enabled substantial progress for women, but they have not been fully effective policy responses to women's subordinate occupational status.

In addition to the question of whether or not laws should be gender neutral, there is the important issue of whether the state's intervention in different realms is justified if it promotes gender equality. This is a question likely to be especially controversial in the realm of religion. Religious freedom, for example, can undermine fair equality of opportunity. The Catholic Church does not ordain women as priests; some nations admit immigrants who practice (and continue to practice) polygamy; some orthodox Jewish schools refuse to admit girls. On their face, these practices are forms of sex discrimination, but the courts, at least in the United States, do not generally subject religious institutions to sex-discrimination law. Advocates of a prohibition on state intervention in such practices typically appeal to the importance of religious freedom and to the idea that this kind of intervention would impose an intolerable burden on many religious beliefs and practices. There is clearly force to this argument but whether it justifies an absolute prohibition on interfering with religious practices that support sex discrimination is another matter (Sunstein 2009). Many people think that it is completely appropriate for the law to regulate practices such as animal sacrifice and the use of peyote, even though such regulation clearly burdens some religions. Additionally, it may be that, in many cases, the burdens imposed are not serious, and there may be ways of ameliorating the conflict between gender equality and other values. In the end, the issue is how one balances claims of liberty and diversity against the claims of equality, a familiar source of tension between more egalitarian and more liberal political philosophies.

On a policy level, there are different proposals for achieving gender justice, proposals that differ considerably on how the choices within diverse institutions that undermine gender equality should be treated. Some feminists prefer to derail such choices *indirectly*, by creating incentives for people to act so as to maintain just social structures or by creating external counterweights to individual actions. Okin (1989) argues, for example, that to offset the disparity of power in marriage, spouses should be equally entitled to earnings, day care should be available to all families, work should be made more flexible, and, in the event of divorce, postdivorce households should enjoy the same standard of living. She believes that reconfiguring structures *outside* the family—the wage system, the childcare system, the availability of parttime work, maternity and paternity leave—is the most appropriate way to shape individual choice *inside* the family. This is because, in part, she views the concept of privacy and a sphere of personal life in which the state's role is limited as "essential" (Okin 1989, 128). Likewise, Anne Philips (1991) has argued for increasing the presence of women in decision-making bodies and Anne Alstott (2004) for publically provided subsidies for childrearing. All of these policies aim to change the context of choice-making without directly interfering with choices themselves. Alternative views give less room for individual choice within the family and are more likely to endorse policies that directly interfere with those choices. Catherine MacKinnon argues that respecting the choices that men and women make with respect to the family and sex and reproduction will continue to sustain the subordination of women and their unequal lives. She trenchantly remarks: "The right of privacy is an injury got up as a gift"(1988, 100). Theorists critical of privacy considerations might be willing to legally mandate shared domestic responsibilities or assign a regulatory agency to oversee the domestic division of labor. Some theorists consider such a remedy worse than the malady it is designed to redress.

3. Conclusion

Although the ideal of gender equality is widely accepted in theory in the developed democracies, this ideal is still contested in many parts of the world. Moreover, in practice in many developing countries women and girls are less likely to be educated, vaccinated, or even fed than males. In India, for example, girls are 50 percent more likely to die before the age of five than boys (Kristof and WuDunn 2009). Girls in South Asia, sub-Saharan Africa, and the Middle East receive fewer than two years of schooling, on average, for every three received by boys. These inequalities cannot be justified by appeal to biology or choice, and they fly in the face of any plausible theory of justice. These are urgent concerns that are changeable. Moreover, they are maintained not only by laws and formal workplace practices: Some of the worst violations take place within the home in the form of unequal access to food, domestic violence, and unequal control over sexuality, which is manifested in the skyrocketing numbers of women affected by AIDS. These concerns cannot be addressed by policies that fail to pay attention to gender.

Even in the societies in which the ideal of gender equality is accepted, men and women do not enjoy equal opportunities. As we have seen, different theories offer different diagnoses of what, if anything, is unjust about unequal opportunity and other inequalities that attach to men and women in societies. I have considered the "there is no choice," "unfairly constrained choice," and "unfair compensation" criticisms of the contemporary gender division of labor in the household and in the wider society. If the gender division of labor is unjust, as feminists say it is and as I have suggested is a claim well supported by empirical evidence, then we need more work identifying what policies can best advance justice in both the affluent democracies and the undeveloped societies around the globe.

NOTES

1. Carole Pateman (1988), for example, has argued that contract theory cannot accommodate the equality of women.

2. The following two paragraphs draw on Satz (2010a).
3. This paragraph draws on Satz (2010a).
4. Thanks to David Estlund for pressing this objection.
5. See the chapters by Pettit and Anderson in this volume.
6. See the chapter by Audi in this volume.

REFERENCES

"Top Women CEOs." 2010. *International Business Times* (May 20).
Alstott, Anne. 2004. *No Exit: What Parents Owe Children and What Society Owes Parents*. Oxford: Oxford University Press.
Anderson, Elizabeth. 1993. *Value in Ethics and Economics*. Cambridge, MA: Harvard University Press.
Bergmann, Barbara. 2002. *The Economic Emergence of Women*, 2d ed. New York: Palgrave/St. Martin's Press.
Chodorow, Nancy. 1978. *The Reproduction of Mothering*. Berkeley: University of California Press.
Correll, Shelley, Stephen Benard, and In Paik. 2007. "Getting a Job: Is There a Motherhood Penalty?" *American Journal of Sociology* 112: 1297–338.
Cudd, Anne. 2006. *Analyzing Oppression*. New York: Oxford University Press.
de Beauvoir, Simone. 1973. *The Second Sex*. New York: Vintage Books. (Originally published 1949)
Dworkin, Ronald. 2000. *Sovereign Virtue: The Theory and Practice of Equality*. Cambridge, MA: Harvard University Press.
Fausto-Sterling, Anne. 1992. *Myths of Gender: Biological Theories about Men and Women*. New York: Basic Books.
Firestone, Shulamith. 1970. *The Dialectic of Sex: The Case for Feminist Revolution*: New York: William Morrow.
Folbre, Nancy. 1994. *Who Pays for the Kids? Gender and the Structures of Constraint*. New York: Routledge.
Gilligan, Carol. 1982. *In a Different Voice*. Cambridge, MA: Harvard University Press.
Glendon, Mary Anne. 1987. *Abortion and Divorce in Western Law*. Cambridge, MA: Harvard University Press.
Gornick, Janet, and Marcia Meyers. 2003. *Families that Work: Policies for Reconciling Parenthood and Employment*. New York: Russell Sage Foundation.
Haslanger, Sally. 2000. "Gender and Race: (What) Are They? (What) Do We Want Them to Be?" *Nous* 34:1: 31–55.
Hochschild, Arlie. 1989. *The Second Shift: Working Parents and the Revolution at Home*. New York: Penguin Books.
Jaggar, Alison. 1983. "Human Biology and Feminist Theory." In *Beyond Domination: New Perspectives on Women*. Edited by Carol Gould. Totowa, NJ: Rowman & Littlefield.
Jaggar, Alison. 1990. "Sexual Difference and Sexual Equality." In *Theoretical Perspectives on Sexual Difference*. Edited by Deborah L. Rhode. New Haven, CT: Yale University Press.
Jarvis, Sarah, and Stephen P. Jenkins. 1999. "Marital Splits and Income Changes: Evidence from the British Household Panel Survey." *Population Studies* 53(2): 237–54.

Joshi, Heather. 1998. "The Opportunity Cost of Childbearing: More Than Mother's Business." *Journal of Population Economics* 11: 161–83.

Kittay, Eva. 1999. *Love's Labor: Essays on Women, Equality and Dependency*. New York: Routledge.

Kristof, Nicholas, and Sheryl WuDunn. 2009. *Half the Sky: Turning Oppression into Opportunity for Women Worldwide*. New York: Knopf.

Kymlicka, Will. 2002. *Contemporary Political Philosophy. An Introduction*, 2nd ed. Oxford: Oxford University Press.

MacKinnon, Catharine. 1988. *Feminism Unmodified*. Cambridge, MA: Harvard University Press.

MacKinnon, Catharine. 1989. *Toward a Feminist Theory of the State*. Cambridge, MA: Harvard University Press.

MacKinnon, Catharine. 1994. *Only Words*. Cambridge, MA: Harvard University Press.

Martell, Richard. 1996. "What Mediates Gender Bias in Work Behavior Ratings?" 35(3/4) *Sex Roles:* 153–69.

Mill, John Stuart. 1988. *The Subjection of Women*. Indianapolis, IN: Hackett Publishing. (Originally published 1869)

Noddings, Nel. 1984. *Caring: A Feminine Approach to Ethics and Moral Education*. Berkeley: University of California Press.

Nussbaum, Martha. 1998. "Whether from Reason or Prejudice: Taking Money for Bodily Services" *Journal of Legal Studies* 27(2): 693–724.

Nussbaum, Martha. 2000. *Women and Human Development: The Capabilities Approach*. Cambridge, UK: Cambridge University Press.

Okin, Susan. 1989. *Justice, Gender and the Family*. New York: Basic Books.

Paludi, Michelle, and Lisa Strayer. 1985. "What's in an Author's Name? Differential Evaluations of Performance as a Function of Author's Name." *Sex Roles* 12(3/4): 353–61.

Pateman, Carole. 1988. *The Sexual Contract*. Stanford, CA: Stanford University Press.

Peterson, Richard. 1996. "A Re-Evaluation of the Economic Consequences of Divorce." *American Sociological Review* (61): 528–36.

Phillips, Anne. 1991. *Engendering Democracy*. Cambridge, MA: Polity Press.

Ruddick, Sara.1990. *Maternal Thinking: Towards a Politics of Peace*. Boston: Beacon Press.

Sandel, Michael. 1998. "What Money Can't Buy: The Moral Limits of Markets." In *The Tanner Lectures on Human Values*. Oxford: Oxford University Press.

Satz, Debra. 2010a. "Feminist Perspectives on Reproduction and the Family." In *Stanford Encyclopedia of Philosophy*, 2012 ed. Edited by Ed Zalta. Available from http://plato.stanford.edu/entries/feminism-family.

Satz, Debra. 2010b. *Why Some Things Should Not Be for Sale: The Moral Limits of Markets*. Oxford: Oxford University Press.

Scott, Joan. 1986. "Gender: A Useful Category of Historical Analysis." *American Historical Review* 91(5): 1053–75.

Sen, Amartya. 1990a. "Gender and Cooperative Conflicts." In *Persistent Inequalities*. Edited by Irene Tinker. New York: Oxford University Press.

Sen, Amartya. 1990b. "More Than 100 Million Women Are Missing." *The New York Review of Books* (December 20).

Shanley, Molly. 2009. "'No More Relevance Than Eye Color': Justice and a Society without Gender." In *Toward a Humanist Justice: The Political Philosophy of Susan Moller Okin*. Edited by Debra Satz and Rob Reich. Oxford: Oxford University Press.

Sunstein, Cass. 2009. "On the Tensions between Sex Equality and Religious Freedom." In *Toward a Humanist Justice: The Political Philosophy of Susan Moller Okin*. Edited by Debra Satz and Rob Reich. Oxford: Oxford University Press.

Valian, Virginia. 1998. *Why So Slow? The Advancement of Women*. Cambridge, MA: MIT Press.

van Parijs, Philippe. 2001. "Real Freedom, the Market and the Family: A Reply to Seven Critics." *Analyse und Kritik* 23(1): 106–31.

Wertheimer, Alan. 1987. *Coercion*. Princeton, NJ: Princeton University Press.

Williams, Joan. 1998. "Do Women Need Special Treatment? Do Feminists Need Equality?" *Journal of Contemporary Legal Issues* 279(9): 279–320.

World Health Organization. 2012. "What Do We Mean by 'Sex' and 'Gender'?" Available from http://www.who.int/gender/whatisgender/en/index.html.

CHAPTER 20

IDEAL AND NONIDEAL THEORY

ZOFIA STEMPLOWSKA AND ADAM SWIFT

THE first Polish encyclopedia, prepared in the eighteenth century by Benedykt Chmielowski, had an entry on "horse" that informed the reader: "what a horse is everyone can see." *Ideal theory* is rather less straightforward. Recent debates have seen the term used in different ways and its critics attacking a variety of different targets. It was coined by Rawls to describe the kind of theory of social justice that he was seeking—one that identified principles to guide the basic institutions of a society in which certain counterfactual, idealized, conditions were satisfied. For Rawls, theory of that kind was an essential first step before we could address the more urgent and pressing questions in *nonideal theory*, about what social justice requires of us in our actual circumstances.

While there has been some productive discussion of Rawls's rather specific methodological claim, the term *ideal theory* has also been used to stand for apparently useless, unrealistic, naïve, utopian—perhaps even ideological or dangerous—currents in contemporary political philosophy, which has muddied the waters somewhat. Others, such as G. A. Cohen, have criticized Rawls from what looks like the other direction: For allowing the principles of his supposedly ideal theory to be influenced by empirical assumptions in a way that, for Cohen, compromises justice. Debate has, then, spilled over from its Rawlsian origins into a dispute about the methods and aims of political philosophy quite generally. Our aim in this chapter is to dispel at least some of the resulting confusion by disentangling various key strands of argument that have arisen, as well as offering our own evaluation of them.

Some of the confusion, we suspect, stems from ambiguities in both "ideal" and "theory." "Ideal," whether used as noun or adjective, has connotations of perfection ("he is my ideal of manliness") but also of impossibility ("idealism" contrasted with "realism"); it can also be used, more loosely, to refer simply to an evaluative standard ("the ideal of gender equality is realized better in Sweden than in Afghanistan"). "Theory" refers both to a method and to its product: Are Rawls's two principles an ideal theory of justice, or is the method he uses to derive them that of ideal theory? More fundamentally, there is uncertainty about what ideal theory is theory of or about. We might think of political philosophy as seeking to tell us what the values that apply to the political sphere are and what they require. But that formulation is ambiguous. It can be given a practical reading, whereby its aim is to identify what actions need to be undertaken to promote, to respect, or fully to realize the values in question, or it can be interpreted epistemically, whereby the goal is systematic knowledge or understanding of the values, which includes but is not confined to knowledge or understanding of what would be required for them to be promoted, respected, or fully realized. Because most of the debate about the relevance or utility of ideal theory has taken place among those who accept the practical aim, we focus on that.

Other factors have compounded the difficulties. Rawls was talking specifically about justice, and much of the subsequent literature has focused on the value, or otherwise, of ideal theory in relation to that particular ideal. Our discussion follows suit, but of course other normative concepts, such as equality, democracy, or legitimacy might also be thought of as ideals, and, because the merits or demerits of ideal theories of (or "ideal theorizing" about) those concepts might be rather different, we address the issues at an appropriate level of generality. This attention to the specificity of the ideal under the spotlight is important because, in our view, even those who have been focusing on what they call "justice" have in fact been talking past one another somewhat. Given these cross-cutting complexities, it should be no surprise that methodological issues in political philosophy have commanded such attention and generated such confusion.

Our endeavor to bring some order to the chaos has the following structure. We first set out Rawls's conception and defense of ideal theory as necessary precursor to the kind of nonideal theory that can guide action in the real world, before considering and evaluating the critique of those, such as Amartya Sen, who insist that knowing what an ideally just society would look like is simply not helpful for that purpose. Having also addressed the complaint that the Rawlsian approach is ideological, and hence worse than useless, our discussion broadens out to compass the more wide-ranging critique of mainstream contemporary political philosophy leveled by so-called political realists. We then turn to Cohen's very different objection—that Rawls's ideal theory of justice is too tailored to empirical circumstance—before concluding with an attempt to identify the variety of different things that might be conceived as nonideal theory. Ideal theory may be understood in many different ways, but nonideal theory fares little better.

1. Ideal Theory in Rawls

For Rawls, ideal theory contrasts with nonideal theory and identifies a limitation in the scope of his theory of justice.[1] Both kinds of theory attempt to identify principles that should regulate basic social institutions for the sake of justice. How do they differ? The first and fundamental difference is that ideal theory assumes "strict compliance," that is, that "(nearly) everyone strictly complies with . . . the principles of justice" (2001, 13). Nonideal theory, by contrast, tells us how to deal with noncompliance. It thus "comprises such topics as the theory of punishment, the doctrine of just war, and the justification of the various ways of opposing unjust regimes, ranging from civil disobedience and conscientious objection to militant resistance and revolution" (1999a, 8).

Rawls gives the impression, at times, that the distinction between ideal and nonideal theory simply reduces to whether a theory assumes strict or only partial compliance. Thus, he speaks of "[i]deal, or strict compliance, theory" (2001, 13) and, even more strikingly, introduces the concept of ideal theory for the first time exclusively with reference to the problem of compliance (1999a, 7–8). However, ideal theory has a second feature: It "assumes strict compliance and works out the principles that characterize a well-ordered society under favorable circumstances" (1999a, 216). The second difference between ideal and nonideal theory, then, is that the former assumes favorable circumstances.

Favorable circumstances are the "conditions that, provided the political will exists, make a constitutional regime possible" (Rawls 2001, 101). They are favorable in that they can sustain a constitutional democracy, which is, for Rawls, what a well-ordered society needs to be. The relevant conditions do not include "political will," but they do include "historical, economic and social conditions," such as "economic means, . . . education, or the many skills needed to run a democratic regime" (2001, 47). Clearly, distinguishing social conditions from political will is no easy task, but Rawls's basic point is clear: Ideal theory can, and should, assume that the broad socioeconomic conditions do not preclude the possibility of a just (well-ordered) society.

The assumptions of strict compliance and favorable conditions can then be seen as jointly necessary to delineate ideal theory. Nonideal theory, in turn, deals with obstacles to a well-ordered society due to injustice (partial compliance) and due to socioeconomic limitations (unfavorable circumstances). Both of the assumptions of ideal theory are idealizing in the sense that they are insensitive to the realities of the world: No matter what facts obtain in the world, ideal theory assumes strict compliance and favorable circumstances. The assumption of strict compliance is, in addition, idealizing in the sense that it is bound to depart from facts about any contemporary society: no society is currently characterized by full compliance with the requirements of justice (or any other norm). Favorable circumstances, by contrast, are thought by Rawls to be relatively prevalent in the modern world.

However, while the two assumptions of ideal theory are insensitive to the actually existing levels of compliance and socioeconomic conditions, Rawls limits how far the assumptions can, in fact, depart from the constraints of the real word. For ideal theory must, as he explains, stay within the realm of what is "realistically practicable" (2001, 13); even if it delineates a distant vision, it must remain a "realistic utopia" (1999b, 11–12). In essence, the assumptions of ideal theory, even when they depart from real-world conditions, must remain within the realm of what is possible.

But Rawls does not stop there. The assumption of strict compliance is not a carte blanche to assume any feasible level of compliance, no matter how psychologically burdensome it might be to comply with the proposed principles. The task of ideal theory is to identify requirements that people can comply with given "merely" their sense of justice, not their capacity for moral heroism. Ideal theory ought to take into account "[t]he general facts of moral psychology" and filter out principles that could be complied with "only with great difficulty" (Rawls 1999a, 126). Rawls distinguishes, in fact, between the requirements of his ideal theory of justice and those of the moralities of "the saint and the hero" (1999a, 419). The assumption of strict compliance is really, then, the assumption of strict nonheroic compliance. Similarly, to assume "favorable circumstances" is by no means to assume "the best possible circumstances"; it is the task of ideal theory to deal with socioeconomic contingencies that make justice harder to achieve.

With this basic account of ideal theory in place, we can ask about its point: why make such idealizing assumptions? One answer is that if our interest is to find out what perfect justice requires, we must assume strict compliance; in the absence of strict compliance with the requirements of justice, perfect justice cannot hold. The assumption of favorable circumstances is then introduced to put aside the problem that a perfectly just society is made impossible by socioeconomic conditions. But this leads to a further question: Why ask what perfect justice requires if our aim is not simply to satisfy our intellectual curiosity but to guide our actions? Rawls's answer is that ideal theory is a necessary precursor to nonideal theory. It provides "the only basis for the systematic grasp of these more pressing problems" (1999a, 8).

It does this in two ways. First, it identifies the objective at which nonideal theory ought to aim and thereby gives nonideal theory its ultimate target (the target role). As Rawls puts it, "until the ideal is identified . . . nonideal theory lacks an objective, an aim, by reference to which its queries can be answered" (1999b, 90). In its target role, then, ideal theory helps nonideal theory answer the question: "What shall we do here and now given the ideal end point that we want to reach?" Second, ideal theory helps us assess the urgency of injustice we face in the real, nonideal world (the urgency role). For Rawls, the most grievous injustices are "identified by the extent of the deviation from perfect justice" (1999a, 216). In its urgency role, then, ideal theory helps nonideal theory answer the question: "Which of the injustices we face here and now are the most urgent?" That said, he is careful not to oversell how well ideal theory can fulfill its urgency role in nonideal circumstances. As he warns us, "Of course, this idea is extremely rough. The measure of departures from the ideal is left importantly to intuition" (1999a, 216).

Rawls's own example can be used to illustrate both roles. He considers the application of the fundamental principle of justice of his ideal theory—that of equal basic liberties for all—in a situation of war. He admits, for example, that a society that had previously shot prisoners of war would do better to agree to hold them as nonhereditary slaves instead. The sacrifices of basic liberty are justified "when this is required to transform a less fortunate society into one in which all the basic liberties can be fully enjoyed." The liberty principle of ideal theory acts here as a target. But it also acts as an evaluative standard—fulfilling the urgency role of ideal theory—for Rawls argues that this system of slavery is not justified by giving up on the ideal of equal liberty but because the new system preserves it, as "all run the risk of capture in war" (1999a, 217–18).

Importantly, Rawls is clear that the requirements of ideal theory are never to be followed without regard for the actual circumstances—as opposed to the conditions assumed by ideal theory—and that the requirements should still inform—while not rigidly prescribing—what is to be done in those circumstances.

2. Is Ideal Theory Useful, Useless, or Worse Than Useless?

Is Rawls right that knowing the content of ideal theory is needed before we can know what is required of us under our actual, nonideal, circumstances? Is ideal theory in any sense a prerequisite for nonideal theory?

Amartya Sen (2006, 2009) thinks not. To judge what justice requires of us here and now, all we need is the ability to compare the relative justice, and injustice, of the options available to us. Knowing what a perfectly just society would look like is neither necessary nor sufficient for that. As he puts it, "[t]he characterization of spotless justice does not entail any delineation whatever of how diverse departures from spotlessness can be compared and ranked" (2006, 220; cf 2009, 99) and "[t]he possibility of having an identifiably perfect alternative does not indicate that it is necessary, or indeed useful, to refer to it in judging the relative merits of two other alternatives" (2009, 102). Nonideal theory involves a *comparative* approach—we need to compare the justice of the different options within the feasible set—rather than a *transcendental* approach, which would involve the assessment of those options in the light of the picture of justice generated under the idealized assumptions. To climb the highest mountain within range, we do not need to know that Everest is the highest mountain in the world but which mountains are within range and how to compare them to each other. Similarly, if justice not mountaineering is our aim, we can easily judge, for example, that the elimination of extreme poverty would constitute progress toward justice without knowing what principles of justice would be recommended by ideal theory.

Directly challenging Rawls's claim (1999a, 8) that ideal theory "provides . . . the only basis for the systematic grasp of these more pressing problems" of nonideal theory, this objection accuses it of irrelevance or redundancy. If we are interested in promoting justice here and now, ideal theory is useless. For Sen,

> The answers that a transcendental approach to justice gives—or can give—are quite distinct and different from the type of concerns that engage people in discussions on injustice and justice in the world, for example, iniquities of hunger, illiteracy, torture, arbitrary incarceration, or medical exclusion as particular social features that need remedying. The focus of these engagements tends to be on the ways and means of advancing justice—or reducing injustice—in the world by remedying these inequities, rather than on looking only for the simultaneous fulfilment of the entire cluster of perfectly just societal arrangements demanded by a particular transcendental theory. (2006, 218)

We address the objection from uselessness shortly, but this passage hints also at a stronger charge: by focusing on "spotless justice," ideal theory distracts attention from these urgent real-world injustices, and is thus actually counterproductive.

This charge is explicitly leveled by Charles W. Mills. He accepts that "the problem does not inhere in exploration of the ideal, since all moral theory necessarily deals with the ideal in some sense. The problem is the exploration of the ideal as an end in itself without ever turning to the question of what is morally required in the context of the radically deviant *non-ideal* actuality" (Pateman and Mills 2007, 118). Mills's "without ever" overstates the case since in fact few theorists completely neglect problems of nonideal theory; some of the most influential contributors to ideal theory have also proposed solutions to real-world problems.[2]

But Mills goes further, claiming that ideal theory, especially the Rawlsian invocation of a hypothetical contract, is ideological: By distracting attention from actually existing injustice—Mills is concerned particularly with racial injustice—such theory conserves the status quo. Wondering how political philosophers in the United States can be, as he alleges, so "indifferent" to flagrant racial injustice, he suggests as a significant contributory cause "the hegemony of 'ideal theory' in political philosophy" (Pateman and Mills 2007, 107); stronger yet is his claim that the effect and the theoretical method are causally related: "[T]he theory was constructed to *evade* these [racial] problems . . . this methodological decision *itself* demonstrates Rawls's lack of concern" (258; emphases in original). Contractualist approaches can be applied to real-world circumstances and yield radical results, but, for Mills, the "conservative deployment [of the contract] is a result not of its intrinsic features but of its use by a privileged white male group hegemonic in political theory who have had no motivation to extrapolate its logic" (104).

Assessing motivational claims of this kind is hazardous, but the suggestion that those not enduring the daily experience of injustice are less likely to be impatient at the prolonged attention to issues in ideal theory, and less likely to be motivated to develop the kind of nonideal theory that directly addresses that injustice, should be taken seriously. The core defense of that prolonged attention, as we have seen, is that ideal theory is the necessary precursor to any serious attempt to engage with the pressing problems of injustice in the real world, which is exactly what Sen denies. We now tackle this crucial issue head on.

Suppose our ideal theory correctly identifies the long-term goal we want to achieve. We know from Rawls that this goal is realistic, in the sense that it is achievable, if only in the long, perhaps very long, run. As he says, ideal theory probes "the limits of practicable political possibility" (2001, 4, 13). Why would knowing this long-term goal be irrelevant to us here and now? It would be irrelevant if we were simply not interested in long-term goals, but this seems implausible. Or it would be irrelevant if we had reason to believe that all roads led, equally quickly and efficiently, to the long-term goal. But, for any given long-term goal, it seems very unlikely that it would be equally well pursued by all incremental short-term reforms. And in any case, how could we have reason to believe that all roads led to it if we had not yet identified what the long-term goal was? As A. J. Simmons (2010) has argued, without knowing our long term goal, a course of action that might appear to advance justice, and might indeed constitute a short-term improvement with respect to justice, might nonetheless make less likely, or perhaps even impossible, achievement of the long-term goal.

There is, then, some ambiguity in what it means for a reform to constitute an improvement with respect to, or progress toward, the ideal. In mountaineering, the climber who myopically takes immediate gains in height wherever she can is less likely to reach the summit than the one who plans her route carefully. The immediate gains do indeed take her higher—with respect to altitude she is closer to the top—but they may also be taking her away from her goal. The same is true of normative ideals. To eliminate an injustice in the world is surely to make the world more just, but it could also be to take us further away from, not closer toward, the achievement of a just society. Rawls, as we have seen, sees ideal theory as having both a "target" role and an "urgency" role, each of which can guide us when we engage in nonideal theory: It tells us where we are trying to get to in the long run, but it also informs our justice-promoting attempts here and now by providing the basis on which to evaluate the relative importance or urgency of the various ways in which the world deviates from the ideal. Even if Sen is right that we do not need ideal theory to do the latter, Simmons is right that we do need it for the former.

We should be clear about the limits of this defense of ideal theory as providing the orientation for nonideal theory. For one thing, we can judge an ideal to be realistic, in Rawls's sense of "probing the limits of practical possibility" without judging its realization to be empirically likely, even in the very long term. It would be irrational to eschew certain immediate progress for the sake of a hugely ambitious vision that, though feasible, was vanishingly unlikely ever to be reached. Furthermore, we may well simply lack the information needed to judge how a potential short-term improvement relates to the long-term goal. Knowing what a realistically-ideally just society would look like is one thing, assembling the social science needed for us to know how to get there is quite another; charting the route to the just society is a good deal more hazardous than mapping the Himalayas. Again, then, skepticism about our capacity to make the relevant empirical predictions would support our taking gains where we can. If ideal theory provides us with a goal that is too remote or unlikely to make a difference to our judgments about what to do here and now, such theory will indeed seem useless in its target-setting role, and Sen's comparative incrementalism will stand as a model for nonideal theory. But we cannot assess the remoteness or (un)likelihood of the realistic ideal without *some* sense of what that realistic ideal is. Perhaps political philosophers have by now done enough work at the level of ideal theory. If so, that does not make ideal theory useless; the claim is rather that we already have (enough of) it.

3. Ideal Theory and Political Realism

More radical criticisms of Rawls's approach have been delivered by a loose grouping of philosophers (and antiphilosophers) united by a concern that the dominant currents in contemporary political philosophy fail adequately to engage with the realities of politics. Not all their claims are formulated as hostile specifically to ideal theory, and even where they are what they mean by that term sometimes bears only a loose relation to what Rawls intends by it. Indeed, although Rawls is standardly presented as the exemplar of the kind of political philosophizing to which they object, their critique encompasses the very different contributions of philosophers such as Nozick and Habermas. Nonetheless, their insistence that the mode of political philosophy that currently holds sway is unrealistic—utopian, naïve, overambitious, idealistic—and, for some, dangerously so, is often treated as a critique of ideal theory (Galston 2010).

In our view, many realist criticisms of ideal theory simply overlook the distinction between ideal and nonideal theory, and end up criticizing the former for not being the latter. Erroneously attributing to their opponents the views that the recommendations delivered by ideal theory should directly guide political action, and serve as bases for the evaluation of political actors, whatever their context and circumstances, they rightly criticize both claims. As we have seen, it's precisely because ideal theory does not immediately translate into such recommendations and evaluative criteria that nonideal theory is needed; it fills the gap, as it were, between the theoretical ideal and political reality. Putting such misguided objections to one side, then, the more interesting and important challenge to the Rawlsian picture goes deeper.

That picture is accused of conceiving political philosophy as "applied ethics" (Geuss 2008) or of what Bernard Williams calls "political moralism," according to which "political theory is something like applied morality" (Williams 2005, 2). The complaint here is not merely that political philosophers fail adequately to acknowledge the resistances afforded by political reality to the realization of their ideal theory, and hence the scale of the challenge facing nonideal theory. There is a deeper skepticism here about the very idea that moral or ethical theorizing can provide justificatory or evaluative criteria relevant to politics. Though often formulated as a critique of ideal theory, this challenges not merely the point of theorizing about an ideally just (or democratic or equal or legitimate) society but doubts the enterprise of political philosophy engaging in the explication of "moral ideals" at all.

One line of argument worries specifically about the application to political conduct of moral or ethical theories developed for individuals in abstraction from distinctively political concerns. Politics, on this view, should not be seen as just another sphere of activity to which such theories can be applied, and in whose terms political agency can be evaluated, but as requiring distinct kinds of conduct, with their own norms. But the specificity of "the political" is in fact a key issue within liberal political philosophy itself. Rawls, for example, explicitly denies that his theory of justice should be understood as "applied moral philosophy," precisely because "[p]olitical philosophy has its own distinctive features and problems" (2001, 14), and his claims about the continuity, or otherwise, between the reasons that can or should guide individuals in their private and in their public or political lives have commanded a good deal of attention. Moreover, realists' emphasis on the dark side of politics, on problems of dirty hands, their skepticism about expansive theories of human rights, and so on, may better be understood as first-order claims within moral or ethical theory than more thoroughgoing doubts about the propriety of bringing moral or ethical standards to bear on politics (Floyd 2010).

How skeptical about political morality do realists want to be? Of those who self-identify as realists, Geuss comes closest to endorsing radical skepticism, since for him, it seems, abstract moral standards, and the intuitions on which they are constructed, are inevitably ideological. Inspecting and interrogating political reality is, for Geuss, the only way to expose power relations and ideological distortions. But entirely to eschew moral standards would be to leave us without the resources needed morally to evaluate both the power relations thereby exposed and the ways of organizing society those allegedly ideologically distorted intuitions recommend. Since Geuss himself makes ethical judgments, and must ultimately appeal to his own ethical intuitions, he cannot wholeheartedly embrace skepticism about such judgments.

Bernard Williams's version of "political realism" is more modest in its skepticism about the moral standards properly applicable to politics. For Williams, "the first political question" is the Hobbesian one: how to secure "order, protection, safety, trust, and the conditions of cooperation" (2005, 3). But not all solutions to that question are "acceptable"; to qualify as legitimate, in order to be more than successful domination, a state must be able to offer a justification of its power to each subject, including to those radically disadvantaged groups within it. Williams does not deny that this "Basic Legitimation Demand" (2005, 4) is itself a moral principle. What it is not, he insists, is a moral principle that is prior to politics. To solve the problem of order by force alone is not to achieve a political solution; politics is, by definition, an alternative to mere force. The trouble with political moralism is not that it asserts moral claims *tout court*, but that it fails to recognize the specificity of the moral issue specific to, or inherent in, politics. Liberals like Rawls may identify the political as a distinct sphere, in which appeal to comprehensive moral doctrines violates the constraints of public reason, but, for Williams, "political liberalism" is itself grounded in an overambitiously moralized, and idealized, conception of political relationships.

This theme of liberal political philosophy's excessive and naïve ambitions pervades realist thinking. Rawls's well-ordered society, in which all citizens comply with the demands of justice and accept as legitimate the state's demands on them, or Habermas's deliberative democratic ideal, which presents democracy as the expression of autonomy or self-government, are seen as utopian, aiming unrealistically high. Political philosophy in ideal theory mode, it is claimed, Quixotically aspires to a society where citizens' inevitable disagreements do not result in conflict, one in which there is universal compliance with demanding norms of political morality; it attributes to political agents cognitive and moral powers far exceeding anything human history could lead us to regard as remotely plausible. Such idealism is not merely futile but positively dangerous. Only at our peril do we neglect the fragility of social order, fail to celebrate less lofty accomplishments as the achievements that they really are (witness Rawls's denigration of a "mere modus vivendi"), and overlook the fact that expecting too much of people tends to tyranny. In seeking the impossible, we risk losing what we have.

But we have already seen that Rawls's ideal theory is intended precisely to identify a "realistic utopia." It is crucial to his view not only that the goal is possible, in the literal sense that it can be achieved by human beings, but that it is possible without assuming heroic motivations. So Rawls takes issues of feasibility to be internal to the ideal theory project. Perhaps realist critics think Rawls is simply wrong about what human beings are capable of; perhaps they think the kind of well-ordered society he describes is simply beyond the feasible set. If so, that would be a coherent objection to the content of his ideal theory; he would indeed be offering as our lodestar a target that we could never achieve, and that might perhaps be unhelpful, or even dangerous. But it would not be an objection to the very project of constructing an ideal theory in his sense.

So we can ask realists how unambitious they think the long-term goal needs to be in order to qualify as "realistic." Do they want to deny that human beings *can* be motivated to comply with (nonheroically demanding) principles of justice? Do they think it *impossible* for them to accept the legitimacy of procedural solutions to their disagreements and conflicts of interests (and to accept those solutions because they accept justifications of the kind offered by political philosophers)? And we can ask them too how conservative or risk-averse they want us to be when, as we switch from ideal to nonideal theory, we evaluate the short-run options, and associated probabilities, within the feasible set. Once we have put to rest the misunderstanding that those who engage in ideal theory intend it directly to apply to existing circumstances, realists are surely going to be in the business of making judgments on the same moral and empirical issues as those they criticize. The content of the judgments may differ—realists may aim lower in the long, medium, and short run. But the differing judgments would confront the same issues.

4. Is Ideal Theory Too Realistic?

For G. A. Cohen, Rawls's ideal theory of justice does not qualify as a philosophically fundamental theory of justice. Rawls's willingness to incorporate empirical facts into his theorizing means that, rather than identifying fundamental principles of justice, he can generate only secondary "principles of regulation." Cohen's argument does not challenge the suggestion that ideal theory in the Rawlsian sense is a necessary precursor to the kind of nonideal theory that should guide our action in the real world. He can happily grant that feasibility constraints should importantly influence both our long-term goal and the principles that should inform our attempts to pursue it. He is interested primarily in the question of how we should understand the structure of the justification of our action-guiding principles. Cohen's critique, then, is misunderstood if it is seen as a contribution to the debate over the merits of ideal theory. Still, the question of the fact sensitivity of principles in political philosophy has become entangled with that debate, so it warrants some attention here.

According to Cohen, rules of regulation are the principles that we should adopt in order to regulate our affairs, and such rules should be sensitive to facts. The principles of justice that are the output of Rawls's ideal theory are rules of this kind and should not be confused with the fundamental normative principles that are necessary to justify these rules. These fundamental principles, argues Cohen, are free of—that is, not grounded in—any (empirical) facts at all; they are principles that hold no matter what the facts are or are assumed to be. Cohen's argument goes like this: Of any principle that is grounded in facts we can ask why the relevant facts ground it, and an intuitively satisfactory answer to this question will require an appeal to a further principle. Only once we reach a principle that is not grounded in any facts can we treat it as fundamental. For example, take the principle P1: "Human bodies should be treated with caution." Why should we accept P1? A plausible answer will invoke the fact F1 that "human bodies are liable to pain." But why is this fact relevant? Surely only because of some further principle P2 according to which "absent other considerations, if a being is liable to pain, one should not cause it pain." P2 is not grounded in F1: If human bodies were not liable to pain, that would not give us reason to abandon P2. That said, some may subscribe not to P2 but to a version of it P2* according to which "absent other considerations, if a human being is liable to pain, one should not cause it pain"; but notice that P2* is also independent of whether F1 is true or false. P2 or P2* might be grounded in further facts, in which case we will need to ask, once more, why these facts ground these principles and in answer, we will need to invoke a further principle. We need to repeat this process until we reach a principle that is not grounded in any facts. That will be the fundamental principle that grounds P2/P2* and P1 (Cohen 2008, 245).

It may be tempting to think of Cohen as insisting on a "super ideal" theory of justice. But, unlike Rawls, Cohen does not ask us to make any idealized assumptions. He is after principles that hold no matter what assumptions about compliance, circumstances, and all other facts, we should make; fundamental principles apply not to circumstances different from ours but to all circumstances, including ours. And he is not suggesting that facts are irrelevant to our reasoning about such principles: His thesis denies that facts can ground fundamental principles, not that reflecting on facts is helpful when we try to discover what these principles are—it is about the structure of normative beliefs, not their genesis. Finally, Cohen's point is not that fundamental principles better fulfill the roles that Rawls accords his ideal theory. He accepts that facts are relevant to the principles that we should adopt to guide our actions and structure our institutions, both here and now *and* in our long-term goal. As he puts it, "facts are of course indispensable to the justification of rules of regulation," and this applies also to the rules to regulate the "ideal" society (Cohen 2008, 265). Cohen simply does not address Rawls's view that consideration of what would be required of us in idealized, counterfactual circumstances is needed before we can properly judge what is required of us here and now. For Cohen, action-guiding principles in both ideal and nonideal theory need to be grounded in fact-insensitive, fundamental principles.

Moreover, much of the apparent disagreement dissolves once we see that Rawls and Cohen understand the term "justice" very differently—or, perhaps, that what they really disagree about is what kind of thing justice *is*. For Cohen, justice is a philosophical ideal truths about which can be identified by careful reflection on intuition; whether, how, and to what extent, it can or even should be realized in the world, given that it conflicts with other values, are all separate and further questions. For Rawls, justice has a "social" or "problem-solving" role; its identification involves all things considered judgments about the relative importance of different kinds of value, and facts about human nature properly enter into the formulation even of our ideal theory of justice. We cannot here assess this far-reaching dispute, but one aspect of it demands discussion. Cohen's claim that fundamental principles of justice should be insensitive to facts implies that truths about what justice is, or about how the world would need to be in order to be just, can be identified quite separately from knowing whether human beings, or the world they find themselves in, are such that justice can be realized. This seems to diverge not only from the Rawlsian conception of ideal theory, which probes the limits of practical possibility but does not—or at least aims not to—exceed them but also from the widely accepted dictum that "ought implies can." If an action, or a state of affairs, is simply not possible, how can it be recommended or required by justice?

The suggestion that ideals as such might be unrealizable is not in itself problematic. Discovering, for example, that it will always be true of some human beings that they simply cannot engage in the kind of reasoning that are central to conceptions of deliberative democracy might well be cause for regret, and it would presumably affect both our conception of the democratic goal and the means by which we might choose to pursue it; but there does not seem to be any incoherence in concluding on that basis that a fully democratic society cannot be realized. The same seems true of the suggestion that we can never fully realize the ideal of equality—maybe we inevitably lack the information we would need for its realization. Perhaps justice can be conceived along similar lines; it is regrettable if the world is such that we can never achieve an ideally just society but, insofar as its unattainability is due to sheer impossibility, that does not mean that anybody is failing to do what they ought to do. We ought, of course—and perhaps we have duties—to do what we can to promote or respect the ideal. And if the world were other than it is, we might indeed have "oughts" or duties to do what is, in our actual circumstances, impossible. But there is no conceptual incoherence in thinking an ideally just society to be unrealizable (Cohen 2008, 254).

The problem with this approach to justice is that we are left with the conceptual possibility of an unjust society in which nobody is doing anything wrong. If no one is failing to do what they can, there can be regret but no complaint—not, at least, against other people. (One may complain about one's fate, and perhaps conceive oneself as the victim of agentless, cosmic, injustice but the "complaint" here is somewhat metaphorical.) To think of a society as unjust when, for example, individuals are not getting their fair distributive share, and the reason they are not getting it is that we cannot make it happen that they do—perhaps we lack the information we would need to assess what their fair share was, perhaps they are simply physically inaccessible to us—is to create a gap between the idea of injustice, on the one hand, and the idea that some are treating others unjustly, on the other. Some will find that too high a price to pay.

5. What Do We Want from Nonideal Theory?

Much hostility to ideal theory is best understood as a demand not merely for more nonideal theory but for more nonideal theory of a specific kind: theory to guide action in our current circumstances. Rawlsian ideal theory involves two key idealizations, or idealizing assumptions—full compliance and favorable circumstances—but in principle there are as many variants of ideal theory, and of nonideal theory, as there are kinds and degrees of constraint that we might assume away or take as given (Hamlin and Stemplowska 2012). We could, for example, theorize nonideally about the requirements of justice (or democracy or equality) in a world where informational problems were soluble but the political will was lacking, or where full compliance was forthcoming but economic conditions were unfavorable. The theories we produced would remain action-guiding in form, even if they were not intended to guide action in our circumstances. Those impatient with ideal theory are not, typically, interested in that kind of counterfactual; they want guidance about what to do here and now.

Rawls's claim that ideal theory is a necessary precursor to nonideal theory is clearly crucial. If he is right, then its critics' impatience is misplaced. Ideal theory may look utopian in the worst sense, and hence useless (or worse), but, as long as the goal it posits is indeed a realistic utopia, then that kind of theory should not be regarded as an optional extra; the intellectual resources devoted to it are not self-indulgent or wasteful. We need to know the goal before we can form an all-things-considered evaluation of transitional steps in its direction; immediate improvements may take us take us further away from our target, in which case we will face difficult trade-offs. Though there are issues about our ability to map possible futures well enough for this kind of consideration to have great weight, though the likelihood of achieving the goal is a very different matter from its possibility, and though it might be argued that we already know enough about the goal to be able to assess whether immediate steps are unambiguously steps in its direction, this defense of ideal theory as setting the target is compelling.

What of the distinct suggestion that we need ideal theory in order to compare options within the feasible set? As Sen has pointed out, it is implausible to think that we need to know what a perfectly just society would be like in order to evaluate the relative justice of any two options. To be sure, we cannot do without philosophy, whatever Geuss may suggest to the contrary (Swift 2008). And when we engage in philosophy particular forms of idealization are extremely useful in helping us to disentangle, clarify, and sometimes to weigh the competing values that can then be applied to the feasible set. We need, that is, "theory of ideals", and idealization helps us get it (Stemplowska 2008, 326–29; Hamlin and Stemplowska 2012); in our view, much philosophical work that is presented as ideal theory can readily be construed as contributing to the theory of ideals. But Sen is right to claim that we can engage in many relevant comparisons without having an ideal theory in Rawls's sense.

Some critics of ideal theory seem to want not merely nonideal theory addressed to our circumstances, but concrete, determinate recommendations about what we should actually *do* given those circumstances (Farrelly 2007). This is itself a very specific demand. It is perfectly possible to work on nonideal theory at the abstract or philosophical level without applying it to particular contexts in a way that yields concrete proposals; such proposals typically involve careful identification of the empirical circumstances and estimates of the probabilities attaching to the consequences of various things that might be done in those circumstances. But one cannot develop concrete proposals without the philosophy—the theory of ideals—to identify the principles that should inform them.[3] Perhaps political philosophers could and should engage in the kind of social scientific research needed to deliver what we suspect that critics of ideal theory really want; perhaps, more weakly, they should at least engage with it (or, more weakly still, present their findings in ways that allow social scientists and policymakers to engage with them; Swift and White 2008). But we should be clear that to demand that political philosophers deliver concrete action-guidance is to ask them to do something more than philosophy.

The two kinds of idealization that characterize Rawls's ideal theory are very different, and there are correspondingly distinct issues for nonideal theory. Situations of partial compliance are those in which some are failing to comply with the demands of justice. Nonideal theory that focuses on the question of "what is the just way to answer injustice" (Rawls 1999a, 215) is crucial, and in our view underexplored, philosophical terrain. But it involves quite distinct issues from those raised by the question of what justice demands in circumstances that are unfavorable in other ways. The same applies to other ideals. We need to think about very different things when addressing people's failure to comply with the justified demands that democracy or equality make on them, on the one hand, and unfavorable circumstances that involve no moral failings, on the other. Insofar as the term "nonideal theory" obscures that distinction, it is liable to yield a confused agenda.

An ambiguity in what it means for a requirement to be "practical" or "action guiding" is also worth clarifying. A requirement remains action guiding even if we can know for certain that it will not be complied with. For, while "ought" does imply "can," it does not imply "is likely." One can correctly identify what it is that agents ought to do while being entirely hopeless about the prospect of their doing it. The practical question of how people ought to act may yield an answer that is not remotely practical in the sense of being something that we should realistically expect them to do. It is realistic for them to do it; we are not demanding the impossible. But, as an empirical prediction about their behavior, it is not realistic to believe they will—indeed, we may be sure that they will not. While of course we will want also to offer recommendations about how people ought to act given that they will not act as they really, or "ideally," ought to—that is the job of nonideal theory—it would be odd for political philosophers to desist from the business of telling people what they should be doing just because they know they are not going to do it (Estlund 2008, 2011a).

What is the point of coming up with action-guiding recommendations that we accept are not actually going to guide people's actions? Such recommendations may be practical in a philosophical sense, but do they have any value? One answer is that they may play an inspirational role. Even where we know that we will not do exactly what we should, knowing what that would be may help us get closer to it. A second answer challenges the conception of value implicit in the question (Estlund 2011b). Most of us accept that the work done by mathematicians, logicians, or historians has some value even where it is of no practical use. To be sure, we can sensibly ask how much value there is to that kind of work, but the idea that useless knowledge, whether in mathematics or political philosophy, has *no* value is deeply implausible. Perhaps learning in what ways the full realization of an ideal such as democracy or equality is beyond our reach tells us simply what we have reason to regret, and perhaps regret will make us sad. But sadness is a small price to pay for enlightenment.

We end with one more distinction—and an exhortation. The complaint that contemporary political philosophy fails to engage sufficiently with our actual empirical circumstances is typically formulated as a request for policies and institutions. But to issue even a specific policy recommendation to citizens generally, or to argue that a particular institutional arrangement is required, is not to recommend a specific action to any actually existing person. Because it is only individuals that act—policies are not enacted and institutions not established without individual human agents doing things to bring them about—such recommendations must be seen as addressed to individuals who know how to solve the relevant coordination problems, including the philosophically crucial issue of the duties to contribute to the bringing about of the collective, political, action that fall on differentially situated individual agents. That is itself a form of idealization. We can know what we collectively should be doing without knowing what any of us individually ought to be doing, so even the kind of nonideal theory that delivers concrete action-guidance for "us" remains unhelpfully ideal if it does that in the form of policies or institutional arrangements (Swift 2008). In our view, the critique of ideal theory will have been especially useful if its exhortation to a more immediately action-guiding role for political philosophy leads more attention to be focused on recommendations addressed to individual agents.

NOTES

We are grateful to David Estlund and Jonathan Quong for comments on a previous draft. Our thinking about these issues owes much to them and to Alice Baderin, Harry Brighouse, Matthew Clayton, G. A. Cohen, Alan Hamlin, Patrick Tomlin, Andrew Williams, and our co-participants in the European Consortium for Political Research Workshop on "Social Justice: Ideal Theory and Nonideal Circumstances," Helsinki, 2007.

1. See A. J. Simmons (2010) for the first and most complete attempt to systematize and defend Rawls's views.

2. For example, Ronald Dworkin is often seen as an arch exemplar of ideal theory, but the same book in which he sets out his highly idealized clam-shell auction explicitly discusses the transition from "the ideal ideal world of fantasy," through the "ideal real world, only somewhat less fantastic" to "the real real world" (Dworkin 2000, 169–80) and applies his ideal theory to pressing issues such as health care and affirmative action.

3. McMahan (2009) is a good example of highly abstract nonideal theory applied to unjust war. Murphy's (2000) book-length treatment of the implications of noncompliance for individuals' duties is conducted at an even higher level of abstraction.

REFERENCES

Cohen, G. A. 2008. *Rescuing Justice and Equality*. Cambridge, MA: Harvard University Press.
Dworkin, Ronald. 2000, *Sovereign Virtue*. Cambridge, MA: Harvard University Press.
Estlund, David. 2008. *Democratic Authority*. Princeton, NJ: Princeton University Press.
Estlund, David. 2011a. "Human Nature and the Limits (If Any) of Political Philosophy." *Philosophy & Public Affairs* 39: 207–37.
Estlund, David. 2011b. *Analyse & Kritik* 33 (2011) 395–416.

Farrelly, Colin. 2007. "Justice in Ideal Theory: A Refutation." *Political Studies* 55: 844–64.
Floyd. Jonathan. 2010. "Should Political Philosophy Be More Realistic?" *Res Publica* 16: 337–47.
Galston, William. 2010, "Realism in Political Theory." *European Journal of Political Theory* 9: 385–411.
Geuss, Raymond. 2008. *Philosophy and Real Politics*. Princeton, NJ: Princeton University Press.
Hamlin, Alan, and Zofia Stemplowska. 2012. "Ideal Theory, Nonideal Theory and the Theory of Ideals." *Political Studies Review* 10: 48–62.
McMahan, Jeff. 2009. *Killing in War*. Oxford: Oxford University Press.
Murphy, Liam. 2000. *Moral Demands in Nonideal Theory*. Oxford: Oxford University Press.
Pateman, Carole, and Charles Mills. 2007. *Contract and Domination*. Cambridge, UK: Polity Press.
Rawls, John. 1999a. *A Theory of Justice*, rev. ed. Cambridge, MA: Harvard University Press.
Rawls, John. 1999b. *The Law of Peoples*. Cambridge, MA: Harvard University Press.
Rawls, John. 2001. *Justice as Fairness: A Restatement*. Edited by Erin Kelly. Cambridge, MA: Harvard University Press.
Sen, Amartya. 2006, "What Do We Want from a Theory of Justice?" *Journal of Philosophy* 103: 215–38.
Sen, Amartya. 2009. *The Idea of Justice*. London: Allen Lane.
Simmons, A. J. 2010. "Ideal and Nonideal Theory." *Philosophy & Public Affairs* 38: 5–36.
Stemplowska, Zofia. 2008. "What's Ideal About Ideal Theory?" *Social Theory and Practice* 34: 319–40.
Swift, Adam. 2008. "The Value of Philosophy in Nonideal Circumstances." *Social Theory and Practice* 34: 363–87.
Swift, Adam, and Stuart White. 2008. "Political Theory, Social Science, and Real Politics." In *Political Theory: Methods and Approaches*. Edited by David Leopold and Marc Stears. Oxford: Oxford University Press.
Williams, Bernard. 2005. *In the Beginning Was the Deed: Realism and Moralism in Political Argument*. Princeton, NJ: Princeton University Press.

PART VI

In Retrospect

CHAPTER 21

RAWLS

LEIF WENAR

Are human beings "largely amoral, if not incurably cynical and self-centered" (Rawls 1993, lxii)? Must they be driven mostly, as Hobbes said, by "a perpetual and restless desire of power after power" (Hobbes 1994, 58)?

For the young John Rawls, whether man can be moral was a question on which human existence turned. In his early 20s, Rawls had been considering the priesthood. Instead, he found himself a soldier in the vicious Pacific theater of World War II. The horrors of the war exploded the foundations of his Christian belief. Rawls could make no sense of a good God who creates beings that are inherently corrupt, much less ones predestined to cause the atrocities he saw around him. A sniper's bullet grazed his skull; his troop train passed through the devastation that had been Hiroshima; he heard early reports about the Holocaust. Was this the world to which human nature condemns us? Or is another future possible for us?

> The great evils of human history—unjust war and oppression, religious persecution and the denial of liberty of conscience, starvation and poverty, not to mention genocide and mass murder—follow from political injustice, with its own cruelties and callousness ... Once the gravest forms of political injustice are eliminated by following just (or at least decent) social policies and establishing just (or at least decent) basic institutions, these great evils will eventually disappear. (Rawls 1999, 6–7)

Rawls devoted the rest of his life to imagining a moral order. Within a just society, Rawls thought, the great evils would no longer torment man. And a world of such societies could at last be at peace with itself.

For justice and peace to be within our reach, our nature must permit them. Humans must be not irredeemably amoral, cynical, self-centered. Rather, "human beings must have a moral nature, not of course a perfect such nature, yet one that can understand, act on, and be sufficiently moved by a reasonable political conception of right and justice to support a society guided by its ideals and principles" (Rawls 1993, lxii). Rawls saw his life's work as imagining a moral order realistic enough to redeem a credence in man's moral nature. Further, as we will see, Rawls held that belief in man's goodness can itself be crucial for keeping human evil from being human destiny.

Hobbes said of himself that he was born twins with fear. After the war, Rawls's constant companion was hope: hope that humans can do the right thing for its own sake, hope that citizens can favor the common over division—and so hope that man can sustain a just society and a peaceable world.

1. Justice as Fairness

Rawls's hope is not that humans will always act rightly (we know they will not) but that in the right circumstances they can act rightly—reliably, and for its own sake. His hope is that there can be a form of society that fosters a *sense of justice* in those growing up within it: a willingness to act fairly toward other people, even at the cost of narrow self-interest.

Rawls calls this the challenge of *stability*. In a stable society citizens' sense of justice will regulate their pursuit of their own interests, and—what is more—citizens will feel that acting justly is part of a good life for them. What would a society be like that will call forth in all its citizens a strong, dependable, and reflectively endorsed desire to do right?

Rawls's answer is that stability can be achieved by a social order that proclaims the value of each and every one of its members—openly, and at the deepest level. "The most stable conception of justice," Rawls says, "is one that is perspicuous to our reason, congruent with our good, and rooted not in abnegation but in affirmation of the self" (1971, 261).

Rawls's description of what such a society would look like—his theory of a just and stable society—is called *justice as fairness*. Justice as fairness is constructed around a moral vision of people and of how people should relate to each other. Rawls hopes that we will see ourselves in this picture and be drawn to its depiction of what our lives together could be. If this vision is accurate and attractive, then the challenge of stability can be met.

The Conceptions of Person and Society

In Rawls's language, the moral vision of people and their proper social relations is built on a *conception of the person* and a *conception of society*, the two most basic ideas of justice as fairness. Individuals are conceived as *free and equal, reasonable and rational*, and society as *a fair scheme of cooperation*.

Citizens in Rawls's vision of the just society are free and equal in that each has political standing in their own name: Citizens are not property (like slaves) or dependents (like children), and their political status does not turn on their membership in some group (like a church). Each person can take responsibility for his or her own life, and all have the same basic abilities to take part in the society's common life.

Rawls describes the just society as a fair scheme of cooperation. This emphasis on cooperation might not resonate with us on a bad day, watching coworkers fighting to climb the ladder and politicians sent into battle by opposed special interests. Immersed in today's struggles, the best we might expect from our society is a predictable system of competition, where self-interest cancels self-interest well enough that no person or group ever gains too much power.

Yet that is the cynical view of humans and society that Rawls is attempting to replace with his more hopeful vision. Rawls accepts that citizens want more good things for themselves—more rights, more freedoms, more authority in their jobs, more money, more respect in their society (these are what Rawls calls *primary goods*). People are, in this sense, *rational*. Yet citizens in Rawls's moral vision are not only rational, they are also *reasonable*. Reasonable citizens are willing to do their part to uphold fair principles so long as others do so. Reasonable citizens will support an overarching system of cooperation, in which any competitive institutions (markets, politics) respect and promote a distribution of primary goods that is fair to all.

In Rawls's moral conception, society is fair at a deep level. First, citizens see each other as fundamentally equal, regardless of accidents of birth. It is unfair for citizens to get more power or opportunities only because they are white or male, for example. It is unfair for citizens to get better jobs or more pay only because they are fortunate enough to be born to parents who could send them to better schools, or only because they happen to have skills that the economy needs right now. The basic rules of society should not favor some citizens over others solely because they have been lucky enough to have wealthy families or to have more potential for developing some marketable skill. This is why, Rawls says, libertarianism must be rejected as an ideal of a just society—its most basic rules for determining "who gets what" track factors irrelevant to the status of equal citizenship, like how much money a child inherits or whether her genes give her movie-star looks.

There is an ongoing effort (known as luck egalitarianism) to base political theory on a Rawlsian negative precept that *it is unfair for social shares to be based on luck* (Lippert-Rasmussen 2009). Yet Rawls uses his negative precept only in a preparatory stage—only to clear the ground of unfairness. The ground so cleared, Rawls then begins his second, substantive stage, setting out his robust positive ideal of fair cooperation. The positive ideal is an ideal of social unity. It is an ideal of a society in which equal citizens "agree to share one another's fates" (Rawls 1971, 102).

In Rawls's ideal, citizens start with a presumption of equality: All are equal, so prima facie all should get the same. Yet in a Rawlsian society, citizens view the natural and social differences among them as a resource for everyone. The social system may offer more rewards to those more fortunately endowed—not because the fortunate merit more in some elemental sense, but because unequal rewards can work to everyone's benefit. For example, raising the salaries of doctors can enable medical students to invest in better training and having better-trained doctors helps everyone in society, including those with the lowest wages. It can be fair for doctors to earn more—not because doctors deserve a reward for their high IQs but because their earning more creates a better society for all citizens.

In Rawls's ideal of a fair system of cooperation, citizens "share one another's fates" in arranging society so that the good fortune of some works to the advantage of all, including the least-advantaged. This is an ideal of citizens who relate to each other as equals on a deep level. Also, returning to the theme of stability, it is an ideal that affirms the value of each citizen on its face.

The Original Position

Rawls's vision is inspiring but abstract—it is not yet clear what it comes to. Many kinds of political theory, after all, claim to be grounded in freedom, equality, and fairness. Rousseauean theories centered on the political powers of the *demos* claim to give expression to freedom and equality, yet so do Lockean theories that emphasize the private rights of the individual. Freedom and equality form the stuff of socialist criticisms of constitutional democracy—and also of conservative critiques of the welfare state (Rawls 2001, 2, 8).

To turn abstract ideals into distinctive principles of justice, Rawls asks us to join him in performing a thought experiment, the *original position*. With the original position, Rawls aims to transform the hard question, "What are fair terms of cooperation among free and equal citizens?" into the more manageable question, "What would free and equal citizens *agree to* under fair conditions?"

Were we all to gather in real life to agree on the basic rules for our society, the resulting agreement would surely not be fair. Some of us would be richer and so could bribe others to shade the rules in our favor; others would be physically stronger and could negotiate with threats. With the original position Rawls asks us to imagine all of these factors disruptive of fairness removed. We imagine a situation in which each citizen is present as truly free and equal, and we carefully control the conditions so that these citizens are situated exactly fairly with respect to each other. When we work out what free and equal people would agree to when fairly situated, we will see this agreement as defining our ideal because it embodies the ideas of freedom, equality, and fairness in their purest forms.

Rawls constructs the original position from the basic idea of a fair system of cooperation among free and equal citizens. Rawls models fairness through blindness with a *veil of ignorance*: No one knows whether they are male or female, young or old, highly talented or not, part of a majority or a minority race. (Here we see Rawls's negative precept at work: Social shares should not be based on luck.) Citizens are free, each speaking in his or her own name, so each person in the original position speaks only for him or herself—not for anyone else or any group. Citizens are equal, and their worth as citizens is not relative to their wealth or strength, so no one in the original position can bribe or threaten another. All of these factors irrelevant to justice are kept out of the original position, leaving only free and equal persons in fair conditions to reach agreement. If each person tries to get the best deal for him or herself when unfairness is impossible, what will the resulting agreement be?

The Choice of Principles

What the persons (or the "parties") in the original position are agreeing on are the most fundamental principles for their society. These principles are much more general than the laws debated on a typical day in a legislature and even more general than most provisions in national constitutions. The parties are agreeing to the foundational terms of citizens' ongoing cooperation—principles by reference to which a constitution should be written and interpreted. They are agreeing to principles for regulating society's *basic structure* of institutions.

Rawls's main concern is whether the parties in the original position would agree to order their society by utilitarian principles. Maximizing utility is a salient aim in today's public policies. The political imperative to increase national economic growth, for example, as well as the pervasive cost-benefit analysis of public policies, are naturally seen as utilitarian in their rationale. Yet Rawls believes that given a choice, the parties would not go for utilitarianism, but rather for a different standard of justice: the principles of justice as fairness.

Justice as fairness is defined by two principles, and Rawls tests each principle against utilitarianism from the perspective of the original position. In the first test, Rawls asks whether the parties would prefer the utilitarian principle whose goal is the highest average level of well-being, or rather his first principle of equal basic rights and liberties:

> **First principle of justice as fairness**: Each person has the same indefeasible claim to a fully adequate scheme of equal basic liberties, which scheme is compatible with the same scheme of liberties for all. (Rawls 2001, 42)

Rawls's first principle requires that each citizen be secured equal rights of free speech and equal liberty of conscience, equal rights to free association as well as equal rights to vote and to hold public office. For these last two rights Rawls's principle requires not just formal political equality, but equally valuable political liberties: Citizens should have the same opportunities to influence the political process, and to hold public office, regardless of their social class (citizens' political liberties should have *fair value* as he puts it). Rawls means to prove that the parties in the original position would prefer his principle of equal basic rights and liberties to the utilitarian alternative of maximum aggregate welfare.

Rawls argues that each party would prefer to secure equal basic rights and liberties, rather than gambling with the utilitarian principle. The parties will rationally *maximin*: optimize the worst outcome that could befall them. While the utilitarian principle aims at the highest *average* level of welfare, it may be that the best way to boost the average is to curtail the liberties of some citizens for the sake of benefits to others. A societal majority might be much happier, for example, if certain minority religious groups were not eligible to hold positions of power in the government. Yet the parties, behind the veil of ignorance and so not knowing whether they are members of any majority or minority group, would not be willing to risk ending up in a society where their liberties are seriously infringed. To do so would not be to take their own deepest commitments seriously. Moreover, they reason that utility-based public discussions on basic rights would breed mutual suspicion and distrust, as different groups would put forward speculative arguments that average utility could be increased by limiting the liberties of other groups. The first principle of justice as fairness takes such divisive debates permanently off the public agenda, by publicly securing each citizen the same basic rights as every other. Each of the parties in the original position will see this fostering of mutual trust as good from a self-regarding perspective.

Having used the original position to confirm his first principle of equal basic rights and liberties, Rawls then uses it to argue for his second principle of justice, which regulates socio-economic goods such as the powers and positions of office, and wealth and income:

Second principle of justice as fairness: Social and economic inequalities are to satisfy two conditions:

a. They are to be attached to offices and positions open to all under conditions of fair equality of opportunity; and
b. They are to be to the greatest benefit of the least-advantaged members of society (the difference principle).

Fair equality of opportunity requires that citizens who have the same talents, and the same willingness to use those talents, should have the same educational and economic opportunities regardless of where they start in life. With this principle in operation, we should expect, for instance, that broad earnings categories come to be filled equally by people born into different social classes (one quarter of people with the highest earnings were born in the poorest quarter of the income distribution; one quarter were born into the richest quarter; and one quarter were born in each of the two classes in the middle).

The difference principle requires that social institutions be arranged so that any inequalities of wealth and income work to the advantage of all, and particularly to those who will be worst off. For example, if four possible economic systems produce the distributions of wealth and income in Table 21.1, the difference principle will favor the third because it is the system in which the least-advantaged do best.

Rawls evaluates his second principle against utilitarianism from the perspective of the original position with a second test. Would the parties prefer his two principles, or would they prefer his first principle plus average utilitarianism, constrained by some "social minimum" that is secured for all citizens (Rawls 2001, 119–34)?

Rawls argues that the parties will prefer his two principles. This time, Rawls says, the argument has nothing at all to do with maximin reasoning (Rawls 2001, 43 n3). Rather, the parties would prefer his second principle because it engenders a

Table 22.1

Economy	Least-Advantaged Group	Middle Group	Most-Advantaged Group
1	20	20	20
2	24	30	50
3	40	60	100
4	34	100	400

sense of reciprocity in society that is better for everyone. The utilitarian principle will be hard on the least-advantaged. They will rightly suspect that their well-being is being sacrificed to give more advantages to those already most favored; this will be hard on their self-respect, and on their willingness to act as fully cooperating members of society. Again, public debates among the classes over which economic policies will increase average utility, and where to set the social minimum, will tend to foment a social discord that dampens the prospects of all. Under the second principle, by contrast, all citizens work toward an economy that is evidently good for each person, with special attention to the good of those who do worst by it. A publicly reciprocal economic order will therefore be more stable. Overall, such an order will best promote the good of each.

The Institutions of Justice as Fairness

Having tested his two principles against utilitarianism and found them superior, Rawls describes institutions that would realize those principles. His ideal is a *property-owning democracy*. In a property-owning democracy, all citizens' basic rights and liberties are secured equally, and measures are taken to maintain roughly equal influence on politics. Public funding of elections, restrictions on campaign contributions, and more equal access to the media keep the public agenda from being captured by the rich. Fair equality of opportunity is promoted by public provision of high-quality education, especially for the least-advantaged, and by an assured minimum income and health care for all. The economic structure works to disperse ownership of productive resources widely among citizens, deterring disruptive concentrations of economic and political power.

Rawls explicitly rejects both the welfare state and laissez-faire capitalism. The welfare state generates a demoralized and disengaged underclass by depriving the worst-off of sufficient political, educational, and employment opportunities while leaving most of the economy in the hands of the wealthy. Laissez-faire capitalism will be at least as bad as the welfare state along those dimensions. The aim of a property owning democracy is to enable all citizens to participate in society and pursue their own ends with robust public support. "The least-advantaged are not, if all goes well, the unfortunate and unlucky—objects of our charity and compassion, much less our pity—but those to whom reciprocity is owed as a matter of basic justice" (Rawls 2001, 139).

Looking over Rawls's original position argument for his two principles, two features of his strategy stand out. One is how the argument pivots from the first principle to the second. Rawls knows that most of us hold strong commitments to the equal basic rights and liberties that his first principle guarantees. His strategy is to show that the perspective used to justify these equal basic rights and liberties (the original position) also points to a socio-economic order that is much more egalitarian than what we have now. Rawls's original position argument says this: When we understand why equal rights and liberties are so important to us, we see (perhaps to our surprise) why fair equality of opportunity and the difference principle should be important to us as well. When we discover the reasons for equal political liberties, Rawls suggests, we will discover that these reasons require social and economic equality too.

Justice and Money

A second notable feature of Rawls's argument for justice as fairness connects his ideal of social equality with the need for stability with which we began. Recall that Rawls is looking to describe a society in which each person growing up develops a strong, dependable, and reflectively endorsed desire to do what is right—a desire to act on the society's principles of justice. Rawls believes that stability can be secured by equality. The egalitarian society he describes is one whose principles proclaim the value of each citizen, publicly and in full voice.

For certain social goods (like political power) it is not logically possible for some people to have more without others having less. For such goods Rawls tries to secure each person an equal share. Other goods (like income) are not zero-sum: It is possible for everyone to be better off by allowing inequalities. For these goods, Rawls's goal is that the overall system publicly aims to work for the good of each—and especially aims to work for those who end up with the least. Inequalities are allowed only because they benefit everyone. Each person develops a strong attachment to these principles of justice, because every person can see how these principles openly affirm their own worth.

Certain of citizens' attitudes within Rawls's stable society are strikingly different from those common within our own society, especially when it comes to the importance of money. This passage merits careful attention:

> It is a mistake to believe that a just and good society must wait upon a high material standard of life. What men want is meaningful work in free association with others, these associations regulating their relations to one another within a framework of just basic institutions. To achieve this state of things great wealth is not necessary. In fact, beyond some point it is more likely to be a positive hindrance, a meaningless distraction at best if not the temptation to indulgence and emptiness. (Rawls 1971, 290)

Society cannot be stable if people base their self-worth on greater wealth, because the goal of having more money than others is not one that everyone can achieve. The "losers" in a system where esteem comes from riches will rightly conclude that their society is not built for them—and will likely, politically, check out.

In Rawls's just society, citizens gain self-respect from seeing their own good publicly affirmed by their institutions. Under the difference principle, even those who end up with the least know that the economy works for their benefit. To return to the positive ideal of community described above, in justice as fairness, citizens view the natural and social differences among them as a shared resource to be employed for the benefit of all. Every person develops an allegiance to the society because they see how its rules encourage citizens not to do each other down but to share each other's fates.

2. Political Liberalism

Rawls maintained throughout his life that that justice as fairness—his vision of free and equal citizens cooperating fairly—is the most just, and the most stable, ideal for a modern constitutional democracy. Yet the way he presented this vision changed dramatically from his first book, *A Theory of Justice* (1971), to his second, *Political Liberalism* (1993). Rawls came to believe that the stability of society depended not only on the justice of its basic institutions, but also on the *legitimacy* of the exercise of coercive power by the state.

Rawls in fact realized that his first presentation of justice as fairness generated a paradox. In *A Theory of Justice*, the grounding conceptions of person and society are presented as simply part of the truth. People *are* free and equal—essentially, metaphysically—so the most just and stable society will treat them in accordance with how they are. In that book Rawls went so far as to sketch a Kantian interpretation of justice as fairness wherein the original position represents the perspective of our autonomous noumenal selves (or perhaps self), undivided by the contingencies of the perceptible world (1971, 251–57). Yet Rawls discovered that such a metaphysical understanding of free and equal persons cannot order a society without contradicting freedom itself.

The metaphysical interpretation of justice as fairness defines what *Political Liberalism* calls a *comprehensive doctrine*—a partisan view on the nature of humans and the highest values in life. Yet in a free society there will be many different comprehensive doctrines: some philosophical, some religious, some neither. None of these doctrines can be coercively imposed on all citizens without risking the great evils that (as we have seen) it is Rawls's primary aim to avoid:

> A continuing shared adherence to one comprehensive doctrine can be maintained only by the oppressive use of state power, with all its official crimes and the inevitable brutality and cruelties, followed by the corruption of religion, philosophy, and science. If we say a political society is a community when it is united in affirming one and the same comprehensive doctrine, then the oppressive use of state power

with all the attendant evils is necessary to maintain political community... In the society of the middle ages, more or less united in affirming the Catholic faith, the Inquisition was not an accident; its suppression of heresy was needed to preserve the shared religious belief. The same holds, we suppose, for any comprehensive philosophical and moral doctrine, even secular ones. (Rawls 2001, 34)

In this passage John Rawls says that shared adherence to any comprehensive political philosophy, even a liberal one, will require state oppression on the order of the Inquisition. It may give philosophers pause.

In a free society, Rawls claims, citizens will come to have quite divergent world views. Some may be Kantians, some may be Catholics, some may be Muslims, some may be militant atheists. This diversity is inevitable and not regrettable: Free minds will reasonably disagree on the most profound issues in life. However, none of these comprehensive doctrines may be imposed on everyone without violating basic freedoms. And in any society there can only be one law. The state must either fund or not fund religious schools; the law must either grant or deny equal rights to women; sodomy and pornography must be either permitted or forbidden; there can only be one set of rules for running the economy at any one time.

The Challenges of Toleration

Rawls here confronts himself with the classic problem of toleration, which he divides into two connected challenges. The first challenge is moral: How can it be right to enforce *one* law on citizens so diverse in their basic outlooks? The second challenge is the familiar one of stability. How can a society that imposes one law on a diverse citizenry gain the willing and lasting cooperation of each of those citizens? Inevitably this one law cannot align with everything every citizen believes is right. So how can a society that enforces one law activate in citizens a strong, dependable, and reflectively endorsed desire to do what the law requires?

In meeting these twin challenges of legitimacy and stability Rawls rejects one option out of hand. Toleration should not rest simply on a social balance of power (a *modus vivendi*). A mere political compromise that allows religious freedom, for example, may not be secure—this freedom may be taken away should the balance of power shift decisively to one religious group or another (or to the militant atheists). More profoundly, in a *modus vivendi* citizens do not tolerate each other's religions because this is the right thing to do, but only as an expedient given their (perhaps temporary) inability to impose their rule on the rest.

A Political Conception of Justice and an Overlapping Consensus

The best way to meet the two challenges of toleration, Rawls claims, is for a society's laws to be based on a *political conception of justice*. A political conception is not presented as true—for citizens have different views about the truth—but as *reasonable* for every citizen to endorse. A political conception is a freestanding module: It is not defined by any particular controversial comprehensive doctrine, and is therefore able to fit within many of them. A political conception can attract the wholehearted and enduring support from each member of a diverse society, because it makes no commitments on the deep issues that divide them—metaphysical, religious, or otherwise.

Because it is free from factional foundations, a political conception can gain the support of citizens with widely different commitments. Citizens support the same conception, and for moral reasons, yet each for their own moral reasons. The Kantian sees how the political conception can flow from her philosophical position, the Catholic affirms the political conception as part of Catholic dogma, the Muslim finds it in the Koran, and so on. In an *overlapping consensus*, every citizen fully endorses the political conception, each from the perspective of her own comprehensive doctrine. An overlapping consensus is more stable than a mere *modus vivendi* because each citizen affirms the political conception as the ultimate and proper basis for the society's laws, whatever the balance of power in society happens to be, or whatever it becomes.

The vision of a society united by an overlapping consensus on a political conception is an ideal, like the vision of a society ordered by the principles of justice as fairness. Rawls gives no guarantee that an overlapping consensus must happen; he only seeks to prove that one is possible. Furthermore, an overlapping consensus can only be possible if people have the right moral psychology—if people can, in fact, be reasonable. Reasonable people do not just insist on their own view, come what may. Rather, reasonable people desire "for its own sake a social world in which they, as free and equal, can cooperate with others on terms that all can accept" (Rawls 1993, 50). Indeed, reasonable people want to live in a society governed by rules that all can accept, even more than they want society to be governed by their own partisan view. Again, Rawls's hopeful view of human psychology does not demand power after power but allows people to prioritize reciprocal relations of mutual respect.

Should an overlapping consensus come about, then the challenges of legitimacy and stability will be met. It is legitimate to enforce one law when that law is acceptable to each reasonable person from within their own point of view. Law based on a political conception is justifiable "at the tribunal of each person's understanding" (Rawls 1993, 391; citing Waldron 1993, 62). Each citizen understands how the law is compatible with their own world view, and how enforcing that law will not impose a sectarian philosophy—their own, or any other's. Each citizen also willingly abides by this law, for this law expresses their own fundamental commitments. The reasonable Kantian sees the law as Kantian, and is motivated to follow it as such—and similarly for the reasonable Catholic who sees the law as Catholic. Every citizen sees good reason to accept society's laws, even when they do not align perfectly with her own preferences, because the reasons she has for accepting those laws are ultimately her own.

Interpreting the Public Political Culture

The structure of Rawls's solution to the problem of toleration—an overlapping consensus focused on a political conception—may be clear enough. Yet the content of that solution is still uncertain. Rawls seems to have deprived his theory of any source from which to derive the substance of the law. When determining the law on, say, the political status of women, we cannot simply turn to Kantian, or Catholic, or Muslim doctrine without reproducing the problem of intolerance with which we began.

Rawls now draws on what he calls the *public political culture* of a liberal society: "The political institutions of a constitutional regime and the public traditions of their interpretation (including those of the judiciary), as well as historic texts and documents that are common knowledge" (1993, 13–14). Deriving the substance of the law from the public culture of society removes the dangers of drawing on any partisan comprehensive doctrine, and it also supports the formation of an overlapping consensus. The major political ideals of society are ideals with which various comprehensive doctrines within society are most likely to have aligned already (e.g., the endorsement of religious freedom as a civil right within the Catholic doctrine of Vatican II). So these are the ideals on which existing comprehensive doctrines are most likely to be able to converge. Moreover, reasonable citizens will see that the public political culture is the only nonpartisan focal point of ideals common to citizens whose personal views divide them.

There are many reasonable interpretations of the public political culture of a modern liberal society, and so there are many political conceptions of justice on which a particular liberal society can base its politics. There are also, however, limits to this interpretative flexibility. Rawls says that any reasonable interpretation of a liberal public culture must have three features:

1. A reasonable interpretation will ascribe to all citizens familiar individual rights and liberties, such as rights of liberty of conscience, free expression, and free choice of occupation;
2. It will give special priority to these rights and liberties, especially over demands to further the general good (e.g., increasing national wealth) or perfectionist values (e.g., the promotion of high culture); and
3. It will assure for all citizens sufficient all-purpose means to make effective use of their freedoms.

These features require certain institutional manifestations. For example, all political conceptions will insist on fair opportunities for all citizens (especially in education and training), a "not excessively unequal" distribution of income and wealth, government as the employer of last resort, basic health care available to all citizens, and public financing of elections. Rawls states that libertarian principles cannot satisfy these conditions: A libertarian basic structure might allow, for example, excessive inequalities of income and wealth. Yet clearly many different political philosophies current in liberal democracies—from the more conservative to the more progressive—can qualify as political conceptions in Rawls's sense.

Justice as Fairness: A Political Conception

This includes Rawls's own justice as fairness. After his "political" turn, Rawls presents the basic ideas of justice as fairness not as secured by metaphysics, but as the most reasonable interpretations of the public political culture of a modern liberal democracy. Justice as fairness—now political, not metaphysical—offers its ideal of free and equal persons cooperating fairly as a *political self-conception* that can fit into any number of philosophical and religious traditions. The theory is thus one (and, Rawls believes, the best one) of a family of political conceptions, any of which can serve as the basis of a legitimate and tolerant social order free from the great evils of state oppression. Which political conception any society will choose—justice as fairness or some other—Rawls leaves to be settled by debate and by democratic procedures, the rules for which are themselves acceptable to all reasonable citizens.

Stepping back from Rawls's vision of a liberal society shows how much he highlights what can unite us, even as he acknowledges what will divide us. Within justice as fairness, Rawls emphasizes citizens' *sense of justice*: their willingness to support fair principles, even at cost to their narrow self-interest. Within political liberalism, Rawls spotlights citizens' *reasonableness*: their desire to be tolerant, even at the price of living under laws that do not express the entirety of what they think is right. Rawls's hopeful vision of humans as capable of transcending their particularities to identify with the universal, and of doing the right thing because it is right, is continuous with the rationalist tradition to which he belongs. Whether one believes that humans can truly be motivated by fairness and toleration—and whether one believes that, under the right social conditions, these motivations can predominate—are matters for further reflection.

3. The Law of Peoples

The wars of the twentieth century, Rawls wrote, "with their extreme violence and increasing destructiveness, culminating in the manic evil of the Holocaust, raise in an acute way the question whether political relations must be governed by power and coercion alone" (1993, lxii). Rawls's third and final monograph, *The Law of Peoples* (1999), returns to the investigations with which the young Rawls began. Is it possible for humans to avert the great evils persistent in their history: "unjust war and oppression, religious persecution and the denial of liberty of conscience, starvation and poverty, not to mention genocide and mass murder" (1999, 6–7)? For such evils to be averted, what must human nature and human society be like?

Liberal and Decent Peoples

As we have seen, Rawls's hope for humanity's future rests on the internal ordering of societies: "Once the gravest forms of political injustice are eliminated by following just (or at least decent) social policies and establishing just (or at least decent) basic institutions, these great evils will eventually disappear" (1999, 6–7). Rawls's hope here rests on two hypotheses: an *internal* thesis that just or decent societies can avoid great evils within their own borders, and an *internal-external* thesis that domestically well-ordered societies will set themselves against the great evils that threaten between states.

Proving the internal thesis for liberal societies—those stably ordered by some political conception of justice such as justice as fairness—requires no extra work. Rawls has already explained how such societies can be tolerant and unified over time, and given favorable conditions, there is every reason to think they can also escape economic disasters like starvation and poverty. What Rawls adds in *The Law of Peoples* is that nonliberal societies can also be part of this moral vision. Nonliberal but "decent" societies can also prevent the great evils internally, and they can also be equal members of a just and peaceful international order.

A decent society may have a public political culture quite different from a liberal society. Basic institutions may be organized to favor a dominant religion, for example. These institutions may exclude women and religious minorities from holding office, and they may have no place for electoral democracy. Still, the government of a decent society regularly consults with representatives of all social groups; it allows protests and responds to them conscientiously; and it permits those who wish to emigrate to do so. A decent government also secures core human rights for all: rights to personal security and property, freedom from slavery and formal equality before the law, rights to subsistence and basic liberty of conscience, and protections against genocidal attacks. Citizens of liberal societies will certainly not see a decent society as just. Yet they will consider decent societies to merit toleration, and indeed some measure of respect, because these societies are internally well-ordered enough to prevent the great evils.

Satisfied Peoples

Rawls's internal-external thesis is one of the most distinctive and under-explored pieces of his international theory. Rawls, as many who were moved to meditate on the Second World War, concluded that the aggression of states flows from their defects within: "The internal institutional structure of these societies made them inherently aggressive and hostile to other states" (Rawls 1999, 8). Writing of early modern Spain and France as well as Nazi Germany, he says,

> Their fault lay in their political traditions and institutions of law, property, and class structure, with their sustaining religious and moral beliefs and underlying culture. It is these things that shape a society's political will. (Rawls 1999, 106)

Indeed Rawls emphasizes domestic human rights violations as precursors to war at least as much as he emphasizes their inherent wrongness.[1] Getting the internal structure of societies right is the key to world peace, and this is where both liberal and decent societies succeed.

Because of their internal structures liberal and decent peoples are *satisfied* peoples: They are intrinsically nonaggressive. Liberal peoples, for example, will not war with one another "simply because they have no cause to" (Rawls 1999, 8). A liberal people has interests in guaranteeing its security and its national boundaries, in protecting its free institutions and its culture, and in maintaining its proper self-respect. But such a society "is not moved by the desire for world power or national glory; nor does it wage war for purposes of economic gain or the acquisition of territory" (Rawls 1971, 379). A liberal people has no national religion that it wishes to spread, and if it wishes to get richer, it will prefer to trade rather than fight. Decent peoples are, Rawls says, likewise satisfied in themselves, having no reason to war with other liberal or decent societies.

Rawls's strong version of liberal internationalism presents a vision wholly different from the dominant theory in international relations, which is realism. In realist theory, the internal political structure of states is largely irrelevant, and, by definition, no state can be satisfied. States from a realist perspective are primarily distinguished by their relative military and economic power, and each state always strives to increase its security and wealth in whatever ways are available. Realist theory is the self-conscious successor to Hobbesian self-interest theory, applied to the international realm. What Rawls presents is a more hopeful vision of moral psychology—this time, of the moral psychology of the collective agents that are peoples.

For Rawls the hope is not that peoples will always act rightly—we know they will not—but that in the right circumstances they can act fairly toward other peoples, even at the cost of their own narrow self-interest. Rawls's description of the self-conception of well-ordered peoples parallels the description of the self-conception of the individual in his domestic theory. Liberal and decent peoples see themselves as free in that they are politically independent of other peoples, and as equal in seeing themselves as equally deserving of respect. Crucially, these peoples are also reasonable: willing to honor fair terms of cooperation as long as others will also do so and unwilling to impose their partisan political ideals on others. Rawlsian peoples are Rawlsian people writ large.[2]

Rawls's International Principles

As in his domestic theory, Rawls sets out an original position thought experiment to transform abstract conceptions into specific principles. This time, the original position aims to discover what fair terms of cooperation would be among free and equal peoples. Rawls declares that this second original position would select eight principles to order the international basic structure:

1. Peoples are free and independent, and their freedom and independence are to be respected by other peoples;
2. Peoples are to observe treaties and undertakings;
3. Peoples are equal and are parties to the agreements that bind them;
4. Peoples are to observe the duty of nonintervention (except to address grave violations of human rights);

5. Peoples have a right of self-defense, but no right to instigate war for reasons other than self-defense;
6. Peoples are to honor human rights;
7. Peoples are to observe certain specified restrictions in the conduct of war; and
8. Peoples have a duty to assist other peoples living under unfavorable conditions that prevent their having a just or decent political and social regime. (Rawls 1999, 37)

Rawls also suggests that peoples might agree to form international institutions to coordinate their political and economic relations, such as idealized versions of the United Nations, World Bank, and World Trade Organization.

Rawls on World Governance

These eight principles (especially 1–7) are familiar from the current international order. Several principles (especially 4–8) acknowledge the possibility of a less-than-ideal world in which not all states are liberal or decent. *Outlaw states* threaten world peace to gain glory or territory, or violate the human rights of those within their borders. Such states may be coerced, always within the bounds of just war, and with the aim of eventually encouraging them to join the society of well-ordered peoples. *Burdened societies* suffer from serious social or economic pathologies (such as overpopulation) that prevent them from achieving or maintaining liberal or decent institutions. The international community has a duty to render assistance to such societies, until they can become members of that community as self-sufficient participants.

This Rawlsian vision of a perpetually peaceful international society is more sanguine than the realist depiction of permanent Hobbesian anarchy among states. Yet Rawls's vision is considerably less ambitious than those that see progressively greater integration and equality across borders, and it is revealing why this is so. Rawls rejects cosmopolitan dreams of a world state out of hand. Like Kant, he holds that such a state would either be despotic or destabilized by peoples struggling to become autonomous.

Rawls also has no truck with proposals to increase democracy across national borders, or to disperse sovereignty away from national governments. One common worry is that these proposals would require dangerous leaps into the unknown, but this is not Rawls's main concern. For Rawls, these proposals cannot even get started. There is, for Rawls, no problem that they solve.

Avoiding the great evils of human history is Rawls's primary aim. Since he believes his society of peoples would achieve this aim, he endorses it and sees no need to go beyond it. He sees the citizens of well-ordered societies—liberal or decent, as may be—as satisfied members of satisfied peoples. Such citizens understand how their social institutions accommodate their own convictions in the context of their country's political traditions, and how their society's basic laws secure their status as participants in a scheme of social cooperation. They are proud of being members of a self-determining political community, deserving of equal respect as such by other states no matter how much more or less populous or powerful these are. They see the principles that the international community puts in place to secure the independence and equal standing of their society, as well as the mutual assistance provisions that help countries fallen on hard times. Why should such citizens want to disperse political power away from their institutions of national self-determination, and why should they want to gain political power at transnational or global levels? What problem would this solve?

One leading answer to this question is that citizens of poorer states should be concerned with their economic condition relative to citizens in richer states, considering their relative disadvantage in wealth and income to be distressingly arbitrary or unfair. Yet this, to Rawls, is again to give a counterproductive emphasis to money instead of justice.

> The final political end of society is to become fully just and stable for the right reasons. Once that end is reached, the Law of Peoples prescribes no further target such as, for example, to raise the standard of living beyond what is necessary to sustain those institutions. Nor is there any justifiable reason for any society's asking for more than is necessary to sustain just institutions, or for further reduction of material inequalities among societies. (1999, 119)

People within satisfied peoples are themselves satisfied. The idea that each nation should always strive to raise its economic level is merely bourgeois ideology: "The thought that real saving and economic growth are to go on indefinitely, upwards and onwards, with no specified goal in sight, is the idea of the business class of a capitalist society" (Rawls 1999, 107 n33). A satisfied people may sometimes opt for economic growth to achieve some particular purpose, but once it has secured liberal or decent institutions it can—and probably should—remain at a stationary state of zero real growth. For nations, as for individuals, beyond some point questing for greater wealth, "is more likely to be a positive hindrance, a meaningless distraction at best if not the temptation to indulge and emptiness." This Rawlsian ideal of nations that no longer aim at limitless growth is noteworthy and may become increasingly attractive in our times.

The Urgency of Hope

The arc of Rawls's thought, from justice through toleration to peace, originated in his urgent need to envision a world not doomed by selfishness and *pleonexia*. The specific historical events that so concentrated Rawls's mind—the wounding of German and Japanese national pride at the 1919 Paris Peace Conference, the decay of these nations' internal politics that turned them into aggressively dissatisfied powers, the cataclysmic war that ensued—are now long past. Yet Rawls's question persists for each of us. We must ask whether we must resign ourselves to a world that is at best a balance of power, or whether we can believe that better is possible. For Rawls, the answer to that question turns on whether people, and peoples, have a moral nature that in some attainable circumstances can dominate their narrow self-interest. For Rawls, the answer is yes.

Rawls believes that his theories describe a world that is the best we can hope for: a "realistic utopia." Rawls tries to show us the urgency of our taking responsibility for our position on such ideals. Whether we believe that human nature makes such visions feasible, or hopelessly naïve, can itself have real political consequences:

> Debates about general philosophical questions cannot be the stuff of daily politics, but that does not make these questions without significance, since what we think their answers are will shape the underlying attitudes of the public culture and the conduct of politics. If we take it for granted that a just and well-ordered democratic society is impossible, then the quality and tone of those attitudes will reflect that knowledge. A cause of the fall of Weimar's constitutional regime was that none of the traditional elites of Germany supported its constitution or were willing to cooperate to make it work. They no longer believed a decent liberal parliamentary regime was possible. (1993, lix)

Whether we hold a realistic hope for a rightful world matters. It matters to whether our own young soldiers will be sent to war, and whether we ourselves will hear a late-night knock on the door.

NOTES

With many thanks to David Estlund, Fabian Freyenhagen, Jon Mandle, and Paul Weithman.

1. Rawls devotes only a footnote (2000, 94–95 n6) to discussing a hypothetical society that violates human rights internally but is peaceful externally.
2. Wenar and Milanovic (2009) critiques Rawls's internal-external thesis.

REFERENCES

Hobbes, T. 1994. *Leviathan*. Indianapolis, IN: Hackett.
Lippert-Rasmussen, K. 2009. "Justice and Bad Luck." In *The Stanford Encyclopedia of Philosophy*. Edited by N. Zalta. Stanford, CA: Stanford University. Available from plato.stanford.edu/entries/justice-bad-luck/.
Rawls, J. 1971. *A Theory of Justice*. Cambridge, MA: Harvard University Press.
Rawls, J. 1993. *Political Liberalism*. New York: Columbia University Press.
Rawls, J. 1999. *The Law of Peoples*. Cambridge, MA: Harvard University Press.
Rawls, J. 2001. *Justice as Fairness: A Restatement*. Edited by Erin Kelly. Cambridge, MA: Harvard University Press.
Waldron, J. 1993. *Liberal Rights*. Cambridge, UK: Cambridge University Press.
Wenar, L., and Milanovic, B. 2009. "Are Liberal Peoples Peaceful?" *Journal of Political Philosophy* 17:462–86.

CHAPTER 22

NOZICK

DAVID SCHMIDTZ AND CHRISTOPHER FREIMAN

> Philosophers often seek to deduce their total view from a few basic principles... One brick is piled upon another to produce a tall philosophical tower, one brick wide.... Instead of the tottering tower, I suggest that our model be the Parthenon.... When the philosophical structure crumbles somewhat, as we should expect on inductive grounds, something of interest and beauty remains standing. (Nozick 1981, 3)

Nozick wanted to see philosophical work, especially his own, as a stage in a maturation process. The final product is not the sole point, perhaps not even the main point. Although Nozick declined to respond to critics, we aim to respect his distinctively exploratory and "non-coercive" approach even while offering a systematic reconstruction that Nozick himself eschewed.

1. WITHOUT FOUNDATIONS?

"Individuals have rights, and there are things no person or group may do to them (without violating their rights)" (Nozick 1974, ix). Thus begins *Anarchy, State, and Utopia*. Many commentators followed Thomas Nagel (1975) in branding Nozick's premise as "libertarianism without foundations," merely assuming what needs proving. For better or for worse, though, Nozick borrowed John Rawls's foundation, accepting Rawls's premise about the separateness and inviolability of persons. As Rawls puts it, "Each person possesses an inviolability founded on justice that even the welfare of society as a whole cannot override... [T]he rights secured by justice are not subject to political bargaining or to the calculus of social interests" (1971,

3–4). Nozick concurs with "[this] root idea, namely, that there are different individuals with separate lives and so no one may be sacrificed for others" (1974, 33). If this is not a foundation, and if foundations are needed, then the lack is as problematic for Rawls's liberalism as for Nozick's.

Nozick and Rawls each assert that justice requires equal protection of basic rights and liberties so as to enable citizens to freely choose and pursue their conceptions of the good. Nozick departs from Rawls only when he treats liberalism's commitment to letting citizens decide for themselves how to speak and assemble as applying equally to decisions about how to truck, barter, and exchange—that is, as considerations that in the normal course of events trump any imperative to redistribute on behalf of the less advantaged.

2. Rawls

Rawls's most luminously undeniable point is that a free society is a mutually advantageous cooperative venture, not a fixed-sum game.[1] That is why, when given a choice, people virtually always choose to live together, for they are better off together. Cooperation enables us all to flourish, but we each want a larger share of cooperation's fruits, so cooperation inevitably involves conflict. One way to resolve the conflict is to distribute the fruits so as to maximize overall utility. However, this proposal fails to acknowledge that individuals entering into cooperative ventures are separate persons contributing to those ventures in pursuit of their own hopes and dreams.

To Rawls, justice is less like utilitarian calculation and more like bargaining. Rational contractors negotiate an institutional structure to govern future interactions, understanding that no one is obliged to sacrifice so that others may prosper. Justice is a kind of fairness. Many things can be fair. Evaluations can be fair, or not. Shares can be fair, or not. Intuitively, a rule of "equal shares" is fair at a sufficiently high level of abstraction. However, we realize we can make the pie bigger by encouraging each other to work harder, which we do by rewarding efforts to make the pie bigger: offering more pie to those who do more work. In essence, we allow inequalities if and when doing so makes us better off. Here is what we call the precursor.

> Precursor: Inequalities are to be arranged to the advantage of everyone affected: everyone should get more than what *would have been* an equal share in a more equal but less productive scheme.[2]

This precursor, though, is "at best an incomplete principle for ordering distributions" (Rawls 1999a, 135). It states that departures from equal shares are just if they make everyone better off. However, "there are indefinitely many ways in which all may be advantaged when the initial arrangement of equality is taken as a benchmark. How then are we to choose among these possibilities?" (Rawls 1971, 65). A complete theory specifies how to divide the gains. Rawls's way of completing the precursor is to target one position and maximize the prospects of persons in that position. Rawls chooses to favor the less advantaged, thus arriving at the difference principle. The core principles of Rawls's theory state:

1. Each person is equally entitled to the most extensive sphere of liberty compatible with a like liberty for all; and
2. Social and economic inequalities are to be arranged so that they are (a) to the greatest advantage of the least advantaged and (b) attached to offices and positions open to all under conditions of fair equality of opportunity. (Rawls 1971, 302)

According to Rawls, the first principle takes precedence: "liberty can be restricted only for the sake of liberty itself" (1971, 244). This primacy of liberty makes Rawls's a liberal view. There has been relatively little discussion of the first principle, and few quarrel with it. The controversy surrounds the second, particularly part (a), the notorious difference principle.

It is easy to envision *skilled* workers objecting, echoing Nozick by saying, "You imagine us negotiating terms of cooperation, then conclude that *fairness* is about someone else getting as much as possible? We never asked you to see us as self-made Robinson Crusoes, only that you grant that our growing up in 'your' society does not affect our status as separate persons, and by itself gives you no claim to any skills we contribute to our various cooperative ventures."

Rawls has two replies. First, he argues, skilled workers are wrong to see themselves as mere means to the ends of the less advantaged. Workers make this mistake if they see their skills as part of them rather than as accidents that befell them. When skilled workers reconceive themselves as undeserving winners in a genetic and social lottery, they will see the distribution of skill as a common asset. They will no longer see themselves as bringing anything to the table qua individuals, other than their interests.

Second, Rawls says, skilled laborers would not complain if they could view the difference principle as what they would choose in a fair bargaining situation. What would be fair? Suppose Jane assesses alternative distributions from behind a *veil of ignorance*, not knowing which position in the distribution she will occupy. If Jane does not know whether she is a manual worker or a mid-level manager, she will not try to bias the arrangement in favor of managers; she will seek an option that is good for all. So why would Jane pick the difference principle, which seems biased in favor of unskilled workers? One reason to see the difference principle as less biased than it may appear is that "least advantaged" is a fluid category. If Joe starts as least advantaged, then a system that works well on his behalf eventually puts him in a better position than Jane, at which point the system turns to doing what it can for Jane, until she is doing well enough to make it someone else's turn, and so on.

Many who reject Rawls, including Nozick, do so out of a belief that Rawls's theory makes too little room for liberty. Likewise, Rawls's defenders tend to brush past his first principle.[3] One reason for believing that Rawls's first principle must truly come first is as follows. Suppose we found that Jim Crow laws work to the benefit of the least advantaged.[4] (It is a historical fact that many blue-collar workers—the paradigm of Rawls's least advantaged class—embraced Jim Crow laws; see Gates and Appiah 1999, 1211.) Such a result would make the difference principle hard to embrace, at least if we said that whether Jim Crow laws are unjust depends on whether they benefit blue-collar workers. So, what if a theory instead began with a principle of maximum equal liberty for all? On that theory—Rawls's theory—the first principle rules out Jim Crow laws from the start. On Rawls's theory, it *doesn't matter* whether such laws satisfy the difference principle.

3. History and Pattern

Nozick distinguished historical from patterned principles of justice. The distinction is simple on the surface, but as Nozick elaborates, the two categories become three, perhaps four, and become not so easily separated. Some of Nozick's statements are difficult to interpret, but the following is roughly what he intended.

Current time-slice principles assess a distribution at a given moment. We look at an array of outcomes. It does not matter to whom those outcomes attach. So, on an egalitarian time-slice principle, if outcomes are unequal, then from that alone we know we have injustice. We need not know who got which outcome, or how they got it.

End-state principles are similar to current time-slice principles but do not stipulate that outcomes are time slices. For example, an egalitarian end-state principle could say we look at lifetime income: If lifetime incomes are unequal, that is all we need to know. The difference between time-slice and end-state principles is this: Suppose the Smiths and the Joneses have the same jobs at the same factory, but the Joneses are three years older, started working three years earlier, and continually get raises by virtue of seniority that the Smiths will not get for another three years. At no time are wages equal, yet lifetime income evens out. We have injustice by time-slice egalitarianism, but an end-state egalitarianism can conclude that the equality required by justice is achieved.

Patterned principles include the above as subsets or examples, but within the broader class are patterns that are neither time-slice nor end-state. "Equal pay for equal work" is an example of an egalitarian principle that is patterned but neither end-state nor time-slice—it prescribes what outcomes should *track* (in this case, labor inputs) but does not prescribe that outcomes be equal.

Historical principles say that what matters most is the process by which outcomes arise. Historical principles are complex; notwithstanding Nozick's intended contrast, patterned principles can have a historical element, and vice versa. "Equal pay for equal work" is both patterned and historical. It prescribes outcomes tracking a pattern of what people have done.

4. A Problem with Patterns

Nozick saw Rawls's difference principle as patterned but not historical (by virtue of prescribing a distribution without regard to the history of what is being distributed). By contrast, what Nozick calls *entitlement theory* is historical but not patterned.

One problem with patterned principles is that liberty upsets patterns. "No end-state principle or distributional patterned principle of justice can be continuously realized without continuous interference with people's lives" (Nozick 1974, 163). Nozick asks us to imagine that society achieves a pattern of perfect justice (by the lights of whatever theory we prefer). Then someone offers Wilt Chamberlain a quarter for the privilege of watching Wilt play basketball (161–64). Before we know it, thousands of people are paying Wilt a quarter each every time Wilt puts on a show. Wilt gets rich. The distribution is no longer equal, and no one complains.

Moreover, we are all like Wilt. Every time we earn a quarter, or spend one, we change the pattern. Nozick asks: If justice is a pattern, achievable at a given moment, what happens if we achieve perfection? Would justice at that point prohibit everything—no further consuming, creating, trading, or even giving—so as not to upset the perfect pattern? Note that Nozick neither argues nor presumes that people can do whatever they please. Nozick's point is, if there is *anything at all* people can do—such as simply giving a coin to an entertainer—then even that tiniest of liberties will, over time, disturb the pattern. It is false, Nozick concludes, to think end-state principles offer all that entitlement principles offer, only better distributed. Entitlement principles recognize realms of choice that end-state principles cannot recognize. None of the resources governed by end-state principles would ever be at a person's (or even a whole nation's) disposal (Nozick 1974, 167).

Although Nozick is correct in seeing a problem with time-slice principles, he seems to assume that in arguing against end-state and time-slice principles, he is undermining patterned principles more generally. Not so. Not all patterns are the same, and not all require major interference. Nozick is right that if we focus on time slices, we focus on isolated moments and take moments too seriously, when what matters is not the pattern of holdings at a moment but the pattern of how people treat each other over time. Even tiny liberties must upset the pattern of a static moment, but liberty need not upset an ongoing pattern of fair treatment.

A moral principle forbidding racial discrimination, for example, prescribes no particular end-state. Such a principle is what Nozick (1974) calls *weakly patterned*. It affects the pattern (as would a purely historical principle) without prescribing a pattern (or more precisely, without prescribing an end-state). If a principle forbidding racial discrimination works its way into a society through cultural progress rather than legal intervention, it need not involve *any* interference.

If we could make Martin Luther King's dream come true, so that his children are judged not by the color of their skin but by the content of their character, what we would be achieving is a fluid, evolving pattern tracking merit rather than skin color. The resulting society would require *less* intervention than the relentlessly coercive, segregated society from which it evolved. Although Nozick sometimes speaks as if his critique applies to all patterns, we should take seriously his concession that "weak" patterns are compatible with liberty. Some may promote liberty, depending on how they are introduced and maintained. The problem lies not with patterned principles in general but specifically with end-state and especially time-slice principles.

If the bare fact of deviating from a time slice were enough to license intervening to correct the deviation, then Nozick would be right to say that time-slice principles license immense and never-ending interference with everyday life. Does Rawls defend such a view? No. To Rawls, it is not the basic structure's job to make every transaction work to the advantage of the working class, let alone each member of the working class. Rawls was more realistic than that. Instead, the trend of a whole society over time is supposed to benefit the working class *as a class*. To be sure, Rawls was an egalitarian, but not a time-slice or even end-state egalitarian, nor did he hold that the pattern called for by the difference principle should be brought about by any means necessary. The pattern Rawls envisioned weaving into the fabric of society was a pattern of equal status, applying not so much to a distribution as to an ongoing relationship.

It would be incorrect, though, to infer that Nozick's critique had no point. Nozick showed what an alternative theory could look like, portraying Wilt Chamberlain as a separate person in a more robust sense (unencumbered by nebulous debts to society) than Rawls could countenance. To Nozick, Wilt's advantages are not what Wilt *finds* on the table; Wilt's advantages are what Wilt *brings* to the table. Respecting what Wilt brings to the table—respecting what he adds when he participates in cooperative ventures—is the exact essence of respecting him as a separate person.

In part due to Nozick, today's egalitarians are realizing that any equality worthy of aspiration will focus less on justice as a property of a time-slice distribution and more on how people are treated—how they are rewarded for their contributions and enabled over time to make contributions worth rewarding.

In passing, the lesson we are supposed to draw from Nozick's Experience Machine parable (which asks why most of us recoil from the idea of plugging into a "Matrix"-type computer that would fool us into believing we were living the most wonderful life imaginable) is that most of us want to *accomplish* something, not just *experience* something. Nozick might have complained that Rawls's original position is, in a way, an "experience machine," because it suggests the following: It does not matter what we accomplish before arriving at the table to choose principles of justice. The separateness about us that matters is our separateness going forward. What we bring to the bargaining table, the basis for our claims and for our choosing principles, are interests, not accomplishments. We may go on to pick principles that treat our accomplishments as a basis for entitlements, but any entitlements we affirm will be outcomes of deliberation by agents trying to serve their (somewhat veiled) interests, not prior entitlements that affirm our separateness, trump mere interests, and limit the scope of deliberation. In essence, we choose principles that respect our separateness as consumers.

Nozick, by contrast, aims to respect our separateness as producers, saying that goods come into the world attached to producers. (Simply denying that we are separate producers—insisting that only Robinson Crusoe would be a genuinely separate producer—is not a way of respecting our separateness; consequently, it is not a way of being liberal either.) If we agree that principles of justice must respect what less advantaged people do, we will be agreeing not only to respect what less advantaged people do from now on, on the grounds that showing such respect is in their interest. We will be choosing to respect what they have been doing all along.

Still, Nozick does not tie rights-claims to our being producers but to our being traders. Why not? Because Nozick imagines traders being asked to *document* their productivity so as to *prove* they deserved their holdings. That would license ongoing, pointless interference. Nozick's ideal here is that people respect each other as separate producers. However, we respect productivity not by appointing a "desert czar" to allocate shares according to proof of productivity, but simply by requiring that trade be consensual. We respect the productivity of separate self-owners by acknowledging their right to say no. Thus, Nozick's theory is an entitlement theory, not a desert theory.

5. Liberalism and Self-Ownership

Nozick says an entitlement theory's principles fall into three categories: initial acquisition, transfer, and rectification. Principles of *initial acquisition* explain how a person or group legitimately could acquire something that was not previously owned.[5] Previously unclaimed land is a historically central example, as are inventions and other intellectual property. Principles of *transfer* explain how ownership legitimately is transferred from one person (or group) to another. Finally, principles of *rectification* specify what to do about cases of illegitimate acquisition or transfer.

Nozick favors a version of entitlement theory, grounded in an ideal of voluntarism. Nozick says a distribution is just if it arises by just steps from a just initial position, where the paradigm of a just step is voluntary exchange.[6] As an exemplar of the kind of society that would accord with his entitlement theory, Nozick offers the ideal of a civil libertarian, free market society governed by a minimal state (roughly, a government that restricts itself to keeping the peace and defending its borders). In such a society, as people interact by consent and on mutually agreeable terms, there will be "strands" of patterns: People amass wealth in proportion to their ability to offer goods at prices that make their customers better off. Employees tend to get promotions when their talents and efforts merit promotion, and so on.[7]

However, although society will be meritocratic to that extent, that pattern will be only one among many. There will be inheritance and philanthropy, too, conferring goods on recipients who may have done nothing to deserve such gifts. Is that a problem? Not to Nozick. Nozick joins Rawls in denying that merit is a principle to which distributions (and transfers) must answer. The question, to Nozick, is whether people deal with each other in a peaceful, consensual way. Rawls says, "A distinctive feature of pure procedural justice is that the procedure for determining the just result must actually be carried out; for in these cases there is no independent criterion by reference to which a definite outcome can be known to be just" (1971, 86). By this definition, Rawls's theory is not a theory of pure procedural justice, but Nozick's theory is. To Nozick, the question is whether proper procedure was followed (literally followed here and now, not just conceived of as having been followed in a thought experiment). It need not lead to a desired outcome, or at least there is no need to guarantee that it will do so. As far as justice is concerned, there is no further question.

Nozick's theory, in a nutshell, is that we need not preordain an outcome. We need not know what pattern will emerge from voluntary exchange. What arises from a just distribution by just steps is just. If people want to pay Wilt Chamberlain for the thrill of watching him play basketball, and if this leads to Wilt having more money than the people around him, that is okay. To respect Wilt and his fans is to respect their decision to trade.

One thing we might say in support of Wilt having a right to live as he does, and our having a right to pay him for doing so, is that Wilt, like us, is a self-owner.[8] One way or another, someone will decide how to use Wilt's athletic skill. Who, if not Wilt, has the right to make that decision?

Rawls and Nozick each acknowledged a gap between (a) stating that Jane owns her talents and (b) stating that Jane owns the cash value of what she produces when she puts her talent to use. Yet, Nozick thought, to view Jane as a separate person is to presuppose her right to make and execute plans of her own, including plans involving the external world. To say Jane can do what she wants, needing our permission only if she wants to alter the external world, or only if she wants to cooperate for mutual advantage, would be to make a joke of self-ownership. Therefore, where Rawls embraced the gap between (a) and (b), Nozick was struggling to bridge the gap when he gestured at a Lockean theory that we acquire bits of an otherwise unowned external world by working on them. We say "gestured" because Nozick himself has unanswered questions about how Lockean theory works at the edges. Must labor add value? Must it be strenuous? If one pours one's tomato juice into the ocean, why doesn't one thereby come to own the ocean?

With similar candor, Nozick admits he is not sure what to say about a case where, through no one's fault, our town has only one remaining water source, and Joe is its sole owner. If it happened by a process that did not violate anyone's rights, would that make the result okay? At first, Joe could sell his water for whatever his customers were willing to pay. After Joe accidentally becomes a monopolist, though, Nozick is not so sure. We cannot take any simple concept of property for granted in such a case. We must ask what a community is for, how property rights (and specific ways of establishing legal title, including more or less ritualistic forms of labor-mixing) enable a community to serve its purpose, and how the role of property rights in serving that purpose is superseded in extraordinary conditions. Perhaps, in extraordinary conditions, something else serves that purpose. There are strands of patterns here, carrying more weight than Nozick's simple story suggests.

6. Rights

Some rights are prerequisites of a society being a cooperative venture for mutual advantage, partly because some rights enable people to know what to expect from each other and to plan their lives accordingly. On this view, what gives rights their foundation also limits their scope. Why do we have rights? Because we cannot live well together unless we treat each other as having rights. Why do we have limited rights? Because we cannot live well together unless we treat our rights as limited. That is how we know Wilt's right to enjoy his property in peace does not include a right to build biological weapons in his garage in an otherwise ordinary neighborhood.

That also is how we know Wilt's right to buy a sports car does not imply a right to drive through school zones as fast as he pleases. A community, guided by a principle that drivers must be allowed to get where they need to go so long as they do not impose undue risk on pedestrians, concludes that anything in the range of 10 to 20 miles per hour is within reason, then picks something in that range. After a community posts a limit, such as 15 miles per hour, drivers no longer have a right to judge for themselves whether twenty is within reason. From that point, pedestrians have a right that drivers observe the posted limit.

Such a right is a *side constraint*. Ordinary drivers in ordinary cases have no right to judge for themselves whether the constraint is outweighed. When the constraint applies, it applies decisively. It may, however, have limited scope. For example, a community may decide that the law does not apply to ambulances. If an ordinary driver is driving his wife to the hospital and is willing to break laws to get her there sooner, he is liable for the penalty that goes with breaking the law, although courts may, at their mercy, waive the penalty. If the driver is in an ambulance, by contrast, he does not need the court's mercy. If the law does not apply to ambulances, then he is within his rights.

7. Freedom as a Zero-Sum Game

G. A. Cohen saw a problem for anyone who, like Nozick, believes that property rights embody a commitment to peaceful cooperation. Property rights require us not to initiate force, but governments back that requirement with a threat of force, which is in itself an initiation of force.

> I want, let us say, to pitch a tent in your large back garden, perhaps just in order to annoy you, or perhaps for the more substantial reason that I have nowhere to live and no land of my own, but I have got hold of a tent, legitimately or otherwise. If I now do this thing that I want to do, the chances are that the state will intervene on your behalf. If it does, I shall suffer a constraint on my freedom. (Cohen 1995, 56)

To Cohen, "The banal truth is that, if the state prevents me from doing something that I want to do, then it places a restriction on my freedom" (1995, 55). His "general point is that incursions against private property which *reduce* owners' freedom by transferring rights over resources to non-owners thereby *increase* the latter's freedom. In advance of further argument, the net effect on freedom of the resource transfer is indeterminate" (p. 57).

There is no denying Cohen's basic point: Even when the state is trying to protect our freedom, its methods are coercive. We would be wrong to infer from this, though, that the net amount of freedom does not change, or even that we will have a problem discerning a change. Suppose Cohen were talking about taking over your body, not your garden. Would my enslaving you make me more and you less free, with indeterminate net effect? Of course not. Where does that leave Cohen's claim? Cohen might insist he was talking about your garden, not your body. Moreover, he did not state that there is no net effect—only that we would need further argument to discern one. So, what further argument would make the net effect on freedom easier to discern?

Suppose we treat the claim that protecting property owners from trespassers has an indeterminate net impact (because it makes would-be trespassers less free at the same time it makes owners more free) not as conceptual point but as a testable empirical hypothesis. What is it like in a country where ownership is not protected? In Zimbabwe, Robert Mugabe and his army pitch tents where they please, and anyone unlucky enough to find Mr. Mugabe in his back garden would rather be elsewhere. No one who knows the catastrophe that is Zimbabwe could believe that as Zimbabwe's property rights crumble, it merely trades one freedom for another, with indeterminate net effect.

Closer to home, being free to drive through a green light comes at a cost of someone being unfree to drive through a red light. Is anything indeterminate about the net effect? Of course not. Moreover, property rights manage traffic on our possessions as traffic lights manage traffic on our roads. Each system helps us to know what to expect from people and to plan accordingly. A good system of traffic regulation makes us all more free to go where we wish, including those of us currently facing red lights. Of course, red lights must turn green from time to time. Further, those who wait must be alert enough to notice when lights turn green. If people are (or even think they are) being asked to wait forever, the system breaks down.

Traffic laws help us to stay out of each other's way. Property laws let us do more; they also help us to engage in trade, with the result that our traffic (our trucking and bartering) leaves fellow travelers not merely unimpeded but enriched. The traffic of a healthy economy is a boon, not merely something to tolerate.

Cohen states that lack of money is lack of freedom (1995, 58). Cohen also says that having money is like having a ticket one can exchange for various things; and, he adds, having such a ticket is a freedom. To be clear, though, in Cohen's analysis, freedom is access to *real* wealth, not merely to pieces of paper. Governments cannot create more seats in a stadium just by printing more tickets and likewise cannot create more wealth just by printing more currency. Work is what creates wealth, and this is not merely a theoretical possibility but is instead our actual history, wherever property rights are secure enough that people can produce without thereby becoming targets.

The bottom line is that a good system of traffic regulation makes everyone more free to go where they wish, even those who currently face red lights. The tradeoff may appear to be zero-sum at first glance. After all, one person's green light is another person's red light. However, if we let the scene unfold, we see that the net result is not zero-sum.[9] The system's purpose is to enable us all (not only those currently facing green lights) to get where we need to go.

8. Rectification: Does Nozick Have a Theory of Just Distribution? Should He?

Nozick's version of entitlement theory embraces an ideal of voluntarism. A distribution is just if it arises by just steps (paradigmatically, voluntary exchange) from a just initial position.

Perhaps Nozick should not have said that. It sets the bar high. What can a historical theory say where few titles have an unblemished history? Or perhaps that is how it is; perhaps there is no way from here to a world where distributions are just. Either way, Nozick may have been mistaken in seeing himself as addressing the topic of justice, since his theory naturally leads in a different direction. His theory is about justice as how we treat each other, not justice as cleansing the world's distributions of original sin.

In other words, the core of Nozick's theory is not as previously reported. Nozick did indeed say a distribution is just if it arises by just steps from a just initial position. Yet, when Nozick said this, he obscured his real contribution. In truth, Nozick has a theory of just *transfer*, not a theory of just *distribution*: A transfer from one person to another is thoroughly just if thoroughly voluntary. Nozick qualifies his theory in several ways, but this is its essence.

Voluntary transfer cannot cleanse a tainted title of original sin, but any injustice in the result will have been preexisting, not created by the transfer. We are fated to live in a world of background injustice, each of us descended from victims and from victimizers, so it is a virtue of Nozick's theory that it does not pretend we can achieve perfect justice if only we can "even the score." Still, it remains possible for people living ordinary lives to abide by a principle of voluntary transfer and to that (admittedly imperfect) extent to have clean hands.

Nozick thought the question, contra patterned principles, is whether a distribution results from peaceful cooperation. More accurately, to avoid encouraging our self-destructive tendency to dwell on histories of injustice, Nozick might have said the real question is whether ongoing changes in distributions result from peaceful cooperation.

In summary, Nozick offers voluntarism as a basis for a theory of just transfer. He gestured at ideas about how to get resources not yet owned into the realm of what could be voluntarily transferred. He also gestured at the idea that rectificatory justice would have to be concerned with undoing wrongful transfers. However, in Nozick's mind, the point of undoing a wrongful transfer is simply to undo a wrongful transfer, not to make current holdings match a favored pattern. Thus, sometimes justice is about returning a stolen wallet to the person from whom it was stolen. Why return the wallet to that person? We do it not to restore a previously fair pattern but to restore the wallet to the person from whom it was stolen. Sometimes, justice is about *returning*, not *distributing*. The wallet's history trumps any thoughts about how it might best be distributed.

It is in the context of rectificatory justice, though, where Cohen's stance—that government protection of property is coercive—has its most plausible application. When victims and victimizers are long dead, and nothing can be done short of transferring property from one innocent descendent to another, that is when enforcing rights does start to look very much like initiating force. Should we enforce rights of long-dead victims at the expense of people who have not themselves initiated force and who themselves turn out to descend from victims if we go back far enough?

The contours of duties of rectification will not be fully specified by philosophical theory. Communities figure out the evolving contours of such duties in the same way they figure out speed limits, as they would have to do even in Utopia. They specify these contours over time, knowing that *dwelling* on the past is wrong for the same reason that *ignoring* the past is wrong; excess in either direction reduces stability in transactions, thus making it harder to go forward in peace. A routine title search when buying a house (to verify that the seller's holding of the deed is in fact uncontested) facilitates society as a cooperative venture. Going back as many centuries as the land has been occupied would do the opposite.

9. When Do We Have a Right to Distribute?

Nozick thought a bias against respecting separate persons lurks in the very idea of justice. The idea leads people to see goods as having been distributed by a mechanism for which we are responsible. Nozick believes in a free society; there is no such mechanism and no such responsibility. "There is no more a distributing or distribution of shares than there is a distributing of mates in a society in which persons choose whom they shall marry" (Nozick 1974, 150).

The lesson: If we have a license to distribute X, then we ought to distribute X fairly, and Rawls gave us a theory about how to do that. However, we lack a license to distribute mates. Thus, we have no right to distribute mates unfairly, and neither do we have a right to distribute mates fairly. Mates are not ours to distribute.

What about inequalities? The same point applies: Unless a particular inequality is ours to arrange, theories about what would be fair are moot. More generally, to show that I have a right to distribute X according to a given plan, we may at some stage need to show that my plan is fair, but before that, we need to show that X's distribution falls within my jurisdiction. In effect, Rawls's principles do not start at the beginning. They tell us how to distribute X, given that the distribution of X is our business, but the latter is not a given.

To Nozick, we do not judge the justice of a distribution of mates by looking at a pattern. We look at history. Did the partners consent?[10] To Nozick, individuals compete, sometimes for mates, sometimes for employment. Some are lucky, but not all. In neither realm, though, does bad luck count as having been wronged. Bad luck per se does not call for rectification (1974, 237). David Miller states that Nozick appears "happy to ride roughshod over many everyday beliefs in the name of a single principle (of rights) claimed to rest on a fundamental moral insight" (1999, 59), yet here as elsewhere Nozick reaches his conclusion not by steamrolling our everyday beliefs but by reconstructing them.

10. Two Kinds of "Arbitrary"

According to Rawls, "Intuitively, the most obvious injustice of the system of natural liberty is that it permits distributive shares to be improperly influenced by these factors so arbitrary from a moral point of view" (1971, 72). He also says, "Once we decide to look for a conception of justice that nullifies the accidents of natural endowment and the contingencies of social circumstance," we see that his two principles "express the result of leaving aside those aspects of the social world that seem arbitrary" (1971, 15).

The word "arbitrary" has two meanings. Natural distributions can be arbitrary, meaning *random*. Or choices can be arbitrary, meaning *capricious*. In one case, no choice is made. In the second, an unprincipled choice is made.[11] There is a difference. In fair lotteries, winners are chosen at random. A *rigged* lottery is unfair because it fails to be arbitrary in the benign sense. It is by failing to be arbitrary in the benign sense that it counts as arbitrary in the bad sense. What about the natural lottery? The natural lottery is arbitrary in the benign sense, of course, but how does that connect to being unfair in the way capricious choice is unfair?

It doesn't. Capricious choice wears impropriety on its sleeve; the natural lottery does not. Consider the difference between a lottery Jane wins by luck of the draw and a lottery rigged to make sure Jane wins. Consider the difference between Joe turning out to be less skilled than Jane versus a situation where Joe deliberately is held back so as to *make sure* Jane will be more skilled. It is the difference between chance and caprice.

Put it this way: Life is about playing the hand you are dealt. Being dealt a bad hand is not the same as facing a stacked deck. A deck is stacked only if a dealer deliberately stacks it, declining to leave the matter to chance.

One might insist that the natural lottery is not unfair and that Rawls never said otherwise. Instead, one might insist, Rawls invited us to think the natural lottery is fair or perhaps that there is a third category between fair and unfair. Either way, though, it takes more than X being random for justice to call for X to be nullified. Even if Rawls never defends the view that the natural lottery is unfair, that is still the view he encourages when he describes the natural lottery as arbitrary. No one translates the above quotation as, "Intuitively, the most obvious injustice of the system of natural liberty is that it permits distributive shares to be improperly influenced by these factors so . . . *random but in no way unfair* from a moral point of view."

In conclusion, if cleft palates ought to be "nullified," it is because cleft palates are bad, not because cleft palates are randomly distributed.

11. Utopia

Nozick's utopia begins with individuals imagining and thereby creating whatever they deem to be the best possible world. They occupy that imagined world until they begin to imagine something better. Worlds are created until no one can conceive of a better world than the one he or she occupies.

According to Nozick, a political system that maximizes the possibility of experimentation approaches this ideal without realizing it perfectly. Such a system encourages progress through trial and error; it allows associations to evolve and dissolve according to members' conceptions of the good. More specifically, if there is arranging to be done, then we ought to arrange society in such a way that individuals are free to create their own institutional structures and to test their solutions against others. He states that "there will not be one kind of community existing and one kind of life led in utopia. Utopia will consist of utopias, of many different and divergent communities in which people lead different kinds of lives under different institutions" (1974, 311–12). Utopia is not a particular community but rather a marketplace of communities. Nozick accepts pluralism: Individuals will disagree about the best life and the best community. How, then, can we justify political structures to these individuals by their own lights? Nozick answers: Let individuals choose, "voting" with their feet. People exercise their right of exit by coming or going on their own terms, switching countries as they might switch supermarkets in search of a better life.

Self-Esteem in Utopia

Nozick's utopia makes no guarantee of material equality. Is it unstable for this reason? One reason for saying yes is that people's self-respect suffers when they compare unfavorably to their peers'. Nozick, though, conjectures that the way to handle this is not by catering to envy along any given dimension of self-evaluation but by multiplying dimensions. Rawls agrees that liberal institutions generate a "plurality of associations . . . each with its secure internal life . . . The various associations in society tend to divide it into so many noncomparing groups" (1971, 536–37). Thus, athletes, scholars, entertainers, artists, and executives vie for standing along different dimensions and assign different weights to the dimensions along which they compete. There may be no common frame of reference that enables us to compare everyone. Citizens position themselves within multiple associations and enjoy multiple opportunities for favorable social comparisons; the size of the pie of social standing is thereby increased, not simply distributed. Basic structures cannot create more standing along a given dimension of interpersonal comparison (only so many can be in the top ten by any given metric), but they can facilitate the multiplication of dimensions. Nozick also states that almost any individual can see himself "as at the upper end of a distribution through the perspective of the particular weights he assigns" (1974, 245).

Societies that disperse decision making also promote stability in another way. The fewer issues subject to political oversight, the less urgent the need for consensus on contentious questions. For example, selecting a "one-size-fits-all" car model is not currently a source of political conflict. Individuals browse a wide variety of cars and buy whatever best suits their needs and budget. No particular car needs to suit every member of the community. Polities do not put the question of the right car or the right shoe size to a popular vote and enforce the majority decision. In conditions of pluralism, we similarly eschew one-size-fits-all solutions to divisive political problems concerning religion, education, medicine, and so on. Nozick's marketplace of communities is shaped by customers' decisions regarding what to buy and where to shop. By contrast, when issues fall within the purview of politics—even democratic politics—minorities risk finding themselves marginalized.[12]

Nozick's utopia is a thought experiment in implementing historical rather than patterned principles. It is a fair experiment. It does not assume that every token of a society's experiments in living will turn out well. Nozick's basic structure ensures only that citizens have a right to exit when their experiments do not go as planned.

Incompleteness as a Theoretical Ideal

Recall Rawls's precursor: An inequality is allowed only if the institution allowing it works to the advantage of everyone. As noted, Rawls worried that such a principle is incomplete. We considered how Rawls proceeded to complete it.

But do we need a theory to be "complete"? We might suspect that all we need is a theory saying what is unjust and that the precursor is complete enough for that. It rules out sacrificing people for the general good, thus enshrining respect for the separateness of persons. Indeed, we might conclude we do not want a "complete" theory. When we ask what we want from basic structure, we realize we need incompleteness. Rawls says bargainers would choose his difference principle but never acknowledges that choosing anything as "complete" as the difference principle may not be a theory's or even a basic structure's job. Rawls acknowledges this in the international arena: We neither need nor want a complete theory, for we view self-determination as a fundamental good for "peoples" (see Rawls 1999b, 85). A basic structure's job is to get a political community off the ground, enabling voters and legislators to define and refine community norms as they go.

Rawls sometimes says that all we do at a level of theory is pick a framework; societies work out details (1996, 377; 1971, 528). Nozick was saying much the same in his discussion of utopia. Most of what makes a society liberal cannot be guaranteed by basic structure but is instead in the hands of people and communities working out their own destinies within basic structures (see Tomasi 2001). In Nozick's utopia, simply preserving the right to exit encompasses most of what the overarching federation's basic structure would try to do. More would be less.

NOTES

Early sections of this essay condense and extend parts of several chapters of Schmidtz (2006). Later sections borrow from Freiman (2011). We are greatly indebted to David Estlund for helpful feedback.

1. See the chapter by Leif Wenar in this volume.
2. See Rawls (1971, 60, 62). Besides entering Rawls's argument as the difference principle's logical precursor, what we call the precursor was temporally prior too. Amazingly, in his first published statement of the two principles, the second principle is not the difference principle.

> The conception of justice which I want to develop may be stated in the form of two principles as follows: first, each person participating in a practice, or affected by it, has an equal right to the most extensive liberty compatible with a like liberty for all; and second, inequalities are arbitrary unless it is reasonable to expect that they will work out for everyone's advantage, and provided the positions and offices to which they attach, or from which they may be gained, are open to all. (Rawls 1999a)

The precursor survives as Rawls's general conception of justice in *A Theory of Justice* (1971, 53).

3. But see Estlund (1996, 73ff).
4. "Jim Crow" refers to a body of law in the southern states aimed at segregating races. So, for example, section 369 of Birmingham's Racial Segregation Ordinances states: "It shall be unlawful to conduct a restaurant or other place for the serving of food in the

city, at which white and colored people are served in the same room, unless such white and colored persons are effectually separated by a solid partition extending from the floor upward to a distance of seven feet or higher, and unless a separate entrance from the street is provided for each compartment." (Source: Courtesy of the Birmingham Civil Rights Institute).

5. Nozick's justification of initial acquisition strikes many as the theory's weak link, but see Schmidtz (1994).

6. But see Section VIII for a revisionist account of what Nozick should have said.

7. Nozick is imagining a competitive market economy where, at equilibrium, scarce talent is paid according to its highest marginal value. He is not talking about the two-person labor market imagined by Cohen (1995).

8. See Peter Vallentyne's "Left-Libertarianism" in this volume.

9. Intellectual property rights raise the same issues. To award a patent is to secure an inventor's claim to profit from an invention, at a cost of denying others the right to reproduce the invention without permission. In the abstract, it is hard to know whether the net effect of a patent system is liberating or stifling, but we can check and see whether societies that respect patents are more inventive and more prosperous than societies that don't.

10. We might also ask, "Were they old enough to consent?" In any case, Nozick was a liberal through and through. Regarding polygamy or gay marriage, we suspect Nozick's only question would be, "Did the partners consent?"

11. When we call a choice arbitrary, we imply not only that it is unjustified, not only that it is wrong, but that it exhibits a certain arrogance: For example, a person's attitude might be "I can do what I want."

12. We thank David Estlund for the thought that, "when a matter is under market direction rather than political control there will still be winners and losers. There's one kind of dissatisfaction bred by losing politically, another kind bred by losing in the market." Our thought is that politics is deciding between, say, two huge shopping carts, one Republican and one Democrat. Both carts are vastly more than we want, but we end up with one of them, and not because we individually chose it. Nearly half of us get our second choice in a field of two. In this case, it is unclear that there are any winners. In a market, by contrast, an item is in our cart only if we want it. Either way, we pay for what is in our carts, but markets empower us to decline what is not worth the price. And in a market society, even the least advantaged can afford enough to give them a life expectancy of eight decades.

REFERENCES

Cohen, G. A. 1995. *Self-Ownership, Freedom, and Equality*. Cambridge, UK: Cambridge University Press.

Cohen, G. A. 2000. "Self-Ownership, World-Ownership, and Equality." In *Vallentyne & Steiner, Left-Libertarianism and Its Critics*, 247–70. New York: Palgrave.

Estlund, David. 1996. "The Survival of Egalitarian Justice in John Rawls's Political Liberalism." *Journal of Political Philosophy* 4:68–78.

Freiman, Christopher. 2011. "Priority and Position." Unpublished manuscript.

Gates, Henry Louis, and Appiah, Anthony. 1999. *Africana: The Encyclopedia of the African and African American Experience*. New York: Basic Civitas Books.

Miller, David. 1999. *Principles of Social Justice*. Cambridge, MA: Harvard University Press.
Nagel, Thomas. 1975. "Libertarianism without Foundations." *Yale Law Journal* 85:136–49.
Nozick, Robert. 1974. *Anarchy, State, and Utopia*. New York: Basic Books.
Nozick, Robert. 1981. *Philosophical Explanations*. Cambridge, MA: Belknap Press.
Rawls, John. 1971. *A Theory of Justice*. Cambridge, MA: Harvard University Press.
Rawls, John. 1996. *Political Liberalism*. New York: Columbia University Press.
Rawls, John. 1999a. *Collected Papers*. Edited by S. Freeman, Cambridge, MA: Harvard University Press.
Rawls, John. 1999b. *The Law of Peoples*. Cambridge, MA: Harvard University Press.
Rawls, John. 2001. *Justice as Fairness: A Restatement*. Cambridge, MA: Harvard University Press.
Schmidtz, David. 1994. "The Institution of Property." *Social Philosophy & Policy* 11:42–62.
Schmidtz, David. 2006. *Elements of Justice*. New York: Cambridge University Press.
Tomasi, John. 2001. *Liberalism Beyond Justice*. Princeton, NJ: Princeton University Press.

Index

action
  authority and reasons for, 32
  right, 59
action guidance
  compliance in, 387
  in ideal theory, 380, 384, 385, 388
  justice and, 376
  of nonideal theory, 374, 383, 384, 385, 387, 388
  in political philosophy, 387–88
activism
  deliberative democracy and political, 214, 216
  religious considerations in public discourse, and privatization vs., 234–37
African Americans
  enduring injustice against, 327–28, 330
  historical injustices against, 319–25, 327–30, 333n2
  racism against, 327, 330
  reparations for, 323, 324, 325, 328, 333n2
  slavery of, 319, 321, 324, 325, 327, 333n2
aggregative democratic theory
  overview, 206, 207
  as schoolyard view of democracy, 206
Althusser, Louis, 170, 183
analytical Marxism
  Cohen, G. A., on, 9, 170, 176, 177
  communism and, 9–10
  on economics, 172, 179
  of Elster, 9, 170, 175
  history of, 170–75
  on justice, 171–72
  liberalism and, 183
  Marx and, 9, 169, 171, 173
  Marxism and, 169–75, 177
  overview, 9, 17n16, 169–70
  political theory and, 179
  rational choice Marxism and, 174–75
  socialism and, 172, 177
  on Soviet Union, 9–10, 17n17
anarchism
  egalitarian camp of, 46, 51
  philosophical, 31, 36
Anarchy, State, and Utopia (Nozick), 8, 61, 93, 129n8, 411
Anscombe, G. E. M., 189
antiracism, 336, 337, 348, 350
arbitrary choice, 423–24, 427n11
Attas, Daniel, 103–5, 109n11, 110n13, 110n17
Augustine, 299
authority. *See also* political authority; practical authority

  autonomy and, 31–32
  concept of, 23–26
  de facto, 25–26, 38n5
  de jure, 25–26, 37n1, 38n2, 38n5
  Hobbes on, 23
  individual irrationality and, 32
  legitimacy and, 26, 28, 33, 34, 35, 36–37, 37n1, 38n2
  reasons for action, and, 32
  theoretical (epistemic), 23–24, 32
autonomy
  authority and, 31–32
  principle in democracy, 194–96

Bartels, Larry, 245
basic liberties, 60, 87, 115, 116, 118, 146, 233, 235, 377, 397, 406
Beitz, Charles, 198, 270–71, 280, 283
  human rights political theory of, 284, 285, 286–87, 296n8
Bentham, Jeremy, 80, 89
Berlin, Isaiah, 9, 78, 79, 80, 82, 88, 89
Brennan, Jason, 125
Buckle, Steven, 98, 108
bundle-of-rights. *See* property rights bundle
Butt, Daniel, 322–23

campaign finance, 242, 244–45, 251
  free expression and, 254, 255
  public financing of elections, 246–47
Canada
  Chinese American discrimination by, 319
  indigenous peoples assimilation, 319
  racism, 319
Caney, Simon, 266, 267–68
capability
  approach, luck egalitarianism, and distributive justice, 64
  democratic equality and, 71
  theories, 296n11
capitalism, 182
  high liberalism on, 127
  historical materialism on, 176
  laissez-faire, 127–28
  Marx on, 173, 176
  neoclassical liberalism on, 127, 128
  state and, 180
Chinese Americans
  discrimination against, 319, 330
  historical injustices against, 319, 328, 330
Chodorow, Nancy, 360

church-state separation, 231, 235
　ecclesiastical political neutrality principle, 235–36, 237, 239n24
　equality principle, 224, 225, 226, 237
　establishment and, 224–25, 237n1
　in liberal democracy, 226
　liberty principle, 224, 237
　neutrality principle, 224, 225, 226–27, 237, 238nn8–9
　overview, 223, 224–27
　religious liberty and, 224, 225
　in U.S., 225, 237n1, 238n8
citizenship. *See also* freedom of citizens
　equal citizenship status, 48
citizenship ethics, 237
　good, 228, 232
　rational disagreement between epistemic peers, and, 233–34, 239n21
civic republicanism, 210
civic republican deliberativism
　liberal deliberativism compared to, 212–13
　overview, 210, 212, 220n15
　radical democratic deliberativism compared to, 213
civic voice, 236–37, 239n25
civil religion, 224, 237n1
class
　historical materialism on, 178, 181
　Marx on, 178, 180, 181–82
　property relations and, 178
　state and, 180
class dictatorship
　bourgeois, 180, 181
　Marx on, 181–82
　proletarian, 181–82
classical just war theory, 300
　conduct of war (*jus in bello*) principles, 299
　just cause in, 299
　natural law theory and, 298
　overview, 298, 299
　resort to war (*jus ad bellum*) principles, 299
　on unjust war, 299
classical liberalism, 128. *See also* libertarianism; neoclassical liberalism
　on economic liberty, 115, 116, 117, 118–19, 126
　high liberalism compared to, 117, 118
　on ideal theory, 127
　on liberty, 120, 121
　on markets, 123, 124
　new liberalism and, 94
　overview and summary, 115–17, 128–29
　on private property rights, 93–94, 105, 106, 107, 108, 109, 110n14, 119
　on social justice, 124–25, 126
classical racialism, 337
coercion
　based statism, 270, 271, 277n8
　coercive conduct *vs.* free expression, 227–28
　gender issues, choice and, 358–65
　liberalization and, 235
　secular rationale principle and, 235
Cohen, Gerald Allen, 13, 46, 173, 174, 419
　analytical Marxism of, 9, 170, 176, 177
　on freedom, 419–20, 421
　on ideal theory, 373, 374, 383–84
　on justice, 384
　on private property, 419, 420, 422
Cohen, I. Andrew, 323–24
Cohen, Joshua, 11, 210, 211, 220n12, 220n19
common good
　in democracy, 144, 190, 194
　in democratic theory, 206, 208
　general will and, 144
　in social contract, 144, 146, 147
communism, 10. *See also* Marxism; socialism
　analytical Marxism and, 9–10
　Marxism and, 170, 176, 177, 182
　socialism and, 181, 182
　Soviet Union, 9–10, 17n17, 171
The Communist Manifesto (Marx), 180
communitarianism, 7–8
conduct of war (*jus in bello*) principles
　classical just war theory, 299
　just war theory, 298–312, 314
　revisionist just war theory, 310, 311, 314
　traditional just war theory, 301–12
consciousness
　historical materialism on economics and, 178–79
　state and, 182–83
Considerations on Representative Government (Mill), 193
Constitution (U.S.), 144, 181, 212, 225, 289
contractarianism, 146, 150. *See also* social contract
control rights. *See also* liberty rights; security rights
　property rights, 104–5, 109nn11–12
convention-based social contracts, 148–49
　of Hume, 135, 148–49
　justice in, 148–49
　overview, 135
cosmopolitan egalitarianism, 14–15, 42, 52
cosmopolitanism, 267, 408
counterterrorism, 15
Covenant on Civil and Political Rights (ICCPR), 279, 281–82, 283, 296n3
Covenant on Economic, Social and Cultural Rights (ICESCR), 279, 281–82, 283, 288, 296n3

deliberation
　in deliberative democracy, 208–19, 219nn5–6
　in democratic theory, 206–8
　about ends, 204, 205–6, 207
　in instrumentalism, 205–6, 207, 208–9
　money in politics, and, 246
　nonrational elements in, 215–16
　overview, 204–6
　political communication and, 16
　practical, 204, 205
　rational considerations for decisions in, 204
　reason in, 204, 205, 206, 215–18
　theoretical, 204–5
deliberative democracy, 192, 382. *See also* civic republican deliberativism; liberal deliberativism; radical democratic deliberativism

civility in, 216–17
deliberation in, 208–19, 219nn5–6
democratic theory, 208
epistemology of, 214–19, 220nn18–19
instrumentalism contrast with, 208–9, 219n9
nondeliberative democracy compared to, 208, 219n5
overview, 10–11, 208–10, 219nn4–6
political activism and, 214, 216
public ignorance and, 218
reason in, 209–10, 215–19, 219nn9–10
republicans on, 212
three styles of, 210–14
deliberativism. *See* deliberative democracy
democracy. *See also* deliberative democracy; liberal democracy; radical democracy; social democracy
autonomy principle in, 194–96
common good in, 144, 190, 194
complexity and representation, 199–201
deliberative democracy compared to nondeliberative, 208, 219n5
direct, 200, 202n14
egalitarian camp of, 46–47, 51–52
in egalitarian society, 52
equal consideration of interests in, 191–92, 211
equality constraint in, 196, 197
equal respect in political realm in, 193–97
freedom and, 89–90
general interest in, 189, 190
individualism and, 188, 189, 190, 191
justice in, 193–94
majority decision in, 189–90, 197–98, 199, 201n4, 202n12
majority in, 189–90, 197
market, 126
overview, 187–88
participatory, 52, 208
of people, 188
people or persons in, 188–91
political authority and, 34–37
political equality in, 191–97, 198–99, 200, 201
procedures and outcomes, 198–99
representative, 200–201, 202n14, 202n16
right-based social contracts, liberalism, and, 133, 134, 135, 141–48
social hierarchy and, 47
social welfare function in, 190, 192, 194
terminology of, 187–88
unanimity principle in, 195–96, 197
U.S., 191, 202n16
utilitarianism on, 201n4
voting in, 188–90, 196–97, 211
democratic equality
capability and, 71
distributive justice, equality of social relations, and, 69–73
luck egalitarianism and, 70, 71–72
democratic societies

money in politics, in, 241
religion and politics in, 235, 237
religion and secularity of, 223
democratic theory. *See also* civic republicanism; deliberative democracy; liberalism; minimalist democratic theory; radical democracy
aggregative, 206, 207
common good in, 206, 208
deliberation in, 206–8
deliberative democracy, 208
instrumentalism in, 206, 207
normative, 207–8
popular will in, 206, 207, 208
dictatorship. *See also* class dictatorship
Marx on, 181
overview, 181, 187–88
of proletariat, 180
state as, 181
discrimination. *See also* racial discrimination
against Chinese Americans, 319, 330
differential treatment and, 343–44
against immigrants, 328, 330
overview, 341–42
sex, 368
wrongful, 341, 342
distributive equality, 10, 40, 41
moral equality and, 267
political equality and, 267
distributive justice, 265, 267, 272. *See also* global justice; justice
benefits and burdens in, 58, 74n2
democratic equality, equality of social relations, and, 69–73
Dworkin's equality of resources doctrine and, 64–66
fair distribution in, 58
inequality and, 423
interpersonal comparisons, welfare, and equality *vs.* sufficiency *vs.* priority, and, 66–69, 72, 74n5
Lockean libertarianism and, 61–63
luck egalitarianism, capabilities approach, and, 64
luck egalitarianism and, 64, 69–72, 73
Nozick on, 62, 421, 422–23, 427n10
overview and conclusion, 58, 73–74, 74nn1–2, 261
social equality and, 73
in utilitarianism, 59–61
utilitarianism critique by Rawls, 60–61
welfare, welfarism, and, 66–69, 74n5
domestic justice
on equality, 267
overview, 262
Rawls on, 265, 271
domination
freedom of the state, interference and, 89–90
high liberalism, neoclassical liberalism, and political, 123, 130nn18–19
issue *vs.* interference, in freedom to exercise choice, 77, 78–83, 87, 89–90
social hierarchies of command or, 42–47

Dworkin, Ronald, 10, 254, 388n2
    distributive justice, and equality of resources
        doctrine of, 64–66

ECHR. *See* European Convention on Human Rights
economics
    analytical Marxism on, 172, 179
    egalitarian society, 51–52
    freedom as opportunity for choice, and, 83–84
    historical materialism on consciousness and, 178–79
    Marxism on, 172, 174, 179
    model of political agency, 10, 11
economic liberty. *See also* property rights
    classical liberalism on, 115, 116, 117, 118–19, 126
    high liberalism on, 115, 117, 118, 119
    left libertarianism on, 116, 117, 129n6
    liberalism on, 115, 116, 117, 118–19
    libertarianism on, 116, 117, 118–19
    neoclassical liberalism on, 117, 118, 119, 125
    Rawls on, 116, 118
    social democracy rankings of, 129n12
egalitarianism, 72–73. *See also* equality; luck egalitarianism
    anarchist camp of, 46, 51
    cosmopolitan, 14–15, 42, 52
    critiques of social hierarchies, 40, 41, 42, 44–51
    democratic camp of, 46–47, 51–52
    on gender inequality, 365
    language of, 10
    Marxism and, 10
    material, 122, 123, 130nn13–14
    on money in politics, 252
    money in politics, and, 252–53
    on moral equality, 45, 46
    remedies, 41, 42
    remedies for social hierarchies, 41, 43
    social democracy camp of, 51–52
    telic, 54–55, 55n6
    of utilitarianism, 59
    views of equality, 40–42
egalitarian liberalism, 94, 125, 329. *See also* new liberalism
egalitarian social movements, 40, 41, 52, 53
egalitarian society, 41. *See also* just society
    competing visions of, 51–53
    democracy in, 52
    economics, 51–52
    transnational and global institutions, 52, 55n5
    workplace in, 52
Elster, Jon, 9, 170, 175
enduring injustice
    against African Americans, 327–28, 330
    criteria of, 328–30
    historical injustice and, 327–32
    against indigenous peoples, 330–32
    liberal justice and, 329, 330, 331–32
    against Native Americans, 330, 331, 332, 333n4
    stolen land and, 330–32

epistemic proceduralism, 220n13
equality. *See also* democratic equality; egalitarianism; gender equality; inequality; moral equality; political equality
    classical Marxism on, 171, 172
    concepts of, 40–42
    distributive, 10, 40, 41, 267
    distributive implications of relational, 53–55
    distributive justice, and sufficiency *vs.* priority *vs.*, 66–67, 72
    as distributive principle or ideal of social relations, 40–42, 52–55
    domestic justice on, 267
    egalitarian views of, 40–42
    equal citizenship status, 48
    fair equality of opportunity, 60–61, 398
    injustice in expanding circle of, 15
    liberalism on freedom and, 115
    Marx and, 9–10
    Marxism and, 9–10
    material, 123, 130nn17–18
    political philosophy on expanding circle of, 14–15
    principle, 66–67, 224, 225, 226, 237
    racial, 336, 350
    of resources doctrine, and distributive justice, 64–66
    Scanlon on, 269
    social, 41–42, 52, 73
    social hierarchy types and, 42–44
    of social relations, democratic equality, and distributive justice, 69–73
equal moral worth
    in human rights philosophical theories, 281, 282, 283, 284, 288, 289, 291
    in human rights political theories, 285
    moral status and, 343
establishment
    church-state separation, and, 224–25, 237n1
    doctrinal, 224, 237n1
    formal, 224, 225, 237n1
    limited, 225
    of religion, 224–25, 237n1
esteem
    Nozick's utopia and self-, 425
    social hierarchies of, 43–44, 45, 46, 47–49
Estlund, David, 216–17, 220n13, 252, 253, 427n12
ethics. *See also* citizenship ethics; morality
    interpersonal ethical ownership, 155
    meta-, 6, 16n8, 206
    standards for law and public policy advocacy, 228–31, 238n15, 238nn12–13
European Convention on Human Rights (ECHR), 279

fair equality of opportunity (FEO), 60–61, 398
fairness. *See also* justice as fairness
    theory of, 68–69
family
    feminist scholarship on, 355
    gender inequality in, 354–55, 358, 359, 360, 361–63

gender roles in, 358–62
women's subordination in, 354, 355
feminism
  on gender differences, 357
  on gender inequality, 355, 356, 357
  on women's subordination, 356, 357
feminist philosophy
  critique of liberalism's individualism, 8
  necessity for, 356, 369n1
  on "personal is political," 8
feminist scholarship
  on family, 355
  on gender differences, 357
FEO. *See* fair equality of opportunity
Filmer, Robert, 28
Fraser, Nancy, 44
freedom. *See also* liberty; individual freedom
  Bentham on, 80, 89
  Berlin on, 78, 79, 80, 82, 88, 89
  Cohen, G. A., on, 419–20, 421
  democracy and, 89–90
  Hobbes on, 78, 79, 86, 89
  liberalism on equality and, 115
  national boundary restrictions on, 273
  overview, 76–77
  positive, 9
  republican concept of, 82, 86, 88, 90, 212, 220n16
  state and, 420
  as zero-sum game, 419–21
freedom as opportunity for choice
  economics and, 83–84
  efficiency argument, 83, 84
  freedom of citizens, and, 86, 87
  freedom to exercise choice, and, 83, 84, 85–86
  overview, 76
freedom of choice. *See also* freedom as opportunity for choice; freedom to exercise choice
  freedom of citizens, and, 86–88, 89
  options, 76–77
freedom of citizens
  freedom of choice, and, 86–88, 89
  freedom of the state, and, 88–89, 90
  overview, 76, 86
freedom of the state
  democracy and, 89–90
  freedom of citizens, and, 88–89, 90
  interference, domination, and, 89–90
  overview, 76
freedom to exercise choice
  freedom as opportunity for choice, and, 83, 84, 85–86
  freedom of citizens, and, 86, 87, 88
  interference *vs.* domination issue, 77, 78–83, 87, 89–90
  nature *vs.* will issue, 77–78
  overview, 76, 77
free expression
  campaign finance and, 254, 255
  coercive conduct *vs.*, 227–28
  for law and public policy advocacy, 227, 228
  in liberal democracy, 227
  money in politics, and, 253–55
  overview, 227–28
  in public discourse, 227
Freeman, Samuel, 117, 265
Friedman, Milton, 119, 125, 129n10
full ownership, 106, 109
  overview, 95–96
  property rights bundle and, 96
full ownership justifications
  instability of, 97–101
  liberty upsetting of, 99–100, 101, 109n7
  problem of restricted justification, 97–99, 100–101, 102
full ownership rights
  control rights over use of entity, 154, 166n6
  overview, 154, 166n6
full self-ownership
  full control self-ownership, 159
  full transfer rights, 159–61
  libertarianism on, 153–61
  liberty rights, 157–59
  moral, 153–54
  overview and summary, 153–56, 165
  powers to authorize use by others, 157, 159, 166n8
  security rights, 156–57, 158, 159
full transfer rights
  full self-ownership, 159–61
  objections to, 159–60

Gaus, Gerald, 123, 126
Gauthier, David, 139–40, 141, 147
gay, 44, 53, 359
gender. *See also* women
  absence in just society, 365
  overview and conclusion, 354–58, 369
  sex and, 356–57, 358, 365
  understandings of, 356–58
  women and, 354–69
gender differences
  choice and coercion in, 358–65
  feminism on, 357
  feminist scholarship on, 357
  gender inequality and, 355–56, 357–63
  gender justice and, 365–66
  sex-based, 357, 358, 360, 365, 366, 367
  understandings of, 356–58
gender equality
  contestation of, 369
  in gender roles, 363
  religion and, 365, 368
  as sameness, 366
  state promotion of, 368
  throughout world, 369
  unequal opportunity and, 369
gender inequality. *See also* women's inequality
  choice and coercion in, 359–65
  egalitarianism on, 365
  in family, 354–55, 358, 359, 360, 361–63

gender inequality (*continued*)
  feminism on, 355, 356, 357
  gender differences and, 355–56, 357–63
  gender roles and, 360–63
  just and unjust, 358
  political philosophy on, 354, 355, 356
  questions about, 355–56
  social justice and, 354, 355, 356
gender justice, 355–56
  choice in, 358–66, 368–69
  ends, 358–66
  gender differences and, 365–66
  gender neutrality in, 366–68
  means, 358, 366–69
  policy, 368–69
  religion and, 368
  state and, 366–68
  for women, 366
gender roles
  choice and coercion in, 358–65
  in family, 358–61
  gender equality in, 363
  gender inequality and, 360–63
  sex and, 360, 365
general interest
  in democracy, 189, 190
  social welfare function and, 190
general will
  common good and, 144
  of Rousseau, 144–45, 146, 150n4
Gilens, Martin, 245
global governance
  globalization and, 263
  global justice and, 263
  Rawls on world governance, 408–9
globalism
  global order and, 264, 276n3
  justice and, 264, 268, 270, 271, 277n4
  on moral equality, 267
  relationism of, 264, 268, 270, 276n3
  state and, 264, 267
  statism and, 264, 268, 270–71
globalization
  global governance and, 263
  global order and, 263
  overview, 263
global justice. *See also* international justice
  climate change and, 14
  cosmopolitanism and, 267
  global governance and, 263
  global order, the poor, and, 272–73
  global order and, 263, 271
  increase in scholarly work on, 13, 17n24
  international justice difference from, 261
  moral equality and, 267
  nonrelationism and, 263, 264, 277n6
  overview and conclusion, 13–14, 261–63, 276
  Rawls on, 265–66
  relationism and, 263
  social justice and, 13
  state and, 261–62, 271

global order, 270
  the poor and, 272–76, 277n12
  globalism and, 264, 276n3
  globalization and, 263
  global justice, the poor, and, 272–73
  global justice and, 263, 271
goodness
  in social hierarchies, 50
  utility and individual good, 59
  as value realm, 44
goods, primary social, 61, 64, 65, 68
Gramsci, Antonio, 183
Greenawalt, Kent, 229, 238n12
Grey, Thomas C., 94, 95, 103, 108
Griffin, James, 287, 296n9
grounding view (GV), 289
  in human rights political theories, 286, 287, 296n8
  justification of, 281–84, 296nn3–4
  normative agency in, 287
  overview, 280–81
guarantees, and liberty, 120–22
Gutmann, Amy, 210, 211
GV. *See* grounding view

Habermas, Jürgen, 11, 209, 210, 238n15
Hayek, Friedrich August, 115, 119, 120, 121, 124–25
Hegel, Georg Wilhelm Friedrich, 101, 174, 176
Hendrix, Burke, 331, 332
high liberalism, 126
  on capitalism, 127
  classical liberalism compared to, 117, 118
  on economic liberty, 115, 117, 118, 119
  on ideal theory, 126, 127, 130n21
  on liberty, 120, 123
  on markets, 124, 128
  on material egalitarianism and material equality, 122, 123, 130n13, 130n18
  neoclassical liberalism and, 128–29
  overview, 115, 117, 128–29
  political domination and, 123, 130nn18–19
  on property rights, 118
history
  Hegel on philosophy of, 174, 176
  mainstream historiography on historical materialism, 173–74
  political philosophy and, 3
historical injustice
  apologies, 319
  compensation, 319, 322–25, 326–27, 333n2
  current injustice and, 320, 322, 325, 327–32
  enduring injustice and, 327–32
  against indigenous peoples, 319, 320, 326, 328–29, 330–32, 333nn4–5
  liberal justice and, 331–32
  overview, 319–20
  rectification, 319, 322–27
  remembering, 319, 320–22
  reparations, 319, 321, 322–25, 327, 328
  responsibility for, 320–22, 332n1
  without responsible agents, 319, 321–22

historical materialism
  on capitalism, 176
  on class, 178, 181
  on economics and consciousness, 178–79
  liberalism and, 177
  mainstream historiography on, 173–74
  of Marx, 173–74, 175–78, 181, 183
  Marxism on, 173–74, 177
  on ownership, 176
  on precapitalism, 176
  on property relations, 177–78
  on socialism, 176, 177
  validity of, 175–76, 177
Hobbes, Thomas, 393
  on authority, 23
  on freedom, 78, 79, 86, 89
  interest-based social contract of, 135–41, 146, 147, 148
  on justice, 139, 141
  Leviathan of, 79, 86, 89, 133, 135, 138
  on political authority, 23, 28, 34
  on practical authority, 26–28, 29
  on the state, 179, 180, 181, 262, 299–300
  traditional just war theory and, 299–300
Hobhouse, L. T., 94
Hohfeld, Wesley N., 25
human rights. *See also* international human rights; moral human rights
  ambiguity in human rights philosophical theories, 280–81
  overview, 279–80
human rights philosophical theories. *See also* human rights political theories
  capability theories, 296n11
  enriched conception of, 290–91
  equal moral worth or dignity in, 281, 282, 283, 284, 288, 289, 291
  grounding view justification, 281–84
  human rights ambiguity in, 280–81
  human rights practice institutional challenges, 289–91
  human rights practice normative challenges, 291–95
  institutions, and scope and conflict problems, 289–91
  interest-based theories, 287–89
  on international legal human rights, 280, 296n1
  limits of traditional, 293
  needs-based theories, 287–89
  overview and conclusion, 279–80, 295
  supremacy issue, 293
  theoretical advances or institutional development, 294–95
human rights political theories. *See also* human rights philosophical theories
  of Beitz, 284, 285, 286–87, 296n8
  equal moral worth or dignity in, 285
  grounding view in, 286, 287, 296n8
  international legal human rights in, 284, 285, 286, 287, 296n8
  moral human rights in, 285, 286, 287, 296n8
  of Rawls, 284, 285–86, 287

human rights practice. *See* international human rights practice
Hume, David, 135, 143, 148–49, 205

ICCPR. *See* Covenant on Civil and Political Rights
ICESCR. *See* Covenant on Economic, Social and Cultural Rights
ideal theory, 388n2. *See also* nonideal theory
  action guidance in, 380, 384, 385, 388
  classical liberalism on, 127
  Cohen, G. A., on, 373, 374, 383–84
  on compliance, 375, 376, 385, 386
  high liberalism on, 126, 127, 130n21
  injustice and, 376, 378–79, 385
  justice and, 374, 375–79, 383, 384–85, 386
  neoclassical liberalism on, 127
  nonideal theory and, 374–80, 382, 383, 385, 386
  overview, 126–27, 373–74, 375
  on political moralism, 382
  political philosophy and, 373, 374, 378, 380–81, 382, 383, 386, 388
  political realism and, 380–82
  Rawls on, 6, 13, 126–28, 373–87
  realism and, 380–82, 383–85, 386
  social justice and, 373
  usefulness and uselessness of, 377–80
immigration, 273, 276
  discrimination against, 328, 330
incidents, 96. *See also* property rights
indigenous peoples. *See also* Native Americans
  assimilation in Canada, 319
  enduring injustice against, 330–32
  historical injustice against, 319, 320, 326, 328–29, 330–32, 333nn4–5
  historical injustice between, 326
individuals, state and, 262
individual freedom
  negative liberty, 9
  nondomination, 9
  political authority and, 30–31, 36
  positive freedom, 9
individualism
  democracy and, 188, 189, 190, 191
  feminist critique of liberalism's, 8
inequality. *See also* equality; gender inequality; social hierarchies
  distributive justice and, 423
  poor and, 274
  Rawls on, 398–99, 412, 413, 423, 426n2
injustice. *See also* enduring injustice; historical injustice
  expanding circle of equality and, 15
  ideal theory and, 376, 378–79, 385
  nonideal theory on, 375, 378, 387
  race and, 337
institutions
  human rights and, 289–92, 294–95
  of justice as fairness, 399–400

institutions (*continued*)
  overview, 340
  transnational and global, 52, 55n5
institutional racism, 339–41, 346
instrumentalism
  deliberation in, 205–6, 207, 208–9
  deliberative democracy contrast with, 208–9, 219n9
  in democratic theory, 206, 207
  overview, 205
  reason in, 205, 206, 209, 219n9
interest-based social contracts
  contemporary, 137–41
  conventional, 137–38
  of Hobbes, 135–41, 146, 147, 148
  justice in, 135–36, 137, 139, 141, 147
  morality in, 135, 136, 137, 139–41, 142
  overview, 135–36, 137–38
  right-based social contracts compared to, 146–48
international human rights. *See also* international legal human rights
  treaties, 279, 293
international human rights practice (the practice), 287
  institutional challenges to, 289–91
  international legal human rights promotion by, 279–80, 291–95
  legal human rights institutional implementation legitimacy, 291–92
  legal human rights norms legitimacy, 291, 292–93
  normative challenges to, 291–95
  overview, 279–80
  supremacy issue, 291, 293
  theoretical advances or institutional development, 294–95
  traditional philosophical theory limits, 293–94
internationalism
  graded, 271–72
  justice and, 271, 272
  monist, 271
  nongraded, 271
  nonrelationalism and, 272
  overview, 271–72
  pluralist, 271, 272
  relationalism and, 272
  state and, 271, 272
international justice, 265. *See also* global justice
  global justice difference from, 261
international legal human rights. *See also* grounding view
  human rights philosophical theories on, 280, 296n1
  in human rights political theories, 284, 285, 286, 287, 296n8
  international human rights practice promotion of, 279–80, 291–95
  in international legal rights, 280
  legitimacy of institutional implementation of, 291–92
  legitimacy of norms of, 292–93

moral human rights and, 280–84, 285, 286, 287, 288, 289, 291, 293, 296nn3–4, 296nn8–9
  overview, 279–80
  social moral epistemology of, 290
  summary of justifications for, 295
international legal rights, 287
  international legal human rights in, 280
international principles, of Rawls, 407–8

Jim Crow, 319
jurisdictions
  property as, 105–8
  wide and narrow senses of liberalism, property, and, 106–8
jus ad bellum. *See* resort to war principles
jus in bello. *See* conduct of war principles
justice. *See also* distributive justice; domestic justice; gender justice; global justice; injustice; liberal justice; racial justice; social justice
  action guidance and, 376
  analytical Marxism on, 171–72
  classical Marxism on, 171, 172
  Cohen, G. A., on, 384
  convention-based social contracts on, 148–49
  corrective, 346
  in democracy, 193–94
  globalism and, 264, 268, 270, 271, 277n4
  grounds of, 263–64, 266–67, 277n4
  Hobbes on, 139, 141
  ideal theory and, 374, 375–79, 383, 384–85, 386
  interest-based social contracts on, 135–36, 137, 139, 141, 147
  internationalism and, 271, 272
  libertarianism on, 152–53, 155
  Marxism on, 171–72
  nonideal theory and, 375, 376, 377, 385, 386–87
  nonrelationism and, 263–64, 266, 268, 272, 277n6, 277nn4–5
  Nozick on, 411–12, 414–18
  overview, 261
  Rawls on, 4, 5, 6, 8, 10, 34, 58, 60–61, 117, 125, 126, 145–46, 150n3, 171, 182, 265–66, 271, 285, 373–77, 381–84, 386, 393–405, 411–12, 418, 423, 426n2
  realism on, 382
  of rectification, 326–27
  rectificatory, 261, 422
  relationism and, 263–64, 265–66, 268–69, 272, 277n4
  right-based social contracts on, 135–36, 141, 142, 144, 145–46, 147
  Schmidtz on, 125–26, 130n20
  social contracts on, 135, 136, 148, 149–50
  state and, 262, 264, 270, 271, 272
  statism and, 264, 268, 271, 276n2, 277n4
justice as fairness
  choice of principles, 397–99
  conception of person, 394–96
  conception of society, 394–96
  difference principle, in, 60, 61, 398

fair equality of opportunity, in, 60–61, 398
first principle, of equal basic rights and liberties, 397–98
institutions of, 399–400
justice and money, and, 400–401
original position and, 396–97, 398, 400, 407
overview, 145–46, 394
political conception of, 404–5
property-owning democracy, in, 399–400
Rawls theory of, 145–46, 394–401, 404–5
second principle, on socio-economic inequalities, 398–99
utilitarianism and, 397, 398–99
just society
gender absence in, 365
of Rawls, 393–401
stable and, 394
theory as justice as fairness, 394
just war theory. *See also* classical just war theory; revisionist just war theory; traditional just war theory
conduct of war (*jus in bello*) principles, 298–312, 314
on humanitarian intervention, 313–14
just cause in, 299, 302, 308, 310, 311, 312–13, 314
on preventive war, 313
resort to war (*jus ad bellum*) principles, 298–302, 310–12, 314
two sets of principles, 298–99

Kant, Immanuel, 31, 34, 48, 101
right-based social contract of, 134, 142, 145
Karl Marx's Theory of History: A Defense (Cohen), 173

Ladenson, Robert, 38n5
law. *See also* natural law theory
property, 420
Rawls on obeying, 6–7
traffic, 420–21
law and public policy advocacy
ethical standards for, 228–31, 238n15, 238nn12–13
free expression for, 227, 228
religious reasons in, 229, 230
secular rationale principle, 229–30, 238n15
The Law of Peoples (Rawls), 265, 266, 405, 406
left libertarianism, 157, 161, 166n16. *See also* libertarianism
on economic liberty, 116, 117, 129n6
equal opportunity, 164–65, 167nn17–18
equal share, 164
joint-ownership, 161–62
overview and summary, 116, 117, 152, 153, 165
rights to use and appropriate natural resources, 161–62, 164
legal human rights. *See* international legal human rights
legal philosophy, 10
legitimacy
authority and, 26, 28, 33, 34, 35, 36–37, 37n1, 38n2
de jure, 37n1, 38n2

Lenin, Vladimir, 179, 181, 182, 183
Leviathan (Hobbes), 79, 86, 89, 133, 135, 138
liberal deliberativism
civic republican deliberativism compared to, 212–13
overview, 210–12
radical democratic deliberativism compared to, 213
liberal democracy. *See also* liberal deliberativism
church-state separation in, 226
free expression in, 227
liberty in, 225, 227, 238n10
money in politics, in, 241
liberalism. *See also* classical liberalism; high liberalism; political liberalism
analytical Marxism and, 183
commitment to toleration, 285–86
communitarian critique of, 7–8
on economic liberty, 115, 116, 117, 118–19
egalitarian, 94, 125, 329
feminist critique of individualism of, 8
on freedom and equality, 115
historical materialism and, 177
on liberty, 116, 120–22, 212
Marxism and, 179, 182, 183
new, 94, 109n2
Nozick on self-ownership and, 417–19
overview, 115–17, 128–29, 210
political theory of, 179–80
right-based social contracts, democracy and, 133, 134, 135, 141–48
state and, 179–80, 181, 182
utilitarianism and, 60, 61
varieties of, 117
wide and narrow senses of property, jurisdictions, and, 106–8
liberalization, and coercion, 235
liberal justice, 124–25, 126, 127
enduring injustice and, 329, 330, 331–32
historical injustice and, 331–32
libertarianism, 128. *See also* full self-ownership; left libertarianism; right libertarianism
on economic liberty, 116, 117, 118–19
on enforceable duties, 152, 153, 155, 158, 166n2
on full self-ownership, 153–61
on justice, 152–53, 155
of Locke, 61–63, 162–64, 166nn13–15
on moral duties that we owe each other, 152–53, 155
natural rights doctrine of, 61, 153
of Nozick, 61–63, 118–19, 129n8, 153, 163, 165, 166n7, 411–12, 417
overview, 116, 117, 129n4, 152–53
on ownership, 153–61
on private property rights, 105, 110n14, 152
Rawls on, 395
on rights, 61–62, 63, 74n3, 166n7
rights to use and appropriate natural resources, 153, 161–65, 166nn11–12
on self-ownership, 9, 61–62, 152, 153–61

libertarianism (*continued*)
  on social justice, 124
  sufficientarian (centrist), 163–64
  unilateralist, 162
liberty. *See also* economic liberty; freedom; political liberty
  basic liberties, 60, 87, 115, 116, 118, 146, 233, 235, 377, 397, 406
  classical liberalism on, 120, 121
  guarantees and, 120, 121
  high liberalism on, 120, 123
  in liberal democracy, 225, 227, 238n10
  liberalism on, 116, 120–22, 212
  Marxism on, 120
  Mill, J. S., on, 101, 116, 224, 225, 238n10
  negative, 9, 120, 121
  neoclassical liberalism on, 120–22
  Nozick on, 8–9, 413, 414, 415
  positive, 120–21
  principle, 224, 237
  religious, 224, 225
  upsetting of full ownership justification, 99–100, 101, 109n7
liberty rights, 25, 38n5
  full ownership, 154
  full self-ownership, 157–59
  powers to authorize use by others and, 157, 159, 166n8
lobbyists, 247–48
Locke, John
  consent thesis, 142, 143
  distributive justice and libertarianism of, 61–63
  libertarianism of, 61–63, 162–64, 166nn13–15
  Lockean proviso, 162–64, 166nn14–15
  on political authority, 28, 29, 34, 37, 134
  on practical authority, 28–30, 38n4
  on property, 97, 98
  right-based social contract of, 133, 134, 135, 136, 141, 142–44, 145
Lomasky, Loren, 99, 100, 103
luck egalitarianism, 395
  criticisms of, 69–70
  democratic equality and, 70, 71–72
  distributive justice, capabilities approach, and, 64
  distributive justice and, 64, 69–72, 73
  social equality and, 73

Mack, Eric, 93, 99
majority decision (MD)
  in democracy, 189–90, 197–98, 199, 201n4, 202n12
  overview, 197–98
  political equality and, 198, 199
markets, 427n12
  classical liberalism on, 123, 124
  high liberalism on, 124, 128
  market democracy, 126
  neoclassical liberalism on, 123, 124, 128
  Nozick on free, 417, 427n7
  spontaneous order of, 123–24
Marx, Karl. *See also* historical materialism
  analytical Marxism and, 9, 169, 171, 173
  on capitalism, 173, 176
  on class, 178, 180, 181–82
  on class dictatorship, 181–82
  on dictatorship, 181
  equality and, 9–10
  historical materialism of, 173–74, 175–78, 181, 183
  Marxism and, 169, 177
  political liberalism and, 182
  political theory and, 179, 180
  on the state, 180–81
Marxism. *See also* analytical Marxism; communism; socialism
  of Althusser, 170, 183
  analytical Marxism and, 169–75, 177
  analytical Marxism and rational choice, 174–75
  classical, 171
  communism and, 170, 176, 177, 182
  on economics, 172, 174, 179
  egalitarianism and, 10
  equality and, 9–10
  on historical materialism, 173–74, 177
  history of, 170–75
  on justice, 171–72
  liberalism and, 179, 182, 183
  on liberty, 120
  Marx and, 169, 177
  as Marxist, 183
  meaning of, 170
  political theory and, 179, 181, 182
  revitalization of, 183
  on socialism, 171, 176, 177
  on social science, 172–73
  on the state, 182–83
material equality, 130n18
  political liberty and, 123, 130n17
McCarthy, Thomas, 320
MD. *See* majority decision
meta-ethics, 6, 16n8, 206
Mill, James, 197, 201n4
Mill, John Stuart, 41, 118, 193, 196–97, 302–3
  on liberty, 101, 116, 224, 225, 238n10
  on women's inequality, 354–55, 362
Mills, Charles W., 378
minimalist democratic theory
  elitism of, 207
  interest-group pluralist, 207
  Madisonian, 207, 219n2
  overview, 207
  shortcomings of, 207–8
miscegenation, 337
modern liberalism, 115. *See also* high liberalism
monarchy, 187–88
money in politics
  campaign finance, 242, 244–45, 246–47, 251, 254, 255
  corruption and, 242–43
  deliberation and, 246
  in democratic societies, 241
  egalitarianism, and, 252–53
  equality and, 250–55

free expression and, 253–55
influence mechanisms, 241–50
in liberal democracy, 241
lobbyists and, 247–48
money as gatekeeper, 244–47, 250, 254–55
money as independent political power, 250
money for votes, 242–44
money to influence opinions, 247–50, 251, 254, 255
overview, 241–42
political equality and, 242, 250–55
scarcity and, 248–50
think tanks, 250
in U.S., 242, 245, 251, 254, 255n5
moral equality. *See also* equal moral worth
distributive equality and, 267
egalitarianism on, 45, 46
globalism on, 267
global justice and, 267
nonrelationism on, 267
political equality and, 267, 273
statism on, 267
moral human rights. *See also* grounding view
in human rights political theories, 285, 286, 287, 296n8
international legal human rights and, 280–84, 285, 286, 287, 288, 289, 291, 293, 296nn3–4, 296nn8–9
normative agency grounding of, 287
overview, 279
morality. *See also* ethics; political moralism
interest-based social contracts on, 135, 136, 137, 139–41, 142
political theory and, 380–81
Rawls on morality, 5, 140, 142, 150n3, 285–86, 393–94
right-based social contracts on, 135, 136, 141–42, 143, 145, 146
of side constraints, 62, 63
moral rights, 25, 26, 61, 63, 142, 143, 154, 225, 238n5. *See also* moral human rights
moral status
equal moral worth and, 343
in racial discrimination, 343

Narveson, Jan, 98, 99
Native Americans
enduring injustice against, 330, 331, 332, 333n4
historical injustice against, 320, 326, 328–32, 333n4
natural law theory, 231
classical just war theory and, 298
on property, 108
natural racial hierarchy, 337
natural reason
overview, 231–32, 239n20
religious identity and, 232–33
religious reasons and, 232
secularity, religious conviction, and, 231–32
secular rationale principle as principle of, 230, 232, 237, 239n18
secular reason and, 239n18

natural resources
libertarianism on rights to use and appropriate, 153, 161–65, 166nn11–12
overview, 161
property rights and, 98, 109n6
natural rights
doctrine of libertarianism, 61, 153
to property, 61, 93, 99
theory of right-based social contracts, 142, 145
neoclassical liberalism, 126
on capitalism, 127, 128
on economic liberty, 117, 118, 119, 125
high liberalism and, 128–29
on ideal theory, 127
on liberty, 120–22
on markets, 123, 124, 128
on material egalitarianism, 122, 123, 130n14
overview, 115, 116–17, 128–29
political domination and, 123, 130n19
on social justice, 125, 127
welfarism, sufficientarianism, and prioritarianism of, 122–23
neutrality principle, 224, 225, 226–27, 237, 238nn8–9
new liberalism, 109n2. *See also* egalitarian liberalism
classical liberalism and, 94
on private property rights, 94
nonideal theory. *See also* ideal theory
action guidance of, 374, 383, 384, 385, 387, 388
on compliance, 375, 376, 386
ideal theory and, 374–80, 382, 383, 385, 386
on injustice, 375, 378, 387
justice and, 375, 376, 377, 385, 386–87
on noncompliance, 375, 388n3
overview, 373, 374, 375
political realism and, 380
Rawls on, 373, 375, 376, 377, 378
realism and, 380, 382
social justice and, 373
what's wanted from, 385–88
nonrelationism. *See also* relationism
global justice and, 263, 264, 277n6
internationalism and, 272
justice and, 263–64, 266, 268, 272, 277n6, 277nn4–5
on moral equality, 267
overview, 263–64, 267–68
relationism and, 263–64, 266, 270, 272
state and, 264, 267
normative agency
in grounding view, 287
moral human rights grounding by, 287
Nozick, Robert, 3, 4, 324–25
Anarchy, State, and Utopia of, 8, 61, 93, 129n8, 411
on distributive justice, 62, 421, 422–23, 427n10
on end-state justice principles, 414, 415
on entitlement theory, 415, 417, 421
on entitlement theory principles, 415, 417
on free markets, 417, 427n7
on historical justice principles, 414, 415

Nozick, Robert (*continued*)
   on initial acquisition principles, 417, 427n5
   on just distribution, 421
   on justice, 411–12, 414–18
   on justice principles, 414–17, 422
   just transfer theory of, 421–22
   on liberalism and self-ownership, 417–19
   libertarianism of, 61–63, 118–19, 129n8, 153, 163, 165, 166n7, 411–12, 417
   libertarianism without foundations, of, 411
   on liberty, 8–9, 413, 414, 415
   on patterned justice principles, 414–17, 422
   on political philosophy, 411
   on property rights, 62, 93, 118–19, 129n8, 418, 419
   Rawls and, 8, 9, 411–14, 415, 417–18
   on rectification principles, 417
   on rectificatory justice, 422
   self-esteem in utopia of, 425
   on time-slice justice principles, 414, 415, 416
   on transfer principles, 417
   utopia of, 424–25, 426
Nussbaum, Martha, 64, 273

Okin, Susan, 365
oligarchy, 187, 188
ownership. *See also* full ownership; property; self-ownership
   Attas on, 103–5, 109n11, 110n13
   fragmentation of, 95–96, 101
   historical materialism on, 176
   interpersonal ethical, 155
   libertarianism on, 153–61
   overview and summary, 108–9, 154
   political, 155
   property defragmentation and logical structure of, 103–5
   property rights bundle, and, 97–103
   property rights bundle structure, and rescuing, 97–103
   retreating to core property rights of, 102–3
   state and, 109n4
ownership rights. *See also* control rights; full ownership rights; transfer rights
   control rights over use of entity, 154, 166nn4–6
   overview, 154

Paley, William, 89
Pareto-efficient, 150n2
Pareto-improvement, 137, 150n2
people. *See also* indigenous peoples
   democracy of, 188
   or persons in democracy, 188–91
   Rawls' law of, 405–10
   Rawls on liberal and decent, 405–6
   Rawls on satisfied, 406–7
persons
   or people in democracy, 188–91
   Rawls' conceptions of, 394–96
   separateness of, 60, 62
   state's harm of, 273

personal property, private property rights and, 94
Pettit, Philip, 9, 212, 213, 220n16
philosophical anarchism, 31, 36
pluralist
   interest-group, 207
   internationalism, 271, 272
Pogge, Thomas, 55n5, 267, 274
politics. *See also* money in politics
   democratic societies, religion, and, 235, 237
   religion and, 235, 237
political agency, economist model of, 10, 11
political authority, 25
   annexation and, 35–37
   arbitration model of, 33–34
   consent-based, 30, 34–35
   de jure, 32–33, 37
   democracy and, 34–37
   grounds of, 29–37, 38n5
   Hobbes on, 23, 28, 34
   individual freedom and, 30–31, 36
   justification of, 33
   Locke on, 28, 29, 34, 37, 134
   moral obligation or duty, and, 33
   political obligations and, 30, 38n5
   Raz on, 32–33, 38nn8–9
   social contract and, 30, 34, 134, 136
political communication, and deliberation, 16
political equality
   in democracy, 191–97, 198–99, 200, 201
   distributive equality and, 267
   equal consideration of interests in, 191–92, 211
   equal respect in political realm in, 193–97
   majority decision and, 198, 199
   money in politics, and, 242, 250–55
   moral equality and, 267, 273
   statism on, 267
political history, political theorists and, 4
political justification
   public reason and, 12
   Rawls on, 12
political liberalism. *See also* liberalism
   Marx and, 182
   political moralism and, 382
   of Rawls, 182, 183, 381–82, 401–5
   realism on, 382
Political Liberalism (Rawls), 5, 8, 12, 401
political liberty. *See also* liberty
   material equality and, 123, 130n17
political moralism
   ideal theory on, 382
   overview, 380, 381–82
   political liberalism and, 382
   realism on, 381
political philosophers
   approaches and methods, 4
   issues of, 3
   other philosophical branches and, 4
   political theorists compared to, 4
political philosophy
   action guidance in, 387–88

disciplines included in, 4
evolving field of, 3
expanding circle of equality in, 14–15
on gender inequality, 354, 355, 356
history and, 3
ideal theory and, 373, 374, 378, 380–81, 382, 383, 386, 388
new directions, 14–16
Nozick on, 411
political theory and, 3
on race, 336–38, 346, 350
state in, 15
political realism. *See also* realism
ideal theory and, 380–82
nonideal theory and, 380
political theory. *See also* democratic theory; human rights political theories; ideal theory; justice as fairness; just war theory; natural law theory
analytical Marxism and, 179
of liberalism, 179–80
Marx and, 179, 180
Marxism and, 179, 181, 182
morality and, 380–81
political philosophy and, 3
political theorists
approaches and methods, 4
political history and, 4
political philosophers compared to, 4
polygamy, 365
poor
global order, global justice, and, 272–73
global order and, 272–76, 277n12
inequality and, 274
postracialism, 348
overview, 348
racial pluralist rejection of, 349
state promotion of, 348–49
power, money as independent political, 250
powers to authorize use by others
full self-ownership and, 157, 159, 166n8
liberty rights and, 157, 159, 166n8
practical authority. *See also* political authority
consent-based, 26–28, 29, 30, 34–35
de facto, 25–26
de jure, 25–26, 28, 29
hierarchical, 26, 38n3
Hobbes on, 26–28, 29
Locke on, 28–30, 38n4
right to act, 24–25
right to obligations of others, 25
theoretical authority compared to, 23–24, 32
varieties of, 26–29
the practice. *See* international human rights practice
precapitalism, historical materialism on, 176
preferences, 192, 206, 209, 210, 341
adaptation of, 80, 82
formation, 11, 66, 241, 251, 255
satisfaction, 10, 11, 69, 80, 83–84, 149
prioritarianism
neoclassical liberalism, 122, 123
overview, 67, 74n4, 123

priority, distributive justice, and equality *vs.* sufficiency *vs.*, 66–67, 72
private property. *See also* property
Cohen, G. A., on, 419, 420, 422
fundamental or passé, 93–95, 108–9
late-20th century reconceptualization of, 94–95
private property rights. *See also* property rights
classical liberalism on, 93–94, 105, 106, 107, 108, 109, 110n14, 119
libertarianism on, 105, 110n14, 152
new liberalism on, 94
personal property and, 94
privatization, religious considerations in public discourse, and activism *vs.*, 234–37
property. *See also* ownership; private property
defragmentation and logical structure of ownership, 103–5
disintegration thesis, 94, 95, 103, 108
fragmentation of, 95, 96, 100, 101, 106
as jurisdictions, 105–8
late-20th century reconceptualization of, 94–95
laws, 420
Locke on, 97, 98
natural law theory on, 108
natural rights to, 61, 93, 99
private property rights and personal, 94
protection of, 420
wide and narrow senses of liberalism, jurisdictions, and, 106–8
property relations
class and, 178
historical materialism on, 177–78
property rights. *See also* private property rights
Attas on, 103–5, 109n11, 110n13, 110n17
control rights, 104–5, 109nn11–12
fragmentation of, 96, 100, 102, 106
high liberalism on, 118
intellectual, 427n9
liability rights, 102–3, 107, 109n10
natural resources and, 98, 109n6
Nozick on, 62, 93, 118–19, 129n8, 418, 419
ownership and retreating to core, 102–3
strong and extensive, 105–6, 107, 110n15
summary, 108–9
property rights bundle, 94, 102, 109n8
fragmentation of, 101
full ownership and, 96
ownership and, 97–103
property-thing rights and, 95
structure and rescuing ownership, 97–103
property-thing rights, 108, 110n16
property rights bundle and, 95
prostitution, 364–65
public discourse
activism *vs.* privatization, and religious considerations in, 234–37
civic voice in, 236–37, 239n25
free expression in, 227
public policy. *See* law and public policy advocacy

public reason
  disputes over, 12
  political justification and, 12
  Rawls and, 11–12, 228–29

race. *See also* postracialism
  debate over reality of, 337
  in good society, 348, 349
  idea of, 337–38
  injustice and, 337
  naturalists on, 337–38
  overview and conclusion, 337, 350
  political philosophy on, 336–38, 346, 350
  social constructionists on, 338
racial determinism, 337
racial discrimination, 336
  based on racial inferiority belief, 343, 344, 350n4
  colorblindness and, 342, 343, 344
  differential treatment and, 343–44, 345–46
  equal respect and treatment, and, 343–44
  as expressive harm, 344–45
  meritocracy and, 345, 347, 348
  moral status in, 343
  overview, 341
  racial injustice based on, 346
  racist basis for, 344, 345
  reaction qualifications in, 345
  social justice and, 341–46
  state and, 342–43
  statistical discrimination, 345–46
  unjust, 342, 343, 344, 345
  wrongful, 342, 343, 344, 347–48
racial equality, 336, 350
racial essentialism, 337
racial identity
  community and, 348–50
  in good society, 348, 349
  racial pluralist valuing of, 349–50
  state and, 348, 349–50
  white and non-white, 349
racial injustice, 378
  based on racism and racial discrimination, 346
  corrective justice for, 346
  disadvantage neutralization response to, 347–48
  harm caused by, 346–48
  Jim Crow laws, 413, 426n4
  rectification for, 347
  reparations for, 346–47, 348, 350n8
  responses to, 346–48
  state responses to, 348
racialism, classical, 337
racial justice. *See also* racial injustice
  in good society, 348
  reaction qualifications and, 345
racial pluralism
  racial identity valuing of, 349–50
  rejection of postracialism, 349
racial skeptics, 337
racism, 336, 337. *See also* antiracism
  against African Americans, 327, 330

  beliefs about, 338–39
  Canadian, 319
  cognitive errors about, 339
  debate over, 338
  extrinsic, 338–39
  institutional, 339–41, 346
  intrinsic, 338, 339
  irrational, 339
  mental states of, 339–40
  overt, 340
  overview, 338–41
  racial discrimination based on, 344, 345
  racial injustice based on, 346
  racist actions, 339
  theories about, 338–39
  unconscious, 339
  U.S., 319, 327, 330
radical democracy, 210, 213
radical democratic deliberativism
  civic republican deliberativism compared to, 213
  liberal deliberativism compared to, 213
  overview, 210, 213–14
rational choice, 30, 84, 136, 139, 142, 149, 174–75
rational disagreement
  between epistemic peers, and citizenship ethics, 233–34, 239n21
  over religion, 233, 239n21
Rawls, John, 3, 46, 140, 150n4, 179, 210, 424. *See also* justice as fairness
  benefit maximization for worst-off social group, 60, 61
  on challenge of stability, 394
  on challenges of toleration, 402
  on controversies, 5–6
  difference principle of, 60, 61, 398, 413, 414, 415, 416, 426, 426n2
  on domestic justice, 265, 271
  on economic liberty, 116, 118
  era of, 4–7
  on fair equality of opportunity, 60–61, 398
  on finding common ground, 5–6
  first original position, 396–97, 398, 400, 407
  first principle, of equal basic rights and liberties, 397–98, 413–14, 423, 426n2
  on global justice, 265–66
  human rights political theory of, 284, 285–86, 287
  on ideal theory, 6, 13, 126–28, 373–87
  on inequality, 398–99, 412, 413, 423, 426n2
  influence of, 4–5, 7
  internal-external thesis, 406
  internal thesis, 405–6
  international principles of, 407–8
  just and stable society of, 394
  on justice, 4, 5, 6, 8, 10, 34, 58, 60–61, 117, 125, 126, 145–46, 150n3, 171, 182, 265–66, 271, 285, 373–77, 381–84, 386, 393–405, 411–12, 418, 423, 426n2
  on justice as fairness, 145–46, 394–401, 404–5
  just society of, 393–401
  law of peoples, 405–10
  The Law of Peoples of, 265, 266, 405, 406

on liberal and decent peoples, 405–6
on libertarianism, 395
on morality, 5, 140, 142, 150n3, 285–86, 393–94
on nonideal theory, 373, 375, 376, 377, 378
Nozick and, 8, 9, 411–14, 415, 417–18
on obeying laws, 6–7
overview, 4–7, 393–94
political conception of justice, of, 402–3
on political justification, 12
political liberalism of, 182, 183, 381–82, 401–5
Political Liberalism of, 5, 8, 12, 401
precursor of, 412–13, 425, 426n2
public political culture of liberal society, 403–4
public reason and, 11–12, 228–29
on reconciliation, 5–6
relationism of, 265–66
right-based social contract of, 134, 140, 142, 145–46, 147
Sandels critique of, 7–8
on satisfied peoples, 406–7
second original position, 407–8
second principle, on socio-economic inequalities, 398–99, 413, 423, 426n2
on social justice, 5, 6, 373, 384
statism of, 265
A Theory of Justice of, 4, 5, 8, 10, 60, 208, 401, 426n2
on urgency of hope, 409–10
on utilitarianism, 6, 10–11, 60–61, 397, 398–99
on world governance, 408–9
Raz, Joseph, 32–33, 38nn8–9
realism. *See also* political realism
 ideal theory and, 380–82, 383–85, 386
 on justice, 382
 nonideal theory and, 380, 382
 on political liberalism, 382
 on political moralism, 381
reason. *See also* natural reason; public reason; religious reasons; secular reason
 in deliberation, 204, 205, 206, 215–18
 in deliberative democracy, 209–10, 215–19, 219nn9–10
 in instrumentalism, 205, 206, 209, 219n9
rectification. *See also* reparations
 arguments against historical injustice, 326–27
 compensation, 326–27, 333n2
 contours of duties of, 422
 historical injustice, 319, 322–27
 just claims, 326
 justice of, 326–27
 Nozick on, 417, 422
 for racial injustice, 347
 rectificatory justice, 261, 422
relationism. *See also* nonrelationism
 defenses of, 268–70
 of globalism, 264, 268, 270, 276n3
 global justice and, 263
 internationalism and, 272
 justice and, 263–64, 265–66, 268–69, 272, 277n4

nonrelationism and, 263–64, 266, 270, 272
overview, 263–64
Rawls, 265–66
of statism, 264, 268, 270
religion. *See also* church-state separation; secularity
 civil, 224, 237n1
 considerations in public discourse, and activism *vs.* privatization, 234–37
 criteria for, 230, 238n17
 democratic societies, politics and, 235, 237
 establishment of, 224–25, 237n1
 gender equality and, 365, 368
 gender justice and, 368
 politics and, 235, 237
 rational disagreement over, 233, 239n21
 secularity and, 230
 secularity of democratic societies, and, 223
religious conviction
 natural reason, secularity, and, 231–32
 secular rationale principle and, 231, 237
religious identity, and natural reason, 232–33
religious liberty, 224, 225
religious rationale principle, 232, 237
religious reasons, 237
 in law and public policy advocacy, 229, 230
 natural reason and, 232
 secular rationale principle and, 230, 232, 234–35, 236, 239n23
 secular reasons and, 232, 233
reparations. *See also* rectification
 for African Americans, 323, 324, 325, 328, 333n2
 arguments, 322, 323–25, 327, 328, 347
 compensation, 322–25
 determining, 322–25
 harm argument for, 347
 for historical injustice, 319, 321, 322–25, 327, 328
 inheritance argument for, 347
 for racial injustice, 346–47, 348, 350n8
 responsible parties for, 324
 unjust enrichment argument for, 347
republicans
 concept of freedom, 82, 86, 88, 90, 212, 220n16
 on deliberative democracy, 212
republicanism, civic. *See* civic republicanism
resort to war (*jus ad bellum*) principles
 classical just war theory, 299
 just war theory, 298–302, 310–12, 314
 revisionist just war theory, 310
 traditional just war theory, 301, 302, 310, 311, 312, 314
resources. *See also* natural resources
 equality doctrine and distributive justice, 64–66
revisionist just war theory
 conduct of war (*jus in bello*) principles, 310, 311, 314
 on humanitarian intervention, 313–14
 just cause in, 310, 311, 314
 overview, 309
 on preventive war, 313
 resort to war (*jus ad bellum*) principles, 310
 self- and other-defense in, 309–10
 on war and other conflicts, 309–10

revolution, 15
rights. *See also* human rights; liberty rights; moral rights; natural rights; ownership rights; property rights; security rights; transfer rights
   to act, and practical authority, 24–25
   libertarianism on, 61–62, 63, 74n3, 156, 166n7
   to obligations of others, and practical authority, 25
   oughts compared to, 228
   overview, 419
   side constraint, 62, 63, 419
   value realm of rightness, 44
   various terminologies of, 25
right action, 59
right-based social contracts
   interest-based social contracts compared to, 146–48
   justice in, 135–36, 141, 142, 144, 145–46, 147
   of Kant, 134, 142, 145
   liberal and democratic traditions, and, 133, 134, 135, 141–48
   of Locke, 133, 134, 135, 136, 141, 142–44, 145
   Locke's consent thesis and, 142, 143
   morality in, 135, 136, 141–42, 143, 145, 146
   natural rights theory of, 142, 145
   overview, 135–36, 141–42
   of Rawls, 134, 140, 142, 145–46, 147
   of Rousseau, 133, 134, 135, 141, 144–45
right libertarianism
   Nozickean, 163
   overview, 152, 153
   radical, 162
Riker, William, 207, 219n2
Roemer, John, 17nn16–17, 170
Rousseau, Jean-Jacques, 31, 47, 48
   general will of, 144–45, 146, 150n4
   right-based social contract of, 133, 134, 135, 141, 144–45
   Social Contract of, 78, 90
   on war, 300

Sandels, Michael, 7–8
   communitarianism of, 7–8
   critique of Rawls, 7–8
Sanders, Lynn, 214, 216
Scanlon, T. M., 150n3, 269
scarcity, 248
   media expression, 248, 249
   message space, 248, 249
   money in politics, and, 248–50
   socially induced cognitive, 248–49
Scheffler, Samuel, 72–73, 270
Schmidtz, David, 102, 122, 125–26, 130n14, 130n20
secularism
   secularity difference from, 231
   spirituality and, 230–31
secularity. *See also* church-state separation; religion
   of democratic societies, and religion, 223
   natural reason, religious conviction, and, 231–32
   religion and, 230

secularism difference from, 231
   spirituality and, 230
secular rationale principle, 229
   coercion and, 235
   in law and public policy advocacy, 229–30, 238n15
   overview and summary, 229–30, 231, 237, 238n15, 239n18
   as principle of natural reason, 230, 232, 237, 239n18
   religious conviction and, 231, 237
   religious reasons and, 230, 232, 234–35, 236, 239n23
   secular reason in, 229–30
secular reason
   natural reason and, 239n18
   religious reasons and, 232, 233
   in secular rationale principle, 229–30
security rights
   full self-ownership, 156–57, 158, 159
   self-ownership, 156–57, 158
self-ownership. *See also* full self-ownership; ownership
   libertarianism on, 9, 61–62, 152, 153–61
   Nozick on liberalism and, 417–19
   partial, 155–56
   security rights, 156–57, 158
Sen, Amartya, 11, 64, 273, 374, 377–78, 386
separateness of persons, 62
   utilitarianism and, 60
sex
   based gender differences, 357, 358, 360, 365, 366, 367
   discrimination, 368
   gender and, 356–57, 358, 360, 365
sexuality, 40, 42, 45, 52, 364, 369
sexual orientation, 14, 43. *See also* gay
Shapiro, Scott, 33–34, 35
Sher, George, 323, 326, 327, 333n2
side constraints, 62, 63, 419
slavery, 322
   U.S. African American, 319, 321, 324, 325, 327, 333n2
Smith, Adam, 125
social choice, 195, 206, 208
social contract. *See also* convention-based social contracts; interest-based social contracts; right-based social contracts
   common good in, 144, 146, 147
   contractarianism and, 146, 150
   general features, 133–36
   justice in, 135, 136, 148, 149–50
   overview and summary of, 133–36, 149–50
   political authority and, 30, 34, 134, 136
   as redundant and unnecessary, 148
   theory, 34
   traditions, 135
Social Contract (Rousseau), 78, 90
social democracy
   economic liberty rankings of, 129n12
   egalitarian camp of, 51–52

ownership and, 109n4
in political philosophy, 15
social insurance *vs.* regulatory, 129n12
social equality
  distributive justice and, 73
  ideals of, 41–42, 52
  luck egalitarianism and, 73
social goods, primary, 61, 64, 65, 68
social hierarchies
  democracy and, 47
  of domination or command, 42–47
  egalitarian critiques of, 40, 41, 42, 44–51
  egalitarian remedies for, 41, 43
  of esteem, 43–44, 45, 46, 47–49
  goodness in, 50
  of standing, 43, 44, 45, 46, 48
  types, 42–44
  virtue in, 46, 47–48, 49–50
socialism, 9, 10, 169, 170. *See also* communism; Marxism
  analytical Marxism and, 172, 177
  communism and, 181, 182
  historical materialism on, 176, 177
  Marxism on, 171, 176, 177
social justice. *See also* ideal theory
  classical liberalism on, 124–25, 126
  gender inequality and, 354, 355
  global justice and, 13
  ideal theory and, 373
  libertarianism on, 124
  neoclassical liberalism on, 125, 127
  nonideal theory and, 373
  racial discrimination and, 341–46
  Rawls on, 5, 6, 373, 384
social moral epistemology
  of international legal human rights, 290–91
  overview, 290
social movements, egalitarian, 40, 41, 52, 53
social relations
  distributive justice, democratic equality, and equality of, 69–73
  equality as distributive principle or ideal of, 40–42, 52–55
social science, and Marxism, 172–73
social welfare function
  in democracy, 190, 192, 194
  general interest and, 190
society. *See also* democratic societies; egalitarian society; just society
  race in good, 348, 349
  Rawls' conception of, 394–96
Soviet Union
  analytical Marxism on, 9–10, 17n17
  communism, 9–10, 17n17, 171
spirituality
  secularism and, 230–31
  secularity and, 230
state. *See also* church-state separation; freedom of the state
  capitalism and, 180

class and, 180
consciousness and, 182–83
as dictatorship, 181
freedom and, 420
gender equality promotion by, 368
gender justice and, 366–68
globalism and, 264, 267
global justice and, 261–62, 271
Hobbes on, 179, 180, 181, 262, 299–300
individuals and, 262
internationalism and, 271, 272
justice and, 262, 264, 270, 271, 272
liberalism and, 179–80, 181, 182
Marxism on, 182–83
Marx on, 180–81
nonrelationism and, 264, 267
persons harmed by, 273
promotion of postracialism, 348–49
racial discrimination and, 342–43
racial identity and, 348, 349–50
responses to racial injustice, 348
statism on the, 264, 270, 271
in war, 299–300, 301, 302, 306, 307–8, 310
world state, 262
statism
  coercion-based, 270, 271, 277n8
  globalism and, 264, 268, 270–71
  justice and, 264, 268, 271, 276n2, 277n4
  on moral equality, 267
  on political equality, 267
  of Rawls, 265
  reciprocity-based, 270, 271, 277n8
  relationism of, 264, 268, 270
  on the state, 264, 270, 271
subversion, 15
sufficiency
  distributive justice, and equality *vs.* priority *vs.*, 66–67, 72
  principle, 66, 72
sufficientarianism
  libertarianism, 163–64
  neoclassical liberalism, 122, 123
  overview, 122
surrogacy, 364–65

Tasioulas, John, 280
terrorism, 15
theory. *See also* political theory
  incompleteness as ideal of, 425–26
A Theory of Justice (Rawls), 4, 5, 8, 10, 60, 208, 401, 426n2
Thompson, Dennis, 211
toleration
  liberalism commitment to, 285–86
  principle, 233–34, 237
  Rawls on challenges of, 402
traditional just war theory
  conduct of war (*jus in bello*) principles, 301–12
  Hobbes and, 299–300
  on humanitarian intervention, 313–14

traditional just war theory (*continued*)
  just cause in, 308, 310, 311, 312–13, 314
  overview, 299–300, 301, 302–9
  on preventive war, 313
  resort to war (*jus ad bellum*) principles, 301, 302, 310, 311, 312, 314
  self- and other-defense in, 302–6, 309, 310
  on unjust war, 302, 303, 308–9
  on war and other conflicts, 306, 307–9
transfer rights, 154
  full, 159–61
Two Treatises of Government (Locke), 28

UDHR. *See* Universal Declaration of Human Rights
United Nations (UN), 262
  Charter, 263, 281, 283, 296n3, 301
  Human Rights Council, 279
United States (U.S.)
  church-state separation in, 225, 237n1, 238n8
  Constitution, 144, 181, 212, 225, 289
  democracy, 191, 202n16
  enduring injustice against Native Americans, 330, 331, 332, 333n4
  Hawaiian overthrow by, 319, 320
  historical injustice against Native Americans, 320, 326, 328–32, 333n4
  historical injustices against African Americans, 319–25, 327–30, 333n2
  historical injustices against Chinese Americans, 319, 328
  money in politics, in, 242, 245, 251, 254, 255n5
  racism, 319, 327, 330
  subordination of women in, 354
Universal Declaration of Human Rights (UDHR), 279, 281, 282, 283, 284, 296nn3–4
utility
  individual good or welfare, as, 59
  maximization, 59, 60
utilitarianism
  on democracy, 201n4
  distributive justice in, 59–61
  egalitarianism of, 59
  justice as fairness, and, 397, 398–99
  liberalism and, 60, 61
  overview, 59
  Rawls on, 6, 10–11, 60–61, 397, 398–99
  right action, 59
  separateness of persons, and, 60
  utility maximization, 59, 60

utopia
  of Nozick, 424–25, 426
  self-esteem in, 425

value realms
  of goodness, 44
  of rightness, 44
  of virtue, 44
van Donselaar, Gijs, 98, 99
virtue
  in social hierarchies, 46, 47–48, 49–50
  value realm of, 44
voting
  in democracy, 188–90, 196–97, 211
  money for, 242–44

Waldron, Jeremy, 326, 327, 331, 332
war, 377. *See also* just war theory
  civil, 306–7
  Rousseau on, 300
  state in, 299–300, 301, 302, 306, 307–8, 310
Weber, Max, 26
Weithman, Paul, 229, 238n13
welfare. *See also* social welfare function
  distributive justice and, 66–69, 74n5
  as utility, 59
  welfarism and, 122
welfarism
  distributive justice and, 66–69, 74n5
  neoclassical liberalism, 122, 123
  overview, 122
  welfare and, 122
Williams, Bernard, 380, 381
Wolff, Robert P., 31, 38n7
Wollstonecraft, Mary, 50
women. *See also* gender
  justice for, 366
  women's inequality and choices of, 358–65
women's inequality, 354, 367. *See also* gender inequality
  Mill, J. S., on, 354–55, 362
  women's choices and, 358–65
women's subordination, 368, 369
  in family, 354, 355
  feminism on, 356, 357
  overview, 354
  polygamy and, 365
World Trade Organization (WTO), 263, 271, 272

Young, Iris, 215–16

CPSIA information can be obtained
at www.ICGtesting.com
Printed in the USA
BVHW080339281218
536256BV00004B/9/P